INSIGHT GUIDES

UNITED STATES ON THE ROAD

APA PUBLICATIONS **L**

Part of the Langenscheidt Publishing Group

✕ INSIGHT GUIDE

UNITED STATES ON THE ROAD

Editorial
Project Editor
Alyse Dar
Art Director
Ian Spick
Picture Manager
Steven Lawrence
Series Manager
Rachel Fox

Distribution

United States
Langenscheidt Publishers, Inc.
36–36 33rd Street 4th Floor
Long Island City, NY 11106
orders@langenscheidt.com

UK & Ireland
GeoCenter International Ltd
Meridian House, Churchill Way West
Basingstoke, Hampshire RG21 6YR
sales@geocenter.co.uk

Australia
Universal Publishers
1 Waterloo Road
Macquarie Park, NSW 2113
sales@universalpublishers.com.au

New Zealand
Hema Maps New Zealand Ltd (HNZ)
Unit 2, 10 Cryers Road
East Tamaki, Auckland 2013
sales.hema@clear.net.nz

Worldwide
Apa Publications GmbH & Co.
Verlag KG (Singapore branch)
38 Joo Koon Road, Singapore 628990
Tel: (65) 6865 1600.
apasin@singnet.com.sg

Printing

Insight Print Services (Pte) Ltd
38 Joo Koon Road, Singapore 628990
Tel: (65) 6865 1600.

©2010 Apa Publications GmbH & Co.
Verlag KG (Singapore branch)
All Rights Reserved

First Edition 2001
Second Edition 2010

CONTACTING THE EDITORS
We would appreciate it if readers
would alert us to errors or out-
dated information by writing to:
**Insight Guides, P.O. Box 7910,
London SE1 1WE, England.**
insight@apaguide.co.uk

www.insightguides.com

Birmingham City Council	
WA	
C2 000 004 394691	
Askews	Feb-2010
917.304	£17.99
WALMLEY	

ABOUT THIS BOOK

The first Insight Guide pio-
neered the use of creative
full-color photography in travel
guides in 1970. Since then, we
have expanded our range to cater
for our readers' need not only for
reliable information about their
chosen destination but also for a
real understanding of the culture
and workings of that destination.
Now, when the internet can supply
inexhaustible (but not always reliable) facts, our books marry text
and pictures to provide those much
more elusive qualities: knowledge
and discernment. To achieve this,
they rely heavily on the authority of
locally based writers and photographers. This book is structured to
convey an understanding of the
United States and its unique on-
the-road culture, as well as to guide
readers through the country's variety of sights and activities:

◆ The **Features** section, indicated
by a pink bar at the top of each page,
covers the history and travel culture
of the United States in a series of
informative essays.
◆ The main **Routes** section, indicated by a blue bar, is a complete
guide to all the sights and areas
worth visiting along five east-west
and north-south routes. Places of
special interest are coordinated by
number with the maps. The route
guides begin, and some end, with
photo features illustrating our rec-
ommendations for short stays in
major "hub" cities.
◆ The **Travel Tips** listings section,
with a yellow bar, provides full information on transportation, hotels,
activities from sports to shopping,
and an A–Z section of essential practical information. A contents list for
Travel Tips is printed on the back flap,
which also serves as a bookmark.

LEFT: driving through Arizona on Route 66.

Veteran Insight Guide contributor **Nicky Leach** was inspired by the discoveries she made on the backroads along the Southern Route: nature artist Walter Anderson's paintings in Ocean Springs, Mississippi; Cajun music at Breaux Bridge; and modern-art-meets-cowboy culture in Marfa, Texas. As well as contributing to the Places chapters, she also compiled the general practical information for the redesigned Travel Tips.

Former Insight Guides editorial director **Brian Bell** updated the New York to Georgia leg of the Atlantic Route; long-standing travel writer, **Ray Bartlett** took the wheel for the Florida section. Bartlett has written for a wide variety of travel publications, including newspapers, magazines, radio, video and travel guides. When not on the road he divides his time between Cape Cod and Baja California Sur in Mexico.

This book builds on the first edition, produced by London-based American **Martha Ellen Zenfell** who commissioned a team of ace writers including **Greg Ward** (Southern Route) and **Paul Karr** (Atlantic and Northern Routes), **John Wilcock** and **Teresa Machan** (Central Route). Wilcock also tackled the Pacific Route, with help from Zenfell, who drew on a trip through Big Sur on a Harley-Davidson to supply that bugs-in-the-teeth realism. **Paul Taylor**, publisher of *Route 66 Magazine*, wrote the feature on the Mother Road.

Thanks also go to **Adam Liptak**, **Robert Seidenberg** and **Rich Taskin**, **Laura Martone**, **Barbara Balletto**, and **Catherine Dreghorn** for their contributions. The book was proofread by **Janet McCann** and **Helen Peters** compiled the index.

The contributors

This new edition was commissioned and edited by **Alyse Dar** at Insight Guides' London office. She enlisted a team of experienced travel writers who covered many thousands of miles to research places of interest and to find the best places to eat, sleep and shop along each route.

Donna Dailey and **Mike Gerrard** drove the Pacific Route as well as parts of the Southern, Central and Northern Routes. They revised the history and features chapters and wrote the new Best of the United States section. Dailey's work appears in magazines, newspapers and websites worldwide. Her Insight Guides include *Step by Step: Orlando* and *Pocket Guide: Denver*. Gerrard has written about travel for many publications including *National Geographic* and *The Times*. Both have won prestigious travel writing awards.

Map Legend

▬▬ ▪ ▪	International Boundary
▬ ▬ ▬	State Boundary
⊖	Border Crossing
▬ ▪ ▬ ▪	National Park/Reserve
▭▭▭	Highway
▭▭▭	Other Multi-lane Highway
▭▭▭	Principal Highway
▭▭▭	Through Highway
▬▬	Other Road
⑤	Interstate Highway
① ㉙	US Highway
㊿ ㉉	Other Highway
⌐	On the Road Routes
✈ ✈	Airport: International/Regional
★	Place of Interest

The main places of interest in the Places section are coordinated by number with a full-color map (eg ❶), and a symbol at the top of every right-hand page tells you where to find the map.

Contents

NATIONAL CONTESTANT

503

JUST HOLLER!

LEFT: rural New England mailboxes framed in autumn foliage.

Maps

THE BEST OF THE UNITED STATES: TOP ATTRACTIONS

From soaring skyscrapers to plunging canyons, and Native American pueblos to gracious Southern mansions, here are some of the most spectacular places in the United States

△ Native American, Hispanic, and Anglo cultures blend together in **Santa Fe**. The nation's oldest capital is a handsome city of adobe-style buildings and Southwestern art, set around its historic plaza. *See pages 214–15*

▽ Spewing geysers, bubbling mudpots, sizzling hot springs, and other geothermal features are scattered amid the spectacular beauty of the Rocky Mountains in **Yellowstone National Park**. *See pages 157–9*

▷ The Colorado River carved out the colorful bluffs, mesas, and rock formations of the **Grand Canyon**, one of the great natural wonders of the world. *See pages 226–7*

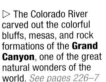

▷ Dripping with Spanish moss and Southern charm, **Savannah** is the jewel of the Old South. Take a carriage ride round its cobbled squares and visit its gracious antebellum mansions. *See pages 78–9*

△ The unique environment of the **Everglades** forms the largest subtropical wilderness in the country. It protects rare and endangered plant and animal species, some found nowhere else in the world. *See pages 88–9*

◁ **New York City** is the nation's capital of art, commerce, fashion, and culture, with world-class museums, restaurants, and shopping. From its skyscraper skyline to the lights of Times Square, it never fails to impress. *See pages 52–3*

△ The thundering cascades of **Niagara Falls** mark the border between the United States and Canada. The boat ride into the mist at the base of the falls is an unforgettable thrill. *See page 120*

▷ Walk among towering ancient trees, lush ferns, and dripping mosses in **Olympic National Park**, which preserves one of the largest areas of temperate rainforest in the country. *See pages 169–70*

▷▷ The rugged cliffs and pounding surf of California's **Big Sur** form one of the most dramatic stretches of the Pacific coast, a road trip you'll never forget. *See pages 344–6*

▷ The **saguaro cactus**, symbol of the American Southwest, is a stunning sight against the backdrop of an Arizona sunset. These prickly giants grow only in the Sonoran Desert. *See page 303–4*

THE BEST OF THE UNITED STATES: EDITOR'S CHOICE

With its magnificent sweeping landscapes, ethnic and regional cultures and cuisines, and an endless capacity for fun, there's always something new to explore on the road in the United States. Here are some of the editor's American favorites:

BEST FOR FAMILIES

- **Orlando**
Nonstop entertainment at Walt Disney World's four theme parks, Universal Studios, the Kennedy Space Center, and a host of family attractions *See page 84.*
- **San Diego**
From SeaWorld and the San Diego Zoo to whale-watching cruises and trolley tours, there's plenty to delight all ages. *See pages 322–3.*
- **Williamsburg**
Step back in time and see how people lived in the early days of the country. *See page 63.*
- **Monterey Bay Aquarium**
One of the best in the world, with mesmerizing exhibits and touch tanks that bring you up close to the undersea world. *See page 347.*
- **Tombstone**
The Wild West lives on in this historic town of boardwalks, Boothill and shoot-outs at the OK Corral. *See page 301–2*
- **Arizona-Sonora Desert Museum**
Watch raptors in flight and observe javelinas, coyote, mountain lions, and other desert creatures in their natural setting. *See page 304.*

BEST SCENIC DRIVES

- **The Pacific Coast Highway**
Highways 1 and 101 take you from California's rugged shores to Oregon's idyllic beaches. *See pages 339–82.*
- **Blue Ridge Mountains**
Enjoy the stunning vistas of this romantic mountain chain along Skyline Drive and the Blue Ridge Parkway. *See pages 66 and 187–90.*
- **Going to the Sun Road**
Traversing Glacier National Park, this is one of the most dramatic drives in the Rocky Mountains. *See pages 162–4.*
- **Atchafalaya Swamp Freeway**
Watch out for alligators as you drive across the largest swamp in the country. *See page 267.*
- **Monument Valley**
These awesome buttes and mesas rising up from the desert floor formed the backdrop for many Hollywood Westerns. *See page 223.*
- **Outer Banks**
Pristine dunes, beaches, islands, and lighthouses along the Atlantic coast are preserved in two national seashores. *See page 70.*
- **The Badlands**
A starkly beautiful landscape of rolling grasslands and twisted rocky canyons stretches right across the windswept plains of South Dakota. *See pages 139–41.*

LEFT: Walt Disney World. **ABOVE:** Monument Valley.

BEST MUSEUMS AND GALLERIES

● **Getty Villa at Malibu**
The re-created 1st-century Roman villa is an impressive home for this collection of Greek and Roman antiquities.
Page 339.
● **Smithsonian Institution**
A group of museums highlighting the nation's best achievements in art, history, and science line the Mall in Washington, DC.
See pages 180–81.
● **National Civil Rights Museum**
The moving story of the Civil Rights movement, set around the

Memphis motel where Martin Luther King, Jr was assassinated. *See page 196.*
● **Heard Museum**
This beautiful collection of Native American arts and crafts in Phoenix, Arizona is among the finest in the country. *See pages 308–9.*
● **New Mexico Museum of Space History**
Fly a space shuttle simulator and follow the story of early pioneers in the space race. *See page 292.*

BEST HISTORICAL SITES

● **Independence National Historical Park**
The United States was founded in these Philadelphia buildings. *See pages 58–9.*
● **Charleston**
The first shots of the Civil War were fired in the harbor of this city of elegant 18th-century houses. *See pages 74–7.*

● **Palace of the Governors**
This adobe jewel is the anchor for the excellent New Mexico History Museum. *See page 214.*
● **The Alamo**
The famous battle that took place here became a rallying cry for Texan independence. *See page 282.*

ABOVE: Art Deco in Miami. **BELOW:** the Chrysler Building.

BEST ARCHITECTURE AND BUILDINGS

● **Miami's Art Deco District**
Pastel-painted hotels and shops with striking nautical motifs line Miami's South Beach. *See pages 92–3.*
● **Hearst Castle**
Filled with exquisite art and furnishings, this opulent hilltop residence was a playground for Hollywood's elite. *See pages 343–4.*
● **Chrysler Building**
The most ornate and arguably the best-loved of Manhattan's skyscrapers. *See page 53.*

● **Las Vegas**
Kitsch is king in Sin City's neon-lit, mind-blowing casinos designed after such world landmarks as the Egyptian pyramids. *See page 229.*
● **Golden Gate Bridge**
Graceful and romantic, this San Francisco landmark is said to be the most photographed bridge in the world. *See pages 350–1.*
● **French Quarter**
Beautiful wrought-iron galleries line the historic buildings in the heart of old New Orleans. *See pages 262–3.*

FLAVORS OF THE USA

● **American Diners**
These 1950s-style eateries are the best places for burgers, milkshakes, and classic casual fare.
● **Buffalo Burgers**
A lean and mean version of the nation's favorite sandwich, served throughout the West.
● **Creole and Cajun Cuisine**
Try jambalaya, crawfish etouffe,

gumbo, and other dishes from the Louisiana bayou.
● **Tex-Mex**
The American take on Mexican dishes includes tacos, burritos, fajitas, and chili con carne.
● **California Wine Country**
Sip your way around the many fine wineries and vineyards in Napa and Sonoma valleys and Paso Robles.

● **Microbrews**
Seek out the growing number of brew-pubs and bars that serve real ales and original beers produced by local microbreweries.

THIS IS AS WE KNEW
IT BOB—MARCH
J.N. MARCHAND
1906

DECISIVE DATES

1492
Explorer Christopher Columbus reaches America, landing at San Salvador.

1607
Jamestown, Virginia settled by the British.

1620
Sixty-six Puritans found Plymouth Colony, Cape Cod Bay.

1773
In the "Boston Tea Party," men dump tea crates into the harbor to protest against taxes.

1775
Paul Revere rides from Boston warning of the arrival of British troops. The American Revolution begins.

1776
On July 4, the Continental Congress, meeting in Philadelphia, adopts the Declaration of Independence, penned by Thomas Jefferson.

1789
George Washington takes the first presidential oath at New York's Federal Hall.

1804
Lewis and Clark set out on their 8,000-mile (13,000km) expedition to the Pacific Coast.

1836
Siege of the Alamo in San Antonio, Texas, results in the death of all 189 American defenders.

1848
Gold is discovered at Sutter's Fort, California, bringing over 200,000 prospectors within the next three years.

1858
After a 25-day journey, John Butterfield's Overland Stage delivers its first sack of mail to the West Coast.

1860
South Carolina secedes from the Union, and the Confederate states are born.

1862
Confederates open fire on Fort Sumter, in the first shots of the Civil War. Abraham Lincoln legally frees all slaves by issuing the Emancipation Proclamation.

1864
The transcontinental telegraph connects Seattle, Washington, with the rest of the US.

1865
The Civil War ends. President Abraham Lincoln is assassinated in Washington, DC.

1869
The Central Pacific and Union Pacific railroads meet in Ogden, Utah, completing the first transcontinental railroad.

1876
General George A. Custer leads his 264 men into battle at Little Bighorn Creek against the Sioux and Cheyenne. All are wiped out in "Custer's Last Stand."

1890
A US Army regiment attacks a camp near Wounded Knee Creek in South Dakota's Pine Ridge Reservation, killing 300 Indians.

1906
A massive earthquake measuring 8.2 on the Richter Scale, followed by a devastating fire, flattens San Francisco.

1908
Henry Ford begins mass production of the Model T car.

1920
Nineteenth Amendment to the Constitution guarantees women's right to vote.

1929
Wall Street crashes, and with it comes the beginning of the Great Depression.

1930s
The "Dust Bowl" forces thousands from farmlands around Oklahoma on a migrant trek west to California in search of work.

1941
Japan attacks Pearl Harbor, and the United States enters World War II.

1945
First atomic bomb detonates in New Mexico; bombs dropped on Hiroshima and Nagasaki. United Nations charter drafted in San Francisco.

1955
Rev. Martin Luther King, Jr leads the Montgomery (Alabama) Bus Boycott.

PRECEDING PAGE: linking the East and West coasts by rail, 1869. FAR LEFT TOP: The Boston Tea Party. FAR LEFT: Paul Revere's midnight ride. NEAR LEFT: American automobile manufacturer, Henry Ford. ABOVE: abandoned Dust Bowl farm. NEAR RIGHT: Neil Armstrong, the first man on the moon. FAR RIGHT TOP: twin beams of light symbolizing the World Trade Center. FAR RIGHT BOTTOM: inauguration of Barack Obama.

1963
President John F. Kennedy is assassinated while touring Dallas, Texas.

1968
James Earl Ray kills Martin Luther King, Jr in Memphis, and Robert F. Kennedy is assassinated in Los Angeles.

1969
Apollo 11 commander Neil Armstrong communicates with Houston from the moon.

1974
Richard M. Nixon, 37th president, resigns after facing impeachment over Watergate.

1980
Mount St Helens in Washington erupts, devastating the surrounding region.

1989
An earthquake (7.1 on the Richter Scale) collapses a freeway and causes chaos and destruction in the San Francisco area.

2000
Incompletely punched ballot cards cause rage in Florida as George W. Bush becomes president.

2001
Four passenger jets hijacked by suicide bombers destroy New York City's World Trade Center.

2005
Hurricane Katrina causes major flooding and destruction in New Orleans and along the Gulf Coast, killing thousands of residents.

2008
Gas prices soar, topping $4 per gallon in California.

2009
Barack Obama is sworn in as the 44th President of the United States, becoming the first African-American to hold the nation's highest office. Chrysler and General Motors file for bankruptcy.

THE TRANSPORTATION REVOLUTION

From wagon trains to the iron horse to today's super-highways, travel is at the heart of America's history

During the 17th and 18th centuries, white settlers in early America followed the network of paths that Native Americans had carved out for themselves, and travel conditions were notoriously wretched. During the time of colonization with Great Britain, it cost less to transport goods across the Atlantic Ocean from London to Philadelphia than to carry those same goods 100 miles (160km) to Lancaster, Pennsylvania. In 1776, news of the Declaration of Independence took 29 days to reach the people of Charleston, South Carolina. No wonder New England delegates at the Constitutional Convention in 1787 had more things in common with their brethren in Britain than with their fellow countrymen down South in the Carolinas and Georgia.

Fifty years later, when Alexis de Tocqueville, Michael Chevalier, and a host of European travelers *(see page 16)* examined the American experiment of self-government, conditions on dry land were little improved. Whereas the Roman Empire made the construction of great roads an important function of its central government, in 19th-century America laissez-faire attitudes predominated, leaving the construction of highways a state and local responsibility. Often, farmers and laborers who were unable to meet their tax obligations ended up doing the little road work that was done.

Tolerance of mud

As a direct consequence of the American belief in "the less government the better," roads suffered from neglect and disrepair. Pioneers, such

---

LEFT: explorer, Meriwether Lewis.
RIGHT: bygone mode of transportation recalled in song.

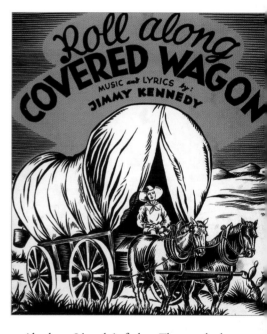

as Abraham Lincoln's father, Thomas, had to possess courage, physical strength, and an incredible tolerance of mud. William Herndon, Lincoln's law partner and biographer, described the Lincoln family's move from Indiana to Illinois in March of 1830 as one which "suited the roving and migratory spirit of Thomas Lincoln." With the "obscure and penniless" 21-year-old Abe commanding a wagon drawn by two oxen, "the journey was a long and tedious one." Basing his literary account of the trip on Lincoln's recollections, Herndon memorably evokes the experience of thousands of similar travelers. "The rude, heavy wagon," he wrote, "with its primitive wheels, creaked and groaned as it crawled through the woods and now and then stalled in the mud. Many were the delays."

In antebellum America, geography created a formidable barrier to migration. Even as late as the 1830s, approximately 80 percent of the American population still continued to reside east of the Allegheny Mountains.

Thomas Jefferson's decision to send those two intrepid travelers, Captain Meriwether Lewis and Lieutenant William Clark, to explore the territories west of the Mississippi River charted the way for settlement of the vast, important region. The president dispatched Lewis and Clark shortly after the Louisiana Pur-

chase in 1803. His motives for asking for a $2,500 appropriation from Congress to finance the expedition were mixed. Even at this late date, it appears Jefferson had not abandoned all hope that a passage to Asia might be found. He was also confident that the explorers would discover trade routes to benefit fur traders. Nor was Jefferson without hope of further expanding what he liked to call the "empire of liberty." But this is not to say that the president was prevaricating when he explained to the Spanish Minister that the purpose of the mission was the "advancement of science." Jefferson, a child of the Enlightenment Era, saw the active study

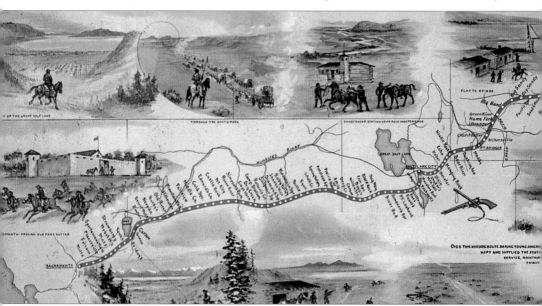

THE PONY EXPRESS

One of the 19th century's most romantic enterprises, the Pony Express, galloped across the western landscape and into the history books in just over 18 months. From April 1860 through October 1861, Express horsemen formed a record-setting, trans-Mississippi relay team that won over the hearts of Americans, if not the pocketbooks of the US Congress. The daring young mail carriers braved rain, snow, sleet, dead of night, and Indian attacks between St Joseph, Missouri, and Sacramento, California, to deliver over 35,000 letters, telegrams, and newspapers. The riders tallied up 650,000 miles (1 milllion km) on the 1,966-mile (3,164km) -long Pony Express Trail. And they lost only one mailbag.

Newspaper ads for Express riders did not mince words: "WANTED – Young, skinny, wiry fellows not over 18. Must be expert riders willing to risk death daily. Orphans preferred." Eighty riders, almost all weighing less than 125 pounds (57kg), were hired initially, including a fatherless 15-year-old named William F. Cody, later known as Buffalo Bill. The pay was attractive, at least $50 a month, plus free lodging and food. Each rider took an oath, agreeing not to use profane language, not to get drunk, and not to fight with other employees. Each horseman also received a copy of the Bible, plus two Colt revolvers, a knife, and a carbine. The journey took 10 days each way.

of the physical universe as an important chapter in the life of the mind.

Lewis and Clark did not disappoint Jefferson. Their voluminous journals provided detailed descriptions of what eventually became the Oregon Trail. Perhaps what is remembered most from sampling their writings are the descriptions of the geology, fauna, and wildlife of the West. Their wide range of learning, courage displayed in the face of physical deprivation, and eloquence are inspiring. Lewis and Clark prepared the way for the invasion of the West that is still in progress today.

In the 1840s, the journalist John O'Sullivan

ley at Fort Sumter to reach San Francisco, but, by the end of the war, the nation was forging the bonds of union. The age of the turnpike, steamboat, and canal had been overtaken by the iron horse; it is widely conceded that the North's superior transportation system played a crucial role in crushing the Southern rebels. In 1863, the

> *Thomas Jefferson thought it would take close to a thousand years to settle the lands west of the Mississippi River; he was mistaken by more than 900 years.*

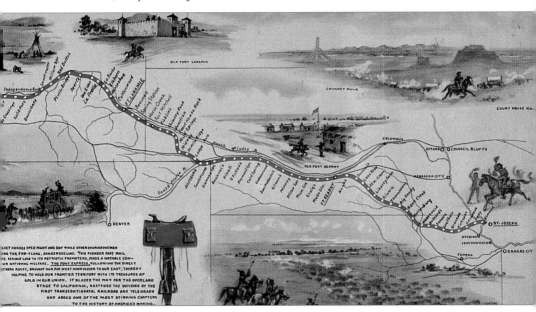

LEFT AND ABOVE: the Pony Express lasted only 18 months, but inspired countless stories.

popularized the phrase "manifest destiny" to describe a widespread expansionist ideology.

Western politicians such as Stephen Douglas based their political fortunes on promoting the future greatness of the West as the ultimate destination and demanded the construction of a transcontinental railroad in order to link the nation's rapidly expanding economy.

Age of the iron horse

Before the Union could be linked by rail, the United States was plunged into the Civil War. It took four weeks for the news of the opening vol-

North was able to transport 25,000 troops by rail from Washington, DC, to Chatanooga, Tennessee, to turn the tide in a major battle.

Mark Twain and Charles Dudley Warner dubbed the final third of the 19th century "the Gilded Age," an era of conspicuous consumption and corruption. Perhaps the age might better be thought of as being the age of the railroad. The railroad barons – the Goulds, Huntingtons, and Vanderbilts – all understood that the railroad was the lubricant of both a booming economy and sleazy politics.

The railroad also made long-distance travel for pleasure a realistic possibility for middle-class Americans. The creation of the Pullman Palace Car Company in 1868 reflected the growing number of Americans interested in taking vacations. Although a period of rest and relaxation did not sit well with those devoted to work, so publicists for the new leisure ethic stressed that Americans were growing unhealthy – both physically and spiritually – as a result of their obsession with success. Regeneration through contact with the great outdoors and the vigorous life was a stock promise from popularizers of the West.

In 1893, the year of the Chicago World's Fair, two bicycle mechanics, Charles and J. Frank Duryea, successfully tested the first automobile on the streets of Springfield, Massachusetts, and a new age began.

Car crazy

Public roads were among the initial benefits of the age of the automobile. The movement to upgrade the quality of highways had begun during the 1880s when bicycling organizations led the call for improved roads. When automobiles began to appear in the streets in greater numbers after 1900, the drive for surfaced roads attracted increasing support. In 1916, President Woodrow Wilson signed a Federal Aid Road Act which was the first of a series of occasions when Federal intrusion into the nation's transportation system met with widespread public approval.

The constituency for such governmental action grew larger with each passing decade. And the person who probably deserves the greatest

share of credit for democratizing the automobile and travel is Henry Ford, who introduced to the industry the assembly line, which revolutionized the production and sale of cars; by 1922, he was selling an astonishing 1.3 million Model Ts. The Tin Lizzie had made the automobile a badge of social distinction as well as a necessity.

The impact of the widespread ownership of cars upon travel cannot be overstated. It was probably the single most important factor in the opening of American life not only to travelers seeking remote scenes, but also to 20th-century movers and migrants.

What would the 1930s have been like, after all, if John Steinbeck's literary Tom Joad and his fellow wandering poor could not have climbed into a car and headed for California where, as a Jimmie Rodgers song promised, the "water tastes like cherry wine"? The increased mobility the automobile offered underscores the judgment of George F. Pierson, who in his book *The Moving American* describes this freedom as "the great American permit to be both more free and more equal than our contemporaries could manage to become in the more static societies of Europe."

But the early years of the new millennium brought a challenge to this American dream. The realities of global warming forced people to look hard at the environmental cost of their transient lifestyle. As developing countries followed in America's footsteps, oil production could not keep up with demand. In 2008, when gas prices topped $4 in California, Americans realized that they could no longer take for granted the cheap transportation that they had enjoyed from birth. At the same time, a world economic recession, brought on by severe problems in the financial and housing sectors, brought further pressures on mobility as the nation faced unemployment, plunging house values, and the near collapse of its automotive industry.

As in the past, Americans are rising to the challenge with the production of ethanol blends that mix grain fuels with gasoline, and the exchange of gas-guzzling SUVs for a new breed of cars that can run partly on electricity. Nearly half a million new hybrids hit American roads in 2009. Indeed, a new transportation revolution is under way – in hearts and minds, as well as on the road. ❏

LEFT: gridlock on a New Jersey highway – with paved roads and cheaper cars came traffic jams.
RIGHT: the West is seen as the ultimate destination.

AMERICAN ARTISTS AND THE ROAD

Novelists, poets, musicians, film-makers – the romance of the open road seduces them all

American artists are perpetually on the run. Their work epitomizes the wanderlust of the American people: the belief in movement for movement's sake. "The sound of a jet," John Steinbeck wrote in 1961, "an engine warming up, even the clopping of shod hooves on pavement brings an ancient shudder, the dry mouth and vacant eye, the hot palms and the churn of stomach high up under the rib cage."

A century before Steinbeck, Herman Melville depicted travel as a balm to a depressed soul. "Whenever I find myself growing grim about the mouth," he mused in the famous first paragraph of *Moby Dick*, "whenever it is a damp, drizzly November in my soul; ...whenever my hypos get such an upper hand of me, that it requires a strong moral principle to prevent me from deliberately stepping into the street, and methodically knocking people's hats off – then, I account it high time to get to sea as soon as I can." In the classic American fiction of Melville, Edgar Allan Poe, James Fenimore Cooper, and Mark Twain, we encounter characters fleeing the inertia of polite society for a jaunt into the wild.

A stay against confusion

The great writers of 19th-century America celebrated the movement away from complex modern life. They viewed travel as a "stay against confusion" in a society committed to material gain. Melville, Nathaniel Hawthorne, and Cooper felt alienated from the climate of the times and sought refuge in foreign travel.

LEFT: Marlon Brando as *The Wild One*, one of the first anti-heroes of the silver screen. **RIGHT:** Tom Hanks as *Forrest Gump*, who runs across America and participates in much of its recent history.

Their despair with the democratic masses stands in marked contrast to one of the greatest American poets of the open road, Walt Whitman. A journey along the open highway suited his desire to comprehend the whole of life: the casual meeting, the encounter between the eye of the seer and the landscape and the timelessness of nature. Whitman saw the open road as the passage to wisdom and fraternity.

The very act of traveling is a democratic gesture to the poet, a source of inspiration, and a symbol of his personal liberty. Not only were the "American people the greatest poem," but the American environment itself was an incubator of freedom and unity. As he wrote in his acclaimed "Song of the Open Road:"

I think all heroic deeds were all conceiv'd
in the open air, and all free poems also,
I think I could stop here myself and do miracles,
I think whatever I shall meet
on the road I shall like, and
whoever beholds me shall like me.
I think whoever I see must be happy.

Mark Twain used the voyage as a metaphor for change. In his novel *The Adventures of Huckleberry Finn*, he made it clear that the voyage was a learning experience and a rebellion against conventional morality. Some of the book's most moving passages are Huck's accounts of life on the river.

of the 1960s and 1970s. Kerouac's prose may impress less now, but his celebration of finding spiritual truths while racing across the continent makes the work transcend conventional literary canons.

> 66 *"I wish for a change of place, The hour is come at last, that I must fly from my home and abandon my farm!"*
> J. Hector St John de Crevecoeur,
> *Letters from an American Farmer* 99

Each time Huck and the escaped slave Jim encounter people on shore, trouble, trickery, and cruelty predominate. The book ends with Huck's famous vow to flee civilization and its hypocrisy. But, of course, the old-fashioned frontier was disappearing when Twain was writing in the 1880s, so Huck's dream of flight belonged to a vanishing world. Still, Huck's words at the close of *Huckleberry Finn* bring to mind another characteristic of American literature: loneliness, and the traveler as a solitary figure.

Since World War II, the accelerated pace of travel has produced a literature equally frenetic. The most famous road book has been Jack Kerouac's *On the Road*, the definitive statement of Beat culture and the cultural radicals

Kerouac's work continued the tradition of writer as pathfinder and spiritual voyager, as did Native American writer William Least Heat-Moon's *Blue Highways*. Heat-Moon traversed the nation in his van "ghost dancing." His report is both a rumination on travel literature and a revealing study of the state of the nation. Richard Grant, a British journalist, fell in love with the American nomadic lifestyle. His *Ghost Riders* tells the story of nomads present (in their own words from boxcar slang to cowboy drawl) and past.

Whereas Kerouac filtered experience through his ahistorical frame of mind, Heat-Moon and Grant, by letting people speak for themselves, capture the diversity of the landscape that often overwhelms the trans-American traveler.

Travel continues to be a method by which writers question where we have come and where we are going, whether collectively as a society, as in Dave Gorman's *American Unchained*, or personally, as in Dan Jackson's *Old Bug: The Spiritual Quest of a Skeptical Guy on a Road Trip Across America with a Long Lost Friend in a Beat-Up Beetle*. Both are comic and touching odysseys of self-discovery.

Today, television, which has replaced literature as the medium for the masses, has picked up the tradition and writers have adapted to a visual role. In *Stephen Fry in America*, the writer and comedian traveled across all 50 states to find the

"the lost highway." Cowboys, singing at night to fight off despair and keep cattle from stampeding, often reworked old Irish and English ballads about murder and betrayal. Much of the music produced under such circumstances was often grim and filled with resignation. In the 1940s and 1950s, cowboy singers such as Roy Rogers evoked the nostalgia of the open range for listeners confined by harsh economic circumstances to lives of poverty and loneliness.

Not all country music is downbeat, however. A whole genre of music has arisen devoted to the lives of the modern riders of the open range: truck drivers. These contemporary folk figures

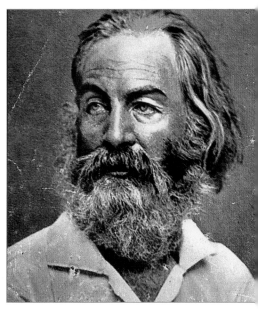

heart and psyche of the nation, while historian Simon Schama took to the road to understand the contemporary political situation in *The American Future*. BBC environmental journalist Justin Rowlatt spent six weeks traveling 6,500 miles (10,400km) across the US on public transportation while reporting on climate change.

Music to their ears

It is not just literary artists who have sung of the loneliness and vagaries of the open road. Country music in particular often focuses on that "lonesome guy" Hank Williams sang about on

*I'm going down that long, lonesome road
And I ain't gonna be treated this a-way.*
Lonesome Road Blues, Bill Monroe

form a loyal audience for country music, and songs like the admired and much-recorded "Six Days on the Road" are pure Walt Whitman-esque whoops of triumph over the law, the cops, and anything that might get in the way.

The theme of the open road extends to rock music and blues as well. Is it any wonder that one of the rock anthems of the 1970s was Bruce

LEFT: Jack Kerouac and Woody Guthrie.
ABOVE: John Steinbeck and Walt Whitman.

Springsteen's "Born to Run"? Ace bluesman Robert Johnson evoked the road as a haunting meeting place. In his highly influential song "Cross Road Blues", the narrator's fear and anguish are clear as he prays at the crossroad for mercy for (so the legend goes) having sold his soul to the devil in exchange for mastery of the guitar.

Surely Woody Guthrie is the "bard of the open road." Even a simple listing of some of his songs – "Dust Bowl Refugees," "I Ain't Got No Home," "Walkin' Down the Railroad Line" – suggests the prominence he assigned to "walkin' down the line." Like Whitman, he attempted to capture the whole of America in the verses of "This Land is Your Land." Guthrie lived the life he wrote about after his family was wrecked by tragedy and disease. His best work is timeless – not surprisingly, many of his tunes borrow heavily from hymns and ballads – and will live as long as there are roads to walk and people to sing.

Sagas of the silver screen

The great road films of Hollywood are the best visual sagas of the open plains. People all over the world think of the United States as a land of wide-open spaces, thanks to the images they receive from the films of directors John Ford and other Western movie-makers. Again we

ON THE ROAD MOVIES

About Schmidt (Alexander Payne, 2002)
Badlands (Terrence Malick, 1973)
Bonnie and Clyde (Arthur Penn, 1967)
Breakdown (Jonathan Mostow, 1997)
Death Proof (Quentin Tarantino, 2007)
Duel (Steven Spielberg, 1971)
Easy Rider (Dennis Hopper, 1969)
Forrest Gump (Robert Zemeckis, 1994)
The Grapes of Wrath (John Ford, 1939)
Joy Ride (John Dahl, 2001)
Little Miss Sunshine (J. Dayton and V. Faris, 2006)
Natural Born Killers (Oliver Stone, 1994)
The Outlaw Josey Wales (Clint Eastwood, 1986)

O Brother, Where Art Thou? (Joel Coen, 2000)
Paris, Texas (Wim Wenders, 1984)
Rain Man (Barry Levinson, 1988)
Sideways (Alexander Payne, 2004)
The Sugarland Express (Steven Spielberg, 1974)
The Searchers (John Ford, 1956)
The Wild One (Laslo Benedek, 1953)
Thelma and Louise (Ridley Scott, 1991)
Transamerica (Duncan Tucker, 2005)
Two Lane Blacktop (Monte Hellman, 1971)
Vanishing Point (Richard C. Sarafian, 1971)
Wild at Heart (David Lynch, 1990)
The Wizard of Oz (Victor Fleming, 1939)

encounter solitary figures in an uncomfortable relationship with polite society. Ready to right wrong wherever they find it, the cowboy must move along in the last reel.

Clint Eastwood's *Pale Rider* attempted to revive this formula in the 1980s, but, since the 1960s, motor-driven outlaws have replaced the cowboy as the stars of road films. From Marlon Brando in the *The Wild One* to Mel Gibson in *The Road Warrior*, films set on the road have focused on wandering antisocial anti-heroes alienated from society. Robert Zemeckis's *Forrest Gump* (1994) added a twist: the main character is too simple to know if he is hero

1969). Those who see the film as a period piece and high camp have no idea how its original viewers saw it. *Rider* was probably the most powerful advertisement for the counter-culture to appear in movie houses throughout the heartland of the nation. To this day, there are middle-aged workers who dream of throwing away their cellphones, mounting a Harley motorcycle, and setting off for Mardi Gras in New Orleans.

Thelma and Louise (Ridley Scott, 1991) updated this story, using cars and women to illustrate the hi-jinks and low life of on-the-road escapism. The final scene, when the women end it all, is in the tradition of the best Westerns of the 1950s.

or anti-hero, or to realize the significance of the events he witnesses.

Bonnie and Clyde (Arthur Penn, 1967) is an example of the perfect tragi-comic road picture. Viewed through the counter-cultural lens of the 1960s, the story of Clyde Barrow and Bonnie Parker seems like a folk tale of the Depression-era 1930s. Bonnie and Clyde rob banks that rob the poor of their dreams and make their getaway to the sound of rebellious country music.

Few films of the recent past inspired more real-life voyages than *Easy Rider* (Dennis Hopper,

LEFT: Dennis Hopper and Peter Fonda hit the open road in *Easy Rider*. **ABOVE:** pursuing a family dream in *Little Miss Sunshine*.

But the public has an appetite for softer films too, which portray the road as an antidote to modern angst. Witness the hit sleepers *Little Miss Sunshine*, which has a dysfunctional family hobbling across the miles in a broken-down VW bus to help a little girl pursue her dream of entering a beauty pageant. Or a man shaking off a midlife crisis in California's wine country in *Sideways*.

The swoop of history follows us down every highway, and the traveler has many teachers to choose from before embarking on an adventure. For William Least Heat-Moon, Walt Whitman served as the model. For Ridley Scott, John Ford was the inspiration. As you head out on the highway, listen to these voices, but be aware that there is no experience like an original one. ❑

ROUTE 66: AMERICA'S MAIN STREET

Quirky motels, mom 'n' pop diners, drive-in movie theaters: in its heyday, many thought this was the most magical road in the world

In 1926, US Highway 66 put down its roots near Lake Michigan at the corner of Michigan Avenue and Jackson Boulevard in Chicago, Illinois. With its catchy double-six road markers, it stretched its 2,448 miles (3,940km) of asphalt and concrete westward through three time zones, across eight states – Illinois, Missouri, Kansas, Oklahoma, Texas, New Mexico, Arizona, and California – to the shores of the Pacific Ocean at Santa Monica. Route 66 was one of the country's first continuous spans of paved highway, linking the eastern part of America with the west.

A stroll on wheels

US Highway 66, with undisputed certainty, reigns as the most storied highway in the United States. A recurring theme in American literature, Route 66 has been the star of more stories, books, songs, movies, and television shows than any other. The road is more popular than Route 1 from Maine to Key West. From the mid-1920s to the mid-1970s, it was more traveled than Highway 101 on the Pacific Coast, and better known than the Pennsylvania Turnpike or the Alcan Highway. And before the advent of the interstate systems, US 66 came closer than any other highway to becoming the National Road. Route 66 was soon known as "the most magical road in all the world." A legend was in the making.

And what a legend it would be. During its glory days, authors, songwriters, and movie moguls all seemed to be headed west on Route

"Hobo" Dick Zimmerman routinely walked Route 66 from California to Michigan, pushing a wheelbarrow, to visit his 101-year-old mother. Dick was 78.

66. Nobody could possibly know how many Americans – from the Dust Bowl famine victims in Oklahoma to the flower children headed for California's Haight Ashbury – would consider Route 66 to be first, and foremost, an invitation for an extended stroll on four wheels.

The nation first became aware of US Highway 66 when the 1928 International Transcontinental

---

LEFT: family outings along Route 66 were common in the 1940s and '50s.

RIGHT: Happy Lou Phillips made headlines by roller-skating from Washington, DC to San Francisco.

Foot Marathon (affectionately known as the Bunion Derby) followed Route 66 from Los Angeles to Chicago, then on to Madison Square Garden in New York, a distance of 3,448 miles (5,548km). The winner was handed $25,000. Andy Payne, a part-Cherokee Indian from Oklahoma, won the purse.

Three decades later, for a fee of $1,500, Peter

> If you ever plan to motor west;
> travel my way, take the highway that's the best.
> Get your kicks on Route Sixty-six!

Another student of perambulating the old highway was "Shopping Cart" Doughtery, who, sporting a white beard and turban, traveled 9 to 16 miles (14 to 26km) a day on Route 66 with all his worldly possessions in a shopping cart. History doesn't tell us the final destination of Doughtery.

Joggers and baton twirlers

In 1972, John Ball, a 45-year-old South African, jogged from California to Chicago on Route 66, and then became a hero on the East Coast. The journey took 54 days.

The Mother Road has also seen its share of

McDonald walked on stilts from New York City to Los Angeles, a distance of 3,200 miles (5,150km). From Chicago to Los Angeles, his way out west was Route 66. Pete was neither the first nor the last to place the road in the public eye – wild, weird, and wondrous celebrants were to follow. Two such celebrities were Happy Lou Phillips and his friend Lucky Jimmy Parker. The pair of intrepid travelers strapped on skates and rolled their way along America's Main Street, as it was called, during their cross-country journey from Washington, DC, to San Francisco. Through the state of Arizona, a newspaper reported, "They walked a great deal, since at that time (1929) Route 66 was only paved through towns."

high school baton twirlers, who have marched along Old 66 setting dubious records.

Route 66 was a highway of flat tires, overheated radiators, motor courts, cars with no air conditioning, tourist traps, treacherous curves, narrow lanes, and detour signs.

In the Roaring Twenties, desperadoes and bootleggers – the likes of John Dillinger, Al Capone, Bugs Moran, Bonnie and Clyde, and Ma Barker and her god-fearing boys – lurched down Old 66, using it as an escape route. Occasionally, the Associated Press warned travelers of the dangers of "the criminally few who mix with the tourist throng."

Route 66 was Burma Shave signs, neon signs, full-service gas stations, mom 'n' pop diners,

blue-plate specials, homemade pies, and waitresses who called everybody "honey," winked at
the kids, and yelled at the cook. Hitchhiking
was safe, and billboards along the highway were
legal. People guzzled Grape Nehi, and summer
lasted longer because of drive-in movies, miniature golf, and slow-pitch softball under the
lights. Motels didn't take reservations. And doc-
tors didn't mind making house calls.

Through good times and hard times, the
highway became a symbol of faith for the
future. Novelist John Steinbeck set the tone of
the highway in his Pulitzer Prize-winning book
The Grapes of Wrath, when he found a nurtur-

different locations throughout her history –
names like the Pontiac Trail, Osage Indian Trail,
Wire Road, Postal Highway, Grand Canyon
Route, National Old Trails Highway, Ozark
Trail, Will Rogers Highway, and, because it went
through the center of so many towns, the Main
Street of America.

All-night radio

Route 66 was hundreds of locally improved and
maintained lanes going from one town to the
next. In Vega, Texas, a story – probably sprinkled
with a little local folklore – is told of the town's
baseball team. They wanted to play the team in

ing quality in Route 66 and called her "the
mother road." It was the "Road of Second
Chance." To some, like the immigrants of the
Dust Bowl, it was the "Glory Road." To architect
Frank Lloyd Wright, it was the chute of a tilt-
ing continent, on which everything loose
seemed to be sliding into Southern California.
And to travel agencies it was the chosen thoroughfare of the growing numbers of discrimi-
nating American tourists.

Route 66 was to carry a sundry of names at

> *It winds from Chicago to L.A.*
> *More than two thousand miles all the way.*
> *Get your kicks on Route Sixty-six!*

a nearby community but there was no connecting road. So the ambitious folks in this small
Texas town built one. Today, that former deep-
rutted path is said to be part of Route 66.

Route 66 was all-night radio out of Del Rio,
Texas, Continental Trailways, and Greyhound
buses, lemonade stands, family reunions, 25¢
haircuts, and a 5¢ cup of coffee. Kids counted
telephone poles on the road, waved at engineers on trains, slept in a wigwam in Holbrook,

LEFT: whimsical establishments like the Iceberg Café
in Albuquerque, New Mexico, have been demolished.
ABOVE: DJ Wolfman Jack was the voice on the radio
accompanying most long-distance drives.

Burma Shave

Exploiting the potential of a captive audience, the verses along the Mother Road entertained the road-weary and accelerated sales.

The Burma Shave company was founded by an imaginative insurance salesman to provide a speedy, brushless shave for the businessman on the go. Clinton Odell, father of the company's former CEO, collaborated with pharmacist Carl

Tho tough
And rough
From wind and wave
Your cheek
Grows sleek with
Burma-Shave

Faces are the most enthusiastic Burma-Shave fans there are. When your face discovers how good Burma-Shave makes it feel, it will say, "Boss, I want to be Burma-Shaved every day—like millions of other lucky faces are!"

IN TUBE OR JAR AT ALL DRUG COUNTERS

Noren to produce an item that became one of the most famous in America by virtue of being seen along every highway.

"By the start of the year we were getting the first repeat orders in the history of the company – all from druggists serving people who traveled these roads," Odell told Frank Rowsome, Jr, who wrote the history of the company.

Does Your Husband/Misbehave/Grunt and Grumble/Rant and Rave/Shoot the Brute Some/ Burma Shave was one of the earliest signs, its lines spaced 100 paces apart – like most of the thousands that followed. In his book, *The Verse by the Side of the Road*, Rowsome explained that, traveling at 35mph, the sequence took 18 seconds to read – "far more time and attention than a news-

paper or magazine advertiser could reasonably expect from the casual viewer." Alexander Woollcott maintained that it was as difficult to read a single sign as it was to eat one salted peanut.

In those early days, rival advertisers soon became jealous. Many of them had been spending thousands on marketing their product, only to see a perky upstart impress its name on the consumer in a way that was remembered long after the signs ceased to exist. Sensing their annoyance, the signs cheekily responded by rubbing it in: *Let's Give the/Clerk a Hand/Who Never/Palms Off/Another Brand*. Burma Shave also knew how to needle the latest electric competition: *A Silky Cheek/Shaved Smooth/And Clean/Is Not Obtained/With a Mowing Machine*.

There were once 35,000 Burma Shave signs, but by 1963 they were removed. By this time, they were costing the company almost a quarter of a million dollars a year and clearly were having a diminishing effect on sales.

"The commercial fortunes of the Burma-Vita Company can be read like tea leaves in the jingles themselves," wrote Rowsome. There were many reasons for the downturn in sales: people were driving too fast, superhighway rights of way frequently banned commercial signs, and possibly people were becoming too sophisticated to regard them as anything more than corny relics.

Most people were sad to see the Burma Shave signs disappear, as their growing insignificance proved to be just one more nail in the coffin of the vibrant Mother Road. As early as 1930, the company had been spending $65,000 a year (prompting $3 million in annual sales), but it was not only passing drivers that enjoyed them: friendly relations had been established with hundreds of farmers on whose land the red-and-white signs appeared. Although rentals rarely topped $25 per year, many farmers were so proud of the signs that they made their own repairs when necessary. Incidentally, horses found them to be perfect back-scratchers – until the company got wise and raised the height of the signs.

There was never a chance that Burma Shave would run out of slogans. An annual contest offering $100 for each jingle used drew more than 50,000 entries. These would be whittled down to the best 1,000 stanzas. Of course, there were thousands of entries that were not considered "appropriate" and hence never used: *Listen, Birds/These Signs Cost Money/So Roost a While/But Don't Get Funny*. ❏

LEFT: Burma Shave verses appreared in magazine advertisements as well as along US highways.

Arizona, and signs in New Mexico promised "Tucumcari Tonight."

"Route 66," Bobby Troup's hit song of 1946, became a highway national anthem. Originally crooned by Nat "King" Cole, the simple tune went on to be immortalized by Bing Crosby, Chuck Berry, The Rolling Stones, and a host of other recording artists – at last count over 100 of them. Nothing captured America's love affair with the road more than this song.

It celebrated the end of World War II, and the end of gas and food rationing. The lyrics invited Americans to get their kicks on Route 66, and millions of motoring adventurers, addicted to

through state maps and plotted a course on the road to adventure – Route 66.

Mom wrote "Wish you were here" messages on picture postcards. The kids bought rich, gooey Pecan Log Rolls at Stuckey's Candy Shoppe while Dad filled the gas tank at 17¢ a gallon and bought the entire family sticky, orange-flavored Popsicles out of the freezer.

The toll fare at the Chain of Rocks Bridge over the mighty Mississippi River was 35¢ per automobile, and brightly colored signs on the outskirts of St Louis, Missouri advertised "the Greatest Show under the Earth" at the nearby Merimac Caverns.

the smell of gasoline and the drone of rubber on the pavement, took Bobby's suggestion to heart.

Itchy feet

Americans with itchy feet were ready to hit the road. They removed the musty canvas that had covered and protected the Plymouth ragtop and the Oldsmobile Woody since the outbreak of the war. And although the cars had been stored on blocks, folks replaced the prewar tires with a set of six-ply Allstate clinchers at a total cost of $43.80. Vacationers shined up their new postwar sedans and thumbed

ABOVE: the 1960s weekly series sold more Corvette sports cars than any TV commercial.

The 1950s saw Route 66 reach genuine celebrity status. Families could leave their homes in the East and Midwest and drive to the Painted Desert or Grand Canyon. They could drive all the way to the Pacific Ocean on a highway that passed through towns where the young outlaw Jesse James robbed banks, where Abraham Lincoln practiced law, and cross the great river Mark Twain wrote about. Tourists could see snake pits and caged wild critters and mysterious caverns and real-life cowboys and Indians, and visit Mickey's Magic Kingdom in Disneyland, California.

Route 66 reached even greater popularity when a nomadic pot-boiler of a book by the same name as the highway became a hit TV show during 1960–64. *route 66* (yes, the "r" was not capitalized in the show title) was the story of two young adventurers, Buz (George Maharis) and Tod (Martin Milner), getting their kicks on Route 66 in a Corvette. Among its 116 episodes, few were actually filmed on Route 66. Sponsored in part by Chevrolet, the show itself inspired more Corvette sales than any TV commercial, and established the Vette as an American icon.

When the Federal Highway Act of 1956 called for the construction of interstate systems throughout the United States, it looked as if the bright lights of fame and fortune that had shone on Route 66 for so many years were beginning to dim.

Little by little, here and there, pieces of Route 66 were replaced by the interstate. Bypassing of the towns that the fabled highway served was a task that took five different superhighways to achieve – Interstate 55 from Chicago to St Louis, Interstate 44 from St Louis to Oklahoma City, Interstate 40 from Oklahoma City to Barstow, Interstate 15 from Barstow to San Bernardino, and Interstate 10 from San Bernardino to Santa Monica.

The last stretch of Route 66 was bypassed in 1984 at Williams, Arizona, when the old highway was replaced by Interstate 40. There was a ceremony, almost a wake. The late Bobby Troup was there to give a speech. As tears streamed from his eyes, he called the occasion "a very sad day."

Wurlitzer jukeboxes

In 1985, US Highway 66 was decertified, giving way to superhighways of diesel fumes and fast-food chains. Because the road is no longer classified as a federal highway, some folks will tell you the road is no longer there. For a while, the route that symbolized America's love affair with the open road seemed destined to live on only in memories and museums.

But progress does not necessarily conquer all. Beyond the endless blandness of the interstates, there is a powerful rhythm in an old two-lane highway that still rises and twists and turns across rolling hills, the mountains, and the deserts. Slowing through quiet towns, then rushing on and up again to the next ridge, you'll find the road waiting to be discovered in each of the eight Route 66 states.

Because Route 66 is no longer marked on most roadmaps, many sections of the old road are often hard to find. But what modern development takes away with one hand it can give back with another. Log on to the website www. historic66.com, and you'll find a turn-by-turn route description of old Route 66 through every state.

In rural areas you may come across abandoned and decaying remnants that pay an evocative tribute to the heyday of Route 66. Elsewhere, however, cafés and roadside attractions have been revived, restored, and reopened. Vintage Wurlitzer jukeboxes blare out old road songs. Folks in classic cars cruise into a drive-in for a hamburger and shake. Service station attendants offer to check under the hood and wash the windshield. Family-owned restaurants serve homemade pie, and a waitress in a starched pink uniform still calls you "Hon!" and yells at the cook. The old road still beckons pilgrims not only from across the US, but from nearly every compass point of the world.

With the car open to the wind, and an AM station riddled with static from a thunderstorm on the horizon, memories flicker in the sweetness of the moment. The miles themselves dissolve every question except the one that matters. What lies waiting, there, just over the next rise of Route 66? ❑

LEFT: vintage Wurlitzer jukeboxes keep the romance of the open road alive in diners along the Mother Road. **RIGHT:** pit stop for a little red Corvette in Santa Rosa, New Mexico.

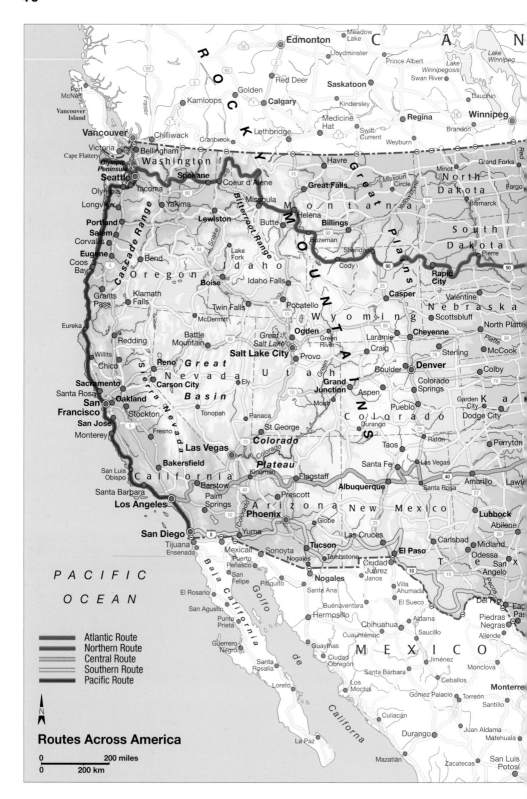

Routes Across America

Atlantic Route
Northern Route
Central Route
Southern Route
Pacific Route

0   200 miles
0   200 km

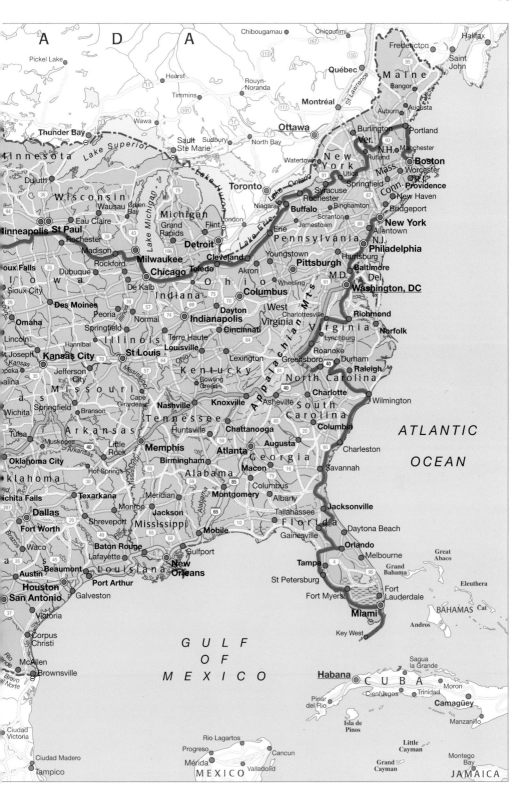

THE ATLANTIC ROUTE

A detailed guide to the attractions of the eastern seaboard, with principal sites cross-referenced by number to the maps

The systematic colonization by the British of America's East Coast was only accomplished once settlers had learned to use its waterways: the Atlantic coastline's bays, the long rivers running out of the Appalachian Mountains and the languid tidal inlets so vital to inland transport in the flat but densely foliated southern states. It was at the mouths of rivers and ports that virtually every important Eastern city sprang up.

Appropriately, then, our route south will rarely stray very far from water. Beginning in New York City, undisputed king of America's cities, we will then pass through a close succession of two more important cities, each with its own distinct personality: Philadelphia, cradle of American independence, and Baltimore, originally a fishing town and one still largely dependent on port activities.

From there, we will move inland to make two exceptionally scenic drives in Virginia, passing at last into North Carolina and examining one of the South's most pleasant states. We will cut east through tobacco fields to the coastline and ride along water once again through South Carolina and Georgia, each time stopping to linger over a beautiful old city or a small, half-forgotten town.

Once in Florida, the weather – and the temperature of the water – will turn steadily warmer as we zigzag south from the nation's oldest settlement, St Augustine on the Atlantic Ocean, to Orlando's lakes, Tampa's mild Gulf of Mexico waters, and past the edge of south Florida to the vast (and moist) natural area known as the Everglades. At long last, we will emerge at the Atlantic coast once more, skimming past Miami and its attached beaches – in order to come back later – to continue on to the Florida Keys, a place where water is more influential and obvious than it is anywhere else, probably, in North America. ❏

PRECEDING PAGES: motorbikes on a Nevada highway; moving house near Santa Fe; the Golden Gate Bridge. **LEFT:** the Blue Ridge Parkway. **TOP RIGHT:** Baltimore Harbor. **ABOVE LEFT:** row houses, Baltimore. **ABOVE RIGHT:** sunbathing in Key West.

A SHORT STAY IN NEW YORK CITY

New York is the city that never sleeps; it has energy and confusion, culture and great charm. Here's a list of the not-to-be-missed attractions:

- Central Park, stretching from 59th to 110th streets, hosts ice skating in winter and outdoor concerts in summer. You can hire a boat on its lake.

- The Art Deco spire of the 1930 Chrysler Building, at 42nd Street and Lexington Avenue, rises 1,046ft (319 meters) like a stainless-steel rocket powered by gargoyles.

- The Ellis Island Immigration Museum provides a visual history of the port that 40 percent of all Americans can trace their roots to, and documents the migration from the world to the United States.

ABOVE AND BELOW CENTER: Panorama of the City. Zoom up to the 102nd-floor observation deck of the Empire State Building for the panorama of Manhattan. The view never fails to impress.

- New York's Museum of Modern Art (MoMA), on West 53rd Street, houses over 150,000 individual pieces of art. Founded in 1929, the world-class institution almost doubled in size between 2002 and 2004.

- Famous for the Rockettes, Radio City Music Hall hosts spectacular music and theater shows. Tours are available during the day.

- Lincoln Center, on the Upper West Side, is home to the New York City Opera, the New York City Ballet, the American Ballet Theater, and the Metropolitan Opera.

- The hub of much of New York City's nightlife, Greenwich Village is still a center for musicians, artists, the eccentric, and the shoppers.

- SoHo and Tribeca, with their art galleries and restaurants, are perfect for Saturday strolling. Chinatown is close by if you're hungry.

- Although its financiers are no longer lords of the universe, Wall Street in historic downtown New York is lined with some notable architecture.

LEFT: Statue of Liberty. Boats from South Ferry take visitors to Liberty Island to view the icon that has greeted immigrants since 1886. Or why not sail by on a sleek 1929 double-master schooner departing from North Cove Marina?

THE BIG APPLE

There is a mix of fantasy and foreignness in New York that is unsurpassed anywhere. You want to have a cocktail on a level with the clouds? Go dancing when the moon is high and the mood overtakes you? Want to go in-line skating, ice skating, or take in that Broadway show? You've come to the right town. New York's skyline is instantly recognizable; its attractions the best in the world. Its cultural life is matched only by its culinary awareness; there are over 15,000 eating places. If there are more ways of making it here, there are also more ways of spending it, so bring a fat wallet and lots of stamina.

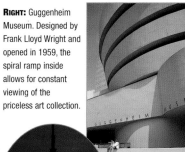

RIGHT: Guggenheim Museum. Designed by Frank Lloyd Wright and opened in 1959, the spiral ramp inside allows for constant viewing of the priceless art collection.

ABOVE RIGHT: Chrysler Building. The Art Deco icon was once the tallest building in the world.

ABOVE LEFT: Chinatown. One of the city's most vibrant areas.

LEFT: Times Square. The bright lights of the renovated square, gateway to Broadway, have made it a tourist magnet once again.

IMPORTANT INFORMATION

Population: 8.3 million
Dialing codes: 212, 646, 347, 718, 917
Website: www.nycgo.com
Tourist information: 810 Seventh Avenue, NY 10019; tel: 212-484-1200

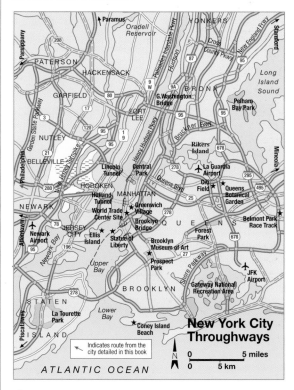

New York City Throughways

NEW YORK TO VIRGINIA

Just beyond the frenzy of New York City lie national historic sites and cities of colonial interest, as well as the green, green hills of Virginia

This first leg of the Atlantic route takes in some of the most historic sites in the United States – places where the Revolutionary and Civil Wars were fought, and where the brash, new nation was conceived. But in order to take this cruise through history, a bit of contemporary, behind-the-wheel negotiation is required first. There are three ways to leave **New York City ①** *(see page 52)* and cross the Hudson River into the neighboring state of New Jersey. Although all – depending on the time of day – can be unnervingly congested (and all charge a toll), the northernmost of these "escapes" from Manhattan is probably also the least unpleasant: across the **George Washington Bridge**. The simplest way to find it, from wherever you are in Manhattan, is to head towards the mighty Hudson until you hit SR 9A (the Henry Hudson Parkway), and head north until it intersects with I-95 and the bridge. If you don't feel like driving north to eventually go south in New Jersey, then your only option is to go *under* the river via the extremely tedious **Lincoln** or **Holland tunnels**, both located more at the southern end of Manhattan.

Whichever way you choose, eventually you'll be steered onto the New Jersey Turnpike (I-95). New Jersey's nickname, the Garden State, seems a cruel joke at first: the early miles reveal nothing more than bleak industrial landscape. Past the factories, ware-houses, and landfills, however, you pass into a more diverse region of some natural beauty and historical significance.

If you've taken the Lincoln Tunnel out of Manhattan, head south on the New Jersey Turnpike. If you have opted for the Holland Tunnel, then head north for a short stretch: your aim is to cut west on I-280 toward the Oranges. Here, the harsh landscape begins to soften. Luxurious greenery replaces the endless drab scrub along the turnpike, and the smoke-belching factories give

Main attractions
NEW YORK CITY
EDISON NATIONAL HISTORIC SITE
PRINCETON
INDEPENDENCE HALL
BALTIMORE
WILLIAMSBURG
MONTICELLO
BLUE RIDGE PARKWAY

LEFT: Mabry Mill near the Blue Ridge Parkway, Virginia.
BELOW: the George Washington Bridge.

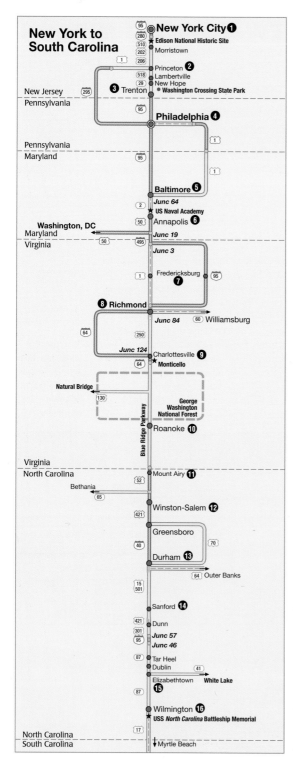

New York to South Carolina

95 · 280 · 510 · 202 — New York City ❶
★ Edison National Historic Site
Morristown

1 · 206
518 — Princeton ❷
29 — Lambertville
New Hope
New Jersey — 295 — ❸ Trenton — Washington Crossing State Park
Pennsylvania
95

Pennsylvania — Philadelphia ❹
1

Pennsylvania
Maryland — 95
1

Baltimore ❺
2 — Junc 64
★ US Naval Academy
Washington, DC — 50 — Annapolis ❻
Maryland — Junc 19
Virginia — 50 · 495 — Junc 3

1 — Fredericksburg — 95 ❼

❽ Richmond
Junc 84 — 60 Williamsburg
64 · 250
Junc 124 — Charlottesville ❾
64 — ★ Monticello

Natural Bridge
130 — George Washington National Forest
Blue Ridge Parkway — Roanoke ❿

Virginia
North Carolina
Bethania — 52 — Mount Airy ⓫
65
Winston-Salem ⓬
421
Greensboro
40 — 70
Durham ⓭
64 Outer Banks
15 · 501
Sanford ⓮
421
Dunn — 301
Junc 57
95 — Junc 46
87 — Tar Heel
Dublin — 41
Elizabethtown — White Lake
87 — ⓯
Wilmington ⓰
★ USS *North Carolina* Battleship Memorial
17
North Carolina
South Carolina — ↓ Myrtle Beach

way to white churches and comfortable middle-class homes.

Edison's experiments

Only 15 minutes out of the Big Apple, small-town life already begins to take the place of the urban crush, and the pace of day-to-day life slows considerably. Get off the freeway at either exit 9 or 10 and head east to connect with Main Street, heading north through the town of **West Orange** past the town hall. You will reach **Glenmont** (tel: 973-736-0550; Fri–Sun, house tours noon–4pm), the 29-room Queen Anne-style mansion in the private residential community of Llewellyn Park that was the home of Thomas Edison (1847–1931), the prolific inventor who created the phonograph and the motion picture camera and revolutionized electric power generation.

Part of the **Edison National Historic Site**, maintained by the National Park Service, the house is half a mile (1km) from Edison's fascinating laboratory complex, sometimes described as "the cradle of American industry" but currently closed for major reconstruction. When it reopens, NPS guides will resume their tours of his historic chemistry lab and the experimental machine shop in which Edison and his associates applied mass production principles to new products. A gorgeous library is on display in the building, lined with thousands of leather-bound volumes in numerous languages.

On the walls hang portraits of Edison, as well as various placards inscribed with sayings of which he was fond: "There is no expedient to which a man will not resort in order to avoid the real labor of thinking" (Sir Joshua Reynolds), and Edison's own famous description of genius as "1 percent inspiration and 99 percent perspiration." Edison supposedly claimed that Reynolds' quotation served as his 1 percent inspiration.

Included on the tour is a walk by a reconstructed version of Black Maria, the world's first film studio, preceded by

a screening of Edison Studios' first feature film, *The Great Train Robbery*, an 11-minute drama produced in 1903. You may well leave the complex filled with a powerful sense of wonder at Edison's artistic vision and technical prowess.

Morristown

Jog south a bit, then turn west onto State 510 through enclaves of great wealth to reach **Morristown**, home to a constellation of Revolutionary War sites. At 230 Morris Street stands the lovely **Jacob Ford Mansion**, the colonial house that General George Washington used as headquarters during the bitter winters of 1777 and 1780.

It is part of the **Morristown National Historical Park** (tel: 973-539-2085; daily). The park includes **Jockey Hollow** (6 miles/10km southwest of Morristown proper in its Fort Nonsense unit), where the Revolutionary army encamped under Washington, and **Wick House**, an 18th-century farmhouse rich with the smell of firewood. On weekends, women and children dressed in colonial garb cook in the kitchen.

Princeton

Head south on US 202 to get more of the country flavor of the Garden State; the road here is verdant and calming. Just after Bridgewater, US 202 continues with a sharp turn to the southwest, but you want to continue due south on US 206. You soon arrive at **Princeton ❷**, home to elegant **Princeton University**. A Gothic architectural style dominates, although there are a few modern structures thrown in for good measure – and you'll also find a fine collection of outdoor sculpture scattered about the grounds. **Nassau Hall**, the oldest building on campus, played host to the Continental Congress in 1783 when mutinous soldiers forced Congress to leave Philadelphia. One-hour campus tours are run year-round, departing from Clio Hall on weekdays and from Frist Campus Center at weekends (www.princeton.edu/main/visiting/tours).

Two American presidents, James Madison and Woodrow Wilson, graduated from Princeton, as did First Lady Michelle Obama.

From here, you've got several options. You can shoot straight down busy US 1

Princeton has one of the most beautiful campuses in the East.

BELOW LEFT: a Princeton graduate. **BELOW:** autumn foliage mirrored in a Morristown, New Jersey lake.

or I-295 to Philadelphia, or – with time on your hands – sidetrack through the lovely **Delaware River Valley**.

To do that, backtrack north up US 206 to State 518, then head west. At the river, you'll pass through quiet **Lambertville** with old inns, antique shops, and a narrow bridge connecting it to **New Hope**, Pennsylvania. Both **Washington Crossing State Park** (tel: 609-737-0623), where General George Washington landed on Christmas Eve in 1776, and the state capital of **Trenton ❸**, where Washington's army captured Hessian soldiers in battle that night, sit directly downriver and can be reached via twisting Route 29. It's a fitting colonial and historical introduction to what awaits in the "City of Brotherly Love" – Philadelphia – just beyond (Route 29 will connect with I-95 just as you get into Trenton; take that south).

Philadelphia

At the time of the American Revolution, **Philadelphia ❹** was the economic and political center of the fledgling United States. During the early years of the Republic, however, the nation's economic heart was transplanted north to New York City while governmental power traveled south to the new city of Washington, DC. This left the city with a bit of an identity crisis. An interesting ethnic mix has sustained the place ever since, however, making it today one of America's most vibrant – and low-profile – large cities.

The nation's fifth most populous city, this is, for tourists and historians – along with Boston – an American city *par excellence*. Film buffs cannot help but feel a swell of emotion, either, when viewing the Art Museum stairs Sylvester Stallone ran up to Bill Conti's soaring score in the 1976 film *Rocky*. Stallone wasn't a local, but his choice of Philly for the *Rocky* screenplay – which sent him to stardom – was apt: this is a gritty, lively, and fascinating place.

Situated at the conjunction of the Schuylkill (pronounced *skoo-kill*) and Delaware rivers, the city was founded in 1682 by the English Quaker William Penn. Penn envisioned a colony in which the right to freedom of religious expression would not be quashed, so it's not surprising that when representatives of the 13 colonies convened to sign the Declaration of Independence on July 4, 1776, they did so here – thereby giving birth to the United States of America.

A nation is born

The best place to start a tour is at the **Independence Visitor Center** (6th and Market streets; tel: 800-537-7676; daily). It has free films about the city's history, computer kiosks with tourist information, costumed interpreters, and a reservation service for many tours and attractions.

It also issues the free tickets necessary between March and December for entry to **Independence Hall** (Chestnut Street between 5th and 6th streets; tel: 215-965-2305; daily), where the Declaration of Independence and the

Constitution were signed. The Assembly Room, which contains the inkstand used by the signers of the Declaration as well as the chair in which George Washington supposedly sat during the drafting of the Constitution, should not be missed.

To the west of Independence Hall is **Congress Hall**, where the US Congress convened between 1790 and 1800 when Philadelphia was briefly the nation's capital. On 6th Street, between Market and Chestnut streets, stands the **Liberty Bell Center**, built in 2003 at a cost of $12.6 million to provide a better space for the ironic icon of freedom and more room for educational exhibitions. Reservations are not necessary, but expect lines at peak times.

On Independence Mall, between Race and Arch streets, is the **National Constitution Center** (tel: 215-409-6600; daily). Using interactive exhibits and live actors, the museum tells the story of the constitution – its creation in early America, its application in history, and its continuing impact on the lives of Americans today.

On Market Street, toward the Delaware River, is **Franklin Court**, site of Ben Franklin's residence. His home no longer exists but is commemorated by an evocative outline of painted white steel beams. Beneath the courtyard, a museum features displays and a film about Franklin's life as an author, traveler, scientist, gastronome, and colonial mover and shaker. **Christ Church**, at Second Street just above Market, was built in 1695 and was the preferred house of worship for the men of the Continental Congress. Plaques mark pews once occupied by George Washington, Ben Franklin, and Betsy Ross. Nearby, **Betsy Ross House** was the place where Ross stitched the new nation's first flag.

High Society

From Independence Hall, wend your way toward South Street via the cobblestone streets and garden paths of **Society Hill**, Philly's original residential district and a place of elegant 300-year-old Federal-style homes.

During the late 1970s, Philadelphia's waterfront – like that of many eastern

Signpost marking an intersection named after two great cities on the Atlantic Route.

BELOW:
National Park Law Enforcement Ranger standing guard at Independence Hall.

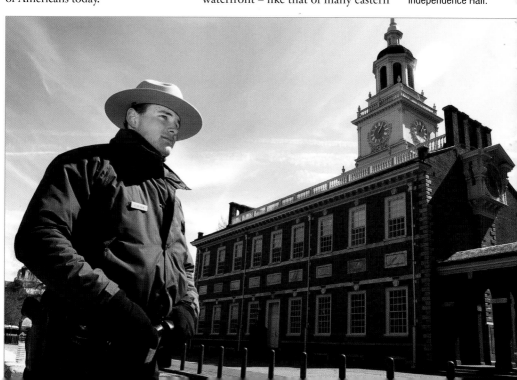

Baltimore: Charm City

Baltimore is a big city with a small-town feel – the home of good food, great baseball, and "The Star Spangled Banner."

The favorite food on most Baltimore tables is the local Maryland blue crab, also found in abundance on the menus of the seafood restaurants of the town's Inner Harbor. At Pier 1, you can tour the historic **USS Constellation** (www.constellation.org; daily 10am–5pm), a 22-gun, three-masted sloop-of-war launched in 1854.

Baseball fans will relish the memorabilia-filled **Babe Ruth Museum** (tel: 410-727-1539; daily) at 216 Emory Street. Ruth, often hailed as the game's greatest ever player, was born in this modest house in 1895.

Afterward, get a look at the bigger picture of the town as seen from the **Top of the World** observation deck, located on the 27th floor of the pentagonal World Trade Center.

Not far away at Pratt Street is the fine **National Aquarium** (tel: 410-576-3800; daily), one of the nation's best, complete with a simulated Amazon rainforest, coral reef display, and 220,000-gallon

(830,000-liter) open ocean tank. Across the harbor in Light Street, the Maryland Science Center (tel: 410-685-5225) has hands-on exhibits on topics such as dinosaurs and space travel.

Fell's Point, Baltimore's first ship-building and maritime center, still has the charm of an old port town. Among the cobbled streets stand more than 350 original Colonial homes, many in perfect condition. Interspersed are old pubs, antique shops, and great places to eat. You can also stroll through the original wooden **Broadway Market**.

The waterfront's best-known attraction is **Fort McHenry** (tel: 410-962-4290; daily). During the war of 1812, this fort withstood a 25-hour bombardment from the British fleet, prompting Francis Scott Key in 1814 to pen the lyrics that in 1931 became America's national anthem, "The Star Spangled Banner."

Mt Vernon Place, designated a National Historic Landmark, features many of Baltimore's oldest and most elegant townhouses, churches, and cultural institutions. At the center of the district stands the **Washington Monument**, the first formal monument to George Washington. Climb the 228 stairs of this 178ft (54-meter) white marble column for another unobstructed view of the city.

Head up Charles Street to Johns Hopkins University, which since the late 19th century has been a major force in medical research. Right next door stands the respected **Baltimore Museum of Art** (tel: 443-573-1700; Wed–Sun), which contains works by Picasso and Matisse, art from Africa, and a beautiful modern sculpture garden. ❑

ABOVE: the National Aquarium overlooks Inner Harbor.
LEFT: Mount Vernon Place.

seaboard cities – underwent considerable rehabilitation. **Penn's Landing**, between Market and Lombard streets along the Delaware River, is where William Penn came ashore in 1682. Today, the area features the **Independence Seaport Museum** (tel: 215-413-8615; daily) – several historic ships moored in the harbor – and views of **Camden**, New Jersey (home to the American poet Walt Whitman), across the river. One block below Lombard at **South Street**, you will find a stimulating array of punk haberdashers as well as chic boutiques.

City Hall, at Broad and Market streets, is the largest municipal building in the US. It was patterned after the Louvre, though it more resembles Paris's Hôtel de Ville. The 37ft (11-meter) -high rooftop statue of William Penn is the tallest atop any building in the world. Until recently, the Philadelphia skyline was capped by an ordinance declaring no structure could exceed the height of Penn's hat.

The **Benjamin Franklin Parkway**, built in the 1920s, was modeled after the Champs-Elysées in Paris. This broad road cuts diagonally through Philly's square grid from City Hall to Fairmount Park. On the parkway at 20th Street, visit the **Franklin Institute** (tel: 215-448-1200; daily), a science museum that is also a memorial to Franklin containing many of his personal possessions. Four floors of science exhibits are sure to amuse and educate all ages. In addition, the **Fels Planetarium** offers several shows daily.

Art in the city

Two blocks away is the **Rodin Museum** (tel: 215-568-6026; Tue–Sun), with an excellent collection of casts and originals by the great French sculptor. Among them is *The Thinker*, one of the world's most beloved statues. At the end of the parkway stands the Rodin Museum's "parent," the **Philadelphia Museum of Art** (tel: 215-763-8100; Tue–Sun), one of the great American art museums. Among the works in its col-

lection are Breughel's *Village Wedding* and Picasso's *Three Musicians*, as well as an extraordinary collection of art and artifacts from the Middle Ages.

After hours spent walking the streets of Philly's historic districts and visiting its museums, the greenery of **Fairmount Park** – the country's largest municipal park – rejuvenates even the most exhausted traveler. In addition to grassy meadows and acres of woodland, the park features a horticultural center, zoo, Japanese house, tea garden, and several historic homes along the banks of the Schuylkill. If you're road-weary, bring a picnic lunch and spend a full day taking in the pleasures of this gorgeous park before taking to the highway again toward **Baltimore** ❺ *(see page 60)*. From Philadelphia, it's no more than an hour's drive down either I-95 or the somewhat quieter US 1 to Maryland: a journey that travels across the Mason-Dixon line which separates, many say, the North from the South.

ON TOWARD VIRGINIA

Leaving Baltimore, take State Route 2 south to Annapolis. As you cross the

TIP

In Baltimore, the Old City Art Association sponsors First Friday. On the first Friday evening of every month, galleries host open houses. The event is followed by First Saturday, when artists, curators, and gallery owners offer workshops, lectures, and other informal get-togethers.

BELOW: Rodin Museum.

Sign on a Civil War battlefield depicting the action.

BELOW:
Confederate flag and Civil War cannon on the Spotsylvania battlefield site.

Severn River, you might well get a view of sailboats crisscrossing a sparkling expanse of water.

Annapolis ❻ sparkles, too, in a way particular to towns built on and sustained by the sea. At dusk, its elegant Georgian houses and winding narrow streets shimmer in the dying light of day. Walking is an easy way to see the town, starting at the top where the **Maryland State House** sits. It was here that the Continental Congress ratified the Treaty of Paris, which officially ended the War of Independence.

Wind your way toward the beautifully preserved 18th-century waterfront to the **US Naval Academy** and its museum at **Preble Hall** (tel: 410-293-2108; daily), with exhibits on maritime life and the history of this venerable institution. You'll be feeling suitably red, white, and blue by the time you climb back into your car and drive the short 30 miles (48km) west along US 50 towards America's capital, **Washington, DC** (*see "Central Route,"* *page 180*). For our purposes on this route, we'll bypass the city using the I-495 loop; take the highway south to connect up with I-95 (or the slower, but more interesting, highway US 1 that runs parallel to it). You are now on your way to the heart of the Confederate South.

Confederate South

Only 52 miles (84km) outside of Washington, DC, and midway between it and the once-opposing capital of Richmond (*see page 63*), it is not surprising that **Fredericksburg ❼** was a major battleground during the Civil War. In fact, with 110,000 casualties occurring during the four major battles fought in the vicinity of the city, it has been said that it is the "bloodiest ground" on the North American continent.

In recognition of the men who died during those battles, in 1927 the US Congress established the 8,400-acre (3,400-hectare) **Fredericksburg and Spotsylvania County Battlefields Memorial National Military Park** (tel: 540-373-6122), the largest military park in the world. The park is located just west of the city on either side of Route 3. Both the Fredericksburg Battlefield and the Chancellorsville

Battlefield have visitor centers that are open daily and feature exhibits and slide programs; historians are also on hand to answer questions.

The park comprises several important historic structures, including **Chatham Manor** (daily), which served as Union headquarters during the battle of Fredericksburg and where Clara Barton and Walt Whitman joined in the efforts to treat hundreds of wounded soldiers. Fredericksburg was also the home of George Washington. **Ferry Farm** (tel: 540-370-0732; daily), where he grew up, is just across the Rappahannock River on Route 3 – it was here that young George allegedly uttered that line, "I cannot tell a lie," and came clean about chopping down a certain cherry tree.

The nation's fifth president, James Monroe, also hailed from here; the **James Monroe Museum and Memorial Library** (tel: 540-654-1043; daily) on Charles Street contains a collection of the personal possessions, furnishings, and papers of Monroe and his wife, Elizabeth.

18th-century tavern life

Today's Fredericksburg still remains rooted in the past, helped along considerably by its large (40-block) **Historic Kenmore** containing not only historic attractions, but antique shops and restaurants. Some buildings, like the elegant **Kenmore Plantation and Gardens** (tel: 540-373-3381; daily) on Washington Avenue, give a taste of how the city's elite lived in bygone days. But everyday life is also represented at places like the **Hugh Mercer Apothecary Shop** (tel: 540-373-3362; daily) – where visitors can hear about how to treat a lady's hysteria – and the **Rising Sun Tavern** (tel: 540-371-1494; daily), which provides an interpretation of 18th-century tavern life. Both are on Charles Street.

Head back down I-95 (or US 1) for another 55 miles (88km) to what locals consider to be the "birthplace of America," **Richmond ❽**. It was here – at pretty **St John's Church** on Broad Street – where the 2nd Virginia Convention was held in 1775, a stirring event that culminated in Patrick Henry's famous "Give Me Liberty, or

James Monroe, president from 1817 to 1825, is remembered today mostly for the Monroe Doctrine, which condemned European meddling in the western hemisphere and became a key element of American foreign policy. But also during his presidency Florida was acquired, Missouri was declared a slave state, and Maine was admitted to the union.

BELOW: demonstrating traditional carpentry methods in Colonial Williamsburg.

Detour – Williamsburg

A 54-mile (87km) drive from Richmond along SR 60 ends at Colonial Williamsburg, which does more than just revive buildings, streets, and gardens: it recreates the everyday life of the nation's infancy. Established in 1633, Williamsburg grew into an outpost of culture, fashion, and festive living. After the state government moved to Richmond in 1780, the city languished until the Rev. W.A.R. Goodwin approached John D. Rockefeller, Jr, in 1926 for funds to save those historic buildings still standing and rebuild others. Using original blueprints and materials, Goodwin resurrected the entire town, from the Congress – where George Mason's Declaration of Rights to the House of Burgesses laid the foundation for the Constitution – to the Raleigh Tavern, where George Washington plotted military strategy in the revolt against Great Britain. Nearly 2,000 "residents" recreate the original Williamsburg community. The blacksmith pounds away at glowing iron as visitors look on; the cabinetmaker carves chair legs while clad in knee breeches and powdered wig; a maid in bonnet and hooped skirt weaves linen at a 200-year-old loom. The baker, the printer, and the glass-blower are all represented, too. For tour information, tel: 757-220-7645.

The Maggie L. Walker House (600 North 2nd Street, Richmond) memorializes the woman who, in 1903, founded the nation's oldest, continuously operated, black-owned bank. Nearby, a statue commemorates Bill "Bojangles" Robinson (1878–1949), the fast-as-lightning local boy who found fame as a tap dancer.

BELOW: the Rotunda, University of Virginia.

Give Me Death" speech. Discovered by British explorers in 1607 and named after a borough of London, the city of Richmond wasn't founded until 1737. Laid out on the fall line of the James River, its location made it a natural center for commerce. By 1779, this more centrally located city had replaced colonial Williamsburg as the capital of Virginia.

Thomas Jefferson designed the striking neoclassical **State Capitol**, which is home to Jean-Antoine Houdon's full-size statue of George Washington, one of America's most valuable pieces of sculpture. During the Civil War, Richmond became the capital of the Confederacy, and about two blocks away from the State Capitol – at 12th and Clay streets in the city's historic **Court End** neighborhood – is the **Museum of the Confederacy** (tel: 804-649-1861; Thur–Tue), consisting of a modern museum and the restored White House of the Confederacy. If it's Civil War artifacts you're interested in, this is the place: it has the world's largest and most comprehensive collection.

Civil War buffs can also fuel their interest in this ever-interesting subject by visiting the **Hollywood Cemetery** on Cherry Street (final resting place of Confederate president Jefferson Davis, US presidents James Monroe and John Tyler, and more than 18,000 Confederate soldiers); **Monument Avenue** (home to – surprise! – a wealth of monuments to various key Civil War figures); and strings of battlefield parks and trails in the area.

Despite its huge historic neighborhoods and attractions, Richmond remains surprisingly untouristy, and also has a pleasant dash of modernity in its skyline and its cosmopolitan atmosphere. The city is renowned for its symphony, opera, and ballet, as well as for the **Virginia Museum of Fine Arts** (tel: 804-340-1400; Wed–Sun) on Grove Avenue.

Land of Jefferson

From Richmond, take I-64 or US 250 west for 74 miles (119km) to **Charlottesville ❾**, site of the University of Virginia and the home of Thomas Jefferson. Although the city now has its fair share of chain restaurants and hotels, it has still managed to retain something of a countrified splendor.

Jefferson designed the original buildings and campus of the **University of Virginia** in the 1820s and claimed, late in life, that it was of this achievement that he was most proud. His architecture is based on European classical style, adapted to local materials such as red brick and painted wood. Daily tours of the university leave from the **Rotunda**, which is modeled after the Roman Pantheon. Looking out from the elevated walkway of the Rotunda, you will see the splendid swath of grass known as "The Lawn," bordered by columned pavilions. Originally, these were the residences of all the students and professors of Jefferson's "academic villages" – now they are inhabited by school officials and top-notch students. **West Range** is on McCormack

Road, where Edgar Allan Poe (1809–49) lived during his unsuccessful undergraduate tenure here. His former room is open to visitors.

Continue down University Avenue to "**The Corner**," a collection of restaurants and shops catering to students, tourists, and local residents, if you want to see the modern-day beneficiaries of Jefferson's dream – a university consistently ranked near the top in lists of public universities in the United States.

Monticello

Even before you arrive at **Monticello** (tel: 434-984-9800; daily), the "little mountain" estate of Thomas Jefferson, you will be familiar with its shape; its image adorns the tail side of the US nickel. This elegant, dome shape is particularly Jeffersonian, for not only does it appear on the Rotunda at the University of Virginia, but also as the roof of the Jefferson Memorial building in Washington, DC. Jefferson designed every aspect of Monticello, and the imprint of his active mind is everywhere apparent.

Try to arrive early, as the wait for the mandatory tour is known to extend up to two hours at midday. The walk takes you through the ground floor of the residence; afterward you're free to wander about the lovely grounds of the mansion. The house's gadgetry is particularly endearing, especially the seven-day clock by the entrance, the double writing machine in Jefferson's study and the dumbwaiter in the dining room. Be sure and ask about the home's extraordinary toilet system. Library walls are lined with leatherbound books, many written by the philosophers of the French Enlightenment who so strongly influenced Jefferson. The former president's grave is visible as you leave the grounds to return to the parking lot.

Jefferson's good friend James Monroe, fifth president of the United States, lived nearby at attractive **Ash Lawn-Highland** (tel: 434-293-9539; daily). Though not nearly as stately as Monticello, Monroe's residence has a friendly charm of its own. As you drive back toward I-64 to continue south, you will pass by **Michie Tavern**, once

Every aspect of Thomas Jefferson's home, Monticello, was designed by the inventive president.

BELOW: derelict car on an East Coast farm.

*The Blue Ridge Park-
way, "America's
Favorite Drive," was
conceived in the
1930s as a Depres-
sion-era public works
project, and driving it
through mountainous
terrain was an engi-
neering challenge
that involved digging
26 tunnels. The last
stretch of parkway
was completed in
1987.*

BELOW: Art Deco
gas station in
Virginia.
RIGHT: star-gazing
in Roanoke.

a pre-Revolutionary watering hole but
now a museum filled with colonial
furniture and artifacts.

The road to Natural Bridge

Take I-64 west to Rockfish Gap, where
the breathtaking 459-mile (739km)
Blue Ridge Parkway begins. Cutting
through the **George Washington
National Forest**, the Parkway – like
its nearby counterpart, the Skyline
Drive *(see page 185)* – was cut into the
side of the Blue Ridge Mountains.
However, as this is not a national park,
you'll note one big difference: this
drive is filled not only with forest and
flowers but also with working farms.
Trees carpet the surrounding mountains, which seem bluer and bluer as
they recede into the distance. If you're
driving alone, don't allow the superb
views to lure your eyes too far from
the road or you'll end up tumbling
over the edge of a cliff.

If you want to experience a ques-
tionable slice of Americana, get off
the Parkway at Mile 61 ("km 98") via
State 130 west to **Natural Bridge** –
and prepare yourself for some of the

crassest come-ons in the whole grand
tour. Billboards blare "See the Natural
Bridge!" and try to lure you into a
wax museum, a haunted house, and a
replica of Stonehenge made from Sty-
rofoam. To get down to the Natural
Bridge, an extraordinary 215ft (66-
meter) high rock formation, you are
forced to pass through a knick-knack
shop as big as a department store,
packed with junky tourist parapher-
nalia. Descend the stairs, walk past
the electronic game room, and begin
the short hike down to the main
attraction.

The Monocan Indians called this
"The Bridge of God," and no doubt
the enormous limestone arch must
have been a place of great wonder in
the past. By the time you arrive there,
however, you may be so queasy from
the overload that it becomes difficult
to conjure up the requisite awe; loudspeakers on high blare recordings of
church bells. Things get even worse
after dark, when a religious film is
projected right onto the stone side of
the bridge.

End of the line

Back on the Parkway, gratefully continue south toward North Carolina.
Below the pretty town of **Roanoke** ❿
(see page 187) the road continues to
climb and dip, winding through attractive farmlands where the hay is gathered and neatly rolled into picturesque
bales. Wooden fences turned silver-gray
by time line the road, keeping the cows
right where they are – grazing languidly in green pastures.

Just before the North Carolina border, the Blue Ridge Parkway ends and
you begin to pass through a stretch of
farmers' markets selling local produce
and religious curios at bargain prices.
The accent of the people is now very
heavy, you will notice, almost incomprehensible to an ear accustomed to
Northerners. If you are beginning to
feel you are entering another country
altogether, you are right. You are entering the Deep South. ❏

NORTH CAROLINA TO SAVANNAH

Pine-scented mountains, sandy beaches, plantation homes, and antebellum cities – the Deep South begins here

New York

Miami

All that remains of the first-known settlement in present-day North Carolina is one word. That word – Croatan – has kept etymologists and philologists busy for centuries, ever since it was found scraped into a tree in the vanished colony of Fort Raleigh on Roanoke Island. Nothing else was left of the "lost colony," which was founded in 1587.

Today, the state is experiencing rapid transformation from a country backwater to a manufacturing and educational power. Jobs and suburbs are sprouting up all along the Interstate 85 corridor, particularly in light industrial trades. Charlotte has become the banking power of the South. And the Raleigh-Durham area contains a very high concentration of quality universities. It's a measure of this success that you can now watch ice hockey in a state where it rarely snows, and professional football, too; both have recently arrived along with the new jobs. Strains of folk and bluegrass music can still be heard in the mountainous Appalachian third of the state, but you've got to hunt a bit for them now.

Weeping willow trees

US 52 takes you over the border from Virginia's Blue Ridge Parkway through trim **Mount Airy ⓫** – birthplace of Carolina hero Andy Griffith, and the model town for his wildly popular classic TV program *Mayberry RFD* – then on down to Winston-Salem (*see page 188*). Take the "King and Tobaccoville" exit and follow the back roads to **Bethania**, a town founded by Moravians who came to the New World to escape religious persecution.

The road is lined with graceful weeping willow trees and leads past fields covered, as you'd expect, with tobacco plants; visit in summer, and they'll be high and big-leafed, but come back in autumn and they'll be a mess of tangled vines burned black.

State 67 east (continue on US 52 if you did not detour to Bethania) leads

Map on page 56

Main attractions
OUTER BANKS
DURHAM
MYRTLE BEACH
PAWLEY'S ISLAND
CHARLESTON
OLD SLAVE MART MUSEUM
BEAUFORT
SAVANNAH

LEFT: family of bears in the Smoky Mountains. **BELOW:** vintage diner table jukebox and a 1932 Ford Model B.

CLOSED
Please Call Again

Winston-Salem man in Moravian costume working with tobacco.

BELOW: an Outer Banks lighthouse.

on to **Winston-Salem** ⑫, home of the R.J. Reynolds tobacco factory, which produces more than 450 million cigarettes daily. The odor of tobacco wafts throughout the town, a constant reminder of the second-largest industry in North Carolina (textiles are first). The Reynolds plant is located, naturally, on Reynolds Boulevard and it's open to visitors during the week. This is also stock-car racing country, an area where many NASCAR greats were reared and still live.

The Salem half of Winston-Salem was founded by Moravians in 1766. The name is derived from the Hebrew word "shalom," meaning peace. In 1913, it was incorporated with its neighbor Winston, and when its old buildings fell into disrepair, a restoration project during the 1930s saved them. The success of this effort can be seen in **Salem Old Town**, which is entered from the Old Salem Road near the center of town. Particularly interesting are the **Mikisch Tobacco Shop**, thought to be the oldest tobacco shop still standing in America; the **Winkler Bakery**, a restored Moravian bakery that produces lovely bread Monday through Saturday; and the **Salem Tavern** with its **Barn and Farm Museum. God's Acre**, a Moravian graveyard nearby, possesses 4,000 graves, many graced with flat marble markers symbolizing the equality of the deceased. (*For more information on Winston-Salem, see page 188.*)

Busy four-lane US 421 leads east through undistinguished country toward growing **Greensboro**, once the home of short story master O. Henry (William Sydney Porter) and long a major producer of textiles; white-collar jobs are now springing up here as well. A Woolworth's store in the central downtown area, now closed, unfortunately, was the site of one of the very first civil rights actions in the South – a sit-in at a soda fountain by local black activists.

Detour – Outer Banks

A leisurely 193-mile (311km) drive along SR 64 from Raleigh leads to the Outer Banks, which emerge like the head of a whale breaching into the Atlantic. Two national seashores, Cape Hatteras and Cape Lookout, preserve 120 miles (190km) of these beaches on Bodie, Hatteras and Ocracoke islands, and Core and Shackleford banks. While most coastal islands lie within 10 miles (16km) of shore, the Outer Banks belong to the realm of the sea; in places, 30 miles (48km) of water separate Hatteras Island from the mainland. The National Seashores of the Outer Banks have personalities unique to the rest of North Carolina. The islands have wide, water-thrashed beaches, while scattered patches of sea oats and beach grasses bind low dunes behind them. Clumps of shrubby marsh elder and bayberry dot the swales. The mainland side of each island hosts extensive tidal marshes of swaying cordgrass. Distinctly patterned lighthouses mark the shores for passing ships, in particular the spiral-painted Cape Hatteras lighthouse. The lighthouse now stands less than 200ft (61 meters) from the shore, although it was built 1,500ft (460 meters) away. For more information, call the Outer Banks Chamber of Commerce on 252-441-8144.

The Research Triangle

Continue along either US 70 or Interstate 40 east to the town of **Durham** ⓭, home of **Duke University**. Along with **Chapel Hill** and **Raleigh**, Durham is part of the Research Triangle, a liberal oasis in the middle of North Carolina which claims to have more Ph.D.s per capita than any other area in the nation. This is also the place to come for top-quality college basketball in winter: North Carolina is a hoops-crazy state, and its Duke Blue Devils, North Carolina Tar Heels, and North Carolina State Wolfpack – all playing in the Triangle – do the state proud. Duke's campus is among the most beautiful in the South, with Gothic and Georgian buildings filling neat quadrangles, and plenty of nice botanical gardens and lawns for picnicking. Figure out a legal place to park, then head for the Duke University Chapel to see the **Benjamin N. Duke Memorial Flentrop Organ**, a 5,000-pipe extravaganza. Walking tours of the university lasting 75 minutes and originating at the Admissions Office are held most afternoons; no booking is needed.

Southern summer evenings

The city is also interesting for its lively mixture of tobacco warehouses and chic restaurants, working-class mill hands and college professors, old Southerners and new Yankee upstarts. **Ninth Street** is the place to go for youth, with plenty of good record shops, bookstores, coffee shops, and eateries.

Also make a point of finding the Durham Bulls' minor-league ballpark, one of the nation's finest and the perfect spot to spend a warm summer evening watching future stars play baseball the way it was meant to be played. Note the outfield bull, which snorts steam when a home run is hit. The Bulls' former ballpark, El Toro Field, was even more authentic – one side consisted of tobacco warehouses, and the steam-snorting bull made its debut here during the filming of the baseball film *Bull Durham* – though the place has lately fallen into disuse; you can still take a look, though, as it is easily walkable from Downtown.

Just to the southwest of Durham, smaller **Chapel Hill** is the home of the

Why is North Carolina known as the Tar Heel state? The prosaic explanation is that workers making tar by burning longleaf pine trees still had the sticky substance on their heels after leaving the woods. The poetic explanation is that, during the Civil War, North Carolina soldiers told a group of retreating troops that they'd put tar on their heels to make them stick in the next battle.

BELOW:
Downtown
Winston-Salem.

A rural mailbox in North Carolina.

BELOW: 1950s stock car, South Carolina.

pleasant **University of North Carolina** campus. UNC is said to have been the first state university chartered in the US. Fans of astronomy will enjoy the **Morehead Planetarium and Science Center** (250 E. Franklin Street; tel: 919-962-1236; for details of shows, visit www.moreheadplanetarium.org).

Toward the coast

Continue along US 15-501 (also known as the Jefferson Davis Highway) south through residential Chapel Hill toward **Sanford ⑭**, where pottery has become a popular cottage industry. At Sanford, change onto US 421, a road lined with fast-food shops, and angle southeast. You are now on the way to Wilmington, principal deep-water port on the North Carolina coast and a refreshing change from this hot and dusty road, where roadside fields are again densely covered with tobacco plants and the occasional weeping willow or algae-covered

pond does little to dispel summer's oppressive heat.

At **Dunn**, turn south on State 301 toward **Fayetteville**. This smaller road runs through farm country, through corn and tobacco fields extending for acres back from the highway. There are innumerable small churches along the road, the majority of which are Baptist; you are truly in the South now.

Use the I-95 to get around Fayetteville, exiting shortly to continue south on State 87, a scenic route to the coast taking you deep into the heart of southeast Carolina. Along the way, you'll pass through the tiny settlements of **Tar Heel** and **Dublin**, but little else of size.

By the time you reach **Elizabethtown ⑮**, you may be so tuckered out from driving that a swim will seem a tantalizing idea. Follow State 41 east to **White Lake**, an oasis in the middle of the Cape Fear region. On the eastern side of the lake is **Goldston's Beach**, a public beach with the requisite tourist shops and thrill rides. The water is warm and soothing, though, and the sandy beach might well prove a haven to muscles weary of driving. The small amusement park nearby has pinball machines from the 1960s and old skee-ball games, which lend an anachronistic air to the place, as though it had been bypassed by 40 years of history. Many of the small towns of the Deep South, you will find, have just this same feeling to them: frozen in another era.

Cape Cod in Carolina

Continue on State 87 to **Wilmington ⑯**, NBA great Michael Jordan's hometown. It's interesting to note that the town's good looks and extremely savvy marketing campaign have created a recent film boom. A number of popular television programs and movies are filmed and produced here in a huge studio lot.

For sightseeing, why not think about visiting the **USS *North Carolina* Battleship Memorial** (tel: 910-

251-5797; daily)? Nicknamed "The Showboat," the ship was commissioned in 1941 and was considered at the time to be the greatest fighting vessel the United States had yet produced. In town, many historic houses are to be seen, among them the **Zebulon Latimer House** at 126 South Third Street and the **Burgwin-Wright House** at Third and Market streets. None appear affected by the high flooding from recent tropical storms and hurricanes.

The Southern grace of Wilmington's finer homes will pique your interest, and prepare you for the even more splendid homes of Charleston and Savannah that lie just to the south.

SOUTH CAROLINA

On December 20, 1860, South Carolina became the first state to secede from the Union. John C. Calhoun's efforts to combat federal laws had not been enough to keep the South's economic and social order – built as it was on the institution of slavery – intact. Knowing its way of life was threatened, South Carolina insisted in 1860 on the right of states to disavow the Federal union. That one step plunged the nation into one of its bloodiest wars: a war with itself.

Even after the Civil War ended in defeat, South Carolina refused to grant the right to vote to its newly freed blacks – a situation that led to the imposition of martial law for a time. This refusal to change with the times kept the state mired in an economic backwater until after World War II, when the state's economy began to switch from an agricultural one to a newly developing industrial base. Textiles, furniture, and chemical industries began to flourish. (Agriculture remains strong, however: this is America's top peach producer and its only producer of tea.)

In succeeding years, the modern industry of tourism also began to gather steam here. Nowhere can this burgeoning industry be better seen – for better and worse – than along the Carolina coast, from Myrtle Beach and the Grand Strand down to Charleston and beyond.

Take US 17 south from Wilmington

Southerners are great storytellers. In Wilmington, ask about the unsolved murder of 1760, which involved a man, a snake ring, and a riderless horse on a rainy night.

BELOW: luxurious houses line the waterfront in Charleston.

Charleston, named America's "best-mannered" city by the late etiquette expert Marjabelle Young Stewart, set up the country's first Livability Court. This is a court of limited jurisdiction which deals with infringements of codes covering the environment, noise, animal control, traffic, and tourism.

BELOW: Myrtle Beach State Park Pier.

into South Carolina, and you will have entered the 55-mile (88km) stretch of beach resort known as the **Grand Strand**. The first oddity you will encounter is the ubiquity of fireworks shops. This is the only East Coast state to have legalized the sale of fireworks, and throughout the area they are big business, hawked perhaps a little too enthusiastically at dozens of roadside stands.

Myrtle Beach ⑰ is the third most popular tourist resort on the East Coast, after Disney World and Atlantic City. The extraordinary commercialization of the area may well overwhelm you, as the grandly named King's Highway (US 17) consists of mile after mile of high-rise condominium developments, miniature golf courses, and honky-tonk shops dispensing the accessories that go with beach culture. The city's **Board-walk**, with amusement parks, fast-food stands, and hordes of tourists, is a typical slice of American beach excess. If you must have excitement, try the Cork-screw, a harrowing roller coaster that turns you upside down at oblique angles and over death-defying humps.

For swimming, you are best advised to eschew the crowded strand at Myrtle Beach in favor of less spoiled beaches to the north or south. **Pawley's Island ⑱** has one particularly beautiful beach where you can enjoy the warm waters and good body-surfing of the Carolina coast minus the throngs and relax in one of the rope hammocks for which the island is famous.

South of Myrtle Beach on US 17, across the Pee Dee River, lies quieter and more genteel **Georgetown ⑲**. An early failed attempt by the Spanish to settle this coast, it today consists mostly of museums, churches, old homes, and plantations. The **Rice Museum** (tel: 843-546-7423; Mon–Sat) gives a look at the crop that sustained this area for much of its early history.

Historic Charleston

South again along US 17, you cross a steep and narrow double set of bridges over the Cooper River before touching down in **Charleston ⑳**. In 1670, English colonists founded Charlest Towne, named after Charles II, on

the Ashley River, 5 miles (8km) from Charleston's present location. This was the first permanent settlement in the Carolinas. After 10 years of battling malaria, heat, flooding, and the Kiawah Indians, they packed up and headed to the peninsula where modern Charleston was built. The prosperity of the city's early days is reflected in elegant 18th-century homes that fill the residential area south of Broad Street. In fact, this is one of America's top walking cities (more compact Savannah, just to the south, is another).

Charleston suffered massive damage when Hurricane Hugo raged onto its shore in September 1989, but fortunately the historic district was spared heavy damage. Amble about the cobbled streets at your leisure, taking in the many museums and monuments here.

Moss-draped walks

The palmetto-lined **Battery** faces Charleston Harbor and is a good place to begin a walking tour of town. In **White Point Gardens**, you can see gorgeous live oak trees with languid Spanish moss hanging from them. At Number 21 East Battery sits the **Edmondston-Alston House**, built around 1828 by a wealthy wharf owner and decorated in Greek Revival style; it offers an unobstructed view of the harbor. Be sure to sit on the "**joggling board**" located behind the house. This board is 16ft (5 meters) long and works as a kind of rocking chair; once thought to have therapeutic properties in the cure of rheumatism, the joggling board is also said to prevent spinsterhood – though scientific studies have never been made to test this theory.

The **Nathaniel Russell House**, at 51 Meeting Street, is also worth a visit – quite elegant, with an impressive flying staircase spiraling unsupported to the top. Both these homes are maintained by the Historic Charleston Foundation (tel: 843-723-1623), a non-profit restoration agency founded in 1947 to protect Downtown's architectural treasures. Informative tours given by

Pineapple-shaped fountain in Waterfront Park, Charleston.

The wedding cake steeple of St Michael's Church, Myrtle Beach.

BELOW: interior of a slave cabin.

the foundation explain the intricacies of design of each home, as well as the histories and customs of the families that have lived in them.

In addition, the Charleston Museum (tel: 843-722-2996; daily) administers guided tours of the very handsome **Heyward-Washington House** (87 Church Street) and the **Joseph Manigault House** (350 Meeting Street), both highly regarded as architectural attractions. The best way to see Charleston's historic homes in one fell swoop is to visit the city during early spring, when the annual Festival of Houses opens many normally private homes to public walking tours. Watch for classic examples of the "Charleston single house" – long, narrow homes with side piazzas and a marked West Indian influence.

Slave market

At the **Old Slave Mart Museum** on Chalmers Street, you can see, among other items, facsimiles of bills of sale used in the slave trade. "A prime gang of 25 negroes accustomed to the culture of Sea Island Cotton and Rice," reads one placard advertising the upcoming sale of 25 human beings into bondage. It is a startling and sobering museum, especially so when one realizes this heinous practice was still in full swing just a century and a half ago. The self-contented opulence south of Broad suddenly appears quite different after a long, thoughtful visit to the slave market.

Charleston is chock-full of historic churches, as well as all its other cultural and social attractions. Two of the more interesting are the **Huguenot Church**, a Gothic structure built by French Protestants, and **St Michael's Episcopal Church** with its 186ft (57-meter) -high steeple. Nearby **Fort Sumter** (tel: 843-883-3123; daily), site of the Confederate attack on Union forces that touched off the Civil War, is accessible from

Charleston Harbor: a 2½-hour tour leaves several times daily from the Municipal Marina.

Plantations aplenty

Three plantations in the vicinity of Charleston are also worth a visit if you have the time. **Magnolia Plantation and Gardens** (tel: 843-571-1266; daily) at 3550 Ashley River Road (State Route 61) has beautiful gardens, a children's petting zoo, an 18th-century herb garden and a 16th-century horticultural maze to lose yourself in. At **Middleton Place** (tel: 843-556-6020; daily), farther up the road, you can see the oldest landscaped gardens in the country – the result of nearly 10 years' labor by 100 slaves. Just north of Charleston on US 17 is **Mount Pleasant**, and the achingly beautiful avenue of live oak trees featured in the movie version of *Gone With the Wind*. At the end of the drive lies **Boone Hall** (1235 Long Point Road; tel 843-884-4371; daily), most people's idea of the perfect antebellum residence. In fact, the house was rebuilt only in 1935, but the nine slave cabins are authentic.

There are house tours, garden tours, and a tram tour of the plantation.

After Charleston, follow US 17 south through the so-called "Low Country" toward the Georgia border. Turn onto State 174 for a ride beneath a canopy of oaks, and in 24 miles (39km) you arrive at **Edisto Island**, a resort community whose commercialism has not yet eliminated its rustic charm. Farther south, turning east onto US 21 from US 17, is **Beaufort** (pronounced *bew-ford*), the second-oldest town in South Carolina and one that's still quite compact and attractive. Hollywood movie producers come calling to use the gorgeous antebellum waterfront homes as set pieces. Indigo and rice cultivation brought wealth during the 18th century, when the majority of these houses (some are inns) were constructed. The best way to experience this town is to wander about, enjoying the friendly talk of residents at any one of the seafood restaurants before moving on south again into Georgia and that beautiful "Southern belle" of a city, **Savannah** ㉑ *(see page 78)*.   ❏

The slave cabins at Boone Hall were built of bricks made on the premises; among several other industries, the plantation had a working brick and tile yard.

BELOW: Magnolia Plantation house and gardens.

Savannah: First City of Georgia

The port of Savannah is a strange, seductive place – equal parts history, treachery, revelry, and oddity.

B est known for its gorgeous, moss-draped live oaks, cobblestone streets, and light, pastel-colored buildings, an air of mystique still hovers over Savannah, Georgia's original settlement.

The saucy, best-selling book *Midnight in the Garden of Good and Evil* made this city a household name, with a corresponding increase in the city's

tourism. Today, a visit is likely to consist of a horse-drawn carriage ride through stately squares, lunch in an outdoor café – and a roaring evening in a gay bar where transvestites waltz across stage. Founding father James Edward Oglethorpe must be turning in his grave.

In 1733, Oglethorpe received a royal charter to establish "the colony of Georgia in America" – and protect the coast from Spanish Florida while producing wine and silk for the Crown. Oglethorpe laid out a grid of broad thoroughfares, punctuated at regular intervals with two dozen spacious public squares. The 20 that remain have been refurbished, forming the nucleus of **Savannah's Historic District** – one of the largest urban national historic landmark districts in the United States, and probably the most beautiful. The district is bounded by the Savannah River to the north and Forsyth Park to the south, covering a 2½-mile (4km) radius in all.

Each square has a distinctive character; Bull Street, running the length of the district north to south, links some of the most beautiful squares to each other. These squares excel in Savannah's most characteristic details: fancy ironwork and atmospheric Spanish moss. They are also enlivened with daily activity – art vendors, hot dog stands, and street performers. Summer brings free jazz concerts to John Square near the river, but early spring is the best time to visit, when the city's azaleas are in full blossom.

The Historic Savannah Foundation has preserved many of the city's treasures. Anyone interested in history or architecture should see the **Owens-Thomas House** (124 Abercorn Street), the **Hamilton-Turner Mansion** at Lafayette Square and the **Cathedral of St John the Baptist**, also by Lafayette Square. One of the nation's most beautiful synagogues is located here. Yet another notable structure is **Juliette Gordon Low's birthplace** at 142 Bull Street, a handsome home that is associated with the founder of the Girl Scouts of America.

Horticulturists should seek out **Trustees' Garden** on East Broad Street, planted in the 1700s as Georgia's first experimental garden; it is now filled with exotic plants from around the world. Afterward, join a jovial crowd upstairs at Hannah's East, where Emma Kelly, a real-life character from the *Midnight* novel, used to play the piano each evening before her death in January 2001.

ABOVE LEFT: tombstone in Bonaventure Cemetery.
LEFT: the grand Forsyth Park fountain.
RIGHT: brightly painted gingerbread row houses.

Several historic buildings in the next few blocks were designed in Regency style by English architect William Jay on his arrival in 1817, most notably the **Alexander Telfair home** (121 Barnard Street) – once the official residence of visiting state governors – and the **William Scarbrough house** (41 West Broad Street), which once hosted President Monroe.

But the most talked-about residence in recent memory is **Mercer Williams House** (429 Bull Street, Monterey Square; www.mercerhouse.com; daily). Built by composer Johnny Mercer's grandfather, it was the home of the late antique dealer Jim Williams, an eccentric millionaire who shot his 22-year-old male companion in 1981. Convicted twice of murder, he was later acquitted; today, his sister occupies the house and conducts lunchtime tours.

For lunch, stop by **The Wilkes' House Dining Room** on Jones Street. Tucked away between stately homes, this Southern-style restaurant serves up fried chicken, bowls overflowing with fresh vegetables, and bottomless glasses of sweet iced tea. Wilkes' round tables comfortably seat 10 to 12 diners at a time; you'll sit elbow-to-elbow with locals and other Savannah fans.

The Historic District's procession of squares ends nicely in beautiful **Forsyth Park**, a 31-acre (13-hectare) setting of constant outdoor activity. At the center of the park stands an elaborate fountain.

Savannah's harborside of old brick warehouses and shipping offices has become a tourist attraction, reached by a series of steep steps; these are now inns, pubs, restaurants, and gift shops that run the length of River Street.

Walking is the best way to see the city, unless the heat is oppressive, in which case the Hyatt Regency Hotel and the **Savannah Visitor Center** (301 Martin Luther King Blvd; tel: 912-944-0455) are your best bets for catching a tour bus. You can choose from a wide selection of transportation, from modern mini-buses to horse-drawn carriages.

Leave Downtown by heading east on Victory Drive in the direction of the coastal islands to visit **Bonaventure Cemetery**, a luxurious final resting place for Savannah's most distinguished citizens. A former plantation, Bonaventure is wistfully beautiful, dripping with moss and overflowing with azaleas, jasmine, magnolias, and live oak trees. The images on several of the gravestones have become synonymous with both the *Midnight* book and the city itself.

Thunderbolt, 6 miles (10km) east of Downtown on US 80, is a shrimping and fishing village on the banks of the Intracoastal Waterway. Continue east along US 80 over a few more bridges to **Skidaway** and **Tybee** islands, where the breeze is as fresh as the seafood in the restaurants alongside the water.   ❏

GEORGIA TO THE FLORIDA KEYS

Small-town ambiance, a tropical paradise, alligators in the Everglades, and the southernmost point in the US highlight the end of the Atlantic Route

The Georgia coast is one of the Southeast's most interesting natural regions, a string of marshes, largely undeveloped islands, and good beaches rarely sought out by the traveler focused solely on getting through the state via Interstate 95 as quickly as possible. No wonder this region is known locally as the Golden Isles. The inattentive traveler's loss, however, has been others' gain: a number of unusual birds live secreted along this coast, and there are also vestiges of African culture from the dark days when slaves were shipped across the Atlantic to work the plantations of the South.

From Savannah, take Victory Drive (US 17) west out of town, where it shortly becomes Ogeechee Road – and also becomes more rural in character. About 25 miles (40km) along, stop in **Midway** ❷ for a look at the small, whitewashed village church, a copy of the original church erected here in the late 1700s by displaced New Englanders. Get its key from the gas station just beside and take a look around, noting the section that was designated specifically for slaves and a gracefully kept cemetery outside. Adjacent to the church stands the small **Midway Museum** (tel: 912-884-5837; Tue–Sun), with a collection of period items.

Small-town life

Past Riceboro, home to an agricultural research station, the highway passes

beneath I-95 again and crosses a bridge over a tidal inlet into McIntosh County. To learn more about the politics, poverty, and small-town intrigue of the county, look for the biting nonfiction book *Praying for Sheetrock*, which won awards for its clear-eyed portrait of local life.

If you make a left just after the bridge onto unnumbered Harris Neck Road, you can find **Harris Neck National Wildlife Refuge**, a pocket of wilderness that was saved from development because a former mili-

LEFT: Naples Florida pier.
BELOW: ripe Georgia peaches at a roadside stand.

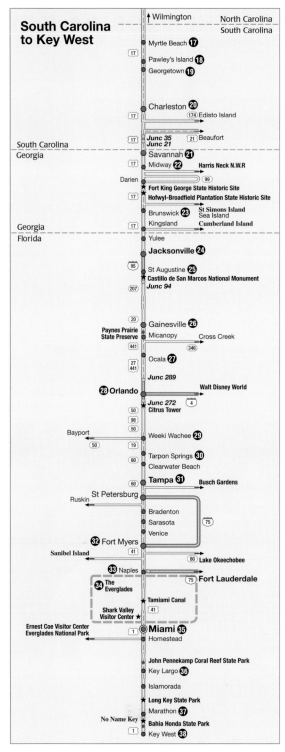

tary airstrip occupied the land. Fishing is the most popular activity here, but you can also drive a one-way dirt loop road for a look at the waterfowl in their natural environs. Just offshore sits St Catherines Island, an off-limits island used by Brooklyn Zoo as a breeding ground for rare birds and animals.

South again on US 17, make a brief detour onto Georgia 99, which reveals some truly old-fashioned towns and dwellings – shacks, mostly, many of them occupied by the modern-day descendants of freed slaves. These small communities – Crescent, Valona, Meridian, Carnigan, and Ridgeville – are fishing and shellfishing communities now.

At **Darien**, rustic Georgia 99 rejoins US 17 again. The **Fort King George State Historic Site** (tel: 912-437-4770; Tue–Sun) here re-creates a Colonial-era blockhouse; this is where the British first settled Georgia and for a brief period administered to the area.

Five miles (8km) south, at the mouth of the Altamaha River, sits the **Hofwyl-Broadfield Plantation** (tel: 912-264-7333; Tue–Sun) – prettifying the story of slavery somewhat as it demonstrates how the know-how of slaves imported from Africa was crucial to the successful cultivation of rice on these islands.

Hold your nose as you enter industrial **Brunswick ㉓**, a major center for paper and chemical production. Despite its industrial character, Brunswick's Downtown is surprisingly slow-paced and old-Southern, with an attractive grid of streets, homes, and moss-draped live oak trees. One such oak tree, the so-called Lover's Oak, is believed to have stood for hundreds – possibly even close to one thousand – years.

The city is also set on a wide, beautiful (if not exactly pure) marsh immortalized by poet Sidney Lanier as the **"Marshes of Glynn"** (for Glynn County). A turnout facing the marshes has information explaining their formation, which provides an opportunity to stretch your legs, take some snapshots, and pick up lots of tourist information.

Lush islands

From the marshes, turn east and cross the toll bridge for a look at lush, though somewhat exclusive, **St Simons Island**. Palm fronds, live oak trees, and flowers cover both sides of the road in perpetual green as you drive through the road to the single attractive harborfront, and you might consider staying the night in these restful environs. A museum in the former lighthouse tells the history of coastal Georgia, and there's a good beach out beyond the main settlement. **Sea Island**, an even more exclusive resort reached via another series of roads on the island, possesses beautiful beaches and a world-class golf course.

South again on US 17, you cross more bridges and then pivot inland through tiny towns. At Kingsland, you can make a turnoff to catch the ferry for elegant **Cumberland Island**, one of the most attractive islands in the Georgia chain. Once the exclusive domain of wealthy families, it is now mostly owned by the US government as a "national seashore," meaning there are a small number of rudimentary campsites available to the public. Spirited jockeying for these few camping spots begins well in advance, however, so don't expect to just waltz in and secure one at the last moment.

FLORIDA

Crossing the St Marys River, a broad watershed that reaches the Okefenokee, you're greeted with a double row of palm trees and, possibly, the presence of police cars: you have reached Florida. The first town you reach is **Yulee**, named for legislator and entrepreneur David Yulee. Mr Yulee built a railroad from coast to Florida coast, and it thrived for a short time, but politics and the Civil War soon did it in and the town is of little consequence today. It isn't very long afterward that the rural roads give way to

sprawl, announcing the outskirts of **Jacksonville** ㉔.

Jacksonville is trying hard to remake itself over as a new urban destination, and corporate headquarters are relocating here to take advantage of the excellent weather and pristine beaches. There are cultural attractions, too – the town is justly proud of its **Riverwalk** and the associated **Museum of Science and History** (tel: 904-396-6674; daily), for example, while the **Cummer Museum of Art and Gardens** (tel: 904-356-6857; Tue–Sun except holidays) stands amid lush gardens right on the St Johns River.

Chances are, you'll want to keep going: move on southward on I-95 to the indisputable jewel of northern Florida, a town small enough to explore in a day: **St Augustine** ㉕. This town, founded by Spanish explorers in 1565 and later occupied by the British, lays claim to being America's oldest continuously occupied city. Most of Downtown's buildings aren't nearly so ancient, but a pleasantly Mediterranean atmosphere has been preserved

Taking it easy on a Georgia beach.

BELOW: salt marshes edging St Simons Island.

Orlando: The World's Best Playground

Not long ago, Orlando was just another agricultural town. Now it's Florida's best success story, a transformation made possible by a cartoon mouse.

Orlando's best known, best loved, and best reviled attraction is just southwest of the city. Walt Disney World (tel: 407-934-7639; daily), with its four enormous complexes of entertainments, is thronged year-round by American and international tourists alike, and similar parks have sprung up around the globe.

The **Magic Kingdom** is Mickey Mouse's domain and the original facility. It still remains the most popular with visitors of all ages, and is divided into four distinctive theme areas – Tomorrowland, Adventureland, Fantasyland, and Frontierland.

Introduced by a glittering "geospherical" dome, the Future World exhibits at **Epcot Center**, the second part of the Disney complex, provide an invigorating look at science past, present, and future. The other half of EPCOT is its World Showcase, where you can "travel the world" in less than a day through a variety of cultural (and culinary) attractions.

Rides and tours in the **Disney-MGM Studios** portion of the Disney World experience give a closer look at "show business," with perspectives as seen from both sides of the cameras. Disney's Animal Kingdom, the most recent addition to the Mickey Mouse empire, invites visitors to explore the world

ABOVE: Mickey's Magic Kingdom.
RIGHT: Disney's Typhoon Lagoon Water Park.

of animals on a safari, in a prehistoric world and at special stage shows held throughout the day.

Not far from Disney World – but a completely separate entity – is **Universal Orlando Resort** (tel: 407-363-8000; daily). Opened the same year as Disney-MGM's facility, this attraction offers a similar experience: a chance to learn more about live television and film production, with a number of exciting movie-themed rides thrown in as well. Look for the spotlights just west of Interstate 4.

There are dozens of similar amusements scattered about the greater Orlando area. Water slides, weird museums, and amusement park rides are especially prevalent, and kids will go crazy with joy as parents just go crazy.

The most intriguing non-Disney non-movie-related non-theme-park attraction nearby isn't within the city limits at all, but is worth traveling the few extra miles to see. About 40 miles (64km) to the east, on a sandy stretch known as Cape Canaveral, the **Kennedy Space Center** (tel: 321-452-2121; daily) provides a fascinating up-close look at the workings of America's space program, and the Astronauts' Hall of Fame. If you're lucky, your visit will coincide with a space shuttle or rocket launch. When it doesn't, you can still tour the same runways, training areas, assembly buildings, and launch pads that NASA uses to prepare the crafts – and their crews – for flight. ❑

with narrow alleys, flowers, shops, and Spanish architecture. A number of museums and attractions compete for the traveler's attention – some boasting rather dubious "oldest this" or "oldest that" claims – and there's also a good set of beaches and state parks just across the Lions Bridge, which can be crossed from the center of town.

Not to miss is the star-shaped **Castillo de San Marcos** fort (tel: 904-829-6506; daily), right on the water, which defended the Spanish town from invaders. Nearby, **The Spanish Quarter** interprets 18th-century Spanish life with blacksmiths, woodworkers, and the like. A series of buildings constructed by oil and railroad magnate Henry Flagler is notable, particularly the **Memorial Presbyterian Church** that Flagler built as a memorial to his daughter. Finally, note the huge round **zero milestone** across the road from the visitors' center: this stone marks the endpoint in a string of Spanish missions that once stretched all the way to San Diego.

Sweet potatoes and greens

From St Augustine, head southwest out of town on Florida 207, passing beneath the interstate and then through fields of sweet potatoes, cabbages, and greens – you are back in deep-Southern farm country – across the broad St Johns River the highway becomes Florida 20. The route passes Newnans Lake, a beautiful spot to stop for a picnic, and comes directly into **Gainesville ㉖**, home to the University of Florida. As a result, there are gardens and nature trails, not to mention a good choice of restaurants and cultural offerings, within city limits.

US 441 exits the city south, shortly cutting right through the middle of **Paynes Prairie State Preserve** (tel: 352-466-3397; daily), a huge expanse of marsh and grassland bridged by the four-lane highway. Though located here in Florida, it aims to preserve some of the great plains species that once thrived in the wild, untamed west.

Home to rare bison and cranes, among other creatures, the park offers glimpses of this lost world either through the viewing tower or from regular park-sponsored tours. Just south is tiny **Micanopy**, a town of dirt roads and simple buildings – an anomaly, something like how the old Florida must have looked.

For an even closer look at the state's recent past, take State Route 346 a few miles east, then follow signs south along Route 325 for a look at **Cross Creek** – a tiny town, not even a town, really, but rather a place strongly identified with Florida author Marjorie Kinnan Rawlings. You can tour Rawlings' former home (tel: 352-466-3672; daily), where she penned her most famous work, *The Yearling*, and endured a tough life of farming and ranching, then dine, if you like, in an incongruously fine upscale restaurant on the premises. Highway 441 continues south through horse country to **Ocala ㉗**, a small Southern market town with a town square and old-fashioned eateries. From Ocala, US 441 gets busy and inches through quiet

Shady porch on a rural Georgia log house.

BELOW:
Castillo de San Marcos, St Augustine, Florida.

Marmalade from local oranges makes a great gift.

BELOW: locally caught sponges for sale, Tarpon Springs.

lake towns, lush citrus groves, and sharp-smelling juice-processing plants. Soon enough, you enter the extensive suburbs announcing the most improbable Florida success story of all, **Orlando ㉘** (*see page 84*).

SOUTH FLORIDA

The vast majority of those travelers heading out from Orlando use the interstates and toll roads, but for more of the real Florida take the state highways a bit longer. Robert Frost's "Road Less Travelled" applies well here. Get off the beaten path (in this case the paved four-lane highway) and you'll see small-town life that hasn't changed for decades. Florida 50 (also called West Colonial Drive) leaves Orlando's city center and cuts due west, shedding the suburbs. In about 15 miles (24km), you come to Clermont, singular for its drab but undeniably tall **Citrus Tower** – you can pay to ride an elevator 23 stories to the top if you fancy a view of the surrounding lakes and hills. Though eclipsed now by far more famous theme parks, the humble Citrus Tower was one of Florida's first tourist attractions.

Florida 50 now passes through the limestone spine of central Florida – a land of scrubby trees and prickly plants, sand dunes, citrus groves heavy with fruit in mid-winter, golf courses, even cowboys working cattle herds. Back-road stands sell everything from bovine medicine to boiled peanuts, and you'll also see a surprising number of adult video stores, and plenty of churches in all the various denominations.

The route continues west, brushing the edge of Withlacoochee State Forest (tel: 352-754-6896; Mon–Fri except holidays) before arriving at whimsically named **Weeki Wachee ㉙**, a town famous with tourists for its natural warm-water spring – and the water park, cruise facility, zoo, and other attractions that have "sprung" up around it. It all requires a certain sense of humor and tolerance for excess to enjoy properly.

If you're in a hurry to get a glimpse of the **Gulf of Mexico**, press west a few additional miles to tiny **Bayport** with its picnic area overlooking the water. Otherwise, turn south down US 19 and prepare for a spell of thick four-lane traffic and plenty of stoplights. Bring your baseball cap – during early spring, this area is home to the training grounds for a number of major league baseball teams.

It's 30 miles (48km) down US 19 to the junction with Alt-19. Take Alt-19 to **Tarpon Springs ㉚**, a harbor community that is fascinating not for its physical appearance but its population: the town is largely Greek. Greeks originally settled this area to dive for the sponges that live abundantly in the warm surrounding seas, and today local shops and restaurants continue to reflect this heritage.

Past Dunedin, take Florida 60 west across the causeway to **Clearwater Beach**, a relaxed town of seafood restaurants and beach homes. It's a fine place to swim in warm water and lie on the beautiful – and public – white sand beaches. The best ones are further south.

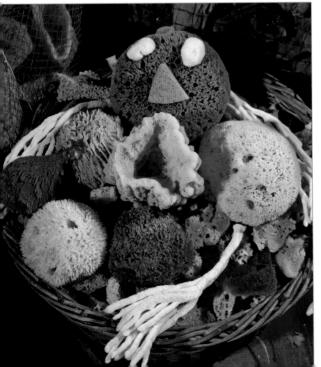

Turn south down the beach road (which eventually becomes Florida 699), crossing several short toll bridges linking the various sandbars. You will pass through more waterfront towns, most with excellent sand but some too overdeveloped for their own good. The finest beach on the entire string is probably the southernmost one, **Passe-a-Grille Beach**, some 20 miles (32km) of slow driving onward from Clearwater. Gawk at the huge and expensive pink **Don Cesar Hotel** (tel: 727-360-1881), an Art Deco masterpiece right beside the blue Gulf waters, then hit the sand.

In central downtown St Petersburg on Third Street you will find the **Salvador Dalí Museum** (tel: 727-823-3767; Mon–Sun), which displays dozens of the artist's paintings – without question the central cultural attraction of the city. East across Tampa Bay via either I-275 or US 92, and set right on the water facing St Pete, is **Tampa ③**. This city's Cuban influence is nowhere clearer than in **Ybor City**, with its concentration of Cuban diners and atmospheric cigar manufacturers. Ybor City was built on empty scrub by a local cigar maker in the late 1800s; now it still retains the Spanish influence, but also sports posh pubs and some hot nightlife, and often hosts movie festivals and other cultural events.

Be a little bit careful here if you come after dark, but that doesn't mean you shouldn't venture out for a taste of what this city has to offer. Other city attractions include a full February slate of events, kicked off by a wild Mardi Gras-like parade, and Tampa Bay itself – best viewed during a stroll along the sidewalk arcing around upscale Bayshore Boulevard, or by zipping over the stunning Sunshine Skyway, a long suspension bridge that spans this beautiful body of water.

Frolicking manatees

Most visitors to Tampa also make a visit to **Busch Gardens** (tel: 888-800-5447; daily), the area's "other" famous theme park, which will appeal to anyone who likes those sorts of things. The park features heart-dropping roller coasters, water slides, and simulated rapids, not to mention world-famous performances of water ballet, waterskiing skills, and the like.

Take US 41 south out of Tampa, stopping a moment outside **Ruskin** where the Little Manatee River empties into the bay. As you'd expect from the name, you can sometimes find manatees frolicking at this inlet in winter, when they swim here to enjoy the warm water. In winter it's not uncommon to see dozens of them clustering around the outflow.

US 41 plunges due south through strings of heavily built-up towns and cities, many catering to elderly retirees. A much faster route would take the parallel Interstate 75.

Bradenton and **Sarasota** are next, twin cities on the Gulf of Mexico, offering very favorable weather, spring baseball and more good sandy beaches with warm ocean water. The beaches continue, in fact, through Siesta Key and Casey Key to **Venice**

Some of the world's best sportfishing happens here, in and around the network of shallow coves and lagoons. Yet this is also prime area for manatees, so boaters should be ever-vigilant and observe the signs and warnings to avoid collisions.

BELOW: head over heels in Busch Gardens, Tampa.

TIP

The best way to explore the Everglades is to rent a canoe or boat, or get in touch with one of the licensed outfitters who also provide guides. Seeing this exotic place only from land does not do justice to its mystery.

BELOW RIGHT:
Seminole children operating an airboat in the Everglades.

and beyond. The highway circles around Charlotte Harbor and crosses the Caloosahatchee River into well-known **Fort Myers ㉜**. The mild climate has made this a popular winter resort town for a very long time; Northerners Thomas Edison and Henry Ford were neighbors on the riverfront, for example, and you can tour both the Edison & Ford Winter Estates (tel: 239-334-7419; daily) on one combined ticket. The highlight is a museum collecting some of Edison's inventions.

If you're in a mood to do some sea-shell collecting (known here as "shelling"), follow signs over the toll bridge to **Sanibel Island**. Sanibel may offer the finest shell collecting in all of America. Devotees come out here so frequently that someone coined a phrase to describe the parade of hunched-over collectors inspecting the backwash of each wave for new finds: they call this posture the "Sanibel stoop." It's possible to find a number of brightly colored shells here in the balmy surf, not to mention fossilized shark's teeth as well.

The route continues south to exclusive **Naples ㉝**, haunt of the rich and the beautiful. Now, you have a choice of routes east between **Alligator Alley**, as the high-speed toll route of Interstate 75 is known, or else older US 41 farther south, cutting alongside the **Tamiami Canal** that connects the Atlantic Ocean with the Gulf of Mexico. Those wanting close-up views of North America's largest reptile will not be disappointed if they take the former route. The animals sun themselves in large numbers all along the swampy canal. Pictures are easy to take, but watch for traffic as you toodle along, and don't get too close to the water either – alligators can move surprisingly fast, and you don't want your last picture to be the one of you getting eaten.

The Everglades

US 41 goes on for miles and miles through the quiet heart of Florida, passing no towns at all save the occasional gas station. There are no towns because you are slowly penetrating the **Everglades ㉞**, a vast pocket of

Lake Okeechobee

A 58-mile (93km) drive along SR 80 from Fort Myers brings you to Lake Okeechobee and its 750 sq miles (1,940 sq km) of crystal waters. Florida's largest lake is as beautiful as it is sad; the lake reflects the damage being done to the sensitive Everglades' environment by the inexorably burgeoning population of Florida. The water from Lake Okeechobee once fed the wide shallow river of the Everglades, but dikes, pumping stations, and canals were constructed to tame this dramatic lake and its flooding waters. While this has made the surrounding area an agricultural paradise (the area produces enough sugar to supply 15 million Americans' sweet tooth for an entire year), the projects have brought ecological hardships to the surrounding environment, and, to some degree, to the residents as well. Both the Everglades and South Florida's cities have been threatened with drought by the dwindling water level of the lake. Excessive pumping of the Everglades' mother waters for the booming population along the Gold Coast is also sucking it dry. Still a popular destination for anglers, fish camps punctuate the lake's perimeter. Okeechobee, the largest town on the north shore of the lake, is the best base if you want to explore the area. Boat trips can be easily arranged.

swampland partially protected by law and difficult, in any case, to build on.

This strange landscape is home to alligators, venomous snakes, sinuous blackwater creeks overhung by lush vegetation, and probably a few desperado-like characters too; it also supplies the bulk of the drinking water to greater Miami. Authors, including Marjory Stoneman Douglas and Peter Matthiessen, have written about the unique people and creatures here in books like *River of Grass* and *Killer Mister Watson*, but the place to this day remains somewhat inscrutable. Susan Orlean's best-seller *The Orchid Thief* touches on this unique landscape and its colorful characters in wonderful detail. You'll see "Jaguar Crossing" road signs, and – if you're really lucky – perhaps even a real-life jaguar. And like all natural parks, the Everglades is a unique and fascinating area with a multitude of outdoor activities, although at certain times of year, the entire plain floods, sometimes by inches, sometimes by feet. It then gradually drains off into the Gulf of Mexico.

Nearby, at the **Miccosukee Indian Reservation**, you can get supplies and even gamble (it's legal within the reservation), but there's little mention of the tribe's history: heroic Seminole warriors like Osceola outfoxed Federal troops in these endless swamps for more than a year rather than surrender. Just a few miles east, the National Park Service has constructed a loop road at **Shark Valley** that can only be toured by bicycle or tram. The tour terminates at an observation tower that allows unhindered views out over miles of the southern Everglades.

FLORIDA KEYS

This string of tiny islands holds some of the world's most unique plant and animal life, and is where noted literati and "glitterati" have visited, put roots down, and decided to stay. The most famous is perhaps Ernest Hemingway, but numerous others have passed through, by, or lived here in the "Conch Republic." Recent decades have made it quite a hit with gay and lesbian travelers, perhaps in part because of the laid-back, carefree attitude that pervades.

A hawksbill turtle "flying" through the ocean just off Florida Keys.

BELOW: the Overseas Highway, Florida Keys.

Florida wildlife is not for feeding.

BELOW: the bronze sculpture *Christ of the Abyss*, off Key Largo, is one of several submerged in the world's seas.

Don't come here expecting to fret and stress during your vacation. Find a beach chair and a spot in the sun, get a beverage of choice, and leave your worries at the doorstep... or better yet, leave your worries back home. Even the light is different here, a mysterious, turquoise shade of blue that reflects off everything it touches. It is a wonder, really, that these disparate islands are connected to each other or the mainland at all. Yet a series of 42 highway bridges does indeed bridge the many gaps between land and water.

From **Miami** ㉟ *(see page 92)* US 1 proceeds south through **Homestead**, a quiet community that now has one of the highest foreclosure rates in the country. A branch road here, Florida 9336, leads through **Everglades National Park** (Ernest Coe Visitor Center in Homestead; tel: 305-242-7700; daily) and offers glimpses of cypress swamp, grassland, mangroves, and more. Be sure to watch out for 'gators, and resist the temptation to put the pedal to the metal – the rangers are polite but zealous about tickets.

Those with a sweet tooth will enjoy sampling Key Lime ice cream at the roadside stands.

Key information

Be sure to allow plenty of time if you're aiming to reach Key West. Much of the drive will be at or around 30mph (48kph). US 1 enters the Keys as the Overseas Highway at **Key Largo** ㊱, immortalized in the Humphrey Bogart/Lauren Bacall film of the same name (which wasn't actually filmed here), and right away you get an opportunity to view the sea up-close. At **John Pennekamp Coral Reef State Park** (tel: 305-451-6300; daily), one of the most popular parks in Florida, you can gaze through glass-bottomed boats at the most incredible formations of coral reef under the sea. Equally compelling are the fish and shellfish swimming and living throughout this delicate ecosystem. Snorkelling and diving are a must.

If this reef is the best place to see the nature of the Keys, the next park, **Long Key State Park** (tel: 305-664-4815; daily), some 30-odd miles (48km) farther along US 1, is your best bet for a swim or reclining in the sun before proceeding west.

For a lesson on what made the Keys into such a unique place, journey 20 more miles (32km) beyond Long Key to the best museum in the region, the **Crane Point Museum** (tel: 305-743-9100; Mon–Sat) in the resort town of **Marathon** ㊲. Marathon itself is more like a big town than an island paradise, and is best used for stocking up on supplies.

The mangrove forests thicken beyond here as nature begins reclaiming the westernmost islands. You'll get plenty of water views on both sides of the car now as you cross **Seven Mile Bridge**, landing briefly on beautiful **No Name Key** and its **Bahia Honda State Park** (tel: 305-872-3210; daily) – yet another wonderful state-run park. The Key Deer are an endangered species well worth

stopping for and relatively easy to see, especially on No Name Key.

Key West

You cross more bridges still, landing on **Big Pine Key**, **Sugarloaf Key**, and **Looe Key**, each with its own personality and laid-back eateries. Eventually, the highway comes to rest upon balmy **Key West** ㊳, last island in the chain – and also the name of the town here that has been drawing interesting characters for a very long time. Today, it's a mixture of fishermen, retirees, Cubans, and tourist tack, as well as a thriving gay and lesbian population.

The writer Ernest Hemingway lived here, and purveying "Papa's" image has become one of the town's hottest cottage industries. To get a taste of how he lived, visit the **Ernest Hemingway Home and Museum** (tel: 305-294-1136; daily), where Hemingway wrote for a decade; notable are the gardens he personally tended and the cats that overrun the place. Most are descended from the writer's own cats; others were strays who happened to know a good thing when they saw it. The bars lining **Duval Street**, including several once frequented by Hemingway, are a lively refreshment spot, and the Hemingway look-alike contest held every year is a highlight of a noisy social season that is busy to begin with. The country's only Gay Chamber of Commerce is located here as well, catering to the many gays and lesbians who winter or vacation here.

The two most popular sights in town, however, are both free. The first is **Mallory Square Dock**, where residents and tourists alike have been turning out every night for decades to cheer the beautiful sunsets over the water. The other free attraction is also a good one: the brightly colored buoy that marks the **southernmost point** in the continental 48 states, which is near the aptly named Southernmost Hotel and Southernmost House (an old private home converted to a quirky museum and guest house; tel: 305-296-3141; daily). Locals claim that on a very clear night you can even faintly make out the lights of Cuba, lying less than 100 miles (160km) away. ❑

No Name Key is one of the best places to see the rare, endangered Key Deer. A subspecies of the larger, mainland White Tail, the diminutive Key Deer's size is an adaptation to life on the Keys. These animals are often struck by cars and speed limits are strictly enforced; even if you are driving slowly however, keep a careful eye out to avoid hitting these unique animals. Other wildlife will also thank you.

BELOW: Ernest Hemingway house.

A Short Stay in Miami

Sensual and warm, spicy and seductive, Miami appeals to the visitor who is longing for escape. Here's a list of the not-to-be-missed attractions:

● Coral Gables is an enchanting Mediterranean-style neighborhood, home to the glorious Biltmore Hotel (1926) and the Venetian Pool, sometimes called "the most beautiful swimming hole in the world."

● The Kampong, the house where David Fairchild lived, is a lush, tropical garden with numerous botanical wonders and Indonesian-inspired architecture and pools.

● Coconut Grove is a vibrant, eclectic neighborhood of funky houses, dense natural greenery, and good shopping at Coco Walk.

● I.M. Pei designed the futuristic International Place, a 47-story building in downtown Miami that changes color at the flick of a switch.

● Wolfsonian features an eclectic collection of art and miscellany that Mitchell Wolfson Jr collected during his lifetime.

● Lummus Park combines the oldest structures in Miami (the William English Slave Plantation House and the William Wagner House) with a white-sand beach stretching along the coastline.

● Little Haiti is home to immigrants from the Caribbean island of Haiti. The area offers great food and an encounter with a rich culture.

● Key Biscayne, an island paradise connected by bridge, offers many water-related recreations, like jet-skiing, windsurfing, and, of course, lying on your back under the sun.

● Bill Baggs Cape Florida State Park, on the very tip of Key Biscayne and with a view of Cape Florida Lighthouse, has few facilities and little shade – just peace and solitude.

LEFT: Metrozoo. This huge, cageless zoo showcases more than 1,300 animals. There's also a kids' zoo and talks by the zookeepers.

CITY OF FANTASY

Miami is everything other cities are not – pastel colors, swaying palms, and Art Deco balconies are not only easy on the eye, but also kind to the disposition: it's impossible to fret when there's a fizzy cocktail on the table, a pink plastic flamingo on the counter, and a three-piece band playing loud and sassy salsa in your eardrums. If you're staying in South Beach, you can also leave your car behind and stretch those weary legs before getting them tanned on the sandy beach across the street. Or give yourself a workout surfing some of this area's best waves. Miami has a lot of things worth discovering. Just don't forget the sunscreen.

ABOVE RIGHT: Mile after mile of golden sands, upscale communities, and the eye-catching architecture of Miami Modernism, known locally as MiMo, mean that Miami Beach is back on the scene.

ABOVE: Art Deco District. Pastel-colored fantasies line Ocean Drive.

LEFT AND RIGHT: Fun in the sun. South Beach is the new American Riviera, where the buff, bronzed, and beautiful come to play.

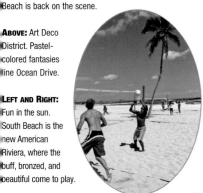

IMPORTANT INFORMATION

Population: 400,000
Dialing code: 305, 786
Website: www.gmcvb.com
Tourist information: Convention & Visitors Bureau, 701 Brickell Avenue, Suite 2700, FL 33131; tel: 305-539-3000

THE NORTHERN ROUTE

A detailed guide from east to west, with
principal sites clearly cross-referenced
by number to the maps

On our northern route between Boston and Washington state's Olympic Peninsula, you will encounter a collage of farmlands, ranches, wilderness, port towns, declining industrial cities, reborn urban centers, and constant reminders of the nation's history.

The first half of the journey is largely marked and guided by water. From Boston, you follow the Atlantic coast through New England up to Maine; later, from the Albany area, your route will swing west alongside the once-busy, now-dormant Erie Canal.

The Great Lakes dominate the next portion of the trip, including Chicago, the great Midwestern crossroads at the southern tip of Lake Michigan. From here to the thriving twin cities of Minneapolis and St Paul, the tour is never far from water, most significantly when it runs right beside the mighty Mississippi. Once you reach western Minnesota, however, the character of the land begins to change. As you cut across South Dakota, the geography overwhelms: rising out of the prairie are the otherworldly Badlands, the Black Hills, and Wounded Knee, a reminder of the nation's brutal treatment of Native Americans. Along a legendary stagecoach route come towns of the notorious Wild West. The sky here is huge and the land seems vast, characterized by small buttes and sagebrush. The route through Wyoming and Montana passes the site of General Custer's last stand against the Indians.

From here, the tour passes into the northern Rocky Mountains with its gorgeous national parks. Crossing the Continental Divide on paths previously traveled by mountain tribes, gold prospectors, and homesteaders, the route cuts through the forests, lakes, and buffalo reserves of Montana, the Idaho panhandle and into the state of Washington, where the land modulates between deserts, canyons, and irrigated farmland.

The final portion of the route runs westward toward the Pacific Ocean through Seattle and the Olympic Peninsula. Suddenly, water is abundant again as you enter America's only rainforest. This wildly beautiful spot is an ideal place to reflect upon your just-completed trans-American journey. ❏

PRECEDING PAGES: open Wyoming range; Chicago blues. **LEFT:** State House Grand Rotunda, Boston. **ABOVE LEFT:** a Montana cowboy. **ABOVE RIGHT:** sidewalk marker.

A SHORT STAY IN BOSTON

The many colleges in this historic and attractive city ensure it retains a youthful, vibrant outlook. Here's a list of the not-to-be-missed attractions:

● Full-scale replicas of three 18th-century ships – *Beaver II, Dartmouth,* and *Eleanor* – sit in the harbor at the Boston Tea Party Ships and Museum. They commemorate the 1773 dunking of taxed tea from Britain, an incident that fueled the flames of the American Revolution.

● Built in 1676, the Paul Revere House is the oldest residence in downtown Boston; Revere lived here from 1770 to 1800. Exhibits include the saddlebags the patriot used on his famous midnight ride to warn of a British attack.

● Since 1877 swan-shaped boats have been plying the Public Garden lagoon. Inspired by *Lohengrin*, the boats, which make lazy figure eights in the water, have been operated by the same family for three generations.

● The oldest botanical garden in America, the Public Garden is Boston's prettiest green space. The focus is the lagoon, surrounded by willow trees and crossed by a mock suspension bridge.

● Trinity Church, H.H. Richardson's 1877 masterpiece in Copley Square, is one of America's finest ecclesiastical buildings. Its wealth of murals, mosaics, carvings, and stained glass makes it Boston's most sumptuous interior space.

● Opened in 1895, the Boston Public Library is designed in the Renaissance Revival style. The interior includes murals by John Singer Sargent; the courtyard is reminiscent of 16th-century Italy.

● The 1903 Isabella Stewart Gardner Museum has many architectural elements, from Venetian window frames to Roman mosaic floor tiles. The galleries hold paintings by Titian, Raphael, Degas, and Rembrandt.

Above: Massachusetts State House. On July 4, 1795, Massachusetts Governor Samuel Adams and Paul Revere laid the cornerstone for the "new" State House. The building overlooks Boston Common and can be explored on a free guided tour.

Right: Downtown. To walk the streets of downtown Boston today is to walk with the ghosts of colonial settlers upon ground now shadowed by modern skyscrapers. Street names have changed but the design is much the same as it was in the 1600s.

Left: Museum of Fine Arts. The museum's permanent collection includes treasures from Old Kingdom Egypt, and works from Asia, Europe, and America.

THE BACK BAY CITY

"I have learned never to argue with a Bostonian," said poet Rudyard Kipling in the early 1900s, and that is still true now. By American standards, Boston is old. Cobbled streets lit by gas-lamps; National Historic Landmarks; individual buildings of great stature and charm. A couple of decades ago, Boston was in danger of becoming a museum of living history, forever trapped in its 1700s and 1800s heyday. Then a change took place: the basin was cleaned, the buildings washed and, due to the high-tech industries of nearby Cambridge, businesses began to flock back. Boston is now modern-minded, so go check it out. And no arguing.

ABOVE RIGHT: USS *Constitution*. Known as "Old Ironsides," the 1797 frigate won all 40 of the battles she fought. Still seaworthy, she is berthed in Charlestown.

LEFT: Nichols House Museum. Housed in a splendid 1804 Federal-style townhouse attributed to Bulfinch. Nichols House is a true Beacon Hill period piece.

IMPORTANT INFORMATION

Population: 600,000
Dialing code: 617, 857
Website: www.bostonusa.com
Tourist information: Greater Boston C&VB, 2 Copley Place, Suite 105, MA 02116; tel: 888-SEE-BOSTON; fax: 617-424-7664

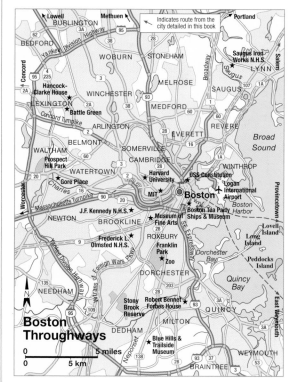

BOSTON TO BUFFALO

Take a drive through the prettiest parts
of New England before beginning a
coast-to-coast trek to the West, starting
with the old route of the Erie Canal

Beginning in downtown **Boston** ❶ *(see page 100)*, the Northern route across the United States starts out by visiting "suburban Boston." This is accomplished by crossing the Charles River into busy **Cambridge** ❷. Cambridge's combination of old-fashioned leafy streets, active squares, and buzzing student life makes it one of Greater Boston's most interesting areas. The activity focuses around triangular **Harvard Square** and more rough-and-tumble but no less vibrant **Central Square**. While here, explore the brick buildings and carefully manicured greens of **Harvard University**, the second-oldest educational institution in the land; it was chartered back in 1636 and remains one of the finest universities in America, with a number of good museums on the quiet campus.

The city's beautifully kept **Mount Auburn Cemetery** is worth seeing as well; its peaceful grounds harbor the remains of such artistic luminaries as Henry Longfellow, Oliver Wendell Holmes, and Winslow Homer.

Keep following signs for 2A, a scenic route that leads out from Massachusetts Avenue into quieter towns. You soon come to **Arlington**, now suburban and high-tech but once a textile community where retreating British soldiers skirmished with local residents known as "Minutemen" (they were said to have been ready at a minute's notice to fight) in April of 1775 as the British backtracked along this road.

Paul Revere's ride

At **Lexington**, about 10 miles (16km) outside Boston proper, turn off 2A into the downtown area for a look at the town green, the main stage of the Battle of Lexington on that fateful April night. A number of statues and monuments commemorate this spirited American defense of their town, considered critical in turning the tide of the American Revolution; silversmith Paul Revere rode his horse here from Boston under cover of night to warn the residents of a British attack. There

Main attractions
BOSTON
SALEM
YORK
NUBBLE LIGHT
NORMAN ROCKWELL
  EXHIBIT
NATIONAL BASEBALL HALL
  OF FAME
NATIONAL WOMEN'S HALL
  OF FAME
NIAGARA FALLS

LEFT: Boston's
Copley Square.
BELOW: Paul Revere,
statue, Boston.

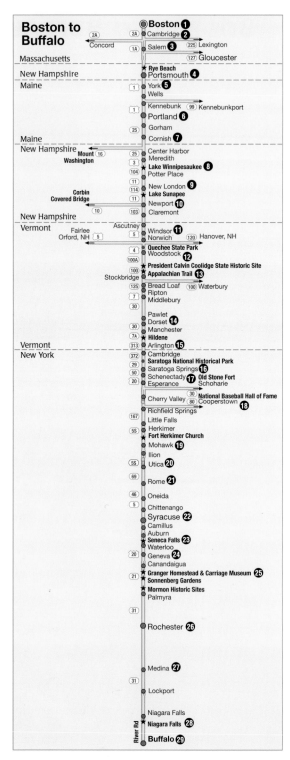

Boston to Buffalo

Massachusetts

New Hampshire

Maine

Maine

New Hampshire

New Hampshire

Vermont

Vermont

New York

◉ Boston ❶
● Cambridge ❷
● Salem ❸ ㉖ Lexington
⑫⑦ Gloucester
★ Rye Beach
● Portsmouth ❹
● York ❺
● Wells
● Kennebunk ㊾ Kennebunkport
● Portland ❻
● Gorham
● Cornish ❼
● Center Harbor
● Meredith
★ Lake Winnipesaukee ❽
● Potter Place
● New London ❾
★ Lake Sunapee
● Newport ❿
● Claremont
● Windsor ⓫
● Norwich ⑫⓪ Hanover, NH
★ Quechee State Park
● Woodstock ⓬
★ President Calvin Coolidge State Historic Site
★ Appalachian Trail ⓭
● Bread Loaf ⑩⓪ Waterbury
● Ripton
● Middlebury
● Pawlet
● Dorset ⓮
● Manchester
★ Hildene
● Arlington ⓯
● Cambridge
Saratoga National Historical Park
● Saratoga Springs ⓰
● Schenectady **Old Stone Fort** ⓱
● Esperance Schoharie
● Cherry Valley ㉚ **National Baseball Hall of Fame**
  ⑧⓪ Cooperstown ⓲
● Richfield Springs
● Little Falls
● Herkimer
★ **Fort Herkimer Church**
● Mohawk ⓳
● Ilion
● Utica ⓴
● Rome ㉑
● Oneida
● Chittenango
● Syracuse ㉒
● Camillus
● Auburn
★ Seneca Falls ㉓
● Waterloo
● Geneva ㉔
● Canandaigua
★ **Granger Homestead & Carriage Museum** ㉕
● Sonnenberg Gardens
★ **Mormon Historic Sites**
● Palmyra
● Rochester ㉖
● Medina ㉗
● Lockport
● Niagara Falls
★ Niagara Falls ㉘
● Buffalo ㉙

Mount Washington ⑯
Corbin Covered Bridge
Fairlee
Orford, NH ⑤
Ascutney
Stockbridge

River Rd

---

are also several old taverns in the area, one of which – Munroe Tavern – served as the makeshift British hospital and command center during the battle.

Continue west along 2A, where American Revolution events are further cataloged in the now-peaceful **Minute Man National Historical Park** (tel: 978-369-6993; daily), which occupies both sides of the highway in a green patch just northwest of the village green.

Concord, the next town, is another significant site. This town was a center of literature and philosophy during the 19th century, as evidenced by such prominent residents as Ralph Waldo Emerson, Henry David Thoreau, and Louisa May Alcott, among others. Alcott's former home, **Orchard House** (tel: 978-369-4118; daily), where she wrote *Little Women*, is first as you approach town, on the right. **Emerson House** (tel: 978-369-2236; mid-Apr–Oct Thur–Sun) comes next, less than half a mile beyond, with items from the life and work of the influential Transcendentalist thinker.

From the center of town, take Walden Street south a short distance to visit **Walden Pond State Reservation** (tel: 978-369-3254), a testament to Henry Thoreau's life, work and unique viewpoint. Thoreau built a simple cabin beside this pond in 1845 and lived there for a time, later writing *Walden* about the experience. "I went to the woods because I wished to live deliberately," he proclaimed, emerging with a view of nature as teacher – rather than slave – of man, and though the book sold poorly in his time, it has since become one of the enduring classics of American literature. The pond isn't nearly as peaceful as it was in his time, but you can still get a sense of what Thoreau must have felt.

ENTERING NEW ENGLAND

Before leaving Boston bound for the wild West, it's worth a short detour north first through the splendors of back-road New England, where America began and a delightful small-town

neighborliness can still be felt today.

Begin, then, by heading north from downtown Boston on State Route 1A (North Street from Downtown) towards **Salem ❸**. This sea town was one of the earliest capitals of the Massachusetts Bay Colony, and is filled with period captains' homes and the like. It's more famous, though, for the **Salem Witch Trials** that began in 1692, an attempt to root out suspected witchcraft among local women and children; nearly two dozen were killed during the height of the frenzy – a symbol, ever after, for misplaced persecution. (The term "witch hunt," broadly applied to political activities, remains in the American lexicon today.) The **Salem Witch Museum** (tel: 978-744-1692; daily), beside the city's large central green, offers an explanation of the trials. Writer Nathaniel Hawthorne was born in one of the houses on the **House of the Seven Gables Historic Site** (tel: 978-744-0991; daily), on the city waterfront nearby; the famed gabled house about which he later penned the well-known novel is also there; its "official" name is the Turner-Ingersoll Mansion.

Route 1A heads due north from Salem and continues on a scenic track through salt marshes, small drawbridges, farmland, and little fishing and commuter towns such as Ipswich, Rowley, and Newbury. Along the way, you may wish to detour east to **Gloucester**, the entrance to lovely Cape Ann and home port to large numbers of fishing and whale-watching boats.

NEW HAMPSHIRE AND MAINE

After entering **New Hampshire**, 1A frees itself from ticky-tacky beach development to reveal the Atlantic itself at **Rye Beach** – your first true glimpse of the open ocean on this tour. Continue a few miles to **Portsmouth ❹**, New Hampshire's most attractive city and one with a salty taste.

Originally known as Strawberry Banke for the wild fruits covering the ground, Portsmouth was ideally situated at the meeting place of a river mouth and the ocean; founded in 1631, it has been a fishing and shipping center ever since. Fine old seamen's homes still crowd the downtown area, and while designer coffee shops and microbreweries are rapidly crowding out the old salts – this is only an hour's commute from Boston, remember – you can still find good clam chowder in the local diners.

North across the Piscataqua River and its bridges lies **Maine**, the "Pine Tree State." Pull off busy US 1 after 6 miles (10km) to visit **York ❺**, Maine's first settlement, which possesses a clutch of old buildings (including an old jail) by the waterfront, all connected by the Cliff Walk coastal track. Most visitors come, however, for the stretch of good beach known as **Long Sands**, framed at one end by a much-photographed lighthouse, the Cape Neddick Light Station, known locally as **Nubble Light**. Buy exceptional locally made ice cream in the summer months from Brown's Old Fashioned

Man dressed as a Civil War sergeant of the 13th Massachusetts Volunteers.

BELOW: the Salem Witch Museum.

Lobsters 2 go.

BELOW: Portland
Head Light, built on
Cape Elizabeth in
1794.

Ice Cream, just uphill of the famous beacon; choose between blueberry, checkerberry (a New England berry tasting of wintergreen) or cinnamon flavors if they're in stock.

North again on US 1, **Wells** is a fairly forgettable beach town, but just north lies the **Wells National Estuarine Reserve** – a protected section of marshland on the sea. It incorporates the National Wildlife Refuge which commemorates scientist Rachel Carson, whose books about the ocean, songbirds, and ecology changed the way Americans thought about the natural world.

Upper crust

Farther north, you hit the Kennebunks, two towns physically joined at the hip by a bridge but quite different in character. **Kennebunk** is more workaday, with an exclusive beach several miles east, while **Kennebunkport** is a slice of quaint, upper-crust New England – all gift shops, designer beers, and fish houses, a bit rich for the blood. Former president George Bush Sr's family compound stands among dramatic shore rocks and crashing waves east of Downtown.

It's 20 more slow miles (32km) north along US 1 (or you can pay to take Interstate 95) to **Portland ⑥**, the state's largest city and cultural center, if rather a humdrum place. At least there's a good collection of beaches, parks, and restaurants to sample before moving along.

Eastern Promenade Park makes a good first stop, with its panoramic view of islands in the bay and part of the city's working waterfront. The **Old Port** district, once a maze of rough streets frequented by sailors, has now been entirely taken over by gift shops, overpriced restaurants, and cut-rate bars aimed at day-trippers; avoid it and go instead for the **Arts District**, where the **Victoria Mansion** (also known as the Morse-Libby House; tel: 207-772-4841; May–Oct) on Danforth Street stands as an excellent example of Victorian architecture. Or take a ferry to tranquil little **Peaks Island** for a closer look at the sea. Back in the center of town, the **Portland Museum of Art** (tel: 207-775-6148; Tue–Sun year-

round, also Mon Oct–May) sometimes hangs good exhibits and has a permanent collection of Winslow Homer's work. Just watch the time on your parking meter: ticketers around town are needlessly ruthless.

From Portland, quieter Route 25 cuts swiftly west through suburbs and then rolling farmland. The town of **Gorham** is little more than a four-way intersection and the rural main campus of the University of Southern Maine; stay on Route 25, proceeding through more small towns. At East Limington, the bridge crosses the Saco River, a superb canoeing river that winds from deep in western Maine to the sea. A free park on the left-hand side of the road here provides a scenic picnic spot; rocks make for good sunning, and a pathway leads downriver to a small swimming beach, out of the sometimes-swift current.

Farther west, the route passes through more countryside to **Cornish** ❼, one of western Maine's very handsome towns. The activity here is focused around a small triangular green space lined with small shops and a hardware store, most in typical whitewashed New England fashion. Each September, an annual apple festival showcases local pies, cider, and other apple products on the town common – with the apple pie contest held on the porch of the venerable Cornish Inn that stands beside the green. The best part comes after the judging, when all pies – winners and losers – are auctioned off to lingering spectators.

Windy heights

Keep to Route 25 as it jogs west into New Hampshire, the "Granite State," then briefly north; if you kept going north on Route 16, you would soon pass **Mount Washington**, at 6,288ft (1,917 meters) the tallest peak east of the Mississippi – and home to the highest recorded winds on the planet.

At West Ossipee, however, make a turn inland again and follow Route 25 through Moultonborough, **Center**

Harbor – whose little general store features New Hampshire's Squamscot soda – and finally **Meredith**, a resort town with the Annalee Doll Museum, set on big, pretty **Lake Winnipesaukee** ❽, New Hampshire's largest body of water.

Head south a short while on US 3 as the road passes right beside the lake. Going uphill as you leave the town, bear right to take state Route 104 through small, typically New Hampshire towns. At Danbury, cut south on US 4 a short distance to Route 11, and then turn west again just after **Potter Place**.

It's only 10 miles (16km) more to the prim town of **New London** ❾ (turn right onto Route 114 just past Elkins), which has a fine central green and good views of the surrounding hills and mountains. This is known locally as a college town, with attractive Colby-Sawyer College located right next to the village green. This former women's college was long one of America's few remaining single-sex institutions of higher education, and became co-educational only in recent years. Connecting with Route 11 from

One mile high (5,271ft/1,606 meters), Mt Katahdin in Maine signals the northern end of the Appalachian Trail.

BELOW: lobster boats in Maine.

The distinctive roof of a New England covered bridge served two purposes: first, to prevent the wood rotting, and second as a method of keeping horses that were pulling carriages from being spooked by the river waters rushing below.

BELOW: a typical New England covered bridge, Vermont.

Route 114, the road passes through the hamlets of Georges Mills (a general store, coves on either side of the road and little more) and the lake town of Sunapee, with a pretty harbor on **Lake Sunapee** – reputedly one of the cleanest lakes in America, and one circled by hills of hardwoods.

Six more miles (10km) east on Route 11, **Newport ⑩** spreads out in the Sugar River Valley, a small textile and arms manufacturing town with an old opera house, wooden covered bridge, and the handsome rectangular "town common" so typical of older New England towns. These green pastures once served as common grazing spaces for local livestock, but today serve mostly as the settings for soccer matches, carnivals, and farmers' markets.

Newport is perhaps best known for Sarah Josepha Buell Hale (1788–1879). Despite early tragedies including the loss of her mother, sister, and husband, Hale rose to prominence in Boston and Philadelphia as one of America's early feminists and female editors. She advocated education and equal opportunity for women, convinced President Abraham Lincoln to create Thanksgiving Day and penned the popular children's nursery rhyme "Mary Had a Little Lamb." Her birth home is on Route 11 a few miles before you enter town, across the street from a once-famous woolen mill.

Bridge to the past

For a look at the **Corbin Covered Bridge**, drive through Newport's main street and continue north on Route 10 for a mile or so, then turn left, passing the town airport and driving through a corridor of pine trees. The bridge at the edge was constructed as a copy to replace the original jewel, which was burned by a thoughtless arsonist in 1993. Such bridges are sprinkled throughout New England, their distinctive design a way to delay the wood rotting as creosote wasn't around. They were also, some say, a method of keeping horses drawing carriages from being spooked by rushing rivers below.

The craftsman who built this particular bridge was such a perfectionist for detail that he copied the original design and then hauled the bridge to its Sugar River home with an oxen team – both to transport it undamaged and to preserve a sense of history.

From central Newport, Route 103 proceeds west through **Claremont**, previously a fading mill city, that is redeveloping its old decaying riverside mill buildings. The historic Opera House located on Opera House Square has year-round performances from opera and theater to comedy and music. Just west of the city, the highway crosses the broad and picturesque Connecticut River dividing New Hampshire from its similar-sized (but very different-thinking) cousin, Vermont.

At **Ascutney**, on the far side of the river, the antenna-topped peak of Mount Ascutney fills the eye; Vermont 5 keeps it to one side and the broad Connecticut River to the other as it heads due north. Shortly thereafter, the road arrives in **Windsor ⑪** – a town that rightly claims itself the

"Birthplace of Vermont." In Elijah West's tavern on Main Street, now known as **Old Constitution House** (tel: 802-672-3773; late May–mid-Oct Sat–Sun), Vermont's Constitution was drafted and signed in 1777, making it for a time an independent republic that was neither British nor American. This independent streak still marks Vermonters today – in the 1990s, they elected and re-elected a Socialist, Bernie Sanders, to sit in the US House of Representatives. And in 2005, Sanders became the first Socialist Senator.

The **Simon Pearce** glassblowing shop, also in Windsor, may be one of the nation's finest such shops. (The establishment also operates a restaurant on Main Street in **Quechee**, serving meals on glassware from the shop.)

Still heading north on Vermont 5, you dip and curve riverside and soon enough come to **Norwich**, a tiny, typical Vermont town with its classic general store – the first of many you'll see on this drive. Near the interstate, the local **King Arthur Flour Baker's Store** sells the company's superior stone-milled flour, plus some top-grade cooking supplies and cookbooks, at a picturesque store on Vermont 5. Outside town, the **Montshire Museum of Science** (tel: 802-649-2200; daily) provides children with a terrific hands-on look at ecology and nature amid riverside fields.

Ivy-clad Dartmouth

Cross the Connecticut River into New Hampshire once more on Route 120 to **Hanover**, an attractive town largely thanks to the elegant, ivy-clad presence of **Dartmouth College**. Dartmouth was founded in 1769 by the Reverend Eleazer Wheelock to educate (and, of course, convert) local Indian children. Now, it is one of America's finest private colleges, with especially strong programs in the sciences, humanities, and Native American studies. The pleasing Dartmouth Green is a center of town life, surrounded on all sides by college buildings, including the **Hopkins Center** performing arts space –

designed by the same architect who later went on to plan New York's Metropolitan Opera House.

The downtown district also features the excellent Dartmouth Bookstore, as well as one of New England's most-beloved natural food cooperatives. It isn't unusual to see haggard, unshaven hikers lugging huge backpacks tramping through town, either, as the bridge from Norwich and downtown Hanover form one of the most civilized stretches of the entire Appalachian Trail *(see page 110)*.

For a little more of New England character before moving west, continue farther north on Vermont 5, which snuggles between the interstate and the river, mostly passing through dairy pastures and cornfields. Several of the small towns have interesting gathering spots, such as the Fairlee Diner in **Fairlee**, Vermont. Across a small bridge from Fairlee, in **Orford**, New Hampshire, beautiful white wooden and red brick homes from the 1900s – not to mention the Orford Social Library and a general store full of local characters – line the town's main street. It was

Famous Dartmouth College alumni include Daniel Webster, Robert Frost, Theodore "Dr" Seuss, and Nelson Rockefeller.

BELOW:
kids love the tour of Ben & Jerry's ice-cream plant in Waterbury, Vermont.

It is estimated that walking the entire length of the Appalachian trail requires 5 million steps.

from here that local car salesman Mel Thomson rose to become a multi-term governor of the state, never straying from his extremely Republican view of things. On summer weekends, the **Mount Cube Sugar House**, in the hills east of Orford down Route 25A, serves huge breakfasts with their own maple syrup: a delicious taste of the region that should not be missed if you are in the area. Locals swear by them.

From Hanover, cross back to Vermont and proceed a short distance south before turning west on US 4 at White River Junction. You soon come to little Quechee, nondescript but for deep **Quechee Gorge**. This 165ft (50-meter) cut in the rock, made by the Ottauquechee River, is accessible from several viewpoints; you can't hike down the steep, narrow walls, but you can hike the woods and camp in a state park across the street. Unfortunately, a small tourist complex has sprung up right beside the gorge.

BELOW: bright autumn foliage heralds in the "leaf-peeper" season.

Woodstock

Ten miles (16km) beyond, compact **Woodstock** ⓬ sits prettily among trees, ridges, and river. On an autumn afternoon, the town is jammed tightly with leaf-peepers touring the area to view the fall foliage, but early October is the time to come – an annual chili cook-off and apple festival and other autumn events compete with the stunning foliage. From Downtown, it is just a few paces to the handsome **Middle Bridge** covered bridge, which is located beside a row of exceptionally fine homes surrounding the village green.

The Woodstock Historical Society leads tours of some of these homes that encircle the central common, and two outstanding museums nearby – the **Billings Farm & Museum** (a look at 19th-century dairy farming; tel: 802-457-2355; May–Oct daily, Nov–Feb Sat–Sun) and the **Vermont Institute of Natural Science** (tel: 802-359-5000; daily, Nov–Apr Wed–Sun), with its good record of nursing birds of prey back to health – provide additional diversion. Just 2 miles (3km) west of town via US 4, the community of **West Woodstock** already has a slightly less manicured feel. The

Appalachian Trail

A pleasant 19-mile (31km) drive along SR 100A, then SR 100, from the town of Bridgewater Corners, Vermont, leads to one of the longest marked footpaths in the world, winding a total of 2,178 miles (3,505km) from Maine to Georgia. Benton MacKaye, who proposed the trail in 1921, wrote about his great project: "The ultimate purpose? There are three things: 1) to walk; 2) to see; 3) to see what you see... Some people like to record how speedily they can traverse the length of the trail, but I would give a prize for the ones who took the longest time." His idea was for a super-trail running the length of the industrialized East Coast. This would be a trail that was wild, yet within reach of major urban centers and the throngs of workers who were alienated from outdoor life. He felt the trail would grace all who spent time on it with the healing tonic of wilderness. Winding from north to south, it traverses the many distinct ranges that make up the Appalachian chain, touching the tops of many of the states it enters. Though not the first of its kind, the Appalachian Trail remains a favorite with outdoors people, enjoying celebrity status among the great hikes of the world. For more information, call the Appalachian Trail Conservancy on 304-535-6331.

seasonal White Cottage Snack Bar serves up fried clams, ice cream, and similar summertime snacks, while the Woodstock Farmers' Market purveys gourmet foods next door. You pass a llama farm (trekking available in summer and fall, tel: 802-295-1573), and go several more miles to **Bridgewater Corners**, home of the Long Trail Brewing Company and its locally popular Long Trail Ale.

Turn left onto Vermont 100A for a beautiful little detour through some of the state's nicest scenery – past haybales and syrup signs, red barns, spotted cows, and grazing horses: pure Vermont. The stretch is particularly beautiful when leaves are changing color. About 6 miles (10km) along, take a right onto the dirt drive for a look at the **President Calvin Coolidge State Historic Site** (tel: 802-672-3773; end of May–mid-Oct daily), the farm homestead where "silent Cal" was raised and to which he periodically returned.

When President Warren G. Harding died in office in 1923, Coolidge was sworn into office on the spot here by his father, a notary public. He remains to this day a hero to Vermonters, symbol of a kind of taciturn, humanistic work ethic that still drives Vermont farmers and politicians alike.

Famed footpaths

Continue on Route 100A until it ends at Route 100, making a right and driving north. You pass numerous B&Bs in the agreeable small towns; if you're in a hurry to get west, turn at **Killington** and cut through the scenic mountains to Rutland. With time to spare, however, you should continue north on Route 100 to its junction with US 4. This is the spot where two of America's famous hiking trails – the **Appalachian Trail ⑬** (*see page 110*) and Vermont's **Long Trail** – diverge. Making a right on 100 north, you can park and take a short stroll on the trail to the left (through Gifford Woods State Park) or the right, around the shore of Kent Pond.

Stay on Route 100 through little **Stockbridge** until it connects with Route 125, then make a choice: food or nature? If you are hungry, continue north up 100 to **Waterbury** and take a tour of the Ben & Jerry's ice-cream factory. We, however, suggest a left turn onto Vermont 125 to begin 13 gorgeous miles (21km) of national forest land. You'll discover why it's been designated a state scenic route as you wind through **Green Mountain National Forest**. Partway along, just before **Ripton**, pull over for a peek at several Robert Frost-related sites.

Frost, one of America's best-loved poets, moved to this area and wrote his finest poetry in a farmhouse here. **Bread Loaf**, the complex of yellow buildings on the right, is a campus of Middlebury College that becomes an internationally famous school of writing each summer; the yellow Bread Loaf Inn offers lodging on-site. The **Robert Frost Interpretive Trail**, on the left, combines passages from his writing with the typical elements – stone walls, maple trees – that inspired it. There are also a number of impressive hikes off the main road, clearly

Although Vermont had almost all of its timber removed in the late 19th century, more than 75 percent of the state's area is now forested.

BELOW:
Killington Resort has reliably good snowfall and a long season.

BELOW: Buskirk Covered Bridge is one of 29 still standing in New York State.

signposted, although to reach them requires driving some rough gravel and dirt roads. The twisty final miles of Route 125 snake down the western slope of the Green Mountains beside the Middlebury River and must be driven carefully, but they are rewarded with a stunning view of the misty stacks of the Adirondacks as the route coasts down into the village of East Middlebury. At US 7, turn right and enter **Middlebury**, a college town with its own handsome buildings and microbrewery.

Now, we head south on Vermont 30, which angles almost due south. It's delightful driving through classic Vermont scenes of grazing spotted cows, rivers, red barns, and the like. You pass several quiet lakes with good camping grounds, then through **Pawlet**, which possesses one of Vermont's best country stores, now called Mach's: among the wooden iceboxes of beer and stacks of rakes and rubber boots, you can actually see the brook running beneath the store through a grate. It was once a hotel, and there's a sepia 1900s photograph of dapper

men with mustaches who once stayed at the place.

Next comes East Rupert, and then **Dorset** ⓮, an attractive town with a downtown golf course close beside classic New England homes, many of which are now characteristic bed-and-breakfast establishments.

Rockwell country

Crowds begin appearing again in **Manchester**, a tourist-filled town nestled on the **Battenkill River**, itself one of the world's finest fly-fishing rivers. You can learn more at the **American Museum of Fly Fishing** (tel: 802-362-3300; Tue–Sat), which displays the rods and gear of famous fishermen like Hemingway and Eisenhower, among others. Not surprisingly, this is also home to the outdoor equipment and clothing manufacturer Orvis and loads of other shops – no longer the real Vermont, despite the presence of Norman Rockwell memorabilia everywhere.

Breeze right through town and continue south down Vermont 7A, here known as "Historic 7A," as it passes Robert Todd Lincoln's former home, **Hildene** (tel: 802-362-1788; daily). This beautiful Georgian Revival mansion features a huge pipe organ. The road then takes in the pleasing ridge of **Mount Equinox**, especially stunning in fall. A toll road rises to the top, if you wish to drive it. Apple orchards, meadows, and cows continue to be the prevailing themes along 7A.

At **Arlington** ⓯, you can have a look at the famed **Norman Rockwell Exhibit** (tel: 802-375-6423; Feb–Dec daily), a collection of the artist's work. The artist lived in two homes in this area, and locals often served as models for his so-American portraits.

Turn west onto Vermont 313, and as you leave town and Vermont, there's one final treat: just before the New York border you pass by the covered **West Arlington Bridge**, a small bridge over the Battenkill with a plain, typical New England church behind – a composition Rockwell himself was said to

have especially loved. As these are a local specialty, this is the last one you'll see on this cross-country trip. Linger awhile contemplating the river – and the New England – you have seen.

NEW YORK STATE

As you greet the sign welcoming you to **New York** state, you have not only crossed a line on a map separating one state from another. You have also crossed an imaginary, but no less real, boundary where yard sales at once become tag sales, tonic becomes soda, beef-on-weck replaces grinders as the favored submarine-style lunch sandwich and where the clipped, shorthand speech of New Englanders becomes the louder, more persistent one of New Yorkers.

Entering on State Route 313, you arrive shortly at a pleasant picnic spot beside the Battenkill River. Then you pass through **Cambridge**, a small town with antiques and an attractive little general store, more form than function these days. You'll also pass the Cambridge Hotel, built in 1885, self-proclaimed home of "pie à la mode." Change to Route 372, join State 29 and

continue driving west. Ten or 12 miles (16–19km) on, the road crosses the **Hudson River** at Schuylerville, unimpressive here since it's split up into so many parts; in fact, the great river seems tame indeed – there is no hint yet of the power and beauty that will soon fill a great valley and inspire countless artists.

It was only a few miles downstream from these banks that the two Battles of Saratoga were fought in 1777, resulting in a crushing defeat of British troops – a crucial momentum swing in the Revolution. A turnoff leads to the **Saratoga National Historical Park** (tel: 518-664-9821; battlefield: daily, tour road: Apr–Nov), commemorating the battles, where you can drive or be guided through the fields.

Continue to **Saratoga Springs** ⑯, long a resort town due to the mineral springs that bubble up from beneath it and more recently a popular weekend town. It is also home to Skidmore College students and faculty, and thus a fair number of coffeehouses, ice-cream shops, and bookstores speckle the downtown district. The Saratoga Performing Arts Center, within a green

Fresh spring water from Saratoga Springs.

BELOW: antiques of all kinds on display at a Main Street Cambridge store.

park on the southern edge of town, frequently hosts big-name concerts. Summertime also brings crowds to the harness track here, where horse racing is king – witness the presence here of the **National Museum of Racing and Hall of Fame** (tel: 518-584-0400; Apr–Oct daily, Nov–Dec Tue–Sun, Jan–Mar Wed–Sun). Finally, don't miss **Caffé Lena**, an upstairs joint on a central street which is said to have been the first American coffeehouse to host regular folk music performances. It still does.

Erie Canal

Route 50 brings you south through Ballston Spa, home of the eccentric **National Bottle Museum** (tel: 518-885-7589; June–Sept daily, Oct–May Mon–Fri), to the Mohawk River and the Erie Canal. Tracing this great inland water route west to Buffalo is not the shortest way to get from here to there, but it is a route that runs rich with American history.

The idea of a canal connecting the port cities of Albany (on the Hudson River) and Buffalo (on Lake Erie) was greeted with skepticism and derision at first. Detractors called it "Clinton's Ditch" after DeWitt Clinton, champion of the project. Completed in 1825, and eventually bypassed in the early 20th century, the Erie Canal was responsible for the settling of the Midwest and the rise of the state of New York. The old canal towns, once the sites of boisterous activity, are quiet now, many down on their luck.

Begin tracing the route in **Schenectady** ⑰. A plaque in this town sums up its early history: "Settled by Van Curler 1661. Burned by French and Indians Feb 8, 1690."

Because it was the farthest west of all Dutch settlements in the New World, the town's settlers built a stockade around the land, which was bounded by the Mohawk River and a branch called the Binne Kill. The stockade is now gone, dismantled during the American Revolution, but the area it protected is still known as the **Stockade** and is now a historic district containing an eclectic array of buildings that spans over three centuries of American life.

Schenectady's strategic riverfront location has historically made it an important center for commerce and transportation. The city supplied Revolutionary troops battling in the Mohawk Valley, and in the 19th century it was a major port. In 1931, it became the terminus of the nation's first passenger steam train, the "DeWitt Clinton," an innovation stimulated by the protracted process of traversing the 23 locks between Albany and Schenectady.

Schenectady has not been exempt from the exodus of industry out of the Northeast. In the 19th century, it progressed from being a center for the manufacture of brooms, to "the city that lights and hauls the world." The Schenectady Locomotive Works (later the American Locomotive Company) opened in 1851, followed by Edison and his Machine Works – which later became General Electric. The Locomo-

BELOW: taking a break by the encampment tents at a Revolutionary War re-enactment in Mohawk Valley.

tive Company pulled out of town in 1969, but the lights are still switched on at GE.

Leatherstocking trails

New York's heartland is generally considered to begin west of the industrial triangle of Albany, Troy and Schenectady. This essentially rural area north of the Catskill Mountains and south of the Adirondacks is also known as the **Leatherstocking District**, after the protective garb once worn by trailblazers. Native son James Fenimore Cooper immortalized the region in his *Leatherstocking Tales* and other works. And the numerous Revolutionary War battles that took place throughout the Mohawk River Valley are the subject of Walter D. Edmonds' historical novel, *Drums Along the Mohawk*.

Schenectady's Broadway leaves town in a southwesterly direction (Route 7). It passes through Rotterdam and Duanesburg, where Route 7, US 20 and I-88 converge. From there, US 20 travels to **Esperance** on Schoharie Creek. This pleasant town features old houses, antique shops and the obligatory country store. About 8 miles (13km) south of here along Route 30, which follows the creek, is the town of **Schoharie**, the third-oldest village upstate. Its **Old Stone Fort Museum Complex** (tel: 518-295-7192; July–Aug daily, May–June and Sept–Oct Tue–Sun) started as a church in 1772, became a fort during the Revolution, and has served as museum and library specializing in early Americana since 1889.

An interesting chapter out of Schoharie's past includes the Middleburgh and Schoharie Railroad, built in the late 1860s. This short, 5.7-mile (9.2km) run down the Schoharie Creek Valley transported hops and other local products. The railroad's president was fond of pointing out that although it wasn't as long as other railroads, it was just as wide. In its last days, the line's single locomotive faltered physically and financially, and operation was finally stopped in 1936.

Take me out to the ball game

US 20 west of Sharon and Sharon Springs is one of the loveliest stretches of road in central New York, providing a panoramic view of **Cherry Valley**, the site of an infamous massacre in 1778, now crimson only in autumn.

It would be a mistake not to detour 10 miles (16km) south at Springfield Center down Route 80 to visit **Cooperstown** ⓲, a charming town with several important attractions. James Fenimore Cooper's house and museum is one, but the main draw is the **National Baseball Hall of Fame** (tel: 607-547-7200; daily) – a tremendous experience of the history of the sport, which has inspired countless novels, films, and even poems. Make time for a visit to the monuments, biographies, and collections here.

Past **Richfield Springs**, known for its sulfur springs and fossil-hunting grounds, State 167 travels north toward **Little Falls**. Not far up this road stands the **Russian Orthodox Holy Trinity Monastery**, startling to the eye in a land of colonial history, 19th-century

The impressive 16-sided Nott Memorial Building on Schenectady's Union College campus integrates symbols from major world religions.

BELOW: tiered fountain with topiary, Cooperstown.

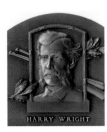

HARRY WRIGHT

Plaque
commemorating one
of the several hundred
star players in the
National Baseball
Hall of Fame,
Cooperstown.

BELOW: patriotic
Paul Revere mural
in Rome, New York.

buildings and rustic farm houses. Little Falls' **Herkimer Home**, former residence of Revolutionary War hero Brigadier General Nicholas Herkimer, provides a glimpse of colonial life, with maple sugar gathering, sheep shearing, and other exhibitions. This canal town once had the world's highest lock, at 41ft (12.5 meters).

West along State 5 is Herkimer, named after the general whose statue still commands attention. The **Herkimer County Courthouse** was the site of the Gillette murder trial, which inspired Theodore Dreiser to write *An American Tragedy*, depicting the dark side of the American dream. George Stevens' film version, *A Place in the Sun*, featured Montgomery Clift, Shelley Winters, and Elizabeth Taylor. Between Herkimer and **Mohawk** ⓳, along Route 5S, stands the **Fort Herkimer Church**, built in 1730.

Ilion, a small industrial pocket, is located just beyond Mohawk. The interesting **Remington Firearms Plant and Museum** (tel: 315-895-3200; museum: Mon–Fri, plant tours: Memorial Day–Labor Day Mon–Fri) here is

devoted to the great guns made by Remington Arms Company, past and present. Continuing west, the road terminates in **Utica** ⓴, the only city of any size you'll have seen since Schenectady.

Utica, once named Fort Schuyler, is rich in colonial and revolutionary history. But the biggest attraction here is the **Munson-Williams-Proctor Arts Institute** (tel: 315-797-0000; Tue–Sun), reputed to have one of the finest collections of 18th- through 20th-century American and European art in the northeast, housed in a building designed by Philip Johnson. On a much less cultural note, Utica's **Matt Brewery** (tel: 315-732-0022; tours run daily June–Aug, Fri–Sat Sept–May) serves its beer up in a Victorian-era tavern built in 1888. It's all part of a brewery tour that culminates in a trolley ride to the tavern.

Erie Canal Village

Route 69 leaves Utica for **Rome** ㉑, best known for its crucial role in the building of the Erie Canal. Beyond this point, there were no continuous

natural water routes westward. This is where excavation began. Commemorating this important chapter in its history is the **Erie Canal Village** (tel: 315-337-3999; Memorial Day–Labor Day Wed–Sun), a reconstructed 1840s village near a refurbished section of the old canal. The biggest tourist attraction here is the *Independence*, a packet boat towed down the canal by horses for a 40-minute ride. When the snow flies, the village also features sleigh rides, a pleasant experience on a crisp, clear day.

The canal brought industry to Rome, some of which remains. Rome has always been serious about America: this, after all, is where native son Francis Bellamy wrote the famous "Pledge of Allegiance" that every American school child learns by heart.

Route 46 takes you from Rome to **Oneida**, still home to the Oneida Indians. The Oneida Community, associated with this town but actually just southeast in Sherrill, was established in the mid-19th century by John Humphrey Noyes and his followers. Calling themselves perfectionists, they adhered to a strict sexual code as part of a community-determined system of selective breeding. In their spare time, they produced high-quality silver-plated flatware. The community was dissolved in 1881, but the silver-plate business continues to thrive.

From Oneida, **Chittenango** is a short drive along Route 5. Don't be surprised, in town, to see a yellow brick sidewalk, for this is "**Oztown, USA.**" The sidewalk is a tribute to L. Frank Baum, author of the beloved *Wizard of Oz*. Stay on Route 5 and it will lead right into Syracuse, the biggest city for miles around in these parts.

Finger Lakes

Busy **Syracuse** ㉒ is the urban gateway to the Finger Lakes. Route 5 becomes Erie Boulevard as it cuts through the heart of the city along a path carved by the Erie Canal. The **Weighlock Building**, built in 1849 in Greek-Revival style, once weighed canal boats for the purpose of toll collection. At the turn of the 20th century, it was converted into an office building, while in its most recent rein-

EAT

Try a *pustie* (short for *pasticciotti* – an Italian custard-filled tart), one of Utica's signature dishes.

BELOW LEFT: globe light fixture at Saratoga Springs City Hall. **BELOW:** tillerman on the rudder at Erie Canal Village.

BIKE ROUTE

Ride a bike along the Seneca Lake Wine Trail that winds around Seneca Lake.

BELOW: the former mansion of George Eastman, who founded Kodak, now houses the International School of Photography.

carnation it serves as the **Erie Canal Museum** (tel: 315-471-0593; daily).

Thanks to the canal, this was once a center for the salt trade, and some still refer to it as "Salt City." The town boomed during the 19th and early 20th centuries on the back of salt and other industries, and its well-preserved architecture testifies to former prosperity. The **Landmark Theatre**, an ornate "fantasy palace" built in the 1920s, now functions as a multi-dimensional entertainment center. But the main draw here today is **Syracuse University**, elevated on a hill above the city, which brings crowds of students, sports fans, and other audiences to its huge **Carrier Dome**. Basketball games are especially well-attended, though football games and rock concerts follow a close second. For the more sedate, the campus also offers the **SUArt Galleries**. Those same art lovers also should not miss the **Everson Museum of Art** (tel: 315-474-6064; Tue–Sun), designed by renowned architect I.M. Pei. Route 5 leaves Syracuse on its way to **Camillus**, where you can canoe and kayak

to your heart's content along 7 miles (11km) of navigable canal in the **Camillus-Erie Canal Park**. Farther along, Route 5 merges with US 20, a route that strings together the northern tips of the largest **Finger Lakes**.

Following close on the heels of the Leatherstocking region, this series of 11 watery depressions was created by scraping glaciers. The region is characterized by vineyards, gracious inns, water pursuits, and hot-air ballooning. The area's vines look especially beautiful when their leaves begin to turn coppery red in late summer, and the colorful balloons are also an attractive sight. The small city of **Auburn**, on US 20/Route 5, isn't quite set on the lakes but does have one site to visit: the **home of Harriet Tubman** (tel: 315-252-2081) on South Street.

Seneca Lake

After Auburn, US 20/Route 5 then passes Cayuga Lake and follows the Seneca River to **Seneca Falls ㉓**, where the first Women's Rights Convention was convened. The site has been developed into a National Historic Site and includes the **National Women's Hall of Fame** (tel: 315-568-8060; May–Sept daily, Oct–Apr Wed–Sat). **Waterloo**, also in between the lake fingers, prides itself on being the birthplace of Memorial Day. The road through here passes by the old Scythe Tree, upon which local farm boys planted their scythes on their way to wars past.

Seneca Lake follows, the town of **Geneva ㉔** its jewel, replete with elegant inns and mansions. This town is also the gateway to a circuit round the lake known as the Seneca Lake Wine Trail; the drive takes in several dozen vintners, including four specializing in champagne and mead (honey wine). It is very pretty in fall, when the grape and maple leaves are changing color. Seneca Lake may seem small and thin, but it's actually one of the deepest freshwater lakes in the world – going down to a depth of more than 600ft (180 meters). The US

Navy used the lake to test depth charges during World War II.

Approximately 20 miles (32km) west of Geneva on US 20/Route 20 is **Canandaigua**, at the northern tip of Canandaigua Lake. Of particular interest here is the Federal-style **Granger Homestead and Carriage Museum** ㉕ (tel: 585-394-1472; late May–late Oct Tue–Fri plus Sat–Sun from June–Sept), built in 1816, with its collection of nearly 70 horse-drawn vehicles. North of town – take Route 21 – are the **Sonnenberg Gardens** (tel: 585-394-4922; mid-May–mid-Oct daily), acres of Victoriana with a mansion incorporating the Wine Center, a collection of gourmet foods and wines from the Finger Lakes region. There is a rotating-inventory tasting bar in the cellar.

Remain on Route 21 and you will pass through Shortsville on the way to **Palmyra**, a pilgrimage site for Mormons. This was the home of Joseph Smith who, according to Mormon belief, received and translated ancient records in the Book of Mormon, buried them here and subsequently founded the Church in the 1820s. Religious sites, the original home built by the Smiths and a replica of Smith's farm homestead are open to the public, as is the **Martin Harris Landmark Cobblestone House**. Built in 1850, the house is typical of the farmers' homes that sprang up along the Erie Canal.

It is approximately 20 miles (32km) from Palmyra to Rochester along Route 31. The names of the towns along the way are perhaps more exotic than the towns: after Palmyra comes Macedon and then Egypt, where the New York State Barge Canal stands in for the Nile.

Pretty as a picture

Like other upstate cities, **Rochester** ㉖ thrived during the canal era and suffered economically with the advent of alternative modes of transportation. But it has adjusted to change better than its siblings and is on the upswing

as a center for high-tech industries, while continuing to preserve much of its 19th-century architectural ambiance. Eastman Kodak is the big name in Rochester, so big they still call it "Picture City."

The former mansion of George Eastman, who founded Kodak, now houses the **International Museum of Photography and Film** (tel: 585-271-3361; Tue–Sun), devoted to the history of this art and science. The **Eastman School of Music** sponsors musical events, from jazz to rock to folk to symphonic works, while the **Eastman Theatre** is the home of the Rochester Philharmonic. For those who still enjoy childish things, the **Strong National Museum of Play** (tel: 585-263-2700; daily) has one of the most extensive collections of dolls and toys in the world, in addition to a butterfly garden and coral reef aquarium. Winters are severe in Rochester, thanks to its northern location on Lake Ontario, the easternmost Great Lake. But in spring, when **Highland Park** is abloom, Rochester really is "pretty as a picture." During May,

TIP

In Auburn, New York, be sure to visit the Harriet Tubman home. Tubman was an escaped slave who coordinated a network called the Underground Railroad to spirit other slaves out of the South.

BELOW:
Seneca Lake.

Sun filtering through a grove of pine trees in photogenic Highland Park, Rochester.

BELOW: suitable attire for viewing the falls. **RIGHT:** Niagara Falls and the *Maid of the Mist* boat tour.

the park (which bills itself as the "Lilac Capital of the World") is the setting for the Lilac Festival featuring the world's largest display of these blossoms.

On to the falls

Route 31 continues along the path of the Erie Canal from Rochester to Niagara Falls. The names of the towns along this route, including Spencerport, Brockport, Middleport, and Gasport, continue to remind the traveler of the canal's former importance. But there are other reminders as well. **Medina** ❷ has its cobblestone buildings and Culvert Road, which passes beneath the canal. **Lockport** also has its share of cobblestone houses, though it is best known for its magnificent flight of five locks.

From Lockport, Route 31 (here called Saunders Settlement Road) travels directly to **Niagara Falls** ❷. Once known as America's "Honeymoon Capital," the town is fond of referring

to itself as an international tourist destination. And, indeed, this remains one of the top tourist draws in all the US despite its endless tackiness. Quite simply, the 700,000 gallons (3 million liters) of water plummeting from top to bottom each second here are a wondrous assault on the senses, something that must be experienced while in America. The magnetic draw of these falls has even inspired some visitors to attempt crossing them on a tightrope or riding them in a barrel, with sometimes-tragic results; both activities are now illegal, though daredevils still occasionally try.

The natural beauty of the site might have been irreparably compromised had it not been for the efforts of landscape architect Frederick Law Olmsted, landscape painter Frederic Church and others. Their "Free Niagara" (from commercialism) campaign resulted in the establishment of the Niagara Reservation in 1885. One of the best ways to experience the falls today is by donning the provided foul-weather gear and taking a boat ride on the *Maid of the Mist*. Alternatively, you might drive across the river to Canada and enjoy what many consider to be a superior view.

River Road hugs the eastern branch of the Niagara River, past the falls and through industrial landscape to **Buffalo** ❷. As with other industrial giants past their prime, New York's second-largest city has acquired a somewhat bad reputation. As the 19th-century terminus of the Erie Canal, Buffalo once served as a funnel through which raw materials, cash, pioneers, and immigrant labor flowed into the Midwestern states. Today, it is a bit ragged. Nevertheless, there are reasons to stop for a visit; you can eat well and cheaply here. A local specialty is spicy chicken wings, which anywhere else are called "Buffalo wings," but here are "wings." You might like to go to the source, the Anchor Bar, whose owner is said to have invented the dish. ❑

CAVE OF THE WINDS TRIP

DownHome MUSIC

GOING TO CHICAGO

USA

Heritage FOLK MUSIC
ESTABLISHED 1962   CITY OF CHICAGO

Mississippi DELTA BLUES

Illinois 8229 AE Land of Lincoln
TRUCK

Kawasaki

BUFFALO TO THE BADLANDS

Follow the shores of Lake Erie into New York,
Pennsylvania, and Ohio, then continue through
the Midwest and the Great Lakes for the
bleak, beautiful hills of the Badlands

Buffalo was an important point of departure for 19th-century settlers heading for the Midwest. From Buffalo, they traveled to major ports of the Great Lakes in order to start their new life. Today, the road from Buffalo to the Midwestern states follows the shore of Lake Erie through New York, Pennsylvania, and Ohio. Although known primarily as an industrial area, there are still some unspoiled stretches of coastline that are remarkable for their beauty. At Toledo, the highway diverges from the shoreline on its way to big, busy, beautiful Chicago.

South of Buffalo along US 62 is the town of **Hamburg**, where the hamburger – perhaps America's greatest contribution to world cuisine – was purportedly invented in 1885. In celebration of the centennial of this event, J. Wellington Wimpy came to town and was honored as the undefeated hamburger-eating champion of the world. Essentially a rural town, Hamburg has been host to America's largest county fair since 1868. It's only about 5 miles (8km) from here to Lake Erie, where you can pick up State 5, a lakeside road that takes you to Ohio.

Antique trail

Lake Erie has suffered more than its sister Great Lakes at the hands of industry, yet miles of its beautiful, sandy, ocean-like shoreline are still unspoiled. The stretch from Silver Creek, New York, to the Pennsylvania border has been called an "antique trail" for the abundance of antique shops located just off the road. But more importantly, it cuts directly across a region devoted to the gentle art of viniculture.

State 5 takes you past terrain blanketed with grape vines and other fruit trees. In **Silver Creek**, go straight to the site of the **Skew Arch Railroad Bridge** on Jackson Street. Built on an angle in 1869, it is one of only two such bridges in the world.

Dunkirk and Fredonia follow, in the

Main attractions
LAKE ERIE STATE PARK
CHAIN O'LAKES STATE PARK
CHICAGO
TALIESIN
WALKER ART CENTER
MINNESOTA STATE FAIR
CORN PALACE
BADLANDS NATIONAL PARK

LEFT: heading to the home of the urban blues: Chicago.
BELOW: sightseeing companions in Downtown Chicago.

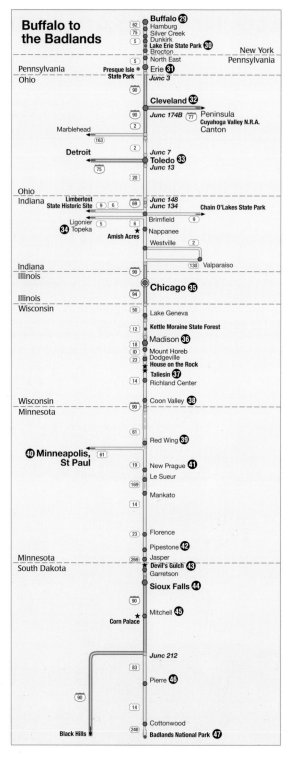

Buffalo to the Badlands

Buffalo **29**
Hamburg
Silver Creek
Dunkirk
Lake Erie State Park **30**
Brocton
North East
Erie **31**
Junc 3
Cleveland **32**
Junc 174B **77** Peninsula
Cuyahoga Valley N.R.A.
Canton
Junc 7
Toledo **33**
Junc 13
Junc 148
Junc 134 Chain O'Lakes State Park
Brimfield
Nappanee
Westville
Valparaiso
Chicago **35**
Lake Geneva
Kettle Moraine State Forest
Madison **36**
Mount Horeb
Dodgeville
House on the Rock
Taliesin **37**
Richland Center
Coon Valley **38**
Red Wing **39**
New Prague **41**
Le Sueur
Mankato
Florence
Pipestone **42**
Jasper
Devil's Gulch **43**
Garretson
Sioux Falls **44**
Mitchell **45**
Corn Palace
Junc 212
Pierre **46**
Cottonwood
Badlands National Park **47**

New York
Pennsylvania

Pennsylvania
Ohio

Presque Isle
State Park

Marblehead
Detroit

Ohio
Indiana Limberlost
State Historic Site
Ligonier
Topeka **34** Amish Acres

Indiana
Illinois

Illinois
Wisconsin

Wisconsin
Minnesota

Minneapolis,
St Paul **40**

Minnesota
South Dakota

Black Hills

heart of the Concord Grape Belt (the world's largest) which extends into Pennsylvania. **Dunkirk**, with its natural harbor, is also a center for boating and the "Chautauqua (County) wine trail." **Fredonia**, to the south, is home to "Grange Number One," the original premises of America's first such farmers' organizations. The Fredonia campus of State University of New York was co-designed and modernized in the late 1960s by renowned architects I.M. Pei and Henry N. Cobb.

Continuing along the lake, the road passes pretty **Lake Erie State Park 30** in **Brocton**, where campers will find a pleasant place to pitch their tents. **Westfield** follows, calling itself "The Grape Juice Capital of the World" and dominated by the various production facilities of a popular grape jelly. Combined with peanut butter and two pieces of bread, this sandwich vies with Hamburg's hamburgers as *the* American food.

There is no obvious transition between New York and its westerly neighbor, Pennsylvania. The landscape remains the same – a sparkling lake on one side and lush vineyards on the other. In season, roadside stands sell the local grapes in every imaginable form. Only 63 miles (101km) of Lake Erie shoreline prevent Pennsylvania from being a landlocked state (an economic decision to do with lake access), and it knows just what to do with it. Past the state line is the town of **North East**, center of the state's tiny wine industry. Several wineries do fairly good business here and all offer tours and tastings.

About 15 miles (24km) west of wine country on State 5 sits the city of **Erie 31**, off whose shores Commander Oliver Hazard Perry's fleet defeated the British in the Battle of Lake Erie during the War of 1812. Despite his motto – "Don't give up the ship!" – the flagship *Niagara* was left to sink in what later became known as **Misery Bay**. That bay is now a quiet fishing cove off Presque Isle, and the ship was rescued a century later. A reconstructed *Niagara* is now docked behind the **Erie Maritime Museum** (tel: 814-452 2744; Apr–Dec daily, Jan–Mar Thur–Sat). When docked here, guided tours onboard are included in the museum's admission price, but be aware that the boat has an active sailing schedule in the summer.

On the other side is Erie's finest physical feature, **Presque Isle**, a claw of land – almost an island, really – reaching out into the lake. You can drive its length, pass Presque Isle Lighthouse, and then loop around along the southern end going past Misery Bay. You'll find lovely sand beaches, wooded trails, fishing holes, and lazy lagoons.

THE TOP OF OHIO

Before you can say "knee high by the Fourth of July," you're in Ohio. Interstate 90 cuts through the gently rolling farmland of this part of the state past Ashtabula, Geneva, and Euclid before reaching the **Cleveland ❸❷** area. Cleveland has its share of high culture – the Cleveland Orchestra and the **Cleveland Museum of Art** (tel: 216-421-

7350; Tue–Sun) – and pop culture – the **Rock and Roll Hall of Fame** (tel: 216-781-ROCK; daily). The latter covers everyone from Louis Jordan to John Lennon, with exhibits including report cards and Jim Morrison's Cub Scout uniform. Hungarian food is a particular specialty of Cleveland, so try some dishes before leaving town.

It's well worth a short detour south from Cleveland to explore the green **Cuyahoga Valley**. The valley's ridges were settled during the late 18th century by the New Englanders who first surveyed its boundaries, and their influence remains today. The town of **Peninsula**, reached by Interstates 77, 80, and 271, is a prime example – all Cape Cod-style whitewashed houses fronted by maple trees. A scenic small-gauge railroad line runs upriver at weekends to the even smaller Boston, and a cycling path runs along the Ohio & Erie canal towpath.

Football Hall of Fame

Sport fans will want to make a brief detour south down I-77, through the smoky industrial city of Akron – tire

Time for lunch: both hamburgers and peanut butter and jelly sandwiches have claims to this part of the US.

BELOW:
Cleveland skyscrapers catching the setting sun.

Classic neon marquee on the 1920s Fox Theater, Detroit.

BELOW: made in Detroit – the mass-produced Ford Model T "put America on wheels."

and rubber capital of America – to the city of **Canton**. Here, the **Pro Football Hall of Fame** (tel: 330-456-8207; daily) offers a look at the heroes of American football. Things peak in August, when an annual game is played here to kick off each season and to celebrate the new class of inductees.

State 2 leaves Cleveland on its way west, diverging from I-90 and running closer to Lake Erie. At Ceylon, it comes right to the lake, loops around Sandusky, then bridges Sandusky Bay to arrive on the Marblehead Peninsula. State 163 takes you out to land's end and reveals the peninsula as a slightly run-down but refreshingly unpretentious place, full of lively harbors, the dinosaur adventure park Prehistoric Forest, orchards, and fruit stands. At its rocky tip is **Marblehead Lighthouse**, which has been in continuous use since 1822, longer than any other beacon on the Great Lakes. It protects ships and boats from this, the most treacherous outcropping along Lake Erie. Looking back south across the bay, you'll see the roller coasters and other thrill rides of

Cedar Point (tel: 419-627-2350; mid-May–Aug daily, Sept–Oct Sat–Sun), a popular 364-acre (147-hectare) amusement park located on the tip of a peninsula accessible from Sandusky. Off the Marblehead Peninsula, State 2 proceeds toward Toledo. This region was once part of the **Black Swamp**, a refuge for wildlife which extended from Sandusky to Detroit. Small remnants of the swamp have managed to survive along this route.

Famous hot dogs

The road emerges from the swamp and continues straight as an arrow to the town of **Toledo** ❸, past bait shops, drive-through liquor stores and drive-in movie theaters. The "Toledo Strip" was once the subject of a border dispute between Ohio and Michigan. When Ohio got the Strip, Michigan got its Upper Peninsula from Wisconsin Territory as compensation – a swap in which Michigan probably made out like a bandit.

At first glance, Toledo seems like an industrial wasteland. Still, there are signs of rejuvenation and redevelop-

Detour – Detroit

A 45-mile (72km) drive beside Lake Erie on I-75 leads from Toledo, Ohio, to Detroit, Michigan – the Motor City. Henry Ford was the single most influential American in motoring history, forming the Ford Motor Company in 1903. Six years later, he had 10,000 orders for his newest car, the Model T, and, by 1919, was selling close to a million cars. His innovations bolstered Detroit's economy, increased the automobile's popularity and gave more people jobs; although shaken by recent bankruptcies and lay-offs, the city still revolves around this industry. The 260-acre (105-hectare) Henry Ford Museum and Greenfield Village complex in the nearby town of Dearborn is the world's largest indoor/outdoor museum, commemorating Ford's contribution to the city. The Ford Museum holds Henry's collection of early automobiles and historic airplanes, while the Village houses recreations of famous businesses and residences, including Thomas Edison's Menlo Park laboratory. Detroit is also the home of Motown records, created by former Ford assembly line worker Berry Gordy, Jr, in 1958, which produced stars of the Detroit Sound such as Smokey Robinson and Diana Ross. The Motown Historical Museum charts the label's influence from the 1960s to the present. The Detroit Visitors Bureau is at 800-338-7648 or www.visitdetroit.com.

ment in the downtown riverfront area along the Maumee. If you've got the time, drop into Tony Packo's Cafe – made famous by Corporal Max Klinger in the long-running TV series *M*A*S*H* – a fun restaurant known for its "Hungarian hot dogs" and quirky collection of hot dog buns autographed by celebrities.

Leaving Toledo and Lake Erie behind at last, US 20 heads due west, cutting straight through Ohio farm country to the Indiana border, a distance of about 60 miles (100km). The road here parallels the Michigan border, which is just a few miles to the north.

INDIANA

They call **Indiana** the Hoosier state, and native Indianans Hoosiers. Some say the name comes from a common inquiry from the pioneer days, "who's yer?" Others say the nickname comes from a canal-builder named Samuel Hoosier, who liked to hire Indiana men over other workers; the workers became known as Hoosiers, and the name stuck. Other versions exist as well, and the question may never be properly settled. Whatever the case, this state has produced such high-profile celebrity residents as basketball star Larry Bird, singer John Mellencamp, and television personality David Letterman.

Meanest man in the world

Ten miles (16km) inside the state at Angola, leave US 20 for I-69 south; you'll immediately note a proliferation of stands selling fireworks, which are illegal in adjoining states but freely available here. Fifteen miles (24km) later, cut over to US 6, which will carry you westward through northern Indiana to Illinois. Fields of golden grain (mostly corn) and silos announce it: you are solidly in the Midwest now. At Brimfield, detour a few miles north up Indiana 9 to the **Limberlost State Historic Site** (tel: 260-368-7428; Apr–mid-Dec Wed–Sun, mid-Dec–Mar Tue–Sat), a log cabin where Gene Stratton-Porter lived and wrote her well-loved books and essays about Midwestern nature. It's a peaceful spot among trees on a lake, perfect for a picnic.

Toni Morrison, Nobel Prize-winning author of Beloved, *was born in Lorain, Ohio. She recently dedicated a bench in Oberlin to mark a stop on the Underground Railroad where slaves on the run received help.*

BELOW:
an Indiana farm.

The Amish splintered off from Swiss Anabaptists in 1693 and settled in Pennsylvania. Now nearly half the states in the US have communities, and the number of followers is growing.

On the other side of Brimfield, south on Indiana 9, sits another fine park – **Chain O' Lakes State Park** is a refreshing string of oases in the middle of Noble County. This county was once home of the "meanest man in the world," according to Indiana's contribution to the 1930s WPA American Guide Series. Legend has it that this man divorced his wife, after which she landed in the poorhouse. In order to get funds, the institution would farm people out to the highest bidders, and when his ex-wife was put on the auction block, the "meanest man" purchased her to do the housework that his second wife had refused to do.

Life in the past lane

Back on US 6, tiny towns punctuate a landscape of corn in this region, known for the productivity of its land and for its considerable Amish population. The Amish have been in this area for more than a century. These inventive, industrious, and deeply religious people go about their business while shunning worldly things such as buttons, zippers, electricity, and motor vehicles. Cut north up Indiana 5 for a look at their farms, homes, and horse-drawn buggies.

First, you pass through **Ligonier**, a real find of a small town with an attractive main street and a number of handsome Victorian mansions. The interesting town clock here was erected by John Cavin, son of local pioneer Isaac Cavin, in memory of the father who laid the town out in 1835. Also have a look at the **Indiana Historic Radio Museum**, with its collection of old radio memorabilia.

Continue north on State 5 and then turn right at a gas station to reach **Topeka ㉞**, a tiny town whose slogan is "Life in the Past Lane." It's the kind of place where Amish buggies line up in parking lots, and hardware and feed stores outnumber banks three-to-one. Amish ride cycles around town, work the counter at restaurants, and just generally blend into life in this farming community. For a more intimate experience, inquire locally about the Amish Country Bed and Breakfast network, or just drive one of the many other county roads in this area. White farmhouses with full clotheslines and

BELOW: a bumper Indiana corn crop.

empty driveways are usually Amish, though you should always check ahead with tourism offices before attempting to visit a private home.

Now, retrace your steps back to US 6 and continue west. **Amish Acres** in **Nappanee** (tel: 800-800-4942; daily, closed Jan–Feb, variable days Mar–Dec), a historic farm homestead which interprets the Amish lifestyle for visitors, is fun though a bit over-commercialized. The round red barn hosts theater performances.

Beyond that, it's more lovely country driving through more fields of corn and occasional stands of maple trees. Drifting along US 6 like the "Windiana winds" through the last of rural Indiana before Chicago's industrial fringe, the route takes you over the Kankakee River (a good fishing stream) and on to **Westville**, home of an annual Pumpkin Festival that brings a carnival – and piles of orange pumpkins, of course – to town early each October.

Old-fashioned atmosphere

If you're hungry, make a quick swing down to US 30, on Indiana 2, and the town of **Valparaiso**, where Schoop's Hamburgers serves up old-fashioned atmosphere in the form of "Green River" sodas. The town was also the home of bow-tied popcorn magnate Orville Redenbacher, and you'll still find occasional popcorn stands in these parts of northern Indiana. In fact, this is a region of America that sometimes appears permanently frozen in 1950 – you are likely to encounter classic cars, crew cuts, and friendly folks. Make the most of it before you reach the sensory assault – and very different pace – of **Chicago** 35 *(see page 130)*.

THE WINDY CITY TO THE TWIN CITIES

Leaving Chicago, take Lake Shore Drive straight north out of the city and follow either US 41 or hop onto I-94 for a spell. Soon enough, you're in **Wisconsin**, the unofficial Cheese Capital of America, a friendly place settled by blond Scandinavians still very much in evidence today.

A few miles inside the state, turn west on Wisconsin 50 to make a lovely country drive past orchards, fruit stands, and

The Amish shun worldliness for small-scale values, with emphasis on the community.

BELOW LEFT: Amish buggy on a rural road.
BELOW: Mexican Independence Day parade, Chicago.

Chicago: The Windy City

Broad-shouldered and big-hearted, Chicago has a long list of aliases: Chitown and Second City are just two.

Although a few people might well dispute the authenticity of some of Chicago's various nicknames, one in particular will remain forever true: Crossroads of the Midwest. Chicago's railroad yards are the largest in the world. O'Hare claims to be the world's busiest airport. Even the famed Art Institute of Chicago straddles train tracks. Visitors get around the city by a light railway known as the El, for "elevated," because it usually is.

The site, at the confluence of the Midwestern prairie, the Chicago River, and Lake Michigan, was an obvious place for a town to spring up. With the building of a canal in the 1840s – essentially linking the Great Lakes with the Mississippi River drainage system – followed by the advent of railroading, Chicago spread like the proverbial wildfire as commerce and masses of immigrants descended upon it.

Then, in 1871, wildfire became a reality. As the story goes, a certain Mrs O'Leary's cow knocked

over a certain lantern, starting a disastrous blaze known as the "Great Chicago Fire." The fire signified the beginning of a new era in Chicago. The city became the workshop of architects like William LeBaron Jenny (the father of the skyscraper), Louis H. Sullivan, Frank Lloyd Wright, and later Ludwig Mies van der Rohe.

From the **Chicago Water Tower and Pumping Station**, the only public building to survive the Great Fire, to the **Sears Tower**, tallest building in America, the city's buildings and skyline are built to impress.

A few remnants of the 19th century have managed to survive, particularly in the **Prairie Avenue Historic District**. Once known as the "Avenue of Avenues," the area experienced a mass exodus during the early part of the 20th century. However, the buildings that remain are now being restored and lovingly protected.

Chicago has made the most of its magnificent lakeshore. A huge front yard encompasses 29 miles (47km) of beaches, wonderful parks with distinct personalities and some of the nation's finest cultural institutions: open daily are the **Museum of Science and Industry** (tel: 773-684-1414) on the South Side; the **Field Museum** (tel: 312-922-9410), the excellent **Shedd Aquarium** (tel: 312-939-2438), and the **Art Institute of Chicago** (tel: 312-443-3600), all in **Grant Park**. The Art Institute is known for its collection of works by the French Impressionists, and is also the home of that famous stoic couple staring out of Grant Wood's painting *American Gothic*.

Chicago is crazy about outdoor sculpture. All the big names are represented – including Olden-

ABOVE: Sears Tower.
LEFT: Lions in front of the Art Institute of Chicago.
RIGHT: Thanksgiving Day parade on State Street.

burg, Calder, Picasso, Miro, and Dubuffet. Chicago is the ultimate *film noir* set piece. Never has a place been so closely associated with gangsters and political corruption, the latter almost an institution. Eternally proud of those things that set it apart, the city has made little attempt to dispel these images even if they are quite unrealistic today. The real life of Chicago is a bit different. Politics are one face of it: black activist Jesse Jackson started his political career here and former mayor Richard J. Daley – gone but never forgotten – pulled the town's strings for so long that time is now measured in years AD ("After Daley").

This is also a writer's town, as articulate as it is brash. A steady stream of writers have interpreted their hometown for the rest of the world, everyone from James T. Farrell and Richard Wright to Saul Bellow, Studs Terkel, David Mamet, and the columnist Mike Royko.

Dark, smoky blues clubs have long been part of the Chicago scene, ever since players and singers from fields in the rural South relocated and invented "electric blues" here. You can hear all about it at **B.L.U.E.S.** on North Halsted or at the relocated **New Checkerboard Lounge** on the city's rougher South Side, where generations of University of Chicago undergraduates have learned about the important things in life from bluesman Muddy Waters.

There's a new brightness to the hip North Side of Chicago, although some locals never wanted the lights to shine – the lights of ivy-walled **Wrigley Field**, that is. After a long and impassioned debate, the home of the Chicago Cubs was the last Major League baseball park to get lights, thereby facilitating night games. Cub fans are fanatics.

The communities flanking Chicago have become part of the silver screen in a number of films poking fun at suburbia. **Glencoe**, to the north, is familiar to many as the home of Joel, the fictional teenager played by Tom Cruise in the movie *Risky Business* who submerges his father's Porsche in Lake Michigan. **Aurora** was the setting for the wacky comedy *Wayne's World*. And Joliet's penitentiary briefly housed John Belushi in *The Blues Brothers*.

Landlocked **Oak Park** is west of Chicago's Loop via I-290, on the other side of the city limits. Ernest Hemingway grew up here, and Frank Lloyd Wright lived and worked in Oak Park during the early part of his career before moving to Wisconsin. He left behind 25 buildings, making this the world's largest repository of his work. Wright's home and studio, built in 1889, is most revealing of his personality and genius: every touch, from the distinctive and renowned streamlined Prairie Style to the Scottish proverb that's carved over a fireplace, bears his characteristic imprint. ❑

Wisconsin's rural road sign is in the shape of the state.

BELOW: scaring the crows away.

small lake towns – one of which is called **Lake Geneva**, attractive if not exactly a match for its counterpart in Switzerland. Turn north on US 12, passing plenty of maple trees, small cafés, burger joints, and rustic roads (so marked by state road signs). You'll also come through **Kettle Moraine State Forest**, named for unusual features of the landscape – ridges of rock and silt, and circular ponds – produced here by the last great glaciation of North America. Rent a cycle from the general store to explore the area at your leisure.

At Whitewater, a small university town, you'll note a preponderance of custard stands serving burgers and frozen custard – a concoction invented in nearby Milwaukee. By state law, custard must contain a certain percentage of cream and a certain number of eggs. It's like ice cream, but sinfully richer; a spoon is barely adequate to pry it from the cup.

US 12 brings you to **Madison** ㊱, Wisconsin's capital and one of the Midwest's most agreeable cities. The city boasts a splendid downtown grid of streets with a capital building at its center, a university district to match and miles of lake frontage popular with joggers, boaters, skiers, and skaters – depending on the season. Snack on "brats" (short for bratwurst, local sausages of German origin) and beer, or enjoy the open-air farmers' market that takes over the city's main square in summer (Wed and Sat), a market purveying everything from organic produce to goat, bison, and emu meat, all produced in the state. There are also a number of museums here.

From Madison, take US 18 west through green pastures and roadcuts revealing the limestone underlying the countryside. This area is an anomaly in the normally flat Midwest, with numerous ridges popping up between you and the horizon; farms top distant hilltops like ships on sea swells. At the little town of **Mount Horeb**, exit onto County Road ID – in Wisconsin, unusually, minor roads are lettered instead of numbered – for a look at two attractions. The National Natural Landmark, **Cave of the Mounds** (tel: 608-437-3038), provides a scenic look below ground; **Little Norway** (tel: 608-437-8211; May–Oct daily) is a somewhat tacky attraction celebrating the Norwegian immigrants who largely settled this state.

Get back onto US 18 and continue to County Road BB, where a short detour south brings you to the **Folklore Village** (tel: 608-924-4000; Tue–Sun), a small complex of period buildings. It offers folk art workshops ranging from cooking to dancing and spinning wool. Call about the culture and recreation programs when in the area. The highlight is a one-room 1882 church, very simple but nicely restored; it was jacked up and moved from a nearby town.

Dodgeville, home to clothier Land's End, is just a few miles on. Take Wisconsin 23 north past the headquarters. On the way out of town you will pass the **Don Q Inn**, an eccentric lodge. Themed rooms include an igloo built for two, a hot-air balloon gondola, and many other options suitable for all levels of taste.

More dips and rises in the road lead to the **House on the Rock** (tel: 608-935-3639; May–Oct daily), Wisconsin's quirkiest must-see attraction. This unique complex of buildings on top of an odd rock formation was built up over a period of decades by inveterate collector Alex Jordan, Jr. Its many attractions include rooms and rooms of art, antiques and oddities, an "Infinity Point" glass bridge with views down a gorge, a huge assemblage of dolls' houses, a collection of rare books, vintage cars, and the world's largest carousel. It's well worth the expensive admission price, if only for a look at the fruits of a single man's manic obsession – you could easily spend the better part of a day roaming around this kitschy complex. If you don't have time for a long visit, there's an attractive spot just north of the entrance to park, walk a spell and get a distant glimpse of the house.

Frank Lloyd Wright's Wisconsin

Wisconsin 23 soon comes to the sandy banks of the Wisconsin River, where you'll be surprised to suddenly come upon Frank Lloyd Wright's **Taliesin** ❸ (tel: 608-588-7900; May–Oct daily, Apr and Nov Sat–Sun). Hillside School, designed by the architect, plus the Romeo & Juliet Windmill Tower and Wright's former home can all be seen; you must be on a guided tour to access this private estate. The setting is peaceful and lovely.

The route continues to the pretty little town of Spring Green, turns west onto US 14 and abruptly flattens before passing through **Richland Center**, the humdrum county seat renowned for being Wright's birth town. Then the road begins climbing and wrinkling again, indicating the approach of the Mississippi River. At **Coon Valley** ❸, neatly tucked within a surprisingly deep valley, you'll marvel at the surroundings and the town's solid Lutheran church. The **Norskedalen** (tel: 608-452-3424; May–Oct daily, rest of year Sun–Fri) complex outside town provides a pleasant look at Norwegian heritage in a quiet natural setting. Speed right through industrial La Crosse, hop onto I-90

Wisconsin was popular with Chicago-based gangsters during the Prohibition and Depression eras. Al Capone and other outlaws established hideouts in isolated areas of the state.

BELOW: a Wisconsin farm.

SLOW!! BUSY STREET AHEAD

Highways have replaced cornfields in many parts of Minnesota.

and take the big bridge across the Mississippi; get off again on the other side at signs for Highway 61, the road Bob Dylan called attention to in the namesake album and song. You have entered **Minnesota** and are now following the **Great River Road** toward the river's source. The route north clings to the bluffs of the Mississippi River, revealing spectacular colors in fall and outstanding river views at any time of the year. Patrons once rode steamboats all the way upriver from St Louis to gaze upon these high, beautiful bluffs.

Highway 61 is mostly grand views and ordinary towns from here to the Twin Cities, but there are a few worthy stops along the way. **Pepin**, back across the great river on the Wisconsin side, is renowned for being the birthplace of Laura Ingalls Wilder of *Little House on the Prairie* fame. There's a copy of the cabin "Little House Wayside" just north of town, and a small museum (mid-May–mid-Oct daily) as well.

North again, **Red Wing ㊴**, with an especially good vista of the valley,

makes a good place for a picnic and a photograph. There's an Indian reservation close by, as well, and it's good to have a look round before plunging into the suburban ring of towns and highways that have replaced what, until very recently, were cornfields but now serve as the suburban bases for legions of commuters into Minneapolis and St Paul.

The Twin Cities

Because of their proximity, **Minneapolis** and **St Paul ㊵**, on opposite sides of the Mississippi, will eternally be known as Minnesota's "Twin Cities." Fraternal rather than identical, they are like sides of the same coin: different, yet inseparable. St Paul, the more conservative, ethnic, and parochial of the two, presents an earthier and more weatherbeaten appearance. There's a more neighborly feel, too, and malt shops, health-food stores, and homes are more common here than the apartments, condos, and skyscrapers across the river.

Minneapolis, more competitive and cosmopolitan, dresses for success while living and breathing the concept of quality time. Local radio humorist Garrison Keillor puts it this way: "The difference between St Paul and Minneapolis is the difference between pumpernickel and Wonder Bread."

Yet together they are responsible for an urban success story, the envy of every overcrowded, and crime-ridden metropolis. Minnesota pioneers were forced by circumstances to cooperate with one another, and a genuine spirit of friendliness toward strangers prevails to this day.

People here put a lot of stock in politics and have developed a rather civic, populist bent: this state nourished the careers of Hubert Humphrey and Walter Mondale, the late Senator Paul Wellstone, and, outrageously, former Governor Jesse "The Body" Ventura, who was once a professional wrestler – continued this populist tradition, if in very different ways.

BELOW: Minneapolis.

MINNESOTA: LAND OF 10,000 LAKES

It always comes back to the lakes. Without its waters, Minnesota wouldn't even be Minnesota; the name itself comes from the Sioux, meaning "sky-blue water." The shore of **Lake Superior** marks the border of its northeast corner and the **Mississippi River** courses down its eastern flank. State license plates affirm "Land of 10,000 Lakes," but there are even more than that in the state.

During the 18th century, French explorers stumbled onto this region and named it *L'Etoile du Nord* – the Star of the North. Over the following 150 years, the Sioux and Ojibwa Indians who originally occupied the territory were frequently set upon by hundreds of white settlers, and violent clashes between the two Indian groups escalated.

In order to protect the early settlers and establish a secure trading station, **Fort Snelling** was built in 1819, high on river bluffs at the site of what is now Minneapolis. As rampaging Indians crossed the plains, white farmers fled to the fort for refuge; thus was the city born. Today, Fort Snelling has been reconstructed and staffed with actors who give visitors a first-hand glimpse of frontier life, *c.* 1825.

An increase in commerce along the river gave birth to the towns of St Paul and Minneapolis. The former sprang up as a local center of navigation and was originally known as Pig's Eye, after "Pig's Eye" Parrent, proprietor of a riverfront saloon. Seeking a better image, its residents renamed it St Paul.

Ever-industrious Minneapolis, "the city of water," evolved upstream around **St Anthony Falls**, source of power for sawmills and gristmills. Both towns were flooded with a wave of immigrants, mostly northern Europeans, on their way to harvest the bounty of the Great North Woods: lumber and iron ore. In the wake of the Homestead Act, more settlers then poured in to help cultivate a sea of wheat.

The Twin Cities' status in the world of agriculture, in fact, is never far from the minds of Minnesotans. Reports from the Minneapolis Grain Exchange, the nation's largest cash market, monopolize the local airwaves; General Mills and Pillsbury are headquartered here. Magnificent grain elevators, standing tall above the Mississippi, vie for attention with the likes of Minneapolis's **Investors Diversified Services** (IDS) building – the tallest one between Chicago and San Francisco – **St Paul's Cathedral** and the handsome **Capitol Building**.

Weather watchers

Characterized by stable neighborhoods and superbly planned public places and open spaces, the Twin Cities run smoothly even in cold weather. They've given a lot of thought to the weather here, after all, and over the years have refined methods of dealing with a winter that is typically cruel and unrelenting. Glass-enclosed skywalks radiate

Canoeing on a Minnesota lake in the morning calm.

BELOW: St Paul's Cathedral.

from the Crystal Court of the IDS building, as they do in downtown St Paul, and the enclosed **Hubert H. Humphrey Metrodome** hosts sports events and concerts year-round – and was the setting for two World Series titles for baseball's Minnesota Twins and success for the football team, the Vikings.

Yet people here are also perversely proud of their ability to withstand record-cold temperatures, and they celebrate the ice and snow at the St Paul's Winter Carnival, an annual event since 1886.

Culture is well endowed and thriving, particularly in Minneapolis. The **Walker Art Center**, along with its sculpture garden, is a forum for contemporary visual and performing arts that *The New York Times* called "one of the best contemporary art exhibition facilities in the world." The **Guthrie Theatre**, sited next to the Mississippi River with great views of St Anthony Falls, is indisputably one of the premier repertory theaters. The **Northrop Dance Season** puts together one of the most impressive dance series. The **American Swedish Institute**

archives and the European collections of the **Minneapolis Institute of Arts** (tel: 612-870-3131; Tue–Sun) are within a short distance of each other; both are terrific.

And there's still more to be found – avant-garde films, classical music, art galleries, jazz. The **Dakota Jazz Club** features the best local and international musicians nightly in downtown Minneapolis.

Famous state fair

The annual **Minnesota State Fair**, the nation's second-largest (behind New York's), should not be missed if you're coming through in late summer. Held at the State Fairgrounds over a week and a half, it is a stream of fishing and farming demonstrations, folk and country music performances, horse shows, special exhibitions for children, and carnival rides – accompanied by every sort of meat or cheese one can imagine, placed onto a stick and fried. The fair celebrated its centenary in 2009 – it's a huge dose of Midwestern popular culture, a little overwhelming but absolutely authentic.

BELOW: take a spin on the Gondola Ferris Wheel, one of the many rides at the Minnesota State Fair.

THE MISSISSIPPI TO THE BADLANDS

The region extending from the Mississippi River in Minnesota to the Missouri River in South Dakota marks the transition from the Midwestern to the Western states – geographically, culturally, and spiritually.

The transition can be subtle. If you listen to the car radio, up-to-the-minute reports from the floor of the Minneapolis Grain Exchange will be heard with progressively less frequency. Western idioms begin to turn up in small farm towns. The changes in geography are more abrupt, as the Missouri River serves as a sharp boundary between the Grain Belt and the true West.

Sodbusters

The region of Minnesota southwest of "The Cities" is unmistakably farm country. This land was settled by European and Scandinavian immigrants during the latter half of the 19th century. Some called them "sodbusters" as they indiscriminately cleared land and penetrated virgin sod, exposing the rich soil of the Midwestern prairie. Many of their grandchildren and great-grandchildren still farm the land here, an occupation known these days as agribusiness.

The founders of **New Prague** ⏶, a town dominated by **St Wenceslaus Church**, clearly had no desire to conceal their Eastern European heritage. West of the town, along State 19, are peculiarly medieval-looking buildings with domed roofs, looking incongruous in the midst of all-American corn country.

Those who believe the Valley of the Jolly Green Giant to be a mythical place created by television advertising executives are mistaken. At **Le Sueur**, renowned for its peas, US 169 intersects the Minnesota River and passes through this lush, green valley, marked by the Green Giant himself sprouting from the top of a billboard.

Branching southwest toward **Mankato**, the road enters Blue Earth country across the **Blue Earth River**. This is some of the most productive farmland in the state, a green expanse interrupted only by lakes. Modern farming is still a family business here, and it isn't unusual to see an entire family out in the fields working various pieces of machinery.

From Mankato, take US 14 west as far as tiny Florence, passing many more farms along the way, and then turn south onto Minnesota 23 for a more scenic stretch. In **Pipestone** ⏶, near the South Dakota border, the strong suit is Sioux quartzite rather than agriculture. Buildings constructed from this local, pinkish stone appear up and down historic Main and Hiawatha streets; significant not only because they are lovely to look at, but because they are among the last of their kind. The use of Sioux quartzite is no longer considered cost-effective.

However, for a period of less than 20 years before the turn of the 19th

Harvested hay bales resting in a Minnesota field.

BELOW: a fiery high-diving act at the Minnesota Fair.

Frequented by arche-ologists and paleon-tologists, South Dakota was where the most complete Tyrannosaurus Rex fossil skeleton was discovered: on the Cheyenne River Sioux Indian Reser-vation near Faith.

century, Pipestone went to town with it – the **County Courthouse**, the **Public Library**, the **National Bank Building**, the **Calumet Historic Inn** and, most impressively, **Moore Block** (1896) are all made of this material. L.H. Moore embellished the block bearing his name with fanciful images of the sun, angels, gargoyles, a jester, and the devil.

Underlying and veining Sioux quartzite is a material called pipestone, which gave the town its name. Longfellow's *The Song of Hiawatha* tells of "the great Red Pipestone Quarry," and the quarries in Pipestone and the land that surrounds them are still sacred ground of the Sioux and other Native Americans today – a land of legend and tradition, and now also a national monument.

To see more, take the **Circle Trail**, a mile loop through the prairie surrounding the quarries. It goes past **Hiawatha Lake**, **Winnewissa Falls**, quartzite cliffs and wind-carved formations known as **Old Stone Face** and the **Oracle**. A stone inscription along the trail documents the past presence

of the Nicollet expedition, members of which traveled through here in 1838 while exploring the lands of the isolated Upper Mississippi region.

Continue south from Pipestone along Minnesota 23, passing through **Jasper** (which also has its share of quartzite buildings). Angle onto Route 269, and in a few miles you will have crossed another state line – and you will be poised exactly halfway between the Atlantic and the Pacific oceans.

THE PINK ROAD TO SOUTH DAKOTA

The South Dakota Department of Highways chose to make use of the locally plentiful quartzite, and so a pink road unfolds at the border of their state. It takes you to **Garretson**, known for its **Devil's Gulch** ❹. The gulch is a sliver in the quartzite cliffs that loom above **Split Rock Creek**. According to one legend, the rocks were split by the Great Spirit's tomahawk. According to another, outlaw Jesse James jumped across the gap while being pursued by a posse. Fortunately for modern travelers, they can

BELOW: prairie sunset. **BELOW RIGHT:** King and Queen Rock, Pallisades State Park in Garretson, South Dakota

now cross the gap over a short bridge. Devil's Gulch lends Garretson an Old West image, but it is primarily a small farming community.

The prairies of eastern South Dakota and the pioneers who settled this land have been immortalized both on canvas and in popular literature. The paintings of Harvey Dunn, son of homesteaders and sodbusters, depict the reality and the dignity of these people. These same themes are mirrored in the work of Laura Ingalls Wilder, author of the beloved *Little House on the Prairie* and other books concerning life in the pioneer era before it was changed by modern times. (The books have now become an enormous industry, with over 50 million volumes having been sold. With the aid of some of Ingalls' descendants, ghostwriters have been employed to continue the series.)

To save time through this stretch of the Great Plains, get onto I-90, which cuts through eastern South Dakota in a nearly straight line through terrain that becomes a bit hillier and less green as rainfall becomes scarcer and the cultivation of hay and wheat mingles with that of corn.

These crops will eventually be taken to busy and industrious **Sioux Falls** ④, the state's commercial center, a city of little interest apart from the waterfalls themselves in Falls Park.

Farther west, in **Mitchell** ⑤, they have created a monument to and with all the amber-colored grains: the **Corn Palace** (tel: 866-273-2676; Dec–Mar Mon–Sat). It's one good reason to stop in Mitchell – the other being to take a much-needed break from the interstate. The Corn Palace is most certainly the world's only Byzantine structure decorated with murals of corn and other grains; each year, the patterns change according to local whim. It is a slice of quintessential Americana.

As I-90 approaches the Missouri River, which divides South Dakota into "East River" and "West River," a very different type of terrain lies ahead.

Where the West begins

Western South Dakota is unquestionably where the West begins. Visually, the Badlands and the Black Hills rise out of the prairie and hit you with a one-two punch; they are equally unexpected and stunning. But there is more to these regions than just their bleak beauty. They have been witnesses to some pretty tumultuous history.

If you're hurrying, stay on I-90 through to these twin wonders, but if you've got the time and inclination to explore rural South Dakota, then meander west instead along US 14, which you can pick up at the rather ordinary state capital of **Pierre** ㊻, reached on US 83 north from Vivian. After crossing the banks of the Missouri River, set your watch back an hour and prepare to traverse mound after mound of prairie grass. This route also coincides with a section of the old **Deadwood Trail**, a legendary wagon-train and stagecoach route.

The wagon-trains and stagecoaches were destined for uncivilized parts of the expanding nation; nevertheless, they had certain rules. "If you must

After crossing the Missouri River, set your watch back by one hour; Central time gives way to Mountain time here.

TIP

BELOW:
the Corn Palace, Mitchell, South Dakota.

drink, share the bottle," was one. Chewing tobacco was permitted, though it was requested the chewer spit "with the wind, not against it." And specified topics of conversation were forbidden: stagecoach robberies and Indian uprisings, to name but two.

US 14 cuts due south and then west again toward **Cottonwood**, foretold by grove after grove of cottonwood trees – the almost magical tree with the ability to "find" water in an arid landscape, and then reproduce in small communities. This tree was the single most useful tool the prairie settlers had: they could build a fence with it, sit under its shade, even cut into its bark to drink a bit of watery pulp in an emergency. Whenever you see the cottonwood's big-toothed leaves in a valley, you know there is water nearby, whether it be in the form of river, stream or some other hidden source.

Continuing west, motorists are besieged by a growing number of signs imploring them to stop at Wall Drug, located in Wall on the northern edge of the Badlands (*see page 143*). Depending on your degree of thirst, hunger, illness or defiance, you can continue west and arrive at Wall in no time at all, or turn south at Cottonwood directly into the Badlands.

This area is also known as the Dakota by the Sioux Indians, which roughly translates as "land bad." French trappers in the early part of the 19th century described it as "a bad land to cross." Many contemporary travelers bypass the Badlands (rarely visible from the interstate) while rushing to the Black Hills and the stone faces of Mount Rushmore, but it is a unique landscape and one that is certainly worth seeing – even if it can be a brutally hot place in summer.

Sand castles and canyon walls

This constantly eroding landscape has often served as a metaphor of youthful malaise and rootlessness: Terence Malick used it as a title for an acclaimed film (*Badlands*, 1973), and Bruce Springsteen later sang about "Badlands" on his 1978 album "Darkness at the Edge of Town." Despite all the discouraging words, there is a rare and striking beauty to be found here – it's well worth a detour off the interstate and the $15 per vehicle charge that it costs to enter the national park.

The Badlands have have been described as "Hell with the fires burned out," but, fire has played no part in it; it has been shaped chiefly by wind and water. Spires, turrets, and ridges form a silent skyline, which changes with each gust of wind and torrential (although infrequent) downpour. **Badlands National Park** ❹⓿ (tel: 605-433-5361) is not a single piece of land, but rather several chunks of territory loosely strung together and carved out of **Buffalo Gap National Grassland** and the **Pine Ridge Indian Reservation**.

It is possible to be driving through rolling grasslands and suddenly be confronted without warning with Badlands terrain: huge sand castles

BELOW: Badlands National Park – a landscape etched by wind and water.

and canyon walls. A 40-mile (64km) loop road traverses the park and provides access to points of geological and paleontological interest, including a number of hikes through the strange terrain.

This was once the stomping ground of ancient camels, three-toed horses, and saber-toothed tigers, whose fossilized remains continue to be uncovered by the elements. Many of these fossils, dating back to the Oligocene epoch, 24 to 34 million years ago, have been preserved by the **South Dakota School of Mines and Technology** and are exhibited at their **Museum of Geology** (tel: 605-394-2467; Mon–Sat in winter) in Rapid City. The largest of the Oligocene mammals was the titanothere, known in Sioux mythology as the Thunderhorse. It was believed by the Sioux that this creature descended from the heavens during thunderstorms and killed buffalo.

Enthusiasts were well on their way toward cleaning out the Badlands of its fossil treasures before the government and Federal protection intervened, and the abundant wildlife that once roamed here was also largely gone by the 1890s – depleted by the throng of humanity en route to the Black Hills in search of "the devil's metal" – gold.

Antelope and buffalo

Thanks to reintroduction and protection, however, the park is today a sanctuary for pronghorn antelope and buffalo. Prairie dogs also thrive here in their own metropolis. These peculiar rodents employ an elaborate system of tunnels, entry holes, and sentries; a shrill "barking" rings throughout the prairie if anyone ventures too closely.

Ranchers neither particularly like these creatures – as cattle can be severely injured by stepping into their holes – nor the weather, which here is as severe as it is unpredictable. Old-timers still talk about the blizzard of May 1905, when the weather progressed from balmy to icy. Thousands of head of cattle and horses drifted south with the wind and eventually fell to their death by pitching over the north wall of the Badlands. ❑

The Badlands have "a rare and striking beauty." For the visual evidence, see page 140.

BELOW: where the buffalo roam – across a road in South Dakota.

THE BADLANDS TO YELLOWSTONE

Drive through the land of Buffalo Bill, Wild Bill
Hickok, Calamity Jane, and the Sundance Kid
to see Mount Rushmore and the tragic
sites of the Indian Wars

L eaving the Badlands behind and heading west through South Dakota on Route 44, you'll come upon tiny Scenic, a ramshackle place named by someone with an extremely wry sense of humor; in exactly the same spirit, a sign along the main road ("Business District") signals your arrival. There's a tiny church here, a few abandoned shacks, several vintage mobile homes, a hole-in-the-wall US Post Office, a heap of junked cars, and, on the edge of town, the place people come here to see: the Longhorn Saloon.

The Longhorn was established in 1906, and the ankle-deep sawdust on the floor has been collecting ever since, as have the bullet holes and cattle brands on the ceiling. In its heyday, it was always the site of a recent shoot-out, and even now discomfort pervades the atmosphere. Tractor seats mounted on metal barrels serve as bar stools. Its facade features longhorn skulls and a weather-beaten sign that originally read "no Indians allowed," the "no" of which has been removed; the staff are often Oglala Sioux from the nearby Pine Ridge Reservation. Route 44 will take you on to Rapid City.

Wounded Knee

The Pine Ridge Reservation surrounds the southern tier of Badlands National Park and coincides with Shannon County, which has the lowest per capita income in the United States. On this bleak land, Wounded Knee Creek bleeds off from the White River to the site of the infamous massacre of December 29, 1890 – when 250 Sioux, mostly unarmed, were slaughtered by the army. Chief Sitting Bull was a casualty of this skirmish – the last tragic episode of the Indian Wars – and the name "Wounded Knee" has become an enduring symbol of unfathomable loss.

Wall Drug, in the town of Wall (located on Interstate 90 after completing a loop of the park), is a one-of-a-kind roadside stop – though it can't possibly live up to the miles of repeated

LEFT: a donkey at Custer State Park.
BELOW: Oglala Lakota boy.

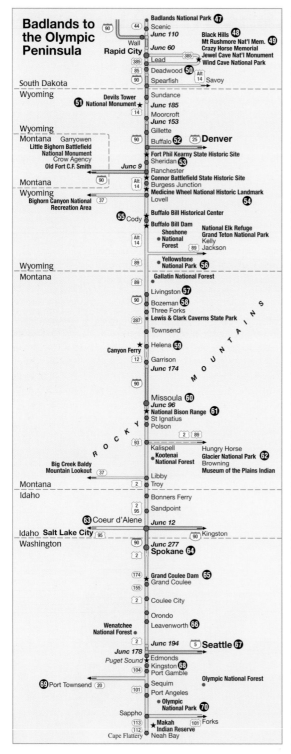

Badlands to the Olympic Peninsula

Badlands National Park 47
Scenic
Junc 110
Wall
Rapid City

South Dakota
Wyoming

Black Hills 48
Mt Rushmore Nat'l Mem. 49
Crazy Horse Memorial
Jewel Cave Nat'l Monument
Wind Cave National Park
Lead
Deadwood 50
Spearfish   Savoy

Devils Tower 51
National Monument ★

Wyoming

Sundance
Junc 185
Moorcroft
Junc 153
Gillette

Wyoming
Montana   Garryowen
Little Bighorn Battlefield
National Monument
Crow Agency
Old Fort C.F. Smith   *Junc 9*

Buffalo 52   Denver
Fort Phil Kearny State Historic Site
Sheridan 53
Ranchester
Connor Battlefield State Historic Site
Burgess Junction
Medicine Wheel National Historic Landmark

Montana
Wyoming
Bighorn Canyon National
Recreation Area

Lovell   54

55 Cody
Buffalo Bill Historical Center
Buffalo Bill Dam   National Elk Refuge
Shoshone   Grand Teton National Park
● National   Kelly
Forest   Jackson

Wyoming
Montana

Yellowstone
National Park 56
Gallatin National Forest
Livingston 57
Bozeman 58
Three Forks
Lewis & Clark Caverns State Park
Townsend
★ Helena 59
Canyon Ferry
Garrison
Junc 174

Missoula 60
Junc 96
★ National Bison Range 61
St Ignatius
Polson

Kalispell   Hungry Horse
Kootenai   Glacier National Park 62
National Forest   Browning
Museum of the Plains Indian
Libby
Troy

Montana
Idaho

Big Creek Baldy
Mountain Lookout

Bonners Ferry
Sandpoint

63 Coeur d'Alene
Junc 12
Idaho Salt Lake City   Kingston
Washington   *Junc 277*
Spokane 64

Grand Coulee Dam 65
Grand Coulee
Coulee City
Orondo
Wenatchee   Leavenworth 66
National Forest
Junc 194   Seattle 67
Junc 178
Puget Sound   Edmonds
69 Port Townsend   Kingston 68
Port Gamble
Sequim   Olympic National Forest
Port Angeles
● Olympic
National Park 70
Sappho
★ Makah   Forks
Indian Reserve
Cape Flattery Neah Bay

ROCKY MOUNTAINS

advertising painted onto abandoned trucks and wooden signs as you come west. Never has there been a more elaborate drugstore: located on the northern wall of the Badlands alongside the interstate, it is difficult to pass through this part of South Dakota without dropping in.

Apothecary Ted Hustead began posting the ubiquitous signs along the highway in the early 1930s, inspired by the old Burma Shave signs. By the time drivers hit the Missouri River, even the most stoic of travelers perceives a need for a glass (or maybe even a jug) of Wall Drug's famous ice water – although it does sell other drinks as well. Hence, what began as the only drugstore in a small, dusty town became famous as the "Ice Water Store" and now takes up most of Main Street.

Wall Drug has, among other things, a chapel for those in need of solace; a clothing and boot shop for those in need of Western duds; a bookstore; jewelry made from Black Hills gold, and a Western art gallery. There is also a staggering assortment of Western "attractions," from a replica of Mount Rushmore (for those tired of driving) to a mythical 6ft (2-meter) "jackalope" (a rabbit with antlers for the uninitiated), a mounted buffalo, and life-sized carvings of Butch Cassidy and the Sundance Kid. Donuts and coffee are free year-round for honeymooners and veterans and during the season for skiers and hunters. Approximately 20,000 folks stop by Wall Drug on a good day. It's the archetypal American success story, and Ted Hustead defines the lesson of his success in this way: "there's absolutely no place on God's earth that's godforsaken."

The ride from Wall to **Rapid City** along I-90 is approximately 50 miles (80km) of rolling, treeless prairie and wheat fields. You'll note black cattle dotting the grasslands, rolling hills slowly increasing in elevation and occasional patches of sunflowers. Rapid City, settled by prospectors in 1876 and slowly becoming a sophisticated place, is the gateway to the Black Hills.

The Black Hills

"... as long as rivers run and grass grows and trees bear leaves, Paha Sapa, the Black Hills of South Dakota, will foreeer be the sacred land of the Sioux Indians."
    excerpt, 1868 Treaty between US Government and Sioux Nation
"There's gold in them thar hills."
    attribuited to US Army scouts, 1874.

These words, taken together, summarize the course of late 19th-Century history in the **Black Hills** ㊽, and indeed throughout the West; an era characterized by greed, deception, and bloodshed. The Sioux were "granted" eternal rights to this land that held little interest for the white man until the discovery of gold. After that, of course, it was a different story.

George Armstrong Custer led an army reconnaissance expedition through here in 1874. The presence of gold was barely confirmed before a deluge of humanity swept through the hills, leaving the treaty of 1868 shredded in its wake. Years of bloodshed followed, and the Sioux would never regain exclusive rights to their sacred

Paha Sapa. A steady stream of travelers continues to flow through the Black Hills today – mostly past Mount Rushmore, the "shrine of democracy" that was never completed.

Going on past Rapid City and all the rampant commercialism of US 16, you'll encounter a road of another color, a 17-mile (27km) corkscrew known as the **Iron Mountain Road**. It is one of the spectacular, specially engineered Black Hills highways built in the 1930s and intended for pleasure driving. The inspiration of Highway Commissioner Peter Norbeck, the roads are characterized by hairpin turns, switchbacks, granite tunnels (placed to provide remarkable vistas) and pigtail bridges using native pine columns in place of steel.

Heads above the rest

Rather than sashaying around the mountain, Iron Mountain Road heads straight for the top. It passes by **Mount Rushmore National Memorial** ㊾ (tel: 605-574-2523; daily), which first appears framed at the end of a tunnel. This sight is akin to watching Hitchcock's *North by Northwest* (1959) on

You are now in rattlesnake country.

BELOW: sculptor Gutzon Borglum began work on Mount Rushmore in 1927, at the age of 60.

Sculptor Korczak Ziolkowski depicted the Native American hero with his left hand pointing in answer to a white man's question, "Where are your lands now?" Crazy Horse replied: "My lands are where my dead lie buried."

BELOW: scale model of the Crazy Horse Memorial, with rock and the work-in-progress in the background.

television from across the room. You may find yourself squinting to see if those specks up there are actually Cary Grant and Eva Marie Saint escaping across the six-story, granite faces.

Rushmore, the (uncarved) mountain, was purportedly named for Charles E. Rushmore, a New York attorney who visited here in 1885. When he asked a local about the name of the (then-nameless) peak, the fellow is said to have obligingly replied, "It is called Mount Rushmore." In the 1920s, Doane Robinson, the official historian of South Dakota, was considering various projects aimed at attracting visitors to the Black Hills. He decided on the concept of a colossal mountain carving, envisioning statues of legendary mountain men such as Jim Bridger, John Colter, and Kit Carson. But the more universally admired presidential subjects (George Washington, Thomas Jefferson, Abraham Lincoln, and, later, Theodore Roosevelt) were finally chosen.

In 1927, sculptor Gutzon Borglum (then 60 years old) was commissioned to do the work. The enormous endeavor took him the remainder of his life, and work on the mountain came to a permanent halt following Borglum's death and then the Japanese attack on Pearl Harbor. It's interesting to note that Borglum had intended the figures to be carved to the waist, and had he begun from the bottom rather than the top, the US would have been left with a rather peculiar shrine to democracy.

The project was always plagued by controversy and a lack of funding, largely as a result of the Depression and Borglum's artistic temperament and egotism. Some say he pushed for the inclusion of Roosevelt because he considered the president's spectacles to be a particular challenge to his skills, for instance. He also planned a 500-word chiseled inscription to be written by President Calvin Coolidge – an idea aborted following a ruthless and undiplomatic edit by Borglum. But the sculptor's ambition and talent were of the highest order, even if he was a difficult man to work with. The stone memorial is a testament to his own peculiar genius, and must be seen simply because it is unique to the United States.

Crazy Horse

Mount Rushmore is not the only mountain carving in the Black Hills. There is also the Crazy Horse Memorial (tel: 605-673-4681; daily), a work-in-progress by the late Korczak Ziolkowski. Whereas Mount Rushmore remains incomplete, Crazy Horse, even more ambitious in scale, is still in its infancy. Ziolkowski left detailed plans and instructions behind, and the grounds – the town of Crazy Horse now – are literally abuzz with workers.

Ziolkowski was engaged to carve this depiction of the great Sioux warrior by Chief Henry Standing Bear so that the white man might know that "the red man had great heroes, too." Although some 8 million tons of rock have been blasted off the mountain since 1949, it is still difficult to visualize a figure on horseback without the aid of a 1/34th scale plaster model. Still, the figure is gradually taking shape. Come for a look at the mountain and also to visit the ever-expanding **Indian Museum of North America**, as well as Ziolkowski's studio. Learning about the sculptor, his life and his ambitions for this place is time well spent. Ziolkowski was a fascinating giant of man, as a father, artist, and humanitarian. He liked to think of himself as a "storyteller in stone," and these are words he personally inscribed on the door of his tomb.

South of Mount Rushmore and Crazy Horse is **Wind Cave**, the first cave to be named a National Park. Wind Cave and **Jewel Cave** (its sister to the west) are the fourth- and second-longest caves in the world, respectively. They are characterized by calcite crystals and honeycomb formations known as "boxwork," found more extensively here than anywhere else in the world.

Supernatural highway

North of Wind Cave in the direction of Lead is Needles Highway, another Black Hills driving experience. The road was built to show off the Needles, granite spires which reach for the sky. The highway meanders and climbs several miles up into the firmament, at times through tiny granite tunnels. You must sound your horn before proceeding and don't let your attention stray too far.

Past Needles Highway, continuing north toward **Lead** on US 385, the aroma of pine pervades the atmosphere as the road passes through thick, dark stands of ponderosa pine. The appearance of these trees from afar gave the Black Hills its name. Lead (pronounced *leed*), named for a lode or vein of ore, is the site of **Homestake Gold Mine**, which produced more gold than any other gold mine in the Western Hemisphere during its 125 years of operation. It's still a company town of pickup truck-driving roughnecks, though tourists now mix curiously with them on the patchwork main street. The town's main tourist attraction is the old "**Open Cut**" – a gash in the side of the mountain where gold was originally discovered in 1876. Locals are proud of their rough-hewn town, and like to point out that it's a mile high, a mile

Cathedral Spires – Needles Highway was built to show them off.

BELOW: an autumn journey through Spearfish Canyon, South Dakota.

Old-style saloon in Deadwood, the "town built by gold." Calamity Jane and Wild Bill Hickok are buried in a cemetery near here.

BELOW: dancing and singing at a South Dakota tribal gathering.

long, a mile wide – and a mile deep.

Deadwood ⑳, three miles (5km) northeast of Lead on US 85, is the other Black Hills town built by gold. In fact, this was the original center of local gold mining activity – called to mind in the Eric Taylor/Nanci Griffith song "Deadwood, South Dakota" – before Lead overtook it. During the 1870s, Deadwood gained a reputation as the quintessential Wild West town thanks to local characters like "Wild Bill" Hickok, Calamity Jane, and others. Wild Bill and Calamity are buried beside each other in **Mount Moriah Cemetery** high above Deadwood, in accordance with Jane's last wishes, but today the place is rather tame and highly overdeveloped, its every nook devoted either to perpetuating a faux-"Wild West" image or to milking tourists out of their cash at one of the many gambling casinos.

If you must, visit **Saloon No. 10**, where Wild Bill was fatally shot by Jack McCall – but you have to find it first, as several bars claim the location. The real one is billed as "Home of the Deadman's Hand" and "The Only Museum in the World With a Bar," but the most interesting attractions of this area lie outside the town as you head further west. Descend from the hills via spectacular **Spearfish Canyon**, reached by driving north from Deadwood on US 85 for a few miles, then west on I-90, then US Alt-14 south. You can turn off onto a still rougher Forest Service road at the town of **Savoy** to glimpse the landscape where part of the movie *Dances With Wolves* was filmed.

Last green oasis

On US Alt-14, the canyon, threaded by the highway, winds down and down right alongside the cool, shaded Spearfish River. You'll have plenty of motorcycles and recreational vehicles for company, but there are a number of pull-offs where you can park and hike up or down the canyon in some solitude, noting the striking high cliffs of sandy-colored rock topped with aspen and pine trees. As this is the last green oasis before some very long and open stretches of forlorn Western country, you'd be well advised to do so.

WYOMING AND SOUTHERN MONTANA

Quite simply, the West is not like the rest of the country. The professional sport of choice here is not football, nor baseball, but rodeo. The sky seems larger than anywhere else, and you'll see frequent references to "Big Sky" country. This is a land of last stands, last chances, lost dreams; it is also a region of sparsely populated open spaces characterized by a wild natural beauty.

And Wyoming and Montana are the quintessential Western states. They lead all others in statistical extremity – the most bars, drive-ins, gas stations, cars, and mobile homes per capita. The myths of the West live on here in the hearts and lives of the people who call this vast country home; theirs is not an easy life, they will tell you, but they would not trade it for anything.

Descending from the Black Hills of South Dakota by way of Spearfish Canyon brings you right to I-90, less than 10 miles (16km) from the **Wyoming** border. The "Cowboy State," known locally as simply "Wyo," greets you with a sign proving you're in the West: while neighboring South Dakota has chosen somber presidential faces for its license plates, Wyoming has opted for a silhouette of a cowboy riding a bucking bronco. You'll notice this icon everywhere you go in the state.

Wyoming has a small piece of the **Black Hills National Forest**, located not far from the border outside of plain **Sundance** – the town "Where the Kid Got His Name." Indeed, Harry Longabaugh, better known as the "Sundance Kid," was said to have shot a deputy sheriff near here and subsequently headed for his infamous "**Hole-in-the-Wall**" hideout about 150 miles (240km) southwest. Once little known outside the West, his memory now lives on – and his name has become a household word – thanks to George Roy Hill and Robert Redford, director and star of the everlastingly popular movie *Butch Cassidy and the Sundance Kid*.

Past Sundance, US 14 loops up toward the Black Hills and **Devils Tower** , the object of obsession in a very different but equally popular film, *Close Encounters of the Third Kind*. Visible from almost 100 miles (160km) away, this 867ft (264-meter) fluted, butte-like rock formation is the tallest of its kind in America. It stands on the other side of the Belle Fourche River, where the Black Hills meet the gullies and grasslands of the plains.

The first white men to explore this region, supposedly misinterpreting a benign name ascribed to it by Native Americans, called it Devils Tower. It held a prominent place in the folklore and legends of the Sioux, and it later served as a landmark for those traveling west, just as it does today.

You can hike around the base of the tower, but beware of rattlesnakes. The majority of visitors simply stare at its almost supernatural shape and size – particularly luminous at sunrise or by the light of the moon. The sight of it so impressed Teddy Roosevelt that he designated it the nation's first national monument in 1906.

> *There's gold in them thar hills.*
>
> US Army scouts, 1874

BELOW:
Devils Tower is well known to fans of *Close Encounters of the Third Kind*.

A bison calf frolicking in the grasslands.

South of the monument, the road loops back onto I-90 at **Moorcroft**, an old cow town. The old Texas Trail made its way through here in the 19th century, trampled by cowboys driving cattle all the way to Montana. Farther west, through and beyond drab **Gillette**, the plains are vast and beautiful, marked only by cattle and the occasional river bottom of aspen and cottonwood trees. Even before crossing the Powder River and its tributary, Crazy Woman Creek, you can see the improbable pile of the Crazy Mountains looming, and then the snow-streaked peaks of the **Bighorn Mountains** in the distance: a tremendous relief for the traveler weary of the Great Plains.

A town called Spotted Horse

If you're taking US 14, you'll go through towns with colorful names such as Spotted Horse and Ucross. Take I-90, though, and you must drive a sparse (if beautiful) 70-mile (113km) stretch without so much as a town or gas pump to interrupt you, only miles of empty ranch lands. The lone break in this stretch is a

BELOW: Denver State Capitol Building.

forlorn rest area among trees at the crossing of the Powder River.

Traveling westward, the Bighorns gradually become closer. They were named for bighorn sheep, once prevalent here but now infrequently seen. As abrupt as they are majestic, the Bighorns foretell the Rocky Mountain ranges just beyond. These eastern foothills are today traversed by I-90 just as they once were by the Bozeman Trail, a bloody short cut in the 19th-century push westward through Sioux, Crow, and Cheyenne Indian hunting grounds.

Buffalo ❷, where the interstate highway bends north for Montana, was actually named after the town in New York and not for the formidable animals that once thundered across the plains. It was one of the earliest settlements in this corner of Wyoming, and its main street was formerly an old trail that negotiated Clear Creek. There's little here to see now besides a short main street, but it is a convenient stocking-up point for excursions into the mountains.

The road from Buffalo to Sheridan passes near the remains – now a state

Detour – Denver

A drive of grand vistas along the base of the Rocky Mountains on I-25 from Buffalo, Wyoming, leads after 388 miles (624km) to Denver, the Mile-High City. Celebrating the Gold Rush that built it is the grand Capitol building, covered in 250 ounces (7 kg) of 28-carat gold leaf. In the mid-1800s, weary, unlucky prospectors flocked to Denver for guns, booze, and women; the gambling halls never closed. Throughout the 1880s, money from silver camps bolstered the economy, and the population increased nearly threefold. The Black American West Museum and the Buffalo Bill's Museum and Grave hark back to these early days. Attractions like the Coors Brewery (free samples) and the Denver Art Museum, specializing in Asian, pre-Columbian, and Native American art, give the area a metropolitan flavor, but for all its culture, the city's natural setting is an easy distraction. Not only do the Rocky Mountains lie less than an hour away, but Denver is in charge of the largest park system in the country. Even its ever-popular concert venue, Red Rocks Amphitheatre, is a natural outdoor wonder, hollowed out of red sandstone on a site high above the city. The Denver Visitors Bureau is at 1-800-233-6837 or www.denver.org.

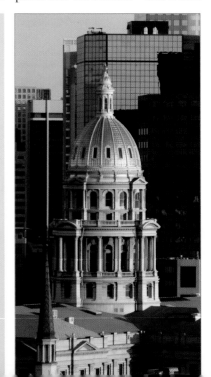

historic site – of **Fort Phil Kearny** (tel: 307-684-7629; daily). This was the most hated army outpost of all along the Bozeman Trail, and when it was finally abandoned in 1868, it was immediately burned to the ground by local Native Americans.

About 20 miles (32km) south of the Montana border lies the small historic city of **Sheridan** ⓢ, where I-90 and US 14 meet, and county seat in a region once inhabited by Crow Indians but now a major cattle-producing area. The railroad came to town in 1890 following the discovery of coal, and continued to play a major role in the development of the city. There are a number of historic homes, but the real pleasure is strolling Main Street among real-life saloons, cowboys, and western-wear stores. Have a drink at the Mint Bar, whose shingle walls are carved with hundreds of brands – each one different – of the cowboys who drank here over the past century. Across the street, through the back of King's Saddlery, is **Don King's Western Museum** (tel: 307-672-2702; Mon–Sat 8am–5pm). You could spend hours perusing this fascinating private collection of Western items, which includes cowboy and Native American memorabilia, historic photos, leatherwork, and around 600 saddles, many with intricately carved decoration.

An important inn

Across the street from the old railroad station is the **Sheridan Inn**, a gracious structure with a long, inviting front porch. It was built in 1893 by the Burlington Railroad and Sheridan Land Company. William F. "Buffalo Bill" Cody once owned part of this inn and made it his second home; it was customary for Cody to sit on the porch and audition acts for his Wild West Show.

Modeled after a Scottish inn, most of the materials used in its construction were shipped from back East by rail. In its day, it was considered to be the finest hotel between Chicago and San Francisco; presidents and such celebrities as Ernest Hemingway, General Pershing, and Will Rogers all stayed the night here, and this was the first building in the area to feature bathtubs and

Buffalo, Wyoming is named for the town of Buffalo, New York, not for the hairy bison that roamed the plains and which can still be seen at Yellowstone.

BELOW: bison (buffalo) in the Black Hills. No longer endangered, their numbers are now thought to be over 250,000.

The Battle of Little Bighorn, also known as "Custer's Last Stand," took place on June 25, 1876. The battle lasted only one hour, during which time the 7th Cavalry lost over 200 soldiers, the Sioux and Cheyenne fewer than 100 men.

electric lights. The lights were powered by an abandoned threshing machine and illuminated from dusk until midnight, when a whistle was blown to warn of impending darkness. Later came a telephone, first in the county, with a direct line to the drugstore. But the inn's pride and joy was its bar, constructed in England from oak and mahogany and hauled from Gillette by ox team. Still in use today, it's known as the "Buffalo Bill Bar."

The hotel is once again open to overnight guests after an extensive renovation in 2009. Have a drink at the famous bar, a bite to eat in the adjoining restaurant, and browse the memorabilia from the hotel's heyday in the reception area and public rooms.

Along I-90 north of Sheridan, as you approach the Montana border, sit two of the most infamous sites of the 1860s "Indian Wars." **Ranchester** is the location of **Connor Battlefield**, where General Patrick E. Connor led a division of more than 300 soldiers in an ambush of an Arapaho encampment. The Arapaho lost 64 of their people and their camp was virtually destroyed.

BELOW: the historic Irma Hotel in Cody.

Women and children were brutally massacred here, and as a result Connor lost his command.

Just north of Ranchester is the **Montana** line – also the beginning of the massive, empty-seeming **Crow Indian Reservation**. I-90 passes right through its heart, through the desolate-looking but neatly kept ranch lands of the reserve.

Battle of Little Bighorn

The town of Garryowen, named after an Irish drinking song, leads you into the legendary **Little Bighorn Battlefield** (tel: 406-638-2621; daily), now a national monument. The Battle of Little Bighorn, better known as "Custer's Last Stand," took about as long as it takes a white man to eat his dinner, according to one observer. But the Sioux and Cheyenne who fought that day were to lose the greater struggle. Two-hundred and sixty white marble stones along with the words of Oglala Chief Black Elk, in Lakota and English: "Know the Power that is Peace" now sanctify the field where Custer's men died.

Beyond the battle site is **Crow Agency**, headquarters of this 2.5 million-acre (1 million-hectare) reservation – far less than the lands outlined in the original treaty, which designated 38 million acres (15 million hectares) as Crow land. This area, bisected by the Bighorn River and characterized by rolling hills, was described by Crow Chief Rotten Belly in the 1830s as being "exactly in the right place. Everything good is to be found there. There is no country like the Crow Country." To get a glimpse of what modern Indian life is like out here today, pull off the interstate and drop into the gas station or grocery store.

Back on the highway, you'll begin to notice the first of many signs indicating "chain up areas" – turnouts where truckers wrap heavy chains around their tires in foul weather to obtain better traction through the treacherous mountain passes that await further inside Montana.

Make time at the northern edge of the Crow reservation, just south of Hardin, for a stop at the **Big Horn County Historical Museum** (tel: 406-665-1671; May–Sept daily, Oct–Apr Mon–Fri). This collection of architectural structures from around the huge, spare county – which is tops in agricultural production for this state – includes a train station, German church, and the original farmhouse and barn that occupied the site. The museum also serves as your first pickup point for Montana information, and its helpful staff can direct you to area attractions such as the superb fishing in **Bighorn Canyon**. Crow guides will take you up the canyon for a price, and if you'd like to stay on the reservation, lodges and motels are thick on the ground in **Fort Smith**.

From Crow Agency to Billings, I-90 skirts the northern boundary of the reservation through towns with names like Big Timber. It doesn't get interesting again until you've reached Livingston and Bozeman. If you wish to see Yellowstone, you can also reach those towns via a scenic – if roundabout – method, by backtracking south a bit to Ranchester, Wyoming.

Towards Yellowstone

Approaching the Bighorn Mountains via I-90 in clear weather, you can sometimes discern a road switch-backing its way up the snow-streaked slopes. Traveling west from Ranchester to Lovell allows you to experience it firsthand. US 14 out of Ranchester ascends Bighorn National Forest past bullet-ridden signposts to Burgess Junction. The road is treacherous beyond this point: several runaway truck ramps and brake-cooling turn-outs help drivers negotiate the steep grades and sharp turns.

About 20 miles (32km) beyond Burgess Junction is a 3-mile (5km) bumpy gravel road leading to the Indian **Medicine Wheel** 54. Although well paved, the road is extremely narrow and winding, at one point crossing a narrow ridge. But the views from these highest reaches of the Bighorns are stupendous, and the immediate countryside is sprinkled with wildflowers. Near its end, the road forks and

Holy Elder at Sioux Pine Ridge Reservation in South Dakota.

BELOW: monuments and graves at Little Big Horn Battlefield, Montana.

Buffalo Bill rose to fame through a series of dime novels based on his character. His Wild West show hit the road in 1883 and by the 1890s was performing in Europe in front of royalty.

BELOW: Buffalo Bill Historical Center, Cody, Wyoming.

presents you with a clear choice: the 20th-century radar facility to the left or the ancient medicine wheel to the right. Go right. This medicine wheel is the most elaborate of a series of stone circles found east of the Rocky Mountains, its 28 spokes forming an almost perfect circle 74ft (23 meters) in diameter. It is thought to be about 600 years old, but its creators and its purpose still remain a mystery. According to Crow legend, the wheel was here when they arrived in the 1770s. Today, it serves a ceremonial function for Native Americans. Perhaps a certain amount of visitors, looking over at the radar station, might wonder how *that* structure will be interpreted centuries from now.

Past the Medicine Wheel, US Alt-14 plunges down the mountain into the **Big Horn Basin**. Protected by the mountains, this region enjoys a milder climate than the rest of Wyoming. It is a prime cattle-producing area that saw one of the last great range wars between cattlemen and sheepherders in the early 20th century.

US Alt-14 travels from Lovell to Cody through Shoshone River Valley. **Lovell**, a well-groomed town, was founded by ranchers in the 1870s and remains identified with cattle, though it is also known as the "Rose Town of Wyoming." Past Garland, the Rocky Mountains loom into view for the first time, with square-topped **Heart Mountain** in the foreground. A short drive from here is Cody, a town named after William F. "Buffalo Bill" Cody.

Buffalo Bill's town

You can't pass through **Cody** ⑮ without confronting the memory of Buffalo Bill, that one-time Pony Express rider, soldier, buffalo hunter, Army Chief of Scouts, rancher, frontiersman, actor, and showman. He has accurately been called a "kaleidoscope of white man's western experience." Through his Wild West Show, his own screen roles and other films that dealt with his character (played by everyone from Roy Rogers to Charlton Heston and Paul Newman), he has, more than any single person, influenced the world view of the West – for better and worse. And he certainly left his mark on Cody.

The place is unquestionably tourist-crazy. When Yellowstone attained national park status, this town jumped in with both feet, billing itself as gateway to the park. Today, there are enough tour buses, tourist attractions, and hoopla in the town that the inclination is to step on the gas. If you can withstand souvenir shops and the phony facade, however, you will discover a bit of the Old West here.

Best is the **Buffalo Bill Historical Center** (tel: 307-587-4771; Apr–Oct daily, Nov–Mar Thur–Sun), which is actually five outstanding museums in one. The **Buffalo Bill Museum** is devoted to the man's vast collection of memorabilia. He was known for his flamboyance and excess, and the collection is all the better for it. The **Whitney Gallery of Western Art** spans the period from the 1800s to the present. All the greats are represented – Catlin,

Bierstadt, Moran, Remington, Russell; Remington's studio has been re-created here, as well. The **Plains Indian Museum** displays perhaps the world's finest collections of Sioux, Cheyenne, Shoshone, Crow, Arapaho, and Blackfoot artifacts. Extremely interesting is a series of precise pictographs executed by Chief Sitting Bull while imprisoned at Fort Randall in 1882. Drawn on Fort Randall stationery, they depict what he considered to be the important events in his life.

Rodeo capital of the world

Cody is also known for its Night Rodeo, a tradition which, along with the annual Fourth of July Cody Stampede, legitimizes the town's claim to be the "Rodeo Capital of the World." Old Trail Town (tel: 307-587-5302; mid-May–mid-Sept daily), which includes the Museum of the Old West, is located west at the original town site. The beloved obsession of Bob and Terry Edgar, this is an impressive collection of authentic frontier buildings, horse-drawn vehicles and other artifacts from Wyoming's past. The

"Hole-in-the-Wall Cabin," used by Butch Cassidy and the Sundance Kid, is also here, marked by a rock with the oldest inscribed date in northern Wyoming (1811).

A number of legendary frontiersmen have been reburied here at the cemetery, among them John "Jeremiah Liver-eating" Johnson, portrayed by Robert Redford in the film *Jeremiah Johnson*. Johnson died in an old soldiers' home far from the mountains where he lived, and his reburial was marked by a moving ceremony attended by Robert Redford and the Utah Mountain Men, who served as pallbearers. The plaque on his grave simply reads "No More Trails."

US 14 west out of Cody follows the Shoshone River, winding through the formations of **Shoshone Canyon** and past the **Buffalo Bill Dam**, the world's first concrete arch dam. It tunnels through **Rattlesnake Mountain** and continues on through the **Shoshone National Forest** (the nation's first). As you take leave, you'll soon find yourself at the entrance to Yellowstone National Park. ❏

Buffalo Bill, claimed by Cody, Wyoming, was actually born in Iowa. The modern artist Jackson Pollock was born in Cody, a fact that is virtually ignored.

BELOW: poster for Buffalo Bill's Wild West show.

YELLOWSTONE TO THE OLYMPIC PENINSULA

The Northern Route concludes its coast-to-coast journey by traveling through several of the most glorious national parks in the land to the far northwestern corner of the US

The national parks of the northern Rockies – Yellowstone, Grand Teton, and Glacier – are regions of breathtaking natural beauty, vignettes from a more primitive North America. These mountain parks all share an abundance of wildlife, but each possesses a distinct personality. Yellowstone has its geysers; Grand Teton encompasses the incomparable Teton Range, rising above cattle country; and Glacier has its spectacular mountain passes.

The route between Yellowstone and Glacier passes through the westernmost **Great Plains**, the traditional hunting grounds of the Plains Indians. First described by Lewis and Clark in the early part of the 19th century, and later depicted by Charles Russell, the landscape is now dominated by cattle ranches and wide-open fields of wheat.

Symbol and sanctuary

Yellowstone National Park **⑤⑥** (tel: 307-344-7381; mid-Apr–Nov daily, weather permitting; most roads closed in winter) is both symbol and sanctuary. Located in the northwest corner of Wyoming, it was the world's first national park – and for many people still the most magnificent. This primitive landscape, forged by fire and water, has been called the "greatest concentration of wonders on the face of the earth," its shapes and colors "beyond the reach of human art." It is a hotbed

of geothermal activity, with more than 10,000 thermal features, as well as being one of the last remaining habitats of the grizzly bear in the continental United States. All this, and enough canyons, cliffs, and cataracts to please the most jaded eye.

Though Native Americans hunted here for centuries, credit for the region's discovery goes to John Colter, the first white man to set foot in what is now Wyoming. Later in the 19th century, trappers and prospectors passed through, among them Jim

Main attractions
YELLOWSTONE NATIONAL PARK
GRAND TETON NATIONAL PARK
NATIONAL ELK REFUGE
MUSEUM OF THE ROCKIES
MONTANA HISTORICAL SOCIETY
NATIONAL BISON RANGE
GLACIER NATIONAL PARK
MUSEUM OF THE PLAINS INDIAN
LAKE PEND D'OREILLE
OLYMPIC NATIONAL PARK
SEATTLE

LEFT: Yellowstone's Old Faithful Geyser. **BELOW:** skiing in the Northern Rockies.

Cowboy country around Yellowstone is also bison, elk, and grizzly bear country.

BELOW: road through Grand Teton National Park.

Bridger, a celebrated mountain man and teller of tall tales. Impressed by the petrified trees of **Specimen Ridge**, he embellished his description a bit, raving of "petrified trees full of petrified birds singing petrified songs." In 1870, Henry Washburn, the Surveyor General of Montana Territory, headed up a more illustrious expedition endeavoring to set the record straight. They returned awestruck and committed to the creation of a "nation's park" – a dream realized in 1872.

Yellowstone encompasses an area of more than 2 million acres (800,000 hectares). Those who prefer being at one with nature can rest assured that 95 percent of this area is backcountry. For the less intrepid, there are nearly 300 miles (480km) of roads. The **Grand Loop Road** provides access to most of the major attractions, from **Yellowstone Lake** and the **Grand Canyon of Yellowstone** to **Mammoth Hot Springs** and **Old Faithful**. They are simply magnificent.

Many visitors view Old Faithful's performance with a sense of obligation. Although not as faithful as it once was, the geyser pleases the crowd regularly – 21 to 23 times daily. This is also a prime location for people-watching; a chance to glimpse a real slice of American life frozen in anticipation.

Don't pet the bears

Some come to Yellowstone primarily to view wildlife, and few depart disappointed. Stopped cars along the road generally indicate that some large mammal is grazing nearby. Unfortunately for both man and beast, visitors tend to forget their natural fear of and respect for these truly wild creatures. A park ranger relates that people who would ordinarily be reluctant to pet a neighbor's dog have no qualms about posing for a snapshot with a wild animal twice their size. Bison gorings are quite common and can be serious. Of ever greater concern to park officials are the bears – both black bears and grizzlies, but the latter are more dangerous and more endangered. One way to avoid bears is to visit the park in winter, a time of hibernation and a season that comes early to Yellowstone.

With the arrival of winter, the Yellowstone elk population leaves the high country and heads for the National Elk Refuge outside of Jackson, Wyoming. Though not exactly following in their hoofprints, US 89 south nevertheless takes you from the southern boundary of Yellowstone Park, through magestic **Grand Teton National Park** (tel: 307-739-3300; daily) and Jackson Hole, alongside the refuge, to Jackson, the perennial boomtown.

If the Rockies are the crown, then the **Teton Range** is its jewel. Exquisitely beautiful, amethyst-tinged, jagged, snowcapped, and hypnotic, they loom above the horizon west of the highway. The **Snake River**, running true to its name, intervenes. The Tetons and **Gros Ventre** ranges encircle the **Jackson Hole** valley. Trappers worked this territory in the early 19th century and it was named for David E. Jackson, a prominent member of the trade. Settlers came in the 1880s as outlaws, homesteaders, and ranchers. This is a gorgeous landscape, never more visually stunning than in the classic 1953 western movie *Shane*, filmed on location here.

It is still cattle country, but tourism has become the economic mainstay now. People flock from all over the country to ski here, especially the well-to-do. Nearby **Rendezvous Mountain**'s claim to fame is its vertical drop – the greatest of any US ski resort, which can be appreciated even in summer by taking a ride on the aerial tram with a sheer ascent of nearly 1 mile (1.6km). The view from the summit is stupendous – across Grand Teton and far beyond.

Million-dollar cowboy bar

The Old West and the New West have converged in **Jackson**, land of condos and cowboys. This is a big-name resort with its share of local color; you just have to look for it. Look beyond the boutiques, the ski chalets, the nightly "shoot-outs" and the stagecoach rides. Bars are generally the best place for this sort of quest, so pull up a saddle (mounted on a bar stool) at the **Million Dollar Cowboy Bar** and hoist a few beers with the locals.

North of Jackson is the **National Elk Refuge** (tel: 307-733-9212; daily), established in 1912 and now the winter habitat of a herd some 5,000 strong. Once victims of starvation and disease, these elk are now protected by law. Regularly scheduled sleigh rides transport visitors briefly into the company of these graceful creatures. In spring, the elk shed their antlers, which are expeditiously retrieved by area Boy Scouts and later auctioned off at a considerable profit.

Gardiner, Montana, sits along US 89 just north of Yellowstone on the southern fringe of **Gallatin National Forest**. Out of Yellowstone, the road passes through barren plains, irrigated farms, and a land of many hot springs – mineral bath resorts are thick on the ground here – before reaching the forest, rich in minerals. The road plays hide-and-seek with the Yellowstone River awhile longer before intersecting with US 191 at Livingston.

TIP

The best way to explore this quintessential winter wonderland is on skis. Snowmobiles and snowcoaches only provide limited access as roads are closed to most vehicles. The thermal areas are good places to spot wildlife warming their hooves and paws.

BELOW: around 5,000 elk spend the winter near Jackson, Wyoming.

BELOW: an unpaved track curving through Gallatin Valley.

Livingston ❺❼ was put on the map by both the Northern Pacific Railroad and its proximity to Yellowstone, just 56 miles (90km) to the south. Retaining some of its pure-West authenticity, it has also been the popular haunt of Western authors and painters such as Russell Chatham and Jim Harrison – not to mention modern movie stars and media types such as Andie Mac-Dowell and Ted Turner, among others. The town consists of a small grid of streets with bars and cafés; its proximity to Bozeman has also brought an increasing number of university students and professors.

A little west along I-90 sits **Bozeman** ❺❽, nestled in the Gallatin Valley beneath 9,000ft (2,700-meter) peaks that seem close enough to touch in the gin-clear air. This was known as the "Valley of Flowers" by the Blackfeet, Crow, Cheyenne, and Snakes who hunted here. William Clark passed through the area with their blessing in 1806 on the return trip of his path-finding expedition. John Bozeman and Jim Bridger later guided wagon trains through in direct violation of treaty, at

considerable risk. The trail became Bonanza Trail, the Bridger Cut-Off, and the Bloody Bozeman – a treacherous short cut for impatient pioneers.

Like so many other Western cities, Bozeman has a historic main street, though several of its century-old buildings were destroyed in a gas explosion in 2009. It also has a state university – which has brought outdoor gear shops, health-food stores, and the like. The Gibson Guitar company manufactures quality guitars at a plant just outside town. You might also care to make a visit to the **Museum of the Rockies** (tel: 406-994-2251; daily), an institution devoted to the physical and cultural heritage of the northern Rockies. Bozeman's own "boot hill" is **Sunset Hills Cemetery**, final resting place of journalist Chet Huntley, pioneer John Bozeman and Nevada miner Henry T.P. Comstock.

Lewis and Clark

Northwest of Bozeman, along Montana 2, sits Manhattan – which doesn't have much of a skyline at all – followed by the town of **Three Forks** across the Madison River. This town was named for the Missouri Headwaters – the Gallatin, Madison, and Jefferson rivers – all named by Lewis and Clark. Meriwether Lewis and William Clark led their historic expedition through here in July 1805, having accepted the challenge of exploring the recently acquired Louisiana Purchase by tracing the Missouri River and its tributaries to (they hoped) the Northwest Passage. By the time they reached the Three Forks area, however, they realized that the Missouri drainage system did not in fact lead to the Pacific. Nevertheless, the success of their expedition remains undisputed. They opened up the West for a generation and for all time; a deluge of exploration – and exploitation – soon followed.

Gone today is the abundant wildlife Lewis and Clark found at the headwaters, although a state park has been

developed to commemorate and interpret its historical significance. Here, you can have a picnic at the very spot where the expedition stopped to have breakfast on July 27, 1805, and then climb up to "**Lewis Rock**," where Lewis sketched a map of the countryside. At the entrance to the park are the remains of a ghost town, **Second Gallatin City**.

The town moved here from across the headwaters so as to sit astride a main stagecoach route, having by that time been abandoned by the steamboat. But its existence was unfortunately short-lived, bypassed by the next wave of transportation – the "iron horse" itself, the mighty railroad.

A few miles west of Three Forks on I-90, the color suddenly changes to the gold of wheat, and US 287 enters, going north toward Helena. Past **Townsend**, **Canyon Ferry Lake** appears to the east of the road like an oasis on the prairie. Behind it stand the **Big Belt Mountains**. US 287 continues north and merges with I-15, skirting **Helena ❺**, Montana's seat of government.

Last Chance Gulch

In Helena, they continue to make Lewis and Clark bourbon, and you still hear talk of Last Chance Gulch – though now it's a pedestrian mall. Fans of cowboy-artist Charles Russell, for whom acclaim runs high in Montana, will want to stop by the **Montana Historical Society** (tel: 406-444-2694; Mon–Sat), which houses a collection of his work.

From Helena, US 12 runs up and over 6,300ft (1,920-meter) MacDonald pass (don't try this if winter is approaching) and the **Continental Divide**. Watersheds from this point flow into the Pacific instead of the Atlantic. To the west of the Divide, at Garrison, you must get back onto I-90 for another stretch of rugged mountains; you are solidly within the Rockies now, with minor ranges such as the Garnet Range to either side of the road. A rest area on the interstate provides a good chance for you (and your vehicle) to rest from

all the mountain-climbing while gazing at the surrounding peaks.

Then it's down to **Missoula ❻**, the state's most liberal-leaning town thanks to the influence of the University of Montana. You will note a giant "M" carved in the hills outside town, and that marks the university. The trail actually runs on campus property and makes for a popular hike. The town boasts the usual rough-and-tumble Western bars, certainly, but also good health-food shops, bookstores, and music – not a bad place to spend the night.

From Missoula, take US 93 due north and begin climbing again, at least for a bit, as you begin to enter the **Flathead Indian Reservation**. Roadside stands and restaurants sell bison burgers and huckleberry shakes, the local twist on fast food. This area was once all Flathead territory by decree of treaty, but the tribal lands were gradually settled by missionaries and sold piecemeal to speculators. Today, a mixture of residents manage to coexist amid lovely, wild scenery.

At the junction of Montana 200, turn west a short ways to tour the

Cowboy-artist Charles Russell's enormous mural, Lewis and Clark Meeting the Flathead Indians at Ross' Hole, *graces the chambers of the House of Representatives in Helena, Montana.*

BELOW: Helena is Montana's seat of government.

The Montana town of Hungry Horse was named for some freight horses that once escaped and nearly starved to death before being discovered and nursed back to health.

National Bison Range ❻ (tel: 406-644-2211; daily, weather permitting), where some 350 to 500 of these magnificent animals – as well as many other species of wildlife – roam over more than 19,000 acres (7,700 hectares) of beautiful grassland and park-like patches of timber. Again, however, remember not to get too close – technically, you are not even supposed to get out of your car while traveling through the range.

A few miles north again on US 93, **St Ignatius** beckons as a turn-off beneath the splendid Mission Mountain range. The town's chief draw today is actually its impressive mission church (tel: 406-745-2768; daily), built in 1854 and possessing some interesting fresco work within. The surrounding mountains are still occupied by Flatheads, and you need tribal permits to fish, hunt or visit. It's a beautiful and rugged country; bears and mountain lions are frequently seen.

North again, US 93 becomes ramrod-straight – one of the most accident-prone stretches of highway in the land, so look sharp. It continues north along-side the mountains to the folksy town of **Polson**, where huge **Flathead Lake** drains through a gorge; then the road bends to circle the lake's western shore. A giant Flathead-owned casino has somewhat marred what was once pristine scenery here, but the lake is still marvelous to contemplate as you climb around it to **Kalispell**, population center of the area and a base for excursions into Glacier National Park. Fittingly, its name means "prairie above the lake."

US 2 turns east to pass through Columbia Falls and then **Hungry Horse**. The highway crosses the middle fork of the Flathead and meanders through the pristine, cathedral-like wilderness of **Flathead National Forest** before finally reaching the natural wonders of the park.

Glacier National Park

Glacier National Park ❻ (tel: 406-888-7800; daily) is more remote and less crowded than Rocky Mountain Park or Yellowstone, yet traffic can still be heavy. Traveling here is therefore most satisfying at off-peak times – at sunrise or sunset or during early summer and autumn. It is generally plowed and fit for driving from mid-June to mid-October, when the Park Service closes it down for the winter.

Near the park's western edge is **McDonald Creek**, a final resting place for kokanee salmon who travel here in late autumn from Flathead Lake to spawn. This event attracts hundreds of bald eagles, which in turn attracts an increasing number of bird-watchers.

The Continental Divide forms Glacier's backbone, crossed by spectacular **Going-to-the-Sun Road** at Logan Pass. Opened in 1933, this is the only road that crosses the park, bisecting it into two nearly equivalent sections. It has been called "the most beautiful stretch of road in the world," its twisting 50 miles (80km) of two-lane pavement climbing from the settlement of West Glacier to the shore of Lake McDonald, to Garden Wall, and finally

BELOW: Going-to-the-Sun Road, Montana, has been called "the most beautiful stretch of road in the world."

crossing Logan Pass and descending to St Mary. The entire road is open mid-June to mid-September, but portions may be closed for roadwork outside this season through 2015.

Along the road, stop for spectacular vistas of the **Hanging Garden Trail**, which leads to vast alpine meadows. Columbian ground squirrels greet hikers at the trail head, which proceeds past deformed trees known as *Krummholz* (the German word for "elfin timber" or "crooked wood") and across the meadow. There is an ever-changing repertoire of glacier lilies, Indian paintbrush, red monkey flowers, and mountain heath. Mountain goats can sometimes be sighted from here, as well as grizzly bears, who feed on the meadow's plentiful bulbs and roots. **The Highline Trail**, across the road from the Hanging Garden, is a more challenging and potentially dangerous trail – not recommended for the faint-hearted. Opportunities for backcountry hiking abound inside the park. Its approximately 50 glaciers, 200 lakes, alpine meadows, and forests are a haven for fishermen, hikers, and wildlife alike. And two rustic stone chalets (called **Granite Park** and **Sperry**), reached only by foot or horseback, offer overnight accommodations; both were built around 1914 by the Great Northern Railroad. The glaciers which created this magnificent park are rapidly disappearing, tragic victims of global warming, and the only way to see many of them is on foot.

At the eastern edge of the park – and Going-to-the-Sun Road – sits the small, friendly town of **St Mary**, which separates Lower St Mary Lake from St Mary Lake proper. Even the drive out of the park along US 89 is dramatically beautiful, descending rapidly from St Mary to Kiowa and winding sharply as it goes, then turning due east out of the mountains. From there, the enticing road goes to **Browning**, headquarters of the **Blackfeet Reservation** and home of the truly interesting **Museum of the Plains Indian** (tel: 406-338-2230; June–Sept daily, Oct–May Mon–Fri), which houses the most comprehensive collection of Blackfeet artifacts in existence.

Western Montana is perfect for mountain biking with many excellent rugged terrain rides only minutes from urban areas.

BELOW: Lake Josephine in beautiful Glacier National Park.

*A Plains Indian
Assiniboine drum.*

Of particular note are the Assiniboine drums, some of which have been painted with wonderful visionary designs suggesting hallucinatory images; it is thought the hallucinations were caused by prolonged fasting.

BEYOND THE GREAT DIVIDE

As waters flow west of the **Continental Divide** toward the Pacific, so too do paths of civilization. The Nez Percé, the Kootenai, the Pend d'Oreille, the Flathead and other mountain tribes lived and hunted here in peace. Later, the Blackfeet came from the plains across the Divide on horse-stealing raids, a journey many have since followed for different reasons.

The first white people to arrive were trappers and traders in the early part of the 19th century, followed by prospectors in search of gold and silver. Homesteaders heading west conquered the Rockies and moved on, some settling in eastern Washington. With the coming of the railroad, the lumber industry found a permanent home in the forests west of the Divide.

BELOW: Mormon re-enactment near Salt Lake City.

Fire! Fire!

From Browning, take US 2 west over **Marias Pass** and skirt the southern edge of Glacier Park, passing through Hungry Horse and Kalispell once more. West of Kalispell, the **Kootenai National Forest** takes over where the Flathead leaves off. Along the highway toward **Libby**, the lumber industry's presence in this area becomes progressively more apparent. Timber has been big business here since 1892, when the Great Northern Railroad arrived. But as with all national forests, the Kootenai is a mixed-use area and within its boundaries (an area nearly three times the size of Rhode Island) lie many acres of wilderness: the habitat of elk, moose, deer, and Rocky Mountain bighorn sheep. A system of observation towers, manned around the clock, was once the primary method of forest fire surveillance. As fire detection methods became more sophisticated, these structures were gradually vacated. The **Canoe Gulch Ranger Station** (tel: 406-293-7773; Mon–Fri) has opened its lookout atop **Big Creek Baldy Mountain** to the

Salt Lake City

A long but beautiful 793-mile (1,276km) journey from Coeur d'Alene, Idaho, on US 95 goes through five national forests on the way to the capital of the Mormon church: Salt Lake City, Utah. Founded in 1847 by Brigham Young, who led Mormons from the persecution in the East to the promised lands of the Utah basin, about 70 percent of Salt Lake's current population belong to the church. The Mormon temple (one of over 100 in the world) is the town's focal point, and is a sacred place for members; the faith reserves the temple for its most special occasions, so it is not open to visitors. However, the immaculate grounds and visitors' center do allow a glimpse into this close and well-ordered religion. The Mormons live by a strict code shunning alcohol, tobacco, and even hot drinks like tea and coffee. There are a number of historic sites to visit, including the Mormon Tabernacle and the Beehive House, and, a few miles west, the phenomenal Great Salt Lake itself. Like many cities in the Southwest, Salt Lake is blessed with a breathtaking setting: mountains in the background offset the desert in the foreground and the strikingly distinctive architecture of this rare religious capital. The Salt Lake Convention and Visitors Bureau can be reached at 801-534-4900 or www.visitsaltlake.com.

public, on a reserve-ahead and pay-ahead basis (tel: 1-877-444-6777; mid-June–Sept). You will be given the combination to the lock and directions, or call the Canoe Gulch Ranger Station for further details. State Highway 37 out of Libby leads to forestry service access roads, the last of which winds its way up to the foot of Big Creek Baldy Lookout. The last mile or so is extremely rough and steeply graded. However, the thrill of making it to the top, mingled with awe upon viewing the panorama that awaits, will take anyone's breath away. And it gets even better after climbing the steps of the 41ft (12-meter) tower.

The 225-sq-ft (21-sq-meter) space with unobstructed windows and an observation deck on all sides contains items essential to survival and comfort and nothing more – save a fire-sighting device smack in the middle of the floor. Below, the tranquil beauty of the forest stretches for many miles in all directions; the wind becomes much more than a whistle, no longer muffled by the trees. This is a solitary, spiritual, romantic place to spend the night.

From Libby, where the **Cabinet Mountains** can be seen from downtown, it is a short drive west along US 2 to the Idaho border along the Kootenai River, passing near lovely and dramatic **Kootenai Falls** and through **Troy**, home of the largest silver mine in the United States. You are leaving a land of cowboy hats and rejoining a land of loggers and miners.

INTO IDAHO

The road enters Boundary County – aptly named, as it borders not just Montana but also British Columbia and Washington – joining US 95 just north of **Bonners Ferry**. Backed by the Selkirk Mountain Range, **Sandpoint** lies on the shores of the huge **Lake Pend d'Oreille**. Here, US 2 splits off to the west, while US 95 crosses the lake on the two-mile Long Bridge on its way southwest toward Coeur

d'Alene. From 1890 to 1910, three transcontinental railroad lines forged their way through this part of Idaho, creating a string of towns that dot the highway.

Before reaching **Coeur d'Alene** ⓺, US 95 greets the interstate. It is worth back-tracking east along I-90 a little here, not only because the road hugs the banks of **Coeur d'Alene lake** for some 11 miles (18km), but primarily because it leads to two vestiges of 19th-century Idaho, both unique in their way.

The **Coeur d'Alene Mission of the Sacred Heart** (also known as the Old Mission; tel: 208-682-3814; daily) stands atop a hill overlooking the main road (I-90). It is the oldest standing building in Idaho, constructed of timber, mud, and wooden pegs in 1853 by Father Anthony Ravalli and the Coeur d'Alene Indians.

The Jesuits came to this part of Idaho knowing they would be welcomed by the Coeur d'Alene Indians, who had been told by neighboring tribes of the great powers of the "Black Robes." Truly a Renaissance man, Ravalli's European training was reflected in the

TIP

Sandpoint makes a fine base for exploring the scenic Idaho panhandle, with its bike paths and hiking trails, boat cruises, and sandy city beaches for a cooling dip in the lake. The city also has around two dozen art galleries.

BELOW: a Northern Rockies cowboy relaxing in front of a traditional log building.

mission's design, perhaps best described as Native American-Italianate. The spacious, cathedral-like interior is decorated with chandeliers made from tin cans, whitewashed newspaper painted with floral motifs, carved pine crosses, a wooden altar painted to resemble marble and many other precious artifacts.

In 1877, the Coeur d'Alene were forced to abandon their beloved mission for a reservation to the south, but they still consider it their mission today and return each August 15 to celebrate the Feast of the Assumption. Due to its location, the mission also became a rendezvous point for mountain men, fur traders and "all sorts of riff-raff," in the words of the cavalrymen who were often called in to maintain peace and order. The annual Historic Skills Fair in July recalls those days with traditional crafts, music, and food.

The Old Mission had no confessional until the late 1800s when one was established, presumably to serve white settlers, some of whom may have sinned at an establishment now called

the **Enaville Resort** (tel: 208-682-3453; daily) located in **Kingston**, east of the mission along I-90 and then north on Coeur d'Alene River Road. It was built in 1880 as an overnight stop en route to gold and silver country, gaining several nicknames over the years – locals still call it the SnakePit. Located across from a lumberyard, a rail crossroads, and a fork of the Coeur d'Alene River, it has served in its time as boomtown bar, hotel, and house of ill repute.

Today, the Enaville is merely a relaxing place to stop for a drink and a bite to eat. Furnishings have piled up over the years and include many pieces hand-wrought by a mysterious man from Finland known only as Mr Egil. His materials were pine burls, antlers, horns, and animal hides; his only recompense was a room, board, and free beer.

WASHINGTON STATE

A short drive west on I-90 takes you out of Idaho and into eastern **Washington**, a land of deserts, canyons, coulees, wheat fields, and irrigated farmland – a sharp contrast to the densely forested terrain of northern Idaho. Historically, this region was home to numerous Native American peoples, most of whom lived along the banks of the Columbia River. Their descendants, members of the Colville Confederated Tribes, live today on a reservation bordered on two sides by the Columbia River. This was uninviting territory for early white explorers. The Grand Coulee itself presented a major obstacle, with few openings through which to pass. In the 1880s, the first white settlers in the region faced enormous hardships. Their numbers remained relatively few until the completion of the Grand Coulee Dam. Built during the height of the Great Depression, the dam and the Columbia Basin irrigation and electrification project changed the face of this region for all time.

Outside **Spokane** ➎, US 2 travels through golden wheat fields toward

BELOW: riding
horseback in
Washington state.

the dam. Road signs become a little confusing as the road approaches not only the Grand Coulee Dam, but the towns of Electric City, Grand Coulee, Grand Coulee Dam, and Coulee City. 'At Wilbur, State 174 goes north to the town of Grand Coulee, where State 155 continues on to the dam. As they say, "You can't miss it." The impact of the **Grand Coulee Dam 65** cannot be overestimated – economically or visually. Its aims, achievements, and sheer size are all on a grand scale, and the design of the dam is of such stylistic integrity that it still looks modern today.

The drive along State 155, from the dam to **Coulee City** and US 2, is surprisingly scenic. The road skirts the lake on one side and the algae-clad coulee walls on the other. West of Coulee City, along US 2, gently sloping fields of wheat, dotted with the occasional farmhouse, give the appearance of a vast desert. Layers of blue mountains appear in the distance like a mirage – the first of the coastal chains.

At **Orondo**, the highway meets, follows and crosses the **Columbia River** and then branches off, tracing its tributary, the Wenatchee, into foothills of the **Cascade Range**. This is orchard country: green patches of fertile land jut into the river and contrast with the golden hills; some of the local stands put out ripe apricots for sale.

Now US 2 climbs and enters a realm of tall timber, passing through the town of **Leavenworth 66** – a self-styled, pseudo-Bavarian ski resort and gateway to the **Wenatchee National Forest**. Over the rushing south fork of the Skykomish River, and through the **Snoqualmie National Forest**, past several small towns with no-nonsense names like Gold Bar and Startup, US 2 continues west, bringing you just to the northeast of **Seattle 67** (see page 172), where you catch the expressway and (hopefully) breeze into one of America's most interesting and attractive cities.

THE OLYMPIC PENINSULA

Before you dig in your heels in Seattle, however, another nearby destination beckons. Washington's **Olympic Peninsula** is the northwesternmost corner of the contiguous 48 states – a remote, exotic, and wildly beautiful region within easy reach of both Seattle and Victoria, British Columbia. It is set apart from these places not merely by Puget (pronounced *pyew-jet*) Sound and the Strait of Juan de Fuca, but by its climate, its geology, the mystery of its peaks and forests and by the natural rhythms that guide the pace of life.

From **Edmonds**, due north of Seattle, a ferry crosses the short, scenic distance across the sound to **Kingston 68** on the peninsula. From here, it is a lovely drive west and north to the peninsula's northeastern tip at the entrance to Puget Sound.

At the heart of the peninsula are the majestic **Olympic Mountains**, snow-streaked even in summer. Long a subject of myth, these mountains remained unexplored until the 1890s, when an expedition from Seattle set off in search of man-eating savages.

The Washington State Ferry system, the largest in the US, runs ferries to the Olympic Peninsula from Seattle.

BELOW: Sol Duc Falls, Olympic Peninsula.

Hiking in the verdant Olympic National Forest.

BELOW: Victorian B&B in Port Townsend, Olympic Peninsula.

Even the peninsula's Native Americans avoided venturing into the interior, fearing the wrath of mighty Thunderbird, who was believed to reside atop Mount Olympus. Today, the mountains are preserved and protected in a near-wilderness state as part of Olympic National Park, which comprises 923,000 acres (374,000 hectares) of the peninsula, most of it inland but also including a 50-mile (80km) strip of Pacific Ocean coastline. Only a few roads venture into the park, and these only peripherally. In fact, the park proper is surrounded by the **Olympic National Forest**, which makes it difficult to reach. Because the peninsula is largely under some form of Federal jurisdiction, there is considerable conflict with the lumber industry.

The Olympic Peninsula sustains the rainforests of the Hoh, Quinault, and Queets river valleys; the glacial peaks of the Olympics; and the rugged Pacific coastline as well as lumber towns, fishing villages, and nine Indian reservations.

Charming **Port Gamble**, the first town along the route, is an authentic

lumber town reflecting a bygone era. Just beyond it, a bridge crosses the Hood Canal – the work of glaciers rather than men. At the town of **Discovery Bay**, State 20 veers off and up to Port Townsend.

Victorian town

Port Townsend ⑨, first settled in 1851, is the peninsula's oldest town and an attractive base. Sea captains and storekeepers from back East made their homes here, and it was quick to become a boomtown, built in anticipation of being linked with the Union Pacific Railroad and consequently becoming the major seaport of the Northwest. All this came to pass – for Seattle, not Port Townsend. After the bust, settlers tore up the train tracks, closed down the banks and departed for more prosperous parts.

Left behind is the best example of a Victorian seacoast town north of San Francisco. Declared a National Historic District, Port Townsend has become a haven for artists and is also the headquarters of the **Northwest School of Wooden Boatbuilding** (tel: 360-385-4948; Mon–Fri), where a dying art has been revived.

US 101 loops around the peninsula like a misshapen horseshoe, open at the bottom. In the north, it passes through Olympic National Forest and on to the lumber towns of the "West End." The region between Discovery Bay and Port Angeles has been called the "banana belt," sitting as it does in the rain shadow of the Olympics. Farmers here see an average rainfall of only 17 inches (43cm) compared with upwards of 140 inches (356cm) on the other side of the mountains. Irrigated farms are a common sight along this stretch, as are madrona trees, twisted and terracotta in color.

Small and distinctive

The towns along the way are small and distinctive. **Blyn** is gone before you can say "Little Brown Church of Blyn," its one and only landmark. Just north

of **Sequim** (pronounced *skwim*), on the Strait of Juan de Fuca (explorer De Fuca thought this was the Northwest Passage), is **Dungeness**, where the Dungeness crabs are landed.

The plants of several major lumber companies are located at **Port Angeles**, and the smell of wood permeates the air; here you can catch big cruise boats to Victoria, British Columbia, on gorgeous Vancouver Island. Port Angeles is the gateway to **Olympic National Park** ⑩ (tel: 360-565-3130; daily). Head up to Hurricane Ridge for stunning views of Mount Olympus and its surrounding glaciers. Heading west, US 101 traces Elwha Creek, enters the National Forest and winds down to crystalline Lake Crescent within the park. The highway is lined with towering evergreens, the roadside carpeted with ferns, as you continue west toward the ocean and the rainfall amounts suddenly begin rising again.

West End

Logging is a way of life in the peninsula's "West End" and evidence of this is everywhere: clearcut hillsides denuded of all trees, reforested plantations, and logging trucks barreling down the roads. Most of the big timber is long since gone now, and what remains is usually – though not always – off-limits to these lumber companies.

US 101 passes through the towns of **Sappho** and **Forks**. The village of **La Push**, on the **Quilayute Indian Reservation**, is reached by way of La Push Road (Route 110) from Forks. Those who live here fish for a living, and those who visit here visit for the fishing. If La Push were not so unpretentious, it would surely proclaim itself driftwood capital of the world: its beach is beautiful at night, a string of warming campfires and sea-stacks visible through the perpetual mist.

The temperate rainforests west of the mountains are the finest of all the sights in the national park. They are the only ones in North America and contain some of the tallest timber in the world. Most accessible of these awe-inspiring forests is the **Hoh River Valley**, located south of Forks and inland on Hoh River Road. Most awesome are the ancient evergreens – western red cedar,

The peninsula's town of Dungeness is the place to find the famous crabs.

BELOW: Second Beach at sunset, Olympic National Park.

Map on page 144

Sitka spruce, Douglas fir, and western hemlock – shrouded with club moss, filtered by light, surrounded by ferns and the sound of the river. It is an eerie, overgrown, magical place, barely touched by the presence of man – with one exception.

John "The Iron Man of Hoh" Huelsdonk came to the Hoh Valley from Iowa in 1891. Discouraged by all who met him, he nevertheless poled his canoe up the wild river and made his home in this forest. What he could not carry by canoe, such as his cast-iron stove, he strapped to his back. Hence the nickname – and the birth of a legend. The Iron Man died and is buried in the forest he so loved, as is his wife.

US 101 continues south to another wide, driftwood-strewn shoreline at **Ruby Beach**; look for rock oysters and starfish clinging to the rocks when the tide is out. On the south side of the park, the **Quinault Rainforest** offers accessible hiking trails through the big trees.

Land's end

You can't get any farther northwest in the continental United States than isolated **Neah Bay**. Forking off the loop of US 101 at Sappho, State 113 and then State 112 winds its way to the ocean along the strait. Vancouver Island is now visible in the distance. Neah Bay is the ancestral and current home of the fine **Makah Indian Nation**, whose presence here for at least 3,000 years has been confirmed by archeologists. Once renowned whale and seal hunters who took to the sea in cedar canoes, the Makah still live off the ocean, though the catch today is more likely to be salmon. On entering town, a sign proclaims: "Makah Nation – a treaty tribe since 1855." The Makah do not underestimate the importance of this treaty, which guarantees their territorial and fishing rights, which to them means survival.

Neah Bay is also a gateway to one of America's most splendid stretches of wilderness coastline. A network of gravel and dirt roads goes part of the distance, but to reach land's end it is necessary to go on foot. If you want some adventure, drive as far as you dare and then hike the precipitous trail down to pretty **Shi-Shi Beach** and simply gaze out to sea. Be aware of time – and tide-tables – as the water rushes in quickly around here.

The trail to **Cape Flattery** is shorter and less dangerous. It descends an intricate stairway of tree roots through the forest, a clearing, and a stand of huckleberry bushes before reaching the cliff's edge. Look out over Cape Flattery, knowing you stand as far northwest as possible in the lower 48 states of the US – and that you have reached the end of a journey that began, thousands of miles ago, beside a different ocean in busy Boston Harbor.

Then retrace your steps back to Seattle, or follow US 101 around the rest of the peninsula and down to the town of Aberdeen, where you can, if you wish, drive all the way to Mexico on US 101 and Highway 1 (*see the Pacific Route, page 382*). ❏

Forks town's status as "logging capital" has been overshadowed by its fame as "vampire capital," since it became the setting for the teen novels and films of Stephanie Meyer's Twilight *series. Fans can pick up a* Twilight *tour packet at the tourist office.*

BELOW AND RIGHT: Henry Wadsworth Longfellow called woods like the Olympic Peninsula's Hoh Rainforest the "forest primeval."

A Short Stay in Seattle

Seattle is youthful and friendly, business-minded, busy, and beautiful: a city of the 21st century. Here's a list of the not-to-be-missed attractions:

● Glide into the Seattle Center, home of the Space Needle, on the monorail and explore its many attractions, from theaters and a children's museum to the excellent Pacific Science Center. It also hosts the famous Bumbershoot music festival each Labor Day weekend.

● The Seattle Aquarium features 200 varieties of fish native to Puget Sound, plus environments simulating rocky reefs, sandy seafloors, eelgrass beds, and tide pools. It's one part of the vibrant Waterfront area, which also has ships, piers, stores, and restaurants.

● Bruce Lee, Seattle's founding fathers and other famous folk lie in the cemetery on Capitol Hill, an eclectic neighborhood of coffee houses, funky shops, hip bars, and restaurants. The renowned Seattle Asian Art Museum stands in Volunteer Park, where there are great city views from the water tower.

● Set in a Frank Gehry building, Experience Music Project (EMP) is a rock music museum conceived by Paul Allen of Microsoft fame, featuring artifacts like Eric Clapton's guitar, state-of-the-art technology, and interactive exhibits. It now stands adjacent to the very cool Science Fiction Museum, whose exhibits are out of this world.

● From spy planes to supersonic jets, explore more than 85 aircraft at the fascinating Museum of Flight. Then head for the Future of Flight Aviation Center in Everett, with hands-on exhibits, and take the Boeing Tour to watch these famous airplanes being assembled.

● "The Mountain" (as it is known by locals) is in Mount Rainier National Park, just outside of the city. A single road loops through miles of parkland and timbered canyons.

ABOVE: Space Needle Skyline. Built for the 1962 World's Fair, the Space Needle offers the best views of the city and surrounding hills.

RIGHT: Monorail. Like the Space Needle, the Monorail dates from the 1962 World's Fair. Trains run between Westlake Center and Downtown.

ABOVE: Seattle Art Museum. Designed by Robert Venturi, the Museum holds a highly regarded collection of Northwest Indian art, paintings by modern artists, and an Australian Aboriginal Gallery.

THE EMERALD CITY

Seattle is constantly rated as one of the most livable cities in the US. With a diverse population, rich cultural life and wealthy industries (Boeing and Microsoft), all situated amid awesome scenery, who wouldn't want to live here? Named for Native American chief Sealth, the laid-back lifestyle associated with the city has long been in place; tribes like the Salish and the Duwamish had been living peacefully in the hills for years. As do its residents now, surrounded by water and mountain peaks, working hard, playing easy, and drinking gallons of strong coffee. If the future of America is anywhere, it is probably right here.

ABOVE: Pioneer Square. The oldest part of the city, Pioneer Square's 19th-century buildings are now showcases for shops and bars.

ABOVE RIGHT: Pike Place Market. Dating from 1907, the market sells local produce, crafts, and more.

RIGHT: Coffee. Visit the Capitol Hill neighborhood to experience Seattle's best coffee houses.

IMPORTANT INFORMATION

Population: 593,000
Dialing code: 206
Website: www.visitseattle.org
Tourist information: One Convention Place, 701 Pike Street, Suite 800, 98101 (no drop in); tel: 206-461-5840

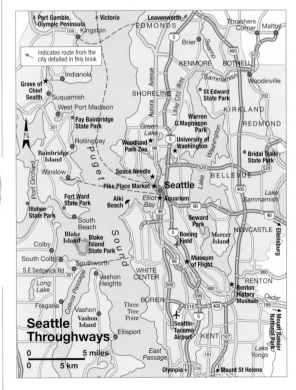

Seattle Throughways

0   5 miles
0   5 km

THE CENTRAL ROUTE

A detailed guide to the Central US, with
principal sites clearly cross-referenced
by number to the maps

t is perhaps fitting to begin a journey across America from
the nation's capital of Washington, DC; the many museums
and landmarks that give a glimpse into the country's past do
much to set the scene for the rest of your trip west. We've chosen
a "south-central" course that combines enough history and
beauty to sate any traveler's appetite.

The history lesson begins as soon as you leave Washington,
heading first west and then sharply south along Skyline Drive
and the Blue Ridge Parkway through the Appalachian Moun-
tains of Virginia. This was Stonewall Jackson territory and the route is sprinkled with Civil War sites. Interstate 40, which we'll be following for much
of the trip, continues into North Carolina and through the Great Smoky
Mountains, taking you past the fine old homes of Knoxville, Tennessee
before reaching Nashville, the capital of Tennessee and of country music.

From there, it's truly into small-town America as you hit Arkansas, stopping in Little Rock, with its impressive state capitol building, historic district, and hot springs. Then into Oklahoma where we pick up Route 66 (see
also "Route 66" essay, page 35). Some know Route 66 from legend, others
from childhood, when every weathered telegraph poles and zany-shaped

motels, was a milestone on a journey into a wonderland
whose roadside attractions included snake pits, live buffaloes,
and Indian dancers.

Oklahoma's piece of Route 66 passes through many interesting small towns, but also some bigger ones, such as Oklahoma City. You'll cross the Texas Panhandle before heading
into New Mexico, visiting the attractive city of Santa Fe. The
state has a wealth of ancient pueblos, homes of early Native
American inhabitants. As you cross into Arizona, you enter
the Navajo Nation; the route passes by the Petrified Forest
National Park before reaching Flagstaff, the gateway for the incomparable
Grand Canyon. You'll cross some desolate countryside in western Arizona,
and again in eastern California's Mojave Desert, before you start seeing signs
of "civilization" as you head into the urban sprawl of Los Angeles. With
some 2,900 miles (4,700km) behind you, the Pacific Ocean beckons. ❑

PRECEDING PAGES: license plates from the 50 states; a rancher. **LEFT:** Washington, DC.
ABOVE LEFT: fuel brand inspired by Route 66. **ABOVE RIGHT:** Civil War memorial.

A Short Stay In Washington, DC

Planned as a city of monuments and memorials, the nation's capital is also one of its most beautiful. Here's a list of the not-to-be-missed attractions:

- Tours of the White House are very restricted, but its Visitor Center at the Department of Commerce, 15th and E streets NW, provides a good sense of the building's history since 1792.

- Whether you wish to retrace the path of Martin Luther King Jr, whose "I Have a Dream" speech came from these steps, or simply take a look at the huge statue of Abraham Lincoln, the Lincoln Memorial celebrates the liberty sought by the founding fathers.

- The Vietnam Veterans Memorial, at Bacon Drive and Constitution Avenue, lists on polished granite the names of more than 58,000 American soldiers killed in the 1960s conflict.

- At first a strategic stronghold in the Civil War, the Arlington National Cemetery contained 16,000 headstones by the end of the struggle. The eternal flame at the grave of John F. Kennedy honors the fallen president, and the Tomb of the Unknowns commemorates the nameless soldiers felled in battles over the past 100 years.

- Exhibits at the National Air and Space Museum range from the Wright Brothers' *Flyer* to the Apollo 11 spacecraft, and includes a planetarium and an IMAX theater.

- The Library of Congress, founded by Thomas Jefferson, is now the largest library in the world. Assistants are sometimes able to give tours to visitors.

- To see where the wealthy lawyers, diplomats, and socialites live, take a stroll through stylish Georgetown and perhaps visit the legendary Blues Alley jazz supper club.

Right: The Smithsonian Institution. Top draws include the National Museum of American History, the National Museum of the American Indian, the National Portrait Gallery, and the National Zoo.

Above: Night-time reflections. From left to right – the Capitol, the Washington Monument, and the Lincoln Memorial.

Left: The Air Force Memorial at Arlington National Cemetery.

Opposite Top: National Gallery of Art. Some of the world's greatest modern paintings, from Picasso to Pollock, are on show in the starkly contemporary East Building.

Right: Main Avenue Fish Market. Dozens of vendors along the Washington Channel hawk fresh seafood. Even if you're not planning feast, savor the scene and enjoy a plate of freshly shucked clams.

THE NATION'S CAPITAL CITY

A visit to Washington, DC, is nothing less than a lesson in history, literally a living history, since the President of the US lives here. The city also has a unique beauty, the credit for which should go to George Washington. The new president insisted on creating a new city as the nation's capital, a place as grand as Paris or London. With this in mind, he hired French architect Pierre Charles L'Enfant to create a "city of magnificent distances." L'Enfant's plan was only partially realized, but Washington *is* magnificent and the distances between monuments deceptively large; bring a good pair of walking shoes.

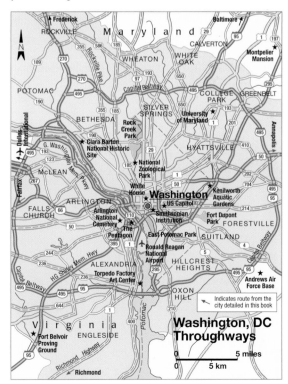

Washington, DC
Throughways

IMPORTANT INFORMATION

Population: 581,500
Dialing code: 202
Website: www.washington.org
Tourist information: 901 7th Street NW, Fourth Floor, Washington, DC, 20001; tel: 800-422-8644

WASHINGTON, DC TO ARKANSAS

From Asheville, North Carolina, to Nashville, Tennessee, and beyond, this route takes in Virginia, Memphis, and the scented highways of Arkansas to Little Rock

Our route begins in **Washington, DC ①** *(see page 180)*, the first leg of which runs to Winston-Salem, North Carolina, along Interstate 66, with a detour along I-81 south as far as New Market. The interstate will take you back to the town of Front Royal and then the Skyline Drive, which runs south along the eastern rampart of the Blue Ridge Mountains – mountains so pine-scented and peaceful we always recommend this drive as the preferred route into North Carolina. On the way to Front Royal, you may want to cruise past the town of **Fairfax**, where, a few miles west, is the **Virginia Visitors' Center** with brochures covering every facet of Virginia tourism. Stop in for schedules of current events and festivals throughout the "Old Dominion."

At some point, if you have time, you can change from I-66 to Virginia 55, which runs parallel, as both roads head for the mountains. The pace of life begins to slow almost immediately as you drive along increasingly serpentine roads with vistas opening to reveal the majestic Blue Ridge Mountains looming in the distance. Cumulus clouds hover over the dark peaks to the west. Small waterfalls slide down rock faces along the road. Beautiful pink and purple crown vetch, dandelions, and goldenrod grow wild on the hillsides.

Manassas

The fast track on I-66 weaves through a tangle of ever-growing suburbs around Washington, DC, practically obscuring a moving site for Southerners. A detour from I-66 onto the smaller SR 234 leads to **Manassas National Battlefield Park ②** (tel: 703-361-1339; daily until dusk), the spot of two great Confederate victories during the Civil War – the First and Second Battles of Manassas (or locally, Bull Run). Ten hours of deadly fighting on July 21, 1861, resulted in a Union defeat, and it was at this battle that General Thomas J. Jackson earned the nickname "Stonewall." The second battle, one year later,

Main attractions
WASHINGTON, DC
MANASSAS NATIONAL BATTLEFIELD
SHENANDOAH NATIONAL PARK
OLD SALEM
GREAT SMOKY MOUNTAINS
  NATIONAL PARK
NASHVILLE
MEMPHIS
LITTLE ROCK CENTRAL HIGH
  SCHOOL NATIONAL HISTORIC SITE
HOT SPRINGS

LEFT: re-enacting a Civil War battle.
BELOW: on stage at the Grand Ole Opry.

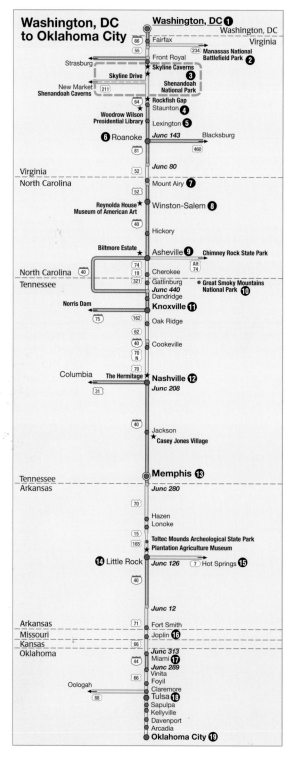

Washington, DC
to Oklahoma City

Washington, DC ❶
Washington, DC
Virginia

66 Fairfax
55 Front Royal
234 Manassas National Battlefield Park ❷
Strasburg
Skyline Caverns ❸
Skyline Drive ★
New Market
Shenandoah Caverns
211
Shenandoah National Park
64 Rockfish Gap
Woodrow Wilson Presidential Library ★
Staunton ❹
Lexington ❺
❻ Roanoke
Junc 143
Blacksburg
81
460
Virginia
North Carolina
52 Junc 80
52 Mount Airy ❼
Reynolda House Museum of American Art
Winston-Salem ❽
40 Hickory
Biltmore Estate ★
Asheville ❾
Chimney Rock State Park
North Carolina
40
74
Alt 74
19 Cherokee
321 Gatlinburg
Junc 440
Dandridge
Great Smoky Mountains National Park ❿
Tennessee
Norris Dam
Knoxville ⓫
75 162 Oak Ridge
62
40
70 N Cookeville
70
Columbia
The Hermitage ★
Nashville ⓬
31 Junc 208
40 Jackson
★ Casey Jones Village
Tennessee
Arkansas
Memphis ⓭
Junc 280
70 Hazen
Lonoke
15 Toltec Mounds Archeological State Park
165 Plantation Agriculture Museum
⓮ Little Rock
Junc 126
7 Hot Springs ⓯
40
Junc 12
Arkansas
Missouri
71 Fort Smith
Joplin ⓰
Kansas
Oklahoma
66 Junc 313
44 Miami ⓱
Junc 289
66 Vinita
Foyil
Oologah
Claremore
88 Tulsa ⓲
Sapulpa
Kellyville
Davenport
Arcadia
Oklahoma City ⓳

proved the genius of Confederate General Robert E. Lee. Driving and walking tours are available, and the visitor center has a museum and orientation film. Be warned, however, that even though the site is well signposted, finding the correct turn-off can be maddeningly confusing – drive slowly and be alert.

The Civil War looms large in these parts, as Virginia was the site for more than half of its major battles (as an example, the Shenandoah Valley town of Winchester changed hands 74 times). At Front Royal visitors' center, you can pick up a guidebook to the Battle of Front Royal or a less descriptive free leaflet of a tour of several Civil War sites. At **Strasburg**, famous since 1761 for its pottery, there's the **Stonewall Jackson Museum** (tel: 540-465-5884; daily). A mix of original artifacts and hands-on reproductions tells the lives of soldiers and civilians during this period.

"There are two things never to be lost sight of by a military commander," General Thomas J. "Stonewall" Jackson declared. "Always mystify, mislead, and surprise the enemy if possible… Such tactics will win every time." The historic **Museum of American Presidents** (tel: 540-465-5999; daily, admission by appointment), eight of whom were Virginians, is also in Strasburg.

From the earth to the sky

Nestled in the foothills of Virginia's Blue Ridge Mountains – amid farms and woodlands, battlefields, riverbeds, streams, and tiny hamlets – are the **Crystal Caverns** (tel: 540-465-5884; daily), one of a series of cave complexes carved out of the limestone cliffs at each side of the valley. The caverns are near the Stonewall Jackson Museum, also on the battlefield of Hupp's Hill. The **Skyline Caverns** (tel: 800-296-4545) are 1 mile south of Front Royal; the **Endless Caverns** (tel: 800-544-2283), **Luray Caverns** (tel: 540-743-6551), and **Shenandoah Caverns** (tel: 540-477-3115) are all open daily and are near **New Market**, whose other attractions include a State Historical Park and museum on the site where Confederate troops routed a superior Union force in 1864, using teenage cadets from the Virginia Military Institute in Lexington.

Front Royal is a fairly ugly little town full of chain stores and fast-food restaurants crammed into a few town blocks. Luckily, you are not far away from the north entrance of **Shenandoah National Park ❸**, where the 105-mile (169km) **Skyline Drive** begins. Established in 1935 after an act of Congress in 1926, the park was an experiment in land reclamation. At the time, the region was overpopulated and the land was eroding. President Franklin Roosevelt ordered the Civilian Conservation Corps to build recreation facilities and complete construction of the Skyline Drive in 1939. During the decades since, the forests have revived and are once again densely overgrown with oak, hickory, pine, and locust trees.

At the **Dickey Ridge Visitor Center** (Apr–Memorial Day and Nov Thur–Mon, late May–Oct daily) you can pick up park maps, guides to local vegetation and wildlife and information about camping and lodging. If the pioneer spirit of "roughing it" doesn't strike your fancy, there are still informative hikes and talks on the natural life of the park led by rangers; you will undoubtedly be tempted to get off the road awhile and hike some of the beautiful forest trails. Even if you don't, at least pack a meal to eat alfresco at one of the seven picnic locations.

Although the earliest access to the Skyline Drive through the park is at Front Royal, the road may be closed in winter, necessitating a drive further south as far as Swift Run Gap, east of **Elkton**, where US 33 crosses southbound US 340.

Oh Shenandoah

Immediately upon entering Shenandoah National Park, the speed limit slows to 35mph (56kph), and the lumbering pace of your fellow cars sets the mood for a leisurely drive. Initially, it's a two-lane, winding road

There are mileposts on the west side of Skyline Drive, beginning with 0.0 at Front Royal and continuing to 105 at the southern end of the park. Park maps use these markers as a reference guide.

BELOW: enjoying the magnificent view from a summit above Shenandoah Valley.

A young spotted fawn taking its first steps in Shenandoah National Park.

BELOW: savoring the Blue Ridge Parkway scenery from Raven's Roost.

covered with dense trees on both sides. As the road ascends, however, you begin to get magnificent glimpses of the **Shenandoah Valley** and **Shenandoah River** to the west. Get out of the car at one of the many overlooks and take in the majesty of the sight. Almost as noticeable as the view is the silence: stop frequently, turn off the engine, and make the most of it. As you continue south, you'll see **Massanutten Mountain** between the north and south forks of the Shenandoah River and then, after about 10 miles (16km) more, the road switches angles to give you an eastern view of Piedmont country.

At Mile 50.7 ("km 82"), stop for a short round-trip hike to **Dark Hollow Falls**, the closest waterfall to the drive. Water tumbles 70ft (21 meters) over its greenstone face. Nearby Harry F. Byrd is – along with Dickey Ridge – one of the two main visitor centers in the park. For those wishing to stay overnight, the **Big Meadows Lodge and Campgrounds** are a convenient stop.

Hundreds of miles of hiking trails lead off the drive into a wilderness dotted with hickory, white pine, red spruce, and chestnut trees, some of which were earlier cleared and planted by the original settlers. After extending their farms onto the hillsides from the fertile Shenandoah Valley, the settlers bragged of being "the breadbasket of the Confederacy."

Natural state

Thousands of tons of grain, leather, and iron were left here to support the Southern forces in the Civil War, nourished by the meat from hogs and cattle and equipped with uniforms from the wool of thousands of sheep. Memories of the Civil War are everywhere, and 400 Confederate soldiers are buried at **Mt Jackson**, a town near the Shenandoah Caverns.

In a novel experiment, almost a century after the conflict, President Franklin D. Roosevelt allowed the over-used foothills to return to their natural state. Pastures and croplands gradually became overgrown with shrubs and trees, creating a wilderness to which hundreds of species of birds, deer, bear, bobcat, and other creatures

returned (although few of these can be seen). The Skyline Drive ends at **Rockfish Gap**, where I-64 leads to **Staunton ❹**, a pleasant former mining town with buildings dating to the 18th century, some of which are B&Bs. Yet another president, also known for his pursuit of peace, is remembered at Staunton, where the **Woodrow Wilson Presidential Library** (tel: 540-885-0897; daily) illustrates local living conditions in the mid-19th century and portrays the 28th president's political career and eight-year (1913–21) White House stint.

West of I-81 is the attractive town of **Lexington ❺**, where ol' Stonewall was teaching cadets at the state-supported Virginia Military Institute (VMI) shortly after its founding in 1831. You can see the **Stonewall Jackson House** (tel: 540-463-2552; daily). Jackson's Confederate colleague General Robert E. Lee also lived in Lexington and taught at the college founded by George Washington, known ever since as Washington and Lee University. Both universities welcome visitors. The latter has a chapel where Lee

is buried plus a museum containing Lee's office and a portrait gallery. VMI's museum includes the raincoat Jackson wore when wounded at Chancellorsville in 1863 and the coat he wore throughout his brilliantly flexible 1862 Valley campaign defending the strategic, highly valuable north–south Shenandoah Valley (an "avenue of invasion") against Federal army troops. This recently renovated museum also features a replica of a cadet room and POW items used by a Vietnam soldier.

Blue Ridge Mountains

Virginia's alluring landscape is a welcome diversion from the trials of the highway. The air is suddenly refreshingly clear, and the famous blue haze shrouding the Blue Ridge Mountains hoves into view. **Roanoke ❻** (pop. 92,000), known as the "Capital of the Blue Ridge" for its proximity to the Blue Ridge Parkway – the connecting link between Shenandoah and Tennessee's Great Smoky Mountains – is a pleasantly relaxed city famous for a **Farmers' Market** that has been operating for 130

TIP

Leave yourself plenty of time to enjoy the walking and hiking excursions offered along the Blue Ridge Parkway; even a tiny walk to a beautiful waterfall can relieve the tedium of driving.

BELOW: the Blue Ridge Parkway was built along the top of the mountains.

Time for a pit stop.

BELOW: bicycling along the Blue Ridge Parkway.

years. Adjoining the market is a multicultural complex known as **Center in the Square** (tel: 540-342-5700), a vibrant collection of restaurants, art and photography galleries, and a planetarium. There are also history and science museums, as well as the **Harrison Museum of African American Culture** (most are closed Mon). Mill Mountain, topped by the huge, illuminated **Roanoke Star**, overlooks the city and is the site of the **Mill Mountain Zoo** (tel: 540-343-3241; daily), whose main attraction is the rare snow leopard.

Interstate 81 continues south, flanked by the vast Jefferson National Forest offering access at **Blacksburg** to the **Cascades National Recreation Trail**, a picturesque gorge that ends in a waterfall (a 4-mile/6km hike, round trip). There's another access point farther along I-81 at Wytheville, where I-77 heads north to a campground in the park. But our route turns south just before that on US 52, which crosses the North Carolina border and takes us through the small town of **Mount Airy** ❼ *(see page 69)*, home of the homespun 1960s TV situation comedy *Mayberry RFD*.

Museum of living history

Continue south on US 52 to **Winston-Salem** ❽ (pop. 227,000), founded by Moravian immigrants in 1766. The area where it all began, **Old Salem**, is now a museum of living history. "After traveling through the woods for many days … the first view of the town is romantic, just as it breaks upon you through the woods; it is pleasantly seated on a rising ground and is surrounded by beautiful meadows, well-cultivated fields, and shady woods," wrote William Loughton Smith in his journal of May 1791.

Arriving in Winston-Salem definitely gives one a sense of having "landed" in North Carolina, and the miles of highway driving start to pay dividends. Old Salem is possibly one of the most authentic and inviting living history towns in the US. Its old tavern is an upscale restaurant, and the simple timber homes contain their original furnishings. The printing shop of John Christian Blum, founding publisher in 1828 of *The Farmers' and Planters' Almanac*, is one of the exhibit buildings. A remarkable timber bridge stands next to the **Frank L. Horton Museum Center**, containing paintings, textiles, ceramics, silver, and other 19th-century creative works. It also houses a **Children's Museum** (closed Sun morning and Mon) with hands-on exhibits. And what of the giant-size metal coffee pot standing on the village green? Built by the sons of Salem's founders, Samuel and Julius Mickey, it was used to advertise their tinsmith's shop.

Costumed guides roam another restored Moravian village, **Historic Bethabara Park** (tel: 336-924-8191; Apr–mid-Dec Tue–Sun), in a pleasant green setting off University Parkway.

The city's **Visitor Center** at 200 Brookstown Avenue (tel: 336-728-

4200) distributes free maps of walking tours that include the **City Market** – where a farmers' market is held on summer Tuesdays and Thursdays – and such interesting structures as the Georgian Revival *Winston-Salem Journal* building (a replica of Philadelphia's Independence Hall), the Renaissance Revival Our Lady of Fatima Chapel and the Art Deco R.J. Reynolds building (which New York architects Shreve and Lamb used as a prototype for their subsequent Empire State Building.) Numerous old brick buildings in nearby streets are being transformed into galleries and artist studios.

Reynolda House Museum of American Art, the former 1917 home of Katharine Smith and Richard Joshua Reynolds (founder of the giant R.J. Reynolds Tobacco Company) – along with its gardens and adjoining Reynolda Village, in which the former buildings have been converted into shops, offices, and restaurants – is open to visitors (tel: 336-758-5005; Tue–Sun). Brendan Gill of *The New Yorker* praised the modesty of the mansion, adding "the intention here is plainly not to show off but to be happy among friends…"

From Winston-Salem, we join I-40, which remains our route for most of the journey. About 73 miles (117km) along the route is the town of **Hickory**, which is famous for its furniture: over 100 such stores are gathered together in one center, and there is even a **Furniture Museum** (tel: 800-462-6278; Mon–Sat).

ASHEVILLE TO NASHVILLE

The Blue Ridge Parkway sweeps across I-40 just before Asheville, home to a popular winery. "More scenery, more music, more country on Country 92 FM," sings the jingle on the car radio, and indeed, when you begin to get a sense of being enveloped by mountains, you've probably arrived. There are vistas around almost every street corner, and the mighty Mount Pisgah

to the west signals the beginning of the Great Smokies.

Exuding a certain amount of small-town charm, **Asheville ❾** is architecturally diverse. Besides Queen Anne, Romanesque, and Revival styles, the town also has one of the largest collections of Art Deco architecture in the Southeast, outside of Miami Beach. You'll find the winery, along with sporting activities, shops, and restaurants, in the immense landscaped gardens of the 250-room **Biltmore Estate** (tel: 800-411-3812; daily), America's largest privately owned home. George Vanderbilt's vision took root in 1887, when he visited Asheville on vacation and became enchanted by the mountain scenery. Vanderbilt set out to create a mansion modeled after the French Loire Valley chateaux, and equipped it with many state-of-the-art luxuries. Today, visitors can enjoy the estate virtually as it was. The estate was a backdrop for *Being There*, one of several movies shot locally, along with *Last of the Mohicans* and *There Will Be Blood*.

Coffee break: this gigantic pot sits on the village green in Old Salem.

BELOW: remember to "pack it in, pack it out" when hiking in the wilderness.

Nicknamed "The Batman Building" for its resemblance to the superhero's mask, the 32-story AT&T Building in Nashville is the tallest in the state of Tennessee.

BELOW: enjoying a day at Knoxville's springtime celebration, The Dogwood Arts Festival.

The natural beauty of Asheville, the largest city near the Blue Ridge Parkway, is emphasized in its botanical gardens, an arboretum with miles of walking trails and guided tours interpreting the area's plant and wildlife, the park-like Riverside Cemetery and the river itself – perfect for white-water activities. Entry to all of these is free (or inexpensive), as is the delightfully named **North Carolina Homespun Museum** (tel: 828-253-7651; Apr–Dec), which offers weaving demonstrations, and the **Folk Art Center** (tel: 828-298-7928; daily).

Muse of the mountain

Asheville's beauty has attracted its fair share of literary giants, including F. Scott Fitzgerald and the influential author Thomas Wolfe. Wolfe spent his childhood in his mother's sprawling Queen Anne-style boarding house on Market Street, which is now the **Thomas Wolfe Memorial** (tel: 828-253-8304; Tue–Sat and Sun afternoon). Despite being banned from

the town's public library for seven years, Wolfe's *Look Homeward, Angel* has never been out of print since it was first published in 1929. Before he died, aged 37, in 1938 he wrote about his old home: "And again, again, in the old house I feel beneath my tread the creak of the old stairs, the worn rail, the whitewashed walls, the feel of darkness and the house asleep, and think, 'I was a child here; here the stairs, here was darkness; this was I, and here is Time.'"

Southeast of Asheville, near the intersection of US 64 and 74A, is **Chimney Rock State Park**, a 1,000-acre (405-hectare) Natural Heritage Site including Chimney Rock itself, and the bottomless pools and waterfalls of majestic **Hickory Nut Falls**, a backdrop for the climactic scenes in the movie *The Last of the Mohicans*. Visitors can take an elevator 26 stories up inside a mountain to emerge on its flat rocky top, 1,200ft (366 meters) above the river, to enjoy spectacular views stretching for up to 75 miles (121km).

THE GREAT SMOKIES

Great Smoky Mountains National Park ⑩, 16 of whose peaks exceed 6,000ft (1,800 meters), sprawls majestically over the North Carolina and Tennessee borders. Access, on the North Carolina side, is gained from the Blue Ridge Mountain Parkway town of **Cherokee**, reached by taking US 74 east from Asheville and then branching off onto US 19 (also eastbound). The highest point in Tennessee, 6,642ft (2,025-meter) **Clingmans Dome** (access closed Dec–Mar), is on the ridge-clinging Appalachian Trail midway between Cherokee and **Gatlinburg**, the Smoky Mountains gateway town on the Tennessee side of the park.

Abundant rainfall keeps the park rich in wildflowers and other plant life; bears and white-tailed deer can sometimes be spotted. An **aerial tramway** (tel: 865-436-5423; daily)

runs from downtown Gatlinburg to Ober Gatlinburg, a ski resort and amusement complex offering fun-but-dumb games and stupendous views. Gatlinburg has become a popular marriage venue, with over 10,000 couples taking their wedding vows here each year.

The more direct route from Asheville into Tennessee is simply to take I-40 north, and then follow it as it turns west toward Knoxville. Just after this turn, on the shore of Douglas Lake, is **Dandridge** (named after George Washington's wife Martha Dandridge), with plenty of boat docks and campgrounds. A scenic route into the Smokies leads from here to Sevierville and Gatlinburg along Route 92 and then US 411.

Just before Knoxville, the **Armstrong-Lockett House** (tel: 865-637-3163; closed Sun morning and Mon), with its collection of 18th-century furniture and ancient English silver, presides over the former Crescent Bend plantation. There are also many interesting old homes in the former state capital, **Knoxville ⓫** – among them

the **Blount Mansion** (tel: 865-525-2375; Tue–Sat), built in 1792 by the governor of the Southwest Territory; the 1797 **Ramsey House Plantation** (tel: 865-546-0745; Tue–Sun); and the 1858 **Mabry-Hazen House** (tel: 865-522-8661; Wed–Sat), which served as headquarters on different occasions for both sides in the Civil War. **James White's Fort** (tel: 865-525-6514; guided tours Apr–Dec Mon–Sat, Jan–Mar Mon–Fri) is the restored home of Knoxville's founder and the region's first pioneer structure.

Celebrating his roots

Victorian art and architecture are plentiful in the serene and rural **Old Gray Cemetery** on North Broadway, named for the English poet, Thomas Gray, author of *Elegy Written in a Country Churchyard*. Tennessean and Pulitzer Prize-winning Alex Haley, best known for *Roots* and *The Autobiography of Malcolm X*, is celebrated with a larger-than-life bronze statue in Morningside Park. Among the many museums, worth noting is the **Women's Basketball Hall of Fame** (tel:

The Ramsey family was one of the first families to settle the Knoxville area. Colonel F.A. Ramsay helped to found Blount College, now the University of Tennessee.

BELOW:
breathtaking view across the summits, Great Smoky Mountains National Park.

*The Hermitage,
Andrew Jackson's
Tennessee home.*

865-633-9000; May 1–Labor Day Mon–Sat, Labor Day–Apr 30 Tue–Sat), where you can watch videos of past moments of glory, as well as shoot some hoops.

North of the city on I-75, the **Norris Dam** was the first to be built by the vast Tennessee Valley Authority, which brought electric power to this region in the 1930s. **Norris Lake**, acclaimed as one of the cleanest in North America, hosts several marinas and supports houseboats, fishing, and jet skiing. There are trails and campgrounds in the surrounding woods, and an 18th-century Rice Grist Mill. The **Museum of Appalachia** (tel: 865-494-7680; seasonal hours) calls itself "a living mountain village" and does a superlative job of interpreting rural Tennessee, with a pioneer school, a dirt-floor cabin (used in the *Young Daniel Boone* TV series), Mark Twain's family cabin and spinning and weaving among its many exhibits.

West of Knoxville, on Route 162, **Oak Ridge**, the "secret city" built in 1942 to work on production of the first atomic bomb, today invites visitors to explore historic sites such as the **Graphite Reactor** (tours June–early Sept Mon–Fri) that formed part of what was known as the Manhattan Project. Somewhat ironic icons are the **International Friendship Bell and Pavilion** intended to serve "as an expression of hope for everlasting peace," and the **New Bethel Church**, which was used as office space for scientists and engineers planning the Big Bang. At **Cookeville**, which is farther west of Knoxville along Route 62, the **Depot Museum** (tel: 931-528-8570; Tue–Sat) occupies a station built by the Tennessee Central RR in 1909. Fun, faded, and aged cabooses are on display in the grounds.

Continue west on US 70N, but consider stopping just before you get into Nashville for a visit to President Andrew Jackson's gracious and beautiful mansion, **The Hermitage** (tel: 615-889-2941; daily), extensively furnished and on whose grounds still stands the pre-existing farmhouse in which Jackson lived before becoming America's seventh president. He died there in 1845.

Nashville

After the peace and tranquility of Virginia and North Carolina, it's into Tennessee and the "country music capital of the world." **Nashville ⑫** isn't too much of a shock to the senses, however, being a compact and pleasant town to walk around, and it's certainly a good stop for a decent cup of coffee after days on the "filter trail." By this stage in the drive, *all* roads, it appears, lead to "the Athens of the South" (as Nashville likes to term itself) where Interstates 40, 24, and 65 intersect.

This moniker is supported by the **Parthenon** (tel: 615-862-8431; Tue–Sat year-round, Sun June–Aug), a same-size replica built for the Tennessee Centennial Exposition in 1897. Originally constructed of wood, it was rebuilt in the 1920s of more sturdy concrete and is used as an art museum

and for other events in the popular Centennial Park. Fifty years before the Centennial, architect William Strickland had anticipated the style with his Greek Revival **State Capitol**, sturdy enough to be used as a fortress during the Civil War. Also worth seeing is the **Athenaeum Rectory** (tel: 931-381-4822; Tue–Sat), which began as a home for President James K. Polk's nephews but later became a school for the affluent female offspring of planters and bankers. Polk's own ancestral home is at **Columbia**, on US 31, southwest of Nashville.

Printers Alley

An ideal city walk takes in the Beaux Arts **Hermitage Hotel**, where suffragist groups and their opponents gathered to lobby the state legislature in 1920 – their target being the 19th Amendment to the US Constitution. This gave women the right to vote and was duly ratified by Tennessee's vote. Also on the route is **Printers Alley**, the pre-World War II center of Nashville nightlife, with venues that later featured Waylon Jennings, Chet Atkins,

Hank Williams and others. There's a life-size bronze statue of the Grammy-award-winning guitarist Chet Atkins outside the Bank of America at 5th and Union streets.

Nashville-born Red Grooms, the whimsical artist and sculptor who made his name in New York, created the city's most popular artwork – a working carousel on the waterfront whose painted figures all depict well-known local characters. They include the late sportscaster Grantland Rice; frontiersman Davy Crockett; musicians the Everly Brothers, and millionaire socialite Adelicia Acklen.

Tennessee State Museum

Centerpiece of the **Tennessee State Museum** (tel: 800-407-4324; Tue–Sun) is an illustrated history of the Civil War – which killed 600,000 Americans – accenting the role that Tennessee, a Confederate state, played in it. Occupying an entire floor are interactive exhibits with sound effects, film, battle flags, a Confederate cannon, Davy Crockett's powder horn, and an old Conestoga wagon in which some

TIP

Take a stroll along the Walk of Fame, found along the 1-mile stretch connecting downtown with Music Row. Star-and-guitar sidewalk markers commemorate Jimi Hendrix, Roy Orbison, and Emmylou Harris, amongst others.

BELOW:
Country Music Hall of Fame.

Lunch break at a Civil War re-enactment event.

BELOW: re-living a Civil War battle in Arkansas.

long-forgotten family from Virginia migrated to the state in about 1800.

Most of the Civil War battles in Tennessee took place along what is now known as the **Antebellum Trail**. A free leaflet listing battlefields (as well as a score of different old mansions) within a 90-mile (145km) round-trip loop, south of Nashville to the Natchez Trace Parkway, is available from the Tennessee Tourism Department (tel: 615-741-2159).

Across the street from the State Museum in the 18-story war memorial building is the **Military Museum**, exhibiting pictures and artifacts from America's subsequent wars. The **Tennessee Historical Commission** operates out of an outstanding 1850s mansion (Mon–Fri). The **Carl Van Vechten Gallery** (tel: 615-329-8720; Tue–Sat) houses the Alfred Stieglitz Collection of modern art and contains African artifacts and a notable collection of photographs and paintings by world-renowned figures.

Nashville's Scarlett O'Hara

Once a famous stud farm and thoroughbred nursery (from which came Iroquois, the 1881 winner of England's Derby), **Belle Meade Plantation** (tel: 615-356-0501; daily) still displays the opulent lifestyles of a century-and-a-half ago, with tour guides in period costume. The 1853 Greek Revival mansion, elegantly restored, presides over what was once a 5,400-acre (2,187-hectare) plantation whose grassy acres now house Nashville's most impressive homes in a multitude of "neo-anything" styles. At one end of the park, **Cheekwood** (tel: 615-356-8000; Tue–Sun), the immense home of the founder of Maxwell House Coffee, has botanical gardens, a restaurant, and an art gallery. Outdoor concerts take place in summer.

Sometimes regarded as the model for Scarlett O'Hara, Nashville's Adelicia Acklen (1817–89) built the Italian-style **Belmont Mansion** (tel: 615-460-5459; daily), now on Belmont University campus, whose grand salon always incites awe and admiration.

Grand Ole Opry

Almost one-third of the 400-plus record companies in the US are situated in Nashville, so it's no surprise the city has a self-proclaimed **Music Valley**, the area lying between Briley Parkway and the Cumberland River. The "valley" contains at least 100 shops, restaurants, hotels, and other attractions, including the famous **Grand Ole Opry House** (tel: 800-733-6779) and its adjoining museum.

Until the 1970s, the Grand Ole Opry – the country's longest-running live radio program, which began in 1925 – was broadcast from Ryman Auditorium ("the Carnegie Hall of the South"), which, since its transfer there in 1943, has played host to everybody from Enrico Caruso, Rudolf Valentino and Mae West to Bruce Springsteen and the Vienna Choirboys. There are four guided tours daily. Behind Ryman Hall were (and still are) a row of honky-tonk bars where the country and western stars would throw back a few beers after a foot-stomping gig.

The **Country Music Hall of Fame** (tel: 615-416-2001; daily) moved from historic premises on tree-lined 16th Avenue (which also housed Studio B, where Elvis Presley cut a platter) to huge, state-of-the-art premises Downtown that span an entire city block. Around three hours is recommended to tour the various galleries, which could begin or end in the 214-seat acoustically excellent Ford Theater. One movie theater shows films featuring today's top country performers, while daily tours of Studio B depart from the museum. In the museum itself, an entire showcase is devoted to Hank Williams who, along with fellow musician Ernest Tubb, is credited with inventing the honky-tonk style developed in roadside taverns and dance-halls prior to World War II.

Other exhibits include Elvis Presley's gold Cadillac and his grand piano; George Strait's hat and jacket; scores of guitars from famous owners, and the 1962 Pontiac – with pistols for door handles and steer horns mounted on the front bumper – owned by Webb Pearce. An enormous two-story wall displays every gold and platinum record to make the country charts (you

Interstate 40, the road that connects Nashville with Memphis, is known as "Music Highway."

BELOW:
country rock star
Charlie Daniels
performing at the
Grand Ole' Opry.

Memphis: Music City USA

The gateway to the Mississippi Delta is the home of blues, Beale Street, and the site of two kings: Elvis and Martin Luther.

The guest list at Memphis's ornate and venerable **Peabody Hotel** (pronounce it *ho*-*tel*) has included US presidents as well as the Confederate hero Robert E. Lee, but infinitely more popular today are the Peabody ducks, who live on the roof. Every day at 11am, they take a ride in the elevator to the lobby, walk across a red carpet and, to the strains of John Philip Sousa, climb into the foun-

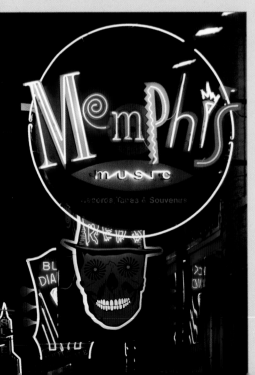

tain, where they remain until 5pm when the performance is repeated in reverse.

Memphis is best known, of course, for **Graceland** (tel: 800-238-2000; Dec–Feb Wed–Mon), about 10 miles (16km) south along Elvis Presley Boulevard, where there are long lines to view the late singer's home and grave.

Sun Studio (tel: 800-441-6249; daily) was where "the King" recorded, but B.B. King, Ike Turner, and many other artists preceded him here. In recent years, Bono, U2, and Paul Simon have been Sun clients. Half-hourly tours are given, and for $30 you can record a song of your own onto CD. The **Stax Museum of American Soul Music** (tel: 901-946-2535; Tue–Sun) celebrates the musicians who lived, worked or are buried in the Memphis area called Soulsville, like Aretha Franklin and Otis Redding, while the **Memphis Rock 'n Soul Museum**, on the corner of Beale Street and Hwy 61, has seven galleries that examine the history of the city's music.

There are plenty of other music venues, among them the **Center for Southern Folklore** (tel: 901-525-3655; Mon–Sat) and B.B. King's Blues Club (tel: 901-524-5464; daily). **Beale Street** is where it all began, and this is where W.C. Handy (1873–1958) set to music the songs of the cotton pickers and "inscribed for ever in the heart of the nation his immortal songs," as the inscription reads on his statue here. The street's bars, nightclubs, and restaurants are all worthwhile. A. **Schwab's**, a store that's been around since 1876, sells hardware, 99¢ neckties, voodoo powders, and tools.

Six blocks south is the **National Civil Rights Museum** (tel: 901-521-9699; Wed–Mon), incorporating the Lorraine Motel where Martin Luther King, Jr was assassinated on April 4, 1968. Even today, the sight of the rumpled bed, breakfast tray, and a few objects in Room 306 – the last things Dr King saw before stepping onto the balcony – bring a tear to the eye. Other rooms focus on the Civil Rights movement. ❑

TOP LEFT: tributes to Elvis, Graceland. **LEFT:** Beale Street music clubs. **ABOVE:** a Music City reminder.

can buy less precious editions of these in the shop). Live entertainment is staged most days.

Southern cookin'

Bronze likenesses of the Hall of Famers themselves – which include promoters and broadcasters as well as performers – are showcased in a huge rotunda "bathed in the natural light admitted by a circle of clerstory windows," proof of how far C&W has come since the humble *Stand By Your Man*. The museum's restaurant serves contemporary Southern cuisine.

If, after this, you're ready to hit the road to visit another famous city of the south, head southwest out of Nashville on I-40. Some 128 miles (206km) farther on, you'll come to **Jackson**, and just beyond that is a great family stop at **Casey Jones Village** (tel: 800-748-9588; daily), with country stores, lavish buffets, an old-fashioned ice-cream parlor, a train museum in Casey Jones' original 1890s home and a replica of a 1900 train station. But if that doesn't suit your fancy, keep headin' on down the highway straight into **Memphis** ⑬ (*see page 196*).

where along the way you will find **Hazen**, with its wildlife preserve, and **Lonoke**, which houses one of the country's largest fish hatcheries. Southwest of Lonoke, just off US 165, are the **Toltec Mounds Archeological State Park** (tel: 501-961-9442; daily), a sprawling prehistoric site, and the **Plantation Agriculture Museum** (tel: 501-961-1409; Tue–Sun), which tells the story of cotton production in the South.

US 165 joins US 70, which turns southwest at Little Rock, heading through **Benton** with its bauxite deposits. This earthy substance from which aluminum is made is responsible for much of the area's wealth – justification enough for the world's only bauxite building to be constructed here.

The Arkansas River carves a gateway between the Ouachita and Ozark mountains to the delta at **Little Rock** ⑭.

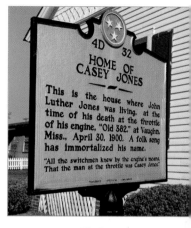

The Casey Jones Village in Jackson honors the locomotive engineer who died while trying to save the lives of his passengers.

BELOW: paddle steamer on the Arkansas River, Little Rock.

ARKANSAS

After the excitement of Nashville and Memphis, the next part of the journey takes us straight back to small-town America, where Interstate 40 crosses the **Mississippi River** and cuts into the middle of Arkansas. Roadsides in Arkansas are often gloriously colorful, testament to the state's extensive wildflower program, which has lined more than 1,000 miles (1,600km) of highway with colorful banks of purple larkspur, black-eyed Susan, Indian paintbrush, goldenrod, pink primrose and bright red cardinal flowers – a native perennial that attracts hummingbirds. The Arkansas highway department claims that almost a quarter million acres of its highways have been graced with 600 species of flowers.

Paralleling the interstate between Memphis and Little Rock is US 70,

The greyhound has been the symbol of US bus travel for many decades.

BELOW: wildflowers on a farm in Ozark Mountain Country.

The city is, therefore, first and foremost a river city; an amalgamation of the Old South and the Southwest. The downtown area of Little Rock extends south from the Arkansas River. Beside it, under the Union Pacific Railroad Bridge, is the "Little Rock" that lent the city its name, and it's also the first visible rock outcrop to hove into view when traveling up from the Gulf of Mexico. **Breckling Riverfront Park**, with its pleasure-boat wharf and extravagant fountain, is the site of an amphitheater and an outdoor film festival.

An extensive area called the **River Market**, flanked at the western end by the Convention Center, comprises businesses, shops, bars and cafés, two hotels, the library, and a Farmers' Market (Tue and Sat May–Oct). There's parking at the eastern end, near the **William J. Clinton Presidential Library** (tel: 501-374-4242; daily), and there are also electric streetcar trolleys downtown, making life even easier for out-of-towners. Heading back inland, the **Convention & Visitors Bureau** at the corner of Markham and Broadway streets (tel: 501-376-4781) is a good starting point to acquire information.

Cast-iron hotel

Across the street is the restored historical **Capital Hotel** where President Ulysses S. Grant stayed shortly after it opened in 1877. The interior and exterior are equally interesting. Note its four-story cast-iron front and an elegant 1908 interior by Little Rock architect George R. Mann. At Second and Center streets is the 10-story Southern Trust Building (now called **Pyramid Place**), the city's first skyscraper when it was built in 1907. Times have changed, and today's Downtown is dominated by the Metropolitan Tower, which American TV and yogurt fans may recognize as once being the old headquarters of "The Country's Best Yogurt."

Located on President Clinton Avenue, the **Museum of Discovery** (tel: 501-396-7050; daily) entices kids and adults with Kewpie collections, over 50 live animal species and more. A number of venerable old buildings

located in downtown streets include the Romanesque Revival **Pulaski County Courthouse** (Markham and Spring streets) with its Classical Revival domed annex, and the **Historic Arkansas Museum** (tel: 501-324-9351; daily). Inside is the **Hinderliter Grog Shop**, the city's oldest building.

The impressive **State Capitol** (tel: 501-682-5080; daily, guided tours Mon–Fri), in which Bill Clinton served five terms as governor, lies at the western end of Capitol Avenue. Its design details include six brass doors purchased from Tiffany's in New York. Flying atop the building is the state flag, which has a diamond shape in the center to mark the fact that Arkansas is the only state with a diamond mine (at Murfreesboro).

Grand old dames

Little Rock is understandably proud of its plethora of wonderful old houses – most of them funded and built by successful bankers, cotton brokers or other wealthy merchants in the 19th century. These interesting mansions are listed in several free books and pamphlets, which offer mapped routes through the various historical districts. A few of the homes have been converted into striking bed-and-breakfasts. Opening times vary and few of the houses are actually open to the public, so if you do have time for a lengthy tour be sure to collect some of this literature from the visitor's bureau before setting out.

A drive around the quiet, tree-lined streets might begin in the **Governor's Mansion Historic District** at the mansion itself (18th and Center streets) and concentrate on the streets between 18th and 15th streets bordered by Louisiana and Gaines. In this area alone, 35 buildings are listed in the Bureau's Tour Number Three. The Queen Anne or Colonial Revival styles, and sometimes a combination of both, predominate in this district, and though varying considerably in appearance, many of the buildings were designed by the same architect, Charles L. Thompson, who practiced in Little Rock from 1885 for more than 50 years. The sumptuous **Governor's Mansion**, where the Clintons lived for

TIP

Stop by the Old State House museum in Little Rock, the place where Bill Clinton gave his election night victory speeches (tel: 501-324-9685; daily).

BELOW: street performers in downtown Little Rock.

The fine old Little Rock house, Villa Marre, narrowly escaped demolition in 1964 when a local furniture store owner purchased it for renovation.

BELOW: Capitol building, Little Rock, where former US president Bill Clinton served five times as governor.

12 years, has a dramatic curving, walnut staircase and is stylishly furnished with Hepplewhite and Chippendale antique furnishings. A bust of Bill sits by the gate. Down the street are the **Cathedral Park Apartments** at 15th and Center, converted from a one-time Episcopal church, and four blocks west on Arch Street is the English Revival-style **Cornish House**, with its magnificent third-floor ballroom in which Ed Cornish, a prominent banker, and his wife staged extravagant parties.

More than bed and breakfast

At 2120 Louisiana Street, the **Hornibrook House** was built by successful saloon owner James Hornibrook who, after a social snub, was determined to build something to make the neighbors gasp. The result is a house known as "The Empress of Little Rock," a Queen Anne-style home with concave

front doors, a stained-glass skylight, turrets, gables, and a wrap-around porch. Inside is a series of luxuriously furnished parlors replete with lace cloths, tasseled lampshades, a dollhouse, antique chairs, and divans. The house now serves as an attractive B&B, with nine octagonal rooms named after some of the state's historical characters – such as John Edward Murray, the youngest general in the Confederate army.

Another B&B worth staying the night for is **Hotze House**, at 1619 Louisiana Street. This one was the monumental home of a cotton broker and has a Colonial Revival exterior with 20ft (6-meter) -high pillars. Beneath the stenciled ceilings are walls covered with tapestry and green damask shot with gold thread.

There are equally impressive homes to be found in the **MacArthur Park** district. The 1881 Italianate **Villa Marre** at 1321 Scott Street was named for another successful saloon keeper, Angelo Marre, about whom one of the local guidebooks writes: "Initially known for his quick temper and shady past, Marre eventually became a respectable member of the City Council." The distinctive **Hanger House** at number 1010 on the same block, which looks like a vision from a fairy tale, owes its earthy shade to Frances Hanger, who remodeled the house herself after researching decorating books. She remarked in a letter to a friend that red seemed to be "about as popular as ever for painting houses."

At 2120 Daisy Bates Drive is the visitor center of the **Little Rock Central High School National Historic Site** (tel: 501-374-1957; daily), across the intersection from the (still operating) school that provoked the dramatic desegregation confrontation of 1957. A refurbished 1957 Mobil gas station (with its pumps frozen at 22.5 cents per gallon) sits opposite the school.

Photos and other visuals depict the scene when Governor Orval Faubus

called out the National Guard to bar admittance to nine black students. Three weeks later President Eisenhower called out the US Army to escort the students into the school. The legal case remained in the courts for an entire year, during which time Little Rock public high schools remained closed. At the time, the Mobil station, with the only pay telephone in the area, was the scene of some unseemly competition among the visiting press.

Hot Springs

About 50 miles (80km) west of Little Rock, in the Diamond Lakes Region off SR 7, is the resort of **Hot Springs** ⓯, which has been a recreational area for hundreds of years. The springs have played a large part in Arkansas politics – not least for being the boyhood home of Bill Clinton. A lakeside resort city surrounded by low-lying mountains, it offers historic buildings, an alligator farm, and petting zoo, spas, ranches, an aquarium, a wax museum, and all of the additional resort amenities. There are hundreds of accommodations ranging from hotels and lakeside cottages to campgrounds and houseboat rentals. (Information from 501-321-2835.) One of the resort hotels claims that although Arkansas is famous for its unspoiled beauty, "we're famous…for our spoiled guests." From Little Rock, I-40 heads northwest and crosses the Oklahoma border at the rather unattractive **Fort Smith**. While the old fort town might be worth a quick visit on the way through, much of the new town of Fort Smith is memorable only for its used car lots and heavy traffic.

Although I-40 will carry you all the way through the state of Oklahoma and on westward, if you're interested in a more colorful journey, we suggest heading north just before Fort Smith on I-540, which becomes US 71 as it crosses into the southwest corner of Missouri and leads you to the city of **Joplin** ⓰, where you can pick up America's "Mother Road" – Route 66. Route 66 will cut across the southeast corner of Kansas before heading into Oklahoma. ❑

BELOW: superheroes greeting their fans at the Annual Hot Springs Bathtub Races, Arkansas.

OKLAHOMA TO NEW MEXICO

Take "a stroll on wheels" along Route 66 through
Oklahoma and the Texas Panhandle, then
cruise through Santa Fe and Albuquerque.
The highway anthem begins here

Oklahoma was the site of one of the most dramatic land rushes in the country. The new towns of Oklahoma City and Guthrie became home to more than 10,000 residents in the space of a day. The state is where we finally get to know the 2,448-mile (3,940-km) -long Route 66 (*see essay on page 35*). If your plan is to follow the "Mother Road" for most or all of the way, a word of advice: time is of the essence. Staying on the road is not as easy as it sounds, and having just enough – or even worse, *not* enough time – as opposed to having ample time could be the difference between a thoroughly enjoyable road trip and a disappointingly frustrating one. Advocates of the famous route claim that half the fun of Route 66 lies in the adventure of finding it, so plan ahead if it is to be a focal point of your drive. On the plus side, dipping in and out of it is relatively easy because of its proximity to the interstate, so even those with less time on their hands should see something of it.

Exile on Main Street

Route 66 is a serious business – "business" being the operative word. Real fanatics will arm themselves with maps and guide books, motel directories, and red-hot tips gleaned avidly from their *Route 66 Magazine* subscription. Some might even drink coffee from their "Main Street, USA" mug while wearing an "I drove the Mother Road" T-shirt.

Fanatic or not, getting lost is inevitable, as you will come across stretches of the route that are maddeningly difficult to find. In some cases, the not-so-trusty brown "Historic US 66" signs vanish, with little or no indication as to where it has gone, or whether it has been subsumed by the nearby interstate. In many places, it runs parallel with the major highway for mile after mile, sometimes marked and sometimes not. Even experienced map-readers will have their competence sorely tested by some of the numerous

Main attractions
STOCKYARDS CITY
COWBOY & WESTERN
  HERITAGE MUSEUM
OKLAHOMA ROUTE 66
  MUSEUM
CADILLAC RANCH
SANTA FE
ALBUQUERQUE OLD TOWN
INDIAN PUEBLO CULTURAL CENTER
ACOMA SKY CITY
EL MORRO NATIONAL MONUMENT

LEFT AND BELOW:
open-road relics
along the Oklahoma
leg of Route 66.

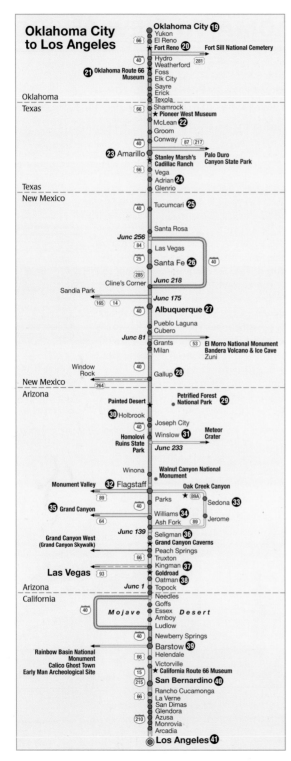

Oklahoma City to Los Angeles

Oklahoma City ⑲
Yukon
66
El Reno
Fort Reno ⑳ · · · · · · Fort Sill National Cemetery
Hydro
40
Weatherford 281
② Oklahoma Route 66 Museum
Foss
Elk City
Sayre
Erick
Oklahoma · · · · · Texola
Texas 66 Shamrock
★ Pioneer West Museum
McLean ㉒
Groom
Conway 87 217
40
② Amarillo Stanley Marsh's Cadillac Ranch
Palo Duro Canyon State Park
66 Vega
Adrian ㉔
Texas · · · · · Glenrio
New Mexico
40 Tucumcari ㉕

Santa Rosa
Junc 256
84 Las Vegas
25 Santa Fe ㉖ 40
285
Cline's Corner Junc 218
Sandia Park
165 14 Junc 175
40 Albuquerque ㉗
Pueblo Laguna
Cubero
Junc 81
Grants 53 El Morro National Monument
Milan Bandera Volcano & Ice Cave
Zuni
Window 40
Rock Gallup ㉘
New Mexico 264
Arizona
Petrified Forest
Painted Desert · National Park ㉙
㉚ Holbrook
Joseph City
40
Homolovi Winslow ㉛ Meteor
Ruins State Crater
Park Junc 233
Winona Walnut Canyon National
Monument
Monument Valley ㉜ Flagstaff Oak Creek Canyon
89 Parks ★ 89A
㉟ Grand Canyon Sedona �33
40 Williams �34 Jerome
64 Ash Fork 89
Junc 139 Seligman �36
Grand Canyon West Grand Canyon Caverns
(Grand Canyon Skywalk) ★ Peach Springs
Truxton
66 Kingman �37
Las Vegas 93 ★ Goldroad
Oatman �38
Arizona Junc 1 Topock
California Needles
Goffs
40 Mojave Essex *Desert*
Amboy
Ludlow
40 Newberry Springs
Barstow �39
Rainbow Basin National Helendale
Monument 66
Calico Ghost Town Victorville
Early Man Archeological Site 15 ★ California Route 66 Museum
215 San Bernardino ㊵
Rancho Cucamonga
66 La Verne
San Dimas
Glendora
210 Azusa
Monrovia
Arcadia
◉ Los Angeles ㊶

maps claiming to trace the entire route. Time, patience, and – at the occasional unmarked crossroad – a little bit of guesswork are the keywords to a successful trip.

Paul Taylor, publisher of the aforementioned and intriguing *Route 66 Magazine*, maintains that with sufficient time to explore, driving the route presents only minor setbacks. Owners of some of the Route 66 landmark attractions and memorabilia stores along the way say that one of the reasons travelers lose their way is because too many people steal the signs. "They are popular souvenirs." So, however tempting – leave that sign alone!

Wondering how long it will take to drive all, or most, of the route? This depends on many factors, not least whether you are what author Tom Snyder defines as: "Late starter, get loster, honky tonker, sensitive browser, coffee hound, museum freak, or postcard looker." A reasonably fast trip, he estimates, would be at least eight days – from its origin in Illinois to the final mile in California.

Route 66 enters Oklahoma at **Quapaw** in the northeast corner, traversing 400 miles (644km) of the state, for much of the way running parallel to (or being replaced by) I-44.

Oklahoma's origins

The creation of the Oklahoma Territory, following the Land Rush 50 years later, shrank Indian Territory by half, forcing Native Americans to abandon communal ownership in favor of small individual plots. Nevertheless, more than 65 Native American tribes are still represented in the state, and one of the first more major towns you'll come to after entering the state, **Miami ⑰**, is named after one of these communities.

One of the earliest sections of the highway is found in the vicinity; you'll also find some Route 66 exhibits in the restored **Coleman Theatre** (tel: 918-540-2425) in the town.

Just after Miami is one of those places where Route 66 sort of "disappears" –

so don't feel you've cheated here by jumping on I-44 for a short stretch. This section of the interstate (up to Tulsa) is also known as the Will Rogers Turnpike (Woody Guthrie wrote a song about it), in memory of the famous homespun comic and No. 1 box office star. You can pick up Route 66 again a little farther on at **Vinita**, which gets its name from Vinnie Ream, who sculpted Washington, DC's Abraham Lincoln statue. The town stages a Will Rogers Memorial Rodeo every August and also lays claim to one of the world's largest (29,135 sq ft/2,707 sq meters) McDonald's.

Farther southwest, in Galloway Park near **Foyil**, is the world's largest totem pole, at 90ft (27 meters) tall. Foyil's main street is named after Andy Payne, $25,000 winner of the 84-day "Bunion Derby" in 1928, whose contestants hiked 2,400 miles (3,862km) from New York to Los Angeles, mostly along Route 66. Less than half of the route had been surfaced by then: it was not until 1938 that the entire route was finally paved. "In those days," Tom Snyder writes, "even Lindbergh's solo flight over the Atlantic was easier than a cross-country trek by automobile in the same year."

A few miles farther on is **Claremore**, with a memorial to Will Rogers; his 1879 birthplace is memorialized at **Oologah**, just to the north. After Foyil, Route 66 continues to head southwest to Tulsa – with the route again joining up with I-44 just as you reach the outskirts of the city.

Tulsa ⑱ (pop. 385,000), with its downtown Art Deco buildings and a wonderful 1950s-style diner, Tally's Good Food Café, on East 11th Street, was once known as the "Oil capital of the world." Here, Cyrus Avery was a co-founder and booster of the fledgling Highway 66 Association.

Continue to follow I-44 out of the city; you can return to Route 66 by getting off at exit 220. The Mother Road again runs parallel to the main highway between Tulsa and Oklahoma City; the interstate on this stretch is also known as the Turner Turnpike. You'll pass through a string of small towns: **Sapulpa**, where aspiring Western star Gene Autry once sang in the local ice-cream parlor, and which has an interesting historical museum; **Kellyville** (look for the Cotton Gin Diner); **Stroud** (head to the 70-year-old Rock Café, which burnt down in 2008 but is getting back on its feet); **Davenport**, with its enormous murals depicting scenes from the early days; and – as you approach Oklahoma City – **Arcadia**, with its distinctive Old Round Barn.

Crystal bridge

Oklahoma City ⑲ blossomed overnight on April 22, 1889, when the Land Rush opened up the adjoining territory to settlement – attracting 50,000 hopeful prospectors. The appeal of today's Oklahoma City owes much to the planning talents of architect I.M. Pei, whose development scheme produced an elegant mix of lakes, parks, landscaped hills, and stylish buildings. The centerpiece is **Myriad Botanical**

Throughout the Southwest, be sure to book rooms way ahead during the summer months.

BELOW: Red Earth festival, Oklahoma City.

Gardens (tel: 405-297-3995; daily), a 17-acre (7-hectare) oasis in the heart of Downtown, its seventh-floor Crystal Bridge housing a plant- and tree-filled tropical conservatory and waterfall.

Oil derricks near the State Capitol are a reminder that the city's wealth stemmed from a major gusher 75 years ago. A score of major producing oil-fields still operate in the state. Cotton was once king here, but it's cattle ranching that predominates today, and this great heritage is celebrated at **Stockyards City**, where ranchers and real cowboys have been coming since its inception in the early 1900s for apparel, equipment, supplies, and a good meal. A "gaslight district" features a variety of western-oriented shops, galleries, and restaurants, but the place is still all about cattle: cattle auctions are held Monday and Tuesday each week, starting at 9am. Tours are offered by Stockyards City's Main Street office, but as this is a one-man office, walking tour maps are provided if the tour leader is unavailable.

More sobering is the site of the April 1995 bombing of the Federal Building at which 168 people were killed. The site has now become a poignant memorial, with 168 empty chairs – reminding visitors of those who died – arranged on a grassy slope under a canopy of trees, facing a shallow reflecting pool.

Cowboys on parade

One of Oklahoma's major attractions is the **National Cowboy & Western Heritage Museum** (tel: 405-478-2250; daily), just north of I-44 as you come into Oklahoma City (exit 129), whose wide, marble-tiled corridors are flanked with giant landscape paintings and photographs depicting cowboy life. This excellent museum has broad appeal, and even those with no interest in the Wild West might find themselves pleasantly surprised. Movie posters of Gene Autry, Tom Mix, and John Wayne decorate one gallery, close to a larger-than-life statue of Ronald Reagan and a huge statue titled *The End of the Trail*, by James Earle Fraser. It is matched by his wife Laura's bas-relief of the Land Rush.

Visitors can stroll through the streets of an old Western town with church, dry goods store, and blacksmith's shop, while children can don chaps, boots, and spurs in the Cowboy Corral, before dismounting and hiding away in a range tent.

Among the hundreds of unique action photographs shot with a con-verted 1880 Graflex camera by rodeo's first professional photographer, Ralph Russell Doubleday (1881–1958), is one of movie cowboy Hopalong Cassidy leading a small-town parade. Postcards of pictures by "Dub," often developed in the bathroom of whatever hotel in which he was staying, sold by the millions.

You can continue to head west either on Route 66 or on I-40 (the two become one some 40 miles/64km out of the city anyway). The Chisholm Trail ran along what is now Ninth Street in tiny **Yukon** – just outside the Oklahoma City limits on Route 66 and

hometown of country star Garth Brooks. Both Sid's Diner in this town and Johnnie's Grill in neighboring **El Reno** claim to be the home of that distinctive Oklahoma treat – the onion-fried hamburger. The El Reno Hotel, built in 1892 when rooms cost all of 50¢ a night, is now part of the Canadian County Historical Museum.

Chisholm Trail

Fort Reno ⓴ (tel: 405-262-3987; daily) displays exhibits from the days when it served as a cavalry post during the Indian Wars. El Reno is now the headquarters for the Cheyenne-Arapaho tribe.

If you take exit 108 off I-40, a short detour north on US 281 leads to **Geary**, bypassed by Route 66 in 1933 despite the locals' work in grading and graveling the road in the hope of enticing the route, and its dollars, through their town. Not far away is **Left Hand Spring Camp**, where Jesse Chisholm, who gave his name to the famous Chisholm Trail, is buried. The trail, which stretched 250 miles (400km) from San Antonio to Abilene, was first laid in 1860 when buffalo still roamed nearby. Twenty years later, when the trail was more or less abandoned, it had seen the passage of more than 10 million cattle. If you head south on US 281, about 78 miles (126km) later, you'll come to **Fort Sill National Cemetery**, where the Apache chief Geronimo died in captivity in 1909.

Driving backwards

Just near where I-40 intersects with US 281 is the 3,944ft (1,202-meter) -long "pony bridge" crossing the South Canadian River, a multiple simple-span bridge typical of the type used in the construction of Route 66. In addition to offering superb vistas of the river, the William H. Murray Bridge starred in a scene in John Ford's 1940 movie version of *The Grapes of Wrath*.

The hill leading up to the bridge is so steep that Model T Fords – their engines generating more power in reverse – had to climb it backward. Continuing west on I-40, just north of exit 88 is Lucille's gas station and store at **Hydro** – Lucille ran the property for 59 years till her death in 2000. It is a

Fancy hood ornament on an antique Ford.

BELOW: Clinton, Oklahoma, has one of the best 66 museums along the historic route.

Giant kachina doll marks the entrance to the National Route 66 Museum in Elk City, Oklahoma.

BELOW: a retro neon welcome to the Oklahoma Route 66 Museum.

favorite with Route 66 regulars, some of whom have been buying gas and groceries here since 1941. Other local landmarks include a building with Greek columns (formerly a bank, now a dress shop) and the century-old Lee Cotter's Blacksmith Shop at **Weatherford**, where the **General Thomas P. Stafford Air and Space Museum** (tel: 580-772-5871; daily), with fighter jets and moon rocks, commemorates Oklahoma's premier astronaut.

One really begins to get a feel of traversing the old road at **Clinton** (pop. 8,833), where the state-sponsored **Oklahoma Route 66 Museum ㉑** (tel: 580-323-7866; closed Sun–Mon Dec–Jan) is the most comprehensive – and memorable – of many similar places found along the famous highway. Each era is presented in its individual room, with photographs of the road's construction in the 1920s. Oklahoma was still "dry" in the 1930s, and the rise of the bootlegger prompted a corresponding increase in the number of law enforcement officers who are pictured in their intimidating uniforms.

Mother Road memories

A typical garage from the same era – with its glass-topped Red Crown gasoline pump – flanks pictures of a few of the three million migrants in their battered trucks bearing "California or Bust" signs. The photos of trucks, crammed with furniture, bedding, pots and pans, and crated chickens, typify the Dust Bowl years, when parched farmlands induced the westward-flight of almost one-fifth of the state's population. "66 is the path of people in flight, refugees from dust and shrinking land," wrote John Steinbeck in the book that produced the 1940 Academy Award-winning *The Grapes of Wrath*.

"We'll go on forever, Pa, cuz we're the people," declared the movie's Ma Joad. A Greyhound bus and a VW bus evoking the hippies-on-the-road era are among the vehicles on show, the "bug" illuminated by fluorescent lighting in a room whose walls display '60s album covers from Sinatra and Dina Shore to Hank Williams and Chuck Berry. A poster promoting a one-time rattlesnake show, a map made by a retired postmaster with franking stamps from every post office along the route, a glass case of souvenirs from long-vanished gift shops, and a video running quaint family movies on an endless loop are also part of the museum tour, which climaxes with an absorbing movie depicting the route's history.

"We heard many years ago in New Zealand Nat King Cole singing 'Get Your Kicks on Route 66'," writes one visitor. "So we came to see it."

Diner lingo

In the museum's replica of a 1950s diner – complete with a 1951 Ford parked out front and interior cozy booths, a jukebox playing Elvis Presley, and plastic donuts and coffee displayed on the Formica counter – is a translation of "diner lingo" – the slang used by waitresses when shouting orders to

the kitchen. Some examples: "Drown one, hold the hail" (Coke, no ice); "Boiled leaves" (hot tea); "Rubber in a bun" (steak sandwich).

Until 1999, Clinton's historic Pop Hick's Restaurant was the oldest continuously operating restaurant along the entire route, but in that year it burned down and owner Howard Nichols has no plans to rebuild. Instead, check out Jiggs Smokehouse, just west on I-40, for delicious barbecue food.

West of Clinton, Route 66 parallels I-40, which is only a stone's throw away, and a facet of traveling along the almost empty Mother Highway is suggested by a Burma Shave aphorism painted on the wall of a local café: *The Guy Who Drives/So Close Behind/Is He Lonesome/Or Just Blind*? (see page 38).

The ghost town of **Foss** and the Old Town Museum complex at **Elk City** of relocated old buildings, plus another Route 66 museum, might draw you off the road after leaving Clinton. When the US Highway 66 Association held its convention in Elk City's Casa Grande Hotel in 1931, more than 20,000 enthusiasts attended. The hotel is now the **Anadarko Basin Museum of Natural History** (tel: 580-243-0437; tours by appointment). Songwriter Jimmy Webb ("Up, Up, and Away") was born here.

Sayre, a little bit farther on, is also alarmingly empty these days, but shows traces of having once been a prominent feature along the route. The town also has a rather grandiloquent courthouse, which featured fleetingly in the movie *The Grapes of Wrath*. The small, fairly ordinary town of **Erick** and the almost deserted town **Texola** have each – at different times by different surveys – been declared to be sitting on the 100th meridian, the longitudinal arcs running through both the North and the South poles that are used as geographical definitions.

On the stretch heading through Erick, Route 66 is renamed Roger Miller Boulevard – a tribute to its song-writing ("King of the Road") native son. Route 66 historian Tom Snyder says that Erick was once one of the nation's worst speed traps, but now behaves itself because its severity caused tourist traffic to dry up.

THE TEXAS PANHANDLE

As you progress west through the high plains of Oklahoma, which merge into the Texas Panhandle, the grass becomes shorter and the hills begin to turn into small buttes and mesas. There's an overwhelming sense of insignificance in the face of the wide, open space stretching as far as the horizon. As might be expected in Texas, there is also a palpable feeling of having arrived in the real West, reflected in the confident pride of most residents. "Character traits, like an independent spirit, found expression in the West," explains the University of Oklahoma's Peter Hassrick. "By going West you escape the social restraints of the East. That same independent spirit could be seen in the mountain man and later the Forty-niners and finally the American cowboy."

Famous Texans include Larry McMurtry, the Pulitzer Prize-winning author of Lonesome Dove, *the definitive Western novel based loosely on real-life people and events.*

BELOW:
Indian handicrafts for sale in Clinton.

Route 66 gas stations were made as pretty as possible in a competitive marketplace.

BELOW: the historic first Phillips gas station in McLean, Texas.

Along this route, you'll perhaps get your first glimpse of the impressive mile-long freight trains snaking their way along the Santa Fe tracks, usually paralleling the road but sometimes causing lengthy delays at road crossings. *Slow Down, Pa/Sakes Alive/Ma Missed Signs/Four and Five*, the Burma Shave signs used to admonish.

At **Shamrock**, Texas – where travelers are invited to experience 4 miles (6km) of historic 66 – is the **Pioneer West Museum** (tel: 806-256-3941; Mon–Fri). Don't miss the lime-green and sand-colored Art Deco masterpiece, the U Drop Inn Café (now a tourism office), and adjoining gas station with matching tower.

Early gas stations had to fight hard for customers in a highly competitive market and the filling pump station took many forms. One, on the site of Albuquerque, New Mexico's present-day Lobo movie theater (now in use as a church) was shaped like a giant chunk of ice. Companies made a big deal of cleanliness. Texaco, for example, established its White Patrol in 1938 – a team of inspectors in white coupés

who toured the highways inspecting the company's rest rooms. The Union Oil Company countered with its Sparkle Corps.

At picturesque, sleepy **McLean** ㉒ (pop. 830), which describes itself as "the heart of old Route 66," an old Phillips 66 gas station has been restored by volunteers, and is one of a surprisingly small number along the route (there are none at all in Arizona). The Phillips Petroleum Company records some of the many erroneous explanations people have offered for the "66" in the company's name, for example: there are 66 books in the Bible; the company's founders were down to their last $66 when they drilled their first successful oil well; or that founder Frank Phillips was 66 years old when he founded the company (he was actually 44).

The Devil's Rope

The **Devil's Rope Museum**, formerly a brassiere factory, is here (tel: 806-779-2225; Tue–Sat) – the "rope" in question being barbed wire, a large rusty ball of which sits outside. Although the museum has a relatively small selection, there are as many as 8,000 different types of barbed wire in existence. Oklahoma's National Cowboy & Western Heritage Museum (*see page 206*) has the largest collection, including the popular "Dodge Spur" with its single line. In the mid-19th century, there were hundreds of competing designs, but it was Joseph F. Glidden's patent for fencing material, consisting of barbs wrapped around a single strand of wire, that eventually predominated.

Towards Amarillo

As you drive out of McLean, look for the large wall mural depicting Elvis performing next to a yellow Cadillac, on whose hood sits a guitar player. The unpaved section of Route 66 between Alanreed and **Groom** has always been a problem for unwary drivers. Bob Moore and Patrick Grauwels, the

acknowledged experts on the road, write that the section, once known as Jericho Gap, "was notorious for bogging down cars and trucks in a black, gumbo mud every time it rained." Their *Illustrated Guidebook to the Mother Road*, with pictures by Yannis Argyropoulos, is indisputably the most comprehensive of the many guides available: a spiral-bound, mile-by-mile summation, it has sold more than 50,000 copies. Moore points out that despite their years of research errors do occur "because Route 66 is still a living entity, and as such, changes are constantly taking place."

The route, which mostly parallels I-40 in this part of Texas, and sometimes merges with it, is hard to follow between here and Amarillo. At the entrance to many towns, it's safer, when in doubt, to take the off-ramp road labeled *Business I-40,* which usually follows the old Route 66 through town. This is the case at **Conway**, recognizable by its huge grain elevators and decrepit motels. Located on the route as you head toward Amarillo is the 24-hour Cattleman's Club & Café,

with a large steer on its sign. An interesting breakfast stop, this place is about as Western as you'll find, with half the customers of both sexes wearing Stetsons, rows of slot machines to keep them occupied and gigantic rubbery omelets big enough to feed a ravenous cowpoke.

Palo Duro Canyon

Just before Amarillo (where local rancher J.F. Glidden invented his barbed wire), you could turn south on US 87 to visit the vast **Palo Duro Canyon**, closely associated with the legendary Charles Goodnight. Goodnight – inventor of the chuckwagon and once owner of the largest ranch in Texas – was the first rancher to move into the Panhandle in the 1870s. A musical named simply *Texas* takes place at the Canyon in summer (tel: 806-655-2181; Mon–Sat) against a steep cliffside backdrop. Chuckwagon tours beginning or ending with "cowboy" breakfast or dinner are offered on the rim of the canyon, where part of an Indiana Jones movie was filmed (tel: 806-488-2227).

Back in 1893 Amarillo's population was recorded as being "between 500–600 humans and 50,000 head of cattle," compared to today's recent population estimate of 185,000 people.

BELOW LEFT AND RIGHT:
Big Texan – that famous "72-ounce steak" eatery in the Texas Panhandle.

TIP

Remember to set your watch back by an hour as you cross the border between Texas and New Mexico and move from the Central to Mountain time zone.

Amarillo ㉓ itself, always a major shipping point for cattle, stages regular rodeos (for information tel: 800-692-1338) and is the home of the **Big Texan Steak Ranch** (tel: 800-657-7177), a world-renowned restaurant offering 72-ounce steaks free to anybody who can eat one within an hour. A unique natural resource found locally is helium, a monument to which sits on Streit Drive near the Botanical Gardens.

The city's one-way traffic system can be confusing, but you'll be back on Route 66 proper if you follow 6th Street, which leads into "**antique row**," where plenty of Route 66 shops and modern cafés entice visitors with their colorful signage, such as the Golden Light Café. It's worth parking the car to take a closer look at some of the brightly colored wall murals harking back to the good ol' days. There are three churches on one block, which ends with the San Jacinto Apartments, San Jacinto Heights being the old name for this particular suburb.

South of I-40 just outside town is **Cadillac Ranch**, the much photographed and often repainted line of ten Cadillacs, their rear ends sticking out of the earth to make some kind of sculptural statement by art financier Stanley Marsh. The Cadillacs are literally in the middle of a field. To get closer, look for a frontage road parallel to the interstate, where you can park free and walk through a gate to take your snapshots of the cars.

Death by highway

There's not much to see at the small town of **Vega**, except the vintage Vega Motel. By 1928, motels were breeding fast along the fledgling Route 66, but in 1956 the creation of the Interstate Highway System sounded the death knell for scores of businesses, which suddenly found themselves bypassed by the traffic that for more than a quarter of a century had brought them prosperity. "As the world changes," says Joe Kisicki of Oklahoma's Route 66 Association, "so do things along the Mother Road. It mirrors life both modern and nostalgic, tacky and clever, restless and changeless."

Tiny and, in parts, dilapidated, **Adrian** ㉔ declares itself to be at the exact center of Route 66, with a sign announcing that it is 1,139 miles (1,833km) to Chicago and 1,139 miles to Los Angeles. There are other, more curiously philosophical signs dotted around its handful of streets – *You Will Never Be the Same* and *If A Man Could Have Half His Wishes He Would Double His Troubles*. Adrian has been the site of Route 66 gatherings and jamborees.

Abandoned buildings such as the "First in Texas/Last in Texas Motel" dot **Glenrio**, the last Texas town you'll come to on this route and another virtual ghost town, although the four-lane Route 66 highway sits invitingly (albeit starting to disintegrate) at the edge of town.

NEW MEXICO

However well prepared you think you might be for New Mexico, no amount of reading can dull the initial, and rather pleasant, shock of finding the

BELOW:
the Cadillac Ranch is just outside Amarillo, Texas.

aesthetic beauty of Spanish South America dropped right in the middle of this vast, though sometimes bland, scenescape. It feels oddly surreal. In some parts of the state, you won't see a gaudy neon sign, motel chain or a pair of golden arches for miles. Make the most of it while you can.

Route 66 is well promoted throughout New Mexico, where it extends more than 300 miles (483km) across the state along I-40. The State Fairgrounds in Albuquerque were the site of the 2001 75th anniversary celebration of Route 66.

An excursion along the route was once made by members of a European travel club in 30 vintage American cars that were shipped from Europe. Rich Williams, past president of the state's Route 66 Association, says the road "still vibrates" and embodies "a kind of mythology, the best of American culture. And everybody wants to experience that – the authentic American spirit that really created this country."

Just across the border in New Mexico the surrounding terrain, the Llano Estacado (Staked Plain) – a high plateau covering 33,000 sq miles (85,430 sq km) – is one of the flattest areas of the continental United States. Spanish explorer Francisco Vasquez de Coronado unsuccessfully combed the region for the fabled Seven Cities of Cibola back in 1540, expecting to uncover unimaginable hoards of gold and silver. Instead, he discovered innumerable Indian pueblos, where the glitter came from beautiful jewelry shaped by native craftspeople. Nineteen of the pueblos still exist and can be visited today.

Route 66 crosses and re-crosses I-40 before running through **Tucumcari** ㉕ ("two miles long and two blocks wide") where the Tee Pee Curio Store (1944) is one of the oldest souvenir shops along the route. Every conceivable type of souvenir item turns up here, and in dozens of independently run shops in one small town after another along the route: pop-up art of paper buildings, old postcards, caps, jackets, scarves, traffic signs,

sheriff's badges, playing cards, mugs, glasses, paperweights, ashtrays, earrings, belt buckles, money clips, and even baby bibs bearing the 66 logo. You'll also find either original or reproduced Burma Shave signs *(see page 38)*: *Be a Modern/Paul Revere/Spread the News/From Ear to Ear/Burma Shave.*

Tucumcari once advertised it had 2,000 motel rooms and watched a nonstop stream of traffic pass by. Not the case today, but keep an eye out for such veterans of the highway as the historic Blue Swallow Motel, with its bright neon signs and old-style garages, and the Safari Motel with its neon sign of a man on a camel.

It's worth turning off Tucumcari's main highway to sip a malted milkshake at the long-standing Big Dipper Café, situated near the Spanish Revival railroad station, and there's a wide variety of fascinating old artifacts and Route 66 memorabilia worth looking at in the **Historical Museum** (tel: 575-461-4201; Mon–Sat).

Don't miss Tinkertown, the amusingly eccentric roadside attraction packed with curiosities. Located a few miles east of Albuquerque on old Route 66.

BELOW: mesas and mountains glimpsed from a Northern New Mexico road.

Santa Fe

Farther along the route, just past **Santa Rosa** at exit 256, you can swing north on US 84, crossing the Pecos River to Las Vegas (not to be confused with the Nevada city of the same name), and then follow the highway as it turns sharply west to **Santa Fe ㉖**, one of the oldest and best-known Western cities by virtue of the Santa Fe Trail. The trail ran from here almost 800 miles (1,290km) to Kansas City and was the major Western trade route in the 18th and 19th centuries. Less a road than a beaten track for freight wagons across the Plains, it segued into El Camino Real, which led into central Mexico. The capital of New Mexico was on the original Route 66 until 1938 when a straighter route superseded it and cut 126 miles (200km) off the journey.

Today Santa Fe's historic central buildings, in matching adobe shades (coated with stucco instead of the traditional, yet fragile, mud plaster) and shaded by arcades, are filled with good restaurants, lively bars, art galleries, and wonderful shops selling Southwestern arts and crafts. Striking Pueblo Revival-style buildings house landmark hotels and fine art museums. Its colorful blend of Native American, Spanish, and Anglo cultures makes it one of the most popular destinations in the Southwest.

Archbishops and artists

The heart of Santa Fe is its central **Plaza**, which dates back to the founding of the city by Spanish settlers from Mexico in 1610. With its bandstand and wrought-iron benches, it's a good place for people-watching. Stretching along the north side is the **Palace of the Governors**; a Native American crafts market operates beneath its portal. The regional government seat for 300 years and the oldest public building in the country, the Palace is now part of the **New Mexico History Museum** (tel: 505-476-5100; Tue–Sun, daily in summer), a fascinating interactive museum which opened in 2009. In the next block is the **New Mexico Museum of Art** (tel: 505-827-4455; Tue–Sun, daily in summer) with works by Southwestern artists. Nearby is the **Georgia O'Keeffe Museum** (tel: 505-946-1000; daily). Inspired by the light and landscapes, the artist made New Mexico her home and the museum holds the largest collection of her works.

To the east of the Plaza is the **Museum of Contemporary Native Arts** (tel: 505-983-8900; Wed–Mon, daily in summer). Formerly called the Institute of American Indian Arts, it features changing exhibitions of Native American paintings, sculptures, and three-dimensional works. Opposite is the landmark **St Francis Cathedral**, whose archbishop, Jean Baptiste Lamy, buried below the altar, was the model for Willa Cather's novel, *Death Comes to the Archbishop*.

The **Old Santa Fe Trail** leads to more historic sites like the lovely **San Miguel Mission** (daily), the **Loretto Chapel** (tel: 505-982-0092; daily) with its "Miraculous Staircase," and the **State Capitol** (tel: 505-986-4589;

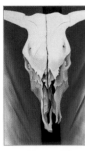

Cow's Skull: Red, White and Blue *by Georgia O'Keeffe; visit a museum devoted to the artist in Santa Fe, New Mexico.*

BELOW: painting the scene on the Taos Road.

Mon–Fri). Even this governmental seat is an art gallery, with works by New Mexico artists surrounding its circular walls.

Artists have always loved Santa Fe, and it is now the nation's second-largest art market after New York. Stroll along **Canyon Road**, off Paseo de Peralta, once a burro track but now lined with exciting art galleries, many housed in historic adobes. Guadalupe Street leads to **The Railyard**, the city's newest arts and entertainment district with a farmers' market, gardens, and **SITE Santa Fe** (tel: 505-989-1199; summer Wed–Sun, winter Thur–Sun), a splendid contemporary art exhibition space. Just beyond the city center, Museum Plaza is home to the delightful **Museum of International Folk Art** (tel: 505-476-1200; Tue–Sun, daily in summer), the impressive **Museum of Indian Arts and Culture** (tel: 505-827-6344; tel: 505-827-4455; Tue–Sun, daily in summer), and other museums.

North of Santa Fe, the eight northern pueblos can easily be visited on a day trip. The city makes a good base for visiting other highlights in northern New Mexico, including the Sanctuario de Chimayo, the Puye cliff dwellings, and those at Bandelier National Monument, and the city of Taos, with more art and history.

Towards Albuquerque

You can take US 285 south to connect up with the main route west again, and just before the intersection with I-40, you'll come to **Cline's Corners**, which founder Roy Cline subsequently described as "the coldest, the meanest, the windiest place on Highway 66." The town features in many of the tales told by Howard Subtle in his *Behind the Wheel on Route 66*. Subtle spent 28 years as a Greyhound bus driver heading back and forth along the highway, and his book is a ragbag of reminiscences about mislaid children, garrulous passengers and the occasional stowaway hiding behind the rear seats. On one occasion, he spotted an elephant tied to a tree; it turned out the beast had not been abandoned, but had been left with food and water after the truck that was transporting it broke down.

The recently installed Rail Runner train links Albuquerque and Santa Fe, New Mexico and connects passengers via bus with Albuquerque International Sunport and Amtrak service.

BELOW:
Christmas Eve in Albuquerque's Old Town.

At Tijeras, east of Albuquerque, is the turn-off through Cedar Crest to the 10,700ft (3,260-meter)-high **Sandia Mountains**, which offer fabulous panoramic views and one of the world's longest (2¾ miles/4km) aerial tramways (tel: 505-856-7325; daily). The Sandia Ranger Station (tel: 505-281-3304; summer Mon–Sat, winter Mon–Fri) has information on the area.

In **Albuquerque ㉗**, the old Route 66 runs along what is now Central Avenue, where the Civic Center, the tourist office, and a handful of vintage buildings lie across the Atchison, Topeka and Santa Fe railroad tracks just past Second Street. A long-term, multi-million dollar revitalization project has transformed this stretch of the route into a vibrant Downtown scene with theaters, nightclubs, and restaurants. A notable landmark is the KiMo Theater, built in 1927 in a fusion of Pueblo Revival and Art Deco styles.

Albuquerque's Old Town

Two miles (3km) further west, on the other side of the Rio Grande, the **Old Town** with its attractive shops and restaurants is one block to the right of Central Avenue, its ancient plaza grandly dominated by the adobe **San Felipe Church** (1706). Five flags have flown over this plaza: Spanish, Mexican, Confederate, the Stars and Stripes, and that of New Mexico. Allow at least an hour to wander around Old Town and try to time it with lunch or an early dinner to take advantage of one of the many cafés.

In the heart of Old Town are the **Albuquerque Museum of Art and History** (tel: 505-243-7255; Tue–Sun), the shuddery **Rattlesnake Museum** (tel: 505-242-6569; daily) and the Turquoise Museum (tel: 505-247-8650; Mon–Sat) which will shed some light on jewelry purchases. Nearby are the **New Mexico Museum of Natural History and Science** (tel: 505-841-2800; daily) with its planetarium, and the **Explora** (tel: 505-224-8300; daily), a hands-on learning center for kids. To the west of Old Town is the **Albuquerque Biological Park** (tel: 505-764-6200; daily) with its aquarium and botanical garden.

The International Balloon Fiesta takes place over nine days in October, with hundreds of balloons lifting off from Albuquerque's Balloon Fiesta Park.

BELOW: lunch on the plaza at La Hacienda, Albuquerque.

Perhaps Albuquerque's finest attraction is the **Indian Pueblo Cultural Center** (tel: 505-843-7270; daily). Its galleries present history and artifacts of the state's 19 pueblos, and there is a gift shop, restaurant, and free traditional dance performances on weekends. At the other end of the spectrum is the **National Museum of Nuclear Science and History** (tel: 505-245-2137; daily). Whatever your politics, it presents an intriguing look at the Atomic Age.

Volcanos and ice caves

Westward, Route 66, running side by side and sometimes absorbed by Interstate 40, passes through **Pueblo Laguna** (tel: 505-552-6654) with its early 18th-century church, and **Cubero**, near which novelist Ernest Hemingway settled in to write *The Old Man and the Sea*. Between the two, a side road runs a few miles south to **Acoma Sky City** which, perched on a mesa 367ft (112 meters) overhead, is the oldest continuously occupied village in the country. Tribal members lead guided tours settting off from the Sky City Cultural Center (tel: 800-747-0181) up to the atmospheric pueblo and explain its fascinating history. The pueblo may be closed for tribal ceremonies, so call ahead.

Grants (named after three brothers) still has the feel of a Route 66 town. In the mid-20th century it was a center for uranium mining, a history that can be explored in the New Mexico Mining Museum (tel: 505-287-4802; Mon–Sat). The Northwest New Mexico visitor center (tel: 505-876-2783) provides information on the unique attractions in this part of the state.

Interesting side trips can be made to the dormant **Bandera Volcano** and nearby **Ice Cave** (tel: 888-423-2283; daily), 25 miles (40km) south on Highway 53; and to **El Morro National Monument** (tel: 505-783-4226; daily), 28 miles (45km) farther along. Also known as Inscription Rock, the sand-

stone pillar is a written history of those who have passed by, from Native Americans, Spanish explorers, and the US Army Camel Corps to pioneers heading west in the mid-19th century. Even older Native American petroglyphs and pictographs can be seen here too.

For most of the way between Grants and Gallup, Route 66 and the interstate are only a few yards apart. Fifteen miles (24km) west of Milan, the Continental Divide is marked by a roadside café of the same name. The **Prewitt Trading Post**, once called the Zuni Mountain Trading Post, dates back to 1946. An unbroken chain of steep, red rock mesas flanks the highway to the north.

Gallup's movie-star hangout

Gallup ❷ is very appealing as a genuine New Mexico town. At first glance, it's not nearly as pretty to look at as picture-perfect Santa Fe or Albuquerque, but it has lots of character and plenty of lingering remnants of the Route 66 era. There's definitely a sense here of a place that gets on with

A 20ft (6-meter) arrow pierces the ground outside a store in Gallup, New Mexico.

BELOW: cheerful modern tepee near Gallup, New Mexico.

everyday life, rather than one which is filled with admiring tourists, or one that is now deserted following the route's demise. One of the high spots for film buffs is the **El Rancho Hotel and Motel**, built in 1937 by Raymond E. Griffith, who passed himself off as the brother of movie pioneer D.W. Griffith. It was a favorite with movie stars from the beginning; by the 1960s, at least 15 movies had been shot using the hotel as headquarters, among them *Sundown*, *Streets of Laredo*, and *The Hallelujah Trail*.

El Rancho is enormous and resembles everybody's dream of a huge ranch house with its Navajo rugs, solid Western furniture, wagon wheels, and mounted moose heads. Its wooden staircase is distinctive enough to bear a designer credit and leads to a balcony decked out with signed photographs from Ronald Reagan, Rosalind Russell, Paulette Goddard, Humphrey Bogart, Jack Benny, and a host of others. Off the immense lobby is a charming restaurant and bar, and burgers and sandwiches are named after the likes of Doris Day, Errol Flynn, and

Burt Lancaster. The "Mae West" sandwich is cheerfully defined as "stacked beef or ham."

Gallup tags itself "where the Indian southwest begins" and remains, as it has always been, a major trading post for the native peoples – these days as many as 200,000 of them – who live on the 17½ million-acre (7,088,000–hectare) **Navajo Nation**. This sprawls across the distinctive **Four Corners** region to the north where the states of New Mexico, Arizona, Colorado, and Utah meet. The percentage of Native-American owned land is second only to Arizona.

Indian territory

The Navajo capital of **Window Rock** is 25 miles (40km) from Gallup (and *just* across the border in Arizona) on State Route 264. **Zuni**, the largest pueblo in the state, with its Our Lady of Guadeloupe Mission dating from 1629, is 40 miles (64km) south on Highway 53. Zuni artisans are famous for their intricate silver jewelry skillfully inlaid with turquoise and coral. If you shop around, you can find Zuni pieces that look surprisingly contemporary. Contact the visitor center (tel: 505-782-7238) before setting off, as the pueblo is sometimes closed for religious ceremonies.

Indian artifacts such as rugs, jewelry, and other crafts can be bought at many stores along Route 66, which happens to be Gallup's main street, the center of town being located in a 12-block area around Hill Avenue and Fourth Street.

The century-old **Rex Hotel** (tel: 505-863-1363) is now a museum, and the historic railroad station is occupied by a cultural center staging ceremonial dances nightly in summer. **Red Rock Museum** (tel: 505-722-3839; Mon–Fri) exhibits Zuni, Hopi, and Navajo pottery, weaving, and other handicrafts. The museum is 20 minutes' drive to the east in the park of the same name. There is a balloon rally in Red Rock Park every December. ❏

ARIZONA TO LOS ANGELES

Wigwam motels, gorgeous gas stations, soda fountains that work – the cruise along Route 66 continues, taking in ghosts and the Grand Canyon along the way

The Mother Road becomes difficult to follow just over the border from New Mexico into Arizona, so if cruising the length of Route 66 is not a priority, you can remain on I-40 through Holbrook, Arizona. Approximately 25 miles (40km) inside the state, exit 330 from I-40 leads into **Petrified Forest National Park ㉙** (tel: 928-524-6228; daily), whose 220,000 acres (89,000 hectares) are littered with giant petrified logs. More than 200 million years ago, the region was a swampy, tropical zone whose mineral-rich soil helped to preserve the fossilized bones of prehistoric animals. In the northern section of the park is the **Painted Desert Inn National Historic Landmark**, now a museum.

Dinosaur statues line the road on the way to **Holbrook ㉚**, whose outstanding attraction is the roadside **Wigwam Motel**, a long-standing favorite (particularly with kids) on Route 66. Each of the 15 cozy rooms is inside its own tall, stone tepee built by owner John Lewis' father in the 1940s from plans by architect Frank Redford. He allowed seven similar motels around the country to be built from his plans, stipulating only that each be equipped with a radio that played 30 minutes for 10¢.

Parked outside the tepees is the family collection of '50s Fords and Buicks, while inside the main building a small museum exhibits chunks of petrified trees, Indian artifacts, and rifles and powder horns from the frontier days. A

Visitor Center and historical museum can be found in the **Historic Navajo County Courthouse** (tel: 928-524-6558; daily), built in 1898, on Navajo Boulevard (Route 66), which runs through the center of town. Indian dances are performed nightly on the courthouse lawn in summer. The local trading posts are a good place to buy Apache baskets, silver and turquoise jewelry, and pottery.

Pony Express

The spirit of the short-lived but legendary Pony Express, whose demise was

LEFT: Frank Lloyd Wright Tower, Scottsdale. **BELOW:** old Route 66 gas station.

TIP

If you want a letter to be carried via the Hashknife Posse, send it, stamped, in the first two weeks of January. Put that envelope in another stamped envelope addressed to the Holbrook Postmaster, Pony Express Ride, Holbrook, AZ, 86025. In the lower left-hand corner write: *Via Pony Express.*

induced by the telegraph system some 150 years ago, is kept alive in Holbrook by the Navajo County Sheriff's posse, who carry mail to Scottsdale (near Phoenix) in late January every year.

Under a contract with the US Postal Service, the 40-strong "Hashknife Posse" carries out a tradition begun in 1954, when a similar posse carried to the state governor an invitation to attend a stampede. An estimated 20,000 letters (sent in by admirers throughout the world) are hand-stamped with the official ride logo and franked with a Pony Express post-mark before being sent off in mail bags relayed by the riders every few miles in the course of the 200-mile (320km) journey.

The posse's name is derived from The Hash Knife Outfit, a branch of the third-largest cattle company in the country, which began shipping out thousands of cattle after 1881 when the life-changing railroad began to go through here.

Holbrook's preserved **Blevins House** across from the Santa Fe depot was the scene of a spectacular shoot-out on September 4, 1857, when the county sheriff went to arrest a horse thief and survived after being shot at by several members of the thief's family. Nearby are the notorious Bucket of Blood Saloon, the 1910 J&J Trading Post and the one-time Campbell's Coffee House (now a Rexall's drug store), which became famous for its "Son of a Bitch stew."

Anasazi ruins

Five miles (8km) off I-40 near **Joseph City** ("Joseph Small Town" would be more appropriate) is the Jackrabbit Trading Post, with its original crouching rabbit sign, while 16 miles (26km) farther on, a turn north on State Route 87 – just before you get to Winslow – will take you to the extensive 14th-century Anasazi site of **Homolovi Ruins State Park** (tel: 928-289-4106; daily). The name Homolovi is the Hopi word for "Place of the Little Hills."

Winslow ㉛ achieved fame from its inclusion in the pop song "Take It Easy" by Jackson Browne. The Eagles' hit single refers to "Standin' on a corner in Winslow, Arizona," and visitors pour into town to do just that at Standin' on the Corner Park (Kinsley and Second streets), where there is a 6ft (2-meter)-high bronze statue of a man with a guitar. The lyric goes: *Well, I'm standing on a corner in Winslow, Arizona/Such a fine sight to see/It's a girl, my Lord/In a flatbed Ford/Slowing down to take a look at me.*

Until the 1960s, Winslow, born with the arrival of the railroad in 1880, was the largest town in northern Arizona, but business began to fade when it was bypassed by the interstate. Its rebirth began with the renovation of Downtown, and, most notably, **La Posada**, the 1930 Fred Harvey railroad hotel (*see pages 225 and 230*).

South of Winslow off SR 99, Anasazi petroglyphs can be admired in **Chevelon Canyon**, west of town, to which tours are conducted from Rock Art Canyon Ranch (tel: 928-288-3260; May–Oct, advance reservations required). Anglers know the area well

BELOW:
Homolovi Ruins
State Park.

for its rainbow and (more enticingly) brown trout that live in the lake and creek here.

About 20 miles (32km) west on I-40, Exit 233 leads south to **Meteor Crater** (tel: 928-289-2362; daily tours), a 600ft (183-meter) deep hole almost a mile across created by the impact of a meteorite nearly 50 centuries ago. Astronauts were trained here before the moon visit, and the Astronaut Park has an Apollo Space Capsule. The new museum has exhibitions documenting the history of meteorites impacting the earth and a theater recreating those impacts as if you were at ground zero. Back on the main road heading west, the ghost town of **Two Guns** sits on an abandoned portion of Route 66.

Although **Winona** features in Bobby Troup's "Route 66" song (it rhymes with "Arizona"), it's actually a dead-end, and what Route 66 historian Tom Snyder calls "a one-blink town." Near Winona, 7 miles (11km) before Flagstaff, is the **Walnut Canyon National Monument** (tel: 928-526-3367; daily), where a short hike down a paved trail reveals ancient cliff dwellings that fell into disuse hundreds of years ago.

Flagstaff

The only large town in northern Arizona, **Flagstaff** ③② is a staging point for trips to the Grand Canyon, 80 miles (129km) to the north. The trip up US 89 and then along State Route 64 is longer, but more scenic, than the shorter route from Williams farther along the highway. Two of Flagstaff's museum attractions, the **Pioneer Museum** (tel: 928-774-6272; Mon–Sat) and the **Museum of Northern Arizona** (tel: 928-774-5213; daily), are not far apart on Fort Valley Road, or from US 180, which also leads to the canyon. Flagstaff's other attractions are either in or near the historic and attractive downtown railroad district, through which Route 66 runs. The city stages a Route 66 Days celebration each September with live music, a

The bones of a sickle claw dinosaur on exhibit at the Museum of Northern Arizona in Flagstaff.

BELOW: the Weatherford Hotel played host to presidents, publishers and

Monument Valley

A 182-mile (293km) journey from Flagstaff, Arizona, leads to one of the most famous sights in the Southwest. Monument Valley (tel: 435-727-5874; daily) is easily recognized from far away thanks to scenes from countless Westerns, especially those by director John Ford, who often used the valley as the backdrop for his movies. With its serene rock formations dominating the surrounding barren desert plains, the valley's mesas were not just attractive to Hollywood, but also served as significant religious monuments for local Native Americans. Medicine men once climbed the Rain God Mesa – home to a sacred burial ground – to pray for rain. The Totem Pole formation served as a center for mythical incidents in folklore, while the Yei-Bi-Chei resembles holy Navajo figures performing a traditional dance. Like the Grand Canyon or Sedona, the timeless mystery of these rocks is humbling in their presence. What seems an impossible creation is the result of ageless erosion of the sandstone and shale, which leaves the harder stone intact. Monument Valley lies entirely within the Navajo Nation reservation, and the tribe conducts tours through its desolate beauty. Catch a sunrise or sunset at the Visitor Center, from which many famous formations can be seen.

Native American sign near Williams, Arizona.

parade of classic cars, and displays of arts and crafts.

On the way into Flagstaff from the direction of the east, be sure to stop by the **Museum Club** (tel: 928-526-9434; daily), a 1931 roadhouse which in Prohibition days began as a "zoo" filled with stuffed animals. Now listed on the National Register of Historic Places, it is a popular dance club by night and dozens of country-western music legends have performed in the Southwest's largest log cabin. Nearer to Downtown are the **Lowell Observatory** (tel: 928-774-2096; daily) and the richly furnished 40-room **Riordan Mansion** (tel: 928-779-4395; daily), set in an attractive park.

Opposite the train station on Leroux Street, you'll find the remarkable **Weatherford Hotel**, which opened its doors on the first day of 1899. That day, it welcomed among its scores of distinguished guests the publisher William Randolph Hearst, President Theodore Roosevelt, and lawman Wyatt Earp. The bar boasts an antique counter that came from Tombstone, and the ballroom is named for Western author

Zane Grey, who stayed here while writing *Call of the Canyon*.

A young reader of Zane Grey's books was one Cecil B. De Mille, who concluded that Flagstaff sounded like a good place to launch his movie career. When he arrived in the town from the East, however, it was snowing, and De Mille decided to continue on the train to Los Angeles, thus altering the course of movie history forever.

An attractive side trip from Flagstaff is along State Highway 89A through the spectacular **Oak Creek Canyon** to the upscale artist community of **Sedona** ㉝, 28 miles (45km) south. It is surrounded by stunning red rock formations that have also been a magnet for film directors, as well as for New Age types who are drawn to its mystical "vortexes." Further south is another artist's haven, **Jerome**, a former ghost town named after a defunct copper mine, with attractive Old West buildings.

Back on Route 66

Between Flagstaff and Williams, Route 66 is mostly unsurfaced and not very

well maintained, but has the distinction of containing the highest point of the route at 7,300ft (2,225 meters) above sea level, about a mile or two before **Parks**. The Parks in the Pines general store has been in business for more than 80 years. Nearby are the remains of the **Beale Wagon Road Historic Trail**, a sturdy 120ft (37-- meter) -wide track constructed in 1857 on which pioneers could safely travel as far as the Colorado River.

Back on I-40, the next town, **Williams ㉞**, as well as its main street on Route 66 and the nearby mountain, were all named after Bill Williams (1787–1849), an early fur trapper whose statue stands at the west end of town. The excellent *Route 66 Magazine* was once published here, the last town on Route 66 to be bypassed by I-40.

Near the Williams railroad depot (which also houses an interesting museum) is the restored **Fray Marcos Hotel** (now the Grand Canyon Railway Hotel; tel: 928-635-4010), originally a unit of the once-ubiquitous Harvey House chain, which an English immigrant, Fred Harvey, established in

the 1880s along the route of the Santa Fe line, revolutionizing the then-abysmal standards of railway food. One of Harvey's basic rules was that the coffee – served by smiling "Harvey Girls" in black dresses and spotless white aprons and bows – was re-made every two hours, even if the urn was still full. For 75¢, customers could choose from seven entrees and take second helpings, too.

A tan-colored 1953 Cadillac and life-size cutouts of James Dean and Marilyn Monroe sit outside **Twisters**, a self-proclaimed "back-to-the '50s diner" that displays hundreds of snapshots of families taken along the route, along with an old glass-topped Sky Chief gasoline pump that has been converted into a holder for typical road souvenirs.

Sit here for 20 minutes or so and immerse yourself in pure, unadulterated kitsch. A menu offers a dozen different shakes, malts, floats, and cherry phosphates. For those seeking more conventional fare, the best-known restaurant in town, **Rod's Steak House**, has been serving customers along Route 66 for more than half a century.

Desert songbird.

BELOW:
Monument Valley is one of the iconic landscapes of the American West and an epicenter of Navajo culture.

TIP

The "almost" ghost town of Chloride (10 miles/16km north of Kingman) is a fitting venue for the Old Miners' Day. Join in the Old West festivities – mock gunfights, pie baking contests, a parade, food booths, and more. Held the last Saturday in June. For further information call 928-565-2204.

BELOW: one of the world's natural wonders, the Grand Canyon was millions of years in the making.

The Grand Canyon

Williams is the main departure point for the **Grand Canyon** ㉟ (tel: 928-638-7888). The Grand Canyon Railway (tel: 800-843-87246) departs here for the canyon every morning. The five-hour round-trip – by vintage steam locomotives in summer, diesel locomotives the rest of the year – allows for three hours' sightseeing at the canyon, but is a worthwhile trip in itself (particularly for families), complete with strolling cowboy musicians and, on the return trip, a "train robbery."

The South Rim of the Grand Canyon, which can also be reached by traveling about 40 miles (64km) north on US 180 from Williams, is open around the clock every day of the year, although the visitor center and most park facilities operate only from 8am to 5pm. A good place to start your visit is at the Canyon View Information Plaza opposite Mather Point. This spacious center has wall-size maps, exhibits, and guides that set the canyon in a larger context and help you get oriented. Park rangers are on hand to answer questions. From here, continue

west to Grand Canyon Village, a hub of tourist facilities.

Free canyon shuttle buses operate from March through November from the village west along the 7-mile (11km) Hermits Rest Route, giving visitors access to nine of the best canyon overlooks and a hiking trail along the canyon rim. Private cars are only allowed along this stretch of road in winter. At **Trailview Point**, you can look back at the village and the **Bright Angel Trail** switchbacking down to the river. In the morning, mule trains plod into the canyon, bearing excited greenhorns who may wish they'd gone on foot when the day is done. Other recommended points along Hermits Road are **Hopi**, **Mohave**, and **Pima**. From each vista different isolated buttes and "temples" present themselves, many with fanciful names bestowed by early explorers. The road ends at **Hermits Rest**, which has a gift shop, concession stand, and restrooms. Returning to the village, another road, **Desert View Drive**, follows the canyon rim for 25 miles (40km) to the east. Over-

looks along the way display still more spectacular canyon scenery.

The Grand Canyon is one of the world's great natural wonders, and it's worth staying at least one night to appreciate the spectacular views at different times of day, when the formations take on different colors and moods. To reserve accommodation at one of the Grand Canyon lodges, call 303-297-2757. Be sure to book early, as rooms are highly prized.

Beyond Williams

From Williams, 19 miles (31km) west along I-40, it's worth getting off the busy road to visit somnolent **Ash Fork**, which was a stage coach depot until the arrival of the railroad in 1882. This was also a regular stop along Route 66 until the town was bypassed by the bigger thoroughfare; a Confederate flag flies over the Route 66 Grill. One of the adorable Harvey Girls *(see page 230)* lived nearby until her death, and she donated several artifacts from the defunct Harvey House chain to a fledgling museum located in a vast, empty warehouse beside the tourist office.

Toward California

Returning briefly to the interstate, it's advisable to leave it again at the Crookton Road exit for the longest and most nostalgic section on the entire Historic 66 Highway. It's quite simple to remain on it all the way to the California border at Topock, a distance of about 180 miles (290km).

You won't miss **Seligman** ⑯, whose main thoroughfare and Route 66 are lined with strangely compelling gift shops devoted to the highway's history, which carry every conceivable type of souvenir, from US 66 highway signs, Mother Road license tags and oil company signs, to old Coca-Cola posters and bottles – as well as the now-familiar inscribed mugs, glasses, and T-shirts. One of these is the Delgadillo Route 66 Gift Shop (tel: 928-422-3352), which also doubles as a visitor center. Here you can pick up a leaflet that will take you on a 20-minute walking tour that takes in colorful remnants of the town's Route 66 heyday. These include the Rusty Bolt Souvenir and Gift Shop with its collection of vintage cars, and Delgadillo's Snow Cap Drive-In, a

Stomachs and gas tanks fueled here.

BELOW: the Snow Cap Drive-In, Seligman.

Clark Gable and Carole Lombard were married in Kingman, Arizona.

Route 66 landmark that serves classic road fare and kitsch in equal measure.

Twenty-five miles (40km) west of Seligman is the deep **Grand Canyon Caverns** (tel: 928-422-3223; daily), into which early visitors paid 25¢ to be lowered 150ft (46 meters) by rope. Today, there's an elevator and illuminated paths on which to walk.

Peach Springs is the tribal headquarters of the Hualapai Nation, whose lands encompass the western end of the Grand Canyon. **Grand Canyon West** (tel: 877-716-9378; daily) is 242 miles (389km) from the entrance at the South Rim – nearly as long as the canyon itself. Here the Hualapai have built the phenomenal Grand Canyon Skywalk, a U-shaped glass-bottomed walkway that extends from the edge of a clifftop out into the air above the canyon, giving visitors a hawks-eye view of the surroundings and the Colorado River, 4,000ft (1,220 meters) below. It's not for those with vertigo, nor for those on a budget. On top of the pricy Skywalk fee, visitors must purchase a Hualapai tour package to gain access to the site, but it's a fun day

of activities and a unique opportunity to walk on air and see the canyon from a new perspective.

Access to Grand Canyon West, 70 miles (112km) north of Kingman, is via minor roads. The last 21 miles (34km) are on unpaved gravel surface, so those with low-clearance vehicles or RVs should use the Park and Ride coach service available at the site.

Kingman ③ is where the tubby, gruff-voiced movie star Andy Devine was born. The main street is named after him, and on this and the adjoining Beale Street are the oldest buildings, including the old Beale Hotel where Clark Gable and Carole Lombard were married in March, 1939.

Kingman's **Route 66 Museum** is located in the visitor center (tel: 928-753-9889; daily), and one of its exhibits is a re-creation of a small-town Main Street, complete with 1950s yellow Studebaker car. The **Mojave Museum of History and Arts** (tel: 928-753-3195; Mon–Sat) displays attractive turquoise jewelry and a re-created Hualapai dwelling, among other historical artifacts.

Heading west, the highway takes on a desolate, rocky wilderness appearance – an indicator of what's to come; be sure you have good brakes. Before long, the road is climbing between jagged peaks in a series of seemingly endless switchbacks and scary, blind curves to the 3,500ft (1,067-meter) -high summit at **Sitgreaves Pass** (named, like the Beale Wagon Trail, for a mid-19th-century Army surveyor), before beginning an equally twisting and turning segment down into the tiny town of Oatman.

Haunted hotel

On the way down into Oatman, you'll pass **Goldroad**, the site of a mine that produced $2-billion-worth of gold in its early years, but closed down in 1907 when gold prices dropped.

Hundreds of wild burros turned loose by early miners roam the mountains, occasionally straying across the highway and wandering into **Oatman 38**, proving irresistible camera fodder for photographers and inspiring the name of the Classy Ass gift shop, next the Oatman Hotel, which sells jewelry made from rocks and sand dollars and other one-of-a-kind gifts. Oatman looks exactly the way you'd imagine an ancient Western town to look, with sagging wooden shacks lining the solitary unpaved street on which amusing mock gunfights are conducted daily.

Across the street from Fast Fanny's (selling clothes, sunglasses, and postcards), a bed on wheels promotes the annual Great Oatman Bed Races, which are held every January. Summer temperatures can reach 118°F (48°C), prompting the annual Sidewalk Egg Fry every Fourth of July.

The worn and characterful 1902 **Oatman Hotel** (tel: 928-768-4408) no longer rents rooms, but it will be forever famous as the place where Clark Gable and Carole Lombard spent their honeymoon night in Room 15, after being married in Kingman, and the simple room is preserved as a sort of shrine to the glamorous Hollywood couple with pictures of the pair on the walls and a pink nightdress draped over a chair. On the ground floor is an ice-cream shop and a bar and restaurant popular with the locals.

It's as though nature tested a man for endurance and constancy to prove whether he was good enough to get to California.

Reference to Mojave Desert, source unknown

BELOW: Viva Las Vegas!

Detour – Las Vegas

A desert drive of 101 miles (163km) from Kingman, Arizona, on US 93 leads straight to Sin City. Each year, 12 million visitors empty their pockets of $4.2 billion in a time-honored homage to frivolity, greed, and gluttony – not to mention plain old fun. For a long time after gambling was legalized in 1931, Las Vegas remained a sleepy desert town. It took visionary underworld hit man Bugsy Siegel to free this seething neon dragon. In 1946, Siegel opened the Flamingo Hotel, sparing no expense in mob finances for its plush interior, which sported a flashing pink neon facade and set a new standard in sheer swank. From a high-roller's point of view, Las Vegas is divided into two parts. First is the Strip, where modern hoteliers vie with each other to offer the latest in accommodation extravaganzas, replicating Venice, Paris, Rome, ocean liners, and Egyptian pyramids. Then there's Downtown – the original Vegas – also known as Glitter Gulch. As for gambling, either way you lose, but Downtown casinos are said to afford better odds. The best advice is simply enjoy it: win, lose or draw, there's nothing quite like the Strip at night, ablaze with electric light and self-indulgence. The Las Vegas Convention and Visitors Authority is at 702-892-0711; www.visitlasvegas.com.

*Don't Take A Curve
At 60 Per We Hate
to Lose A Customer.*

Burma Shave

Twenty miles (32km) of desert scrub land lies between Oatman and **Topock**, where the Colorado River marks the California border. Route 66 comes to a dead-end at Moabi Regional Park with its lake and boat rentals – a refreshing stop after the long drive in the hot sun.

CALIFORNIA

As the car heads ever closer toward the setting sun, spare a thought for those migrants from the early days of Route 66 for whom crossing the border into the "promised land" became an ordeal. Faced with an influx of refugees from the Dust Bowl states, Californians were worried about the impact on property prices and already poorly paid jobs. In some places guards were posted at the border and scores of exhausted migrants were turned away. It's a story that is still familiar today, albeit at a different border.

Sadly, once in California, much of the old Route 66, apart from a few parched stretches through the Mojave Desert, has been largely supplanted and is submerged beneath a welter of busy freeways to re-emerge only in occasional short stretches or as the main routes through towns such as Barstow, Victorville, and Rancho Cucamonga.

Needles

In the first town you'll come to in California, **Needles**, Route 66 passes through the business section and along Broadway. Past the Amtrak terminal, the defunct 1906 Fred Harvey House, known as El Garces and regarded as the crown jewel of the chain, is now just a part of the station. Harvey Girls lived in the upper floors. Trained in neatness and courtesy, the girls signed a contract of employment agreeing not to marry for a year, and lived on the upper floors of the hotel.

The **Needles Regional Museum** (tel: 760-326-5678; Mon–Sat) has a fanciful collection of stuff guaranteed to raise a grin: vintage clothes, old jars and bottles, obsolete currency, pictures curling with sepia, cartridge shells, and Indian artifacts. The **Mojave Tribal Center** with its **Indian Village** sits near the Needles Bridge, and there's a marina park and golf course near the river.

In World War II, General George Patton established an army training center in the Mojave, realizing that a familiarity with its harsh terrain would prepare the troops for the forthcoming Africa campaign, and indeed, conditions are similar. The US Army National Training Center is still headquartered at Barstow, 145 miles (233km) due west of Needles.

The route from Needles to Barstow can be traveled swiftly on I-40, but the old Route 66 runs north of the interstate and heads through **Goffs** before diverting south through the barely existing communities of Essex, Amboy, and Bagdad (famous for its landmark café and, earlier, another Harvey House). Bob Moore recalls in his guidebook that tiny **Essex** featured on NBC's *Tonight Show* in 1977, claiming to be the only town in America with-

BELOW: a classic Mother Road motel sign.

out television. A Pennsylvania company promptly donated the necessary equipment. About a mile from **Amboy** (now a ghost town owned by preservationist Albert Okura and featuring a closed-down café and gas station, once a favorite with filmmakers) is an extinct volcano known as the **Amboy Crater**.

Ludlow, where Route 66 links up once more with the interstate, was once a boom town served not only by the Santa Fe railroad, but also by two others (local lines bearing ore from Death Valley), and in fact was named for a Central Pacific repairman. The 1940s Ludlow Cafe building is derelict, as is the abandoned Ludlow Mercantile Building (1908) down by the railroad tracks, but the newer Ludlow Coffee Shop is usually bustling with activity. Water, always scarce in these parts, was at one time brought in to fill the steam trains by tank cars from **Newberry Springs**, 40 miles (64km) to the west (filming site of the cult movie *Bagdad Café*). There really are springs here, and they supplement the water supply from the region's numerous artesian wells.

The State Agricultural Inspection Station, which tended to hassle visitors in the early days, more often than not these days just waves cars through. Just before Barstow is **Daggett**, whose landmark **Stone Hotel** (currently closed for renovation) was popular with Tom Mix and other movie cowboys. On show in the small Daggett Museum (tel: 760-254-2629; Sat–Sun) is a scale model of the California Edison Company's Solar One thermal plant out in the desert. Giant mirrors focused the sun's energy on tanks of nitrate salt intended to convert water into the steam required to power a turbine generator.

Barstow

The Mojave Desert was a forbidding yet paradoxically inviting place in the 1870s when gold, silver, and borax were among the valuable metals and minerals that drew prospectors and miners from all over the country. The arrival of the Santa Fe railroad in 1883 connected up – and in many cases created – isolated small towns, and the Mediterranean-style Santa Fe

Keep your eyes peeled for snakes when hiking in the desert – and be aware that a rattler taken by surprise may not give you a warning before striking.

BELOW: "As the world changes, so do things along the Mother Road. It mirrors life both modern and nostalgic..."

Depot at **Barstow** ❸❾ and renovated 1911 Casa del Desierto, a former Harvey House and now a route 66 Museum, give some idea of the forgotten splendor of the times. Gift shops and a McDonald's, at which customers eat in converted railroad cars, are among the station's attractions. Among the exhibits in the Route 66 "Mother Road" Museum (tel: 760-255-1890; Fri–Sun) are archival and contemporary prints by photographers who have captured images of the road and its icons. Many are available for purchase.

With the arrival of the pre-World War II National Old Trails Highway, the predecessor to Route 66, Barstow's importance as a transportation center was quite literally cemented. Sitting at the major junction of I-15 and I-40, it has shown little sign of decline. Midway between Los Angeles and Las Vegas, it is a convenient rest stop for drivers on their way to and from the resort city. The older Route 66 motels are to the west end of town. Watch for the splendid El Rancho, built with railroad tiles, and whose 100ft (30-meter)

-high neon sign has been a landmark since the early days of the highway.

The **Mojave River Valley Museum** (tel: 760-256-5452; daily) and the **Desert Discovery Center** (tel: 760-252-6060; Tue–Sat) will together answer all your questions about the desert – past and present.

Side trips from Barstow

One worthwhile side trip from Barstow is to the **Rainbow Basin** (tel: 760-252-6000; daily) where a 4-mile (6km) loop road circles an area filled with fossilized animal remains and fringed by multicolored cliffs; another is to **Calico Ghost Town** (tel: 800-8622-5426; daily), 11 miles (18km) to the east, whose prosperity between 1881–96 came from mining a $12-million seam of silver, a boom that was supplemented by the discovery of borax nearby.

When both "cash crops" gave out, the town's 22 saloons closed one after another as the population drifted to other areas to seek their fortunes, but many of the old buildings have been rehabilitated, and such tourist attractions as wagon rides, mock gunfights, and gold panning were introduced. A few miles to the east at the town of **Calico**, the **Early Man Archeological Site** (tel: 760-254-2248; Wed–Sun) displays relics from the Pleistocene era, which was approximately 50,000 years ago.

Hula Ville

It's an uneventful 40-mile (64km) drive on a good road (which parallels I-15) to Victorville, where Route 66 is merely another city street. **Victorville** began as a mining camp in the 19th century and became a magnet during Hollywood's golden age for moviemakers attracted by its "Western" feel. For a while, it also attracted the Roy Rogers-Dale Evans Museum, where the galleries glittered with the husband-and-wife cowboy stars' sequined costumes, before the museum moved to the country-music town of Branson, Missouri.

BELOW: the old schoolhouse of Calico.

The **California Route 66 Museum** (tel: 760-951-0436; Thur–Mon) offers a final chance for westbound travelers who haven't yet had their fill of ephemera from the Mother Road to dose-up; the museum building itself was once a road house called the Red Rooster Cafe. Its premier exhibit is Hula Ville, an example of the folksy roadside attractions once found all along Route 66. In the mid-1950s, a man named Miles Mahan decided to drive nails into fence posts and hang from them all the bottles left behind by transients. Later, he rescued a huge metal sign of a dancing hula girl and arranged for her to tower over the fences, practically stopping traffic along the route. Locals began to donate other items to Mahan's "Cactus Garden," and in time Hula Ville became a Route 66 high desert legend.

San Bernardino

South of Victorville, I-15 heads over the 4,300ft (1,310-meter) Cajon Summit, which, after taking the Oak Hill exit, brings you to Mariposa Road and the **Summit Inn**, a longtime Route 66 landmark that has been serving diners since 1952. Apart from a brief stretch, I-15 has subsumed much of the old route, but you're on it if you follow Cajon Boulevard into **San Bernardino 40**, a Mormon town in the 1850s, and once a major citrus center. It's the gateway to the mountainous **San Bernardino National Forest**, more than 600,000 acres (243,000 hectares) of wilderness dominated by 11,500ft (3,505-meter) -high Mt San Gorgonio, the highest in Southern California. Deep in the forest are the well-known resorts of **Big Bear** and **Lake Arrowhead**, long hideaways for Hollywood stars. State Route 18, romantically known as the Rim of the World Drive, is the lofty 40-mile (64km) highway that leads to these destinations.

Rim of the World Drive

With panoramic views, switchback turns and lots of overlooks, **Rim of the World Drive** is particularly exhilarating to do on a motorcycle. The best stretch is the 25-mile (40km) run from Redlands up the hill towards **Big Bear Lake**.

Darkling beetles are tough enough to endure the white-hot Mojave sands.

BELOW:
the Mojave Desert was a forbidding place when gold was discovered in the 1870s.

Back down on the ground in San Bernardino itself, the classy old (1928) **California Theater**, on West Fourth Street, is worth noting. Head out of town on Mt Vernon Avenue past some aged motels and a hard-to-miss Santa Fe railroad smokestack, and eventually you will pass the tepees of another Wigwam Motel (1950) along Foothill Boulevard. This leads into **Rancho Cucamonga** and begins with a series of large and anonymous shopping malls, but at the corner of Vineyard Avenue there is a glimpse of earlier times, with an old-fashioned Mobil station from the 1920s sitting on the opposite corner to the historic Thomas Winery building. Once a popular stop on Route 66, the winery is a state landmark, designated as the oldest commercial winery in California and the second-oldest in the country. Sadly, the Thomas vineyards fell victim to development in the 1960s, but the premises is now occupied, appropriately, by The Wine Tailor which sells custom wines.

Further down is the historic **Sycamore Inn**, a huge, rustic log palace and steak house on the site of an 1848 trailside inn that catered to the Gold Rush adventurers. In 1858, it became a stop along the route of the Butterfield Stage.

Past **Claremont**, where the old route suddenly moves upscale with a grassy median and eucalyptus trees, are a few eating places that old-timers might remember. There's Wilson's restaurant (now La Paloma) at **La Verne**; the Pinnacle Peak Steak House, where they cut off customers' ties, at **San Dimas**; and the Golden Spur Restaurant (which began as a hamburger stand over 80 years ago) in **Glendora**.

There are many old motels and eateries along this part of Route 66, including the Derby Restaurant and Rod's Grill in **Arcadia**, and in **Monrovia**, the distinctive one-story Aztec Hotel. This hotel dates from 1925, when it was built by architect Robert Stacy-Judd in a pseudo-Mayan style to catch the attention of motorists along the route.

The end of the road

Just before **Los Angeles ㊶** proper (*see page 236*), Route 66 becomes what is now the Pasadena Freeway, but which started life in the closing days of 1940 as the Arroyo Seco Parkway, the first freeway in a bold, new experiment that was eventually to cover the entire state of California with a network of similarly fast motorways. Continue driving and take the Sunset Boulevard exit, then head west along Sunset until it joins Santa Monica Boulevard, which runs all the way to the Pacific Ocean. Here, in Palisades Park overlooking the beach, a modest plaque commemorates the western terminus of this famous American road.

Nobody can recall seeing a Burma Shave sign in Santa Monica itself, where Route 66 ends, but if the company had ever put one there it would probably have been the one that read *If You/Don't Know/Whose Signs/These Are/You Can't Have/Driven Very Far!* ❏

BELOW: sleeping rattlesnake.
RIGHT: mementos of the Mother Road.

A Short Stay in Los Angeles

The city of fantasy and film, LA has endless sun, an easy ambiance, and, of course, Hollywood. Here's a list of the not-to-be-missed attractions:

● The Hollywood Museum is the place to pay homage to the achievements of the silver screen. Included are displays on history, personalities, and Max Factor innovations.

● Part amusement park, part working film studio, Universal Studios Hollywood is one of the most visited sites in LA. Go behind the scenes to see sensational stunts and special effects, or face dinosaurs and vengeful mummies on heart-pounding thrill rides.

● Lined with jewelers, designer studios, upmarket fashion, and accessories boutiques, Rodeo Drive in Beverly Hills is one of the most exclusive shopping addresses in the world.

● Watch a parade of stars – the celestial kind – at the landmark Griffith Observatory. Like the famous Hollywood sign, it stands in Griffith Park which extends for miles and has far-reaching views over LA and the San Fernando Valley.

● The GRAMMY Museum celebrates modern music, with four floors of interactive exhibits about popular artists and songs and their impact on the world.

● Art lovers should not miss the Los Angeles County Museum of Art. Its displays of costumes, pottery, silverware, and decorative arts, as well as paintings and sculpture from all eras, are augmented by the new Broad Contemporary Art Museum on campus, designed by Renzo Piano.

● L.A. Live is the city's hottest entertainment destination, with the Nokia Theatre, music clubs, restaurants, and more, next to Downtown's premier sports venue, the Staples Center.

● Historic and modern-day injustices of racism and prejudice are the focus of the thoughtful Museum of Tolerance on West Pico Boulevard.

ABOVE AND LEFT: A touch of Chinese. Sidney Grauman, who "invented" the movie premiere, designed Grauman's Chinese Theatre in the 1920s. Its main attraction is the forecourt, with stars' hand- and foot-prints.

LEFT: Sunset Boulevard. Made famous by Billy Wilder's magnificent melodrama, Sunset Boulevard is an important avenue in the evolution of Hollywood.

CITY OF ANGELS

In 1781, Father Junípero Serra named a dry, dusty settlement after St Francis of Assisi's first church, St Mary of the Angels. No one could have conceived that hot, arid place would turn into glittering Los Angeles, the capital of moviedom and a world-famous synonym for glamor and fun. Residents of most big cities pretend to be blasé in the presence of celebrities, but Angelenos really are: movie stars are the stock-in-trade here, as common as scarlet-suited guardsmen in London or yellow cabs in New York. LA is also a city of adventure and innovation: Disneyland, rollerblading, beach culture, rap music – it all started here.

ABOVE RIGHT: Point of view. Drive into the Hollywood Hills to consider the prospect of a city without a center.

ABOVE FAR RIGHT: Getty Center. Architect Richard Meier's fabulous building on top of a hill with stunning views almost distracts from the collection of treasures inside.

IMPORTANT INFORMATION

Population: 3.8 million
Dialing codes: 213, 310, 323, 562, 626, 714, 818, 949
Website: www.lacvb.com
Tourist information: LA Visitor Info Center, 685 S. Figueroa Street, CA 90017; tel: 213-689-8822; fax: 213-624-1992

Map: Los Angeles Throughways

SANTA CLARITA · Cogswell Reservoir · SAN GABRIEL MOUNTAINS · Angeles Crest Hwy · 118 · 405 · 210 · Angeles National Forest · San Gabriel Reservoir · La Verne · GLENDALE · PASADENA · Foothill Freeway · 66 · 101 · Ventura Freeway · 170 · 5 · 2 · Universal Studios · Griffith Observatory · 210 · 605 · 10 · POMONA · Getty Center · Hollywood Bowl · EL MONTE · 19 · San Bernardino · BEVERLY HILLS · 101 · Paramount Studios · Staples Center · 91 · Pomona Freeway · CHINO HILLS · SANTA MONICA · 10 · EAST LOS ANGELES · HACIENDA HEIGHTS · 72 · 55 · 142 · Malibu · Venice Beach · INGLEWOOD · 42 · 710 · 95 · Chino Hills State Park · 91 · 105 · COMPTON · FULLERTON · 90 · 91 · Los Angeles International Airport · 107 · 91 · 605 · Knott's Berry Farm · ANAHEIM · 241 · Santa Monica Bay · TORRANCE · 110 · 405 · GARDEN GROVE · ORANGE · Disneyland · 261 · 241 · Palos Verdes Peninsula · LONG BEACH · 22 · SANTA ANA · Santa Ana Fwy · Wayfarers Chapel · Queen Mary · HUNTINGTON BEACH · 1 · 405 · San Pedro Bay · IRVINE · 73 · 5 · PACIFIC OCEAN · Pacific Coast Highway · Crystal Cove State Park · Oceanside · Aliso Wood Canyons Regional Park · 1

N

Los Angeles Throughways

0 — 10 miles
0 — 10 km

Indicates route from the city detailed in this book

THE SOUTHERN ROUTE

A guide to the South and the Southwest, with principal sites clearly cross-referenced by number to the maps

Sit back, relax, and enjoy the ride if you've chosen the Southern route across the continent. Even if you're not ready to, you'll probably adapt to the leisurely pace soon enough as you meander down a Georgia street lined with Spanish-moss draped trees, relax on a Texas beach or kick up your cowboy boots in a Tombstone, Arizona saloon.

Our nearly 2,500-mile (3,900km) journey through America's South sets off in Atlanta, unofficial capital of the "New South," dynamic home to some well-known global corporations but still blessed with enough of the equally well-known "Southern hospitality" to make it a pleasant and very liveable city. After a detour in Macon – to get a taste of the "Old South" – your trip west begins, moseying through Alabama and its true southern cities of Montgomery and Mobile and on into Mississippi before hitting Louisiana and its belle of a city: New Orleans, full of fabulous food, unforgettable music, and unique architecture – despite the destruction and spiritual defeat left behind by Hurricane Katrina.

Our route then cuts across the boggy bayous of Louisiana and across America's largest swamp before Texas, so that you can dip your toes into the warm Gulf of Mexico on one of Galveston's beaches. Then we jog north to Houston, known for its space connections but with much more to please the visitor, before continuing west to Austin, the Texas capital, and charming San Antonio, with its history and River Walk.

It's a long haul to the next major city – El Paso – but we keep things interesting by following the winding Rio Grande at the Mexican border. There's a worthy detour on the way to beautiful Big Bend National Park before you hit El Paso and its "sister city," Ciudad Juárez, across the border.

New Mexico's next, with its high-tech weaponry and missile sites, but also home to the natural beauty of White Sands National Monument and some ancient cliff dwelling sites. You'll cross the Continental Divide before entering Arizona, where the "Old West" really comes to life in places like Tombstone and Bisbee. The state's "big cities" of Tucson and Phoenix also have much to keep you busy before continuing on west into California to your ultimate destination: sunny San Diego.   ❏

PRECEDING PAGES: plantation house; a natural hay farmer surveys his day's work.
LEFT: Texas rancher. **TOP:** an all-American classic. **RIGHT:** happy in the swamp.

A Short Stay in Atlanta

Atlanta is bold, brash, and self-confident, a cosmopolitan island surrounded by rural Georgia. Here's a list of the not-to-be-missed attractions:

● Atlanta's main attractions are walkable, clustered around the small 1996 Centennial Olympic Park in Downtown. There's plenty for families at the dynamic Georgia Aquarium, which has the world's largest fish tank; Imagine It! The Children's Museum of Atlanta; and the New World of Coca-Cola. The worthwhile Inside CNN Atlanta tour offers a fascinating behind-the-scenes look at newscasting.

● Underground Atlanta is filled with shops and watering holes and stretches six blocks above and below ground. Little Five Points, meanwhile, has shops specializing in everything from New Age crystals and vintage clothes to music and books and serves as the hub for Atlanta's excellent MARTA transportation system.

● Midtown, centered on 10th and Peachtree streets, is Atlanta's fast-growing arts district. Highlights are the light-filled High Museum of Art, designed by Richard Meier, showcasing Rodin sculptures, works by Picasso and Matisse, and big traveling exhibits; the 1929 Fox Theatre, a Moorish-style movie palace, best seen on a tour with the Atlanta Preservation Society.

● *Gone With the Wind* author Margaret Mitchell is a hometown literary hero. The modest apartment where the pioneering journalist wrote her one masterpiece is a mecca for avid fans and is open daily for tours.

● Piedmont Park, surrounded by tree-shaded streets and old homes, is a Midtown favorite. Its northside has a newly expanded Botanical Garden while the south side hosts a Saturday Green Market and annual Dogwood Festival.

● Uptown's ritzy Buckhead district contains beautiful homes, restaurants, and a Whole Foods Market. The Atlanta History Center is a hidden gem. Nestled amid 33 acres (13 hectares) of wooded trails and gardens, it covers the Civil War and other local history and offers tours of the Tullie Smith Farmhouse and Swan House mansion.

ABOVE: The fun New World of Coca-Cola where you can sample 70 products and enjoy classic memorabilia.

BELOW: Martin Luther King, Jr. Learn about the Civil Rights leader at Martin Luther King National Historic Site. The four-block Sweet Auburn District includes King's birth home *(shown)*, his tomb and the church in which the King family preached.

CAPITAL OF THE NEW SOUTH

Atlanta is a city alert to opportunity. This is not just because it was burned down during the Civil War – Atlanta has always been this way. Winning the bid for the 1996 Olympics was just the beginning; now Atlanta is an urban phenomenon, exuding prosperity, self-confidence, self-absorption, and constant reinvention. Don't be fooled by all the construction, though: Atlanta retains a Southern graciousness and is very welcoming. Its population is diverse – it has the second-largest gay population in the US – and, once you get used to navigating streets without good signs, you'll quickly feel at home and want to linger.

ABOVE LEFT:
Skyscraper City. Atlanta's skyline is filled with gleaming, state-of-the-art skyscrapers.

ABOVE RIGHT:
CNN. A studio tour shows the professionals at work.

RIGHT: Buckhead District. The center of Atlanta's nightlife.

IMPORTANT INFORMATION

Population: City: 519,145; Metro: 5,138,223
Dialing codes: 404, 770
Website: www.atlanta.net
Tourist information: Atlanta C & V Bureau, 233 Peachtree Street, Suite 1400, GA 30303; tel: 404-521-6619; fax: 404-577-3293

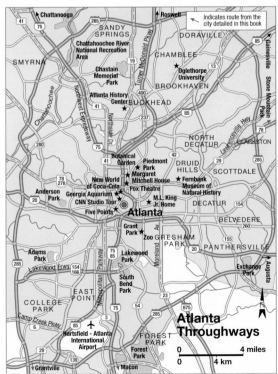

Atlanta Throughways

ATLANTA TO NEW ORLEANS

The mournful whistle of freight trains, small towns on hot summer nights, and grand, glorious antebellum towns highlight this trip through Georgia and Alabama

For more than a century after its cataclysmic encounter with historical destiny – as the focus of the Confederacy during the American Civil War (1861–65) – the South set itself apart from its conquerors (the Federal Government, or Union), stubbornly continuing to identify with the antebellum days on the Cotton Belt. Finally – and in part unwillingly, as a result of the changes forced upon it by the civil rights campaigns of the 1950s and 1960s – a "New South" is emerging. While there is still truth in the popular image of the region as a poor, undeveloped, and uneducated rural backwater, many of its urban communities have recast themselves beyond recognition, as high-tech high-achievers to match any in the nation.

Georgia on my mind

Nowhere is that more true than in the cities of Georgia, particularly its dynamic capital **Atlanta ❶** *(see page 244)*, on the broad Piedmont Plateau of its north-central region. Home to global corporations from Coca-Cola to CNN, Atlanta justly claims to be the heart of the "New South." Nonetheless, it has managed to retain the more appealing aspects of its past, such as the South's traditional mannered gentility and famed flair for hospitality. Macon, too, on the "fall line" that runs from Augusta to Columbus separating northern Georgia from the Coastal Plain, has pros-

pered without losing sight of its heritage, while Savannah, on the Savannah River close to the Atlantic Ocean, surrounds its stunning, antebellum city center with modern industry and shipping activity *(see "Atlantic Route," page 78)*.

Banking, manufacturing, media, military installations, and tourism may have come to dominate its cities, but much of the rest of Georgia remains rural. Agricultural produce such as the state's trademark peaches and sweet Vidalia onions, together with lumber,

Main attractions
HAY HOUSE
LITTLE WHITE HOUSE STATE PARK
CARVER MUSEUM, TUSKEGEE INSTITUTE
CIVIL RIGHTS MEMORIAL
BELLINGRATH GARDENS
WALTER M. ANDERSON MUSEUM OF ART
BEAUVOIR
THE FRENCH QUARTER

LEFT: Stone Mountain Park, outside Atlanta.
BELOW: a Mississippi paddle steamer.

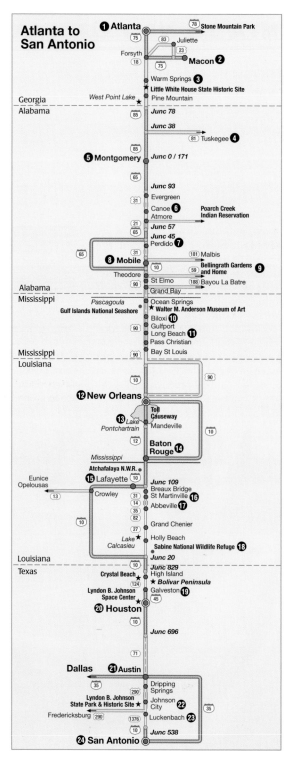

cattle, and poultry, continue to figure prominently in the economy.

Throughout Georgia, expect hot days and pleasant nights from May through September, temperate comfort in April and October and cool to cold temperatures November through March, with occasional frigid northerly winds, even snow. Georgia blooms most beautifully in the spring, which is ideal visiting season. Southern Georgia, on the Coastal Plain, is balmiest, often sweltering in summer.

If finding parking in downtown Atlanta leaves you crying for escape, take a trip 7 miles (11km) east of I-285 on US 78 to **Stone Mountain Park** (tel: 770-498-5690; daily), a recreation complex with seasonal attractions, including an ice rink, golf course, campground, hotels, waterslides, boating, fishing, tennis, wildlife trail, "Scenic Railroad" ride, and reconstructed plantation. Stone Mountain's plantation showcases buildings from throughout the state.

The park sprawls around its eponymous landmark: **Stone Mountain**. The exposed portion of this granite giant occupies a volume of 7.5 trillion cubic ft (213 million cubic meters) and is thought to be almost 3 million years old. Its gestation period was long, as igneous rock struggled to push through the surface. Stone Mountain's thrust to the sky is a fine metaphor for the concrete explosion of modern Atlanta after its razing by the Union army.

The mountain itself, smooth but for light pocks in the surface, is spectacle enough. Its focus, however, is the **Stone Mountain carving**, over 50 years in production, depicting Confederate leaders Jefferson Davis, Robert E. Lee, and "Stonewall" Jackson. The sculpture, which spreads 147ft (45 meters) across and towers 400ft (122 meters) above the ground, was completed in 1972.

Macon

Heading southeast out of Atlanta on I-75, you'll begin to encounter what the Federal Writers' Project called "the rolling character of the land [which] makes for undulations in the roadways, the fields, and the pine forests that border them. The clay hills are deeply gullied by erosion and their red color against the dark pines of the wooded regions creates a perpetually vivid landscape." Some 80 miles (129km) after leaving the "big city," I-75 takes a sharp turn to the south and straight into the heart of **Macon ❷** (it rhymes with "bacon"); you can venture into the city from either I-75 or I-16, which continues southeast to Savannah. Don't expect any classic skyline views: downtown Macon has long since ceased to be the commercial center. But in recent years, Downtown has experienced something of a cultural resurgence, sparked not only by the largest number of listed historic antebellum mansions and civic buildings in Georgia but also Macon's deserved reputation as a music mecca: it is the hometown of rock-and-roll legends Little Richard, Otis Redding, the Allman Brothers, and REM, among others.

The Old South

Macon's marvelous historic buildings were spared destruction during the Civil War by a simple ruse. In 1864, when General Sherman and his troops fired into the city across the Ocmulgee River, the return fire suggested a substantial resistance. But the troops that diverted Sherman and his all-too-tragic torch toward Savannah were not Confederate regulars, just old men and young children.

The architecture that has been preserved and restored is incredibly diverse, yet thoroughly Southern. As one resident puts it: "When people from outside the South come to find the 'Old South,' it's not in Atlanta, which is too new, nor is it in Savannah, which by virtue of its settlers and design is closer to a European city. The Old South is right here in Macon."

During the "cotton boom" of the early 19th century, cotton kings built lavish homes in the early Federal style with classical touches. These were followed by structures in the Greek Temple style adapted to the climate. Over the years, waves of commercial expansion inspired forays into new styles for mansions and civic and commercial buildings. Italianate Revival, Roman

More than 100 streets in Atlanta include the name Peachtree, named for Georgia's famed peaches. Peachtree Street is the main north-south thoroughfare in Atlanta.

BELOW: Macon is the epitome of the Old South.

TIP

Jarrell Plantation State Historic Site preserves an old family homestead and mill and offers bed-and-breakfast in a backwoods setting. It's close to the Whistle Stop Cafe and Piedmont National Wildlife Refuge. To reach it, drive US 23 north of Macon and watch for signs.

Revival and Academic Revival experiments carried through to the 1920s. Among fine examples open daily to visitors are the huge **Hay House** (tel: 478-742-8155) on Georgia Avenue, and **Cannonball House** (tel: 478-745-5982) on Mulberry Street, scarred by a shot from Sherman's artillery and now appropriately housing a **Confederate Museum**.

All can be enjoyed at their best in March each year, when the Cherry Blossom Festival celebrates the simultaneous flowering of Macon's pride and joy, the incredible 300,000 Japanese cherry trees that have been planted along the downtown streets.

The new Macon Visitor Center on Martin Luther King Boulevard has a film introducing Macon narrated by Little Richard, interactive exhibits, and offers walking tours of Macon's historic homes and museums. Nearby, the **Georgia Music Hall of Fame** (tel: 478-750-8555; daily) celebrates Georgia's musical heritage with its Tune Town permanent exhibit showcasing different musical styles, from gospel to R&B.

A bridge honoring Macon's best-known hometown musical legend, Otis Redding, leads away from Downtown across the Ocmulgee River to **Ocmulgee National Monument** (tel: 478-752-8257; daily). This small, peaceful national park doesn't do much to toot its own horn but is one of Macon's undiscovered treasures. It preserves ceremonial mounds, cornfields, and other remnants of the powerful Mississippian Mound Building culture that thrived here between AD 900 and 1100.

A museum inside the 1930s Art Moderne visitor center along with trailside exhibits interpret the lifeways of the Mississippians. Children will enjoy going inside the 42ft (12.8-meter) -diameter reconstructed earthlodge. With its thunderbird-shaped altar, firepit, and banquette seating, the semi-subterranean structure resembles the great kivas found at Chaco Canyon in New Mexico, one of the Mississippians' far-flung trading partners.

Backwoods whistle-stop

Taking US 23, which winds northward from Macon along the Ocmulgee River, enables you to get an appealing taste of rural Georgia. Tiny **Juliette**, 20 miles (32km) along, was reinvigorated in the early 1990s, when its air of picturesque deep-woods dereliction made it the perfect location for the movie *Fried Green Tomatoes at the Whistle Stop Cafe*. The actual **Whistle Stop Cafe** – built for the film beside a still-used country railroad station – was almost destroyed by a flood a few years ago. It's definitely seen better days but is still wildly popular with locals and tourists making a pilgrimage to eat the tempura-style green tomatoes that made it famous.

From Juliette, pick up State 83 east, then State 18, which winds all the way to the Georgia-Alabama border. The buccolic town of **Warm Springs** ❸, approximately an hour east of Juliette, is nestled amid the foothills of Pine Mountain. It grew to fame as a therapeutic center for polio suffer-

BELOW: the Italianate Revival Hay House, Macon.

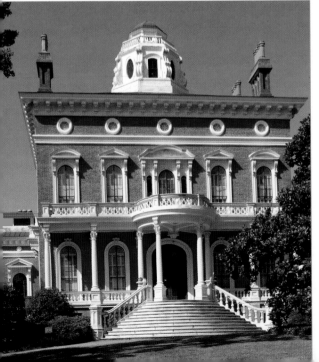

ers in the 1920s, when then-New York Governor Franklin Roosevelt, who suffered from polio himself, began using the warm mineral springs to ease his symptoms. Roosevelt opened a hospital with therapeutic pools, now a private internationally recognized polio facility (the pools are not open to the public).

In 1932, the year before winning the presidency, Roosevelt built a six-room cottage at Warm Springs that served as a regular retreat, where he took the waters, formulated his New Deal policies, and eventually died on April 12, 1945. **Little White House State Park** (tel: 706-655-5870; daily) has a museum on FDR and makes a fascinating stop. This part of Georgia is worth savoring. Using Warm Springs or nearby FDR State Park as a base, you can hike, camp, fish, horse-back ride, and rest up before entering Alabama, a short way to the west on I-85.

ATLANTA TO SOUTHWEST ALABAMA

Alabama and much of the land to its west passed through several hands before it was taken over by the United States in the late 18th century. Labyrinthine Colonial struggles involving the Indian "Five Nations" (Cherokee, Seminole, Muscogee, Chickasaw, and Choctaw) mark Alabama's early history, and its coat of arms displays the emblems of the five non-native nations that successively held sovereignty over it: France, Great Britain, the United States, the Confederacy, and again the United States.

The last two of these regimes, of course, have left the clearest stamp on Alabama, named for the Alabama River, itself named after an Indian tribe. Alabama rose to its economic apex during the cotton boom of the 19th century, and has been markedly reluctant to let go of the memory of its Confederate heyday. Only following bitter campaigns in the 1990s did the state capitol building in Montgomery finally cease to fly the Confederate flag. The state has seen better days, economically and socially, but its natural resources, hard-working citizenry, and enduring pride refuse to admit decline.

Georgia Time

Georgia's best-loved local hero, Ray Charles.

BELOW LEFT: scene from the movie *Fried Green Tomatoes at the Whistle Stop Cafe.* **BELOW:** the earth lodge at Ocmulgee National Monument.

Sign of the South: This climbing vine, known as kudzu, was brought from Asia and used by the government to stop soil erosion. It is now virtually unstoppable, smothering thousands of acres of land.

BELOW: bust of George Washington Carver at the Carver Museum in Tuskegee, Alabama.

Although in principle the **Chattahoochee River** delineates the boundaries of Georgia and Alabama, in fact at this point you cross the Alabama state line a short way west of the river. Even then, you don't join the rest of Alabama on Central Time – one hour earlier – until you're beyond the Lanett Valley here.

After rolling through a forested area along I-85 westbound, you can turn off at exit 38 to **Tuskegee ❹** via State 81 south and State 126 west. Tuskegee is the site of Booker T. Washington's **Tuskegee Normal and Industrial Institute**, which is one of the few institutions of higher learning for American blacks that existed during the 19th century.

Tuskegee and black education

In the words of the leading black intellectual, W.E.B. DuBois, Washington was "the greatest man the South produced since the Civil War." Handsome, politically deft, and enormously inspired, Washington believed in cooperation with the ruling whites and in practical education to serve the needs

of the black masses concentrated in the South. Washington's policy of avoiding confrontation made enemies among other educated blacks and "liberal whites," but he kept Tuskegee alive from 1881 to 1915.

While the institute remains very much active, much of its historic campus has been preserved with the aid of the National Park Service. Its centerpiece is the **Carver Museum** (tel: 334-727-3200; daily), named after the black agricultural chemist George Washington Carver, who worked and taught on campus from 1896 until his retirement to The Oaks in Tuskegee, where he died in 1943.

A former slave, Carver had abandoned artistic aspirations to forge the pioneer science of industrial agriculture. His discoveries saved the Southern economy from collapse after the boll weevil infestation of 1919 destroyed the cotton industry. Many of his "bulletins" are displayed in the museum; through such works as *How To Grow The Peanut and 105 Ways of Preparing It for Human Consumption*, a black man saved a region whose elite had oppressed and would continue to oppress his race. The museum also shows two 30-minute films about Carver and Washington that detail the history of the institution and of their struggles without shying away from the controversies that surround them.

Among Carver's interests were polio therapies, which brought him to the attention of Franklin Roosevelt. In 1939, Roosevelt visited Tuskegee, and shortly thereafter, Tuskegee became the pilot training base for the first all-African-American 99th Pursuit Squadron. In 1998, Moton Field was redesignated **Tuskegee Airmen National Historic Site** (tel: 334-724-0922; daily) to celebrate the lives of these unsung heroes of World War II. A small temporary visitor center has exhibits and five films on the airmen as well as views of the airfield. An annual Tuskegee Airmen Fly-In is held here every Memorial Day weekend,

GEORGE W. CARVER

DONATED BY HIS MANY FRIENDS

featuring historic aircraft, aeronautical displays, and exhibits.

Old Acres and Pecan Grove

Back on I-85 south, travel 41 miles (66km) from Tuskegee to the boundary of **Montgomery ❺**. Alabama's capital city consists of a small, surprisingly quiet downtown area surrounded by wide outlying neighborhoods whose names smack of agricultural gentility. While the prairie muds are still rich, Montgomery bases its livelihood on government services, construction, and manufacturing. It also benefits from the patronage of the US Air Force, whose elite members are frequently assigned to **Maxwell Air Force Base** on the site of famed aviators Wilbur and Orville Wright's flight school.

The state government complex on Goat Hill has several extraordinary public buildings in the gleaming white antebellum style that simply take your breath away. The marble-columned **State Capitol** (tel: 334-242-3935; Mon–Sat) is one of the country's only state capitols designated a national historic landmark: the place where Confederate president Jefferson Davis took his oath of office.

Two grand structures stand across Washington Street from the Capitol: the **First White House of the Confederacy** (tel: 334-242-1861; Mon–Fri) and the imposing **Alabama Department of Archives and History** building (tel: 334-242-4363; Mon–Sat). The White House, relocated from its original site at Bibb and Catoma streets, was the home of Confederate president Jefferson Davis during Montgomery's stint as first capital of the Confederate States of America. This rebel nation was comprised of the 13 states and territories that seceded from the United States in 1860 and 1861 over the issue of states' rights – among them the right to maintain slavery. Davis has been eclipsed in history by Confederate General Robert E. Lee, but in the South he is still revered as an emblem of distinction and self-

determination, as evidenced by the bumper sticker "Don't Blame Me – I Voted For Jefferson Davis."

Civil rights sites

The neoclassical Archives Building is a rich storehouse of Native American arts, Confederate history, and state development. It once housed a diverse collection of performing outfits belonging to home-town music legend Hank Williams, Sr. They, and Williams' baby-blue 1952 Cadillac, now take center stage at the enormously popular **Hank Williams Museum** on Commerce Street (tel: 334-242-3600; daily). Literature buffs won't want to miss the delightful **F. Scott and Zelda Fitzgerald Museum** (tel: 334-264-4222; Wed–Sun) where the author of *The Great Gatsby* and his Jazz Age wife lived after meeting in Montgomery during World War I.

Barely a hundred yards down from the Capitol is **Dexter Avenue King Memorial Baptist Church**, whose 26-year-old pastor, Rev. Martin Luther King, Jr, was thrust somewhat unwillingly into the limelight in December 1955, when he was invited to spearhead

Dr Martin Luther King delivered a stirring speech from the top of the Montgomery State Capitol Building at the end of the Selma-to-Montgomery Civil Rights march in 1965.

BELOW:
Civil Rights Memorial, Montgomery.

Malbis Memorial Greek Orthodox Church.

BELOW: a quiet spot on a Gulf coast beach.

the civil rights campaign known as the Montgomery Bus Boycott after Montgomery resident Rosa Parks refused to give up her seat to a white man. A mural inside the church, "Montgomery to Memphis, 1955–1968," commemorates the long struggle for dignity and equality. Outside the Southern Poverty Law Center nearby, the powerful **Civil Rights Memorial**, designed by Maya Lin (who was also responsible for the celebrated Vietnam Veterans Memorial in Washington, DC), honors King and 40 other martyrs of the movement; a small but well-thought-out visitor center has a stirring audio-visual presentation and an interesting bookstore.

Another Alabama

I-85 into Montgomery dovetails into I-65 and continues south into the rural glades of southwestern Alabama. Along the way, the radio bands are striped with black contemporary music, pop, country, gospel, sermons, and jazz. The soil deepens again to red where it had been sandy and gray in the "Black Belt" through the midsection of the state.

Deeper exploration of rural Alabama is definitely recommended, and US 31 is a good place to start. Branching away from the interstate near the cute little town of **Evergreen**, US 31 arcs through Escambia and Baldwin counties, grazing the northwesternmost edge of Florida near Atmore and Perdido. The land surrounding towns such as Castleberry – "Home of the Alabama Strawberry" – is dotted with small green ponds and spread with groves of pine and oak. Cattle graze on the muddy soil, and farmhouses call forth images of peaceful backwaters.

Before reaching **Atmore**, you pass through **Canoe ❻**, where you might see a horse and buggy along one side of the road as a 100-car-long freight train whistles by on the other. Atmore is weary-palmed, open-fielded, and railroad-tied, with churches signposted in all directions off the highway. Eight miles (13km) north of Atmore, you'll find the 2,340-member **Poarch Creek Indian Reservation**, the only Indian reservation in Alabama and the only one whose members have never been forcibly moved from their original homeland. You can learn more about Poarch Creek

history and culture at its eye-catching new **Wind Creek Casino** (tel: 251-446-4200) near the interstate, which has gambling, four restaurants, and a hotel.

'Bama wine

Continue on I-65 along a 13-mile (21km) stretch before the next exit (exit 45) to **Perdido ❼**. Just south of the highway, the fruit of Jim and Marianne Eddins' gumption and perseverance continues to thrive: **Perdido Vineyards** (tel: 251-937-9463; Mon–Sat). Winemaking in Alabama, once a great domestic industry, was effectively killed by Prohibition. Even afterward, Baptist leaders maintained that drinking – let alone manufacturing – alcohol was next to ungodliness. The Eddins family dared the opposition and began their muscadine vineyard in 1971, marketing the grapes to a Florida winemaker. When that arrangement fell through, Perdido Vineyards began producing its own wine in 1979.

The muscadine varieties grown at Perdido – scuppernongs, higgins, nobles, and magnolias – are from a tough vine indigenous to the southeastern United States. Perdido's table wines, which may be sampled at the vineyard, are mostly sweet wines with a few drier varieties, including an extra-dry white that is reminiscent of some California wines. The Perdido venture met with initial hostility from the community, but its success and the subsequent attention it brought to Baldwin County considerably warmed their reception.

Baldwin County is subject to a "pressure-cooker" climate, hot and prone to extremes of humidity. Nature has been hard on American farmers for centuries, but the environment was very attractive to a settlement of Greeks who came to the shores of Mobile Bay before World War II. Under the leadership of a Greek Orthodox priest named Malbis, the community established the lushest plantation in the county. When Malbis died in Nazi hands after he returned to Greece, the community carried out his plan to build an Ortho-

dox Church in what is now the town of **Malbis**, between US 31 and I-10, 4 miles (6km) east of Mobile Bay. The church was constructed from materials imported from Greece and includes stunning tile work and stained glass.

MOBILE TO NEW ORLEANS

The coastline of the Gulf of Mexico, arcing from northwest Florida to southeast Texas, can well lay claim to the title of "the American Riviera" – though less reverently, it's also known as "the Redneck Riviera." Not so much a Cote d'Azur as a Cote de Blanc, the Gulf Coast spreads its white sands beside warm waters stocked with fine shrimp, oysters, and other delicacies. While never quite ranking as an international destination, the superb beaches of Gulf-Coast Alabama, Mississippi, and Texas have attracted vacationers from the South and Midwest since the mid-19th century. Tourism, gambling, and fishing are the economic mainstays of the region, but they have been impinged upon by hurricanes and the growth of the oil industry, which often drills and

Mobile's historic Downtown features many Victorian architectural gems designed by Rudolph Benz in the early 1900s. A historic walking tour booklet for the area around Dauphin Street includes a number of these buildings, many of which have filigree ironwork similar to that found in New Orleans' French Quarter.

BELOW: strolling on the pristine Alabama gulf shore.

Crest of the Historic Development Commission in Mobile, Alabama.

explores within sight of the sunbathers. Whatever the ecological effects of oil retrieval may be, the petrochemical industry has been crucial to the survival of cities such as Mobile, Alabama.

Former French capital

Interstates 10 and 65 and US 90 (which pick up from US 31) all straddle the mouth of the Mobile River as they cross westward from Baldwin County into the port of **Mobile ❽** (pronounced *Mo-beel*). Mobile's locale on river and gulf has made it the most contested area in all of Alabama's twisted power struggles, and to this day it feels resolutely atypical of a state that outsiders regard as the most insular in the South. That sense of cosmopolitan diversity is hardly surprising; after all, Mobile began life in 1703 as the capital of the French colony of Louisiana, which covered a far larger, if not all that precisely defined, area than the modern state of the same name.

Although a pair of illuminated skyscraper spires make up a distinctive skyline, Mobile's Colonial past remains evident everywhere. Parallels with Louisiana in general, and New Orleans in particular, range from the intricate iron grillwork that adorns the city's balconies to the oysters and gumbo sold in its restaurants. Most striking of all is Mobile's Mardi Gras, which pre-dates its more famous counterpart in New Orleans. Arrive in the week before Lent, and you'll be dazzled by the parades and costumes, but throughout the year tell-tale strings of colored Mardi Gras beads festoon the live oaks and telephone wires in Downtown.

A stroll along downtown avenues such as lower **Government**, **Church**, and **Dauphin streets** is much the best way to get a flavor of Mobile. Pick up a historic walking tour brochure at the south end of Royal Street, at the city's visitor center, which is housed in a partial replica of 1724 **Fort Condé** (tel: 251-208-7569; daily) whose cannons now point forlornly across a concrete underpass. Across the street, **Mobile Museum of History** (tel: 251-208-7569; daily) is housed in an Italianate building and has good exhibits on local history. From there, a short walk

will take you through stately historic districts that flourish with magnolia, azalea, and oak, all of which thrive in the semi-tropical climate. Yet again, serious commerce has fled to the outlying malls, so the old department stores have closed down. Downtown does, however, have a plethora of hip cafés, clubs, and restaurants, and in 2007, after extensive restoration, trumpeted the reopening of one of its *grande dame* hotels – the 1852 Beaux Arts-style **Battle House** – established on the site of Andrew Jackson's military headquarters during the War of 1812.

Semi-tropical jungle

Government Street becomes US 90 as it pulls away from Mobile Bay and widens into the usual mall-motel-and-fast-food sprawl. On reaching the town of **Theodore**, you'll spot a huge billboard directing you south on State 59 to **Bellingrath Gardens and Home ❾** (tel: 251-973-2217; daily), "The Garden For all Seasons." All the hype – "Incomparable," "One of the World's Most Beautiful Year-Round Gardens" – turns out to be pretty much true. Originally a semi-

tropical jungle on the Isle-aux-Dies River, the land was purchased by Walter Bellingrath, who made his fortune as the first bottler of Coca-Cola in Alabama. Mr and Mrs Bellingrath landscaped 65 acres (26 hectares) of the 905-acre (367-hectare) plot, sculpting an evolving, living work of art to surround their magnificent riverfront home. Azaleas, roses, hibiscus, chenille, chrysanthemums, poinsettias, lilies, violets, and dogwood are all part of the "rapturous floral beauty." The Oriental-American Garden, honking geese, flamingos, and teeming bayou will charm where the gift shop and restaurant depress; renting a taped tour is an unnecessary distraction. This attraction is out of the way. Allow half a day for a visit.

Town life in the Deep South

US 90 is the "old highway" along the Gulf Coast from Florida to Louisiana, but you'll have to decide for yourself whether the potted roads, frequent traffic lights, dreary trailer parks, and gritty fishing ports such as Grand Bay and Bayou La Batre close to Mobile merit taking the slow route the whole

TIP

The popular Blessing of the Shrimp Fleet takes place in early May in Bayou La Batre, a fishing town near Mobile.

BELOW:
Overlook Lake, Bellingrath Gardens.

TIP

Gulf Islands National Seashore offers a rare unspoiled look at the natural history of the gulf in charming Ocean Springs, an arts town near Biloxi, Mississippi. Ospreys nest near the visitor center and boardwalk trail through the bayous and gulf shore.

BELOW: born again in the eyes of the Lord.

way or whether you want to drive the more efficient and pleasantly grassy freeway some of the way and get off at US 90 communities that interest you.

If you're taking I-10, **Pascagoula** is your best bet to exit and pick up US 90 as it heads west through Biloxi and Gulfport. Just before reaching Biloxi, you'll pass through the delightful beach town of **Ocean Springs**, a cultural mecca with the intimate feel of California's Carmel that seems almost out of place amid the working-class towns of the Gulf. The pretty, compact Downtown – a haven for artists – offers a variety of unique boutiques, eateries, cafés, and art galleries and makes a relaxing spot to linger over lunch or a cup of coffee.

If you only visit one small-town art museum on this whole Southern Route, make it Ocean Springs' super **Walter M. Anderson Museum of Art** (tel: 228-872-3164; daily). Local boy Anderson (1903–65), a classically trained artist who developed mental problems, was a passionate recorder of the natural treasures along the Gulf Coast shoreline. His moving artwork combines an inner turmoil reminiscent of Van Gogh with the subtly colored but detailed natural forms found in Georgia O'Keeffe's artwork, all of it expressed in thousands of jewel-like watercolors of his beloved Mississippi Gulf Coast. A huge mural in the adjoining community center, containing numerous spiritual references and natural motifs, was designated a National Treasure in 2005. It was damaged by Hurricane Katrina but is gradually being restored. Also on display are ceramics by Walter's brothers Peter, founder of Shearwater Pottery, and James, a noted painter and ceramist.

At the east end of Ocean Springs, you'll find the Mississippi branch of **Gulf Islands National Seashore** (tel: 228-875-9057; daily) – the other branch is in Florida. Its pleasant boardwalk trail offers glimpses of the Gulf and bayous that so entranced Anderson. The visitor center has exhibits and information. This is a good place for nature lovers hoping to view ospreys and other birds and relax in an unspoiled setting.

Mississippi resort

Just across the bridge from Ocean Springs is **Biloxi**  (pronounced locally: *Bluxi*), the second base of operations for the French government of the Louisiana Territory, following Mobile. Founded in 1699 across the Biloxi Bay from its present location, the city sits on a peninsula cut by two bays and the Gulf of Mexico, providing a brilliant and popular beach. The 19th-century bayou-front stately homes on which Biloxi's reputation as a posh winter resort had rested have largely disappeared. Most of the credit for that rests with a succession of severe storms that have swept in from the Gulf. Severe damage was wrought by the vicious onslaught of Hurricane Camille in 1969; a head-on hit from Hurricane Georges in 1998 also caused widespread destruction. But Hurricane Katrina, which made a direct hit on Biloxi in August 2005, surely wreaked the most havoc, killing residents and uprooting homes and businesses, including the new Hard Rock Hotel and Casino – which had been open only a matter of days when the storm hit.

The Hard Rock and other major gambling resorts quickly reopened, demonstrating the strong corporate incentives at play here, as well as fierce North-versus-South politics that has seen Republican governors like Mississippi's Haley Barbour and Louisiana's Bobby Jindahl emphasizing recovery through private enterprise rather than long-delayed government handouts. Today, the Gulf beachfront, from Biloxi to Long Beach, is all business – a hive of construction activity, most of it bulldozing vast quantities of gold sand to recreate the artificial beach that has long been a trademark.

Gambling in Biloxi is so hedged around with arcane restrictions it is a peculiar hybrid here. First of all, casinos can only be built on existing commercial property, so long swathes of pristine beach still survive, and in the quest for room to build, some of the largest casinos have located themselves facing inland on the previously sleepy Back Bay.

Secondly, state laws only allow for gambling on boats, not on land, so the huge structures you see from the road

Mailbox with tiny Confederate flag in the deep South.

BELOW: fat crabs from the warm waters of the Gulf.

Pass Christian was named for a nearby deepwater pass commemorating Nicholas Christian L'Adnier who lived on nearby Cat Island in 1746.

are in fact just the hotel and restaurant segments of the operation, while the actual gaming takes place on "barges" situated behind. Once inside, however, you can't tell where building ends and barge begins. As with much of the Gulf, the appeal of Biloxi remains more for weekenders from adjoining states than international travelers.

Gulfport and Long Beach

Thankfully, Biloxi still holds one genuine historical attraction – though it, too, suffered enormous damage during Hurricane Katrina and only reopened in 2008. The white-columned 1852 oceanfront mansion of **Beauvoir** (tel: 228-388-4400; daily), the last home of Confederate president Jefferson Davis, serves as a showcase for his possessions, and also as a wide-ranging Confederate museum. Five of the seven buildings on the 51-acre (20-hectare) estate were destroyed by Katrina, restoration of the home continues, and the visitor center is now in a trailer. But Davis's continuing appeal for diehard Southerners is demonstrated daily by the huge outpouring of support for restoring the

home and rebuilding its **Jefferson Davis Presidential Library** on the site of the old one. Guides here offer eyewitness accounts of Hurricane Katrina destruction and mince no words in expressing their feelings about the proud South and Beauvoir's historic importance. A visit here is truly an education for any outsider.

If it's beach fun you're after, continue along the coast on US 90, where the golden strands of **Gulfport** and **Long Beach** ⓫ are lined with kiosks that rent out jet-skis, beach tractors with inflatable wheels or simply multicolored beach parasols. One final community, the intriguingly named **Pass Christian**, once harked back to more gracious days in Mississippi, with the Gulf on one side of US 90 and an avenue of live oaks whose branches intertwined above the highway to create a cool green tunnel. It was a popular retirement community until Hurricane Katrina destroyed over 2,000 homes, permanently altering the town. Recovery here is still a long way off, and as with Gulfport and Long Beach, if you're looking for a non-chain hotel or restaurant, you're pretty much out of luck.

US 90 then curves sharply away from the coast and crosses the Bay of St Louis, where a bridge terminates in lovely **Bay St Louis**, "Gateway to the Gulf Coast." With little warning, the road forks: State 609 takes the northwestern way toward I-10 and a National Aeronautics and Space Administration (NASA) test site; US 90 slides southwestward. Both bring you shortly to Louisiana. Eight miles (13km) of bridges form Interstate 10 from shore to shore – from St Tammany "Parish" (as counties are called in Louisiana) into Orleans Parish. As the car crosses on **Lake Pontchartrain Causeway** (see page 265), you feel you're dipping and climbing through the water itself. Suddenly, wistful **New Orleans** ⓬ (see page 262) rises from the opposite shore of **Lake Pontchartrain** ⓭, a crescent of skyscrapers amid a green lake of oak. ❏

BELOW: Beauvior Mansion, Biloxi.
RIGHT: the Lake Pontchartrain Causeway, gateway to New Orleans.

New Orleans: The Big Easy

Anchor of the Gulf Coast, cradle of jazz, home of exotic food – this is without doubt the most fascinating city in the South.

C urling around a mighty bend in the Mississippi, New Orleans (Noo-*Orlens*) is known as the "Crescent City" – the home of jazz, blues, and complex Creole food, blending French, Latin, and Caribbean influences. Since 1857, it's also been synonymous with Mardi Gras, whose private balls, flamboyant float parades, masks, and glittering costume jewelry capture the towering gothic spirit of this unique American city.

Not even the devastating Category 5 Hurricane Katrina, which narrowly missed hitting New Orleans in August 2005, stopped Carnival the following year. But it came close. The levees that protect New Orleans from the surrounding watery domain failed in more than 50 places during the subsequent storm surge, flooding 80 percent of the city for weeks. Remarkably, the Vieux Carre, or **French Quarter**, and other historic areas along the river, the high ground on which the French government had wisely built the original walled city in the 1700s, were spared.

Several Katrina Disaster Tours, guided by locals who witnessed the storm first-hand, escort visitors to view the damage at levees along the canals and slow rebuilding efforts in neighborhoods that one lakeside resident describes as being like Beirut. Many of the 1,836 fatalities were in the Ninth Ward, the poorest part of the city, where residents couldn't afford to leave. Thousands of displaced residents remain in FEMA trailers; many more have left for good, radically reducing the population. If you are interested in volunteering while here, visit www.volunteerlouisiana.gov.

In the French Quarter, between Canal Street and Esplanade, though, it's business as usual – an eerie contrast with outlying neighborhoods. The heart of the French Quarter is **Jackson Square**, fronted by **St Louis Cathedral** (1794). The sidewalks here are the domain of street musicians, portrait artists, and fortune tellers – not to mention the "Lucky Dog" hotdog sellers, their carts shaped like garish giant sausages, immortalized in John Kennedy Toole's comic masterpiece *A Confederacy of Dunces*. To either side are the red-brick **Pontalba Buildings** (1849), the oldest apartment buildings in the US. The **Cabildo** and **Presbytere** (tel: 504-568-6968; daily), two excellent state museums, flank the cathedral itself, housed in cupola-topped Colonial structures. Among their treasures are Napoleon's death mask and the room in which the 1803 Louisiana Purchase was signed.

The main drag (in every sense) is Bourbon Street, a pedestrian circus at all hours. In contrast to Bourbon, one block toward the river, parallel Royal Street hosts an array of classy galleries and antique shops as well as formal restaurants such as **Brennan's** – legendary for its breakfasts – and the Court of **Two Sisters**, whose shaded courtyard is a perfect "jazz brunch spot."

Along **Decatur Street**, the riverfront thoroughfare, tourist dollars are mined enthusiastically at

ABOVE: open all hours. **LEFT:** Jazz Fest in the spring is the best time to hear the best music. **RIGHT:** St Louis Cathedral. **FAR RIGHT:** French Quarter jazz club.

souvenir shops and restaurants and the mall-ified **French Market** and **Jackson Brewery**. It's all accompanied by the deafening blare of tunes played on the whistle of the **Steamboat** *Natchez*, which offers daily sightseeing cruises on the Mississippi. For an appealing half-mile or so, the aptly named "Big Muddy" is lined first by a wooden boardwalk known as the "Moonwalk," then by grassy parks, one of which contains the well-stocked Aquarium of the Americas (tel: 800-774-7394; Tue–Sun). A small free ferry crisscrosses the river to the island of **Algiers**, an interesting vantage point on the city.

Lafitte's Blacksmith Shop at 941 Bourbon Street, the tumbledown brick smithy where the pirate Lafitte plotted many a high-seas escapade, is an atmospheric if almost impenetrably gloomy bar that makes an appropriate starting point for nightly walking tours of "Haunted New Orleans," while the stately Napoleon House at 500 Chartres Street, allegedly the focus of a scheme to rescue the exiled emperor from St Helena and bring him to the United States, is another ravishingly Stygian bar with its own courtyard café.

All along Bourbon Street, talented house bands entertain diners at cafés and restaurants. *The* spot for traditional jazz is Preservation Hall (tel: 504-522-2841), a tiny, dilapidated hall on St Peter Street whose appearance belies the famous musicians who nightly toot their horns here. At legendary clubs like Tipitina's (tel: 504-566-7095), featured in Jim Jarmusch's movie *Down by Law*, you'll see local bands like the Radiators tearing up the dance floor.

Best with spicy gumbo, jambalaya, and crawfish etouffee is ice-cold Abita beer, Louisiana's own brew. The definitive local liquor drinks are Sazerac and Ramos Gin Fizz; a rum-based Hurricane at Pat O'Brien's; or a cooling Pimm's Cup at the Napoleon House. New Orleans is famous for its chicory coffee. It's traditional to enjoy creamy café au lait with beignets – donuts drowned in powdered sugar – at the 24-hour sidewalk **Café du Monde** in the French Market, a great people-watching spot.

West of the Vieux Carré, the **Warehouse District** is New Orleans' up-and-coming arts district. Among its boutique hotels and contemporary restaurants like Cochon (tel: 504-588-2123; Mon–Sat), whose Cajun Southern pork dishes celebrate everything but the squeal, you'll find art galleries and the **Louisiana Children's Museum** (tel: 504-523-1357), and the **National World War II Museum** (tel: 504-527-6012). Beyond the Central Business District, the home of the **Louisiana Superdome** – a good trip to take by tram – is the lush and wealthy **Garden District**, where you can find antebellum houses standing amid the azalea and dogwood, and baroque oak trees shading marvelous structures built in Greek Revival, Renaissance, and Victorian styles. ❑

NEW ORLEANS TO SAN ANTONIO

Cruising across what claims to be "the longest
bridge in the world," take an alligator-enhanced
trip through Cajun Country and end up
in cowboy country

This route from New Orleans to
the Texas border takes in, first,
Cajun country and then the state's
capital. Leaving the city and driving
north, Lake Pontchartrain is spanned
by **Lake Pontchartrain Causeway**,
"the world's longest bridge." The causeway is a 24-mile (39km) double stripe
of highway propped above the surface
of the lake. For miles, nothing can be
seen on the horizon, and the camelback plunge into the void is akin to
crossing the barren yet subtle plains of
Texas *(see picture on page 261)*.

On the trip north over the causeway
to **Mandeville**, land initially appears as
a thin blue sliver on the horizon, an airy
gray-blue strip melting off the murky
waters into the sky. Gradually, the land
becomes more distinct, broader, and
deeper in color until it becomes the
interface of two great azure bodies: sea
and sky. If you choose to cross the Lake
Pontchartrain Causeway, it might be
best to do when leaving the city.

A round-trip across the lake may be
a little overwhelming, and concentration sometimes tends to falter on the
second stretch. When the Causeway
touches land in Mandeville, it becomes
US 190. Four miles (6km) north of the
lakeshore, it interchanges with I-12,
which runs 61 miles (98km) west to
the capital of Louisiana, Baton Rouge.

Acadian bayous

Alternatively, if you follow the efficient
but gritty I-10 out of New Orleans, you
cut through the boggy, baroque bayou
country on the southwest bank of Lake
Pontchartrain in St Charles and St
John the Baptist parishes. The highway
is stilted out of grass-fringed still water
where the thin trunks that disappear
into the mire mimic the somber poles
that support the parallel powerlines.

Bayous – narrow, sluggish rivers usually surrounded by wetlands – run in
veins throughout southern Louisiana,
otherwise known as Acadiana. This
expansive region is named after the
Acadians, Catholic French refugees

Main attractions
LAKE PONTCHARTRAIN CAUSEWAY
NEW CAPITOL
ATCHAFALAYA SWAMP
BREAUX BRIDGE
JEAN LAFITTE SCENIC BYWAY
ST MARTINVILLE
PORT BOLIVAR FERRY
BISHOP'S PALACE
TEXAS STATE CAPITOL
LYNDON B. JOHNSON STATE PARK
LUCKENBACH

LEFT: Cajun
musician. **BELOW:**
big catch at a
country store in
Vacherie, Louisiana.

driven out of Nova Scotia by the British in the late 18th century. Settling the Louisiana lowlands, mostly Spanish dominions, they were joined by Frenchmen fleeing the Revolution, and created a culture known as "Cajun" (a corruption of "Acadian").

Acadiana, stretching along the Gulf Coast to Texas and west from the Mississippi River up to Avoyelles Parish, has been described as "South of the South," although in many ways it's more conspicuously akin to the societies of the French and Spanish West Indies than to the traditional American South.

The land of the Kingfish

I-10 meets the Mississippi River at the city of **Baton Rouge** ⓮, capital of Louisiana and the state's major port. That name, in French, means "red stick." It's generally agreed that the "stick" was a tree, red either from the blood of animals hung there by Indians or from the stripping of its bark. In the latter case, the tree may have been used to mark the boundary of Houma and Bayou Goula Indian land.

BELOW: the Old State Capitol, Baton Rouge.

Although Baton Rouge abuts Acadiana, it has little to do with it, except for governing it and shipping its oil. The ambience is definitely "Southern," and you'll notice, in comparison to New Orleans, a deepening of accent and of provincial ways. The rather quiet, laid-back tempo of the streets belies the intense industry and politicking at the city's heart.

The principal sights of Baton Rouge are the old and new trappings of government. The **Old State Capitol** (tel: 225-342-0500; daily), a Gothic folly constructed beside the Mississippi in 1849, attracted the full force of Mark Twain's considerable scorn. Blaming the "debilitating influence" of Sir Walter Scott for the antebellum South's obsession with notions of "chivalry," he charged "It is pathetic enough that a whitewashed castle, with turrets and things, should ever have been built in this otherwise honorable place; but it is much more pathetic to see this architectural falsehood undergoing restoration and perpetuation in our day, when it would have been so easy to let dynamite finish what a charitable fire began."

In contrast, the 34-story Art Deco **New Capitol** (tel: 225-342-7317; daily free tours), a national historic landmark, bestrides the north end of town. Resembling a scaled-down Empire State Building, the skyscraper was built in 1932 by Louisiana's infamous governor Huey Long, the so-called "Kingfish" who reigned supreme throughout the Great Depression. By all accounts a distasteful and corrupt man, Long was nevertheless an enlightened despot who brooked no opposition to his semi-socialistic rule for the "common man." Highways, schools, and hospitals were built; the unemployed put to work; the privileged heavily taxed. He was gunned down in the capitol in 1935 – a case of memorabilia on the exact spot admits that he may have been killed by his own bodyguards as they panicked in the face of a supposed assassin who never fired a shot – and is now buried in the adjacent garden, alongside a larger-than-life statue.

The twin foundations of the city's wealth appear as you leave. From the huge **Baton Rouge Bridge**, on which I-10 crosses the river, you can see belching petrochemical refineries stretching into the distance. Down below stands Baton Rouge's port, the fourth most active in the nation thanks to being the farthest inland of all deep-water ports serving the Gulf of Mexico. That status was not achieved by chance; one of Long's most brilliant ploys to boost his own state was to build this very bridge too low for ocean-going vessels to continue any farther upstream.

West of the Mississippi, you re-enter Acadiana in West Baton Rouge Parish, and soon pass beyond into Iberville Parish. For the first time in this trip – but not for the last, as you head toward the open spaces of the West – you're treated to spectacular scenery without having to leave the interstate. Here, it becomes the **Atchafalaya Swamp Freeway**, crossing America's largest swamp, dividing into two separate highways, supported on precarious concrete stilts and separated by an expanse of soupy open water that holds lozenge-shaped islets.

Drowned forests

To either side, the landscape is a magical melding of water and drowned forest, punctuated by clumps of trees, telegraph poles, and strangely shaped cypress "knees" (those parts of the root systems of cypress trees that poke out of the morass). Locals fish sedately, or even race speedboats, just below the highway, and every unidentified piece of flotsam may potentially be an alligator. On the far side of the 20-mile (32km) -wide swamp, you find yourself safely back on terra firma. Louisiana natives draw a distinction between the Prairie Cajuns, who farm the soil of south-central Louisiana, and the Bayou Cajuns, the "half-man, half-gator" shrimp-fishing river-dwellers of the marshlands closer to the Gulf. In terms of what the rest of the world thinks of as being Cajun culture, like the accordion- and fiddle-based Cajun music, or the spicy food, the two are not far apart.

Now crossing alligator land, Atchafalaya Swamp, Louisiana.

BELOW: 'gator in a glade, Atchafalaya.

Lafayette 15 50 miles (80km) west of Baton Rouge, is the largest city in Acadiana, and, standing close to the hypothetical line that divides the prairies from the bayous, makes an ideal hub for exploring the region. It is a sprawling city, but, in addition to a number of excellent restaurant-cum-music-clubs, such as **Prejean's** and **Randol's**, it also holds a couple of entertainingly informative "living museums." The best, Vermilionville (tel: 337-233-4077; Tue–Sun), consists of an idealized village of restored and transplanted 19th-century buildings where experts demonstrate traditional Cajun crafts.

Land of the Cajuns

The Texas border is barely 100 miles (160km) west of Lafayette. but the temptation to explore Cajun country in more depth is liable to prove irresistible, as this is one of the most fascinating and culturally rich areas on the whole route. A short excursion north, for example, leads to the welcoming real-life prairie town of **Eunice**, and to **Opelousas**, home of

Cajun music's blacker, bluesier counterpart, zydeco.

If it's a perfect taste of Acadiana you want, plan on leaving I-10 at exit 109 before you get to Lafayette and visit the delightful town of **Breaux Bridge**, which calls itself the Crawfish Capital of the World and has an almost English feel to it, with its tiny bridge, main street cafés, and antique shops. If you're here on a Saturday morning, don't miss the lively zydeco music and Cajun brunch at the famed **Café Des Amis** (tel: 337-332-5273; daily). Around the corner, on Main Street (State 31), at the **Coffee Break** café (tel: 337-442-6607; daily), there's a freewheeling Cajun jam session that attracts musicians young and old, a great place to pass the time as you load up on java for the drive ahead.

Driving the Jean Lafitte Scenic Byway

More ambitious travelers can continue on a long detour south to pick up State 82 to parallel the more interesting coast along the **Jean Lafitte Scenic Byway**. From Breaux Bridge, State 31

follows Bayou Teche another 11 miles (18km) south to **St Martinville** ⓰, one of the most unspoiled towns you will find in your travels in America. A former indigo plantation and Spanish holding, it was populated by Acadians and Frenchmen in the late 18th and 19th centuries, an era when its culture was so rich that its inhabitants nicknamed it "Petit Paris." After its transformation to a minor port on the bayou, St Martinville settled into its current form of small agrarian center, with visible Cajun and French roots.

Locals are glad to recite half-remembered and half-invented histories in small cafés, which might serve Coca-Cola and catfish *etouffée*. The town is thoroughly infused with the legend of Evangeline (subject of a well-known Henry Wadsworth Longfellow poem), who allegedly walked from Nova Scotia to St Martinville in search of her lover.

The venerable **Evangeline Oak** next to the **St Martin de Tours** church (1765), where she arrived only to receive the news that her faithless sweetheart had married another, is now a riverside beauty spot where Cajun couples hold their wedding services, while the **Longfellow-Evangeline State Commemorative Area** preserves Acadian history in the interesting Acadian House Museum.

South of St Martinville, State 675 and then State 14 will take you west into Vermilion Parish and the attractive parish seat, **Abbeville** ⓱. Home to the Giant Omelette Celebration (www.giantomelette.org) in November, Abbeville consists of three interlocking and very sleepy squares, as well as a couple of oyster restaurants.

Grazing cattle indicate solid ground, but the next field along may be a waterlogged rice paddy through which cranes and herons meticulously pick their long-legged way. Locals fish in the channels that run alongside the roadway, or wade through with shrimping nets.

The farther you go, the fewer signs of human life there are along this bleak and windswept drive, but the birds are a constant source of delight. The trees are bent at ever more acute angles as you approach the Gulf, and in places it

Bayou Teche is 125 miles (200km) long and was once the main tributary of the Mississippi River. Teche is an Indian word meaning "snake."

BELOW:
St Martin de Tours Catholic church.

Spanish moss is found draped over live oak trees. It is not really Spanish nor is it really moss; it is an air plant and a member of the pineapple family.

BELOW: cruising a bayou in a traditional Louisiana wooden boat.

feels as though you're having to force yourself through the thick tangles of Spanish moss that hang from overhead. This wispy, gray, romantic shroud is not a parasite but an epiphyte, an air plant, which draws no sustenance from its host, and is therefore equally at home dangling from telephone wires. Turn on the radio for company, and you'll find French- and English-language stations in equal measure, together with Spanish baseball commentaries from Houston as you come within earshot of that city.

Marsh trail

Seventy-two miles (116km) from Abbeville, highway signs announce that you're arriving in **Grand Chenier**, but apart from a few trailer parks, and a Catholic church surrounded by praying statues, no recognizable town ever appears. Another 30 miles (48km) on, beyond a straggle of run-down motels and rudimentary restaurants catering to workers in the occasionally glimpsed oil refineries, the highway is interrupted by an on-demand platform ferry that shuttles a dozen vehicles at a

time across the outlet of **Lake Calcasieu**. On the far side, the open ocean lies barely 50 yards (46 meters) off to your right, and mighty drilling rigs are visible far out to sea. It's said that early Spanish explorers would beach their vessels here to caulk their hulls with the mysterious black substance found oozing on the beaches; a boon for Louisiana, perhaps, but no incentive for a quick dip at **Holly Beach**. In any case, it's time to turn your wheel back inland. The coastal road ahead has been closed by one Gulf storm too many, and to reach Texas you'll have to head 35 miles (56km) north to rejoin the interstate.

One final highlight remains, however, in the shape of the **Sabine National Wildlife Refuge** ⑱ (tel: 337-762-3816; daily), 9 miles (15km) up State 27. Exhibits in the visitor center and along the Wetland Walkway are a major draw. The trail starts beside the **Intracoastal Waterway** – a mind-boggling canal that spans almost the entire length of the state. The best times of year to see alligators sunning themselves along the Wetland Walkway are spring and fall.

EAST TEXAS TO SAN ANTONIO

Everyone has at least one picture of Texas. Tumbleweeds and cacti, oilfields, cowboy millionaires, humming border towns, cattle ranches: popular culture has disseminated a rugged, romantic vision of the largest of the "lower 48" states. Such familiar cultural snapshots, however, both over- and underestimate the sprawling diversity and vitality of Texas. This *is* where the West begins, but it's a West with no coherent definition. At the risk of oversimplifying, one can think of a passage through Texas as a microcosmic passage from East to West, with the point of transition coming at San Antonio, the westernmost of the state's major cities.

Within the compact urban triangle of Houston, Dallas-Fort Worth, and San Antonio is centered Texas' vast wealth and power. From Galveston through Houston to Austin, the Southern tour arcs through the heart of East Texas – its resort, its port and the state capital. Wherever you go, note the change in the triangular yellow signs that elsewhere in the South advise motorists to "Drive Safely." Here, they read: "Drive Friendly." The name "Texas," after all, is derived from "Tejas," meaning "friendly" – the name given by the Spanish to the American Indians they encountered.

Port Bolivar ferry

From the moment you enter Texas on I-10 from Louisiana, highway signs start to count down the mileage to New Mexico. The magnitude of what lies ahead is clear; shortly after the state line, exit 877 branches off to the town of Orange, and the first sign you'll see for El Paso shows it as an incomprehensible 857 miles (1,379km) distant. The chances are, however, that you'll feel ready to leave this nondescript stretch of highway long before the first city of any size – Houston, 110 miles (177km) in. The best, and most obvious alternative, is to return to the Gulf coast as soon as possible,

and head for the resort community of **Galveston ⑲**.

Halfway to Houston, as you approach exit 829, look out for the billboard that lets drivers know whether the free 20-minute Port Bolivar ferry across Galveston Bay is in operation. Assuming that it is, take the scenic island route to Galveston rather than the straight-shot I-45 from Houston to reach Galveston. Pick up State 124 at Winnie, which runs due south to the ocean. En route, as you cross first Spindletop Bayou and then Elm Bayou, little about this marshy landscape suggests that you've left Louisiana. Rice and even crawfish farms stand on either side of the highway, while indefatigable little oil pumps diligently bob away, atop mounds of scrubby gulf vegetation. About 20 miles (32km) south, a humpback bridge crosses the Intracoastal Waterway at **High Island**. High Island's unique salt-dome geography allows trees to grow that serve as stopovers for thousands of neotropical migratory birds during spring migrations. This tiny hamlet is a birding hotspot with

2008's Hurricane Ike was the third costliest storm in US history, after Hurricanes Andrew and Katrina, doing $28.26 billion of damage in the US alone.

BELOW: the "drowned forests" of Louisiana's swamplands.

BELOW: flock of pelicans flying over wooden beach houses, Galveston.
BELOW RIGHT: dolphin statue, on a Galveston beach.

no less than four bird sanctuaries run by Texas Audubon.

State 87 runs the 27-mile (43-km) length of Bolivar Peninsula to dead-end at the ferry terminal for Galveston. This once was a wild barrier island, a boon for those with a taste for nature in the rough. Sparsely inhabited on its eastern end and growing rapidly into a high-end resort community on its west end, by 2008, Bolivar Peninsula had a permanent population of 3,800 residents and attracted thousands of local vacationers.

All that ended abruptly in September 2008, when Hurricane Ike, a category 2 storm with winds up to 110mph (178kph), made a direct hit on East Galveston, creating a massive storm surge that inundated the Bolivar Peninsula. The destruction on Bolivar was almost total, flattening homes and businesses and blowing debris into Galveston Bay. The historic Bolivar lighthouse, which survived the Great Storm of 1900, was destroyed. By early 2009, the peninsula remained a hushed, haunting, Hiroshima-like landscape covered in sand and rubble.

Residents – many of whom rode out the storm against advice from officials – are determined to rebuild. New construction and For Sale signs are appearing, and the island went ahead with its Mardi Gras celebration in 2009. But it's anyone's guess when the island will come back.

Pirate on the beach

Galveston grew to prominence during the early 1800s as a seaport and headquarters for the pirate Jean Lafitte, of New Orleans fame. In the local economic boom that followed the Civil War, it flowered into a fully fledged city, becoming Texas' leading manufacturing center and, by 1899, the largest cotton port in the world. Galveston had the first telephone system in Texas, the first newspaper, electric lights, golf course, brewery, and Ford dealership, while the Strand (named after the street in London), thanks to its profusion of great commercial houses, was renowned as "The Wall Street of the Southwest."

Houston's port has entirely overshadowed the island's, but Galveston

remains an active shipping center and is heavily involved with the vacation industry. Of its 32 miles (51km) of beach, the most popular stretch lies on the Gulf side of the island, along Seawall Boulevard. This broad thoroughfare is lined on its inland side by numerous sprawling motels and fast-food restaurants, while the beach itself is interrupted by a succession of privately owned piers that jut out into the ocean.

There's lots of family-style entertainment in Galveston. In Downtown, you'll find **Texas Seaport Museum**, featuring the **Tall Ship** *Elissa*, and **Galveston County Historical Museum**, which shows a fascinating movie on the Great Storm of 1900. **Ocean Star Offshore Drilling Rig** has a unique working replica of an offshore oil rig. The **Railroad Museum**, at the foot of the Strand, is located in a looming early 20th-century skyscraper, the former home of American National Insurance Company founded by wealthy Galvestonian William Moody Jr.

Moody's name is associated with several places on the island. On Broadway, the 1895 **Moody Mansion** (tel: 409-762-7668; daily), built in a Romanesque style, was the family home for 50 years. While over on the island's quieter northwest side, a family bequest created **Moody Gardens** (tel: 1-800-582-4673; daily), a 242-acre (98-hectare) educational complex used heavily by Texas schools. It has three themed glass pyramids containing a Rainforest, Aquarium, and a Museum/IMAX theater; landscaped waterfront gardens; and a huge hotel/convention complex.

Old wealth

The historic Strand has undergone the familiar renovation-into-tourist-attraction, arguably losing its soul in the process, but the East End Historical District, bounded roughly by Broadway, Mechanic, 19th and 11th streets, remains unspoiled. Here, Victorian homes stand, intermixed with buildings that betray neoclassical, Renaissance, and Italianate influences. Bungalows rest in the shade cast by oleanders, oaks, maples, and palms and are slightly raised from the

The Tall Ship Elissa, *built in 1877 by Alexander Hall & Co. in Aberdeen, Scotland, is now part of the Texas Seaport Museum in Galveston.*

BELOW: the Moody Gardens educational complex seen from Galveston Bay.

Houston: Space-Age City

Once an oil town, Houston now houses a wide range of high-tech industries and quintessentially Texan self-confidence.

Houston, the nation's fourth largest city, boasts that the first word uttered by the first man on the moon was – you guessed it – "Houston." Mission Control Center is the city's prime tourist attraction. Space Center Houston, the official visitors' center for **Johnson Space Center** (tel: 281-244-2100; daily), is located on NASA Road 1 off I-45, about 25 miles (40km) south of Houston. A guided tram tour takes visitors through a campus of structures containing moon rocks and astronauts, into the Mission Control Center and full-scale replicas of the Space Shuttle used for training. Named for the Sea of Tranquility, the base for the 1969 *Apollo* moonshot, Tranquility Park, in downtown Houston, at Bagby and Walker streets is landscaped to look like Tranquility Base, with craters and mounds, fountains, reflecting pools, and copper tubes representing rockets taking off.

More deserving of the name "Tranquility" is the hushed art temple of **Rothko Chapel** (tel: 713-

524-9839; daily), located on Sul Ross in the Museum District. American abstract expressionist Mark Rothko was commissioned by collectors Dominique and John de Menil to create 14 of his oversized trademark colorwash paintings for this chapel for non-denominational worship and meditation. More of the couple's extensive art collection can be seen at the gorgeous **Menil Collection** (tel: 713-525-9400; Wed–Sun), which houses arts and artifacts of mankind from the earliest days in the Near East to contemporary abstract pieces.

The galleries of Houston show how "black gold" has enriched the state through the purchase of works of art. The Matisse bronzes that turn their backs to you at the **Museum of Fine Arts Houston** (tel: 713-639-7300; Tue–Sun) at Main and Bissonet streets make their case about Houston's attitude toward the norm. The collection is particularly strong in American paintings. Across the street is the **Contemporary Arts Museum Houston** (tel: 713-284-8250; Tue–Sun), dedicated to current works. At Hermann Park is the **Museum of Natural Science** (tel: 713-639-4629; daily), with a walk-through greenhouse aflutter with butterflies.

An emblem of Houston's appreciation for huge size is the unbelievable **Astrodomain**, comprised of the Astrodome stadium (one of the various structures labeled as the "Eighth Wonder of the World"); Astroworld (a 100-ride amusement park); and Astrohall (the world's largest one-level convention facility). The discount booklet CityPass includes entry to eight major Houston attractions, and is widely available. For more information, log on to www.visithoustontexas.com. ❏

LEFT: Johnson Space Center on NASA Parkway.
ABOVE: Houston skyline view from a winding trail in City Park.

ground out of respect for the gulf. Post Office and Church streets are particularly lovely. Several of the town's best contemporary eateries are located on 14th Street. On the corner of Broadway and 14th is **Bishop's Palace** (tel: 409-762-2475; daily), a turreted Gothic fantasy rated as one of the top historic buildings in the US by the American Institute of Architects. It was built for the wealthy Gresham family in 1886 by famed Galveston architect Nicholas Clayton.

From a glance at the map, Galveston appears to lie a full 50 miles (80km) south of Houston. In fact, the build-up to the megalopolis begins as soon as you cross back to the mainland on the I-45 Causeway, to be confronted by massed ranks of smoke-belching oil refineries.

From there on in, strip malls and garish billboards line the interstate for the full 27 miles (43km) up to the Sam Houston Tollway, which circles the entire city at a distance of around 20 miles (32km). As you pass beneath its stacked and spiraling freeways and connecting concrete loops, the futuristic downtown skyline of **Houston** ⓴ *(see page 274)* finally rises on the northern horizon.

Well-sheltered Austin

If you see Texas as a microcosm of the whole country, then it's as you head west of Houston that you leave the South behind and enter the Great Plains. The state capital, **Austin** ㉑, is approximately 150 miles (240km) west, but as I-10 runs directly to San Antonio instead, along a slightly more southerly route, reaching Austin entails at least 40 miles (64km) of driving off the interstate. Whichever route you choose will be much the same, a relaxing cruise through the lush plains and gently rolling hills of the German- and Czech-influenced "ranch country" that lies within the Houston–Dallas–San Antonio triangle. Probably the most bucolic option is to leave I-10 at exit 696, near little Columbus, and join State 71 as it meanders back and forth across the equally sinuous Colorado River (not the one that carved the Grand Canyon) all the way up to Austin.

EAT

Austin's premier barbecue restaurant is the family-run Salt Lick (tel: 512-858-4959), famous for smoked pork ribs, sausage, and brisket from family recipes.

BELOW: night-time view over Austin.

The interfaith Rothko Chapel in Houston is an intimate sanctuary open to all.

Austin itself nestles amid verdant woodland in the middle of an agricultural paradise that's unique among the many Texan climates and terrains. Sheltered from the humid heat that sweeps in waves over Houston, this locale is ideal for ranching and recreation. Unlike Houston, and despite having experienced similarly phenomenal growth, Austin is fairly well contained. Exit between Martin Luther King, Jr. Boulevard and Eighth–Third streets from I-35, and you'll be in the middle of a walkable Downtown. For most visitors, the experience of the city is confined to the area from First Street and the Colorado River up to 24th Street and the heart of the **University of Texas** (UT) at Austin along Guadalupe Avenue.

High tech and outlaws

Austin manages the difficult double act of being not only Texas' political capital but also its true cultural capital.

BELOW: Austin's Sixth Street is for entertainment and shopping trips.

Having attained that distinction during the 1960s, when it was a hippie mecca, it went on to spearhead the "outlaw country" movement of the 1970s, when musicians such as Willie Nelson, Waylon Jennings, and Jerry Jeff Walker first came to prominence. Its reputation as a center for live music and the arts no doubt contributed to its 1980s growth as "the Silicon Valley of Texas," when more and more high-tech and financial firms relocated here. That process, of course, brought with it an influx of young urban professionals, and one need look no farther than **Sixth Street** to see the impact of aggressive consumerism on the culture. Experiencing the same gentrification as San Francisco's Haight Street, formerly gay-dominated Sixth Street is still a good place to bar-hop, but not nearly as much of a community as it used to be. Construction, moreover, has become a constant in Downtown – so much so that locals joke Austin's native bird is the "crane."

Despite its changing face, Austin retains much of its laid-back, tolerant spirit. At the University of Texas –

Detour – Dallas

A 195-mile (314km) drive along I-35 from Austin leads to glittering Dallas. With 1.2 million residents, Dallas attracts visitors with its sky-high architecture, quality art collections, and high-class shopping malls. The city grew up around a cabin built by trapper John Neely Bryan beside the Trinity River, which Bryan believed to be navigable for trade all the way to the Gulf of Mexico. It wasn't, but the Houston and Texas Railroad brought people and commerce soon enough. The pioneer era comes alive at woodsy Dallas Heritage Village, which preserves 38 historic structures in a living history museum. The most extravagant local institution is Neiman Marcus department store, whose Christmas catalog once contained a page entitled "how to spend a million dollars." Fortunately, the penchant for extravagance extends to wonderful art collections, such as the Meadows Museum, home to the largest collection of Spanish art outside Spain. Darker history also plagues Dallas: the most visited site is the former Texas School Book Depository, where Lee Harvey Oswald shot President John F. Kennedy in 1963. The Sixth Floor Museum overlooks Dealey Plaza, where the president was assassinated. Dallas Convention and Visitors Bureau (tel: 214-571-1000; www.visitdallas.com).

with over 50,000 students, the largest university campus in the state – the counter-cultural element will always have its place. At heart, it's still got long hair and a beard, though it might also have a Mercedes, a top-of-the-line road bike, and a kid. Hardly surprising, then, that Austin is home base for **Whole Foods Market**, the natural foods giant whose luxurious new headquarters in Downtown has become a tourist destination in itself, and champion bicyclist Lance Armstrong. Armstrong's own new enterprise – a bike rental shop cum café called **Mellow Johnny's** (tel: 512-473-0222) – is rapidly becoming Austin's hippest hangout.

Austin is the Live Music Capital of the US. Some 200 venues offer everything from hard-edged country, "new music," ska, classical, and blues to R&B and jazz. Theater and literary events are numerous, while good bookstores, record stores, cafés, and Tiffany-glass restaurants intermix with low-down, funkier spots. Above all, local legends have persisted despite the changes – for example, **Scholz Garden**. "The most historic restaurant and beer garden in Texas," Scholz Garden was founded in 1866, 16 years before construction began on the Capitol building. You can find good food here with unpretentious charm and heartfelt – if stumbling – music.

Lone star capitol

Scholz Garden is a few blocks from the **State Capitol** (tel: 512-463-0063; daily tours) and the lower edges of UT, two major sources of business. The Capitol itself is unmistakable, a local pink-granite version of the nation's Capitol in Washington, DC. Its white, classical interior focuses on the great rotunda, commemorating the six governments that reigned supreme over Texas (Spain, France, Mexico, the Confederate States, the United States, and, most proudly, the Republic of Texas). Above, at the apex of the dome, is the lone star that is the state's emblem: independence, self-determination, and singularity.

Just north of the Capitol is the **Bob Bullock Texas State History Museum**

Acoustic band playing at the Continental Club in Austin.

BELOW:
Texas State Capitol building guarded by a Texas Ranger statue.

Exhibit from the LBJ Library, Austin. This part of Texas is full of tributes to the locally born 36th President of the US.

(tel: 512-936-8746; daily), an attractive modern building constructed from the same pink granite as the Capitol. Its soaring atrium contains three floors of well-presented audiovisual exhibits covering Texas's Native American, Spanish, and American history, as well as an IMAX theater.

Hill Country

Historic San Antonio is barely an hour's drive southwest of Austin on I-35, but there's a diverting half-day's sightseeing to be had if you make your way between the two along the **Texas Hill Country Trail** to the west instead. At first, leaving Austin, the "trail" – in reality, US 290 – crosses a somewhat dreary Western landscape of thin grassland.

Beyond **Dripping Springs**, however, which calls itself the "Gateway to the Hill Country" but has nothing more to offer than an ugly stone-clad high school, the road starts to climb through a rich rolling terrain of open meadows, scattered with a delightful profusion of wildflowers. When it reaches **Johnson City** ㉒, 50 miles

(80km) west of Austin, it's undulating through pastoral countryside. Johnson City acquired its name long before local boy Lyndon Baines Johnson became the 36th President of the United States, following the assassination of John F. Kennedy in 1963. However, the downtown birthplace of "LBJ," who shared his initials with his wife Lady Bird Johnson, and the nearby LBJ Ranch in Stonewall, to which they retired after the Vietnam War put an end to his political career, are now part of **Lyndon B. Johnson State Park and Historic Site** (tel: 830-644-2252; bus tours of ranch and birthplace daily).

This very middle-European region must have seemed almost heavenly to early European immigrants, and it's hardly surprising that it attracted hundreds of German settlers during the 19th century. The Main Street of the very touristy town of **Fredericksburg**, another 32 miles (51km) west, for example, is labeled "Haupstrasse" and lined with pseudo-Teutonic beer gardens and bakeries, while numerous German-named farms along the inter-

vening highway, like "Der peach garten," sell German-style wines and liquors.

To get a real feel for the best of the Hill Country, take the lesser State 1376 down to San Antonio. Cutting away south from US 290 just south of the Pedernales River, 4 miles (6km) east of Fredericksburg, this route passes within a few feet of the tiny village of **Luckenbach** ❷, another 4 miles (6km) on. Unless you know where to look, however, you'll miss it altogether; the unmarked turning comes immediately before South Grape Creek. A much-loved ghost town – more of a joke town, really – Luckenbach was bought in its entirety by humorist Hondo Crouch in 1970, and made famous by a No. 1 Country & Western hit, recorded in 1976 by Willie Nelson and Waylon Jennings, that featured the refrain "Let's Go To Luckenbach Texas."

Country music town

Hundreds of country fans now do just that, to while away an afternoon in the bar inside the diminutive post office as the postmaster cracks corny jokes and

sings songs, and perhaps buy a souvenir such as a stuffed armadillo drinking a bottle of Luckenbach beer. Willie Nelson hosts a picnic here on July 4th each year, while most summer weekends there's some sort of large-scale concert in the dancehall. From Luckenbach, State 1376 continues south toward San Antonio by way of some beautiful hills, where you're liable to startle wild deer grazing beside the highway. Ten miles (16km) northeast of the city limits, it meets I-10/US87 at Boerne.

San Antonio ❷ at first seems deceptively pastoral; not far from the interstate, luxurious Italianate villas perch on isolated rocky knobs that look like Tuscan hill towns. Soon enough, however, you're forced to run the gauntlet of manic freeways entailed in reaching every large American city; just before it finally spits you out into Downtown, the interstate for no reason splits alarmingly into two separate highways, one stacked on top of the other.   ❑

Luckenbach musician, Levi Darr, leading a local session.

SAN ANTONIO TO SOUTHERN NEW MEXICO

Davy Crockett and Billy the Kid are only two of the people who left their mark on the lands that border Mexico and the Rio Grande

San Diego

Main attractions
THE ALAMO
BIG BEND NATIONAL PARK
CHINATI FOUNDATION
ALPINE
CHAMIZAL NAT'L MEMORIAL
WHITE SANDS
CLOUDCROFT
MESCALERO APACHE
  INDIAN RESERVATION
LA MESILLA PLAZA
GILA CLIFF DWELLINGS

LEFT: a New Mexico coyote.
BELOW: tribal ceremonial, Gallup.

O f all the major cities in Texas, El Paso and San Antonio are the oldest. El Paso began as the first Spanish mission in the future state, while it was in San Antonio that American Texas was born and nearly slaughtered by the Mexicans at the Alamo. Stretching between the two is the vast expanse of **Trans-Peco Texas**, a largely barren yet subtly beautiful mountainous desert. There is a timeless quality to the landscape that stands in marked contrast to the booming spectacle of the metropolitan east.

In the anchor cities, Hispanic culture consistently revitalizes itself much more effectively than in Galveston, Houston or Austin. El Paso and adjoining Ciudad Juárez are bound as a Mexican/American metropolis, a popular gateway to the American Southwest.

Cradle of Texas liberty

San Antonio ㉔, the "Cradle of Texas Liberty," was the Spanish capital of Texas before Mexico won its independence from Spain in 1821. Mexico was essentially an absentee landlord. It began opening the territory of New Spain to settlement by anyone who would develop the land, including immigrants from the fledgling United States. American Stephen F. Austin, whose father Moses had received a land grant from Spain in 1820, inherited it and, in 1822, led a group dubbed the Old Three Hundred to settle Los Brazos River. Before Austin's pilgrim-

age, there were 3,500 persons of European descent in San Antonio and La Bahia. By 1836, 30,000 Anglos, 5,000 black slaves, and 4,000 Mexicans populated Texas.

In the late 1860s, when Spaniards first came to the San Antonio River Valley, which cradles modern San Antonio, they found it occupied by the Payaya Indians, hunters who supplemented their catches with the fruits of the pecan and mesquite trees and prickly pear cactus. The Payaya cooperated readily with the Europeans, but

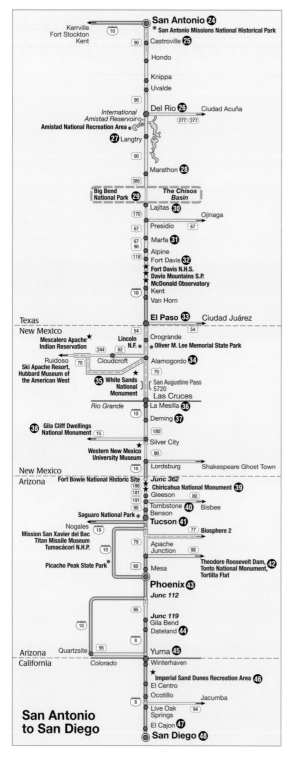

San Antonio to San Diego

the Apache, who controlled the plains to the north, took more convincing, and the nomadic Comanche were always a threat.

Intent on securing their claims in the area and on taming the godless heathens, the Spanish established a military barracks, or *presidio*, and a mission on the west bank of the San Antonio River in 1718. Mission San Antonio de Valero, later known as **The Alamo** (tel: 210-225-1391; daily), was relocated to the east bank. By 1793, San Antonio de Valero had been secularized. Mexican troops were transferred to San Antonio to protect the pueblo that had grown around the riverbanks. Renamed *El Alamo* (the Cottonwood), it became a crucial fortification.

The infamy of the converted mission arises from an ill-conceived standoff with the forces of Mexican president General Antonio Lopez de Santa Anna, the self-styled "Napoleon of the West," on March 6, 1836. Mexico's 5,000 troops were met by 187 (or 186, depending on who you ask) "Texian" martyrs-to-be. In the words of memorializer Frank J. Davis, "All dead within one sanguinary hour; yet the heroes of the Alamo are deathless."

Remember the Alamo

"Remember the Alamo!" was adopted as the Texan battle cry, and revenge came swiftly. Seven weeks later, Santa Anna was defeated in a mere 18 minutes at the Battle of San Jacinto, whereupon the Texas Revolution culminated with the declaration of the newly independent Republic of Texas.

Riddled though it is with as many contradictions as bullet holes, the Alamo, preserved with four other lesser-known missions as **San Antonio Missions National Historical Park** (tel: 210-932-1001; daily), is an essential destination. Its defenders during the battle were, after all, recent arrivals from foreign countries that included England, Ireland, Scotland, even Denmark – as well as the United States – while their 26-year-old commander,

William B. Travis from South Carolina, wrote three days before he died that "the citizens of this municipality are all our enemies."

Davy Crockett

His associates included opportunists such as Jim Bowie, remembered for his namesake knife (though the museum here can only rustle up one of his less-celebrated spoons), and the legendary Davy Crockett, a three-term Congressman from Kentucky who sought his fortune in the West after the evaporation of his presidential ambitions. The independent Texas for which they fought and died survived just nine years before being subsumed by the United States.

A plaque on the front door of the graffiti-etched **Alamo Shrine**, originally the mission's chapel, requests "Be quiet friend, here heroes died to blaze a trail for other men." Most visitors focus on taking photos of the famous exterior of the shrine, then repair first to the lovely garden, shaded by everything from myrtles to a mescal bean tree, then the all-important

souvenir shop. On sale are such reverent mementos as Alamo mugs, belts, patches, playing cards, pencils, plaques, postcards, dishware, license-plate frames, pins, coasters, caps, tote-bags, and erasers.

A river runs through it

Though San Antonio is in truth an enormous desert city, you'd never know it as you amble along the lively, pedestrianized **Paseo del Rio**, or River Walk, an inspired tourist attraction that has done wonders for the rough-around-the-edges Downtown. A highly original and elegantly simple concept, River Walk was instigated in 1939 as part of Franklin Roosevelt's New Deal. The plan called for confining the San Antonio River into a tight and very narrow little channel as it loops through the city center, paving and landscaping both banks, and garnishing them liberally with restaurants, patio cafés, stores, and gardens.

River Walk stands roughly 10ft (3 meters) lower than the busy Downtown streets. Flat-bottomed cruise boats ply gently along the river itself,

Mural along the River Walk in San Antonio.

BELOW: the Alamo, symbol of the Republic of Texas.

BELOW: San Antonio's River Walk at night-time.

and at night, in particular, when it's all low-lit, the effect is magical. There's even an open-air theater, the ingenious **Arneson River Theatre**, where the stage is arranged on one side of the river while the audience watches from a stucco Spanish-style amphitheater of benches on the opposite bank.

Downtown San Antonio holds several other worthwhile attractions. The beautifully restored **Spanish Governor's Palace** (tel: 210-224-0601; daily), a tranquil gem, is located near the original site of Spain's Presidio de Bexar (1722), the **Plaza de Armas**, where a sign notes that in the Republican era (1836–45), the grounds had already become a busy market teeming with "noisy vendors of vegetables, fresh eggs, chili peppers, and live chickens…."

UTSA Institute of Texan Cultures (tel: 210-458-2300; Tue–Sun), in Hemisfair Park, takes an entertaining look at the many different peoples, from Comanches to Czechs, who have contributed to the cosmopolitan blend of modern Texas. There's also a glorious evocation of the cowboy past; one early African-American *vaquero* is quoted as saying "we loved to work cattle so much we'd just be sittin' around cryin' for daylight to come."

Miles, mesas and mountains

It's an exhausting 500-mile (800km) long-haul between San Antonio and El Paso, not recommended as a one-day drive. It's quickest and easiest to stick to I-10, which plots a northerly course across the barren plains. But you'll get a better feel for the desolate border country by taking US 90 right out of San Antonio and heading south toward Del Rio, where the legendary Rio Grande forms the US-Mexico border. Plan on taking two or three days and exploring the dusty backcountry that lies to the south of the interstate such as the artsy Big Bend towns in the Alpine-Marathon-Marfa-Fort Davis quadrangle and nearby Big Bend National Park, one of the country's most remote yet stunning national parks.

As you leave San Antonio, there's a parched quality to roadside grasslands that presages desiccation ahead. At

first, however, agriculture maintains a foothold. Historic **Castroville** ㉕, 15 miles (24km) along on US 90, proclaims itself to be "The Little Alsace of Texas," and has several Alsatian restaurants. **Hondo** just beyond feels like the Great Plains, with huge fields of corn and wheat, while **Knippa** – "Go Ahead and Blink, Knippa is Bigger than You Think" – is devoted to stone quarrying.

There's more going on in **Uvalde**. It has an excellent bird sanctuary and its own small river walk. The Great Depression hit Southwest Texas pretty badly, but Uvalde was fortunate to have President Franklin Roosevelt's vice president, John Garner, as a hometown boy. The 1920 **John Nance Garner Home and Museum** contains Garner's papers and effects. Among Garner's local projects were **Garner State Park**, a riverfront park created in 1941 by the Civilian Conservation Corps (CCC), and the **Aviation Museum at Garner Field**, a World War II training base that displays old bombers and other aircraft.

The Rio Grande

By now, you've almost certainly logged your first sighting of the US Border Patrol, an ever-vigilant presence. Across most of Texas, the desert makes a far more effective barrier against illegal entrants from Mexico than does the Rio Grande. Rather than monitor every inch of the river, therefore, Border Patrol simply erects roadblocks along the few highways that lead away from it; be sure to have citizenship papers in hand at all times.

Past Uvalde, US 90 dwindles to a single lane in either direction. **Del Rio** ㉖ itself comes as an anticlimax; it's home to the large Laughlin Air Force base, and any number of shopping malls catering to daytrippers from the adjacent Mexican town of **Ciudad Acuña**, but apart from a couple of 19th-century buildings, there's not much to divert tourists.

A further 12 miles (19km) northwest, **Amistad National Recreation Area** (tel: 830-775-7491; daily), the

"third-largest international man-made lake in the world," was created by the completion of Amistad Dam, a huge curving wall of concrete jointly dedicated by the presidents of the US and Mexico in 1969. Above this point, the Rio Grande is officially designated as a "Wild and Scenic River," but you won't get any glimpses of the "wild" river until you reach Langtry and beyond in Big Bend.

Another 30 miles (48km) northwest, the highest highway bridge in Texas crosses the deep gorge of the Pecos River, just before its confluence with the Rio Grande. The stern "No Diving From Bridge" signs seem somewhat superfluous, but it's worth stopping to admire this first of the many western canyons, to come and, to envy the eagles and falcons that soar so majestically above it.

Beyond the Pecos, there's no longer any doubt that you've reached true desert, while confirmation that you're in the Wild West soon comes with your arrival in **Langtry** ㉗. This semi ghost town was home to Judge Roy Bean, a storekeeper who was appointed Justice of the Peace here in 1882. Known as the

The hand-operated Los Ebanos Ferry is the last of its kind on the Rio Grande.

BELOW:
morning on the big border river – the Rio Grande is known as the Rio Bravo in Mexico.

British actress Lily Langtry, for whom it's said the eccentric Judge Roy Bean named the tiny Texas town of Langtry.

"Law West of the Pecos," Judge Bean exacted swift frontier justice, despite an ignorance of all legal matters. His saloon-cum-courtroom, a hundred yards shy of the dry-as-bones canyon of the **Rio Grande**, is now a tiny state-run museum and information center. A dusty store offers lukewarm coffee and snacks. Take advantage: this is the only available sustenance in the 120 empty miles (193km) between Langtry and Marathon.

Until you come to **Marathon ㉘**, you've added time but no extra mileage to your trip by taking US 90 rather than I-10. This is where you'll have to decide whether to detour down to Big Bend – a decision best contemplated after a night in the luxury of the restored **Gage Hotel**, the first really appealing accommodation since San Antonio.

Bears and mountain lions

It would be hard to recommend **Big Bend National Park ㉙** (tel: 432-477-2370; daily) too highly. For maximum effect, the 40-mile (64km) drive south to the park entrance on US 385 is best done at sunset or early morning, when the long shadows play over a landscape as entrancing as Shangri La. You head straight toward a mysteriously misty wall of mountains, centering on one giant pyramidal peak, only to shimmy around them at the last minute to find yourself confronted by another equally alluring range on the horizon.

Once inside the park, watch for the small and cute desert boar known as javelinas crossing the road: they have very poor eyesight. Thirty more miles (48km) brings you to the main visitor center, an essential information stop, and one of only two places in this vast park where you can fill up with gas during business hours. The prime destination, the **Chisos Basin**, lies another 12 miles (19km) beyond. A glorious dead-end road – too narrow for large RVs – climbs steeply into the park's central cluster of mountains. Tall yucca plants stand sentry as the road picks its way through a labyrinth of towering rocks, where eye-popping pink-blossomed cacti and other desert succulents dot talus slopes. Finally, you drop down a succession of hairpin bends into the basin itself, a grassy bowl ringed by mountains that holds the park's lodge, campground, and general store. This is bear and mountain lion country, so you may prefer to stay close to your motel-style room, but even in these there's a risk you'll find a rattlesnake coiled on your doorstep. The highest elevation in the park, Chisos Basin is the park's premier hiking area. From the campground, a superb hike takes you on a 4.4-mile (7km) round-trip trail to the **Window**, a gap in the mountains with views across an eerie desert landscape of buttes and mesas.

River-rafting trips

State 170 west of the park, the **River Road**, is one of Texas' most attractive highways – a rare opportunity to drive along the Rio Grande in all its glory. It reaches the river 17 miles (27km) south of the Terlingua/Study Butte

turn-off, at the small resort of **Lajitas** ➌, which specializes in river-rafting trips through high-walled Santa Elena Canyon into the park. For 50 miles (80km) from Lajitas, the River Road sticks close to the river, sometimes scrambling over high sandstone outcrops, at other times meandering through well-watered fields. Cattle can often be seen grazing in Chihuahua, Mexico, and in several places the river is shallow enough for them to wade across. There's another chance to cross into Mexico at **Presidio**, where **Ojinaga** on the far side holds a couple of seafood restaurants plus cut-rate opticians and pharmacies.

Big Bend country

From Presidio, a 61-mile (98km) drive north on US 67 returns you to US 90 at **Marfa** ➊. The ranch town is celebrated as the location for the 1956 movie **Giant** – James Dean, Elizabeth Taylor, and other stars took over Downtown's charming **El Paisano** hotel as headquarters. In the 1970s, Marfa gained a new kind of fame when the late New York-born artist Donald Judd began installing overscaled art projects in historic buildings around town. Judd's legacy is now safeguarded by the **Chinati Foundation** (tel: 432-729-4362), which offers twice-daily tours by reservation to installations. The town has become a haven for hip East Coast urban artists, many of whom have sensitively restored historic buildings for art galleries, eateries, bookstores, even a local public radio station. The wail of locomotives flying through town is often the only sound in this quiet West Texas backwater.

There's more art and a greater selection of restaurants and lodgings in the small college town of **Alpine**, 25 miles (42km) east of Marfa. The excellent little **Museum of the Big Bend** on the campus of Sul Ross State University (tel: 432-837-8730; Tue–Sun) has exhibits on the natural and cultural history of the Big Bend area.

State 17 heads north of Marfa to **Fort Davis** ➋, in the Davis Mountains. **Fort Davis National Historic Site** is the best-preserved 19th-century fort in the West. It's linked to **Davis Mountains State Park**, a pretty valley

Marfa is known for its mysterious colored lights, which appear nightly west of town, moving, splitting apart, and twinkling. Residents think they are UFOs but scientists suspect they are a phenomenon similar to a mirage caused by the interaction of cold and warm air that bends the light. View the lights from an attractive roadside viewing building, 9 miles (14km) east of Marfa.

BELOW:
backpackers on a Big Bend trail.

with lovely oak-shaded campgrounds. From here, it's a beautiful drive through the mountains on State 118 to pick up I-10 again at Kent, passing right by the entrance to **McDonald Observatory**, one of the largest astronomical observatories in the world.

Border town

Once on 1-10, it's roughly two and a half hours to El Paso, gaining an hour as you enter Mountain Time. On the way, you will pass through **Van Horn**, an historic crossroads of the old Bankhead Highway and the Old Spanish Trail. **El Paso** ㉝, a gritty, working-class city of 600,000, which spreads around the base of the Franklin Mountains, lies in the oldest European-settled area of Texas. In the 16th century, Spaniards first crossing the Rio Grande to explore their territories in New Mexico headed along El Paso del Norte – the Pass of the North – which sent the river through a break in the mountain ranges. Soon the trading route of El Camino Real (The Royal Road) was extended from south of Chihuahua City, Mexico, to what is now Santa Fe, New Mexico, by conquistador Juan de Oñate.

When the Spanish colonists were driven out of Santa Fe by the Pueblo Indian Revolt of 1680, a dispirited column of refugees regrouped here, around an adobe Franciscan mission they called Ysleta del Sur, whose founder, Fray Garcia, is commemorated in Downtown's Pioneer Plaza with a 14ft (4-meter) statue by internationally known sculptor David Houser.

It took 12 years before the Spaniards reconquered New Mexico, during which time the towns of Ysleta and El Paso had sprung up around the mission. El Paso gradually absorbed Ysleta, but was itself split in two after the designation of the Rio Grande as the United States–Mexico border. The US city remained El Paso and the Mexican city was dubbed Ciudad Juárez. El Paso's strategic location has made it a travelers' stop for centuries. The Gold Rush '49ers passed through on their way to fortune in California. Refugees, desperados, and tourists have all met here. Today, it is best known as a major gateway to Mexico (*see Mexico Detour box, below*).

TIP

Daytrippers to Ciudad Juárez will do better to walk across one of the three footbridges to Mexico. Driving across the border requires the purchase of additional Mexican insurance.

BELOW RIGHT: Our Lady of Guadalupe Mission, Ciudad Juárez, Mexico.

Detour – Mexico

Ciudad Juárez, across the bridge from El Paso, Texas, is probably the most interesting Mexican border town outside of Tijuana, south of San Diego. But whereas San Diego is sleek and efficient, confirming the US's superior grasp of the modern world, the difference between El Paso and Ciudad Juárez is definitely in Mexico's favor. El Paso is a rather desolate, depressing city, whereas Juárez, the biggest city in the state of Chihuahua, is vibrant and colorful. Bullfights and bright souvenirs make a strong impression right away, as does lush Chamizal Park, a counterpart to El Paso's memorial. Juárez Museum of History, occupying a dazzling historic building, traces the area's development, with special attention paid to the Mexican Revolution and the Mexican hero Pancho Villa. Our Lady of Guadalupe Mission explores the rich religious tapestry of the country. Juárez's food is wonderful and spicy, but don't drink the water, or eat ice cream or ice cubes. It's certainly worth a day trip to experience another country, but make sure you have all valid documents: a passport or proof of citizenship with photo and a green card to re-enter the US, if necessary. If you stay in Mexico more than 72 hours, or travel beyond the border zone (La Frontera), you'll need a Tourist Card, available at the border.

Dust devils and tumbleweed

Much of El Paso's commemorated history invokes gunfights, with the notorious Marshall Dallas Stoudenmire and John Wesley Hardin on many a winning end before finally biting the dust. There's a lot of dust to bite. El Paso's climate is singularly dry, although rain is not unknown. The city is uniformly beige in look and feel. Its shanty dwellings clinging to barren hillsides have more in common with nearby Mexico than the United States.

El Paso is an inexpensive city but there's little here to justify it as a destination. Tourism is mainly channeled to its environs and up to **Ranger Peak** in the Franklin Mountains. The **Tigua Indian Reservation**, a living pueblo of the oldest identifiable Indian tribe in Texas, is on the eastern edge of the city, while **Ysleta Mission**, one of three 17th–19th-century missions in El Paso restored and run by The Mission Trail Foundation (tel: 915-851-9997; daily tours), is in the Ysleta neighborhood in western El Paso. **Fort Bliss Military Reservation**, in the northeast, is the site of the largest Air Defense School in the "free world," and also home to the **National Border Patrol Museum** (tel: 915-759-6060; Tue–Sat), a monument to the US's constant search for secure borders.

Cross-cultural relations

The Rio Grande is more of a fortified moat than a river in El Paso, but its political role as the natural boundary between Mexico and the US is important. That interesting story is told well at **Chamizal National Memorial** (tel: 915-532-7273; daily), a little-known unit of the National Park System overlooking the river. The memorial was established to commemorate the Chamizal Convention of 1963, a milestone in diplomatic relations between Mexico and the United States, which resulted in the peaceful settlement of a century-long boundary dispute. It wholeheartedly celebrates Mexico, with art and museum exhibits, regular cul-

tural performances such as folkloric dance and mariachi music, and thoughtful ranger talks. For visitors in town for just a few hours, it's a safe way of experiencing a little of Mexico's infectious *Viva La Vida*, especially if you have neither the time nor the inclination to cross into Mexico itself.

El Paso – notorious as one of the weakest links in the "Tortilla Curtain" between the United States and Mexico – has a decidedly uneasy, schizophrenic relationship with its sister city across El Rio. That friction has been exacerbated by a recent rapid escalation in drug-related gun violence and crime in Ciudad Juárez, prompting the US Consulate in Mexico to issue a Travel Alert to travelers. Since January 2008 more than 1,800 people – some of them innocent bystanders caught in crossfire – have been killed in the city of 1.6 million, and more than 17,000 car thefts and 1,650 carjackings have been reported.

A major symbol of the tension between the US and Mexico is the construction of a 670-mile (1,078km) -long fence along the US-Mexico border – a $2.6 billion, 18ft (5-meter)

Only a bridge over the Rio Grande separates El Paso, Texas, and Mexico's Ciudad Juárez.

BELOW: corner café in a Mexican border town.

BELOW: the New Mexico Museum of Space History tells the story of the international space race.

-high, steel-and-mesh behemoth that passes straight through neighborhoods in El Paso, blocking the view of Mexico and invoking the Berlin Wall. The fence has been an effective barrier to illegal entry. Once, some 2,000 illegal aliens per day were caught and repatriated, but that figure has dwindled to almost nothing these days.

Still, with thousands of people crossing the border on the city's three foot and road bridges daily, it can feel decidedly like running the gauntlet of Checkpoint Charlie to simply enjoy a day out in Mexico. Weigh the risks against the many pleasures of a quick visit: the vast majority of Mexican citizens are hard-working, law-abiding, and hospitable people, equally terrorized by violence, whose livelihood from tourism on La Frontera is being seriously undermined by a tiny minority. Expect a high military presence in Juárez: thousands of troops have been sent in by the Mexican government in a major crackdown.

NEW MEXICO

Exiting El Paso, US 54 east skirts the eastern slopes of the Franklin Mountains. New Mexico arrives, with the minimum of ceremony, 10 miles (16km) out of El Paso, at which point US 54 contracts to a two-lane undivided highway with virtually no services the entire 83-mile (134km) stretch to Alamogordo and the Tularosa Valley.

New Mexico is among the youngest US states (the 47th admitted to the Union), but it has one of the longest histories. At its eastern edge, near Clovis, archeologists have dug up beautifully carved arrowheads dating back 12,000 years. By the time the first Spanish *conquistadores* reached the valley of the Rio Grande, in 1540, the Rio Grande Valley held some 150 separate villages, or *pueblos,* each home to a distinct clan-based group specializing in certain handicrafts and trade items. The Spaniards named the infant colony New Mexico in the misplaced hope that it might yield similar treasures to the Aztec empire of Mexico.

By the late 16th century, *El Camino Real* (now US 85) extended along the Rio Grande from Mexico to Santa Fe, site of the oldest government building in North America and the oldest US capital. However, although New Mexico covered an area far greater than the modern state, including all of modern Arizona and much of Nevada, California, and Utah, until the Yankees arrived in 1846 it remained an impoverished provincial backwater, whose farmers had to battle against not only the unforgiving desert environment but also Navajo, Apache, and Comanche raiders.

Under American rule, New Mexico has attended to its somewhat mundane motto: *Crescit Eunde* ("It grows as it goes"). Railroading, ranching, and mining have all thrived on the state's rocky surface, warm valleys, and subterranean waters. A deliberate US policy during World War II of siting defense installations in remote landlocked locations has also brought unexpected dividends. It was in New Mexico that scientists developed and tested the first atomic bombs, and

military facilities continue to play a major part in the state's economy. New Mexico is sparsely populated by approximately 1.9 million people, roughly 16 per sq mile (6 per sq km), most of them clustered in the major cities of Albuquerque, Santa Fe, and Las Cruces. Among its notable residents have been sworn enemies Pat Garrett and Billy the Kid, "king of the innkeepers" Conrad Hilton, novelist D.H. Lawrence, artist Georgia O'Keeffe and firefighting legend Smokey Bear.

New Mexico's affecting natural beauty and mesmerizing landscape have captivated all who come here, from prehistoric Indians, via generations of Hispanics, to modern new-age tourists drawn to cities such as Santa Fe, Albuquerque, and Taos. Even little green men from outer space seem to love it here; supposedly drawn by the first signs of mankind's nuclear capability, they've been flocking to places such as Roswell ever since.

Apaches and settlers

As you drive the gorge between the Organ Mountains to the west and the Hueco Mountains to the east, you nick the edge of **White Sands Missile Range**. Roadside signs warn of unexploded ammunition lying in the desert, and advise you not to leave the highway. Just south of Alamogordo, in the Sacramento Mountain foothills, is **Oliver M. Lee Memorial State Park**, named for a state legislator with a colorful past. An immaculate 50-site campground makes a good base to explore scenic Dog Canyon and Lee's ranch, once the largest in New Mexico.

After all that emptiness, **Alamogordo ③④** itself feels positively urban. It's actually a small desert town – 35,500 on the 2000 census – but counting among its population international rocket scientists, astronomers, and military brass, it has a sophistication all its own. Alamogordo is built atop a large 11th-century Indian pueblo that was abandoned in the 1300s when a long drought and Apache raiding made life too difficult. Earlier, the Jornada branch of the Mogollon culture left behind some 21,000 extraordinary petroglyphs, or incised rock art, on basaltic boulders at **Three Rivers**

Bright and shiny customized Harley-Davidson.

BELOW: the courthouse where Billy the Kid was sentenced is now a gift shop. **BELOW LEFT:** Apache crown dancer.

BELOW: the Southern New Mexico Ski Apache resort is located on the Mescalero Apache Indian Reservation.

Petroglyph Site, north of Alamogordo, many of which have, sadly, now been defaced. The Mogollon were the first to learn farming, pottery, and masonry architecture from Mexico. They were subsumed into the more powerful Ancestral Pueblo (Anasazi) trading culture to the north by AD 1000.

Spaniards passed through, naming the valley for its "fat" (gordo) cottonwood trees. They settled on the Tularosa River and founded a presidio and mission in 1719 at **La Luz**, but Apache raiding soon forced them to move on. The arrival of the US Army at **Fort Stanton** in 1855 was the beginning of the end for Apache warriors. In the 1880s, they were forced to make peace and move to a reservation at nearby Ruidoso, allowing Anglo settlement in the Tularosa Basin.

In 1898, C.B. and John A. Eddy founded Alamogordo as a stop on their railroad line. Seduced by the forested valley and its commercial potential for lumber, the Eddys sold the railroad and settled down in Alamogordo to make their fortune from indigenous resources. Alamogordo grew as a trade center, but the development of White Sands Proving Ground and nearby Holloman Air Force Base radically recast the contours of the city. In the words of one local historian, "No longer was it a sleepy, peaceful land of *mañana* [tomorrow], but a hustling, bustling, fast-growing city."

Today, Alamogordo is dominated by the high-tech weaponry community. It also harbors a tribute to the peaceful uses of technology in the exploration of space, in the shape of the **New Mexico Museum of Space History** (tel: 505-437-2840; daily), standing prominently on the foothills at the edge of the valley. This well-conceived museum chronicles the international race for the stars, featuring a "Hall of Fame" of pioneers in space exploration, from early dreamers to the moon-walking astronauts of NASA's *Apollo* missions. After admiring space shuttle models, a lunar TV camera and samples of foods brought aboard *Apollo* and *Skylab* missions (eg canned vanilla ice cream and dehydrated peach ambrosia), you can watch a video presentation of highlights from the *Apollo* 11, 12, and 14 moon landings.

Cool forests and sunspots

In summer, the 12,000ft (3,657-meter) Sacramento Mountains, east of Alamogordo, provide welcome relief from the 100°F (37.7°C) heat of the plains, attracting visitors from southeastern New Mexico and west Texas. Scenic US 82 climbs abruptly from 4,350ft (1,325 meters) at Alamogordo to almost 9,000ft (2,740 meters) to reach **Cloudcroft** in Lincoln National Forest just 20 miles (32km) later. Hiking, cross-country skiing, and camping are popular in the cool, piney national forest.

The quaint alpine village of Cloudcroft is known for its rental log cabins and hiking trails. Historic **Cloudcroft Lodge**, built in 1899 in the Bavarian style, is a must-see: it even has a resident ghost. Sixteen miles (26km) south of Cloudcroft, in tiny Sunspot, is the **National Solar Observatory and Apache Point Observatory** (tel: 505-

434-7190; May–Oct daily). Take a Saturday tour to find out how astronomers safely view the sun, using telescopes like the Dunn Solar Telescope, a rotating instrument that rises 330ft (100 meters) from a subterranean chamber.

Just north of Cloudcroft is the **Mescalero Apache Indian Reservation**. A 28-mile (45km) drive through the reservation on State 244 passes through bucolic scenery, with shimmering little lakes and flower-filled meadows, and Apache cowboys riding the range. Any notions you may have of Indian reservations as desolate or depressing places will evaporate. See if you can catch a rodeo in July.

The Mescalero are prosperous entrepreneurs; while parts of the reservation are closed to outsiders, the tribe operates successful commercial enterprises on adjoining lands. These include the region's grand resort, the recently rebuilt **Inn of the Mountain Gods**, which shares its lovely lakeside setting with glitzy **Casino Apache**. The tribe's luxury winter-sports venue, **Ski Apache**, is set above busy little **Ruidoso**, home to Ruidoso Downs racetrack and **Hub-**

bard **Museum of the American West** (tel: 505-378-4142; daily), an affiliate of the Smithsonian. From Ruidoso, US 70 drops back down to the Tularosa Valley to tribal headquarters at **Mescalero**, best known for its restored 1939 **St Joseph Apache Mission**. From here, Alamogordo is 46 miles (74km).

Blinding white gypsum

Taking the optional detour described above, you'll enjoy mountain-top views of the most spectacular feature of the region: **White Sands National Monument ㉟**. Located 15 miles (24km) southwest of Alamogordo, this stunning 144,458-acre (58,505-hectare) expanse is made up of gypsum sand blown in between the San Andreas and Sacramento mountain ranges and deposited as shifting dunes on this corner of the otherwise off-limits White Sands Missile Range. The only access road, US 70–82, is regularly closed for up to two hours at a time so that military personnel can drive their strange top-secret cargoes along it in peace; inquire at local visitor centers before you set off. As you approach White

Would-be cowboys should visit the Hubbard Museum of the American West in Ruidoso.

BELOW: White Sands National Monument.

Sierra Blanca is the highest peak in Southern New Mexico at 12,005ft (3,659 meters).

BELOW: Trinity Site monument marking the location of the first atomic bomb test.

Sands, you may see eerie V-shaped stealth jets silently speeding through brilliant blue skies, as the glowing dunes rise from the base of the San Andreas Mountains.

The historic visitor center has wonderful Pueblo-style historic architecture and is a good place to pick up information before taking the 16-mile (26km) paved scenic drive that loops through the dunes. The deeper it penetrates into the heart of White Sands, the more the road surface is obscured by drifts of gypsum sand. The effect is both disorienting and remarkable. Gypsum is one of the most common compounds found on earth, but it's rarely seen on the surface because it dissolves readily in water. Surface sand elsewhere is almost always composed of quartz.

At midday, the sands are a blinding, pure white, reflecting so strongly they sting the naked eye. As you clamber over the dunes, occasionally pocked by the slither marks and pawprints of nocturnal wanderers, periodically remove your sunglasses to appreciate the hallucinatory expanse fully. As the afternoon cedes to evening, the sands refract the light, breaking it down into a rainbow. The park is open until 10pm, a good time to hunker down quietly and hope to see some of the 500 different animals that populate the dunes, from coyotes and roadrunners to owls and skunks. There is also a sparse scattering of beautiful plant life, including the hedgehog cactus with its brilliant red flowers.

Concealed amid the roadless wastes to the north, **Trinity Site** is the awesome crater that was created in July 1945, when the United States detonated the first atomic bomb. Public access to this sobering site is only permitted on the first Saturdays in April and October, when convoys of vehicles set off from an inconspicuous gateway north of Alamogordo. Check with the town's visitor center for details.

The Wild West

US 70 southwest slowly but surely rises out of the Tularosa Valley toward Las Cruces. For almost 30 miles (48km), as you head straight toward the sheer wall of the San Andreas range, a route through these mottled peaks seems like an impossibility. Eventually, the highway jinks to the right and climbs to its apex at **San Augustine Pass**, 5,720ft (1,740 meters) high and overlooking the valley that holds Las Cruces. Summiting the pass, you plunge down an exhilarating 3-mile (5km) slope to find yourself back in the beautiful low valley of the Rio Grande, where greens and browns evolve through shades and mixtures below the pearly blue peaks in the distance.

The route briefly engages **Las Cruces** before hooking into I-10 to Deming. Las Cruces – "the crosses" – acquired its name in 1830, after a caravan of travelers coming from Taos were ambushed and slaughtered, and white crosses were erected to mark their graves. Las Cruces is a typically unruly mix of subdivisions and malls around an unremarkable Downtown, but it's now New Mexico's fastest-growing city. The regenerated Downtown offers two good art museums: the **Branigan Cultural**

Center (tel: 505-541-2155; daily) and **Museum of Fine Arts and Culture** (tel: 505-541-2155; Tue–Sun). Its most interesting attraction may be the **New Mexico Farm & Ranch Museum** (tel: 505-522-4100; daily), on the outskirts of town. Highlighting 3,000 years of farming and ranching in the area, Spanish churro sheep, burros, longhorn cattle, and other traditional livestock are kept on the grounds. Demonstrations of weaving, candle making, and other pioneer skills are presented regularly.

The lovely town of **La Mesilla ㊱**, a short hop from downtown Las Cruces on State 28 and State 292 (Motel Boulevard), attracts the most tourism in the area. Its restored historic **Plaza**, dominated by an old gazebo, evokes the color and sounds of Old Mexico. This was where the Gadsden Purchase was sealed in 1854, establishing the current boundaries of Mexico and the United States, while a gift store in one corner was originally the courthouse where the notorious outlaw Billy the Kid was tried and sentenced to hang for murder in 1881. The Kid managed to escape before his hanging, but subsequently met his maker at the hands of Pat Garrett, near Fort Sumner; Garrett was himself murdered near Las Cruces in 1908. Vendors create a Mexican *mercado* (market) atmosphere and will be happy to sell you rugs, pottery, Indian jewelry, ceramics, and other souvenirs. One of Mesilla's most important annual events is April's **Border Book Festival**. Founded by renowned Hispanic author Denise Chavez, it highlights the rich literature of the borderlands and is headquartered in the **Cultural Center of Mesilla** bookshop (tel: 505-523-3988; Fri–Sun), a former Mexican garrison dating to the 1840s. Look for the **Double Eagle Restaurant**, set in a registered historic building and filled with antiques, and have a drink in its elegant Imperial Bar.

Across the Great Divide

A short distance out of Las Cruces on I-10 west, a double ribbon of landscaped orchards lines the narrow Rio Grande, which flows here from its source in Colorado by way of Taos and Albuquerque. Beyond the shallow sandy ridge on the far side, the highway levels

Billy the Kid's tombstone in Fort Sumner, New Mexico.

BELOW: La Mesilla town square.

BELOW: Gila Cliff Dwellings National Monument.

out to cross the windblown chapparal of Luna County, where more and more specimens of the ostrich-like state plant, the yucca, scrutinize travelers as they make their way westward. From here to the Arizona state line, freeway exits are commonly lined with frontier-style outlets for supposedly characteristic goods. Behind false facades spring a trading post, Wild West town or tepee where moccasins, cactus jelly, and plant candy are available to tourists.

Fifty-six miles (90km) out of Las Cruces, in New Mexico's "bootheel," is the truck-stop town of **Deming** ❸❼, encircled by four short mountain ranges. Deming was of great strategic importance to railroad magnate Charles Crocker, who joined his Southern Pacific line to the Santa Fe Railroad. Early settlers included soldiers, professionals, merchants, and a large population of gunmen who dominated local affairs until the town was "cleaned up" in 1883. In the town centre, housed in a historic 1917 armory building, the **Deming Luna Mimbres Museum** (tel: 575-546-2382; daily) is a fine museum of local history with Mimbres crafts and artifacts of the Mogollon culture in the former **National Guard Armory** (1916). One exhibit re-creates frontier life, which, in the words of a guide, was "as you can see just by looking around, not easy here. This wasn't a luxury place." Today, Deming is a homely desert town of about 14,000, where retirees drive and walk slowly, shade trees shield against a fierce sun, and the smell of roasting green chili from nearby Hatch perfumes the air each August.

Relics of the Mimbres

Rather than stay on dreary I-10 for the 60 miles (97km) west to Lordsburg, it makes sense to veer northward on US 180 towards the Gila Mountains. Between the 10th and 12th centuries, this region was home to the Mimbres branch of the Mogollon culture, the highland people who took ceramics from its earliest expression in the Southwest to an exquisite, and now highly collectable, artform – a precious trade item throughout North and Central America. Early archeologist and Mogollon specialist Jesse W. Fewkes has claimed that "no Southwestern pottery, ancient or modern, surpasses that of the Mimbres; and its naturalistic figures are unexcelled in any pottery from prehistoric America."

The Mimbres take their name from the Mimbres River, which at lower elevations remains a bone-dry sandy *arroyo* (wash) most of the year. US 180 crosses it repeatedly en route to Silver City, 53 miles (85km) north of Deming. Now one of New Mexico's most popular historic art towns, **Silver City** has successively been the base for Indian turquoise miners, Hispanic silver miners, modern copper conglomerates and now artists and nature lovers. Billy the Kid lived here as a child, but most of the town he knew was wiped out by a cataclysmic flood in 1895.

Western New Mexico University Museum (tel: 575-538-6386; daily), 12th and Alabama streets, holds the world's finest collection of Mimbres pottery, decorated with black-on-white snakes, parrots, and other animal designs as well as abstract patterns. Each pot is thought to have belonged to a single individual, and to have been buried with its owner, having first had a symbolic "kill hole" punched through its base.

Allow a whole day to make the lengthy, winding, 88-mile (142km) round trip into the Gila Mountains State Road 15 to visit **Gila Cliff Dwellings National Monument** 38 (tel: 575-536-9461; daily), where intact adobe cliff dwellings built by the Mogollon people cluster in caves above the Gila River. A moderate 1-mile (1.7km) trail leads to the dwellings, where rangers conduct regular tours. Be sure to bring water and food: there's none at this remote spot.

State 90 runs 44 miles (71km) southwest from Silver City to rejoin I-10 at **Lordsburg**. Along the way, it crosses the Continental Divide, then descends slowly and gloriously to the vast sagebrush sea in which Lordsburg seems to float alone. The largest settlement in Hidalgo County, Lordsburg sprawls languidly beside the interstate and the

Southern Pacific railroad tracks at the northern edge of the Pyramid Mountains. The train tracks themselves tell the story of modern Lordsburg, which eventually eclipsed neighboring **Shakespeare**. Shakespeare had been a stop on the great Butterfield Stagecoach Line run by the post office from St Louis, Missouri, to San Francisco, California, at the time Charles Crocker laid his railroad tracks.

This town's got ghosts

Today, Shakespeare is a ghost town, preserved in its current state of decay after being abandoned for more profitable pastures. Shakespeare, a short drive south on Main Street from Lordsburg, is the genuine item, although it *is* inhabited by surviving residents and owners Janaloo and Manny Hough who open up the town for two weekends each month, conducting folksy two-hour tours at 10am and 2pm. Several notable characters are known to have graced the dining room of its **Stratford Hotel**, including an escapee from Silver City jail: Billy the Kid.   ❏

Near the town of Shakespeare is a cemetery that claims to be the oldest of its kind in the Southwest. According to a handpainted sign, one of its "residents" is the outlaw Sandy King, convicted of being a "damned nuisance" and hung by committee.

BELOW:
abandoned automobiles and gas pump in Mogollon, a ghost town near Silver City.

SOUTHERN ARIZONA TO SAN DIEGO

From its ponderosa pine forests and saguaro-studded deserts to modern cities and historic settlements, this part of the Southwest is fascinating to explore

To most English speakers, the word "Arizona" suggests one image: aridity. Yes, water is indeed precious here – "Arizona's most precious resource, next to its people" – but the name has nothing to do with lack of water. It is in fact derived from a far less familiar tongue – either from the Pima Indian word for "little spring place," or from the Basque *arritza onac*, meaning "valuable rocky places." The latter perhaps rings truer, as Arizona's first industry was silver mining.

But there *are* "little spring places" in Arizona, as well as just about every climatic, topographic, and ecological variant known to America. From its ponderosa pine forests and saguaro-studded deserts to modern cities and reservations unchanged since ancient times, exquisite Arizona has made the most of its natural gifts.

Arizona would not be what it is today, however, without irrigation and air conditioning. Technology has tamed the desert, although a great deal of arid land remains untouched. Though beautiful, the desert can be unbearable in the summer. Winter is "the season" in most parts of Arizona, particularly in the south and west, although prices tend to rise, also.

Stone spirits

Leaving Lordsburg, New Mexico, on Interstate 10, there's one final 20-mile (32km) stretch of desiccated grassland to cross before you reach the Arizona state line. The serried ranks of mountains that then confront you on the western horizon were, in the 19th century, the stronghold of the Chiricahua Apache, whose chief, Cochise, memorably declared "When I was young I walked all over this country, east and west, and saw no other people than the Apaches."

Two sites indelibly associated with the tragic confrontation between the Apache and the US Army stand just inside the border: Fort Bowie and Chiricahua National Monument. Both

Main attractions
CHIRICAHUA NAT'L MONUMENT
TOMBSTONE
AMERIND FOUNDATION
SAGUARO NATIONAL PARK
ARIZONA-SONORA DESERT
 MUSEUM
MISSION SAN XAVIER DEL BAC
TITAN MISSILE MUSEUM
BIOSPHERE 2
HEARD MUSEUM, PHOENIX
YUMA TERRITORIAL PRISON STATE
 HISTORIC PARK

LEFT: desert plants at Biosphere 2.
BELOW: the Heard Museum, Phoenix.

An empty road curving through Saguaro National Park. The tall, slim saguaro cactus flowers in the springtime with blossoms opening only in the cool desert night air.

BELOW: real-life victims of the OK Corral shootout are buried in Tombstone's Boothill Graveyard.

can be reached by taking exit 366 from I-10 at the run-down little pit-stop of Bowie, then heading south on Apache Pass Road. For its first 3 miles (5km), this skirts some meticulously groomed pistachio orchards, but it then climbs through much scrubbier ranching country, to become an unpaved but well-maintained gravel road 12 miles (19km) out of Bowie.

Soon after that, a small parking lot marks the start of the wonderful hiking trail up to **Fort Bowie** (tel: 520-847-2500; daily). Built in 1886 following two bloody clashes between the Route Army and the Chiricahua, the fort was the headquarters for the next 25 years of a campaign that eventually drove the Apache from this region altogether. As you walk the 3 miles (5km) up to its evocative ruined adobe walls, you seem at first to be in a dry, bowl-shaped depression entirely ringed by mountains. Eventually, however, you come to tranquil, well-wooded Apache Spring, teeming with wildlife, which made this spot so precious to the Apache, and then to the fort, commanding wonderful views out across the valley below.

Stacks of rocks

Another 8 miles (13km) of easy driving beyond the parking lot, the unpaved road reaches State 186. Head west from here to I-10 if you're in a hurry to reach Tombstone, by way of Willcox and Benson, but **Chiricahua National Monument** ❸ (tel: 520-824-3560; daily) lies a mere 14 miles (23km) east. Chiricahua may be a little off the beaten track, but it's a magnificent spot, ideal for hiking, camping, and scenic drives. From the informative visitor center close to the park entrance, Bonita Canyon Drive climbs to an elevation of 6,870ft (2,090 meters). All the way up, alarmingly balanced stacks of rock loom precariously above the road, while the viewpoint at the top surveys a panorama of bizarrely shaped stone towers and columns. This unique landscape has taken shape over a period of 27 million years, as deposits of ash left by volcanic eruptions have been eroded by water, wind, and ice. Benefitting from twice the rainfall received by the yellowed, dusty plains and gorges below, the Chiricahua highlands provide a rich environment for juniper, fir, piñon, yucca, oak, cypress, and sycamore, and harbor many rare species of birds and animals. This petrified maelstrom can be explored along several well-marked hiking trails; an easy half-hour stroll along **Echo Canyon Trail**, for example, will take you through a forest of weird formations.

The most direct route between Chiricahua and Tombstone is to thread your way steadily westwards on State 181, which has the advantage of passing the rattlesnake craft shops, saloons, and crumbling buildings on the main drag of an old copper-mining town called **Gleeson**. Just outside of town on the opposite side of a curvy hillside,

BILLY CLANTON
TOM McLAURY
FRANK McLAURY
MURDERED
ON
THE STREETS
OF
TOMBSTONE
1881

TOM
McLAURY
KILLED
OCT. 26, 1881

the town of **Tombstone** ⑩ can be seen shining in the distance.

Tales from Tombstone

Tombstone was whimsically named by founder Edward Schieffelin after he was advised that the only thing he would find on his mad hunt for silver would be exactly that, his own tombstone. The most famous of "Wild West" mining towns, Tombstone did indeed sit in the heart of lands rich in silver. Its dizzying growth and wealth in the early 1880s attracted more than its share of troublemakers, but Tombstone's decline was every bit as precipitous. Its main silver mine was flooded in 1886, and the town has barely changed since then. Today, it's a tacky but undeniably endearing tourist trap, happy to provide visitors with a sanitized and glamorized taste of the lawless days of the Wild West.

Tombstone might well be forgotten now, had it not played host to the quintessential frontier "showdown" at the **OK Corral** (tel: 520-457-3456; daily), which pitted Wyatt Earp, his brothers and the consumptive dentist

Doc Holliday against the Clanton and McLaury brothers. The latter were at the forefront of a "cowboy" gang that allegedly engineered a series of stagecoach robberies, while the Earps – themselves no angels – represented "establishment" Tombstone. Political and personal clashes culminated in the legendary, bloody "Shootout at the OK Corral" on October 26, 1881, which left three men dead.

The OK Corral

The OK Corral still stands on Allen Street, preserved as it looked on the fateful day. Mannequins of the various participants pose in its yard, guns in hand, despite the general agreement of historians that the shootout in fact took place on neighboring Fremont Street. Nonetheless, staged gunfights take place here every afternoon, with actors re-creating the showdown and keeping the legend alive. Alongside,

Tombstone actors ready for a showdown.

BELOW:
Tombstone's history is recalled in local watering hole, Big Nose Kate's Saloon.

the former studio of Wild West photographer Camillus Fly showcases some of his finest work, including shots of Apache warrior Geronimo. Stagecoaches clatter evocatively past landmarks like the Bird Cage Theatre and Tombstone Courthouse, as well as some very ritzy galleries of Western art. The real-life victims of the shootout rest in **Boothill Cemetery** at the edge of town, on a dusty hillside where the peace of their slumbers is disturbed by loudspeakers concealed amid the boulders that play mournful country music.

Another 24 miles (39km) south of Tombstone on State 80, the more sedate but equally attractive former mining town of **Bisbee** squeezes into a cleft in the Dragoon Mountains. Those of its Victorian mansions that don't house comfortable hotels and B&Bs are instead home to intriguing little crafts and antique stores. The one drawback is having to negotiate all the steep stairways that connect streets at widely varying elevations. The **Queen Mine Tour** (tel: 1-866-432-2071; daily) takes you deep underground to see one of the most productive copper mines of the 20th century.

From Bisbee, you can either retrace your steps along State 80 (through Tombstone) or take State 90 (which initially heads west and then takes a jog north in Sierra Vista) to meet up with I-10 at **Benson**. Whichever way you choose, a worthy stop before you head off down the highway is a unique Arizona attraction: **Kartchner Caverns State Park** (tel: 520-586-4100; daily), just 9 miles (14km) south of I-10 off State 90. Hailed by many to be the best of Arizona's state parks, its focal point is the recently discovered (1974) "living" cavern – its formations inside are still growing – with its miles of surveyed passages.

Tours are given daily, but numbers are limited so as to protect the cave's environment, so it is necessary to book ahead (tel: 520-586-2283). In addition to the cave, there is a world-class Discovery Center, 5 miles (8km) of hiking trails, a picnic area and campground, and a hummingbird garden.

A few miles east of Benson is the **Amerind Foundation** (tel: 520-586-

3666; Tue–Sun), which displays an outstanding collection of Native American art and archeology. Adjoining it is the Fulton-Hayden Memorial Art Gallery, featuring works by western artists including Frederic Remington and William Leigh.

Tucson

From Benson, there are another 43 miles (69km) to go before you reach the city of **Tucson** ❹ (pronounced *too-sawn*) to the west. Tucson is a classic sprawling "boom" city, which has had so much room to expand in the prosperous years since World War II that it has been able to do so without destroying the evidence of its 18th-century Hispanic origins. Having been founded in 1776, it's exactly the same age as the United States, though it only passed into American hands with the Gadsden Purchase of 1854.

Downtown Tucson still centers on the narrow area that was originally contained within the adobe walls of the Spanish *presidio*. This delightfully spacious area is now dotted with artisans' shops, cafés, several good shade trees, and some extremely interesting architecture, anchored by **St Augustine Cathedral**, built in 1897, and the **Pima County Courthouse** with its mosaic tile dome. Five historic homes stand on the grounds of the **Tucson Museum of Art** (tel: 520-624-2333; Tue–Sun), whose collection features pre-Columbian, Hispanic, western, and modern art.

Emblem of the West

For many visitors, Tucson's greatest appeal lies in the fantastic scenery that surrounds it. **Saguaro National Park** (tel: 520-733-5153; daily) occupies two separate tracts of land to either side of the city proper. As its name suggests, it was established to protect dramatic expanses of multi-armed saguaro (pronounced *sah-WA-row*) cacti. Although it's often considered emblematic of the Wild West, the saguaro – which can live for 200 years, and grow to the height of 50ft (15 meters) – is in fact a native of the Sonoran Desert, only a small portion of which extends into Arizona from Mexico. Tucson is thus one of the few places in the US where

Car advertising a cowboy museum, Arizona.

BELOW: the long arm of the desert.

The purple prickly pear cactus is native to the Sonoran Desert.

you can see this fascinating cactus. The western segment of the park, the **Tucson Mountain District** (tel: 520-733-5158), holds an extraordinary "forest" of towering saguaros, which take on an otherworldly magnificence at sunset.

Nearby, the **Arizona-Sonora Desert Museum** (tel: 520-883-2702; daily) holds showpiece gardens of cacti and desert plants of all kinds, as well as desert mammals from prairie dogs to mountain lions. Its real highlights, however, are its walk-through aviaries alive with darting, iridescent hummingbirds, and the raptor free-flight demonstrations that take place twice a day from late October to mid-April.

The Mexican border at Nogales is 65 miles (105km) south of Tucson, but even if you don't want to cross, it's worth venturing at least a short distance down the **Mission Trail** that served as the city's original lifeline. Just

9 miles (14km) out of Downtown on I-19, you'll see the gleaming towers of **Mission San Xavier del Bac** (tel: 520-294-2624; daily), renowned as the most beautiful of all the Spanish missions in North America. Known as the "White Dove of the Desert," it was established at the end of the 17th century to minister to a people the Spanish called the Pima – who are now known by the name they call themselves, Tohono O'odham. The ornate whitewashed mission church dates from around 1783. Both its resplendent facade and its intricately painted interior have been restored to their full glory.

Missions and missiles

There's another wonderful mission church, this time abandoned in ruins, at **Tumacácori National Historical Park** (tel: 520-398-2341; daily), 40 miles (64km) south on I-19. It's massive adobe walls are impressive, while the small museum on the grounds details what mission life was like in the time of the Spanish padres. On the way to the park, you'll pass the delightful artists' colony of **Tubac**, which also

preserves historic buildings in its former presidio grounds. Much closer at hand, however, is a relic from more recent times. The **Titan Missile Museum** (tel: 520-625-7736; daily), near Green Valley 16 miles (26km) south of San Xavier, preserves the only one of the 27 US Titan Missile II sites not to have been dismantled at the end of the Cold War. In the 20 years between going into operation in July, 1963, and being decommissioned in November, 1982, it held two missiles, capable of being fired over 5,000 miles (8,000km) in less than 20 minutes. Gung-ho guides lead equally gung-ho tour parties down into the underground silo and through subterranean passages to reach its control room, which was designed to remain functional even in the event of a direct nuclear hit on the surface above. What they can't tell you, however, is where the missiles were aimed; each was trained on a specific, unchanged target for all its active life, but that information remains Top Secret. The whole installation is eerie and unsettling, and nowhere more so than its restrooms, which feature prominent "watch for rattlesnakes" signs.

Onward to Mars

For lovers of the truly bizarre, the Tucson area has one final, unmissable curiosity to offer: **Biosphere 2** (tel: 520-838-6200; daily), just outside **Oracle**, 32 miles (51km) north of the city on State 77. Completed in 1991, Biosphere 2 was designed as an hermetically sealed replica of Biosphere 1 – the planet Earth – albeit cunningly disguised as a giant greenhouse. Its aim was nothing less than to pave the way for the colonization of Mars. To that end, a group of ex-actors and scientists were locked into it for two full years, to see whether they could survive in a closed and self-sufficient environment. The ambitious experiment met with mixed results.

Now operated by the University of Arizona, Biosphere 2 holds no permanent residents today, and is used for more closely controlled scientific programs. All the publicity, however, has turned it into a major tourist attraction. Tours are inevitably less exciting

The unique Yaqui Easter celebration in Tucson blends a lenten all-night fiesta featuring a Yaqui deer dancer and Holy Week ceremonies including matachine dancers and a maypole.

BELOW:
Biosphere 2, a hermetically sealed environment, was home to ex-actors and scientists for two years.

Dutch prospector Jacob Walz allegedly struck a lode of gold in the Superstition Mountains, but no one from his mining expedition was ever seen again; the Lost Dutchman Mine remains hidden to this day.

now that there are no "Biospherians" to be glimpsed through the windows, but you can now go inside the huge and oddly beautiful structure, including its luxurious living quarters, and explore its multiple environments.

The Apache Trail

The most direct route between Tucson and Phoenix is I-10, on which the long, flat 100-mile (160km) drive takes well under two hours. The main visual distraction along the way, **Picacho Peak**, looks like a double-pronged molar tooth as it looms up 30 miles (48km) out of Tucson, but then resolves into two separate sharp fangs. At its foot, the **Rooster Cogburn Ostrich Farm** just off the highway provides an unexpected photo opportunity, selling bags of seed that you can feed to the aggressive and ungainly birds, as well as feather dusters and colossal eggs.

Alternatively, State 79 sets off from close to Biosphere 2 to follow a parallel and similar course that ends up by approaching Phoenix from the east rather than the south. Known as the **Pinal Pioneer Parkway**, it's lush with

native vegetation, from the prickly pear and saguaro cactus to the catclaw and mesquite tree.

It eventually brings you to **Apache Junction**, due east of central Phoenix, which is the start of the **Apache Trail**. This modern road was constructed in 1905 to provide access to **Theodore Roosevelt Dam ㊷**, the first of the great dams of the West, built to quench the ever-growing thirst of nearby Phoenix. Named the Apache Trail in the hope of encouraging tourism, it was hailed by President Teddy Roosevelt, when he dedicated the dam in 1911, as combining "the grandeur of the Alps, the glory of the Rockies, and the magnificence of the Grand Canyon." Although the president made a wide-sweeping overstatement, it is indeed a ravishing drive.

Shortly after leaving Apache Junction, the Apache Trail passes the enjoyably (albeit touristy) ramshackle **Goldfield Ghost Town**, where you can take horse or jeep rides amid the abandoned mine machinery and false-front stores, or simply pick up a snack at the bakery. Beyond that comes your first clear sighting of the **Superstition Mountains**. The Spanish called these peaks the "Mountains of Foam" because of their effusive volcanic ridges, but they're best known for the legends that surround the Dutch prospector Jacob Walz. He seems to have struck a huge lode of gold in the Superstitions in the late 19th century, but no one who followed him on his expeditions was ever seen again, and the "Lost Dutchman Mine" remains hidden to this day. The Superstition Mountains have taken the life of many an overly curious fortune-seeker.

The Apache Trail cuts into **Tonto National Forest**, where vistas and foot trails skirt the highway. The fun really begins as it winds its narrow way into the highlands. Drivers beware: you'll have to keep your eyes more on the road than the alpine rises, glorious vistas, and lush canyons. Saguaros and mesquite, dry riverbeds, and wave upon

BELOW: petroglyph rock art found near Tucson.

wave of mountain ridges follow a scenic overlook of the **Canyon River**. When you descend into the valley, pull up and strip down, because the blue waters are irresistible.

The trail is well paved for the 18 miles (29km) up to **Tortilla Flat**, a required stop for lovers of desert lore and witty western character. The essence of Tortilla Flat is sold in two forms: a postcard reading *Tortilla Flat/ Pop. 6/30 Miles from Water/2 Feet from Hell!*; and the hokey cans of Jack Rabbit Milk, "a balanced diet for unbalanced people."

Best chili in the West

A hotel, post office, café/restaurant, gift shop, riding stable, curio shop, a legend, and a marvelous view – Tortilla Flat is a great place to stop for "the best chili in the West" and a "Howdy" from "the friendliest town in America." Admire the hundreds of dollar-bills tacked under business cards on the ceiling and walls of the café before you exit back to the sun-drenched desert. Roosevelt Dam lies another 30 miles (48km) up the precipitous but passable dirt road

beyond Tortilla Flat. Above and behind it spreads **Roosevelt Lake**, the reservoir it created. The best views are from a steep hiking trail in **Tonto National Monument** (tel: 928-467-2241; daily), just west of the dam on State 88.

That short but grueling hike culminates in a "cliff-dwelling" once occupied by the Salado Indians, who disappeared from this area before the Apache arrived. Retrack State 88 back into the valley. You'll pass through two unique suburbs, as State 88 becomes Main Street in Mesa, then Apache Boulevard in Tempe. **Mesa** contains Arizona's largest Mormon community and you'll pass by the beautiful **Latter Day Saint Temple**. Things change as you pass into **Tempe**, home of Arizona State University, and its young student population (over 40,000). Turning left on University, you'll come to I-10, which quickly whisks you into the heart of **Phoenix** ⑱ *(see page 308).*

A staple ingredient in this region, chilis are frequently hung in bundles to dry in the red-hot sun.

BELOW: dining on the patio at El Charro, Arizona's oldest Mexican restaurant.

Phoenix: Valley of the Sun

Business is booming in Phoenix, with plenty of industry, tourism, and golf courses. Just be sure to come in winter.

P hoenix may not have had any real ashes to rise from, but its founders were inspired by the knowledge that the merciless heat of the Salt River Valley had been overcome before. Between approximately 1100 and 1450, the Hohokam people successfully irrigated this region by means of a network of over 300 miles (480km) of canals, while Jack Swilling, in 1867, established modern Phoenix by simply re-digging the waterways.

In World War II, the military, utilizing the desert for aviation training, revolutionized Phoenician life further with air conditioning. Suddenly, life in the great hot desert became a year-round possibility, and the great migration was on. Now, Phoenix, with a metropolitan area population of nearly 3.5 million people, is booming.

It's hard not to be impressed by the city's setting. To the east soar the massive Four Peaks and Superstition Mountains, while the Sierra Estrella

rides the southeast horizon. Hemming in the city north and south are lower mountain ranges, framing Camelback Mountain. All of these make for excellent day-hikes, and provide the visitor with an opportunity to witness the beauty (and silence) of the Sonoran desert.

But beware: the average high temperature June through August is 103°F (39°C); May and September aren't much better. Peak tourist season is the winter, when daily maximum temperatures hover around 70°F (21°C) and the valley's resorts and 190 golf courses fill up with tourists.

Phoenix is easily divided into urban districts. Downtown holds the skyscrapers, and the modern **Arizona Center** mall, home to the city's main visitor center. Once lacking a strong downtown character, Phoenix invested considerable energy in locating museums and cultural venues in the city center.

Heritage Square, just east of the Civic Plaza, remains from the city's Victorian days and forms part of Downtown's **Heritage and Science Park** (tel: 602-262-5029; Tue–Sun). Rosson House, a striking red Victorian home built in 1895, stands out from the square's 11 buildings.

The **Phoenix Museum of History** (tel: 602-253-2734; Tue–Sat), with interactive exhibits of the city's development, and the **Arizona Science Center** (tel: 602-716-2000; daily), a $50-million hands-on funhouse of science, embellished with a planetarium, attract the scientific and the simply curious to Heritage Square.

The beautifully designed and organized **Heard Museum** (tel: 602-252-8848; daily) is near Downtown at 2301 North Central Avenue. The Heard focuses on Native American arts and crafts, both ancient and modern. Extensive galleries cover the long-vanished Anasazi, Hohokam, and Mogollon groups as well as the still-thriving Navajo and Apache tribes. Former Republican senator Barry

LEFT: one of the skyscrapers in downtown Phoenix.
ABOVE: African savanna re-created at Phoenix Zoo.
RIGHT: the Arizona Biltmore Resort and Spa.

Goldwater gathered and donated the exquisite and fascinating collection of Hopi *kachina* dolls. The museum complex is worth visiting in its own right, with its older structures arrayed around a quiet courtyard planted with orange trees which manage to blend seamlessly with the newer state-of-the-art facilities.

If you see nothing else, visit the **Arizona Biltmore Resort** (tel: 602-955-6600) at 24th Street and Missouri, 5 miles (8km) northeast of Heritage Park. Phoenix owes the arrival of the renowned American architect Frank Lloyd Wright to this hotel. Built in 1929, Albert Chase McArthur, a former student of Wright, originally designed the building, but found himself in trouble and summoned the master for help.

Wright probably gave more help than required, for the hotel is a delightful masterpiece from Wright's middle period. Gutted by fire in June 1973, refurbished furniture and textile designs from all periods of Wright's career now decorate the interior.

Wright stayed on in Phoenix to found his architectural school and residence, **Taliesin West** (tel: 480-860-2700; daily), hidden in the desert beyond the upscale suburb of Scottsdale, in the northeast.

Wright intended the buildings and facilities to be an ongoing, hands-on educational exercise for architectural and design students. A variety of different tours gives visitors an insight into Wright's visionary architectural style, as well as the facility's interesting "apprentice" program.

Scottsdale is known for its abundance of luxury resorts, such as the ravishing **Phoenician** at the foot of Camelback Mountain, which caters to travelers visiting Arizona for sun and sport rather than pure scenery. Scottsdale also spawned some swish shopping malls, like **Fashion Square**, while its "Hometown USA" central streets are, in fact, filled with expensive galleries of so-called Western Art.

At the southern end of Scottsdale lies the **Phoenix Zoo** (tel: 602-273-1341; daily) as well as the compelling **Desert Botanical Gardens** (tel: 480-941-1225; daily). The arid gardens, located in **Papago Park**, display plants from the world's deserts, including half the known species of cactus. The excellent landscaping, and the exotic power of these acres cannot fail to impress.

South of the zoo and gardens lies **Tempe**. Home of Arizona State University and an artificial lake under a picturesque old (but still in use) railroad bridge, Tempe is perhaps the most attractive of all of Phoenix's areas, and definitely the most self-contained. The city's active nightlife centers on Mill Avenue, which is within easy walking distance of both the hotels and the lake. ❑

PHOENIX TO SAN DIEGO

The 150 miles (240km) between Phoenix and the Colorado River, which marks the border with California, include some of the bleakest desert terrain in the entire Southwest. Taking the southern route to San Diego, you have a choice between sticking with I-10 as far as Quartzsite and then changing to US 95 south, or dropping south much earlier, to meet I-8 at Gila Bend. Either way, your final destination in Arizona will be Yuma, which is even hotter than Phoenix and Tucson.

Quartzsite is only really worth visiting if you're passing through in January or February, when up to 750,000 sun-seeking, northern "snowbirds" (most in RVs) descend on the town for a sort of mineralists' convention – a huge, open-air "flea market" for seekers and sellers of precious, semi-precious and not-under-any-circumstances-even-slightly-precious stones and gems of various shapes and sizes. In a miracle on a par with the loaves and the fishes, Quartzsite's handful of motels and restaurants somehow copes with this rock-hungry throng of oldsters.

Otherwise, you'd do better to turn off I-10 25 miles (40km) west from Phoenix, and take State 85 down to the I-8 truckstop of **Gila Bend**. (For that matter, if you're in a hurry to get to the beach from Tucson, I-8 enables you to bypass Phoenix altogether.) Named, logically enough, for its location on a big bend in the Gila River, Gila Bend holds a predictable array of fast-food restaurants and motels, plus one outstanding exception. The **Best Western Space Age Lodge** is a marvelous 1950s-style folly, kitted out with kitsch Sputnik-shaped neon signs. Its **Outer Limits Restaurant**, which features a dazzling lunar-exploration mural, is well worth a stop for a bite to eat. The visitor center nearby, which doubles as a museum of local history, will confirm your suspicions that not a lot happens in Gila Bend.

Signs on the interstate near Gila Bend warn that this is a "Blowing Dust Area," while bridges repeatedly cross "rivers" that are in truth little more than scrubby strips of sand. Somehow, however, **Dateland** ㊹, 50 miles (80km) west of Gila Bend, manages to grow a

bumper annual crop of dates. If you're desperate for a diversion, stop for a date shake or whatever other date-related product may strike your fancy in Dateland's solitary diner.

The Devil's road

Soon you begin to be aware that you're approaching **Yuma** ⓯. The city avenues are numbered a mile apart, corresponding to the signs on the interstate that count the mileage down to California, and thus you pass an Avenue 51E that's a full 50 miles (80km) east of downtown Yuma. In reality, Yuma is large, but it's not *that* large. There's still a long way to go, including the final climb over the ridge of the Gila Mountains and descent into the Colorado River Valley, before there's any sign of life. That is, apart from the low-flying jets that screech overhead. Southwest Arizona is another proving ground for the US military, and the latest top-secret warplanes are constantly being tested above the barren desert that lies between I-8 and the Mexican border.

When Padre Eusebio Kino, the most tireless of all Spanish missionaries to the American Southwest, opened a trail in 1699 from Sonoita, Mexico, to what is now Yuma, he called the trail *El Camino del Diablo* – the Devil's Road. It seemingly led straight into the inferno. The town subsequently gained a long-standing reputation as one of the worst hell-holes in the Wild West. Yuma smolders to this day, but it's been tamed by the air conditioner into a city fit for human beings. With some 339 days of sunshine and less than 4 inches (10cm) of rainfall annually, it made the *Guinness Book of World Records* as the "sunniest place on earth." All that heat has made Yuma a Mecca for sun-seekers, and the gigantic sprawl of recreational vehicle parks as you approach town in winter just might make you agree with Kino's description.

Starry-eyed gold diggers

Set just below the confluence of the Gila and Colorado rivers, Yuma has been known for centuries as the site of the only natural ford on the southern trail to the Pacific. As such, it was a crucial way-station on the road to

Space cowboys should take a break from the road at the Outer Limits Restaurant, part of the Best Western Space Age Lodge, Gila Bend.

BELOW: watermelon-eating contest; no spitting allowed.

Prison gate at the Yuma Prison Historic Park.

BELOW: Mexican workers harvesting lettuce on a large farm in Yuma.

California even before the Gold Rush of 1849. Originally, local Quechan Indians kept a monopoly on the lucrative river crossing, but as ever greater numbers of starry-eyed miners demanded to be ferried across into gold country, control was wrested away in some astonishingly bloodthirsty conflicts. When gold was discovered to the *east* of Yuma as well, in 1858, the city duly blossomed as a port, where ore was transported by steamboat down the Colorado River and into the Gulf of California.

After the mines dried up and the river was dammed, Yuma converted itself into an agricultural center, with help from irrigation technology. Those vast fields bordering the town produce several crops of lettuce a year, making Yuma the "bagged salad capital of the world." But it's still a crossroads, where Interstate 8 from San Diego meets US 95.

Thanks to diminished water flow, the Gila and Colorado now meet 5 miles (8km) upstream from downtown Yuma. The bluff that once overlooked their intersection remains occupied by the surprisingly interesting **Yuma Territorial Prison State Historic Park.** This museum (tel: 928-783-4771; daily) preserves the remaining structures of the infamous prison of the Arizona Territory, which closed in 1909 three years before Arizona achieved statehood. These include its guard house, courtyards, cell block, and notorious "Dark Cell" for solitary confinement.

Rogues' gallery

All the lawlessness of Arizona a hundred years ago is on show in the rogues' gallery of former inmates that decorates the central building. Larcenists, adulterers, manslaughterers, outright murderers, rapists, and criminals "against nature" all found a home here by the Colorado. You can rest assured the cells weren't air-conditioned, so Yuma Prison must have been a fate so dreaded that at least a few desperadoes thought twice before pulling the trigger.

Below the prison, the Yuma Wetlands Project is gradually restoring the river's flood plain to its natural state, and birds and wildlife are returning along with native plants and trees.

With over 1,400 acres (560 hectares) targeted, it is the largest-scale restoration project of its kind. Volunteers give free walks through the wetlands on Saturday mornings.

The gray railroad bridge that spans the Colorado close to the prison was completed in 1915 as the "Ocean to Ocean" bridge that finally spared travelers the ferry ride across the river. But it was built for Model-Ts, not four-wheel-drive vehicles, and the narrow bridge takes today's traffic one direction at a time. The point from which the ferries once set off, down below on the fringes of Downtown, is now occupied by **Gateway Park**, whose multi-use pathways provide a pleasant spot for strolling or cycling along the riverbank, linking the West and East Wetlands and other points of interest.

At the core of downtown Yuma, "**Old Yuma**" consists of a few blocks of sleepy but atmospheric Victorian-era buildings, such as the Sanguinetti House. Lutes Casino, on South Main Street, resembles a featureless barn on the outside, but you'll find the interior is positively busting with memorabilia

and bric-a-brac, as well as dispensing drinks and snacks. A novel way to see the sights is on a **Segway Tour** (tel: 928-342-1969), which takes you onto the bridge, along the river and through Downtown on an upright scooter that is simply a blast to ride.

Camel Farm

Outside town is a surprising bit of Yuma history. Camels. Camels have been a feature of the Western landscape since the late 1850s, when the US Army imported a batch of the beasts to see whether they were any better equipped than horses and mules to negotiate Arizona's rough terrain. Though the camels produced amazingly high scores on their "endurance tests," they were prone to stampede, and smelled atrocious. After the Civil War put them out of a job, they were set free, and became a nuisance until camel hunting became a brief but effective fad. Today **The Camel Farm** (tel: 928-627-7511; Mon–Sat Oct–May) breeds a herd of drooling, slobbering, one-humped dromedaries along with other exotic animals.

The slow road to Yuma – camels have been in the Wild West since the 1850s.

BELOW:
camels were brought to the West by the US Army, to test whether they fared better than horses in the harsh terrain.

> *A grand garden,*
> *the like of which in*
> *sheer pattern does*
> *not exist, I think,*
> *in the world.*
>
> Frank Lloyd Wright
> about the desert

BELOW:
rippling sand dunes
in the Algodones
wilderness, the
center of which has
no vegetation
whatsoever.

EUREKA! CALIFORNIA

Over the Colorado River, the down-at-heel community of **Winterhaven** provides a deceptively low-key introduction to California, the third-largest and most populous state in the nation. Northwest of here, the **Imperial Valley** – thanks to extensive damming and irrigation – is one of the most agriculturally productive regions on earth. As you follow I-8 to the coast, however, where the Pacific laps on the forever-sunny beaches, it takes a while before the myth of California begins to be fulfilled. First, there is the desert to deal with.

This vast expanse has room for even the biggest of visions. Exit 164 leads to the **Center of the World** (tel: 760-572-0100), a unique attraction inspired by a children's book. Its French-born author, Jacques-Andre Istel, founded the nearby town of Felicity and created the incredible **Museum of History in Granite**, an ongoing project that captures the history of mankind on massive etched granite panels spread out beneath the desert sky. The drawings are amazingly detailed, and it would take you five hours to read every word.

The **Algodones Dunes**, immediately west of the Colorado, were every bit as much of an obstacle to early travelers as the river itself. This strip of deep, shifting sands stretches 40 miles (64km) north to south. It's only around 6 miles (10km) wide at this point, but for the first motorists to attempt to cross, this might as well have been the Sahara Desert. In 1915, a **"Plank Road"** of railroad ties was laid down to enable automobiles to rumble their way over. By 1925, when as many as 30 cars were using the road each day, it had deteriorated alarmingly. A two-lane paved highway, California State Route 80, finally opened in August 1926, and has long since been superseded in turn by I-8.

A small segment of the original plank road can still be seen by leaving the interstate 20 miles (32km) west of Yuma on Grays Well Road, to enter the **Imperial Sand Dunes Recreation Area** ⓭ immediately south. Roughly 4 miles (6km) along, parallel to the interstate and also to the very long **All American Canal**, the dried-out old planks descend a short slope. These arid dunes are now a raucous playground for the Californian youths who race their dune buggies and other off-road vehicles over the razor-edged inclines, while older "snowbirds" tan themselves sleepily beside their RVs.

Islands of irrigated green, dotted with palms, spell "oasis" at the end of the 58-mile (93km) tumble from Yuma to **El Centro**. Supposedly the largest city below sea level in the western hemisphere, and definitely the birthplace of the entertainer Cher, El Centro prospers quietly as a supply center for the Imperial Valley.

To the west, high winds howl across the valley, kicking up a dusty haze around the straggling palms. Beyond the reach of the canals, the vegetation all but disappears, and you enter the bare **Yuma Desert**. Scattered with only the occasional 14ft (4-meter) orange-blossomed ocotillo cactus, the desert floor appears to have undergone an

unsuccessful hair transplant. The appropriately named **Ocotillo**, 28 miles (45km) west of El Centro, is no more than a flyblown little hamlet.

The mountain ranges that sweep down from the northwest just past Ocotillo are at first obscured by the dust, but soon you find yourself embarking on the very steep climb up their rocky flanks. The east- and west-bound lanes of the interstate divide at this point, each plotting its own course across a terrain that consists of no more than piles of rust-colored boulders. Every few hundred yards stand road-side barrels filled with "Radiator Water," as the risk of overheating is so high. Atop a minor eminence at an elevation of 3,000ft (914 meters), 5 miles (8km) out of Ocotillo, the **Desert View Tower** commands a stunning view back across Imperial Valley. Constructed in 1922 using blocks of hewn granite, it holds an enjoyable jumble of exhibits on local history. Entering San Diego County at Mountain Spring, I-8 pulls south to skirt the Mexican border; a minor turn-off leads to the border town of **Jacumba**.

San Diego revealed

Near **Live Oak Springs**, 27 miles (43km) west of Ocotillo, the winds die down and the rises level off. Interstate 8 soon swoops to green valleys and into the **Cleveland National Forest**, winding through Pine Valley and Alpine. As you drop toward Alpine, you should get your first glimpse of the Pacific Ocean, glinting on the horizon ahead. **El Cajon** ㊼, 43 miles (69km) beyond Live Oak Springs, is a nicely landscaped city that marks the first major outpost of the San Diego metropolitan area. **La Mesa** follows, set picturesquely amid the hills that rise on El Cajon's western outskirts.

Past La Mesa, traffic on I-8 becomes increasingly congested; the overpass of I-15 is the portal to San Diego. As the interstate pushes out to the Pacific beaches, its shoulders open up onto shopping malls and numerous sky-scraper hotels. A little further to the south, buildings arched by trees glimmer on the slopes. Behind them lies the sunny border city of **San Diego** ㊽ (*see page 322*). ❑

El Centro is an oasis surrounded by the California desert. The singer Cher is from El Centro.

BELOW: performing at a Cinco de Mayo celebration.

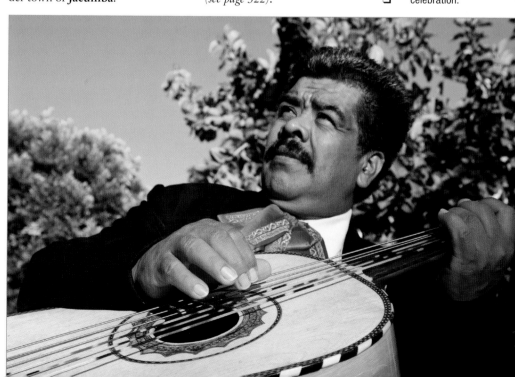

THE PACIFIC ROUTE

A guide to the Pacific Coast, with principal sites
cross-referenced by number to the maps

America's historic US 101 – which stretched from San Diego all the way up the coast through Oregon and Washington to the Canadian border, and eventually became, in part, today's California Highway 1 – has a history that is comparable with its more famous companion, Route 66. Until 1909, it had been a narrow, bumpy, dirt-surfaced track on which horse-drawn wagons and primitive autos competed for space. Then a concrete and macadam road began stretching north from the cities of San Diego and Oceanside.

The spiffy new road stimulated the rise of a phenomenon known as "car culture," epitomized in sunny California, and which spawned all the enterprises that subsequently came to be associated with travel along the highway, such as gas stations, car dealers, motels, diners, and auto laundries.

The highway led visitors from all parts of the Pacific Coast to San Diego's Balboa Park for the 1915–16 Panama-California Exposition, enticed Hollywood movie stars and others to its pristine beaches, and lured those in search of a good time during Prohibition to Mexico's Tijuana.

In 1925, the road officially became US 101. Increased traffic spelled its doom, however, and by the end of the war a new four-lane highway, eventually to become Interstate 5, bypassed the old route. Today, the Pacific Coast Highway, often abbreviated to "PCH," and also known as the El Cabrillo Trail, is a sometimes-scrappy, often sea-scented mixture of the old US 101, California Highway 1 and roaring, ever-busy Interstate 5. We have followed it here as faithfully as possible, stopping off at breathtaking sites like California's Big Sur and Hearst Castle and sometimes diverting inland and away from its charms to visit vibrant cities like Portland and Seattle. Along the way there are quaint Victorian-era towns, wineries, giant redwoods, romantic windswept beaches, historic sites such as San Juan Capistrano Mission, and countless opportunities to see a fascinating array of wildlife.

The Pacific Coast Highway's villages and towns – as well as much of its old structure – are still here, and for those who have time, and a romantic desire to reclaim an earlier America, following Highway 1 and historic 101 along to Seattle can lead to unimaginable pleasures.   ❏

PRECEDING PAGES: fog enveloping the Golden Gate Bridge; rolling into Hollywood.
LEFT: the California dream, on wheels. **ABOVE AND LEFT:** on the road in California.

A SHORT STAY IN SAN DIEGO

San Diego is a busy, elegant harbor town with a history unsurpassed in the state of California. Here's a list of the not-to-be-missed attractions:

● The Mission San Diego (1769) offers a peaceful sanctuary with fragrant gardens. A museum and walking tour tell the story of the "Mother of the Missions", while Mass is still celebrated in the basilica.

● Old Town State Historic Park preserves much of the original settlement where Spanish soldiers and their families lived until the 1800s. Its historic adobe structures now house interesting small museums and shops, offering a glimpse of California as it was in the Mexican and early American periods.

● Thar she blows! Board a Hornblower yacht at Broadway Pier for whale- and dolphin-watching excursions in season (December–March), and scenic harbor and dinner cruises throughout the year.

LEFT: The Cabrillo National Monument. The statue on Point Loma commemorates the first European landing on the West Coast.

BELOW: Hotel del Coronado. A dozen presidents have stayed in this characterful Victorian resort.

● From Dixieland jazz to haute cuisine, the old, restored Gaslamp Quarter offers some of the city's best entertainment and nightlife, as well as interesting Victorian architecture. Shopaholics should make a beeline for nearby Horton Plaza, which has around 150 upmarket shops.

● In the heart of San Diego, Balboa Park covers over 1,000 acres (400 hectares) with 17 museums, theaters, beautiful gardens, art galleries, and more. A pass from the park's Visitor Center allows admission to most of the museums, some of which are housed in ornate old buildings. Have lunch at the rose garden, visit the Spanish Village Art Center and, afterward, soak up some culture at the Starlight Bowl or The Old Globe theater.

● Hire a convertible and take the 59-Mile Scenic Drive which takes you through Downtown, Balboa Park, the beaches, La Jolla, and out to the Cabrillo National Monument on Point Loma for fabulous views of the city and the open ocean.

THE BIRTHPLACE OF CALIFORNIA

California began at San Diego's Presidio Hill on July 16, 1769, when Father Junípero Serra conducted a Mass dedicating the newly created Mission San Diego de Alcalá; the mission was moved to its present site in Mission Valley only five years later. History and luxury can be found in many parts of this harbor city, which has plenty of upscale shops, plus at least 80 golf courses. Although San Diego's harborfront, the Embarcadero, can be touristy, there are enough historic sites, cultural attractions, fine restaurants, shady walks, harbor cruises, and sandy beaches to appeal to the most discerning of visitors.

ABOVE: San Diego Bay. Vessels of all sizes line the natural harbor, from yachts to the USS *Midway* aircraft carrier, now a museum.

ABOVE RIGHT: Beach life. Swim, surf, and sunbathe on San Diego's sandy beaches.

RIGHT: San Diego Zoo. This highly regarded zoo is home to over 800 species of animals including cute pandas and a rainforest aviary.

IMPORTANT INFORMATION

Population: 1.26 million
Dialing codes: 619, 760, 858
Website: www.sandiego.org
Tourist information: San Diego International Visitor Information Center, West Broadway At Harbor Drive, San Diego, CA 92101; tel: 619-236-1212; fax: 619-230-7084

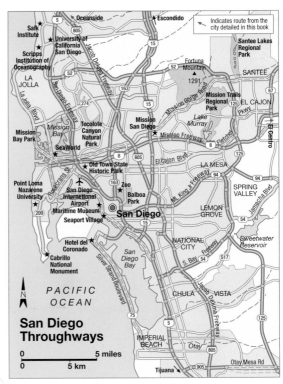

San Diego
Throughways

PACIFIC
OCEAN

0   5 miles
0   5 km

SAN DIEGO TO LOS ANGELES

Beach towns, beach facilities, and beaches themselves – more than 20 of them – line this short stretch of coastline. Is it any wonder the bikini first became famous here?

The journey from seaside **San Diego ❶** (*see page 322*) to glittering Los Angeles is only around 125 miles (200km), but following the ragged coastal roads can take much longer than that short distance implies. It's also much more rewarding, as the coastal route meanders past Southern California's best beaches, prettiest towns, and most exclusive residential areas. For navigational purposes, the road signs along the way go by a variety of names – Highway 1, US 101, I-5 – but to most Californians, this mix of roads paralleling the ocean is known simply as the Pacific Coast Highway.

LA JOLLA TO OCEANSIDE

The first stop out of San Diego is **La Jolla ❷** (pronounced *la-hoy-ya*), a seaside community that once boasted "the richest zip code in America." This college community and upscale town can be reached in a few minutes by heading north up I-5, but a more scenic way is to start the drive to Los Angeles as you intend to proceed – using water as your navigator. From SeaWorld, take the road called SeaWorld Drive to West Mission Bay Drive, routes that curl along the bottom of **Mission Bay** itself. The road turns north (changing into Mission Boulevard) to parallel Mission Beach, then the livelier Pacific Beach, before rolling into La Jolla. La Jolla has beautiful homes and a downtown area – which calls itself "the vil-

lage" – filled with expensive shops, as well as a branch of San Diego's **Museum of Contemporary Art** (tel: 858-454-3541; Thur–Tue). Described by writer Raymond Chandler as "a nice place for old people and their parents," La Jolla featured in Tom Wolfe's 1960s surfer novel *The Pump House Gang*. On the campus of the University of California is the La Jolla Playhouse, whose forerunner was founded by the late actor Gregory Peck. The caves carved into its coastal bluffs have long been a paradise for both deep-sea divers and

Main attractions
SAN DIEGO
LA JOLLA
BIRCH AQUARIUM
OCEANSIDE
CAPISTRANO MISSION
LAGUNA BEACH
NEWPORT BEACH
HUNTINGTON BEACH
LONG BEACH
VENICE BEACH
SANTA MONICA

LEFT: ways to keep fit at Venice Beach.
BELOW: Legoland, Carlsbad, California, near San Diego.

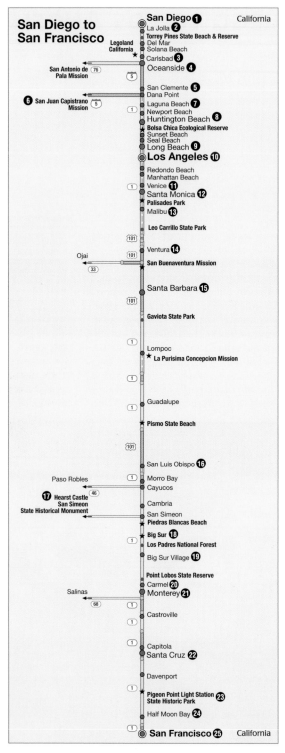

San Diego to San Francisco

Legoland California ★

San Antonio de (76)
Pala Mission

(5)

⑥ San Juan Capistrano Mission (5)

(1)

Ojai (101)
◄————
(33)

(101)

Paso Robles (1)

⑰ Hearst Castle (46)
San Simeon
State Historical Monument

(1)

Salinas
◄————
(68) (1)

(1)

(1)

(1)

(1)

San Diego ❶　California
La Jolla ❷
Torrey Pines State Beach & Reserve
Del Mar
Solana Beach
Carlsbad ❸
Oceanside ❹

San Clemente ❺
Dana Point
Laguna Beach ❼
Newport Beach
Huntington Beach ❽
Bolsa Chica Ecological Reserve
Sunset Beach
Seal Beach
Long Beach ❾
Los Angeles ❿
Redondo Beach
Manhattan Beach
Venice ⓫
Santa Monica ⓬
Palisades Park
Malibu ⓭

Leo Carrillo State Park

Ventura ⓮
San Buenaventura Mission

Santa Barbara ⓯

Gaviota State Park

Lompoc
★ La Purisima Concepcion Mission

Guadalupe

★ Pismo State Beach

San Luis Obispo ⓰
Morro Bay
Cayucos

Cambria
San Simeon
Piedras Blancas Beach
★ Big Sur ⓲
Los Padres National Forest
Big Sur Village ⓳

Point Lobos State Reserve
Carmel ⓴
Monterey ㉑

Castroville

Capitola
Santa Cruz ㉒

Davenport

Pigeon Point Light Station ㉓
State Historic Park
Half Moon Bay ㉔
San Francisco ㉕　California

---

cliff divers, and nearby **Black's Beach** was once legally – and is now illegally – a nudist beach.

Architecturally awesome

At the north end of town above Point La Jolla is the renowned **Scripps Institution of Oceanography**, whose well-stocked **Birch Aquarium** (tel: 858-534-3474; daily) offers whale-watching cruises in season. Among the 33 sea-filled tanks is a two-story tank that replicates a kelp bed with all its familiar and unfamiliar creatures. Farther north and also by the sea is the **Salk Institute**, designed by the late Louis I. Kahn, perhaps one of America's most admired contemporary architects. The institute is named after its famous resident scientist, Jonas Salk, who devised the polio vaccine.

La Jolla Shores Drive parallels Torrey Pines Road, a winding hill out of La Jolla through the affluent suburb of the same name where the trees are environmentally protected. The road gives access to **Torrey Pines Scenic Drive**, off which is a windswept hillside used by flying enthusiasts for launching gliders over the ocean since the 1930s. The **Torrey Pines Gliderport** (tel: 858-452-9858; daily) offers introductory lessons in paragliding; spectators are welcome. There's also a restaurant and flight sport shop at the site. The **Torrey Pines State Reserve** (tel: 858-755-2063; daily) and **Torrey Pines State Beach** are two places perfect for picnics.

Del Mar and Solana Beach

A series of small coastal roads, which together make up US 101, parallels I-5 as far as the town of Oceanside, where the mighty interstate takes over until it reaches Dana Point. From then on, the Pacific Coast Highway becomes Highway 1, and more or less stays Highway 1 until San Francisco.

Both the coast road and the inter-state lead to the community of **Del Mar**, which has an Amtrak Station and has attracted crowds since the

1930s with its famous racetrack (tel: 858-755-1141), which was rescued from collapse by actor Pat O'Brien and singer Bing Crosby. The entertainers turned the track into one of America's most popular racing circuit venues. The season begins in July, a week after Del Mar's big fair ends, and runs until mid-September.

The track's sandy-colored main building, in a sort of California-meets-Mediterranean style, can be glimpsed from the interstate, but much of the town itself lies farther down the hill beside the coast road. Head for Camino del Mar, with its art galleries, boutiques, and outdoor dining with oceanside views.

The communities of **Solana Beach** – with its futuristic-looking railroad station – Cardiff-by-the-Sea, Encinitas, and Leucadia run into each other along this stretch of coast, and a profusion of stop signs and red lights can slow progress. Otherwise, it is a pleasant stretch to drive with plenty of roadside trees, the beach and the railroad track both near the road, and here and there a "Historic US 101"

sign. The sweet-smelling **Quail Botanical Gardens** (tel: 760-436-3036; daily) at **Encinitas** may be worth a stop to admire the waterfall and extensive collection of exotic plants. The **San Dieguito Heritage Museum** (tel: 760-632-9711; Wed–Fri and last Sat of the month) specializes in the history of the area – from the Diegueno Indians of 10,000 years ago to the present day – and includes a fine collection of more than 8,000 photographs. The beach is a few blocks away; the railroad parallels the road to the east. At the north end of the community are the golden domes of the Self Realization Fellowship temple.

Making music

At **Carlsbad ❸**, the road runs along the beach and through the pretty downtown village with antiques stores and the historic Carlsbad Mineral Water Spa (tel: 760-434-1887), which reflects the heritage of its spa-town namesake in the Czech Republic. The region is known for flowers, its bulbs being sold widely throughout the country, and almost 50 hill-

BELOW: these waters form part of the migratory path for whales.

side acres (20 hectares) are resplendent with bright colors. (To visit the Flower Fields, call 760-431-0352.) The **Museum of Making Music** (tel: 760-438-5996; Tue–Sun) spans a century of music-making in America. Exhibits include vintage instruments, samples of music from each era, and photographs and paintings.

Carlsbad's 128-acre (52-hectare) **Legoland California** (tel: 760-918-5346; Thur–Mon and daily June–Aug) was the first of these theme parks in the US. It used 120 million of its signature toy plastic bricks to depict such scaled-down landmarks as New York City and Washington, DC – as well as Castle Hill with an "enchanted walk" where children can search for hidden treasure. Also on the grounds is the SEA LIFE Aquarium.

Let's go surfing now

With almost 4 miles (6km) of white, sandy beaches and "world-class surf," **Oceanside** ❹ is an appropriate place to find the **California Surf Museum** (tel: 760-721-6876; daily), which displays the evolution of surfboards from 16-footers weighing 200 pounds (90kg) to fiberglass creations known as potato-chip boards. There's a huge market among surfing dudes for memorabilia and thus much of the museum's collection is priceless. Surfing veterans such as Olympic-medal swimmer Duke Kahanamoka are honored here.

Other interesting museums include that of the **Historical Society** (tel: 760-722-4786; Thur–Sat); **Oceanside Museum of Art** (tel: 760-721-2787; Tue–Sun) and **Buena Vista Audubon** (tel: 760-439-2473; Tue–Sun) beside a lazy lagoon on the highway south of town. Four miles (6km) inland from the beach is the lovely **Mission San Luis Rey de Francia** (tel: 760-757-3651; daily), the largest of the California missions. Nearby is **Heritage Park** (tel: 760-433-8297; park daily, buildings Sun), whose old buildings include the cottage that was once Oceanside's post office.

Watch for the 101 Cafe as you drive through Oceanside. While the bright mural on its outside wall is a contemporary tribute to the glory days of

BELOW: surf's up in Oceanside.

Highway 101, the diner itself is the real thing. Built in 1928, it is the town's oldest restaurant and is filled with memorabilia. Oceanside has more cafés and shops located in a pleasant man-made harbor, with a lighthouse that serves as a marina for several hundred boats at the north end. From here, boats run across to **Santa Catalina Island** (for information, contact the Catalina Island Chamber of Commerce and Visitors Bureau, tel: 310-510-1520). Oceanside's pier, just north of Mission Avenue, is the longest recreational wooden pier on the West Coast. Hundreds of downtown walkways are marked with the mysterious O.U. MIRACLE, the name of contractor Orville Ullman Miracle, whose construction company submitted the winning bid in the 1920s to improve the community's streets.

OCEANSIDE TO LOS ANGELES

An interesting diversion from Oceanside is to drive inland along State Route 76 for a few miles to **San Antonio de Pala Mission** (tel: 760-742-3317; daily) on the Pala Indian Reservation. This is the only Californian mission still serving Native Americans. San Antonio has celebrated its Corpus Christi Festival, with an open-air mass, dances, and games, on the first Sunday of every June since 1816.

The United States Marine Corps occupies the coastal area north of Oceanside, where the coast road is incorporated into I-5 and the sea is half a mile away. Just north of the controversial San Onofre Nuclear Power Plant is **San Clemente** ❺, where former US president Richard Nixon, an Orange County native, set up a western White House on his 25-acre (10-hectare) estate. This attractive town, with its Spanish-looking tiled roofs and white stucco walls, prompted the *Los Angeles Times* to write in 1927: "If the charms of this place could be shown to the poor, snow-bound, wind-beaten people back East, there would

be an exodus so great the hills above San Clemente would be covered like mushrooms."

In 1925 the town's founder, a former mayor of Seattle named Ole Hanson, purchased and designed the community on what was then empty space. He is memorialized in **Casa Romantica** (tel: 949-498-2139; Tue–Sun), his old home near the Parque Del Mar, as well as the Ole Hanson Beach Club and Ole's Tavern.

Writing in the *San Clemente Journal*, Ann Batty claimed that it was San Clemente designers who first popularized the bikini on local beaches, of which there are many (bikinis *and* beaches). San Clemente and Doheny beaches allow camping for a small fee, and Doheny, Dana Point, Laguna Niguel, Irvine Coast, and Newport Beach all have marine life preserves (patrolled by state fish and game wardens) that are open to the public.

Festival of Whales

Capistrano Beach and Doheny State Beach lie astride the San Juan Creek just before **Dana Point**, where most of

Southern Californian hot-dogger waiting for a wave.

BELOW:
a vintage surfer "wave wagon."

Sometimes it's pigeons, rather than swallows, that arrive at Capistrano.

BELOW: flower-covered cliffs along the Laguna Beach coastline.

the buildings in the harbor complex are a lot younger than they look – although the overall effect is quite attractive. There are dozens of places to shop and eat, and whale-watching excursions depart from here in season (December–March). Dana Point's annual Festival of Whales is an amusing event with its imaginative whale costumes, and a parade of clowns, jugglers, and antique cars, as well as a lively street fair.

The **Ocean Institute** (tel: 949-496-2274; Sat–Sun) at the northern end of the harbor commemorates Richard Henry Dana, whose seafaring exploits from here resulted in the novel *Two Years Before the Mast*, which became a 1946 movie starring Alan Ladd. **Santa Catalina Island** can be reached from here, too, in daily trips that take 90 minutes each way (tel: 877-447-5263).

San Juan Capistrano

Interstate 5 now veers away from the coast and heads inland to the town of San Juan Capistrano. Following it into town, Del Obispo Street leads to Camino Capistrano, on which sits the famous **San Juan Capistrano Mission** ❻ (tel: 949-234-1330; daily), seventh in the chain of 21 established by Franciscan padres late in the 18th century. There's a statue of Father Junípero Serra, who founded this and eight other California missions.

The Serra chapel behind the church is the oldest building still in use within the state of California. Pick up a free map that identifies and dates the chapel's treasures, including the bells to the left of the church, and also tells where the swallows' nests can be found during their residence between their scheduled arrival on St Joseph's Day (March 19) and their departure for the warmer climate of Argentina on October 23. By some mysterious alchemy, the swallows have almost always been on time; their arrival here is marked by a week-long festival with mariachi bands leading a parade. Nevertheless, disappointed tourists sometimes arrive to find only pigeons.

Highway 1

Back on the coast, the Pacific Coast Highway now officially becomes Highway 1. It's been a while since the long-gone Serpentarium at **Laguna Beach** ❼ used to advertise that *rattlesnake à la Maryland* would be on the reptile zoo's menu, and today this upscale beach community is full of art galleries and chic shops. Laguna was always a favorite of Hollywood's movie colony, and Mary Pickford, Bette Davis, Judy Garland, and Rudolph Valentino were just a few of the movie stars who maintained homes here.

The resort has established a worldwide reputation with its annual **Pageant of the Masters** each summer, at which well-rehearsed volunteers take up their roles in living reproductions of famous paintings.

On the first Thursday of each month, the popular **Laguna Art Museum** (tel: 949-494-8971; daily) organizes the Art Walk, which visits some 40 local galleries. The Visitors Bureau located at 252 Broadway (tel:

949-497-9229; Mon–Fri) offers guidance on numerous other "heritage tours," which might include the **Murphy-Smith Historical Bungalow** (tel: 949-497-6834; Fri–Sun), one of the few houses in downtown Laguna Beach remaining from the 1920s.

For lovers of the outdoor life, there are many choices in addition to the annual whale-watching safaris. These include the **Laguna Coast Wilderness Park** (tel: 949-923-2235), a native plant and wildlife refuge on Laguna Canyon Road; the worthwhile **Pacific Marine Mammal Center** for sick and injured seals (tel: 949-494-3050; daily); **Laguna Outdoors** (tel: 949-874-6620) which offers scenic trail hiking along the coast; and the **Glenn E. Vedder Ecological Reserve** (tel: 949-497-6571) at the north section of the main beach, where marine life can be explored by divers. There are also thousands of acres of wilderness parks surrounding Laguna Beach, and maps are available at the Visitors Bureau.

Balboa peninsula

The upscale **Balboa peninsula**, with its 6 miles (10km) of sandy shore, encloses a harbor that is usually filled with yachts, with a large paddle-wheeler moored beside the highway bridge. Given pride of place on Main Street, it's hard to miss the **Balboa Pavilion**, built in 1905 as a railroad terminal, with its distinctive but totally unnecessary steeple. Behind it, if you get here early enough, you'll find fishing boats unloading their daily catch. Almost as old is the ferry that makes the 3-minute trip from the end of Palm Street to **Balboa Island**, with its million-dollar homes and classy shops and cafés. The hour-long walk around the island on the sidewalk hugging the water's edge is enjoyable, particularly just before twilight, not only for the fiery sunset, but for the evening lights reflected across the water from the Balboa Pavilion.

On your way back across the narrow channel, someone will surely point out, on nearby islands, the former homes of John Wayne and cowboy hero Roy Rogers. From **Balboa Pier**, you can admire the kite-flyers, frisbee-throwers, and bodysurfers. Check out the restaurant at the end of the pier before finishing up at the Balboa Fun Zone with its rides and video arcades.

Waves cascade over the breakwater in pretty **Newport Beach**, so it's not a great place for swimming; expert bodysurfers are the only people to truly excel in the water. The town does have other things to offer visitors, including the **Newport Harbor Nautical Museum** (tel: 949-675-8915; Wed–Sun), the well-stocked **Orange County Museum of Art** (tel: 949-759-1122; Wed–Sun) and the huge shopping paradise of **Fashion Island**, which is unmissable on the right-hand side of the road. You can also reach Santa Catalina from Newport Beach on the *Catalina Flyer*; check with the tourist office (tel: 800-942-6278). In **Corona del Mar**, just to the south, the gardens of the Sherman Library and Roger's Gardens are pleasant places to pause.

The upscale neighborhood of Newport Beach, Orange County, was the setting for the popular teenage drama television series The O.C., *which ran from 2003 to 2007, and propelled Mischa Barton into the limelight. However, most of the series was actually shot in Redondo Beach and Hermosa Beach.*

BELOW:
Spanish-style Balboa peninsula architecture.

Beaches and birdwatching

Many of the communities around here are in dispute about which most deserves the desirable Southern California title "Surf City," but **Huntington Beach ❽** claims to have the best case; in 1994, the town inaugurated a sidewalk **Surfers Walk of Fame** in the presence of its surf-fanatical congressman, Dana Rohrabacher. There's also an International Surfing Museum (tel: 714-960-3483; daily).

The highway heads along the coast past Huntington State Beach and the state's longest municipal pier, rebuilt in concrete after the original was destroyed by a fierce storm. Three blocks up Main Street and directly opposite the pier is Plaza Almeria, with an attractive collection of shops, restaurants and homes. Farther uptown, another old mall, the Huntington Beach Center, is an entertainment and shopping complex. Rail tycoon Henry Huntington first brought the railroad here late in the 19th century, and a subsequent oil boom introduced prosperity to a town that ironically is now best known for

its environmental awareness. Its 350-acre (140-hectare) Central Park, 50 percent of which is devoted to wildlife and greenery, is nothing but a taster compared with the sprawling **Bolsa Chica Ecological Reserve**, a vast coastal salt marsh that serves as a resting place for birds migrating between North and South America.

The best spot for birdwatchers is on the inland side of the highway between Golden West Street and Warner Avenue, opposite the entrance to the state beach. There are walking trails and plenty of parking. The **Interpretive Center** (tel: 714-846-1114; daily), which offers bird checklists, is at Warner Avenue. Not far away, between Warner and Heil avenues, is the **Monarch Butterfly Habitat**, where rare butterflies gather in the eucalyptus trees between November and March. Passing through the small, waterside community of **Sunset Beach**, you cannot help but notice a huge wooden water tower beside the highway that became a residence some years ago. Although the tower is private, it is a local landmark for miles around.

Life's a beach

At the Los Angeles County line, **Seal Beach**, an unspoiled enclave with an 80-year-old inn and a lengthy pier uncluttered with modern diversions, is the last place at which the ocean can be seen from the highway for many miles. To the right of the highway at **Belmont Shore**, you can make a diversion along Second Street, which skirts the beach of Alamitos Bay. **Gondola Getaway** on East Ocean Beach Boulevard (tel: 562-433-9595; daily) operates hour-long tours in real gondolas along canals that pass the elegant homes of neighboring **Naples**.

Highway 1 goes inland here, bypassing Long Beach, San Pedro, and the Palo Verdes Peninsula to hit the coast again just south of Redondo Beach.

Long live the *Queen*

Although the Pacific Coast Highway bypasses **Long Beach ❾**, it's worth passing through town to see some of its attractions, which include the world's largest mural, a panorama of marine life that covers the entire surface of the Long Beach Arena on Ocean Boulevard. Other sights include the magnificent **Aquarium of the Pacific** (tel: 562-590-3100; daily) and the venerable ship the *Queen Mary* (tel: 800-437-2934 or 562-435-3511; daily) – which made 1,000 transatlantic crossings and was a heroine of World War II before ending her journey here – moored in the harbor. The ship's history is a starry one, having been the carrier of choice for both celebrities and royalty; visitors can pretend to be the same by staying overnight in a cabin, or dine in the elegantly restored Art Deco restaurant.

Long Beach has positioned itself as a sleek, modern city in recent years, and it certainly has a number of architecturally chic new structures. But it's also anxious to promote its historic downtown buildings from the early part of the 20th century. A walking tour map of more than 40 of these landmarks is available from the Visitors Bureau (tel: 800-452-7829). Anyone traveling with kids might like to know that State Highway 22 east from Long Beach hooks up with I-5 and leads to Anaheim, where the attractions include **Disneyland**, Knotts Berry Farm, Adventure City, and Medieval Times.

Harbor tours

Headquarters of Southern California's fishing fleet, **San Pedro** once carried the distinction of being a genuine fishing port. The old town is now long gone, replaced by an imaginatively designed pseudo-19th-century construction called Ports O'Call Village. Several blocks of saltbox-type weathered-looking shops and numerous restaurants are a pleasure to walk around. Harbor tours and fishing trips leave from here (as well as the *Catalina Express* and a beautiful classic sailing ship), and there's masses of free parking space. Green and white trolleys run along the waterfront, stopping at the World Cruise center, the maritime museum, Ports O'Call Village and the Frank Gehry-designed **Cabrillo Marine Aquarium** (tel: 310-548-7562; Tue–Sun).

The famous Art Deco ocean liner, the Queen Mary, is now a restaurant and hotel in Long Beach.

BELOW: last summer ride.

Santa Monica rollerblader.

BELOW: wheeling along the Venice Beach bike path.

San Pedro's **Cabrillo Beach** has earned a reputation as one of the best places in the area to go windsurfing, and beginners especially favor the sheltered waters inside the harbor breakwater. Between March and September – twice a month, like clockwork – milky-white grunion fish ride in by the thousand on the tide to deposit their eggs in the sand.

On the **Palos Verdes** peninsula are multi-million-dollar Italianate villas and French chateaux overlooking the ocean. Abalone Cove, the beach west of Narcissa Drive, is an ecological preserve at the end of a steep path, perfect for divers and tide-poolers. Just past the Golden Shores mall is a lighthouse beside which, at the **Point Vicente Interpretive Center** (tel: 310-541-0334; daily), are long-lens telescopes for sighting passing whales (December to April), and an exhibit in which visitors can don earphones to hear the mournful voices of these loveable mammals.

About a mile farther on is the wood-and-glass **Wayfarers Chapel** (daily), designed by Frank Lloyd Wright's son, whose inspiration is said to have been Northern California's majestic redwood trees. The chapel was built in 1951 as a memorial to the 18th-century Swedish theologian Emmanuel Swedenborg. Walking around the peaceful gardens to the sound of songbirds, a fountain, and the gurgling stream is a very tranquil experience. There are services in the chapel at 11am every Sunday.

Walking on water

By now we are well and truly in **Los Angeles ❿** *(see page 236)*, although most of this sprawling city's inland tourist attractions lie quite a ways farther north. LA's southern beaches are varied and linked by a combination of Highway 1 and minor roads. After its chances of becoming a major port were wrecked by its vulnerability to severe storms, **Redondo Beach** turned its attention to tourism. A Pacific Electric Railway developer hired a Hawaiian teenager to demonstrate surfing, and before long visitors were flocking to watch "the man who can walk on water."

In the 1930s, even bigger crowds were lured by the gambling ships moored offshore – the most famous being the *Rex* – which could accommodate 1,500 customers, who took 25¢ rides out to the boat from the town pier. Offshore gaming was outlawed by Congress in 1946, but a pier remains at the center of the town's colorful boardwalk. The current pier is horseshoe-shaped, after several predecessors were destroyed by storms, while Redondo Beach itself is a big draw for bodybuilders.

Following Catalina Avenue from Redondo Pier leads to **Hermosa Beach**, an inland road leading past Kings Harbor Marina, opposite which an enormous ocean mural is painted on the wall of the power plant. Hermosa Avenue continues for quite a way one block from the beach. The beach itself stretches for 8 sandy miles (13km) between Kings Harbor and **Marina Del Rey**, the longest uninterrupted stretch in Los Angeles County. There are pedestrian-only streets leading from Hermosa Avenue to the beach at every block.

At 22nd Street, a good neighborhood place to sit outside and watch the locals while drinking a cup of coffee is Martha's Corner. Hermosa is known for its nightclubs, Marina Del Rey for its child-friendly beaches.

In between the two is **Manhattan Beach**, whose name came about because of a homesick New Yorker, who was living in the area in 1902 when just a dozen families made up the community. Its population grew dramatically during World War II when aircraft plants sprang up along Avalon Boulevard. In recent years, the Disney company has constructed a dozen enormous sound stages in what is still largely a commuter community of LA.

But in the last few years, this part of Orange County has become second only to Hollywood as a venue for moviemakers, with its coastal piers especially attractive to the makers of television commercials. The scene down by the water resembles an old episode of *Baywatch*, with plenty of bronzed and beautiful joggers, rollerbladers, and volleyball players.

Manhattan Beach was named by a homesick New Yorker in 1902. Hermosa Beach stretches for 8 miles (13km) between Kings Harbor and Marina Del Rey, making it the longest in LA County.

BELOW:
Pacific surfer on a misty shore.

Venice

Just north of Marina Del Rey, the long pedestrian and bicycle path linking **Venice ❶** (and **Venice Beach**) with Santa Monica is a lively hub of activity, especially in Venice itself, where you'll encounter rollerbladers of both sexes, rainbow-haired punks, magicians, fortune tellers, itinerant musicians, and pumped-up bodybuilders flexing their biceps at **Muscle Beach**. You can rent rollerblades on Windward Avenue or a bicycle on Washington Street (opposite the abandoned pier) or just sit at one of the sidewalk cafés and admire the passing parade. The most interesting place to grab a snack in Venice is probably the art- and artist-filled Rose Café on Rose Avenue. If you feel like getting away from the noise and the relentless body-beautiful activities, this is also a good spot from which to begin exploring Venice proper, which is surprisingly different from the image normally associated with the place.

Canals near the coast

The lesser-visited town of Venice is much more charming than the beach.

Take a stroll through the residential area around the inland canals, where a proliferation of bright flowers tumbles over sagging fences and ducks nestle under upturned boats on tiny jetties. Visitors can pick their way along rutted paths, over gentle humpbacked bridges and past lovingly tended gardens, admiring the variegated architecture, numerous birds, and floral displays.

More than 70 years after the death of Abbott Kinney, who acquired and reclaimed what was worthless marshland in anticipation of creating an "Italy in California," some of his vision still remains in what is probably the most pleasant walk in urban Los Angeles.

The original circulation system for the canals – which envisaged seawater pulsing through 30-inch (76cm) pipes with every fresh tide – proved unworkable, and the canals themselves became sand-clogged and stagnant. In 1993, a $6 million overhaul dredged and refilled the canals, repaired the adjoining paths, and rebuilt some of the bridges.

LA's Auto Museum

Lovers of automobiles and travel will want to make a sidetrip into Los Angeles to visit the Petersen Automotive Museum, one of the world's largest museums devoted exclusively to the history and cultural impact of the car. For when it comes to vehicles, no city knows them like Los Angeles, and no one can know Los Angeles without a vehicle. This city, unlike few others, was designed for the car, and its endless miles of freeway tie it together the way rivers tie together London or Paris. With a board of advisors comprising high-profile enthusiasts like racing ace Parnelli Jones, the four floors of this $40 million museum detail everything you ever wanted to know about four wheels, and the culture that rides above them. The second floor houses racing and classic cars, hot rods, movie-star cars, and vintage motorcycles. But the Petersen is not just about transportation; it's also about style. Although the museum has yet to host an exhibition on why balding old men buy flashy red sports cars, it does have rotating cultural exhibitions covering such novelties as low-riding cars, and the history of that quintessential American icon: the pick-up truck. The Petersen Museum is at 6060 Wilshire Boulevard, tel: 323-930-2277; Tue–Sun.

Movie-star coast

Santa Monica ⑫ is a seaside resort where Los Angeles' West Side meets the ocean. In the streets behind and the canyons above lie the most famous of LA's attractions: Hollywood, Beverly Hills, Rodeo Drive. But down near the waterside, the "Bay City" of Raymond Chandler's novels is a pleasant place to be. The boulevards and side streets are attractive places to stroll and shop. The trendy **Third Street** pedestrian mall, lined with restaurants, stores, bars, and movie theaters, is usually filled with street performers by day and nightlife seekers after dark.

The town's landmark is the century-old **Santa Monica Pier**, which has an assortment of amusement arcades, fairground rides, souvenir stands, snack bars, and sedentary fishermen along its lengthy boardwalk. There's also a wonderful carousel with 44 hand-carved horses which featured in the 1973 film *The Sting*. On either side is the wide, sandy beach bordered by a busy bicycle path.

The clifftop **Palisades Park**, a euca-lyptus-fringed grassy stretch along Ocean Avenue, overlooks the beach and offers views of boats and sunsets. In recent years, the park has proved to be a popular venue for the homeless – although their presence should not deter you from visiting. To one side is an information cabin for bro-chures and useful tips on where to catch local buses. Main Street, with its murals, shops and numerous excel-lent restaurants, is also worth exploring. Looming over the corner with Rose Avenue is Jonathan Borofsky's giant sculpture, *Ballerina Clown*.

One of the many colorful beach houses in Santa Monica.

The mansions along the seashore at the northern end of Santa Monica were mostly built by moviedom's former elite. The grandest, at 415 Pacific Coast Highway, was the 118-room compound designed for William Randolph Hearst and his paramour, Marion Davies. The house was sold to the owner of the Hotel Bel Air, who turned it into a beach hotel and club. ❏

BELOW:
reflections at dusk,
Santa Monica Pier.

LOS ANGELES TO SAN FRANCISCO

This legendary stretch of Highway 1 takes in the California coast's most famous attractions: extravagant Hearst Castle and fog-shrouded Big Sur

The distance from Los Angeles to San Francisco is 380 miles (611km). Taking Interstate 5 all the way means a city-to-city trip can be accomplished in around six hours, but that would be a pity. Highway 1 hugs the coast almost the entire way, presenting heart-stopping curves, breathtaking scenery, pretty inns, scenic sites, and two of California's best attractions – Hearst Castle and Big Sur. With all of this to savor, allowing two days rather than six hours makes far more sense.

LOS ANGELES TO SANTA BARBARA

The Pacific Coast Highway out of Los Angeles cruises along **Malibu** ⑬ with the ease that community's name implies. Despite its worldwide reputation for hijinks and hedonism, the area is largely a private residential community where much of the beach has been cordoned off (at the junction with Webb Way) into the exclusive Malibu Colony. The must-see place is **Getty Villa** (tel: 310-440-7300, Thur–Mon). The original home of the Getty Museum was fashioned after an ancient Roman villa and now houses the Getty Center's (see page 237) superb collection of Greek, Roman and Etruscan antiquities. Also worth visiting is **Adamson House** (tel: 310-456-8432; tours Wed–Sat), built in 1929 for May Ridge, the widow of the man who bought most of what now comprises Malibu back in 1897. The

richly decorated house, replete with tiles from the Ridges' short-lived Malibu Pottery, is a fascinating repository of history about the early Hollywood crowd, who were perfectly content with ocean-front shacks.

North of Malibu, the beaches are more accessible and there's a string of them – **Point Dume**, **Zuma**, and **Leo Carrillo** – until the highway turns inland toward Ventura. Highway 1 is submerged into US 101 here, and you must leave it to visit **Ventura** ⑭ itself, which has a huge city hall perched on

Main attractions
MALIBU
SANTA BARBARA
PISMO STATE BEACH
SAN LUIS OBISPO
MORRO BAY
CAMBRIA
PASO ROBLES WINE REGION
HEARST CASTLE
PIEDRAS BLANCAS BEACH
BIG SUR
CARMEL
MONTEREY

LEFT: view of San Francisco.
BELOW: Steller's sea lions, Monterey.

BELOW:
Santa Barbara Mission – an example of the "myth of tradition" created by the city's architects.

the hillside and a heavily restored "Olde Towne." The 1782 **San Buenaventura Mission** (tel: 805-643-4318; daily) is pretty and worth a visit, and Ventura's harbor area has lots of seafood restaurants. Most of the town's sites are connected by trolley.

Inland along State Route 150, hidden away on the edge of the Los Padres National Forest, is **Ojai** (pronounced *O-hi*), a sleepy artists' and writers' colony near which the 1926 movie *Lost Horizon* was filmed. The town is centered around a main street on which a graceful tower offsets a row of unpretentious shops built under a covered veranda. Artifacts in the Historical Society Museum include those from Chumash Indian times through the ranching period to the days when heavyweight champion Jack Dempsey cleared rocks from what became "Pop" Soper's training ranch. Dozens of boxers trained here, including hero Dempsey himself, while preparing for his fight against Gene Tunney in 1926. On the outskirts of Santa Barbara, the **Montecito Inn** (tel: 805-969-7854) has been popular with discerning refugees

from Hollywood since the 1920s, when one of its original owners was Charlie Chaplin and guests included Fatty Arbuckle, Fred Astaire, and Will Rogers. More than 1,000 two-reeler movies were shot in the Santa Barbara area, most of them between 1913 and 1918; Chicago producer Samuel S. Hutchinson's Flying A Studios alone brought in such silent-screen film celebrities as Mary Pickford and D.W. Griffith. Because of its lower costs and proximity to Los Angeles, many movies and television shows continue to be shot in the region today.

Montecito's legendary **San Ysidro Ranch** (tel: 805-969-5046), in a canyon lined with sycamore and eucalyptus trees, was where John F. Kennedy honeymooned with his wife Jackie; where Lauren Bacall says she fell in love with Humphrey Bogart; and where Laurence Olivier and Vivien Leigh had a midnight wedding in 1940.

Santa Barbara

The most striking aspect of **Santa Barbara ⑮** is its distinctive Mediterranean architecture: the white-washed

adobe, tiled roofing, and iron grill-work permeate a city in which, as one local writer noted, "its architects were able to create a myth of a tradition, which turned out to be far more believable than the realities of factual history." It boasts miles of enticing wide beaches and the **Santa Barbara Mission** (tel: 805-682-4713; daily), the coast's "queen of the missions," arguably the most beautiful in the state. Another highlight is historic **Stearns Wharf**, the oldest pier on the California coast. The pier contains an aquarium, wine-tasting rooms, harbor cruises, fishing facilities, and seafood stands. A waterfront shuttle tram operates between the wharf, Downtown, and the zoo, for easy access to the beaches and palm-lined promenade along the shore.

Downtown Santa Barbara is best explored on foot on the self-guided Red Tile walking tour; pick up a map at the visitor center on Cabrillo Boulevard (tel: 805-965-3021; daily). It takes you along State Street, the city center's attractive shopping street, and over to the handsome 1929 Spanish-Moorish

Court House (tel: 805-962-6464; daily). Its lobby is lined with mosaics and murals, and there's a lovely view from the top of gently sloping roofs and the multi-level lawn below. The route winds through the area where the city began around the old **Presidio.** Inspect 18th-century adobes, and have lunch in the charming, cobbled street called **El Paseo**, where the local theater once featured a dancer named Rita Cansino, later to become better known as Rita Hayworth.

Channel Islands

Between Christmas and late March, there are daily excursions into the offshore Santa Barbara Channel for whale watching. Year-round trips are also made to Santa Barbara Island, whose 640 acres (260 hectares) are a haven for birds, sea lions, 10,000 breeding seals, and other marine life. None of the **Channel Islands** (tel: 805-658-5730), run by the National Park Service, is inhabited, but overnight camping is allowed and island rangers conduct tours. For more information, go to www.nps.gov/chis.

The Santa Lucia mountain range is a successful wine-producing region.

BELOW:
a brown pelican watches over Pismo Beach.

NO OVERHEAD CASTING

SANTA BARBARA TO BIG SUR

After meandering through **Gaviota State Park** (tel: 805-968-1033; daily), Highways 1 and 101 split apart, but both turn inland. It's most fun to continue driving on Highway 1, the road nearest the coast, which heads through sleepy **Lompoc**, ennobled by the presence of **La Purisima Concepcion** (tel: 805-733-3713; daily), the state's 11th mission. North of town, the road passes through an immense area of agri-business-dominated land, irrigated fields used for growing broccoli, cauliflower, and strawberries as well as extensive fields of flowers, which in season offer an extraordinary display of magentas, pinks, golds, and purples. These supply most of the floral seeds that color the fields of the entire US.

Vast fields continue past **Guadalupe**, a quiet, old-fashioned town with an Amtrak station and one-story buildings dating to the turn of the 20th century. Eighteen miles (29km) north, **Pismo State Beach**, once famous for its huge clams (still celebrated with a Clam Festival every October), has fabulous sandy shores stretching all around the bay and leads directly into San Luis Obispo, which is more or less the midway point between Los Angeles and San Francisco. Pismo is one of the few beaches where driving is allowed, so look out for dune buggies. Just before San Luis Obispo, keep an eye open for the extraordinary **Madonna Inn** (tel: 805-543-3000), each of whose 109 rooms are individually decorated in memorably kitsch fashion.

The attractive, low-key college town of **San Luis Obispo ⓰** (SLO) also has an 18th-century mission (tel: 805-781-8220; daily), with a downtown community located around its plaza. There's an Art Center (tel: 805-543-8562; Wed–Mon) and, across from the mission, the County Historical Museum (Wed–Sun, daily in summer).

Morro Bay

Morro Bay is dominated by its 576ft (176-meter) -high rock, whose aeries now shelter the endangered peregrine falcon, the 175mph (282kph) dive-bomber that feeds on live game. There's an excellent beach, and the restaurant-

BELOW: Morro Rock – a volcanic plug in the bay.

fringed harbor is an attractive place to walk around – but be aware that the harbor drive dead-ends in both directions and parking can be difficult. Follow it to the end below Morro Rock, where you can see seal lions and watch playful sea otters wrapping themselves in kelp. The beach is busy long before the tourists arrive, however – ubiquitous is the coastal snowy plover, a threatened species. The **Museum of Natural History** (tel: 805-772-2694; daily) contains exhibits that deal with coastal animal, marine, and plant life, including the Monarch butterfly. This short-lived beauty, with its amber and black wings, can be seen near Pacific Grove (up by Monterey) during the winter months.

Thirteen miles (21km) north, beyond the pretty town of **Cayucos**, is the laid-back town of **Cambria**, set below the hills with its lovely Moonstone Beach. In between the two towns, State Highway 46 winds east through the barren but beautiful hills of the Santa Lucia mountain range, linking up to US 101 and **Paso Robles**. This is a charming, small, wine-producing region where most of the wineries offer free daily tastings. A map of local wineries is available from the Visitor and Conference Bureau (tel: 805-238-0506) in Paso Robles, not far from the **Paso Robles Pioneer Museum** (tel: 805-239-4556; Thur–Sun afternoons), which provides a little lesson in local history.

Hearst Castle

Back on the coast, the hamlet of **San Simeon** is the nearest community to the house of San Simeon, more famously known as **Hearst Castle** ⑰ (daily). For many years, Hearst Castle was the largest private residence in the US; now it vies with Disneyland for the title of "the state's most popular attraction." Perched over the sea on a hill so high the house is often wreathed in fog, its construction began in 1919, financed by newspaper and movie tycoon William Randolph Hearst. Craftsmen labored for 28 years to create the twin-towered home on *La Cuesta Encantada*, "the Enchanted Hill," which Hearst then filled with carvings, furnishings, and works of art from European castles and cathedrals. (Dur-

> *She was very nice and I liked her. She didn't have an awful lot to say...all the men used to flock around her. She was very attractive in an evening dress because she never wore anything under it.*
>
> Marion Davies on Jean Harlow

BELOW:
Hearst Castle.

ing his lifetime, Hearst accumulated one of the largest collections of private art in the world, with a value measured in the hundreds of millions of dollars.) All materials for the house had to be brought up the coast by steamer, then hauled up that impossible hill. San Simeon's grounds were stocked with animals from all over the world, and Hollywood's elite, like Jean Harlow and Clark Gable, were invited to stroll through the beautiful gardens or enjoy the magnificent indoor and outdoor swimming pools.

Reservations for Hearst Castle (tel: 800-444-4445) are virtually mandatory to secure a place on one of the five daily tours, some of which include the home movies of Hearst, whose lonely, lavish lifestyle was the subject of Orson Welles' most celebrated movie, *Citizen Kane*. Tour 1 is probably the best for first-time visitors, as it gives the best overview of the castle and main rooms. Although Hearst Castle is extremely busy, especially during the summer months, the estate is efficiently run, and timed entry means you can go away and have a picnic on the beach

below if the wait proves to be a long one. Unmissable.

Four miles (6km) north, Piedras Blancas is the birthplace each January of thousands of elephant seals. Well into spring, from the walkway overlooking the beach, you can watch the young pups learning to swim. The sheer number of these long-nosed creatures is amazing, and nowhere else on the coast can you see them this close.

Big Sur

The 94-mile (151km) stretch of coastline between San Simeon and the Monterey Peninsula is known as **Big Sur** ⑱, a legendary wilderness of holistic healing retreats and remote homesteads inhabited by third-generation pioneers. The area was barely accessible to traffic until 1937, and even now the sheer cliffs of the Santa Lucia Mountains hugged by the highway occasionally slide into the sea, leaving residents in complete isolation until the road is rebuilt. There are no roads inland between Cambria and Monterey, so it is wise to check the situation before proceeding. And fill

up your tank, preferably in Morro Bay as prices leap in Cambria and gas stations beyond are few – and expensive – along this stretch.

The dark, thicketed mountains rise steeply to the right; the foamy sea to the left constantly changes shape and color. Only the two-lane road separates the two, which means the curling ribbon of road has its own distinct weather pattern. For this read: fog. Although the sun may be shining brightly on the other side of the mountain, and can often be seen slatted through the trees, Highway 1 can be distinctly chilly, and the fog comes on quickly, obliterating the world for unexpected moments. Infrequent guard rails, looking suspiciously flimsy, are small comfort in the face of the menacing rocks below. Driving along Big Sur is not for the faint-hearted, but for those with a sense of adventure and time on their side, this stretch of the California coastline is one of the most exhilarating routes in the US. For added excitement, try it in a convertible or on a motorcycle. Traveling nonstop with good weather, you could

arrive in Carmel in about 3 hours, but the best way is to pause, then pause again, then stay at least for lunch or dinner. This is especially important for the person at the wheel, as the view is so fabulous, but the road so hazardous, it can be frustrating if frequent stops are not taken. Luckily, scenic overlooks are numerous.

Coming from San Simeon, the hills begin gently enough, and the road is fairly easy to navigate. The first sight on the right is **Los Padres National Forest**, the southern tip of the coastal redwood belt, which contains several almost preternaturally beautiful state parks. **Julia Pfeiffer Burns State Park** and **Pfeiffer Big Sur State Park** have wonderful trails that lead up into the mountains or down toward the sea, the former park with a waterfall near McWay Cove that rewards the completion of a (non-demanding) hike.

The long and winding road

As the road twists and turns northward, anybody on a motorcycle will wish they had worn a heavy sweater. Arriving at **Big Sur Village** ⑲ confirms it is

Highway 1 runs almost the entire length of California. The Big Sur stretch is not for the faint-hearted.

BELOW: the stunning rocky coastline of Big Sur.

really little more than a huddle of shops and a post office. Places to stay are few and far between; if you're planning to be in Big Sur overnight during the summer months or on *any* weekend, be sure to book well in advance. The accommodations range from private campgrounds to luxury inns.

Big Sur has always attracted unusual people. Until 1945, it was mainly populated by ranchers, loggers, and miners, but soon after, literary people turned up to stay. The **Henry Miller Memorial Library** (tel: 831-667-2574; Wed–Mon), near **Nepenthe restaurant**, where everybody goes for sunset, has works by and about this local literary hero, who called the area "the face of the earth as the creator intended it to look." In the 1960s, New Agers began communing at the hot spring called Esalen, named after the Native Americans who discovered it. Now the spring is owned by the **Esalen Institute**, where New Agers still congregate. North of the village is the area's crowning manmade achievement, the **Bixby Bridge**. Spanning the steep walls of Bixby Canyon and often obscured by fog, the bridge was called an engineering marvel when it was constructed in 1932.

BIG SUR TO SAN FRANCISCO

Leaving the lush lands of Big Sur for the cities on the Monterey Peninsula can be a shock to the system. A way to ease this uncomfortable transition is to visit one last natural wonder on the way, the undramatic but still lovely **Point Lobos State Reserve** (tel: 831-624-4909; daily). Miles of trails with glimpses of deer, rabbits, sea lions, and sea otters are gentle features that children will love. So did Robert Louis Stevenson, who is said to have been inspired to write *Treasure Island* while at Point Lobos. Several short footpaths traverse the rock-strewn headland, on which is one of two existing groves of ghostly Monterey Cypress trees.

Carmel and Monterey

Carmel ❷⁰ the "Gateway to the Monterey Peninsula" has gained a reputation as being something of an artists' and writers' haven, but – owing to

BELOW: lone tree on a rocky outcrop, Carmel.

the cost of local real estate – is really more a place for selling creative works than making them. Carmel is a classically beautiful little town that has outlawed high-rises, neon signs, traffic lights, parking meters – anything possessing the foul taint of city life, including artificial house plants. Its residents include Hollywood's Clint Eastwood, who famously did a stint as the town's mayor, and Doris Day. The downtown streets are lined with upscale shops and galleries. **Carmel Mission** (tel: 831-624-1271; daily) and **Carmel Beach** are very appealing, and just to the north is justly famous **Pebble Beach**, home to the challenging golf course of the same name.

Motorcyclists are not allowed on the peninsula's **17-Mile Drive**, which even charges a hefty entrance fee to drive around admiring its luxurious private homes. These look, in fact, much like any other affluent American neighborhood, and given the proximity to the exquisite Big Sur coast, the shoreline along this private road is pretty expendable.

Cannery Row in **Monterey** ㉑ at the north end of the peninsula basks in the glow of John Steinbeck's brilliant novel of the same name. Steinbeck's world withered with the mysterious disappearance of the sardines in the mid-1940s, and today the district is a tacky tourist trap.

A visit is redeemed, however, by a few hours spent at the excellent **Monterey Bay Aquarium** (tel: 831-648-4888; daily), California's finest and one of the best in the world, which explores to admirable effect the marine life found in a Grand Canyon-sized trench just offshore. Wall-length tanks house sharks, regal salmon, and schools of tiny fish amid beds of kelp that writhe with the simulated tides. Highlights include the new Seahorses exhibit and the scheduled feeding times – the sea otters are especially amusing. If possible, time your visit to coincide with feeding time, when keepers in wet suits climb into the glass tanks and talk to spectators through underwater microphones.

Cormorants nesting on the California coast.

BELOW: humorous Carmel-by-the-Sea town plan by muralist, Bill Bates.

TIP

From the boardwalk behind the fog signal building at Pigeon Point Lighthouse (whose grounds are open to the public), keep an eye out for gray whales on their annual migration from January through April.

Fisherman's Wharf is a delightful pier lined with tourist shops, restaurants, and stands selling clam chowder in bread bowls. In the boat-filled harbor you'll see – and hear – resident seals. Inland from the pier, Monterey State Historic Park has a cluster of interesting museums and buildings from the town's early days. The self-guided Path of History walking tour leads to many more in the town center. In nearby **Salinas**, Steinbeck's life is celebrated at the **National Steinbeck Center** (tel: 831-796-3833; daily). Traffic on the stretch of coast north towards San Francisco can sometimes be horrendous. If so, you may wish to detour on State Highway 183 to **Castroville**, the "Artichoke Capital of the World," where the Giant Artichoke Restaurant serves the delicious deep-fried leaves.

Half-moons and lighthouses

Highway 1 is bordered by flat agricultural fields, with the freshest of produce sold along the roadside: California's finest artichokes, cherries, and strawberries. The cute, colorful beach town of **Capitola** is a pleasant

place for a stroll, its beach wall decorated with bright tiles seemingly made by local children. The university city of **Santa Cruz** ㉒ is famous for its century-old Beach Boardwalk, with a popular amusement park, thrilling roller coaster, and arcade games alongside the beach. Dine on yummy Dungeness crab in season in one of the restaurants on the pier, then drive along West Cliff Drive, lined with beautiful homes, to see surfers hitting the waves below the cliffs near the Santa Cruz Surfing Museum.

Further up the coast through fields of artichokes is the attractive wide beach at **Scott Creek**, north of **Davenport**. Tan, black, and white cows graze together in fields high up on the cliffs before Highway 1 swoops down to **Waddell Creek** and the driftwood-lined beaches (such as Bean Hollow State Beach and Pescadero State Beach) all the way up to the Santa Cruz county line. Thin slivers of fog can sometimes obscure the view, but when it shifts (which it does every few minutes), drivers are rewarded by views of **Pigeon Point Lighthouse** ㉓, which can be seen from the highway in both directions. At 115ft (35 meters), it is one of the tallest lighthouses in the country and has been in use since 1872.

Heading toward San Francisco, wide, flat fields lie between the highway and the coast. Attractive **Half Moon Bay** ㉔ is only half an hour's drive from the city, and is famous not only for its pumpkins but for the huge waves that pound its shores. Surfers from all around come to tackle the big ones – up to 40ft (12 meters) high – and the talk in the bars is all of "mavericks" and "tubes." Sunday lunchtimes at Half Moon often include jazz or rock concerts.

With the suburbs of the city on the horizon, the coastline becomes rocky and untrafficked again. **Gray Whale Cove State Beach** or **Big Basin Park** are peaceful places for a final walk or picnic before hitting the big time – **San Francisco** (see page 350). ❏

BELOW: Beach Boardwalk amusement park, Santa Cruz.
RIGHT: Bixby Bridge, Big Sur, was called an engineering marvel in 1932.

San Francisco: City By The Bay

Fisherman's Wharf, Chinatown, the Golden Gate Bridge – this city wins hearts straightaway and effortlessly.

Each visitor takes a different memory away from San Francisco: the steep street that drops off toward the bay, the fog drifting through the Golden Gate Bridge, the dishes expertly blended making the perfect meal or the simple fun of a cable-car ride, admiring Victorian houses along the way.

Begin at **Union Square**, where a winged statue commemorates Admiral George Dewey's naval victory over the Spanish in 1898. **Chinatown Gate** appears just to the northeast. While it is no secret to tourists, crowds of Chinese residents vying for space on the sidewalk show the area still caters to locals. Tiny herb shops in mysterious alleys promise everything from rheumatism relief to the restoration of sexual prowess.

Chinatown ends where **North Beach** begins. While a few seedy clubs still promise lap dances, critically acclaimed restaurants, and posh nightclubs entice a different crowd altogether. But this traditional Italian neighborhood still attracts writers and artists, particularly to the **City Lights** bookstore.

To the east, **Telegraph Hill** rises above North Beach, offering spectacular views across San Francisco Bay. **Coit Tower** (tel: 415-362-0808; daily), with its momentous views and frescoes, crowns the hill and can be climbed. Follow Columbus Avenue to **Fisherman's Wharf.** The fishing boats put out before dawn; their catch determines the "special of the day" at the numerous restaurants clustered around the wharf. Lined with shops and ready to please tourists, this is a "must" stop for all; locals eat here too, even if they do not shop here.

At the opposite end of the Embarcadero is another San Francisco landmark. Built in 1903, the **Ferry Building** survived the Great Fire and in its heyday was a hub for water transport between the bay communities. It has now been renovated to house the Ferry Building Marketplace, a foodie's heaven with a fantastic farmers' market and stalls selling gourmet foodstuffs. From here you can ride the vintage electric streetcars of the F-line to Fisherman's Wharf or along Market Street to the Castro district.

A mile offshore from San Francisco is windswept **Alcatraz** (boat tickets – tel: 415-981-7625; daily). Once home to such hardened criminals as Al Capone and the notorious Machine Gun Kelley, officials closed the prison in 1963 when repair

costs grew too great. A tour of the prison is surprisingly rewarding; be sure to bring a sweater for the breezy boat ride over.

A ride on the **Powell-Hyde cable car** begins two blocks inland from Hyde Street Pier, offering a tour of Russian Hill's high-rise apartments and mansions. The cable car passes near the curvy section of Lombard Street often seen in movies and continues on to **Nob Hill**, called the "hill of palaces" by Robert Louis Stevenson.

At the corner of Washington and Mason streets, the **Cable Car Museum** (tel: 415-474-1887; daily) exhibits the city's transit history alongside the operating machinery that pulls the glamorous transportation through town.

The Financial District holds three impressive landmarks. The **Embarcadero Center**, the **Bank of America building** – so tall its roof sometimes disappears in the fog, and the distinctive **Transamerica Pyramid**, with 48 floors the tallest building in San Francisco.

"South of Market," or **SoMa**, is a focal point for art galleries, cafés, nightclubs, and local theaters. The **San Francisco Museum of Modern Art** (tel: 415-357-4000; Thur–Tue) spearheads the attractions, which also include the Yerba Buena Gardens, the Center for the Arts, the Cartoon Art Museum, the Museum of the California Historical Society, and the Foto-Grafix bookshop which sells Ansel Adams books and prints. The **Asian Art Museum** (tel: 415-581-3500; Tue–Sun) is located in the Civic Center district. It contains 10,000 artifacts dating back 3,500 years.

Mission Street heads south into the heart of the Mission district, San Francisco's melting pot of Latin American cultures. The thick adobe walls of Mission Dolores, built in 1776, still form the oldest building in San Francisco, which can be visited.

To the west lies the celebrated gay community of **Castro**. Same-sex couples and rainbow flags fill the streets lined with table-hopping bars. It's a lively, fun, and light-hearted area, regardless of your gender.

Farther west is the **Haight-Ashbury** district. Haight Street was once so gaudy and bizarre that tour buses full of goggle-eyed tourists ran up and down it. Like most such radical departures from the social norm, the hippie experiment fell victim to time and fashion. The neighborhood retains its anti-establishment roots, but today piercing shops

and tattoo parlors replace flower power. It's still a fun stretch, however, with great shopping and a wide range of inexpensive restaurants and cafés.

Golden Gate Park (tel: 415-831-2700), 3 miles (5km) long and almost half a mile wide, consists of tree groves dotted with lakes, meadows, windmills, and dells. Despite the thousands of visitors, it's easy to find tranquility here. In addition to peace, the Conservatory of Flowers offers sweet scents and botanical beauty, and the Music Concourse holds Sunday concerts.

The **California Academy of Sciences** (tel: 415-379-8000; daily) includes animal dioramas, 16,000 specimens of marine life at the Steinhart Aquarium and a laser light show at the Morrison Planetarium. The Japanese Tea Garden claims to be the birthplace of the fortune cookie.

The beautiful and neoclassical **Legion of Honor** (tel: 415-750-3600; Tue–Sun) is unmissable. At the entrance is one of five bronze casts of Rodin's *The Thinker*.

The **Golden Gate Bridge** extends beyond the wonderful Golden Gate National Recreation Area. A promenade goes through Crissy Field, an airfield-turned-picnic area that belongs to the 1,480-acre (600-hectare) **Presidio**. In it stands the Plaster Palace, the classic rococo rotunda of the Palace of Fine Arts, housing the hands-on exhibits of the **Exploratorium** (tel: 415-561-0360; Tue–Sun). ❏

LEFT: a cable car trundles up Nob Hill; the landmark Transamerica Pyramid was ridiculed when it was built in 1972. **RIGHT:** classic car and residential architecture.

SAN FRANCISCO TO OREGON

The Pacific Coast Highway threads its way past golden beaches, hot-tub hideaways, good wineries, and the tallest living things on earth

From San Francisco to the town of Crescent City, which is itself about half an hour's drive from the Oregon border, is 363 miles (584km). Coastal beaches, wineries, and redwood forests are the attractions of this beautiful journey, with trees so massive you can even drive through a few of them.

A trio of "goldens" marks the contributions of **San Francisco** ㉕ to the Pacific Coast Highway, as Highway 1 passes straight through the city's Golden Gate Park, across the Golden Gate Bridge, and flirts with the southeastern edge of the Golden Gate National Recreation Area. The pretty little harbor of **Sausalito** ㉖ is located just off the highway, over the famous orange-red bridge, with a turn-off to the right. The waterside shops, the warrens of pricey but perfect boutiques, and the houses perched behind them on a steep slope draw comparisons to Mediterranean villas of the Riviera. As there is little to do except stroll around or eat and drink, Sausalito might best be visited on a day trip by ferry from San Francisco, leaving you free to cruise westward toward the coast, passing near **Mount Tamalpais**, with its gorgeous views of the city in the far distance; the giant redwoods of 300-acre (120-hectare) **Muir Woods**; and **Stinson Beach**, the city's favorite destination on the few occasions it gets hot enough to swim. The slow, winding coast road bypasses the town of **Boli-** nas, on a thin sliver of a peninsula, which tries so hard not to attract visitors that a hard-core body of locals keeps stealing the highway signs.

The gorgeous **Point Reyes National Seashore** stretches northward for miles along a peninsula off which is the **Point Reyes Lighthouse** (tel: 415-669-1534; visitor center and lighthouse stairs: Thur–Mon). The scenic road out to the lighthouse passes through attractive **Inverness**, which has several inns, restaurants, and a good deli and bakery.

Main attractions
POINT REYES NATIONAL
  SEASHORE
SONOMA VALLEY
NAPA VALLEY
BODEGA BAY
MENDOCINO
AVENUE OF THE GIANTS
FERNDALE
EUREKA
REDWOOD NATIONAL PARK

LEFT: Muir Woods National Monument.
BELOW: a Russian River Valley winery.

San Francisco to Seattle

San Francisco ㉕ California

Sausalito ㉖
Point Reyes National Seashore

116 Petaluma
1
12 121

Napa Sonoma
12 116

29 Santa Rosa Salt Point State Park
Inverness

Bodega
Bodega Bay ㉗
Jenner
★ Fort Ross State Historic Park
Stewarts Point

Gualala
★ Point Arena Lighthouse ㉘
Elk
Albion

Van Damme State Park Mendocino ㉙
Fort Bragg ㉚

Westport

Leggett Lost Coast
Garberville

㉛ Avenue of the Giants - Humboldt Redwoods S.P.
101 Phillipsville Cape Mendocino Lighthouse
Scotia
211 Ferndale ㉜

Humboldt Bay National Wildlife Refuge
Fortuna

Eureka ㉝

Arcata
McKinleyville
101 Patrick's Point State Park Trinidad ㉞

Orick

Redwood N.P.

Jedediah Smith Redwoods State Park
Klamath ㉟
★ Trees of Mystery
Gasquet 199 Crescent City ㊱

California
Oregon

Harris Beach State Park Brookings-Harbor ㊲

101 Samuel H. Boardman State Park
Gold Beach
Humbug Mountain State Park

Cape Blanco Lighthouse Port Orford ㊳
Langlois

Bandon Marsh National Wildlife Refuge Bandon ㊴

Coos Bay Charleston
North Bend ● Shore Acres State Park

Oregon Dunes National Recreation Area ㊵
101
★ Umpqua Lighthouse
Reedsport
Gardiner
Florence
★ Sea Lion Caves
Yachats ㊶
Waldport ㊷

㊸ Yaquina Head Lighthouse ★ Newport ㊸
Devil's Punchbowl ★ Lincoln City ㊺
Devil's Lake State Recreation Area
● Siuslaw National Forest
101 Cloverdale
Cape Meares Lighthouse Tillamook ㊻
6 Portland ㊼
Garibaldi
Rockaway Beach
Oswald West State Park Manzanita
Cannon Beach ㊽
101 Seaside ㊾
Warrenton
Oregon Lewis and Clark National Historical Park Astoria ㊿
Washington Columbia Lewis and Clark National Wildlife Refuge
Ilwaco
★ Willapa Bay 103 Long Beach
Oysterville

South Bend ㊿①
Raymond

105 Grayland

㊿③ Seattle Aberdeen ㊿②
101
Olympic Peninsula

Wine country

For a popular diversion from the coast, take the road east from Point Reyes Station (alternatively, take Highway 101 north from Sausalito through Novato) to Petaluma, turning east on Highway 116. After the upscale communities crowded around the bay, the beautifully open, rolling hills and farmland come as a surprise, but Marin County is largely agricultural. The Marin French Cheese Company, beside a small lake and picnic area, makes a pretty stop. Or visit the Cowgirl Creamery in Point Reyes Station to watch local cheeses being made.

At Petaluma, turn east on Highway 116 for **Sonoma**, hub of the Sonoma Valley wine country. Its central plaza and several historic buildings date from the era of Mexican rule in the mid-19th century. With around 40 wineries spread out through the valley, Sonoma feels less hectic than its famous neighbor. Highlights include the Gloria Ferrer Champagne Caves, Château St Jean, and the Buena Vista Winery, California's oldest winery dating from 1857. A guide to wine-tasting throughout the valley is available from the Sonoma Valley Visitors Bureau on First Street (tel: 866-996-1090; daily).

On the eastern side of the mountains, Highway 29 runs through America's most renowned wine region, **Napa Valley**. Some 300 wineries lie cheek by jowl in this beautiful rolling landscape, ranging from boutique winemakers to vast corporate operations. It can be a little overwhelming for first-time visitors, so stop by the Napa Valley visitor center (tel: 707-226-7459; daily) in **Napa** town center for a guide to tastings and tours.

There are tasting rooms in Napa itself, an attractive riverside town with good restaurants, gourmet food shops, and galleries. Pretty **St Helena**, with its lovely old homes and upscale shopping, is a favorite base. At the northern end of the valley, **Calistoga** is most appealing of all, with its mineral baths, arcaded Victorian-era main street, and casual air.

Coastal drama

Back on the coast, Highway 1 winds along beautiful Tomales Bay, passing oyster farms and rustic hamlets such as Olema and Tomales with its 1850s wooden buildings.

It's no coincidence that Alfred Hitchcock filmed his 1963 movie *The Birds* around **Bodega Bay** ㉗, where hundreds of bird species can be found. Brown pelicans are especially abundant. Just to the south and slightly inland, in the separate village of **Bodega**, you can see the schoolhouse and St Teresa's church which featured in the movie.

After **Sonoma Coast State Beach**, another really dramatic portion of the California coast begins, where Rivers End sits overlooking the mouth of the Russian River at **Jenner**. For miles, Highway 1 snakes around the canyon at ascending levels. The top of a subsequent canyon has been plugged with stone, making a bridge on which to site the road.

The road goes right past the timbered stockade of **Fort Ross** (tel: 707-847-3286; daily), but for history buffs it's worth exploring the cannon-studded fort with its church and blockhouses – if only to muse on how those early 19th-century Russian otter hunters withstood the rugged winters in flimsy wooden buildings on one of the windiest parts of the coast. So well fortified were they that their Indian and Spanish neighbors left them strictly alone until, in 1842, after 30 years of relentless otter hunting (for furs), they sold the place to rancher John Sutter and left.

At **Salt Point State Park**, the trees march down to the water's edge as you drive through this lovely pine-scented stretch. Off the highway, other beaches abound – such as Stump Beach and Fisk Mill Cove. Much of the time, you'll find yourself a solitary visitor, as swimming is unsafe because of rip tides and what the coast guards call "sleeper waves." **Stewarts Point** was once a "doghole" for schooners, so-called because of its anchorages, so tiny "only a dog could fit into them." After Pebble Beach, Stengel Beach and 8 more miles (13km) of a

Russian Orthodox priest at Fort Ross.

BELOW:
spending the day canoeing and picnicking on Russian River.

winding two-lane road, a bridge across the Gualala River marks the end of Sonoma County.

Mendonoma

Mendonoma, a name derived from the adjoining counties of Sonoma and Mendocino, identifies the coastal region between the Russian River at Jenner and the Navarro River, north of Point Arena. A heterogeneous mix of Russians, Germans, and Spaniards settled **Gualala** (pronounced *wah-lah-lah*) in the 1800s, which by the middle of the last century had four sawmills and four bars. Wells Fargo and Western Union had offices in the Gualala Hotel, built by the town's founder in 1903 when rooms with bath and ocean view cost $5. The writer Jack London stayed here a century ago, and things don't appear to have altered much. Since the last mill closed, tourism has filled the gap.

The town's name is a local Indian word that translates as "where the waters flow down," and you can paddle up the estuary of the Gualala River in a canoe or kayak, looking for osprey, heron, kingfishers, and river otters that make their homes here. Many local artists reside in and around the town, which has numerous galleries, shops, and a full program of concerts and theatrical performances at the Gualala Arts Center (tel: 707-884-1138). Art and nature come together in the Art in the Redwoods festival in August and the Redwood Coast Whale and Jazz Festival in April.

A wooden Olde West structure with a tower marks a general merchandise store at **Anchor Bay**. After this, the coast-hugging, sometimes lonely road seems mostly deserted. Fifteen miles (24km) of winding two-lane highway allow ample time to contemplate that state law decreeing that slow-moving vehicles must use a turn-off if five or more vehicles back up behind them.

Beyond the cute town of Point Arena, one of the truly great coastal experiences is **Point Arena Lighthouse** ㉘ (tel: 707-882-2777; daily), the tip of which can be spotted at the beginning of the 2-mile (3km) diversion. A classically beautiful 111ft (34-meter) -high white tower with 145 steps, it replaced an earlier lighthouse damaged by the 1906 San Francisco earthquake. Its 2-ton (1,800kg) French-made Fresnel lens (floating on a tub of mercury) was itself replaced in the 1970s with an aircraft-type beacon. It is maintained by a non-profit group of local citizens and takes around 5 minutes to climb to the top.

Miles of open pasture dotted with ramshackle barns and grazing cows follow Point Arena. Then the road dips, turns, climbs, and dives, winding through tiny **Elk** and **Albion**, pretty roadside communities on either side of the Navarro River, with sloping tracks down to the beach. Look down as the road crosses the Albion River Bridge for a lovely view of the river flowing out to meet the sea, with big rock outcrops framing the river's mouth just offshore. There's another pretty crossing at Little River as the highway twists and turns around high

BELOW: beautiful Bodega Bay – known for its birdlife.

cliffs before descending to a leafy stretch past **Van Damme State Park** (which contains a "pygmy forest" of pines and cypresses), offering occasional glimpses of the sea.

Mendocino

The lovely old town of **Mendocino 29**, which lacks motels, supermarkets, and fast-food joints, is one of the most admired places on the coast and thus is usually filled with tourists, most of whom are just passing through. If you choose to stay the night after they have gone, you'll be rewarded with great restaurants (some with health-conscious menus) and numerous small bed-and-breakfast inns, as well as art galleries jewelry and gift shops, and quaint cafés. The entire village, established by New England whalers, is on the National Register of Historic Places. Among several Victorian homes, the 1854 **Ford House** (tel: 707-937-5397; daily) and the 1861 **Kelley House** (tel: 707-937-5791; June–Aug Thur–Tue, rest of the year Fri–Mon) each contain small museums. The Mendocino Art Center (tel: 707-937-5818; Wed–Sun) show-

cases work by local and national artists. Paths lead along the cliffs overlooking Mendocino Bay with lovely views. Be warned: parking spaces in Mendocino are as rare as gold dust.

North of Caspar, the delightful **Mendocino Coast Botanical Gardens** (tel: 707-964-4352; daily) are worth a stop if only to walk through the aromatic pine forest to the sea, enjoying the interplay between light and shade. It's a good place for whale-watching in season. Plants can be bought here, too. Next comes Noyo Harbor, once the biggest lumber port between Eureka and San Francisco and now a marina for sports fishing boats along with a "fisherman's village" and plenty of restaurants.

Shipwrecks and microbreweries

An 1820 shipwreck led to the founding of **Fort Bragg 30**, when treasure seekers came to loot the wreckage and discovered the redwoods. A fort was built and the Bureau of Indian Affairs established a reservation for the Pomo Indians. Lumber mills sprang up, along with a railroad to transport their product.

The "Skunk Train" at Fort Bragg once carried timber; now it transports tourists through enormous redwood groves.

BELOW LEFT: breaking for breakfast in Mendocino County. **BELOW:** art for sale at one of the many Mendocino galleries.

TIP

If you don't feel like making the fairly arduous 4–5-hour round-trip drive to see the hidden attractions of the Lost Coast, you can hire a guide in Ferndale; inquire locally for details.

When the 1906 earthquake devastated so much of San Francisco, it was Fort Bragg's mills that provided the wood for rebuilding. The famous old "**Skunk Train**" (tel: 866-457-5865) that once carried timber across the mountains to the sawmill at Willits has been a tourist favorite for years, and it still follows the same picturesque route along the Noyo River and through redwood groves.

What remains of the original fort, along with surviving Victorian buildings, can be seen one block east of Main Street (Highway 1) near the Skunk Train depot at Laurel and Franklin. Both the **Guest House Museum** (tel: 707-964-4251; Thur–Sun), with displays on local history, and the **North Coast Brewing Company** (tel: 707-964-3400, free tours on Sat), one of America's best microbreweries, are on Main Street. Fort Bragg is an unpretentious working town that also blossoms with nurseries, one of which grows millions of trees for reforestation projects.

The Lost Coast

Pretty hamlets and gorgeous views of crashing breakers and surf mark the winding coastal road beyond Fort Bragg. North of **Westport**, after 22 miles (35km) of dramatic, picturesque coastline, Highway 1 takes a final look at the sea before heading 25 miles (40km) inland. Here, it merges with US 101 at Leggett and – apart from a brief stretch near Eureka – disappears forever.

The relatively inaccessible (and often unpaved) coastal road leads up through the evocatively named Sinkyone Wilderness and beyond, onto the justly celebrated **Lost Coast**, which has gloriously and almost uniquely escaped development. It's an area of "black sand beaches and old-growth forests on a wall of windswept peaks," as one writer noted. There are 80 miles (129km) of trails and six campgrounds under the aegis of the Bureau of Land Management.

Once projected for an extension of Highway 1, the coast can be visited via a loop road picked up at the town of Weott, north of Leggett. The narrow side road crosses the Mattole River at Honeydew, heads through Petrolia, the site of the state's first but disappoint-

BELOW: bright wildflowers along a Lost Coast trail.

ingly unproductive oil strike, and follows the coast north to Ferndale, where it veers inland again to rejoin US 101 *(see page 361 for more about the Lost Coast)*.

Avenue of the Giants

South again, Highway 1 climbs through redwood forest and merges into US 101 at **Leggett**. Gift shops selling carved wooden figures (Big Foot is a favorite) and gimmicky attractions such as the circular house carved from a single redwood log and **Confusion Hill** (tel: 707-925-6456; daily) vie for attention. The latter really is pretty weird: water runs uphill here; there's also a wooden shack in which a golf ball climbs a slope and a chair prevents you from getting up without using your arms.

The guy who bought Confusion Hill discovered these apparent paradoxes when he first tried to build his home on the hillside, and although some of the effects are obviously optical illusions, the owner says there are things he still hasn't figured out. There's also a funicular ride up the mountain.

Containing several restaurants and motels, **Garberville** is a pleasant little place to break your journey before heading into redwood country proper. Farther north, at **Phillipsville**, the 31-mile (50km) **Avenue of the Giants** ❸ offers an irresistible alternative to US 101, to which it runs parallel, allowing occasional on-off access. There are trees here more than 300ft (91 meters) tall and up to 20ft (6 meters) in diameter. "From them comes silence," wrote John Steinbeck.

A handful of buildings are all that remain of two small towns that once straddled the route until they were washed away by floods in 1964. Otherwise, the route in this stupendously awesome 50,000-acre (20,250-hectare) forest is untrammeled by human life. A series of small groves is dedicated to various groups and individuals that have fought to preserve this magnificent enclave. They are places for contemplation. "We do not see nature with our eyes," wrote William Hazlitt, "but with our understandings and our hearts." Many of the trees on the east side were planted in the 1980s under

Drive Thru, the Chandelier tree in Leggett.

BELOW: the Avenue of the Giants is a scenic drive of many miles.

> *I never saw a discontented tree. They grip the ground as though they liked it, and though fast rooted they travel about as far as we do.*
>
> John Muir

BELOW:
walking through the majestic groves in Humboldt Redwoods State Park.

reforestation projects. Near the town of **Myers Flat** is the **Drive-Thru Tree**, a favorite with children and tourists. Before Weott, the **Humboldt Redwoods State Park Visitor Center** (tel: 707-946-2263; daily) is filled with explanatory exhibits about the magnificent redwoods, which attract tree fans from around the world.

All about trees

Redwood has long been prized for its density and deep color, and despite slumps in the building industry and competition from more common trees such as cedar, it remains in demand. The logging industry, born in tandem with the Gold Rush, made hardly a dent in the redwood belt until the advent of power saws in the 1940s, which made it possible to clear acres in a single day. It takes 40 years to raise a stand of redwoods for such uses as pulp and press board, and 500 years to develop the fine grain and blood-red tint that have made the wood so popular: virgin forest remains at a premium. Conservationists estimate that trees are logged at two and a half times the rate of regeneration.

Conservationist and writer John Muir was not a friend to lumbermen. "Any fool can destroy trees," he commented. "They cannot defend themselves or run away... It took more than 3,000 years to make some of the oldest of the sequoias, trees that are still standing in perfect strength and beauty, waving and singing in the mighty forests of the Sierra."

The redwoods inspire not only passing tourists, but also the entire livelihood of the Humboldt community. Sculptors carve timbers into life-sized grizzly bears for sale at the roadside. Others, for a pretty hefty admission fee, show off the stout trunks growing in their backyards. Huge logging trucks carrying both raw timber and finished boards along the highway are a constant reminder that the trees in this area are an economic necessity as well as a natural wonder.

Fortuna's **Depot Museum** (tel: 707-725-7645; June–Aug daily, Thur–Sun rest of the year) features local logging and railroading history. Located on a back road between Fortuna and Eureka is minuscule **Loleta**, celebrated for cheese and ice-cream production. Its factory, which starred in the 1982 movie *Hallowe'en III: the Season of the Witch*, makes supermarket ice cream in loads of varieties for 11 different companies.

Fascinating Ferndale

The fascination of **Ferndale** ㉜, on the Eel River west of US 101 (reached by turning west off the highway just north of Fortuna), stems from its large numbers of garishly hued Victorian stores and houses, many of which have been converted into enticing bed-and-breakfasts. The whole town, designated a State Historical Landmark, naturally attracts tourists by the thousands. The elaborately turreted and gabled **Gingerbread Mansion Inn** on Berding Street is outstanding, and the town's oldest building, the 18-room **Shaw House Inn**, is fashioned after Nathaniel Hawthorne's *House of the Seven*

Gables. The year-round mild climate encourages productive gardening, and one is apt to see tamed cypresses shaped like giant gumdrops, or other evidence of extensive topiary work. At the head of Main Street is the 110-year-old **Victorian Inn;**" also notable is the **Ferndale Emporium**, farther down the street, which serves genteel afternoon teas from Thursday to Saturday. You can learn more about the town's history in the Ferndale Museum (tel: 707-786-4466; June–Sept Tue–Sat, rest of the year Wed–Sat).

A top-hatted driver offers rides around town in a horse and carriage, while there's a genuine soda fountain on Main Street. Understandably, Ferndale attracts moviemakers, who use its setting for movie and TV dramas. The town is also the birthplace of the delightful Kinetic Sculpture Race, which sees its people-powered models competing in the annual three-day race from Arcata.

Wildcat Road

The drive south along the Lost Coast from Ferndale follows the old stage-coach route that's known locally as Wildcat Road, climbs high into the hills and then, after 30 miles (48km) of twists and turns, descends to cross the Bear River and arrives at the defunct community of Capetown. Off the deserted black sand beach is the immense Sugarloaf Rock and nearby Steamboat Rock, which resembles a big tanker stranded at sea.

Cape Mendocino is the western-most point in California. The **Cape Mendocino Lighthouse** was completed in 1868 only after a two-year struggle to bring materials in by sea and haul them up the steep cliff. Although it warned countless vessels of the treacherous waters, at least nine ships were wrecked off this rugged shore during its 83-year history. Decommissioned in 1951, the wind and sea would have claimed the lighthouse too, but it was rescued and restored in 1999 and now stands in a park at the edge of Point Delgado (Memorial Day–Labor Day when guides are available).

Back on the main road, Highway 101 returns to the coast at Humboldt

Ferndale's Victorian architecture.

BELOW:
the Gingerbread Mansion Inn in Ferndale is named for the lavishly ornamented style of Victorian architecture.

The highly embellished Carson Mansion in Eureka was designed by San Francisco architects, Samuel and Joseph Newsome.

BELOW: tall ship in full sail near the Eureka shoreline.

Bay, where it passes sections of the **Humboldt Bay National Wildlife Refuge**. As a key stop on the Pacific Flyway, it provides protected wetland habitat for tens of thousands of migratory water birds, including Aleutian cackling geese and shorebirds.

The biggest coastal city on the California coast north of San Francisco, **Eureka** ㉝ (pop. 26,000) and its **Old Town** area on the waterfront has often stood in for the Bay Area city in movies. The landmark **Eureka Inn**, a massive Tudor Revival mansion built in 1922, has been closed for several years awaiting renovation. Its early guests included Laurel and Hardy, Shirley Temple, John Barrymore, and Britain's Winston Churchill, who stopped by Eureka to visit an old friend who was editing the local paper. The town's distinctive 1886 **Carson Mansion** – built by a lumber baron with a yen for gables, towers, and turrets – is generally regarded as the handsomest Victorian building in the state, if not in the entire West. It is now a private club.

At the **Blue Ox Millworks** (tel: 707-444-3437; Mon–Sat), a working Victorian sawmill, visitors can watch craftsmen at work and see how much of the characteristic "gingerbread" ornamentation for such houses was crafted. The old Carnegie Library, with its wonderful balconies and redwood pillars, has been converted into an art museum; other attractions include the **Humboldt Bay Maritime Museum** (tel: 707-444-9440; Tue–Wed, Fri–Sat) with its lighthouse memorabilia, and the **Clarke Historical Museum** (tel: 707-443-1947; Wed–Sat) with its collection of weapons, Native American crafts, and Victoriana.

Across the bay on a peninsula is the famous **Samoa Cookhouse** (tel: 707-442-1659; daily), which is the last remaining example of the 1890s lumber camp cookhouses, whose rules included eating as much as you could for a fixed price and helping yourself to anything within reach as long as one foot remained on the ground. Today, huge meals are served family style at long tables – and the same rules apply.

EUREKA TO OREGON

Just north of Eureka, with a reputation for being "the Galapagos of North America," **Arcata** is famous for its bird-watching opportunities. Its variety of bird life is greater than anywhere else in the state, and Marbled Godwit, White-tailed Kite, and Cinnamon Teal are frequently observed. The Chamber of Commerce on G. Street, two blocks north of the plaza, publishes a free leaflet detailing all the different bird species and where to find them, as well as a self-guided walking map of old Victorian homes. Such establishments as Rookery Books and a coffee company advertising "our coffee is for the birds," are an indication of the level of interest in our feathered friends.

Birdwatchers from all over the country converge on the town for the annual Godwit Days in April to go on field trips and attend workshops with such intriguing titles as "Advanced Identification," and "Intermediate Owls." Adjoining the filtration plant on Arcata Bay (which produces more than half of California's oyster crop) is the main center of birding activity, the **Arcata Marsh and Wildlife Sanctuary** (tel: 707-826-2359; daily). Aleutian geese, once down to less than 1,000 in number, are now abundant after years of protection under the Endangered Species Act.

The town of Arcata, founded by a group of miners from the Trinity River region in 1849, grew up around the **Jacoby Building** on the plaza. It was built in 1857 of masonry, when wood usually sufficed, by a far-sighted merchant whose pack trains serviced the goldmines upriver. Elegantly restored and refitted, it now houses stylish shops, a railroad museum, and two of the town's best restaurants.

Humboldt State University's **Natural History Museum** (tel: 707-826-4479; Tue–Sat) exhibits everything from butterflies to dinosaur tails. **McKinleyville**, the fastest growing town in Humboldt County, is also the nearest one to the misnamed Eureka-Arcata airport. It claims to have the world's tallest single-

tree totem pole (at the shopping center). Its 30-acre (12-hectare) **Azalea Reserve**, which blooms in spring, can be reached via a trail off North Bank Road (Central Avenue exit from US 101; tel: 707-488-2041; daily).

Moonshine Beach and Wedding Rock

At **Moonshine Beach**, just north of the airport, Highway 1 detaches itself from US 101, under which it has been submerged for the past 100 miles (161km). For a delightful stretch of 20 miles (32km) or so, it runs along the coast through the lovely clifftop village of **Trinidad ③④** (pop. 500), named by a Spanish explorer in 1775 and the site of a small museum. It is also the last gas station for 20 miles (32km). Farther north is the entrance of **Patrick's Point State Park** (tel: 707-677-3570; daily), named for an Indian scout who settled here in 1851. Seals can be admired basking on the rocks off Rocky Point, and at low tide there are tide pools to explore.

Farther north, **Wedding Rock** is a popular site for marriages conducted to

BELOW:
a collection of bumper stickers at the North County Fair, Arcata.

BELOW: the fast-moving Klamath River from a high scenic overlook.

the accompaniment of crashing waves below. The rock got its name from the park's first caretaker, Vieggo Andersen, whose marriage there to his housekeeper in 1933 began a popular custom. Scenes from Steven Spielberg's *Lost World* were filmed in the parking lot. Nearer to the highway, by the site of the old Yurok village, is an old canoe hollowed out by fire from a tree trunk, which sits near a native garden of indigenous plants. Camping is allowed and *yurts* (highly comfortable, wooden-floor tents) can be rented by the night.

About 14 miles (22km) north of Patrick's Point on the highway before Orick, the **Redwood Information Center** (tel: 707-464-6101) distributes free maps depicting the various trails and camping sites of the redwood forests that extend northward to Crescent City. They are protected in **Redwood National Park** and several adjoining state parklands. Seldom-seen black bears roam through the parks – as well as Roosevelt elk, which occasionally emerge onto the highway, but for the most part it's trees, trees, trees – the tallest living things on earth, which

can reach heights of more than 360ft (110 meters). Fossil records indicate that millions of years ago they blanketed the northern hemisphere when the climate was warmer and wetter. Today, only isolated patches of redwoods remain – mainly in California and China.

Judging by the stalls along the road, the main industry of **Orick**, once a major logging center, appears to be the sale of "burl slabs," which are grotesquely shaped redwood roots. When driving along, take the signposted Newton B. Drury Scenic Parkway through **Prairie Creek Redwoods State Park** (tel: 707-464-6101), a long avenue of incredibly tall trees. Somewhere along the way, you'll probably see the resident herd of Roosevelt elk, which has a tendency to graze beside the highway. These animals should be treated with respect because they can be unpredictably dangerous. A worthwhile sidetrip is to drive down the narrow, potholed Coastal Trail along **Golden Bluffs Beach** through dense woodland to **Fern Canyon**, a ravine bordered on either side by sheer, fern-carpeted cliffs.

Trees of Mystery

For a few miles before **Klamath** ㉟, US 101 runs alongside the broad **Klamath River**, crossed by a bridge marked at each end by life-size statues of golden bears. For a spectacular view of where the river meets the ocean, take the Requa Road on your left to an overlook 600ft (183 meters) above the water. (This side road dead-ends after a few miles.) Gold mines farther up the Klamath River were once served via Klamath from steamers that brought supplies up the coast from San Francisco. Today, the river is popular for jetboat tours from Klamath to see such wildlife as elk and bears. Huge figures of legendary lumberjack Paul Bunyan and his blue ox, Babe, herald the **Trees of Mystery** (tel: 800-638-3389; daily). A trail leads past some unusual groupings: nine trees growing from one root structure to form

the so-called **Cathedral Tree**; a dozen others growing from a single Sitka Spruce trunk. Admission is charged to each trail, but the absorbing museum, with its large collection of Indian costumes and crafts, is free.

US 101 hugs the coast around many attractive bays before beginning a lengthy climb where traffic along the narrow road is controlled by solar-powered lights. Tall trees flank most of the final 10 miles (16km) into Crescent City, until the sea comes into view once again just before town.

Tallest living things on earth

Crescent City ❸❻, named for the shape of the bay on which it sits, sprawls somewhat unattractively behind an interesting harbor replete with restaurants, a seafood market and the **Northcoast Marine Mammal Center** (tel: 707-465-6265) where distressed seals and sea lions are rehabilitated. West of the harbor, the **Battery Point Lighthouse** (tel: 707-464-3089; summer daily, Oct–Apr Sat–Sun) can be visited at low tide and contains a museum with photographs of some of the ship-

wrecks off this treacherous coast. When John Muir visited Crescent City in 1896, he went out on a logging train to see "the work of ruin going on." Some of the trees, he observed, were up to 200ft (61 meters) high and 20ft (6 meters) in diameter and yet two men could chop them down in a single day. His experiences doubtless led him to fight for the redwoods' preservation. The vast **Jedediah Smith Redwoods State Park** (tel: 707-458-3018) to the east is named after Jedediah Smith, the fur trapper who first explored the region in the 1820s. The spectacular and turbulent Smith River, which runs through 300 miles (483km) of wild scenery, offers white-water rafting between soaring canyon walls. At **Gasquet**, on US 199, which runs through the **Smith River National Recreation Area**, a Forest Service office (tel: 707-457-3131) provides maps, general information and the opportunity to book a night in a remote fire-lookout cabin atop Bear Basin Butte. Whether you head north from Crescent City or Gasquet, in less than 25 miles (40km), you'll be in **Oregon**. ❑

BELOW LEFT: Paul Bunyan welcoming visitors to the Trees of Mystery. **BELOW:** the historic Battery Point Lighthouse in Crescent City.

OREGON TO WASHINGTON

Oregon's rugged coastline stretches for 400 miles, offering wilderness glimpses of deer, elk, and bald eagles, before heading into the state of Washington for more of the same

Trusty US 101 trundles all the way up the Oregon coast and into the state of Washington, serving the same function that Highway 1 served in California – offering some of the best coastal scenery in the United States. Rural and more rugged than much of its southern neighbor, Oregon's section of US 101, which is signposted as the Pacific Coast Scenic Highway, offers tantalizing views of elk and bald eagles.

BROOKINGS-HARBOR TO WALDPORT

The southern part of the Oregon Coast – the **Siskiyou Coast** – begins calmly enough; a drive taking the car through relatively peaceful farmland after the turbulence of the Smith River near the state border. Ships pop up on dry land, first a huge one beached beside the appropriately named Ship Ashore Motel, and then an old tugboat beached and converted into a souvenir store just south of **Brookings-Harbor** ㊲. This is the town (although technically "towns": Brookings is the larger of the two side-by-side communities) where the sports fishing fleet anchors, and it also contains the local Visitor Information Bureau (tel: 800-535-9469).

At the mouth of the Chetco River, Brookings is a popular retirement spot because of its reputation as being in the "banana belt," with winter temperatures often reaching 65°F (18°C). The technical explanation for its moderate climate is that the town's southeast to northwest geographical layout combines with constant low-pressure thermal troughs that pull down the highly compressed air following a storm system. One consequence is that the region produces most of the country's Easter lilies, and visitors swarm in to see **Azalea Park** (tel: 541-469-1100) in the springtime when the flowers are in bloom. There's an Azalea Festival on Memorial Day weekend. Some of the most spectacular coastal scenery is to

Main attractions
BOARDMAN STATE PARK
GOLD BEACH
COQUILLE RIVER
  LIGHTHOUSE
COOS BAY
OREGON DUNES
SEA LION CAVES
YACHATS
NEWPORT
PORTLAND
CANNON BEACH

LEFT: an Oregon cattleman riding a Quarter Horse.
BELOW: Crater Lake.

Gold Beach dates its name from 1850, when prospectors discovered that the sands surrounding the rock were sprinkled with gold dust.

be found in **Samuel H. Boardman State Park** just north of town. It runs for about 12 miles (19km) past rugged cliffs, sparkling coves, and offshore rock formations such as Arch Rock and Natural Bridges. March brings daffodils, May the wild azaleas and July the snow lilies, while every month of the year brings eager photographers.

Anyone for gas?

As Oregon's coastline stretches for almost 400 miles (644km), you won't be in the state for long before discovering that state law prohibits customers pumping their own gas, ostensibly to "boost the economy" by providing more jobs, but also because it is supposedly unsafe. This particular part of the Oregon Statute (unpopular with locals) cites 20 potential hazards, including the fact that customers are not trained in the safe handling of flammable liquids and that exposure to toxic fumes is a health hazard.

North of town past the large, green barns of the South Coast Lumber Company, and near the **Harris Beach State Park** (tel: 541-469-2021), are

numerous parking bays beside the highway from which to gaze at the ocean. Harris is one of 30 places on the Oregon coast designated as a whale-watching site, and is attended by trained volunteers on winter mornings to assist visitors.

Around 100 gray whales spend the summer feeding off the Siskiyou coast; the smaller mammals often nursing a calf. Larger gray whales can reach 45ft (14 meters) in length – bigger than a Greyhound bus – and weigh up to 45 tons (45,720kg). Their annual migration between the Bering Sea and Mexico is a grueling 10,000-mile (16,000km) round trip at a speed of around 5mph (8kph) heading southbound.

Kissing Rock

US 101 soon crosses the **Thomas Creek Bridge**, the state's highest at 345ft (105 meters), then a string of dune-backed beaches begins just before Pistol River. The best of these are around the rather eye-catching **Kissing Rock**, popular with windsurfers, between Meyers Creek and Gold

BELOW: a view of the coastline at Brookings-Harbor.

Beach. The latter's name dates from the 1850s, when prospectors discovered that the sands around the mouth of the Rogue River were salted with gold dust.

Today, several companies offer excursions in powerful hydro jetboats up this wild and scenic river through a beautiful, pristine landscape teeming with wildlife; its upper reaches encompass dramatic canyons hundreds of feet deep. Sport fishing for salmon and steelhead trout can be arranged, as well as ocean fishing, and horses can be rented for riding on the beach. At **Gold Beach**, a pleasant, laid-back town large enough for a couple of good restaurants that are open year-round, make time to visit the Curry County Historical Museum (tel: 541-247-9396; Feb–Dec Tue–Sat). Highway 101 then crosses the graceful Patterson Memorial Bridge over the Rogue River to continue up the coast.

Seven miles (11km) north at **Nesika Beach**, the highway levels with the shoreline. Low-lying, tree-covered hills flank the right-hand side and marshland sits between road and sea. Massive moss and lichen-covered rocks stick out of the water, and around **Humbug Mountain** the scenery is particularly stunning. Towering mountains taper down to the road, which flanks a series of bays enlivened by crashing white surf. "The mountains are fountains of men as well as of rivers, of glaciers, of fertile soil," wrote John Muir. "The great poets, philosophers, prophets, able men whose thoughts and deeds have moved the world, have come down from the mountains – mountain dwellers have grown strong there with the forest trees in Nature's workshop."

Oregon license plate on a 1949 classic.

Westernmost city

Keep an eye out on the right for the painted dinosaur outside the **Prehistoric Gardens** in the rainforest. Perched on scenic bluffs, **Port Orford** ❸❽ is the westernmost city in the contiguous United States, and was a major lumber shipping port more than a

BELOW: a Stegosaurus exhibit at Prehistoric Gardens.

STEGOSAURUS
pronounced: steg-o-SAWR-us
literally, 'roofed lizard'

century ago. Just offshore, past the battered Shack Art Studio, is a wooded island called **Battle Rock**. In 1851, the island's original party of settlers was besieged by local Indians who resented their claim to the land. A month later, a larger white group arrived and took possession.

There's a beautiful view of the coast from here back to Humbug Mountain. Take a lingering look at Port Orford's lovely bay, because it will be your last uninterrupted view of the ocean for nearly 100 miles (161km), although frequent "Coastal Access" signs dot the highway. Northeast of town on Elk River Road is the **Elk River Fish Hatchery**, where salmon smelts are raised.

Lighthouses and lazy countryside

A 6-mile (10km) side trip can be made to the cliffs of **Cape Blanco** to inspect the 1870 lighthouse (tel: 541-756-0100; Tue–Sun in summer), which sits 245ft (75 meters) above the sea and is operated by the Bureau of Land Management. Next comes **Langlois**, located in

serene countryside filled with cows and sheep. There's a wool factory outlet among its small shops. In the surrounding hills are many lonely sheep ranches. Miles of bright yellow gorse line the approach to **Bandon** ❸❾, twice destroyed by fire in the last century; a brick chimney on the site of the old bakery stands as a memorial just off the highway. Artists' homes and studios along with craft shops cluster around Bandon's **Old Town** area. The Bandon Historical Society Museum (tel: 541-347-2164; Mon–Sat) includes an exhibit about cranberry cultivation. This has been taking place in nearby bogs for more than a century, ever since the early settlers learned the technique from the Indians. The town celebrates with a Cranberry Festival every fall, and cranberry farms can be toured by appointment. Near Bandon is another lighthouse, the **Coquille River Lighthouse** (tel: 541-347-3501; mid-Apr–May Wed–Sun, June–Oct daily), accessed through Bullards Beach State Park. Across the river is the **Bandon Marsh National Wildlife Refuge**, one of the best birding areas along the coast.

Coos Bay is a major lumber shipping port, with warehouses and stacked timber lining the road. Even its Mill Casino, run by the Coquille Indians, is set in a converted saw mill. Back in 1850, Captain Asa Simpson established a sawmill and shipyard here, which built about 50 vessels before the end of the century. On a smaller scale, you can tour the **Oregon Connection** factory (tel: 541-267-7804), where myrtlewood logs are fashioned into bowls, goblets, and other products. To the east is **Golden and Silver Falls State Park** with its 100ft (30-meter) waterfalls. On the coast, the fishing village of **Charleston** is a good place for fresh crab and seafood at Fisherman's Wharf. Continue south on the scenic Cape Arago Beach Loop for stunning sea views and vantage points for spotting seals, sea lions, and whales. The Arago Cape is the home of the elephant seal, a deep-

BELOW: fresh seafood is plentiful in the coastal town of Bandon.

diving mammal that has been known to reach depths of 4,000ft (1,200 meters). The drive encompasses three state parks, including **Shore Acres State Park**, once the gardens of the spacious house of lumber baron Louis J. Simpson, Asa's son.

Dune walk

Across the long bridge spanning the Hayes Inlet is Coos Bay's neighbor, **North Bend**, where the useful Visitors Information Bureau (tel: 541-756-4613) sits opposite the ancient steam locomotive outside the Coos Historical and Maritime Museum (tel: 541-756-6320; Tue–Sat).

The **Oregon Dunes National Recreation Area** 40 begins at North Bend, a huge expanse of sand that blocks easy access to the sea for 40 miles (64km) of coast. There are 11 different places offering beach access, at least one of which, **Spinreel** (watch for the highway sign) offers a chance to rent dune buggies (tel: 541-759-3313) and cavort in the sandy wilderness; dune tours are also available. These dunes reach heights of several hundred feet, giving

refuge to many types of flora and fauna, and are constantly sculpted into different shapes by wind and water. In addition to campgrounds and hiking trails, they are rife with wildlife and birds, as well as red and yellow salmonberries, thimble berries (similar to raspberries), wild strawberries and, in the fall, huckleberries.

Lower **Umpqua Bay** is said to be the most fertile place for big soft-shell clams, some weighing around half a pound (220 grams). The delicious Dungeness crab is found in the Winchester Bay area, where the Umpqua River meets the ocean. Shops sell crabbing equipment and bait.

At the Umpqua Dunes Trailhead (watch for the highway sign), you can park the car and climb the dunes. Camp facilities here includes spacious *yurts*: structurally supported domed tents with plywood floors, lockable doors, comfortable beds and light and heating. They are designed to withstand high winds and retain heat in winter. You'll find them throughout the state of Oregon park system, from rustic to deluxe (tel: 800-551-6949 for

Enjoying a dune buggy ride along the Southern Oregon coast.

BELOW:
Oregon Dunes National Recreation Area.

Many people not born near the sea confuse sea lions with seals. Sea lions have external ears, and can rotate their hind flippers to walk on land. Seals live exclusively on the edge of – or in – the water.

information). In summer you might care to take a 5-mile (8km) side trip to visit the **Umpqua Lighthouse** (Wed–Sat afternoons), an 1894 replacement for the first one that had been built on the Oregon coast 37 years previously.

Rusty frogs and bald eagles

Just before **Salmon Harbor** (unsurprisingly the largest salmon fishing port on the Oregon coast), keep an eye out for the Rusty Frog Gallery to your right and then cross the bridge into **Reedsport**, where an interpretive facility called the **Umpqua Discovery Center** (tel: 541-271-4816; daily) explains the dunes and much else besides. An additional source is the **Oregon Dunes Visitor Center** on US 101, which publicizes preservation efforts, issues bird checklists (there are five different types of seagull alone) and books campground sites (tel: 541-271-3611). A mile or two to the east on State Road 38, visitors can admire herds of Roosevelt elk at the pleasant **Dean Creek Elk Viewing Area**, which is also a haven for bald eagles, osprey, and blue herons.

Continuing north, Highway 101 passes through **Gardiner**, with a historic district of cute, quaint buildings and a pioneer cemetery. The Tsunami Art Gallery is aptly named, given the number of "tsunami hazard zone" signs along the coast. Glimpses of lakes and mountains appear through the pines along the pretty forest-lined road. There are numerous campgrounds and the dunes continue all the way to Florence.

Sea lion lair

Florence has a picturesque harbor backdropped by some ancient buildings; it's especially pretty when the rhododendrons display their vivid pink blossoms in late spring. In the Old Town, the **Siuslaw Pioneer Museum** (tel: 541-997-7884; Tue–Sun) displays old photographs and household items. When landslides block US 101 to the north (as happened for months early in 2000), it's the last chance to turn inland before Waldport. If traffic conditions have been bad, check with the Oregon Department of Transportation (tel: 888-275-6368), because even when the road is "closed," it's sometimes open for an hour or two each day, usually early morning and early evening.

Eleven miles (18km) north of Florence is the **Heceta Head Lighthouse**, which has been beaming its warning to mariners since 1894. The interpretive center in the keeper's house (tel: 1-866-547-3696; Memorial Day–Labor Day weekend Thur–Mon) offers tours. Shortly before the lighthouse is the fascinating **Sea Lion Caves** (tel: 541-547-3111; daily) at the bottom of cliffs accessed by an elevator. Only a wire screen separates visitors from hundreds of Steller's sea lions, the closest you'll get to their underground lair. Harbor seals (which have spotted coats) and elephant seals are the types most commonly found on this coast; neither has external ears – as opposed to sea lions. The latter can also rotate their hind flippers and thus walk on land.

BELOW: strolling in downtown Florence.

Cape Perpetua is the highest point (803ft/245 meters above sea level) on the coast, and has a helpful **Visitor Center** (tel: 541-547-3289) that provides maps and advice for hikers bound for explorations along the trails of Siuslaw National Forest. From its overlook, the highway looks like a thin sliver of silver ribbon threading along the coast.

The curiously named **Yachats** ④, an attractive and laid-back resort town nestled between the mountains and the sea, has beach trails, rewarding tide pools, and good fishing. Once known for the multitude of smelts (a silvery sardine-like fish) that spawned here, the numbers have steadily declined in recent years and the community now has to import the fish from California for its annual Smelt Fry in July.

Waldport ④ lies at the mouth of the Alsea River, which arrives at the ocean from its origin in Siuslaw National Forest, and US 101 enters the town over the huge bay bridge. Waldport is mainly known for its fishing, crabbing and clamming. It's also a particularly good base for hiking.

WALDPORT TO SEASIDE

Look to the right while crossing Yaquina Bay into the town of **Newport** ④. The section below the bridge is Newport's **Historic Bayfront**, whose attractions include old taverns, gift shops, a harbor filled with fishing boats and a trio of commercial attractions including the Undersea Gardens (tel: 541-265-2206; daily), a below-the-surface aquarium where divers cavort behind glass. Across the bay, **South Beach** has the larger **Oregon Coast Aquarium** (tel: 541-867-3474; daily), whose famous former resident, Keiko the Orca whale, starred in the film *Free Willy*.

To reach the Bayfront, turn off the main street at the traffic light (opposite the Mazatlan Mexican Restaurant in a gray, wooden building) and head down Hurburt Street. Farther on through town, several streets lead west to the

seaport with its pedestrian promenade and historic murals. One block farther, Third Street leads to **Nye Beach**, at one time the Oregon Coast's major draw. The Visual Arts Center (tel: 541-265-6540; Tue–Sun) is also here. On Hwy 101, opposite the visitor center (tel: 541-265-8801), a boarding house from the 1890s forms part of the Lincoln County Historical Society Museum.

Just outside Newport is the much loved and much photographed **Yaquina Head Lighthouse** ④, built in 1873. Composer Earnest Block spent the last decades of his life at his home near here, and a memorial to him has been constructed. There is an interpretive center (daily) and weekend tours.

About 5 miles (8km) farther north of Newport, don't miss the signs for the **Devil's Punchbowl**, a couple of hundred yards off the highway. This is

Yachats covered bridge crosses the North Forks of Yachats River in Lincoln County Oregon.

BELOW:
Heceta Head Lighthouse has been beaming its warning to mariners since 1894.

The Blue Heron French Cheese Company in Tillamook has a gift shop, a deli, a petting farm, and also offers wine and cheese tastings.

where a huge stone basin fills dramatically – and noisily – as the tide crashes in. Waves are higher in the Pacific than the Atlantic because the wind blows uninterruptedly over a larger distance, and the study of waves – whose height is measured as the distance between the highest point (crest) and lowest point (trough) – is understandably one of great interest to coastal communities. Tide tables are listed around here in local phone directories. A tide could be regarded as a very slow wave, with high tide representing the crest, and low tide the trough.

Festival of glass

Cape Foulweather was named in 1778 by the British navigator Captain James Cook. It was his first sighting of the American mainland following his return from discovering Hawaii. The winds here, 500ft (152 meters) above the ocean, can reach 100mph (161kph).

The small gift shop sells the much-prized green glass bubbles that have drifted here from fishermen's nets all the way from Japan. Lincoln City launches its own floats every year at its Festival of Glass.

The coastal views from these cliffs and capes are spectacular, and sometimes whales can be spotted on their 12,000-mile (19,300km) round trip between Alaska and Baja California. The awesome cliffs and headlands are basalt, formed by molten lava hitting the ocean aeons ago and hardening instantly. Sometimes, this instant cooling creates oddly shaped rock structures known as pillow basalt, which can be seen offshore near Cape Foulweather and at **Depoe Bay**, a pretty resort that claims to be the world's smallest navigable harbor.

At high tide, seawater shoots skyward through two rock formations known locally as the **Spouting Horns**. Visitors get a close-up look at the wave action just by walking along the sea wall, which runs the full length of the town. When a storm is about to hit, everyone heads to a Depoe Bay restaurant for a full-frontal view, complete with sound effects.

Pink starfish

Trawling for glass floats, collecting driftwood and studying tide pools are all popular pastimes along this stretch of low-key coast. Tide pools could be regarded as miniature ocean habitats, where some creatures wait in anticipation for the waves to wash in their lunch. Orange and pink starfish, urchins and sea anemones can usually be seen among the tiny fish that dart about the shallows, while rocky residents such as long-tapered mussels and white barnacles cluster on the rocks.

Lincoln City ㊺, which has 7 miles (11km) of beaches beginning with a half-mile-deep strand when the tide is out at Siletz Bay, also has a cluster of antique stores and second-hand bookstores. There is the Chinook Winds Casino for night-time action and a fac-

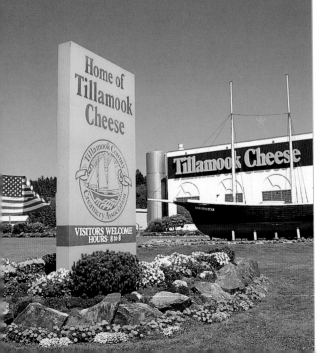

tory outlet center for daytime shopping, which draws tourists in droves for great bargains. The tiny D River links nearby **Devil's Lake** with the ocean, providing both freshwater and oceanside fun.

North of town, **Cascade Head** is the home of such raptors as falcons, hawks, and bald eagles – predators that deploy keen eyesight, outstanding hearing, and amazing speed to hunt and eat other mammals with their large clawed feet and hooked bills. Birdwatching is a popular local pastime.

Cows versus people

The highway traverses wonderful, fresh-scented **Siuslaw National Forest**, its highest peak, Mount Hebo, ascending to 3,000ft (914 meters). It skirts residential **Neskowin** and then heads inland, passing meadows of grazing cows (which outnumber people in this very pastoral county) owned by the 180 working farms that provide the milk for the delectable Tillamook cheese. After **Cloverdale**, with its colorful rustic buildings, sturdy wooden barns and springtime

daffodils catch the eye before the towns of Hebo and Beaver appear.

Cheesy town

The **Tillamook Air Museum** (tel: 503-842-1130; daily), a couple of miles south of town, is housed in an enormous hangar containing World War II vintage planes and a welcome 1940s-style café. **Tillamook** ❹❻ is justly famous for its huge, pristine Tillamook Cheese factory (tel: 503-815-1300; daily), which offers a free tour to inspect the manufacturing process and admire a life-size, painted plaster cow, beribboned with a computer chip that has replaced the old cow bell. A wall chart lists "udderly amazing" facts such as that 2,600 pints of blood pass through the udder to produce one pint of milk and that a cow yields 10,000 gallons of milk in her lifetime. Help yourself to the free cheese samples, because it's a sure bet that you're bound to buy something in the tempting Aladdin's Cave that calls itself a gift shop. Not to be outdone, the **Blue Heron French Cheese Company** (tel: 503-842-8281; daily)

TIP

Stop off at the Depoe Bay Whale Center (tel: 541-765-3304), the central location for whale viewing on the Oregon coast. The whales migrate north past Oregon from March through June and migrate south from December through January, although a pod (social group) remains along the Oregon coast to feed throughout summer.

BELOW:
built on the site of the former Union Fish Cannery, rooms at the Cannery Pier Hotel have fabulous Columbia River views.

Portland: City of Roses

A ride-for-free transit system, stunning scenery, and micro-breweries everywhere – no wonder Portland smells like roses.

Portland, voted one of America's best walking towns, has always prided itself on its pedestrian friendliness and trees-and-parks image. Its **Forest Park** is the largest urban wilderness in the US, and in the metro area alone there are 37,000 acres (15,000 hectares) of parks and gardens.

The Metropolitan Art Commission and Art Media (tel: 503-223-3724) have brochures locating museums and art galleries; the Portland Development Commission (tel: 503-823-3200) has a map showing interesting historical and architectural sites, and private guided walking tours are also available (tel: 503-774-4522).

Downtown Portland is focused around **Pioneer Courthouse Square**, where the Weather Machine, an earth-shaped sphere by local artist Terence O'Donnell on a 25ft (8-meter) column, comes to life with a musical fanfare at noon each day. Portland's efficient transit system is centered around a 300-block "Fareless Square" Downtown, the area where passengers ride free on buses or the light rail system. Washington Park subway is within easy access of many major attractions. These include the **Oregon Zoo**, the **World Forestry Center**, the **Hoyt Arboretum**, and the **Children's Museum**.

A streetcar system links the downtown area with the Pearl District (an area colonized by local artists) and the **Nob Hill** neighborhood with its fine Victorian and Georgian mansions. In the historic **Skidmore District**, there's a large weekend open-air market with live entertainment. Portland also has more microbreweries and brew pubs than any other city in the nation.

The state's history comes to life in the **Oregon Historical Society Museum** (tel: 503-222-1741; Tue–Sun) and in the **Pittock Mansion** (tel: 503-823-3623), the 1914 home of the founder of Portland's well-regarded daily newspaper, The Oregonian. Various tour boats operate along the river, some venturing as far as the Bonneville Lock and Dam, 40 miles (64km) to the east. At the **Oregon Museum of Science and Industry** (tel: 503-797-4000; Tue–Sun and Mon during school holidays) you can experience a simulated earthquake or board a jetboat for a worthwhile river excursion.

Top art spots include the **Portland Art Museum** (tel: 503-226-2811; Tue–Sun) and the **Museum of Contemporary Craft** (tel: 503-223-2654; Tue–Sun). Portland's quirkiest attraction is the **Church of Elvis** (24 hours), a coin-operated shrine offering marriage counseling and more. ❑

LEFT: view over Portland. **ABOVE:** a serene corner of the lovely Portland Japanese Gardens.

offers wine with its cheese tastings. Needless to say, the Dairy Parade is a major event each June.

West of Tillamook a side-trip could be made along the 20-mile (32km) **Three Capes Scenic Drive** to view the "Octopus Tree" – a Sitka spruce with multiple trunks – and the **Cape Meares Lighthouse**, built in 1890 with a lens imported from Paris. An early lighthouse keeper wrote of the harrowing all-night horse-and-buggy trip required to reach a doctor in Tillamook, a trip that today takes about 16 minutes.

Two miles (3km) out to sea is the **Tillamook Lighthouse**, situated on a solitary rock amid crashing waves that in 1934 roared into a maelstrom, climbing more than 100ft (30 meters) high to engulf the entire building. "Terrible Tilly" was how lighthouse keepers used to describe the building. Life on the rock was too hazardous to allow families to accompany staff to their jobs, who were routed every three weeks and allowed 96 days' leave each year to recover. It was decommissioned in 1980.

For a taste of big-city life, take a detour from Tillamook along State Route 6 east to the "City of Roses," otherwise known as **Portland** ⏣ *(see page 376)*. Past Tillamook, the highway hugs the 13-sq-mile (34-sq-km) shallow bay, which is rarely deeper than 6ft (2 meters). Estuaries such as this, where fresh water mingles with that of the ocean, are especially inviting to plant and marine life. Eelgrass provides shelter and nourishment to crabs as well as young salmon and other small fish; mudflats harbor gourmet treats for the stately great blue heron, which can often be seen rummaging.

Garibaldi and ghosts

Next on the Pacific Coast Scenic Highway, preceded by a giant, abandoned smokestack, comes **Garibaldi** (named for the 19th-century Italian liberator), which has a battered Ghost Hole Tavern, a Lumberman's Memorial Park and Garibaldi Museum (tel: 503-322-8411; May–Oct Thur–Mon) and the annual Crab Races, which presumably take place sideways.

At the cute, old-fashioned resort of **Rockaway Beach**, a red caboose beside

Portland is the hometown of Matt Groening, creator of the long-running TV series The Simpsons. *A number of the animated characters are named after city sites and streets.*

BELOW:
poles at the ready on a sports fishing boat in Garibaldi Harbor.

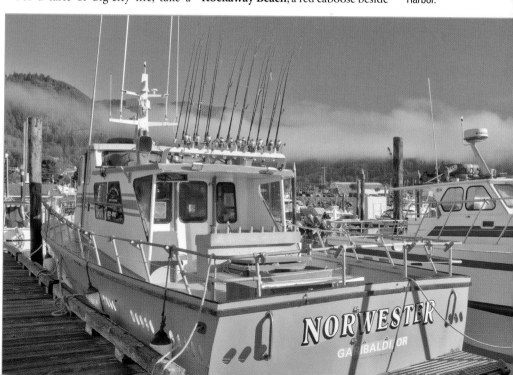

Haystack Rock at Cannon Beach.

the highway is the tourist office (tel: 503-355-8108; Mon–Fri, albeit sporadically). Freight trains loaded with lumber can occasionally be seen running on the roadside track, which follows the course of the Nehalem River. Tiny **Wheeler** has antiques shops and a wildlife viewing area along the bay in the town center.

After the long climb from **Manzanita**, there are spectacular views from an overlook above the sea where the **Oswald West State Park** begins. Down to the trestle bridge over the canyon, Tillamook County (which bills itself as "the land of cheese, trees, and gentle breeze") comes to an end just before the tunnel.

An unmistakable landmark at **Cannon Beach** ⓸ is 235ft (72-meter) -high **Haystack Rock**, offshore. It is home to tufted puffins which nest here in spring and summer. The very active community, an artists' haven with over a dozen visual arts studios and galleries, is named after a cannon washed ashore after an 1846 shipwreck. It is another kite-flying paradise, and the vision of colorful stunt

kites soaring overhead is matched only by the tranquil scene of families and friends gathering round campfires on the beach as the silhouetted rock fades into the sunset.

The town sponsors an annual Sandcastle Day in June and a dog show on the beach in October with contests for best bark, Frisbee catch and owner/dog lookalike. There's even a Stormy Weather Arts Festival (indoors) in November. The visitors' center (tel: 503-436-2623) on 2nd Street can suggest plenty of things to do, but the biggest attraction here is simply strolling along the beach and investigating the tidepools on this magnificent section of the Oregon coast.

Seaside

On the north side of town, Ecola State Park has beautiful views of the coastline and Haystack Rock. Eight miles (13km) north of Cannon Beach, US 101 descends into the town of **Seaside** ⓴ (pop. 6,000), the first and largest resort on the Oregon Coast. It is bisected by the Necanicum River, with its historic downtown area on the western side of Broadway. A wide sandy beach is flanked by a pedestrian promenade, along which is the **Aquarium** (tel: 503-738-6211; daily). Three blocks farther north is Seaside's **Historical Society Museum** (tel: 503-738-7065; daily).

It was at Seaside that members of the Lewis and Clark exploration party set up a camp to make salt by boiling seawater. For that first cold, wet winter of 1805 the expedition established **Fort Clatsop** southeast of what is now Warrenton, naming it for a local tribe of Indians who brought whale meat to trade (Clark cooked and ate some, describing it as "very palatable and tender").

A replica of the fort (tel: 503-861-2471; daily) – a 50-sq-ft (5-sq-meter) stockade with a parade ground and two rows of small cabins – helps visitors to visualize the conditions. There's also a summer program in which

buckskin-clad rangers offer demonstrations. Nearby **Fort Stevens** in the state park was built to defend the mouth of the Columbia River in the Civil War.

ASTORIA TO ABERDEEN

Astoria 🐠 – 22 miles (35km) north of Seaside – was once known as "the salmon canning capital of the world," and in an 1872 book, Frances Fuller Victor was able to write: "The immense numbers of all kinds of salmon, which ascend the Columbia annually, is something wonderful. They seem to be seeking quiet and safe places to deposit their spawn, and thousands of them never stop until they can reach the great falls of the Snake River, more than 600 miles (966km) from the sea." As late as 1915, fishermen were taking 21,000 tons of salmon from the river. But then came the giant dams. The protest by the Cayuse Indians that it would abrogate their rights by eliminating most of the salmon sadly turned out to be true. Some salmon runs have declined 85 percent from what they once were, despite the pro-

duction of 170 million fish each year by artificial hatcheries. In this place alone, at its mouth, is the Columbia River unchanged.

The mighty Columbia

Here, at its most powerful, the river thrusts 150 billion gallons (682 billion litres) of water a day through the sandbars into the Pacific Ocean, a torrent that has capsized at least 2,000 boats in the two centuries since John Jacob Astor's Pacific Fur Company created the first American settlement on shore. In recent years, the Federal government has dredged a 40ft (12-meter) channel and placed long jetties at each side to narrow the channel, but despite constant dredging and other attempts to tame the river at its mouth, it remains one of the most dangerous in the world. The weather so consistently stirs up stormy seas that the Coast Guard set up its National Motor Lifeboat School at the tip of Cape Disappointment; at times the waves reach as high as 30ft (9 meters). Nevertheless, cruise boats regularly call at Astoria, depositing hundreds of passengers at the 17th

John Jacob Astor was a German immigrant who became the first multi-millionaire in the States. He made his fortune from real estate, opium, and fur trading, from which he created the Pacific Fur Company.

BELOW:
view over the gorgeous gorge of the Columbia River.

TIP

Waikiki Beach is where the North Jetty meets the cape in Cape Disappointment State Park. This is an ideal place for storm watching as the waves crash into the cliffs with Cape Disappointment lighthouse in the background. Only a few miles from Ilwaco and great for photos.

BELOW: shoving off for a kayaking trip on Long Island Slough, Willapa National Wildlife Refuge.

Street Dock, used regularly by Coast Guard cutters.

The **Columbia River Maritime Museum** (tel: 503-325-2323; daily) is all about shipwrecks, lighthouses, fishing, navigation, and naval history. Much of Astoria's history is reflected in its handsome old houses, which fall into particular styles: Italianate, whose overhanging eaves have decorative brackets and tall or paired windows and doors, or Queen Anne (multiple roof lines, towers and turrets, paneled doors, and stained glass). An interesting example of the latter is the **Captain George Flavel House**, dating from the 1880s, on Eighth Street (tel: 503-325-2203; daily).

It's a steep, winding drive past old Victorian houses up the hill on which sits the **Astoria Column**, with its 164 winding steps, each one individually sponsored. The Great Northern Railroad and Vincent Astor, great-grandson of fur-trading tycoon and town founder Jacob Astor, were responsible for the 125ft (38-meter) -high tower that was completed in 1926. The views, of course, are stupendous, but once back

on the ground you'll be glad to warm up in the hut as you buy a postcard.

WASHINGTON STATE'S DISCOVERY COAST

It was three weeks before the Lewis and Clark exploration party managed to cross the wide Columbia River, setting up another camp near today's **Chinook** on Washington state's west coast (called the Discovery Coast). The 4-mile (6km) -long bridge that crosses from Oregon into Washington state is one of the great thrills of driving the Pacific Coast route, even (or perhaps especially) in a fog. It climbs steeply above the water as seagulls swoop overhead with keening cries and the wind is almost gale force.

US 101 continues past a bird-filled wildlife refuge to the attractive, unspoiled town of **Ilwaco** with its murals and **Heritage Museum** (tel: 360-642-3446; Tue–Sun). The expedition stayed for three lonely months in this isolated area.

Ilwaco sits at the bottom of the Long Beach peninsula – 28 miles (45km) of uninterrupted sandy beach – which

gets nicer the farther north you go. In the southwest corner, **Fort Canby** guarded the mouth of the Columbia for almost a century before becoming a state park in 1957. It houses a very interesting **Lewis and Clark Interpretive Center** (daily) where you can study biographies of members of the original party and entries from the actual journals they kept. **Cape Disappointment Lighthouse**, built in 1856, is less than a mile away at the southwesternmost tip, but such was the continuing toll of wrecked ships that it had to be supplemented before the century was out by another lighthouse at nearby **North Head**. This can be toured in summer (tel: 360-902-8844 for times).

Long Beach itself is a rather déclassé resort – its main street lined with tatty souvenir stores, a Ripley-style "museum," uninteresting restaurants and numerous inexpensive motels. But it does have a pleasant boardwalk, as well as a 2-mile (3km) Dune Trail. The peninsula's beaches are popular for clamming. **Nahcotta** and **Oysterville** at the northern end became prosperous from

oyster gathering before the crop was over-harvested, but some fine Victorian homes remain from those days, and the **Willapa Bay Interpretive Center** (Fri–Sun in summer) at Nahcotta explains the history of it all. Leadbetter Park, at the northern tip, is also a wildlife refuge where birds stop over on their way south.

Oyster capital

Back on "the mainland," US 101 crosses the Naselle River and a number of sloughs (inlets) before arriving at **South Bend** ⑤, which sits on a bay at the mouth of the Willapa River. Signs announcing oysters for sale in what calls itself the "oyster capital of the world" are a reminder that a century ago tons of these succulent bivalves were harvested by Native Americans, which all now find a ready and willing market in the gourmet restaurants of Seattle, Portland, and San Francisco. Also in search of the same is the black oystercatcher, a bird whose long red bill helps it open the shellfish once it has found them.

Two ancient wooden warehouses

Pacific Ocean fish and oysters find a ready market in the watering holes of Seattle and Portland.

BELOW LEFT:
Pacific Northwest winemaker.
BELOW:
catch of the day.

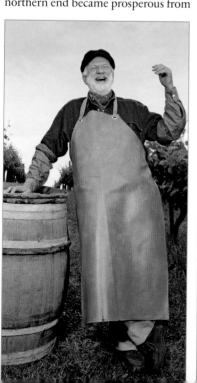

BELOW: freshly caught Pacific crab for lunch.
RIGHT: metal figures along the Wildlife-Heritage Sculpture Corridor in Raymond.

contain a shipwright and an iron works in South Bend, which stages its annual Oyster Stampede every May. South Bend's near neighbor **Raymond** is an unspoiled, un-touristy sort of place with a library built in the style of a timbered English cottage – its art-glass panes depicting fairy-tale characters.

Reckless extravagance

Architecturally, Raymond's pride and joy is the old courthouse, with its spiral staircase and stained-glass dome. "A gilded palace of reckless extravagance" was how the local paper described it when the courthouse first went up in 1910. Life-size metal silhouettes of sculptured animals and historical figures form the Wildlife-Heritage Sculpture Corridor which runs through the town on along Highway 101. Four miles (6km) east of Raymond on State Route 6 is the (marked) grave of Willie Kiel, a 19-year-old who died of malaria just before the family wagon train left Missouri in 1855. Preserved in whisky in a lead casket by his doctor father, the body came along for the trip and was

buried atop a grassy knoll, which is now crowned with towering cedars.

Access to west-coast beaches is via State Route 105, which runs past the Shoalwater Indian Reservation and the cranberry bogs between North Cove and Grayland. Cranberries blossom in late June, and **Grayland** holds its annual cranberry festival in October, following the harvest.

Between Raymond and Aberdeen, US 105 bends and twists through a forest of mist-shrouded pines, but large tracts have been devastated by logging while others are covered with recent plantations. It emerges beside the smoke-belching, century-old Weyerhaeuser lumber plant, a mile or two south of town. When the bridge over the broad Chehalis River is raised, vehicles must wait to continue their journey.

Aberdeen ⑤②, a major lumber port for more than a century, is, like its Scottish namesake, at the meeting of two rivers. It is known for **Grays Harbor**, the seaport around which the town grew after Robert Gray sailed in on the *Lady Washington* in 1788 to help arrange fur trading between the Pacific Northwest and China. A replica of the 170-ton ship is used for educational trips, but is usually on show in the harbor, and more about the town's early days can be explored in the **Aberdeen Museum of History** (tel: 360-533-1976; Tue–Sun). By the time the first mill was built in 1852, the government was making treaties with the Indians of the region and Aberdeen was developing into a rowdy, honky-tonk shipping town.

San Diego to Seattle

US 101 reaches the end of the journey that began all the way south in sunny San Diego with a flourishy loop around the magnificent Olympic Peninsula *(see the Northern Route, page 167)*, ending up not far from Seattle. Alternatively, head straight for **Seattle** ⑤③ *(see page 172)* from Aberdeen by taking US 12 to **Olympia**, then Interstate 5. ❑

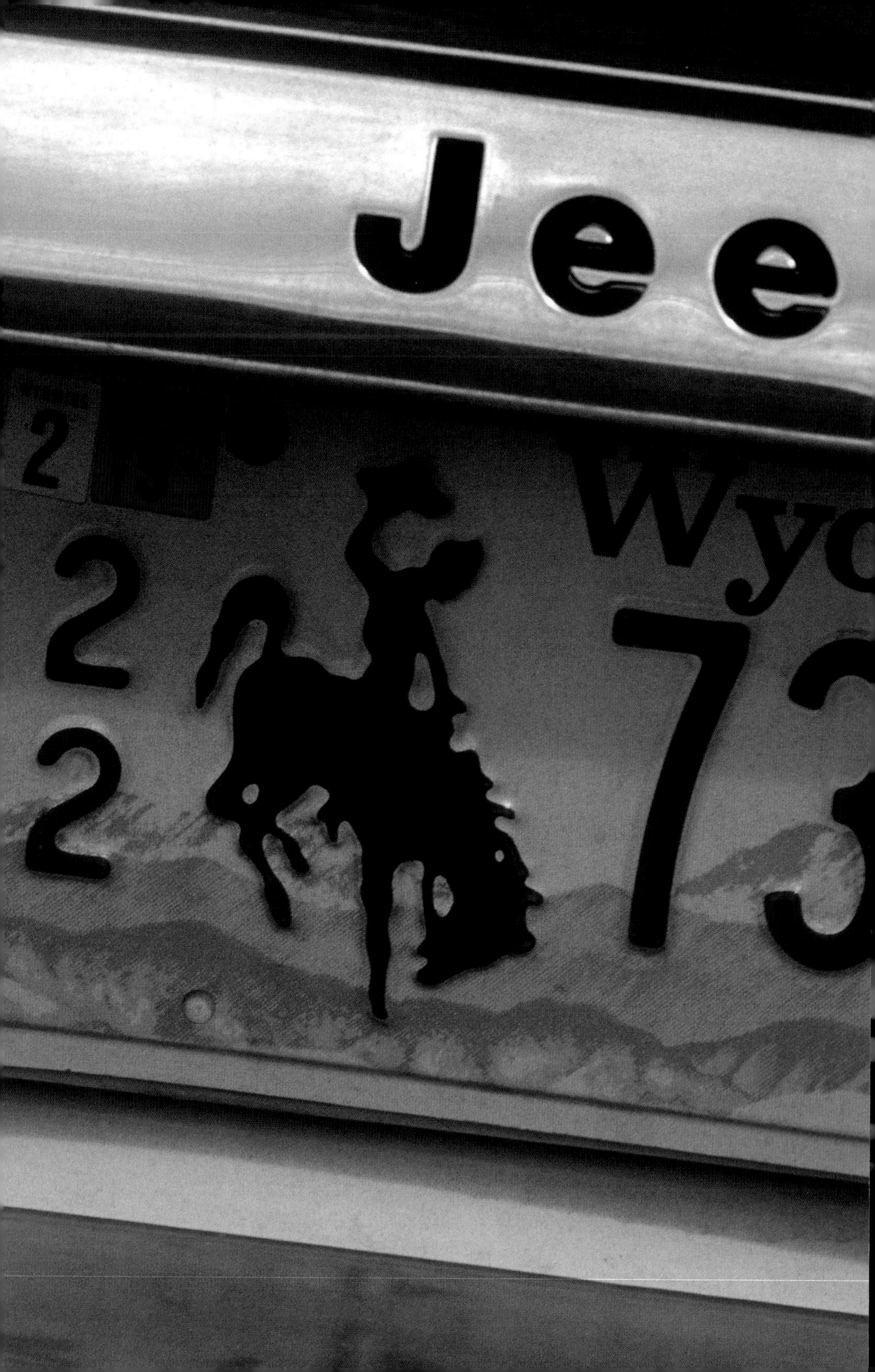
Jee
2
Wyo
22
73

✹INSIGHT GUIDES   TRAVEL TIPS

UNITED STATES ON THE ROAD

TRANSPORTATION

GETTING **T**HERE AND **G**ETTING **A**ROUND

GETTING **T**HERE

Most travelers arriving in the United States do so by air. The routes in this book begin and end at major US cities with international airports: New York to Miami (Atlantic route); Boston to Seattle (Northern Route); Washington, DC to Los Angeles (Central Route); Atlanta to San Diego (Southern Route); Los Angeles to San Diego (Pacific Route). From here, connecting flights can be made all over the US to secondary cities and towns. It is also possible to arrive by ship. Seattle, San Francisco, San Diego, Los Angeles, New York, Boston, Fort Lauderdale, Miami, and Baton Rouge, Houston, and Tampa on the Gulf of Mexico are major deep-water port cities in the US.

Important Note: As of January 12, 2009, non-US residents from Visa Waiver countries such as the UK are required to submit information about themselves online to the Department of Homeland Security and be pre-approved for travel to the US at least three days before they travel *(see Visas and Entry, page 453)*.

Atlanta

Hartsfield-Jackson Atlanta International Airport, located 10 miles (16km) from Atlanta, is the world's busiest. International passengers arrive at Concourse E. The terminal has six concourses with 151 domestic and 28 international gates; international passengers arrive at Concourse E. There are over 200 food and beverage, retail and high-end outlets, with more planned in the future.

Boston

Logan International Airport handles more than 1,100 flights daily, with more than 30 carriers serving the airport. It is the northern terminal of the world's busiest airline market: the Boston–New York–Washington, DC run. Delta Airlines, US Airways, and JetBlue run shuttles between these airports. Logan has five terminals (A–E). Note that domestic and international flights of the same airline do not necessarily use the same terminal. There is a free shuttle bus service between the terminals.

Los Angeles

Los Angeles International Airport (LAX) is the city's main airport. It is the sixth-busiest airport in the world and serves most of the world's major airlines. LAX is 17 miles (27km) from Downtown and a short drive to Santa Monica and other locations along the coast. Free shuttle buses connect its nine terminals. An information booth is located on the departure level of the Tom Bradley International Terminal, which offers a language translation link for non-English speakers. Other convenient airports serving the metro area with domestic flights include **Bob Hope Airport** (BUR) serving the San Fernando Valley; **John Wayne (Orange County) Airport** (SNA) is 35 miles (56km) south of Los Angeles in Santa Ana, convenient for Disneyland; and **Long Beach Municipal Airport** (LGB).

Miami

Miami International Airport is the city's primary airport. It is often also called Wilcox Field, and is one of the key airports serving the Southern United States as well as other Central and Latin American destinations. Miami International is about a 30-minute drive from Downtown, though traffic congestion at peak times can lengthen this considerably. Currently, there are eleven concourses that serve almost all major domestic and international carriers. Information booths have Miami maps and can provide info about buses and shuttles to and from the airport via the train and Tri-Rail lines. Alternately, the Fort Lauderdale airport in Broward County (FLL) can be used and is only 30 minutes north of Miami. Other airports are inconveniently distant, making Miami International or Fort Lauderdale the best choices for incoming travelers.

New York City

New York's two major airports, **John F. Kennedy International** (JFK) and **LaGuardia**, are both in Queens, east of Manhattan on Long Island, respectively 15 and 8 miles (24km and 13km) from Midtown. Driving time to/from Kennedy is estimated at 90 minutes, but heavy traffic can often double this, so leave lots of time if you're catching a flight. LaGuardia is used only for shorter US domestic and some Canadian routes, and does not have any intercontinental flights.

San Diego

San Diego International Airport (SAN) (tel: 619-400-2404; www.san.org), also called Lindbergh Field, is 3 miles (5km) northwest of downtown San Diego, about a 5-minute drive from the city center. It is served by all the major domestic carriers and many international airlines. Free transportation between the airport's three terminals is provided on the Red Bus transport system. Volunteer Airport Ambassadors in green polo shirts provide assistance to travelers around the airport and at the information booths in the baggage claim areas in Terminal 1 (tel: 619-231-7361) and Terminal 2 (tel: 619-231-5230) from 6am to 11pm daily.

Seattle

Seattle-Tacoma International Airport (SEA) (tel: 206-433-5388; www.portseattle.org/seatac), known locally as Sea-Tac, is served by domestic carriers and several major international airlines. It is 14 miles (22km) south of Seattle city center, about a 25-minute drive depending on traffic. The airport has a central terminal and two satellite terminals for international flights, which are linked by a rail transit system. An airport information booth is located in the baggage claim area across from carousel 12 and is open daily from 6am until 2am.

Washington, DC

The city is served by three regional airports. **Ronald Reagan Washington National Airport** (or simply National,

Airlines

Air Canada: tel: 888-247-2262; www.aircanada.com
AirTran Airways: tel: 800-247-8726; www.ata.com
American: tel: 800-433-7300; www.aa.com
British Airways: tel: 800-247-9297; www.british-airways.com
Continental: tel: 800-523-3273; www.continental.com
Delta: tel: 800-221-1212; www.delta-air.com
Frontier Airlines: tel: 800-432-1359; www.flyfrontier.com
Lufthansa: tel: 800-645-3880; www.lufthansa.com
Northwest-KLM: tel: 800-225-2525; www.nwa.com
Southwest Airlines: tel: 800-435-9792; www.southwest.com
Spirit Airlines: tel: 800-772-7117; www.spiritair.com
United Airlines: tel: 800-225-5833; www.ual.com
US Airways: tel: 800-428-4322; www.usairways.com
Virgin Atlantic: tel: 800-862-8621; www.virginatlantic.com

as it's often still called) is closest to the city, just 4 miles (6.4km) across the Potomac in Virginia. **Dulles Airport** is also in Virginia, 26 miles (42km) from DC. **Baltimore-Washington International Airport** (or BWI) is 40 miles (64km) north in the city of Baltimore in Maryland and about an hour by car. **Reagan National** offers mostly domestic service and also flights to and from some Canadian cities. Dulles and BWI are both international airports.

GETTING AROUND

The United States is so huge that, for most people, the only logical way to get around is by flying. Many flights connect through hub cities, served by major airlines. A number of regional airlines fly into smaller cities. A large road network of rapid **interstate** and **US highways**, **scenic state routes**, and **slow county**, **forest**, and **Indian reservation backroads** offers a variety of driving options.

Federal and state highways are paved and kept free of snow by snow plows in winter; local backroads are often unmaintained and may consist of anything from graded gravel to four-wheel-drive routes, many of which become impassable during rainstorms and snow. Other transportation options include **trains**, operated nationally by Amtrak, and light rail within and between local cities. **Buses** operated by Greyhound crisscross the country, usually operating out of an easily accessible downtown depot with links to local transport.

By Air

If it is too impractical because of long distances to drive to the destinations listed here, an easy alternative is to fly. Airlines that serve the airports in the major hub cities include American, Delta, Continental, Northwest, Southwest, United, and US Airways.

You can also fly into cities along the routes, including Charleston, Savannah, and Tampa; Mobile, New Orleans, Houston, and Phoenix, San Francisco, and Portland; Buffalo, Chicago, Minneapolis/St Paul, Sioux Falls, Spokane. Smaller cities are often served by regional airlines.

Airport Security

Since September 11, 2001, air travel in the US has changed drastically. Expect delays departing US airports

due to recent Homeland Security anti-terrorism rules. These are apt to change, so check before flying. Pack items for both carry-on and checked luggage in clear bags, leave gifts unwrapped, and take laptops out of bags for inspection by Transportation Security Administration (TSA) personnel. Consider wearing slip-on shoes as all footwear must be removed and scanned by x-ray machines.

Passengers are allowed one carry-on resealable 1-quart (1-liter) clear plastic bag, which can contain liquids, gels, or aerosols in containers of 3 ounces or less. The contents in the plastic bag must be sealed and may be subjected to x-ray inspection separate from the carry-on bag.

Allow plenty of time at the airport to clear security, expect searches and questions to be asked, and do not attempt to carry any sharp objects in your hand luggage. This includes scissors, nailclippers, pen-knives, and other seemingly innocuous items.

By Train

Although passenger services were greatly curtailed in the latter part of the 20th century, it is still possible to travel the length and breadth of the continent by rail. **Amtrak** is the major rail passenger carrier in the US. Its network links many cities, but sadly bypasses many more. However, there are still some excellent trans-continental and coastal routes that glide through breathtaking scenery and often feature on-board entertainment, such as Indian storytellers and local historians. It's also possible to find Amtrak trains that allow you to take your car with you, such as the Auto Train between Lorton, Virginia, near Washington, DC, and Sanford, north of Orlando. You will also find an increasing number of light-rail options once you arrive in major cities.

Train passes

Passes for unlimited travel on Amtrak over a fixed period of time are available only from a travel agent in a foreign country. Proof of non-US residency is required. For information about Amtrak's services, call 800-872-7245 or visit: www.amtrak.com.

By Bus

The national bus line, Greyhound, as well as a number of smaller charter companies, provide an impressive network of ground travel throughout the country, offering daily service to major towns and cities. Routes and schedules are subject to change; it is a good idea to check all arrangements with local stations in advance.

Most cities also have municipal bus systems. As both Greyhound and municipal stations are often situated in somewhat squalid areas, try to stay alert and do not wander too far, particularly after dark. Plan your journey for daylight arrival if possible. On the whole, the buses themselves are safe and reasonably comfortable; choosing a seat near to the driver may discourage unwanted attention.

For reservations and local bus station details, telephone 800-229-9424, or visit www.greyhound.com.

Bus passes

A Greyhound Ameripass offers unlimited travel to 2,600 destinations within 68 consecutive days. The pass may be purchased only outside the US. Details are available from Greyhound and most foreign travel agents.

By Car

The American love affair with the car is reflected in the excellent network of roads that has sprung up since World War II creating access to the remotest areas. If you're in a hurry, the larger interstates are your best bet, with their fast, direct routes, 24-hour services, and year-round maintenance. But you'll see more of the real America and its people if you drive at least some of the time on its folksy "blue highways." This book's routes offer a combination of both experiences.

Car rental agencies are located at all airports, in cities, and large towns; they are very hard to find in more remote areas of the US West. In most places you must be at least 21 years old (25 at some locations) to rent a car and you must have a valid driver's license and at least one major credit card. More agencies are accepting debit cards these days, but may hold back as much as $500 on the card to cover rental. Inquire at the time of reservation to avoid nasty surprises.

Be sure to check insurance provisions before signing anything. Cover is usually $15–25 per day. You may already be covered by your own auto insurance or credit card company, however, so check with them first. **Loss Damage Waiver** (LDW) or **Collision Damage Waiver** (CDW) is essential. Without it, you'll be liable for any damage done to your vehicle, regardless of fault. You are advised to pay for supplementary liability insurance on top of standard

Car Rental Companies

Contact details for major nationwide car rental agencies are listed below. Check the *Yellow Pages* for a full list of firms.
Alamo, tel: 800-327-9633; www.goalamo.com
Avis, tel: 800-831-2847; www.avis.com
Budget, tel: 800-527-0700; www.budget.com
Dollar, tel: 800-800-4000; www.dollar.com
Enterprise, tel: 800-325-8007; www.enterprise.com
Hertz, tel: 800-654-3131; www.hertz.com
National, tel: 800-227-7368; www.nationalcar.com
Thrifty, tel: 800-367-2277; www.thrifty.com

third-party insurance. Be sure to walk around the rental car slowly, check it for existing damage, and make a careful note of any dents or dings before leaving the lot.

US rental car rates are excellent ($35/day average for a compact), if you return the car to the original location. One-way rentals are much more expensive: $100/day average. Good deals may be found in the US by checking online and booking through either a company or travel website.

Distances and Driving Times

The routes in this book are not designed to be driven straight through, so how long you take to drive them is entirely up to you: preferably, the slower the better. If you do decide to drive the whole route at once, allow two weeks for coastal routes and a month for cross-country routes so that you can spend 2–3 nights at major destinations and single nights in between. Where possible, the drives in this book are planned so that there are reasonable driving distances between towns and cities. Driving no more than 200 miles (320km)/day or 4 hours allows you to get the driving done in the morning, allowing you some of the afternoon to see the sights.

On cross-country routes across the West, you will inevitably have a few days of 500-mile (800km) pushes across empty highway to reach the next destination. Do a bit of planning and try to find a way of breaking up the journey to avoid burning out and having roads and towns start to blur into one another.

Not counting stops, visits to attractions, side trips, traffic delays,

and low-speed highways, the routes in this book could, theoretically, be driven Jack Kerouac–style straight through in the following time frames:
Atlantic Route: New York to Key West (1,761 miles/2,836km, allow 32 driving hours minimum)
Northern Route: Boston to Cape Flattery (4,095 miles/6,590km, allow 55 driving hours minimum)
Central Route: Washington, DC to Los Angeles (2,922 miles/4,702km, allow 42 driving hours minimum)
Southern Route: Atlanta to San Diego (2,572 miles/4,139km, allow 40 driving hours minimum)
Pacific Route: San Diego to Seattle (1,399 miles/2,251km, allow 30 driving hours minimum).

For detailed information on mileage between key cities along the route, see mileage charts on page 464.

RV Rentals

No special license is necessary to operate a motor home (or recreational vehicle – RV for short), but they aren't cheap. When you add up the cost of rental fees, insurance, gas, and campgrounds, you may find that renting a car and staying in motels or tent camping is less expensive. Keep in mind, too, that RVs are large and slow and may be difficult to handle on narrow mountain roads. If parking space is tight, driving an RV may be very inconvenient. Access to some roads may be limited. For additional information about RV rentals, call the **Recreational Vehicle Rental Association**, tel 800-336-0355.

Open Road Survival Skills

It is essential to inform yourself properly about the area you are traveling in, including weather and road conditions, and be prepared to change your plans at the first hint of potential danger, such as blizzards, heavy thunder storms, and tornadoes.

Traveling in remote backcountry on foot is not recommended for solo women, but if you do, leave a note inside the car about your planned return time and don't hike off-trail or otherwise invite problems. It helps to know a few survival skills suitable for the terrain, including first aid, if you're traveling alone, especially in desert and mountain areas of the West.

It goes without saying that you should drive a reliable vehicle and carry plenty of supplies, including any medications, first aid kit, spare tire and gas, a gallon of water per day, nutritious food, emergency flares, warm clothing, and a cellphone.

Desert travelers: the single most important precaution you can take is to tell someone your destination, route and expected time of arrival. Check tires carefully before long stretches of desert driving. Heat builds pressure, so keep them at slightly below normal air pressure. The desert's arid climate makes carrying extra water – both for passengers and vehicles – essential. Carry at least one gallon per person per day. Keep an eye on the gas gauge. It's a good idea to gas up whenever you have an opportunity and have more than you think you need. Remember, if you should have car trouble or become lost, do not strike out on foot. A car, visible from the air and presumably on a road, is easier to spot than a person, and it affords shelter from the weather. Wait to be found. Mountain drivers are advised to be equally vigilant. Winter storms in California's Sierra Nevada and Washington's Cascades occasionally close major roads, and at times chains are required on tires. Conditions often change fast, so check the weather forecast regularly and phone ahead for road conditions before you depart.

AAA Membership

Anyone spending a significant amount of time driving US highways is strongly advised to join the Automobile Association of America (AAA or Triple A). Benefits include emergency breakdown service, excellent road maps, travel literature, and personalized trip planning. Premier level offers towing up to 200 miles (320km) from breakdown site – important if you are in the middle of nowhere – and lockout, refueling, and jumpstart service. Insurance is also available through the association, which has a reciprocal arrangement with some of the automobile associations in other countries. Telephone 800-874-7532 or visit www.aaa.com.

By Motorbike

For those with *Easy Rider* dreams, touring by motorbike may be an inspiring option. Harley-Davidson and other major motorbike vendors also offer rentals in some locations in the US. If you do decide to ride a motorbike on any of the routes in this book, be conservative: you won't be able to cover as much ground as in a car in a day (probably no more than 250–300 miles/320–480km) to allow plenty of time for visiting attractions. And inevitably, you'll be riding on scenic highways and backroads off the Interstate, so factor that in, too. Vital clothing includes a helmet, stiff boots, and, in cool weather, leather chaps to cut down on road abrasion, should you take a spill. There are several organizations for enthusiasts of particular motorbike makes, from Harley-Davidson to BMW. Several homegrown websites offer ideas on US motorcycle traveling.

By Bicycle

Bicycle touring is gaining in popularity in the US. It's definitely the slow option of seeing the country, but that's not a bad thing in this age of rapid transit. Most cyclists average little more than 10–15mph (16–24kmh), so your best bet is to cover a short scenic segment of any of the routes in this book, if you choose the bicycle option, and stick to areas with clustered attractions, scenery, and lodging/food services.

Hub Cities

Atlanta
Public Transportation
From the airport: Hartsfield-Jackson Atlanta International Airport is 10 miles (16km) from Downtown, further to Midtown and Buckhead on the north side. Many hotels offer courtesy buses from the airport. Shared-ride shuttles provide service into the city: $16.50/one way. Contact The Atlanta Link, tel: 404-564-0607 or 404-524-3400; www.theatlantalink.com.

Public transportation from the airport to the city and within the metropolitan area is much cheaper and extremely safe, clean, and reliable.
Rapid Transportation/buses: MARTA (Metropolitan Rapid Transit Authority) is a rapid-rail and bus system comprising north–south and east–west rail lines intersecting at the main Five Points Station in downtown Atlanta. Stations are designated N, S, E, W, or P, denoting their compass points (P represents the current single station Proctor Creek line). The Hartsfield International Airport Station is designated Airport S7 and is the final stop on the South line. The trip to downtown Atlanta takes just 17 minutes. Trains operate daily 5am–1am. A one-way Breeze ticket costs $1.75. A weekly visitor pass costs $13. In addition to rail links, MARTA offers local bus service throughout Atlanta; cost is the same.
National buses: Greyhound operates from the depot at 81 International Boulevard NW, tel: 800-229-7245.

National rail: Amtrak trains run from Peachtree Station, 1688 Peachtree Street NW, tel: 800-872-7245.

Private Transportation
Atlanta – sprawling, suburban and subject to extremes of weather – is not ideally suited for extensive walking tours.
Car rental: agencies may be found at the airport, and/or Downtown.
Taxis: Taxi companies are numerous. Ask at a hotel for assistance; hotels are always good places to find a taxi. Flat-rate fares within Downtown, Midtown, or Buckhead zones are $8, $2 each additional person. Outside the Business District, the following fares apply: first 1/8 mile, $2.50; each additional 1/8 mile, 25 cents; waiting, $21 an hour. Flat-rate fare from the airport to Downtown: $25, to Buckhead: $40. Fares are subject to 6 percent tax. Tel: 404-762-6087 for more information.

Boston
Public Transportation
From the airport: Logan International Airport, just 3 miles (5km) from downtown Boston, is closer to town than any other major airport in the nation: this refers to distance and not to time. Traffic can back up at the tunnels under the harbor connecting the airport and city. The Massachusetts Bay Transportation Authority's (MBTA) Blue Line from Airport Station is the fastest way to Downtown (about 10 minutes) and to many other places as well. Free shuttle buses run between all the airport terminals and the subway station. Cabs can be found outside each terminal. Fares to Downtown should average about $20, including tip, providing there are no major traffic jams. Airways Transportation buses leave all terminals every half hour for downtown and Back Bay hotels, and several major bus companies, including Bonanza, Concord Trailways, Peter Pan, and Vermont Transit, serve many outlying suburbs and distant destinations.
Rapid transit: Boston's subway system (the "T") offers good value. The Boston Passport, offering one, three or seven days of unlimited rides, can be purchased at the Boston Common Visitor Information Center at 147 Tremont Street, tel: 617-426-3115.
City buses: The majority of the MBTA's 160-plus bus routes operate feeder services linking subway stations to neighborhoods not directly served by the rapid transit system. Some

crosstown routes connect stations on different subway lines without going into Downtown. Only a few MBTA buses actually enter downtown Boston, and most of these are express buses from outlying areas. The basic MBTA bus fare is under $1.50.

Intercity buses: Several intercity bus companies serve Boston. The two largest, Greyhound (800-229-9424), and Peter Pan (800-237-8747), have frequent daily services from New York City and Albany, NY, as well as services from points within New England.

Commuter rail: The MBTA Commuter Rail extends from downtown Boston to as far as 60 miles (100km) away and serves such tourist destinations as Concord, Lowell, Salem, Ipswich, Gloucester, and Rockport. Trains to the north and northwest of Boston depart from North Station; trains to points south and west of the city leave from South Station. All south side commuter trains, except the Fairmount Line, also stop at the Back Bay Station. For information on trains from any of these stations, telephone 617-222-3200.

National rail: Amtrak Passenger trains arrive at South Station (Atlantic Avenue and Summer Street, 800-872-7245; tdd: 800-523-6590) from New York, Washington, DC, and Philadelphia with connections from all points in the nationwide Amtrak system. They also stop at Back Bay Station (145 Dartmouth Street).

Private Transportation
Boston, it is justly claimed, is a walker's city – a good thing, for it is certainly not a driver's city. Early city planners laid streets along cow paths, Native American trails, and colonial wagon tracks, linked by crooked little alleys. However, in the middle of the 19th century, impeccable grid systems were introduced in the Back Bay, South End, and, to a lesser degree, South Boston. If you attempt to drive, be aware that being stuck in a traffic jam, getting lost, and then being unable to find a parking space is about par for the course. Public parking facilities are found at Government Center; Post Office Square; the Public Garden; the Prudential Center; on Clarendon Street near the John Hancock Tower; and elsewhere. Private lots are scattered here and there.

Car rental: Most agencies have offices at the airport and/or Downtown.

Taxis: Taxi stands are common at popular tourist sites. Companies to call include: Checker Taxi, tel: 617-536-7500; Red Cab, tel: 617-734-5000; Town Taxi, tel: 617-536-5000.

Los Angeles
Public Transportation
From the airport: Public transportation is found on LAX's lower level, which is where arriving passengers claim baggage. At this level, there are stops for taxis, LAX shuttles, buses, courtesy trams, and vans in front of each airline terminal. Information boards about ground transport are located in all the baggage claim areas and they are very easy to understand. Shuttles from the airport are reasonably priced; the fare varies depending on your destination. Among the companies operating 24 hours a day are Flyaway Bus Service, tel: 866-435-9529; Prime Time Shuttle, tel: 310-536-7922; and The SuperShuttle, tel: 310-782-6600 or 800-258-3826. Hopping in a taxi at LAX should be avoided if at all possible. Los Angeles' cabs are very expensive – more so than most US cities – and are almost never found driving the streets looking for customers. Free shuttle service is now provided to the Metro Green Line's Aviation Station. Pick up is on the Lower/Arrival level under the LAX Shuttle sign. Check out the Metro Bus and Metro Rail routes and schedules at www.metro.net.

Metro: Los Angeles County Metropolitan Transportation Authority, known as **Metro**, serves an area of 1,433 sq miles (3,711 sq km). With around 2,200 buses and four rail lines. Metro Rail currently operates over 73 miles (117km) of subway and light rail lines, with 62 stations stretching from North Hollywood south to Long Beach, and from the coast east to Pasadena, serving many key visitor destinations. The Metro Red Line subway serves Hollywood, Universal Studios, and several downtown locations. The Metro Blue Line runs from Downtown to Long Beach. The Metro Gold Line connects with the Red Line and runs to Pasadena. The Metro Green Line serves Los Angeles Airport. The Metro Orange Line serves the San Fernando Valley with Metroliner buses.

For information on **Metro Rail** and **Metro Bus**, tel: 800-COMMUTE (226-6883) or use the trip planner on their website: www.metro.net. The base fare is $1.25 plus 30 cents for transfers. Bus drivers do not give change, so you must have the exact fare or a token. The **Metro Day Pass**, which allows unlimited bus and rail journeys, is good value at $5. You can buy them on the bus, or at vending machines in rail stations. Buses and rail lines operate from 4am to after midnight, though night services are less frequent.

The **DASH shuttle system** (tel: 213-808-2273; www.ladottransit.com) operates Downtown during daytime hours, linking major businesses and the civic and entertainment centers. It costs 25 cents per ride and transfers are free. Separate DASH systems operate around Hollywood and other parts of the city, while the Runabout is a similar service operating in Long Beach.

Private Transportation
The most efficient way to get around Los Angeles is to rent a car. Rental agencies may be found at the airport, your hotel and in various locations around the city. Cars often can be delivered to you. Car rental companies all charge basically the same price.

Taxis: Taxis are fairly expensive and you will rarely find them cruising the streets but they can be ordered or found at airports, train stations, bus terminals, and at major hotels. Try: Yellow Cab Co, tel: 310-851-5022 or Independent Taxi, tel: 213-666-0040. The LA Checker Cab Co, tel: 213-482-3456 also offers vans with wheelchair lifts. An average fare from the Los Angeles Airport to downtown Los Angeles would be at least $46.

Miami
Public Transportation
From the airport: Miami International Airport is 7 miles (12km) from Downtown. SuperShuttle (tel: 305-871-2000) operates between the airport and major hotels. Metrobus service departs from Level 1 next to Concourse E. A taxi fare to Downtown costs less than $30 and takes about 30 minutes.

Rapid transit: Metrorail is an elevated rapid transit system connecting Downtown with Dadeland and Hialeah. The Metromover monorail system circles the Downtown area. Metro-Dade Transit runs both (tel: 305-770-3131). Single fares under $2.

City buses: Metro-Dade Transit also runs the Metrobus fleet from stops indicated by distinctive blue and green signs. Single fares under $2.

Intercity buses: The main Greyhound terminal is at Bayside Station, 700 Biscayne Boulevard (tel: 800-231-2222).

Commuter rail: The Tri-Rail (tel: 800-874-7245) service links Miami-Dade with Palm Beach and Broward.

Trains: Amtrak trains run from the Miami Terminal (tel: 800-872-7245).

Private Transportation
Miami is not a difficult city to negotiate by car but try to avoid weekday rush-hour snarls. Parking in the Miami Beach area can be scarce

and restrictions are stringently imposed by a fleet of super-efficient tow-trucks. Fortunately, Miami Beach is a delightful place to explore by foot. Most of the car rental companies have offices at Miami International airport or Downtown. Check the *Yellow Pages* for a full list of firms.

Ports: Florida has several major cruise ship ports, with Miami and Port Everglades leading with the most sailings. Others include Port Canaveral, Palm Beach, St Petersburg, Tampa, Port Manatee (in Tampa Bay), and Madeira Beach and Treasure Island (just north of St Pete Beach). The Port of Miami is the largest cruise port in the world. Seven cruise lines carry more than 1.5 million passengers a year into the port, which represents over two-thirds of all cruise passengers worldwide. The port is just a five-minute ride from Downtown and Miami Beach. Tel: 305 371-7678.

Taxis: Taxis are relatively plentiful in South Beach with fares under $3 per mile (1.6km). They can also be found at airports, train stations, bus terminals and the major hotels, or ordered by telephone. Call Yellow Cab Co (tel: 305-633-1111); Metro Cab (tel: 305-888-8888); or Flamingo Taxi (tel: 305-759-8100).

New York City
Public Transportation
From the airport: AirTrain is an airport rail system that connects JFK and Newark airports with the subway and rail networks, at Howard Beach (A train) and Sutphin Boulevard (E, J, and Z train) subways and at Jamaica Long Island Railroad station for JFK, and at a special airport rail station in Newark. At each airport, AirTrain runs every few minutes and takes about 10 minutes from each terminal. Traveling between JFK and Midtown Manhattan by AirTrain and subway takes about one hour; traveling from Newark (by AirTrain and then Amtrak or NJ Transit train to Penn Station) can take only 30–45 minutes. For AirTrain information contact (JFK) tel: 877-535-2478; www.airtrainjfk.com; (Newark) tel: 888-397-4636; information: tel: 888-397-4636; www.panynj.gov/airtrainnewark.

New York Airport Service (tel: 212-875-8200; www.nyairportservice.com) buses run between both JFK and LaGuardia airports and Manhattan. Pick-up and drop-off points include: Port Authority Bus Terminal, Penn Station, and Grand Central Terminal, with a transfer service available to or from Midtown hotels. Buses from JFK run 6.15am–11.10pm.

From LaGuardia, the M60 bus to upper Manhattan subway stations operates 5–1am, while **Triboro Coach** bus Q-33 runs to 74th St subway stop in Jackson Heights, Queens, from which various trains run to Manhattan.

Newark Liberty Airport Express (tel: 877-8NEWARK; www.coachusa.com) operates express buses daily between Newark airport and Manhattan, stopping at the Port Authority Bus Terminal, Grand Central, and Fifth Ave, at 42nd Street. Buses run 4am–1am.

There are several minibus services from all three airports to Manhattan. A big plus is that they take you door-to-door, direct to hotels or private addresses, but this can be slow, with many stops. SuperShuttle (tel: 212-258-3826; www.supershuttle.com) offers a frequent service. It can be booked online, at airport ground transportation centers or from courtesy phones at the airports.

Rapid transit and buses: Subways and buses run 24 hours, less frequently after midnight, with the fare payable by token or (buses only) exact change, as well as by MetroCard pass (available at subway ticket booths), which allows free transfers within two hours of use. Unlimited-ride passes are good for seven days or 30 day-passes are also available, as is a day pass sold at news-stands, hotels, and electronic kiosks in some subway stations. For general bus and subway information and for other details about the MetroCard pass call: 718-330-1234. Greyhound buses run from the Port Authority bus terminal, 41st, and Eighth Avenue (tel: 800-229-9424).

Trains: National rail trains arrive and depart from Manhattan's two railroad terminals: Grand Central Terminal and Pennsylvania Station. City buses stop outside each terminal and each sits atop a subway station. Amtrak information, tel: 800-872-7245.

Private Transportation
Car Rental: Driving around Manhattan is not much fun although, should the need arise, there is a wide range of firms available at airports from which cars can be rented.

Taxis: All are metered, cruise the streets randomly and must be hailed, although there are official taxi stands at places like Grand Central Terminal. Be sure to hail an official yellow cab, not an unlicensed "gypsy" cab. One fare covers all passengers up to four (five in a few of the larger cabs). After 8pm there is a 50¢ surcharge on all taxi rides. Telephone 212-302-8294 for lost property or to make a complaint.

San Diego
Public Transportation
From the airport: Various shuttle services operate from San Diego International Airport to the city center and are reasonablly priced. Shuttle service companies include the SuperShuttle, tel: 800-974-8885, Advanced Shuttle, tel: 800-719-3499 or 619-466-6885, and SeaBreeze Shuttle, tel: 800-777-0585 or 619-297-7463. The Metropolitan Transit System bus route 992 travels from the airport to Downtown.

City buses and trolleys: City buses and the San Diego Trolley are run by San Diego Metropolitan Transit System (tel: 619-685-4900; www.transit.511sd.com). Fares start at $1 for buses and $1.25 for trolleys; exact change is required. Day passes are available from $5 that include both bus and trolley routes. The **San Diego Trolley System** has three lines; the Blue Line travels from Downtown to the Mexican border at San Ysidro. Trolleys operate daily from 5am until midnight. Some bus services run later but routes vary.

Trains: Amtrak (tel: 800-872-7245; www.amtrak.com) trains run from the Santa Fe Depot at 10850 Kettner Boulevard to Los Angeles with stops along the coast. **The Coaster** (tel: 800-262-7837; www.transit.511sd.com) is an express rail commuter service that runs between downtown San Diego and Oceanside.

Private Transportation
Unlike Los Angeles, San Diego is a relatively easy city to explore either with or without a car. However, as in most big cities, journeys are best planned around the weekday early morning and late afternoon crush. Parking is generally easy to find and for the most part moderately priced. Most of the major car rental agencies have offices at the airport and in the downtown area.

Taxis: Try any of the following companies or check the *Yellow Pages* for a full list of firms – Orange Cab, tel: 619-291-3333; San Diego Cab, tel: 619-226-8294; Yellow Cab, tel: 619-234-6161.

Traveling to Tijuana/Baja
Although in the past US citizens did not need a passport to travel to Tijuana for the day, border security has changed significantly in recent years. Now, US citizens as well as non-citizens must have a valid passport and, if applicable, green card, to re-enter the country.

US insurance is not valid in Mexico. You are strongly advised to obtain short-term insurance at one of the many sales offices just north of the border. Crossing into Mexico is easy, with immigration officers at both sides usually just waving you along.

Because driving is not easy in Tijuana for those unfamiliar with the city (and the Spanish language), many drivers park in San Diego's San Ysidro, crossing into Tijuana via the elevated pedestrian walkway. Avoid leaving your car in the parking places of merchants unless you want to have it towed away by police. There's an all-day secure lot off the "Last Exit US parking" ramp – turn right at the stop sign to the Tijuana side. Cheap taxis and buses are available.

Crossing Back: The return to California can be more tense than the entry into Mexico, as US officers take much more interest in who's coming into the country. Expect long lines, especially in busy vacation periods.

Seattle
Public Transportation
From the airport: Access to Sea-Tac is via I-5 (exit 154 from south I-5 or exit 152 from north I-5), or via Highway 99/509 and 518. Stop-and-go traffic on I-5 is not uncommon, especially during rush hours, so the alternate route on the highway is often quicker. Buses provide the least costly method of transportation. The 194 is the most direct, bringing passengers downtown in about 30 minutes. The 174 makes local stops on its way downtown. At the time of writing, a light rail link between downtown Seattle and Sea-Tac was under construction, due for completion in late 2009. Bus or van companies that link the airport with metropolitan Seattle or Bellevue include:
The Gray Line Downtown Airporter (tel: 800-426-7532)
Shuttle Express (tel: 425-981-7000)
Capital Aeroporter (tel: 253-838-7431)
Quick Shuttle (tel:, 800-665-2122)
STITA (tel: 206-246-9999) provides a taxi service to and from the airport. From the airport to Downtown (or vice versa) costs about $35.
National buses: The Greyhound terminal is located at 811 Stewart Street (tel: 800-231-2222).
National trains: The Amtrak station is at Third Avenue and S. Jackson Street (tel: 800-872-7245)
Commuter trains: Metro Transit (tel: 206-553-3000; http://transit.metrokc.gov) provides a "Ride Free Area" in the downtown core bordered by the I-5 to the east, the waterfront to the west, Jackson Street to the south, and Battery Street to the north.

Streetcar: Metro also operates a 1927 vintage trolley which runs 1½ miles (3km) along the waterfront every 20–30 minutes from Myrtle, and from Edwards Park to the Pioneer Square district. The trolley has been temporarily suspended owing to construction work in the area, but a free bus service has been provided.
Monorail: The Monorail tel: 206-905-2620; www.seattlemonorail.com), which was built for the 1962 World Fair, runs every 15 minutes between Seattle Center and Fourth and Pine streets to Westlake Center. The ride is just under 1 mile (2km) and takes only 90 seconds. It's clean and spacious with large windows.
Ferries: The Washington State Ferry system (tel: 800-843-3779; www.wsdot.wa.gov/ferries), the largest in the country, covers the Puget Sound area, linking Seattle (at Pier 52) with the Olympic Peninsula via Bremerton and Bainbridge Island. State ferries also depart from West Seattle to Vashon Island and Southworth and from Edmonds, 7 miles (11km) north of Seattle, to Kingston on Kitsap Peninsula. They also go from Anacortes, 90 miles (145km) northwest of Seattle, through the San Juan Islands to Victoria, on Canada's Vancouver Island. Passengers to Canada need a passport. The Black Ball Ferry (tel: 360-457-4491) departs from Port Angeles on the Olympic Peninsula to Victoria, BC, four times a day in summer and twice daily the rest of the year. Ferries carry cars.

Private Transportation
When the weather is fine, Seattle is a very pleasant city to walk about in – it is hilly, but many of the sights may be toured comfortably on foot. Heavy traffic congestion and scarce, expensive parking make driving in the center a less attractive option. Many of the major car rental agencies have offices at Seattle-Tacoma Airport or in the downtown area. Consult the *Yellow Pages* phone book for a full listing of rental firms.

Washington, DC
Public Transportation
From National: There's a Metro subway station here, easily accessible from the airport terminal with quick service into DC (about $6). You can also take a taxi, available curbside when you pick up your bags, with fares that range from $10 to $30.
From Dulles: Take a Washington Flyer Taxi directly into the city, which will cost about $50. Bus service runs about every 30 minutes and costs $8.

Buy your bus ticket at the kiosk on the airport Arrivals level.
From BWI: A taxi from this airport, which you can hail at the curb near the baggage claim, will cost about $60 into DC. You can also take the free shuttle bus to the nearby Amtrak rail station (800-872-7245, or visit www.amtrak.com) and take the train into DC's Union Station for about $30, but you may have a wait, depending on the train schedule.
SuperShuttle: You can pick up one of these dependable blue mini-vans at any of the airports and share a ride into the city. Cost from Dulles and BWI into DC is about $50, from National about $20. When you're ready to fly home, schedule a pickup to the airport by phoning 800-258-3826.
International Limousine is one of the city's oldest limo services, available 24 hours. Tel: 202-388-6800 or visit www.internationallimo.com.
Metro: A $7.80 one-day Metrorail pass provides all-day subway travel after 9.30am.
City buses: Metrobus (tel: 202-637-7000) operates a comprehensive but confusing network of routes covering the city and outlying areas. You need exact change to board.
National buses: Greyhound buses operate out of the station at 1005 First Street NE (800-231-2222).
National rail: Amtrak runs from Union Station, 60 Massachusetts Avenue NE (800-872-7245).

Private Transportation
Washington, DC is compact enough to make it one of the best cities in the country for exploring on foot.
Car rental: Another good way to get around – particularly if you are interested in some of the worthwhile day trips – is to rent a car. You can do this at the airport, your hotel, or any car rental agency.
Parking: Most hotels (but not all) offer free parking for their guests; if staying in the city for any length of time, leave your car in the garage. Parking around DC is difficult on the street and expensive in car parks. All have numerous offices around the city, so consult the phone directory for the one nearest you.
Taxis: Long-distance taxi fares are steep, but traveling inside Washington is cheaper than in other American cities and much cheaper than in some European capitals. For planned trips, reserve a taxi at least an hour in advance of departure. Two of the major taxi cab companies are: Diamond Cab, tel: 202-387-6200 and Yellow Cab, tel: 202-544-1212.

A CCOMMODATIONS

HOTELS, YOUTH HOSTELS, BED AND BREAKFAST

Choosing Accommodation

Hotels and Motels

Chain hotels and motels are reliable, convenient, and often reasonably priced, but tend to lack character. In general, prices range from $50 to $150 depending on the location, the season, and additional amenities. Resorts and large hotels are often located on spacious properties outside Downtown and cater to guests who want everything onsite, from pools, spas, health centers, and sporting facilities to restaurants and snack shops, high-end shopping, ATM machines, business and meeting facilities, and in-room amenities such as fridges, microwaves, and coffeemakers. Their friendly, all-in anonymity is may be just what you need when your nervous system needs to come down from the occasionally overwhelming sensory input of a long road trip.

Boutique inns and small historic hotels, on the other hand, are often located in converted historic buildings in Downtown. They offer B&B-like charm along with big-hotel sophistication and a surprising number of amenities, such as spas, fine dining, and in-room extras like jacuzzi baths and robes. Their downtown location can make them a bit noisier than outlying hotels, and you'll usually pay more. But it's definitely worth it, if your budget allows, as these unique inns tend to be memorable and offer a quick way of getting to know more about the history and ambiance of a town – a boon if you're only in an area for one night.

Watch for hidden fees at luxury hotel chains. Most lodgings – even small ones – offer wireless internet in rooms but beware of hefty access fees (up to $12.95/day) at major hotels. Phone connection charges are also often charged. You can usually access wireless internet for free in the lobby and use a pay phone there, if you don't have a cellphone.

Reservations made on the internet generally offer the best deal, but you can also call and ask specifically about special weekend or corporate rates and "package deals." Motels, such as Best Western, offer a discount for AAA members. Book your room by credit card and secure a guaranteed late arrival, in case of any delays in your travel plans. A list of telephone numbers to make reservations at major chains in the US follows.

Bed and Breakfasts

B&Bs tend to be more personal than hotels. In some cases, you're a guest at a person's home where the accommodations are fairly simple and may involve a lot of interaction with family and other guests; in others, the rooms are in separate (large) historic homes or inns decorated with antiques, quilts, art, and other period furnishings. Most do not allow smoking. Before booking, also ask whether the room has a private bathroom, telephone, television, and wireless internet access. Inquire about breakfast, too. The morning meal is included in the price but may be anything from a couple of muffins to a multicourse feast. For more information contact:

Bed-and-Breakfast Inns ONLINE
909 N. Sepulveda Boulevard, 11th Floor, El Segundo, CA 90245.
Tel: 800-215-7365 or 310-280-4363

Budget Accommodations
Hostelling International
2nd Floor, Gate House, Fretherne Road, Welwyn Garden City, Herts, AL8 6RD, England
Tel: 01707-324170
Hostelling International/American Youth Hostels
8401 Colesville Road, Suite 600, Silver Spring, MD 20910
Tel: 301-495-1240
www.hiusa.org
YMCA
YMCA of the USA
Association Advancement, 101 N. Wacker Drive, Chicago, IL 60606
Tel: 800-872-9622
www.ymca.netoo
YWCA
1015 18th Street NW, Suite 1100, Washington DC 20036
Tel: 202-467-0801
www.ywca.org

Chain Hotels and Motels

Best Western, tel: 800-780-7234
Budget Host Inns, tel: 800-283-4678
Choice Hotels, tel: 877-424-6423
Days Inns of America, tel: 800-329-7466
Hampton Inns, tel: 800-426-7866
Hilton, tel: 800-445-8667
Holiday Inn, tel: 800-465-4329
Hyatt, tel: 800-633-7313
La Quinta, tel: 866-753-3757
Marriott, tel: 888-236-2427
Motel 6, tel: 800-466-8356
Radisson, tel: 888-201-1719
Ramada, tel: 800-272-6232
Red Roof Inns, tel: 800-733-7663
Starwood, tel: 888-625-5144

National Parks

Lodgings inside popular parks such as Grand Canyon, Yosemite, and Yellowstone sell out a year in advance, so it's essential to book as soon as possible. Reservations are handled through the park's concessionaire, a company operating under license with the National Park Service to manage accommodations, food service, gift shops, tours, and other services. Major concessionaires include **Xanterra** and **Amfac**. Information is available on the park's website or by calling direct. For general park information, contact:
National Park Service
Department of the Interior
1849 C Street NW, Washington, DC 20240
Tel: 202-208-6843
www.nps.gov

Campgrounds

Most state and national parks, US Forest Service areas, and some Bureau of Land Management sites have developed campgrounds. National Park Service campgrounds typically offer groomed tent and RV campsites with water, hookups, barbecue grate, picnic table, and a restroom with flush toilets; state parks usually also offer showers,

ABOVE: Beach camping, North Carolina.

electrical hookups, campstore, and other facilities.

Fees average $14 per site. You'll often find "primitive" campgrounds in remote areas of national parks and national forests, where there may be designated campsites but only a pit toilet and often no water or other facilities. Such sites are usually less expensive ($5–10).

National forests also allow free "dispersed camping" away from trails and destinations. At primitive sites, expect no facilities and bring everything you need, including a gallon of water per person per day, nutritious food, and the means to practice "leave no trace" camping.

If you plan on overnighting in national park backcountry or wilder-

ness, you'll need to register with the park's backcountry office in person to receive a permit and a designated campsite. This may be free (although not necessarily): rangers use it to restrict backcountry numbers, safeguarding the resource and visitor experience of solitude. Most campgrounds are busy from mid-June to September (winter in Florida). Be sure to make advance reservations for popular coastal state park campgrounds, especially those in California and Florida and the Northwest. Reservations for state park campgrounds and those under National Park Service or US Forest Service management may be made by logging onto www.reserve america.com or www.recreation.gov; tel: 877-444-6777; International: 518-885-3639. Reservations may be made up to 6 months in advance. Note: most NPS campgrounds still operate on a first-come, first-served basis, so be sure to arrive early in the day to get a spot.

Private RV campgrounds are typically very developed and more expensive and offer additional facilities such as coin laundries, pools, playgrounds, and restaurants. An extensive nationwide network of such sites is run by **Kampgrounds of America (KOA)**; Tel: 406-248-7444; www.koa.com.

ACCOMMODATIONS LISTINGS

ATLANTIC ROUTE

New York

New York City

The Carlyle
35 E. 76th Street
Tel: 744-1600
www.thecarlyle.com
Posh, reserved, and serene in its elegance, The Carlyle remains one of the city's most highly acclaimed luxury hotels. Home of Café Carlyle and Bemelmans Bar, two of the city's most enduring and upscale evening spots. The Carlyle is a favorite with visiting royalty. $$$

The Chelsea Hotel
204 W. 23rd Street
Tel: 929-9353
A red-brick, Victorian landmark of bohemian decadence, home to beatnik

poets, then Warhol drag queens, then Sid Vicious, and now… some of all of the above. Accommodations vary from a few inexpensive "student rooms" to suites. **$$–$$$**

Hotel Pennsylvania
401 Seventh Avenue (at 33rd Street)
Tel: 736-5000
Vast hotel, with 1,700 rooms, across from Madison Square Garden and Penn Station, donated its phone number to the 1938 Big Band hit *Pennsylvania 6-5000* and offers good-value packages with few frills. $$$

La Quinta Manhattan
17 W. 32nd Street
Tel: 736-1600
www.applecorehotels.com
Like others in the Apple

Core Hotels group (Quality Hotel East Side, etc.), rates at this 176-room hotel, a short walk from Macy's and Madison Square Garden, are extremely reasonable, especially considering that the comfortable rooms come with such conveniences as data ports and voice mail. There's also a lobby café with entertainment, a restaurant with room service, and an open-air rooftop bar where music and snacks can be enjoyed in summer, along with views of the Empire State Building. $$$

Murray Hill East Suites
149 E. 39th Street
Tel: 661-2100
Good value for longer stays. Each suite has a kitchen,

which you can stock inexpensively from local stores. $$

New York International Youth Hostel
891 Amsterdam Avenue
(at W. 103rd Street)
Tel: 932-2300
Accommodations in dormitory-style rooms range from $29 upwards per person per night; $3 less for IYH members. $

Washington Square Hotel
103 Waverly Place, NY 10011
Tel: 777-9515
www.wshotel.com
An almost century-old hotel that offers the perfect Village locale. The rooms are small but nicely appointed. In a former incarnation, this was the seedy Hotel Earle, where Papa John wrote the 1960s rock classic *California Dreaming*. **$$**

New Jersey
Lambertville
Apple Inn
31 York Street, NJ 08530
Tel: 973-764-3735
Well-kept Victorian-style bed and full breakfast in the heart of Lambertville. Five nice rooms with private baths. **$$$**
Chimney Hill Farm Estate
207 Goat Hill Road, NJ 08530
Tel: 609-397-1516
www.chimneyhillinn.com
An impressive gabled field-stone house located in the hills 5 miles (8km) from Lambertville. Candlelit country breakfasts and many other nice touches. **$$–$$$**

Morristown
The Madison Hotel
1 Convent Road, NJ 07960
Tel: 973-285-1800
www.themadisonhotel.com
Central, luxury accommodation with indoor heated swimming pool, jacuzzi, and sauna. Disabled access. **$$**
The Westin Governor Morris
2 Whippany Road, NY 07960
Tel: 973-539-7300
www.westin.com
Large, recently renovated hotel in the heart of Morristown. Facilities include 200 attractive guest rooms, two restaurants, and two lounges. **$$**

Trenton
Best Western Bordentown Inn
1068 Rt 206 Dunsmill, NJ 08505
Tel: 609-298-8000
www.bestwesternnewjersey.com
This inn features attractive, spacious rooms with movies, cable TV, HBO, and refrigerators. Other amenities include an attractive indoor pool, exercise room, sauna, bar, free parking, and fishing. **$$$**
Laurel Notch Motor Lodge
US 206, Bordentown, NJ 08505
Tel: 609-298-6500
Simple but very clean rooms. Close to local attractions. **$**

Pennsylvania
Lancaster
Strasburg Village Inn
1 W. Main Street, Strasburg, PA 17579
Tel: 717-687-0900
Fully renovated 18th-century bed-and-breakfast inn with Colonial decor in the center of town. Amenities include: private bath, some rooms with jacuzzi, complimentary full breakfast, air conditioning, TV, free parking. **$–$$**

Philadelphia
Alexander Inn
12th and Spruce streets, PA 19107
Tel: 215-923-3535
www.alexanderinn.com
Popular city-center boutique hotel with 48 designer rooms; recently renovated. **$$$**
Omni Hotel at Independence Park
401 Chestnut Street, PA 19106
Tel: 215-925-0000
www.omnihotels.com
Plush hotel located in Old City adjacent to Independence National Park. Featuring Azalea, a gourmet restaurant and lounge; indoor pool, health club, and sauna. **$$$**
Thomas Bond House
129 S. 2nd Street, PA 19106
Tel: 215-923-8523
www.winston-salem-inn.com/philadelphia
A handsome, Federal-style B&B maintained by the National Park Service with 10 rooms and two suites in the heart of the historic district. Amenities: private and shared bath, some rooms with fireplace, whirlpool, sofa bed, free continental breakfast. **$$–$$$**

Maryland
Annapolis
Maryland Inn
16 Church Circle, MD 21401
Tel: 410-263-2641
www.historicinnsofannapolis.com
A pub and tavern with splendid rooms, many dating to the revolutionary era. The wooden porches,and marble tiled lobby are Victorian. **$–$$**

Baltimore
Admiral Fell Inn
888 S. Broadway, MD 21231
Tel: 410-522-7377
www.admiralfell.com
Pleasing proportions and custom-crafted Federal-style furnishings characterize this well-preserved Fells Point inn. The Admiral Fell has received many accolades for its New American cuisine and award-winning wine cellar. Guests are offered free parking and transportation to local attractions. **$$**
Henderson's Wharf Inn
1000 Fell Street, MD 21231
Tel: 410-522-7777
www.hendersonswharf.com
Great marina views and all modern conveniences including satellite TV and free internet access in old warehouse. **$$$**
Inn at the Colonnade
4 W. University Parkway
Tel: 410-235-5400
www.colonnadebaltimore.com
Just across from Johns Hopkins University, this is a businessman's haunt in a land of students. **$$$**
Mount Vernon Hotel
24 W. Franklin Street, MD 21201
Tel: 410-727-2000
www.mountvernonbaltimore.com
Located in Baltimore's mid-town areas, you are very near the Peabody Conservatory and other attractions. **$$$**

Virginia
Blacksburg
The Inn at Virginia Tech
901 Prices Fork Road, VA 24061
Tel: 540-231-8000
www.theinnatvirginia tech.com
Convenient location on the campus of Virginia Tech;

147 rooms with upscale amenities. **$$$**

Charlottesville
Cavalier Inn
1613 Emmett Street, VA 22905
Tel: 434-296-8111
www.cavalierinn.com
Standard motel rooms in the university district. Complimentary breakfast, courtesy shuttle, seasonal outdoor pool, and restaurant. **$**
Clifton – The Country Inn
1296 Clifton Inn Drive, VA 22911
Tel: 434-971-1800
www.cliftoninn.net
Elegant Federal and colonial revival-style historic manor house surrounded by 40 wooded acres (17 hectares). Guest rooms are furnished with antiques and a wood-burning fireplace. Facilities include clay tennis courts, pool, whirlpool, and award-winning cuisine. **$$–$$$**
Silver Thatch Inn
3001 Hollymead Drive, VA 22911
Tel: 434-978-4686
www.silverthatch.com
This delightful clapboard home is one of the oldest buildings in central Virginia. Accommodations comprise seven guest rooms all with private baths and several with canopy beds and fireplaces. The uniquely appointed rooms are named after early Virginian-born presidents. There are three dining rooms and a bar. **$$**

Lexington
B&B at Llewellyn Lodge
603 Main Street, VA 24450
Tel/fax: 540-463-3235
www.llodge.com
Six comfortable, individually decorated rooms in an attractive gray brick colonial building. This inn is known for its tempting breakfast menu featuring the innkeeper's award-winning omelets. A health-conscious menu is also available.

PRICE CATEGORIES

Price categories are based on the average cost of a double room for one night:
$ = under $110
$$ = $110–250
$$$ = more than $250

Other features include four-poster beds, ceiling fans, and a porch swing. Situated close to Downtown, this is the ideal base for visiting Lexington's attractions. **$$$**

Historic Country Inns
11 N. Main Street, VA 24450
Tel: 877-283-9680
www.lexingtonhistoricinns.com
This firm runs three inns in the area: two in the Lexington Historic District – the Alexander Withrow House and McCampbell Inn – and Maple Hall 6 miles (9km) to the north on 56 acres (22 hectares). All inns feature fireplaces, fine dining, trails, and pool. **$–$$**

Richmond

West-Bocock House
1107 Grove Avenue, VA 23220
Tel: 804-358-6174
This elegant 19th-century historic house is well placed for visiting the city's attractions. Guest rooms have private baths, fresh flowers, and French linen. **$$**

North Carolina

Chapel Hill

Carolina Inn
211 Pittsboro Street, NC 27516
Tel: 919-933-2001
www.carolinainn.com
This elegantly furnished historic inn provides a good base for exploring downtown Chapel Hill and the shops and restaurants of Franklin Street. Extras include complimentary breakfast and newspaper. The inn's Crossroads restaurant has been awarded a four diamond rating by the AAA. **$$$**

Durham

Carolina Duke Motor Inn
2517 Guess Road, NC 27705
Tel/fax: 919-286-0771
Very reasonable, well-decorated rooms (180). Amenities include pool and area transportation. **$**

Greensboro

Microtel Inn
4304 Big Tree Way, NC 27409
Tel: 336-547-7007
Clean, comfortable, good-value motor inn. **$**

Manteo

Tranquil House Inn
405 Queen Elizabeth Street, NC 27954
Tel: 252-473-1404
www.1587.com
A pleasant waterfront inn with suites, rooms, and a deck. Extras include a complimentary breakfast and wine & cheese evening. A good place to relax and renew. **$$–$$$**

Mount Airy

Mayberry Motor Inn
1001 US Highway 52N, NC 27030
Tel: 336-786-4109
www.mayberrymotorinn.com
Well-kept, comfortable rooms. Very good value. Continental breakfast. Nearby jogging and nature trail. **$**

Nags Head

Carolinian Hotel
10.5 Mile Post Beach Road, NC 27959
Tel: 252-441-7171
A rustic waterfront hotel with 86 rooms, cooking facilities. Amenities include exercise and game rooms, lounge, restaurant, and pool. **$$$**

First Colony Inn
6720S.Virginia Dare Trail, NC 27959
Tel: 252-441-2343
www.firstcolonyinn.com
Handsome older inn, carefully restored and furnished with antiques. Babysitting services, two jacuzzis, pool. **$$**

Ocracoke

The Island Inn and Dining Room
PO Box 9, NC 27960
Tel: 252-928-4351
www.ocracokeislandinn.com
The characterful older section (c.1901) offers rooms with antiques, private baths, and a heated outdoor pool. The newer motel-style section also has a pool and welcomes families. Villa "full efficiencies" with cooking facilities are also available. The inn's dining room is known for its fresh, well-cooked seafood and hush puppies. Guests may use the inn's canoes, boats, and rafts. **$$$**

Wilmington

Carolinian Inn
2916 Market Street, NC 28403
Tel: 910-763-4653
www.thecarolinianinn.com
Between Downtown and the Atlantic beaches. Recently remodeled incorporating de luxe amenities, and lovely mature gardens. Free continental breakfast. **$$**

The Inn on Orange B&B
410 Orange Street, NC 28401
Tel: 910-815-0035
www.innonorange.com
An historic Italianate Victorian home located within walking distance of the riverside and close to Downtown. The inn features ceiling fans, fireplaces, and TVs on request. Full breakfast is served on the weekends; continental breakfast is available on weekdays. There is a two-night minimum stay on the weekend. **$$–$$$**

Winston-Salem

Best Western Salem Inn
127 S. Cherry Street, NC 27101
Tel: 800-533-8760
www.saleminn.com
Well-maintained budget inn with exercise room, lounge, pool, jogging, and nature trail. Continental breakfast provided. **$**

Brookstown Inn
200 Brookstown Avenue, NC 27101
Tel: 336-725-1120
www.brookstowninn.com
Exposed brick walls and wooden beams reveal its 1837 origins as a textile mill. Free wine and cheese reception each evening adds to its charm. A short walk from the restored Moravian village of Old Salem. **$$$**

South Carolina

Beaufort

Rhett House
1009 Craven Street, SC 29902
Tel: 843-524-9030
Plantation house bordering the Intercoastal waterway. Built in 1820 and restored following the Civil War, the inn features stately white columns, broad verandas, rocking chairs, and period decor. Many rooms have fireplaces, private balconies, and whirlpool baths. Afternoon tea. **$$**

Charleston

Governor's House Inn
117 Broad Street, SC 29401
Tel: 843-720-2070
www.governorshouse.com
Attention to detail, elegant decor, and exceptional service are hallmarks of this historic inn. Originally the residence of Governor Edward Rutledge, the youngest signer of the Declaration of Independence, the house still retains an air of tradition with its broad veranda, chandeliers, numerous fireplaces, and spacious rooms. In the center of the historic district and close to many land-marks and restaurants. **$$$**

Vendue Inn
19 Vendue Range, SC 29401
Tel: 843-577-7970
www.vendueinn.com
Luxurious boutique hotel in heart of Historic District, with fine harbor view from a rooftop restaurant. **$$$**

Georgetown

Carolinian Inn
706 Church Street, SC 29440
Tel: 803-546-5191
www.carolinianinn.com
Spacious and affordable rooms. Pool. **$**

Harbor House Bed and Breakfast
15 Cannon Street, SC 29440
Tel: 843-546-6532
www.harborhouse.com
Large waterfront inn with distinctive red roof. Built in 1740 as a shipping warehouse. Lovely, spacious rooms. **$$$**

Myrtle Beach

Compass Cove
2311 S.Ocean Boulevard, SC 29577
Tel: 843-448-8373
www.compasscove.com
Large family-friendly resort situated 2½ miles (4km) from the Pavilion with ocean-front rooms. The complex has pools, jacuzzis, restaurant, and lounge. **$$**

Coral Beach Resort
1105 S. Ocean Boulevard,
SC 29577
Tel: 843-448-8412
www.coral-beach.com
Full service oceanfront resort with nicely furnished guest rooms and public areas. Facilities include indoor and outdoor pools, saunas, whirlpool, restaurant, and lounge. Disabled access. **$$$**

Georgia

Brunswick

Hostel in the Forest
PO Box 1496, GA 31521
Tel: 912-264-9738
www.foresthostel.com
Since 1975, this hostel has offered beds in tree houses or geodesic domes. Amenities include tranquility and natural beauty. **$**

St Simons Island

The Lodge on Little St Simons Island
PO Box 21078, GA 31522-0578
Tel: 912-638-7472
www.littlestsimonsisland.com
This unique lodge, set on an unspoiled barrier, hosts only 30 overnight guests. The only way there is by boat. Price includes three Southern meals and on-island activities. Idyllic. **$$$**

Savannah

East Bay Inn
225 E. Bay Street, GA 31401
Tel: 912-238-1225
www.eastbayinn.com
An historic bed-and-breakfast, this 28-unit restored 1853 warehouse features large, Georgian-style rooms. **$$**
The Gastonian
220 E. Gaston Street, GA 31401
Tel: 912-232-2869
www.gastonian.com
This 16-unit historic B&B consists of restored, connected late-1800s houses. Six rooms with whirlpool bath. No pets allowed. **$$**
The Marshall House
123 E. Broughton Street, GA 31401
Tel: 912-644-7896
www.marshallhouse.com

The city's first hotel in 1851, it was later used as a Civil War hospital (hence its rumored ghosts) and has been recently renovated. **$–$$**
Olde Harbour Inn
508 E. Factors Walk, GA 31401
Tel: 912-234-4100
www.oldeharbourinn.com
A 24-unit historic bed-and-breakfast in the riverfront district. River-view suites with fully equipped kitchens. **$$**

Florida

Bahia Honda State Recreation Area

For information about the park, tel: 305-872-2353
Campsites **$** Cabins **$$**
http://www.floridastateparks.org/
bahiahonda/default.cfm
Big Pine Key Fishing Lodge
33000 Overseas Highway, Big Pine Key, FL 33043
Tel: 305-872-2351
Spick and span lodge rooms and five canal-side motel rooms with cooking facilities. **$**
Deer Run Bed & Breakfast
Long Beach Road, FL 33043
Tel: 305-872-2015
www.deerrunfloridabb.com
Spacious guest rooms with ocean views located in two houses near the bay. Deer roam the surrounding native wooded land (also a good birdwatching area). Amenities include a full vegetarian breakfast, jacuzzi on the beach, porches, and private balconies. **$$$**

Bradenton

Silver Surf Gulf Beach Resort
1301 Gulf Drive N., FL 34217
Tel: 941-778-6626
www.silverresorts.com
A deluxe waterfront hotel featuring panoramic Gulf views, pool, and private sandy beach. **$$**

Clearwater Beach

Amber Tides Motel
420 Hamden Drive, FL 33767
Tel: 727-445-1145
www.ambertides-motel.com
Small, German-run motel with clean and cozy rooms,

ABOVE: the historic East Bay Inn in Savannah, Georgia.

a nice pool and courtyard. Bike rental and fishing trips also available. Note: a minimum 3-night stay is required. **$**
Belleview Biltmore
25 Belleview Boulevard, FL 33756
Tel: 727-442-6171
www.belleviewbiltmore.com
Currently being remodeled, this grand old four-season resort has been welcoming guests since 1897. Recreational facilities include red clay tennis courts, an excellent golf course, a de luxe spa, and fitness center. **$$**

Fort Myers

Mantanzas Inn
414 Crescent Street, FL 33931
Tel: 239-463-9258
www.matanzasinn.com
Nicely decorated rooms and close to the beach. Facilities include pool and restaurant. **$**

Homestead

Everglades Motel
605 S. Krome Avenue, FL 33030
Tel: 305-247-4117
Fourteen tidy rooms with pool and laundry facilities. **$**

Islamorada

Lime Tree Bay Resort Motel
PO Box 839, Limekey FL 33001
Tel: 305-664-4740
www.limetreebayresort.com
Delightful cottages, apartments and tastefully decorated motel rooms. Amenities include a private sandy area with beach chairs, hot tub, pool, small watersports rental conces-

sion, and snorkeling. **$–$$**

Key Largo

Jule's Undersea Lodge
From 51 Shoreland Drive, off MM 103.2, FL 33037
Tel: 305-451-2353
www.jul.com
A unique two-bedroomed lodge 22ft (7 meters) beneath the sea. Originally a research facility, accommodations are basic, but comfortable. Each of the two bedrooms has a 42-inch (107cm) round window looking into the sea, hot and cold shower, and TV/VCR. The only way to get there is by scuba diving. The price includes all gear and unlimited diving. Reserve well in advance. **$$$**
Kona Kai Resort
97802 Overseas Highway, FL 33037
Tel: 305-852-7200
www.konakairesort.com
Waterfront resort with full kitchen facilities. **$$**

Key West

Hostelling International – Key West
718 S. Street, FL 33040
Tel: 305-296-5719
www.keywesthostel.com
Located two blocks from the beach, this hostel offers scuba diving lessons, and

snorkeling. There is an outdoor courtyard, barbecue pit, pool table, and laundry facilities. **$**

The Marquesa Hotel
600 Fleming Street, FL 33040
Tel: 305-292-1919
www.marquesa.com
This late 19th-century landmark has been lovingly restored to its original splendor. Tucked in the heart of Key West's Historic District, four handsome buildings encircle two swimming pools and luxurious tropical gardens. Amenities include marble baths and fine dining in the adjoining Café Marquesa. **$$$**

Southernmost Hotel
1319 Duval Street, FL 33040
Tel: 305-296-6577
127 guest rooms in a beautiful old home. Two large pools and poolside bars, jacuzzi, public beach access, bicycle moped rental, and warm, friendly service. **$$**

Kissimmee

Sevilla Inn
4640 W. Irlo Bronson Highway, FL 34746
Tel: 407-396-4135
www.sevillainn.net
A well-maintained motor inn with pool. **$**

Miami

Astor
956 Washington Avenue, Miami Beach, FL 33139
Tel: 305-531-8081
www.hotelastor.com
Understated stylishness is the hallmark of this trendy Art Deco hotel. Bedrooms – mostly suites – and their wall-to-wall marble bathrooms come in muted creams and beiges. The pool is striking, and Maizon d'Azur is one of South Beach's top restaurants. **$$**

Cardozo
1300 Ocean Drive, Miami Beach, FL 33139
Tel: 305-535-6500
www.cardozohotel.com
Owned by Gloria Estefan, a Streamline Moderne Art Deco masterpiece that is bathed in purple neon at night. A lively bar, seductive dining terrace, and eye-

catching bedrooms with hardwood floors, iron beds, and zebra-striped furniture. **$$**

Clay Hotel Hostelling International – Miami Beach
1438 Washington Avenue, FL 33139
Tel: 305-534-2988
www.clayhotel.com
Great location in the heart of the Old Miami Beach Art Deco District. Amenities include kitchen, laundry facilities, lockers/baggage storage, and restaurant. **$**

Marlin
1200 Collins Avenue, Miami Beach, FL 33139
Tel: 305-531 8800
This much-photographed lilac-colored Art Deco building is currently undergoing remodeling, but it is a very hip hotel. U2 and Aerosmith have made albums here, as it is also a recording studio. The Opium Den bar often has live music in the evenings. **$$**

The Tides
1220 Ocean Drive, Miami Beach, FL 33139
Tel: 305-604-5070
www.tidessouthbeach.com
This sleek white oceanfront block contains a small luxury hotel of immaculate taste. The giant, minimalist bedrooms have mischievous postcards with the message "Let's make love at The Tides," and each has uninterrupted views of the

ocean and the beach, with telescopes for birding... or to spy on sunbathers. Also a good-sized swimming pool. **$$$**

Micanopy

Knights Inns
17110 SE CR 234, FL 32667
Tel: 352-466-3163
Squeaky-clean budget rooms and a restaurant. **$**

Orlando

Embassy Suites – Lake Buena Vista
8100 Lake Avenue, FL 32836
Tel: 407-239-1144
www.embassy-suites.com
Spacious suites with in-room movies, fitness center, whirlpool, steam room, and family fun center. Free breakfast and transportation to Walt Disney World. **$$**

Walt Disney World All-Star Resorts
The cheapest rooms within Walt Disney World.
All Star Movies Resort
Tel: 407-939-7000. **$**
All Star Music Resort
Tel: 407-939-6000. **$**
All Star Sports Resort
Tel: 407-939-5000. **$**

St Augustine

Kenwood Inn
38 Marine Street, FL 32084
Tel: 904-824-2116
www.thekenwoodinn.com
This time-honored Victorian hotel is close to the seafront

BELOW: Disney All Star Music Resort.

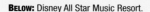

and other attractions, plus excellent breakfasts and an attractive cocktail hour. **$$**

St Petersburg

Coral Reef Beach Resort
5800 Gulf Boulevard, FL 33714
Tel: 727-360-0821
A first-class resort with de luxe suites and nicely appointed rooms. The pool is enormous. Beach bar and restaurant. **$$**

Sanibel Island

South Seas Island Resort
5400 South Seas Plantation Road, FL 33924
Tel: 866-565-5089
www.southseas.com
Sprawling resort occupying most of the island and Sanibel's first. Guests can choose from condominium style and well-fitted standard guest rooms. **$$**

Tampa

East Lake Inn
6529 E. Hillsborough Avenue, FL 33610
Tel: 813-622-8339
www.eastlakeinn.biz
Clean and comfortable rooms. **$**

Holiday Inn Express Hotel Suites – Tampa USF-Busch Gardens
2807 E. Busch Boulevard, FL 33612
Tel: 813-936-8200
www.ichotelsgroup.com
Modern and clean rooms, a good pool and close to tourist attractions and restaurants. **$$**

Quorum Hotel Tampa
700 N.Westshore Boulevard, FL 33609
Tel: 813-289-8200
www.quorumtampa.com
Convenient location with a good on-site restaurant and spacious rooms. Also close to the airport, stores, and restaurants. **$$**

Tarpon Springs

Tarpon Shores Inn
40346 US Highway 19N, FL 34689
Tel: 727-938-2483
www.tarponshoresinn.com
Good-value rooms, some with microwaves and refrigerators. Facilities include pool, jacuzzi and laundry facilities. **$**

Massachusetts

Boston

Boston Harbor Hotel
70 Rowes Wharf, MA 02110
Tel: 617-439-7000
www.bhh.com
Board the airport water
shuttle at Logan and, seven
minutes later, step into the
luxury of the city's foremost
waterside hotel. Bedrooms
all have either harbor or
skyline views. Eighteen
rooms are specially
designed for the disabled
guests. A museum-quality
art collection decorates the
public areas. **$$$**

Lenox Hotel
61 Exeter Street at Boylston, Back
Bay, MA 02116
Tel: 617-536-5300
www.lenoxhotel.com
Modest and moderate
traditional family hotel built
in 1900. Bedrooms, some
with functional fireplaces,
have been redecorated in
French Provincial, Oriental
or colonial decor. Just a few
steps from the Prudential
Center and a block from the
subway. **$$**

Omni Parker House
60 School Street, MA 02018
Tel: 617-227-8600
www.omnihotels.com
Reportedly the oldest
continuously operating hotel
in America (since 1854);
yet, the frequently
renovated present building
dates only from 1927. Some
rooms have showers only.
Malcolm X and (allegedly)
Ho Chi Minh both worked
here, they claim. **$$$**

Cambridge

The Charles Hotel
1 Bennett Street, MA 02138
Tel: 617-864-1200
www.charleshotel.com
A modern hotel with 294
rooms in Harvard Square,
with airy, neo-traditional
rooms, some overlooking
the river. Home to the
popular Regattabar jazz
club which draws nationally
known jazz artists. **$$$**

Harvard Square Hotel
110 Mount Auburn Street,
MA 02138

Tel: 617-864-5200
www.harvardsquarehotel.com
A six-floor motel in the heart
of Harvard Square. All
rooms with picture windows.
On-site parking available
but there is a charge. **$$**

Mary Prentiss Inn
6 Prentiss Street, MA 02140
Tel: 617-661-2929
www.maryprentissinn.com
Tastefully appointed Greek
Revival B&B. Some of the
20 rooms have antique
armoires and four-poster
beds. Made-to-order
breakfasts served outside
on the terrace in summer.
Situated on a residential
street between Harvard and
Porter Squares. Free Wi-fi
and parking. **$$–$$$**

Concord

Colonial Inn
48 Monument Square, MA 01742
Tel: 978-369-9200
www.concordscolonialinn.com
The historic main inn and its
newer wing, a guesthouse, a
cottage and two other
houses offer 56 rooms, the
latter three more suited to
longer stays. The main
1716 inn on Concord's town
common has 15 rooms and
the Village Forge Lounge,
where live entertainment
takes place on Thur–Sat
evenings. **$$**

Longfellow's Wayside Inn
72 Wayside Inn Road, Sudbury,
MA 01776
Tel: 978-443-1776
www.wayside.org
A mid-18th-century tavern,
operating as an inn since
1716, with 10 rooms, near
Concord. Lunch and dinner
available daily. **$$**

Deerfield

Deerfield Inn
81 Main Street, MA 01342
Tel: 413-774-5587
www.deerfieldinn.
A traditional inn surrounded
by historic houses; 24 large
rooms furnished with
antiques and period
reproductions. Continental
breakfast available. The
tavern is open daily, serving
locally brewed beer as well
as dinner Thur–Mon. **$$**

Gloucester

Bass Rocks Ocean Inn
107 Atlantic Road, MA 01930
Tel: 978-283-7600
www.bassrocksoceaninn.com
Stay in one of the 51 rooms
in the Oceanfront, Seaside
or Stacy Houses, whose
rooms all look out to sea.
Balcony or patio attached to
rooms in the Oceanfront
and Seaside Houses. Free
bicycle use, heated pool,
and complimentary
breakfast. **$$–$$$**

Harborview Inn
Stacey Boulevard,
71 Western Avenue, MA 01930
Tel: 978-283-2277
www.harborviewinn.com
A comfortable house-
turned-B&B near the
Fisherman Memorial statue.
Three rooms and three
suites, some with an ocean
view. Complimentary
continental breakfast.
$–$$

Greenfield

Brandt House
29 Highland Drive, MA 01301
Tel: 413-774-3329
www.brandthouse.com
Eight comfortable, simply
decorated rooms, plus two-
storey penthouse suite with
balcony. House has a
wraparound porch, library,
and living room with fire.
$–$$

New Hampshire

Claremont

Claremont Motor Lodge
16 Beauregard Street, NH 03743
Tel: 603-542-2540
www.claremontmotel.com
Rooms have cable TV and
internet access; some also
include kitchen facilities.
Free continental breakfast
and pets allowed. **$**

Portsmouth

Inn at Strawbery Banke
314 Court Street, NH 03801
Tel: 603-436-7242
www.innatstrawberybanke.com
An elegant older house with
seven well-proportioned
rooms spread over two
floors, both with a sitting
room. **$–$$**

Wolfeboro

Wolfeboro Inn
90 N. Main Street, NH 03894
Tel: 603-569-3016
www.wolfeboroinn.com
Renovated in 2009, this is a
picturesque 19th-century
waterfront inn with an
inviting tavern. Stay in the
modern, rather than
historic, part of the inn if you
want a balcony overlooking
Wolfeboro Bay. Guests can
dine on the patio in summer.
$$

Maine

Cape Elizabeth

Inn by the Sea
40 Bowery Beach Road, ME 04107
Tel: 207-799-3134
www.innbythesea.com
Large, rambling carbon-
neutral coastal resort with
57 luxury rooms, suites, and
cottages, all with porch or
deck with ocean view.
Rooms come with flatscreen
TVs. Offers spa, gym, pool,
bar, and restaurant serving
fresh, local produce. The
whole place is set in five
acres of grounds certified as
a wildlife sanctuary. Strong
green credentials. Pet-
friendly. **$$$+**

Cornish

Cornish Inn
2 High Road, PO Box 266, MA 04020
Tel: 207-625-8501
www.cornishinn.com
Lovely colonial house at the
base of the White
Mountains *(see page 107)*.

PRICE CATEGORIES

Price categories are based
on the average cost of a
double room for one night:
$ = under $110
$$ = $110–250
$$$ = more than $250

Has a restaurant and bar. Breakfast included. **$–$$**

Kennebunkport
1802 House B&B
15 Locke Street, ME 04046
Tel: 207-967-5632
www.1802inn.com
Six warm, intimate guest rooms with wood-burning fireplaces, antiques, and original artwork. The private tiled bathrooms feature whirlpool baths. Secluded hideaway minutes from central Dock Square and next to Cape Arundel golf course. Three-course breakfast served. **$$–$$$**

Ogunquit Beach
The Beachmere Inn
62 Beachmere Place, ME 03907
Tel: 207-646-2021
www.beachmereinn.com
Intimate, stylish, and eco-friendly Victorian inn with wonderful coastal views and a small private beach. Many rooms have private balconies or decks and four also have wood-burning fireplaces. **$–$$**
The Dunes on the Waterfront
PO Box 917, 518 Main Street, ME 03907

BELOW: Dockside Guest Quarters in York, Maine.

www.dunesonthewaterfront.com
Established in 1936, The Dunes features 17 well-kept guest rooms and 19 traditional New England cottages set in trim open grounds overlooking the tidal river. Heated outdoor pool. Seasonal opening. **$$**

Portland
Inn on Carleton
46 Carleton Street, ME 04102
Tel: 207-775-1910
www.innoncarleton.com
A beautifully restored Victorian home in the center of Portland's historical district. This B&B has six rooms, four with private baths and showers, two with showers only. **$–$$**
Pomegranate Inn
49 Neal Street, ME 04102
Tel: 207-772-1006
www.pomegranateinn.com
A tranquil hideaway set in the Western Promenade historical district. Five of the eight rooms have working fireplaces, all have private bathrooms and contemporary Maine and international art is displayed. Room on the first floor comes with access to a private garden. **$$–$$$**

York
Dockside Guest Quarters
22 Harris Island Road, ME 03909
Tel: 207-363-2868
www.docksidegq.com
Situated on a private peninsula surrounded by sweeping views of Maine's scenic beauty. Maine House has large balconies but rooms and suites are located in several buildings across the seven acres. Dockside restaurant. Buffet breakfast included in the price. **$$**

Vermont

Arlington
Arlington Inn
Route 7A, VT 05250
Tel: 802-375-6532
www.arlingtoninn.com
An elegant B&B Greek Revival mansion with comfortable Victorian-style interior furnishings in the five guest rooms. More rooms available in the Carriage House, some with jacuzzis, and in the Old Parsonage, some with private porches. Restaurant and gardens. Located between Bennington and Manchester. **$–$$$**
West Mountain Inn
River Road (off Route 313), VT 05250
Tel: 802-375-6516
www.westmountaininn.com
A family-friendly 1840s farmhouse turned 14-room inn with mountain views on 150 country acres. Trails for hiking or cross-country skiing, game room, fishing, and the resident llama ranch amuse all ages. **$$–$$$**

Bridgewater Corners
October Country Inn B&B
362 Upper Road, PO Box 66, VT 05035
Tel: 802-672-3412
www.octobercountryinn.com
A cozy farmhouse with 10 rooms on a back road, about 5 miles (8km) from the Killington ski area. Outdoor pool. Dinner available. Closed in April and November. **$$** (for 2 people)

ABOVE: Fly Fishing at Mountain Meadows Lodge.

Dorset
Barrows House
Route 30, VT 05251
Tel: 802-867-4455
www.barrowshouse.com
An 18th-century Federal-style inn (plus eight other buildings) with homey touches in the 28 rooms and a well-regarded restaurant. Outdoor pool, tennis courts. Bicycle and cross-country ski hire available. Located 6 miles (10km) north of Manchester. **$$**
Dorset Inn
8 Church St (Route 30), VT 05251
Tel: 802-867-5500
www.dorsetinn.com
One of the state's oldest – and reliably enjoyable – inns, opened in 1796, with 25 rooms, spa, and award-winning restaurant. Pet-friendly. **$$–$$$** (includes breakfast)

Fairlee
Silver Maple Lodge and Cottages
520 US Rt 5 S., VT 05045
Tel: 802-333-4326
www.silvermaplelodge.com
A handsome old farmhouse with eight comfortable lodge rooms and a futher seven rooms in well-fitted rustic, knotty-pine cabins. Thirteen rooms have private bathrooms. **$**

Killington
Inn of the Six Mountains
2617 Killington Road, VT 05751
Tel: 802-422-4302
www.sixmountains.com
A 103-room modern resort hotel with a Rockies feel; everything, including the central fieldstone hearth, is

lavishly overscale. Close to skiing and hiking trails. Two pools, hot tubs, and spa. **$–$$**

Mountain Meadows Lodge
285 Thundering Brook Road, VT 05751
Tel: 802-775-1010
www.mountainmeadowslodge.com
A large, eco-friendly lakeside farmhouse offering 17 rooms, with extensive cross-country trails (the Appalachian Trail crosses the property). Farm animals wander the grounds and rowing boats, canoes and kayaks can be hired. Children under 12 years of age stay free. **$$**

Manchester

1811 House (owned by Equinox Resort)
3567 Main Street, Route 7A, VT 05254
Tel: 877-854-7625
(Inns at Equinox)
www.equinoxresort.com/accommodations
A Federal manse that is the former home of Abraham Lincoln's granddaughter. Thirteen spacious, antiques-filled guest rooms, some with canopied beds, all with flatscreen TVs. The three cottage rooms have wood-burning fireplaces. Located at the north end of Manchester Village. Access to resort's spa and pool. **$$$**

The Equinox
3567 Main Street, Route 7A, VT 05254
www.equinoxresort.com
A grand old hotel with 195 rooms, recently renovated and stylishly furnished. Three restaurants, bar, and tavern. Plenty of sporting activities: choose from off-road driving instruction, fly fishing, golf, falconry, archery, and clay target shooting. **$$$+**

Middlebury

Swift House Inn
25 Stewart Lane, VT 05753
Tel: 802-388-9925
www.swifthouseinn.com
An elegantly detailed 1814 Federal house with 20 luxurious guest rooms; the

Carriage House features spacious rooms with whirlpool baths and the Gate House has a wraparound porch. Restaurant, steam room and sauna. **$$** (includes breakfast)

Quechee

Quechee Inn at Marshland Farm
Quechee Main Street, VT 05059
Tel: 802-295-3133
www.quecheeinn.com
With wilderness trails, cross-country skiing, biking, and canoeing, this inn has much to offer those seeking an active holiday. Reservations for dinner recommended. **$–$$** (includes buffet breakfast)

Ripton

The Chipman Inn
Rt 125, VT 05766
Tel: 802-388-2390
www.chipmaninn.com
Small, gracious historic B&B inn with eight appealing rooms and tranquil atmosphere. Main lounge has a private bar. **$–$$**

Windsor

Juniper Hill Inn
153 Pembroke Road, VT 05089
Tel: 802-674-5273
www.juniperhillinn.com
A 107-year-old Greek Revival mansion B&B set on a broad lawn. Sixteen elegantly appointed rooms furnished with Queen Anne and Edwardian pieces. Dine on the restaurant's regional specialities in the same room Teddy Roosevelt did. Hilltop setting near Ascutney Mountain, outdoor pool. No children under 12. **$$–$$$**

Woodstock

Kedron Valley Inn
10671 S. Road, South Woodstock, VT 10671
Tel: 802-457-1473
www.kedronvalleyinn.com
Rooms in this B&B are spread throughout the main inn, tavern building and a log cabin, many of which feature fireplaces, jacuzzis or private decks. The restaurant is

exceptional – book in advance if you want dinner. The ski lodge-style building behind the main inn attracts families, who also enjoy the two-acre swimming pond. **$$**

Woodstock Inn & Resort
14 The Green (Route 4), VT 05091
Tel: 802-457-1100
www.woodstockinn.com
The Rockefellers' homage to country inns past includes 142 bedrooms, a library and three restaurants. The decor is corporate/country with modern furniture. Facilities include indoor and outdoor pools, tennis courts, golf, health club, racquet ball and squash courts, and a downhill ski area. **$$$**

New York

Buffalo

Lenox Hotel and Suites
140 N. Street, NY 14201
Tel: 716-884-1700
www.lenoxhotelandsuites.com
Historic hotel offering guest rooms and luxury suites. Rooms come equipped with refrigerators and microwaves, while some of the suites contain kitchens. **$$**

Lord Amherst Motor Hotel
5000 Main Street, NY 14226
Tel: 716-839-2200
www.lordamherst.com
Well-maintained motel close to shopping malls. Exercise room, heated outdoor pool, restaurant, and free Wi-fi. **$**

Cambridge

Cambridge Hotel
4 W. Main Street, NY 12816
Tel: 518-677-5626
Attractive B&B with gorgeous upper and lower verandas. 17 rooms decorated in either a Victorian or country style, with private bathrooms and internet access. Massage and reflexology practitioners visit the hotel for guest appointments. **$$**

Canandaigua

Morgan Samuels Inn
2920 Smith Road, NY 14424
Tel: 585-394-9232

www.morgansamuelsinn.com
This stately English-style mansion with tree-lined approach invites you to unwind in civilized comfort. The inn stands in extensive wooded grounds and is furnished with oil paintings and antiques. **$$**

Cooperstown

The Inn at Cooperstown
16 Chestnut Street, NY 13326
Tel: 607-547-5756
www.inatcooperstown.com
A distinctive Second Empire-style inn designed by Henry J. Hardenbergh, known for his New York City projects – the Dakota Apartments and Plaza Hotel. Built in 1874 as an annex to the plush Hotel Fenimore. 18 spotless, modern rooms and suites. Central location. **$–$$** (includes buffet breakfast)

Fredonia

The White Inn
52 E. Main Street, NY 14063
Tel: 716-672-2103
www.whiteinn.com
Dignified older inn furnished with antiques and reproductions. Restaurant offers excellent American cuisine with top-quality, fresh ingredients. **$–$$**

Geneva

Belhurst Castle
4069 Route 14 S., NY 14456
Tel: 315-781-0201
www.belhurst.com
A choice of 14 rooms, some with jacuzzis, in a 19th-century castle overlooking Seneca Lake. Property has two restaurants and its own winery. **$–$$**

Niagara Falls

Crowne Plaza
300 Third Street, NY 14303
Tel: 0871-423-4942
www.crowneplaza.com
Swanky and central. Renovated in 2007, this

PRICE CATEGORIES

Price categories are based on the average cost of a double room for one night:
$ = under $110
$$ = $110–250
$$$ = more than $250

huge hotel has nearly 400 rooms available, a Grille serving breakfast and a Sports Bar serving lunch and dinner. Facilities include a small gym, indoor pool and casino. **$$**

Hostelling International – Niagara Falls
1101 Ferry Avenue, NY 14301
Tel: 716-282-3700
www.hihostels.com
The hostel occupies a historic Georgian-style home within walking distance of the Falls. Amenities include kitchen, internet access, on-site parking, laundry facilities, and luggage and bike storage. **$**

Rome
Quality Inn Rome
200 S. James St at Erie Boulevard, NY 13440
Tel: 315-336-4300
Good location. Rooms come with microwaves and refrigerators. Laundry facilities, outdoor pool, exercise room, restaurant, and free internet access. Disabled access rooms. **$**

Saratoga Springs
Batcheller Mansion Inn
20 Circular Street, NY 12866
Tel: 518-584-7012
www.batchellermansioninn.com
A marvelous High Victorian Gothic inn, impeccably preserved. This fantastic B&B features 8 elegantly appointed rooms and 1 suite, a living room with grand piano and French windows, and shaded porches. Price includes hot breakfast, but be aware weekend rates are higher during the racing season

BELOW: it's smart to reserve ahead during peak season.

(July–Sept). No guests under 16. **$$**

Syracuse
Hostelling International – Syracuse
535 Oak Street, NY 13203
Tel: 315-472-5788
Attractive hostel occupies an enormous old house in the center of Syracuse. Amenities include self-catering kitchen, laundry facilities, and baggage storage. **$**

Park View Hotel
713 E. Genesee Street, NY 13210
Tel: 315-701-2600
www.theparkviewhotel.com
Centrally located opposite Foreman Park, with spacious rooms, a gym, coffee and wine bar, and the elegant 1060 restaurant. **$$**

Utica
Red Roof Inn
20 Weaver Street, NY 13502
Tel: 315-724-7128
www.redroof.com
Spotless, well-fitted rooms and friendly service. Restaurants and shopping close by. Children under 17 stay free when sharing a room with an adult family member. **$**

Westfield
The William Seward Inn
6645 S.Portage Road, NY 14787
Tel: 716-326-4151
www.williamsewardinn.com
Fine old B&B furnished with antiques and famed for its fine dining, available Thur–Mon. The 12 rooms all have private bathrooms and internet access. Made-to-order breakfast. No children under 10. Resident dog. **$$**

Pennsylvania
Erie
Downtown Erie Hotel
18 W. 18th Street, PA 16501
Tel: 814-456-2961
www.downtowneriehotel.com
Central location, with cable TV in the rooms and internet access in the lobby and lounge. Outdoor pool and complimentary continental breakfast. **$**

Ohio
Cleveland
Glidden House Hotel
1901 Ford Drive, OH 44106
Tel: 216-231-8900
www.gliddenhouse.com
Attractive historic hotel on the Case Western Reserve University campus and close to the city's museums. Stylish rooms with plasma screen TVs. Dine on Mediterranean cuisine in the Carriage House restaurant, often accompanied by live music. Wheelchair-accessible rooms. **$$**

Wyndham Cleveland Hotel at Playhouse Square
1260 Euclid Avenue, OH 44115
Tel: 216-615-7500
Convenient location and adjacent to the theater district. Newly renovated, with nicely decorated rooms, restaurant, lounge, indoor pool, and fitness center. Wheelchair-accessible rooms. Complimentary shuttle service to local attractions. **$$**

Sandusky
Hampton Inn Sandusky-Central
6100 Milan Road, OH 44870
Tel: 419-609-9000
50 comfortable rooms with free internet access plus the usual amenities, close to Cedar Point Amusement Park, the safari park, and indoor and outdoor water parks. Complimentary hot breakfast, fitness room, indoor pool, and jacuzzi. **$$**

Toledo
Mansion View Inn
2035 Collingwood Boulevard, OH 43620
Tel: 419-244-5676
www.mansionviewtoledo.com
Located in the historic old west end district, this striking 1887 mansion has four B&B rooms decorated in Victorian style. Sitting room has DVDs, videos, TV, and books. **$$**

Indiana
Nappanee
Inn at Amish Acres
1234 W. Market Street, IN 46550

Tel: 574-773-2011
www.amishacres.com
A chance to enjoy some of life's quiet pleasures: porch rockers, checker boards, and twining flowers. All rooms have cable TV and Amish patterned quilts; 16 have hot tubs. Disabled-access rooms. Outdoor pool, free internet access, and continental breakfast served. **$–$$**

South Bend
The Oliver Inn
630 W. Washington Street, IN 46601
Tel: 574-232-4545
www.oliverinn.com
B&B in a very pretty early 20th-century house with corner porches, bay windows, and trim gardens. The wood-burning fireplace and live piano music add to the flavor of the common areas. **$–$$**

Valparaiso
The Inn at Aberdeen
3158 S. SR 2, IN 46385
Tel: 219-465-3753
www.innataberdeen.com
Comfortable guest rooms with jacuzzis and balconies. Full gourmet breakfast, evening dessert, unlimited beverages, and snacks. Garden has a gazebo. **$$**

Michigan
Dearborn
Victory Inn
23730 Michigan Avenue, MI 48124
Tel: 313-565-7250
All rooms in this Downtown inn come with cable TV, free internet access, refrigerator, and microwave. Outdoor pool. Free continental breakfast. **$**

Illinois
Chicago
Cass Hotel
640 N. Wabash Avenue, IL 60611
Tel: 312-787-4030
www.casshotel.com
Great location on the Magnificent Mile for this boutique-type hotel. Stylish rooms come with free internet access, high-definition flatscreen TV, and

complimentary breakfast.
$$
The Drake Hotel
140 E. Walton Place, IL 60611
Tel: 312-787-2200
www.thedrakehotel.com
This sophisticated, elegant
landmark hotel has hosted
everyone from the Queen of
England to Japanese
emperors, heads of state to
Pope John Paul II. Luxurious
rooms with Italian marble
bathrooms, two ballrooms,
a gym, and a shopping
arcade featuring Chanel and
the jewelry designer Georg
Jensen. Four restaurants,
including the nautically
themed, celeb-favorite,
seafood specialty Cape Cod
Room, where Marilyn
Monroe carved her initials in
the bar – reservation
recommended. **$$$**
The Whitehall Hotel
105 E. Delaware Place, IL 60611
Tel: 312-944-6300
Perfectly located, European-
style hotel restored to its
original 1920s beauty.
Rooms have mahogany
furniture and 300-thread
count Egyptian cotton
sheets. Italian restaurant,
pizza bar and lounge where
the Beatles once drank.
$$$

Wisconsin

Dodgeville
**Best Western Quiet House
& Suites**
1130 N.Johns Street, WI 53533
Tel: 608-935-7739
Located only 3 miles (5km)
from a state park, this
hotel's rooms come with
cable TV, internet access,
microwave, and refrigerator.
Free continental breakfast,
indoor and outdoor pools.
$-$$
Don Q Inn
3658 SR 23 N., WI 53533
Tel: 608-935-2321
www.fantasuite.com
21 themed rooms (**$-$$**),
from geisha to safari, tacky
to random, plus 35
standard rooms (**$**). Pool
and free continental
breakfast. *(see page 132).*
House on the Rock Inn
3591 Highway 23, WI 53533
Tel: 608-935-3711

www.thehouseontherock.com
A modern inn situated 7
miles (11km) south of the
unique House on the Rock,
echoing some of its features.
An attractive lounge opens
onto a deck overlooking the
outdoor pool. Indoor pool
includes children's play area.
Continental breakfast
included. **$-$$**

Madison
Madison Concourse Hotel
1 W. Dayton Street, WI 53703
Tel: 608-257-6000
www.concoursehotel.com
A smart, downtown hotel
with indoor pool, fitness
center, game room, bar, and
restaurant. **$$**
Mansion Hill Inn
424 N. Pinckney Street,
WI 53703
Tel: 608-255-0172
www.mansionhillinn.com
A mid 19th-century
Romanesque Revival
mansion situated in the
historic district. Tastefully
furnished with fine antiques.
Expect a warm welcome and
attentive service. No
children under 13. **$$$**

Richland Center
Park View Motel
511 W. 6th Street, WI 53581
Tel: 608-647-6354
www.pvrcmotel.com
Fifteen basic but well-
maintained units with
refrigerator, microwave, TV,
and wireless internet.
Opposite a public park and
pool. **$**
Prairie House Motel
E. 4884, Highway 14,
Spring Green, WI 53588
Tel: 608-588-2088
www.theprairiehousemotel.com
Spacious rooms, fitness
center, whirlpool, sauna,
and lounge area. **$**

Minnesota

Bloomington
Hotel Sofitel
5601 W. 78 Street, MN 55439
Tel: 952-835-1900
Luxury, contemporary-style
accommodation close to the
Mall of America, with an
impressive French
restaurant, bar, and fitness
center. **$$**

ABOVE: hotels and shops line Chicago's Magnificent Mile.

Le Sueur
Cosgrove House
228 S. 2nd Street, MN 56058
Tel: 507-665-2500
Four B&B rooms, each with
their own bath. Equipped
with air-con and laundry
facilities, and serves a full
breakfast. **$-$$**

Mankato
Riverfront Inn
1727 N.Riverfront Dr, MN 56001
Tel: 507-388-1638
www.riverfrontinnofmankato.com
All 19 rooms come with
internet, microwave, and
refrigerator. Suites also
have hot tubs and sauna.
No stairs plus some
wheelchair-accessible
rooms. **$**

Minneapolis
The Depot Renaissance
225 S. 3rd Avenue, MN 55401
Tel: 612-375-1700
www.marriott.com
Well-maintained,
comfortable rooms near city
center. Housed in a restored
train depot, close to the
Light Rail, with restaurant,
bar, gym, indoor waterpark,
and seasonal indoor skating
rink. **$$**
Evelo's B&B
2301 Bryant Ave S, MN 55405
Tel: 612-374-9656
Pleasant bed and breakfast

in well-preserved Victorian
house. Four rooms, all with
air-con and TV, share two
bathrooms. No children. **$**
The Marquette Hotel
710 Marquette Avenue, MN 55402
Tel: 612-333-4545
www.marquettehotel.com
Newly renovated boutique-
style hotel located in the IDS
Center. Huge rooms with
high-definition flatscreen
TVs. Gym, restaurant,
lounge bar, and discounted
rates for the nearby YMCA
pool. **$**
Nicollet Island Inn
95 Merriam Street, MN 55401
Tel: 612-331-1800
www.nicolletislandinn.com
Prime riverside location. 24
individually appointed
rooms and top-notch
restaurant featuring local
cuisine. The bread and
desserts are prepared daily
on-site. **$$**

Pipestone
Historic Calumet Inn
104 W. Main Street, MN 56164
Tel: 507-825-5871

PRICE CATEGORIES

Price categories are based
on the average cost of a
double room for one night:
$ = under $110
$$ = $110–250
$$$ = more than $250

www.calumetinn.com
(see page 137) **$$**

St Paul
The St Paul Hotel
350 Market Street, MN 55102
Tel: 651-292-9292
www.saintpaulhotel.com
Historic, landmark hotel
located in city center,
overlooking Rice Park.
Luxurious rooms,
restaurant, café and lobby
bar, rooftop fitness center,
and complimentary local
transport. **$$$**

South Dakota

Badlands National Park
Cedar Pass Lodge
20681 SD Highway 240, SD 57750
Tel: 877-386-4383
Escape from life's hectic
pace and stay in a cabin
with air-con and bathroom
but no phone or TV to
distract you. Buffalo tacos
served in the restaurant.
Located just past the Ben
Reifel park visitor center.
Open mid-April to mid-
October. **$**

Deadwood
Bullock Hotel
633 Main Street, SD 57732
Tel: 800-336-1876
Well-restored Victorian hotel
in historic town with
24-hour gaming, 28 rooms,
and breakfast and brunch
available. Reputedly
haunted by Seth Bullock,
Deadwood's first Sheriff! **$$**
Franklin Historic Hotel
700 Main Street, SD 57732
Tel: 605-578-3670
www.silveradofranklin.com
Located on Deadwood's
historic Main Street, this
lovely old hotel was built in
1903 and is now thoroughly
restored. Amenities: air
conditioning, television,
parking, restaurant, bars,
casino. **$**
Penny Motel
818 Upper Main Street, SD 57732
Tel/fax: 605-578-1842
www.pennymotel.com
Minutes from historic
Downtown. Amenities
include internet, laundry
facilities, parking, and
patios with gas grills. Casino
and restaurant located next

door. Continental breakfast
offered. **$**

Interior
**Circle View Guest Ranch
B&B**
20055 E. Highway 44, SD 57780
Tel: 605-433-5582
www.circleviewranch.com
Stay on this third-
generation, family-run,
3,000-acre (1,214-hectare)
working cattle ranch,
located on top of a butte
with amazing views of the
stunning scenery. Eight
rooms with private
bathrooms. Guest kitchen
and games room. Cooked
breakfast. **$**

Mitchell
Kelly Inn & Suites
1010 Cabela Drive, SD 57301
Tel: 605-995-0500
www.kellyinnmitchell.com
Good value for money. All
rooms have refrigerators,
microwaves, and internet
access. Some family and
wheelchair-accessible
rooms. Exercise room and
indoor pool. **$**

Pierre
River Lodge
713 W. Sioux Avenue, SD 57501
Tel: 605-224-4140
www.riverlodgesd.com
Convenient, family-owned,
and situated only one block
away from the river.
Continental breakfast
included. Freezer space for
fishermen's catches.
Cookies await your arrival. **$**

Rapid City
**Best Western Ramkota
Hotel**
2111 N. LaCrosse Street, SD 57701
Tel: 605-343-8550
Spacious rooms plus 33
two-room suites for
families. Free internet
access and parking. Indoor
pool, fitness room,
restaurant and bar, and
indoor waterpark. **$$**
Hotel Alex Johnson
523 Sixth Street, SD 57701
Tel: 605-342-1210
www.alexjohnson.com
Commissioned by rail
tycoon, Alex Johnson, said
to be a great admirer of
Native American culture. An

intriguing blend of German
and Plains Indian
influences. Don't miss the
chandelier fashioned from
war lances. Restaurant
open during the summer.
$$

Sioux Falls
Brimark Inn
3200 W. Russell Street, SD 57107
Tel/fax: 605-332-2000
www.brimarkinn.com
Good, owner-operated
motor inn with outdoor pool.
Close to Elmwood golf
course. **$**

Spearfish
Spearfish Canyon Lodge
10619 Roughlock Falls Road, Lead,
SD 57754
Tel: 605-584-3435
www.spfcanyon.com
54 rooms in a stone and
wood, old west-style lodge
nestled against cliffs. Hot
tub on the balcony, lounge,
bar, and restaurant. Ideal
for outdoor types, with
fishing, snowmobiling,
birdwatching, and hiking
opportunities on the
doorstep. **$$**

Wall
America's Best Value Inn
201 S. Boulevard, SD 57790
Tel: 605-279-2127
Save the pennies and stay
in these clean and
comfortable rooms fitted
with cable TV and wireless
internet. Continental
breakfast and heated
outdoor pool. **$**

Wyoming

Big Horn
**Spahn's Big Horn Mountain
Bed and Breakfast**
PO Box 579, WY 82833
Tel: 307-674-8150
www.bighorn-wyoming.com
This traditional mountain
lodge has a peaceful
location on the side of a
mountain, with stunning
views of the surrounding Big
Horn range. Guest
bedrooms in the main
house are decorated with
country quilts and oak
furniture, and there are cozy
cabins with front porches.
$$

Cody
Irma Hotel
1192 Sheridan Avenue, WY 82414
Tel: 307-587-4221
www.irmahotel.com
Built in 1902 by Buffalo Bill
Cody for his daughter, Irma,
the hotel still retains the
flavor of the Old West.
Amenities include air
conditioning, television,
restaurant. **$–$$**

Gillette
White House Inn B&B
2708 Ridgecrest Drive,
WY 82718
Tel: 307-687-1240
Email: whitehouseinn@vcn.com
Attractive, compact inn with
columned front porch.
$–$$

Grand Teton National Park
**Jackson Lake Lodge
Grand Teton Lodge Co.**
PO Box 240, Moran, WY 83013
Tel: 307-543-2811
www.gtlc.com
An eco-friendly, luxury lodge
with stunning views of the
lake and the Teton Range
from its huge lobby
windows, this large resort
has 385 rooms in the main
lodge and surrounding
cottages. It has a swimming
pool, playground, Western
art, and other amenities.
$$–$$$
Signal Mountain Lodge
Inner Teton Park Road, Moran,
WY 83013
Tel: 307-543-2831
Set right on the shores of
Jackson Lake,
accommodation is in
country-style rooms in the
main lodge, modern
bungalows and rustic log
cabins with pine furniture.
Deluxe lakefront units are
also available **$$–$$$**

Greybull
Yellowstone Motel
247 Greybull Avenue, WY 82426
Tel: 307-765-4456
www.yellowstonemotel.net
Warm, comfortable rooms
and suites at the base of
the Big Horn Mountains,
100 miles (160km) east of
Yellowstone National Park.
Amenities include a putting
green, heated pool, and
restaurant next door. **$–$$**

Jackson

Buckrail Lodge
110 E. Karns Avenue, WY 83001
Tel: 307-733-2079
www.buckraillodge.com
Large, comfortable cedar-log room with cathedral ceilings and western decor. Set in spacious grounds in quiet residential neighborhood. Good views. jacuzzi, cable TV. **$–$$**

Rustic Inn at Jackson Hole
435 N.Cache Street, WY 83001
Tel: 307-733-2357
www.rusticinnatjh.com
Luxury log cabins in peaceful park setting near a quiet elk refuge but also convenient to Town Square. Amenities include a restaurant and wine bar, heated outdoor pool and jacuzzi, spa, gym, and complimentary Wi-fi. **$$$**

Lovell

TX Ranch
PO Box 194, WY 82431
Tel: 406-484-6415
www.txranch.com
Guests help out with duties on this working cattle ranch situated at the foot of Pryor Mountain. Tents, horses, gear, and food provided. **$$**

Sheridan

Historic Sheridan Inn
Fifth and Broadway, WY 82801
Tel: 307-673-2777
Once part-owned by Buffalo Bill, this landmark inn *(see page 157)* is welcoming guests once more after a major renovation. Gracious rooms reflect the decor and comforts the great showman would have expected, and you can have a drink at the same mahogany bar which he once frequented, or a bite to eat in the adjoining 1893 Grille. **$$**

Trail's End Motel
2125 N.Main Street, WY 82801
Tel: 307-672-2477
www.trailsendmotelwy.com
A few blocks from Downtown, the Trail's End an excellent budget choice, having been renovated to a high standard by new owners. The spacious rooms are spread over several buildings, and the

complimentary breakfast is better than you'd get in many more expensive hotels. There's also a lively bar (non-smoking) and a restaurant, both of which are popular with locals. **$**

Montana

Bozeman

Mountain Sky Guest Ranch
Box 1219, Emigrant, MT 59027
Tel: 406-333-4911
www.mtnsky.com
The ranch overlooks the lovely Paradise Valley about 30 miles (48km) from Yellowstone National Park in southwestern Montana. Amenities include horseback riding and instruction, children's counselors, fishing, tennis, pool, hot tub. **$$$**

Columbia Falls

Meadow Lake Resort
100 St Andrews Dr, MT 59912
Tel: 406-892-8700 or toll-free 800-689-6579
www.meadowlake.com
Luxurious resort comprising vacation homes, combos, and inn rooms. Amenities include golf course, tennis and fitness center, Amtrak and ski shuttles, indoor and outdoor pools, restaurant, and lounge. **$$$**

Coram

A Wild Rose
10280 Highway 2 E., MT 59913
Tel: 406-387-4900
Cradled in stunning mountain scenery bordering Glacier National Park, this inn provides tranquility and pampering services with therapeutic spa and massage, whirlpool suites, and gourmet breakfasts. **$$**

Helena

Appleton Inn B&B
1999 Euclid Avenue, MT 59601
Tel: 406-449-7492
Restored 1890s Victorian house listed on the National Historic Register. It's now a comfortable bed-and-breakfast inn. **$–$$**

Elkhorn Mountain Inn
1 Jackson Creek Road. Montana City, MT 59634

ABOVE: long hours on the open road merit a luxury stopover.

Tel: 406-442-6625
www.elkhorninn.com
Elk antlers adorn the lobby of this rustic inn outside Helena at the base of the Elkhorn mountains. Rooms and 3 suites are attractively furnished and affordable. There is a recreation area with trails behind the hotel. **$–$$**

Kalispell

Kalispell Grand Hotel
100 Main Street, MT 59901
Tel: 406-755-8100
www.kalispellgrand.com
In this fine old historic hotel in downtown Kalispell, a grand oak staircase leads to comfortably furnished modern rooms. There are larger family rooms and some suites with jetted tubs. **$–$$**

Livingston

63 Ranch
Box 979, MT 59047
Tel: 406-222-0570
www.63ranch.com
Founded in 1929, this working ranch is set on 2,000 acres (810 hectares) in the Absaroka Mountains about 50 miles (81km) north of Yellowstone National Park and is listed on the National Register of Historic Places. Amenities include horseback riding and instruction, fishing, overnight trips. **$$$**

Missoula

Goldsmith's Bed and Breakfast Inn
809 E. Front, MT 59802
Tel: 406-728-1585
www.goldsmithsinn.com
A quiet riverside B&B in an older house, just a pleasant stroll away from Downtown. Rooms have individual amenities such as a fireplace, hot tub or deck. **$$**

Mountain Valley Inn
420 W. Broadway, MT 59802
Tel: 406-728-4500
www.mountainvalleyinnmissoula.com
The Mountain Valley Inn is a simple, pleasant, and inexpensive motel in the center of Missoula, just a few blocks' walk or drive from the main downtown shops, restaurants, and bars. It has lots of free amenities: covered parking, breakfast, coffee throughout the day, afternoon cookies, wireless internet, and a small exercise room. **$**

Polson

Best Western KwaTaqNuk Resort
49708 Highway 93, MT 59860

PRICE CATEGORIES

Price categories are based on the average cost of a double room for one night:
$ = under $110
$$ = $110–250
$$$ = more than $250

Tel: 406-883-3636
www.kwataqnuk.com
This waterfront resort on Flathead Lake has many first-rate facilities including two pools, whirlpool, fine dining restaurant, and gift shop. The resort's marina offers cruises on the lake. **$$$**

St Ignatius
Sunset Motel
32670 Highway 93, MT 59865
Tel: 406-745-3900
www.stignatiussunsetmotel.com
Well placed in the beautiful Mission Valley, this small hotel has spacious rooms decorated in "mountain theme." Cable TV, free high-speed internet, and kitchenettes. **$**

Whitefish
Duck Inn Lodge
1305 Columbia Avenue, MT 59937
Tel: 406-862-3825
www.duckinn.com
This is a pretty lodge by the river and an easy walk to Downtown. The pretty rooms are individually decorated and many have fireplaces, patios, jacuzzi, deep soak tubs; breakfast included. **$–$$**

Idaho

Bonners Ferry
Best Western Kootenai River Inn and Casino
7169 Plaza Street, ID 83805
Tel: 208-267-8511
www.kootenairiverinn.com
Spacious rooms and suites with private balconies, the better to enjoy the beautiful view over the river. Pool, hot tub, waterfront access, exercise room, spa. **$–$$$**

Coeur d'Alene
The Coeur d'Alene Resort
115 S. 2nd Street, ID 83814
Tel: 208-765-4000
www.cdaresort.com
Luxury resort on scenic Lake Coeur d'Alene. The many first-rate amenities include a floating moveable golf green. Close to fishing, skiing, and other area attractions. **$$$**

Sandpoint
The Lodge at Sandpoint
41 Lakeshore Drive, Sagle, ID 83860
Tel: 208-263-2211
www.lodgeatsandpoint.com
On the shores of Lake Pend Oreille, the lodge was only built in 2007 but combines an old-fashioned wooden rustic look with all the modern comforts like hot tubs, internet, movie library, art works on the walls, and a terrific bar and breakfast room. The great room has a roaring fire and magnificent views. **$–$$$**

Washington

Ellensburg
The I-90 Inn Motel
1390 Dollar Way, WA 98926
Tel: 509-925-9844
www.i-90inn.com
The I-90 is not only conveniently located just off I-90's exit 106, and a 5-minute drive from Downtown, it is also the kind of motel you dream of finding – comfortable, bright, nicely decorated, very clean, and with a friendly staff, good-sized rooms, and inexpensive. **$**

Forks
Kalaloch Lodge
157151 Highway 101, WA 98331
Tel: 866-525-2562
www.visitkalaloch.com
The Kalaloch Lodge, located 35 miles (56km) south of Forks, offers very simple accommodation either in the main Lodge building or in rustic log cabins in the grounds. Go for the Bluff Cabins with their Pacific Ocean views. There's a full-service restaurant and small shop, but with no internet or cellphone reception, this is for those who really like getting away from it all. **$–$$$**

La Push
La Push Ocean Park Resort
PO Box 67, WA 98350
Tel: 360-374-5267
There are beautiful seaside views from this resort complex with nicely

decorated cabins and guest rooms, some with fireplaces. No TV or cell-phone access. **$$**

Leavenworth
Alpenrose Inn
500 Alpine Place, WA 98826
Tel: 509-548-3000
www.alpenroseinn.com
Intimate Bavarian-style B&B inn in scenic alpine setting. **$$**

Haus Rohrbach Pension
12882 Ranger Road, WA 98826
Tel: 509-548-7024
www.hausrohrbach.com
Cozy and convivial European-style pension. High on a hill with views across the valley. **$–$$**

Port Angeles
Red Lion Hotel
221 N. Lincoln Street, WA 98362
Tel: 360-452-9215
www.redlionportangeles.com
Waterfront location with harbor view. Some rooms have balconies. Facilities include dining room, valet service, and laundry. **$$**

Port Townsend
Palace Hotel
1004 Water Street, WA 98368
Tel: 360-385-0773
or 800-962-0741
www.palacehotelpt.com
A nicely restored historic Downtown edifice which was built by a retired sea captain in 1889. It has been decorated in original Victorian style. **$–$$**

The Tides Inn
1807 Water Street, WA 98368
Tel: 360-385-0595
www.tides-inn.com
Charming hotel on the waterfront overlooking the beach and the bay, with view of the Cascades and Olympic Mountains. Several rooms have private jacuzzis on the decks. **$–$$$**

Seattle
The Edgewater Inn
Pier 67, 2411 Alaskan Way, WA 98101
Tel: 206-728-7000
Seattle's only luxury downtown waterfront hotel, with an atrium lobby, stone fireplaces, and mountain lodge decor. The restaurant

features northwestern cuisine. Rates vary depending on water- or city-view rooms. **$$–$$$**

Inn At The Market
Pike Place Market, 86 Pine Street, WA 98101
Tel: 206-443-3600
www.innatthemarket.com
In Pike Place Market with splendid views of Elliott Bay, the hotel is surrounded by trendy shops, spa, and restaurant. Rooms have spacious bathrooms and free Wi-fi. Free downtown shuttle. **$$–$$$**

Shafer-Baillie Mansion
907 14th Avenue E., WA 98112
Tel: 206-322-4654or
800-985-4654
www.sbmansion.com
Antique-furnished B&B in a Tudor-Revival mansion, set in spacious grounds on Seattle's Capitol Hill. Rooms have rich oak and mahogany woodwork, antique and reproduction furniture, and Oriental rugs. Gourmet breakfast is included. **$$**

University Plaza Hotel
400 NE 45th Street, WA 98105
Tel: 206-634-0100
In the heart of the University District, with 135 rooms. Pool, fitness center, beauty salon, laundry service, restaurant, lounge with entertainment. **$**

Quinault
Lake Quinault Lodge
345 S. Shore Road, WA 98575
Tel: 360-288-2900
www.visitlakequinault.com
Right on the shores of Lake Quinault and surrounded by the magnificent forests of the Olympic National Park, the Lake Quinault Lodge offers a range of simple but comfortable accommodations aimed at those who come here to hike the trails and enjoy the scenery and the wildlife. The smart Roosevelt Restaurant is named for FDR who was staying here in 1937 when the idea of creating this National Park was suggested over lunch. **$$–$$$**

CENTRAL ROUTE

Washington, DC

Allen Lee Hotel
2224 F Street NW, 20037
Tel: 202-331-1224
Simple but clean hotel – some rooms share baths. Great for the young. Amenities: free coffee and cookies in lobby on Sunday mornings, maid service daily. All rooms have TV; some have baths. **$$**

The Channel Inn
650 Water Street SW, 20024
Tel: 202-554-2400
www.channelinn.com
Washington's only waterfront hotel, close to the marina restaurants, with large and simple but comfortable rooms. Amenities: good seafood restaurant, coffee shop, outdoor pool, plus the Arena Stage, golf course, indoor and outdoor tennis courts are close by. **$$**

The Jefferson
1200 16th Street NW, 20036
Tel: 202-347-2200
www.jeffersondc.com
A relatively small hotel, offering discreet and sensitive service in elegant surroundings. Amenities: restaurant, Saturday jazz, high tea, bathrobes, hair dryers, exercise, and swimming facilities at University Club opposite, laundry, one-hour pressing, valet parking, pets accepted. **$$$**

Virginia

Front Royal

Relax Inn
1801 N. Shenandoah Avenue, VA 22630
Tel: 540-635-4101
www.relaxinnfrontroyal.com
Situated on the Shenandoah River 2 miles (1.6km) from the entrance to the Shenandoah Parkway, all 20 guest rooms in this well-maintained older motel have double beds, bathroom, refrigerator, microwave, and TV. There is an outdoor pool and pleasant picnic area. **$**

Luray

Mayne View B&B
439 Mechanic Street, VA 22835
Tel: 540-743-7921
www.mayneview.com
This former hunting lodge was built by one of the discoverers of the Luray Caverns and was used as a stop on the Underground Railroad towards the end of the Civil War. Five rooms with private bathrooms. Hot tub on the deck. Located in 3 acres (1.2 hectares) of grounds with fine mountain views. **$–$$**

New Market

Blue Ridge Inn
2251 Old Valley Pike, VA 22844
Tel: 540-740-4136
www.blueridgeinn.com
Pleasant with cable TV and refrigerators. Set in 4 acres (1.6 hectares) of grounds, with a picnic area, barbecue, and play area. **$**

Strasburg

Hotel Strasburg
213 S. Holliday Street, VA 22657
Tel: 540-465-9191
www.hotelstrasburg.com
Massanutten Mountain forms the backdrop for this former hospital, converted into a lovely hotel in 1915. Featuring creative Southern-style fine dining. **$–$$**

North Carolina

Asheville

Richmond Hill Inn
87 Richmond Hill Drive, NC 28806
Tel: 828-252-7313
www.richmondhillinn.com
This romantic 19th-century mansion commands fine panoramic views from atop a wooded hill. Stay in rooms in quiet cottages overlooking the beautiful garden or surrounding the croquet lawn. Spa, porch rockers, and fine dining featuring an extensive wine list. Breakfast, afternoon tea, and soft drinks included in the price. A peaceful haven. **$$$**

Cherokee

Best Western Great Smokies Inn
Highway 441 North and Acquoni Road, NC 28719
Tel: 828-497-2020
www.greatsmokiesinn.com
Well-fitted guest rooms and suites, outdoor pool, and laundry. Restaurant open Apr–early Nov. Complimentary continental breakfast served mid-Nov–Mar. One mile outside the national park. **$**

Tennessee

Dandridge

Goose Creek Farm B&B
621 Highway 139, TN 37725
Tel: 865-397-6166
www.goosecreekfarm-bed-n-breakfast.com
Restored farmhouse set in 12 acres (4.8 hectares) of grounds, with wraparound porch on which breakfast (full or continental) is sometimes served. Three rooms with bathrooms. No children under 12 years of age. Kennels for canine companions. **$$**

Mountain Harbor Inn
1199 Highway 139, TN 37725
Tel: 865-397-1313
www.mountainharborinn.com
Nicely decorated rooms, all with breathtaking mountain and lake views. Room price includes breakfast buffet and sunset cruise. Boat and jet ski rental available. **$$**

Knoxville

Hilton Knoxville
501 W. Church Avenue, TN 37902
Tel: 865-523-2300
All amenities you'd expect, plus a Starbucks, cyber café, bar, and two restaurants, one serving breakfast and lunch, the other dinner only. Children's video rental available. Outdoor pool. Request a room with views of the Smokies or the Tennessee River. Cheaper if you book online. **$–$$**

Hotel St Oliver
407 Union Avenue, TN 37902
Tel: 865-521-0050
www.hotelstolivertn.com
Located on Market Square in the centre of Downtown, the hotel features period furniture and antiques. Built in 1876 to serve as a bakery, this tastefully decorated building has 24 rooms complete with bathrooms, refrigerators and TVs, and a library. **$**

Memphis

The Bridgewater House B&B
7015 Raleigh LaGrange Road, Cordova, TN 38018
Tel: 901-384-0080
Email: mistilis@bellsouth.net
This intimate B&B is housed in a century-old former schoolhouse shaded by 2 wooded acres (1 hectare) of mature oaks. Many pampering extras including bathrobes, down comforters, and a full gourmet breakfast. Ceiling fans, antiques, and hardwood floors. No children. **$$**

Heartbreak Hotel
3677 Elvis Presley Boulevard, TN 38116
Tel: 901-332-1000
www.elvis.com/epheartbreakhotel
Opened in 1999, adjacent to Graceland, owned and operated by Elvis Presley Enterprises, Inc. Features 1950s decor, in-room Elvis movies and heart-shaped outdoor pool. Packages include Graceland tours. **$$**

The Peabody
149 Union Avenue, TN 38103
Tel: 901-529-4000
www.peabodymemphis.com
(see page 196) **$$**

PRICE CATEGORIES

Price categories are based on the average cost of a double room for one night:
$ = under $110
$$ = $110–250
$$$ = more than $250

River Inn at Harbor Town
50 Harbor Town Square
Tel: 901-260-3333
www.riverinnmemphis.com
This inviting boutique inn overlooking trails along the Mississippi green belt anchors a new development on Muddy Island and feels miles from busy downtown Memphis. Windows in the 28 rooms and suites frame stunning sunsets and include walnut armoires, floaty four-poster beds, desks, and Wi-fi. Guests are spoiled with Champagne on arrival, homemade truffles, and port before bed, hot beverages in library sitting areas, gourmet dining, and silver-service breakfasts. **$$$**

Nashville
Daisy Hill Bed & Breakfast
2816 Blair Boulevard, TN 37212
Tel: 615-297-9795
www.daisyhillbedandbreakfast.com
Tudor Revival-style house with three guestrooms with bathrooms. Beautifully decorated, with a communal living room, dining room, library, sun room, porch, and garden. Full breakfast served. No children under 12. **$–$$**
Gaylord Opryland Hotel
2800 Opryland Drive, TN 37214
Tel: 615-889-1000
A Music City extravaganza with Vegas-Disney overtones and 9 acres (3.6 hectares) of indoor gardens. Vast, showy, and very pricey. **$$$+**
The Hermitage Hotel
231 6th Avenue N., TN 37219
Tel: 615-244-3121
www.historichotels.org
(see page 193) **$$$**

Oak Ridge
DoubleTree Hotel
215 S. Illinois Avenue,
TN 37830
Tel: 865-481-2468
www.doubletreeoakridge.com
King bed, two double bed, suite and wheelchair-accessible rooms, with refrigerators, internet access, and continental breakfast. The hotel's facilities include indoor/outdoor pools, lounge, bar, and a good restaurant. Pet-friendly. **$$**

Sevierville
Blue Mountain Mist Country Inn & Cottages
1811 Pullen Road, TN 37862
Tel: 865-428-2335
Twelve rooms in the attractive main building, plus five cottages with kitchenettes and porches ideal for couples, and a two-bedroom guesthouse. This B&B establishment is furnished with antiques and sits in 60-acre (24-hectare) grounds amidst beautiful mountain scenery. Hammocks in the garden. **$$**

Arkansas

Hot Springs
The Arlington Resort Hotel and Spa
239 Central Avenue, AR 71901
Tel: 501-623-7771
www.arlingtonhotel.com
This full-service resort has been pampering visitors since 1875; previous guests include Al Capone. Facilities include an on-premises bath house with thermal water baths and massages (book well in advance!), three restaurants and beauty salon. **$–$$**
Wildwood 1884 B&B Inn
808 Park Avenue, AR 71901
Tel: 501-624-4267
www.wildwood1884.com
Carefully restored 1884 Queen Anne mansion with original woodwork, antiques, and stained glass. Some of the five rooms have porches. Ideal for couples due to the romantic focus. **$$**

Little Rock
Capital Hotel
Louisiana and Markham streets,
AR 72201
Tel: 501-374-7474
www.capitalhotel.com
Handsome Victorian hotel. Lavish architecture, two restaurants, and free admission to the gym across the street *(see page 198)*. **$$**
The Empress of Little Rock
2120 S. Louisiana Street,
AR 72206
Tel: 501-374-7966
www.theempress.com

Impressive Gothic Queen Anne house featuring elegant double stairway. Additional rooms in the carriage house. Gourmet breakfast *(see page 200)*. **$$**
Rosemont B&B
515 W. 15th Street, AR 72202
Tel: 501-374-7456
www.rosemontoflittlerock.com
Comfortable, unfussy, en suite Victorian rooms, most with fireplaces or jacuzzis. Swing and chairs on the porch, garden, library. Vegetarian, diabetic, and lactose-intolerant guests catered for at breakfast. **$–$$**

Oklahoma

Chandler
Lincoln Motel
740 E. First Street, OK 74834
Tel: 405-258-0200
A well-maintained vintage Route 66 motor inn. **$**

Clinton
Best Western Elk City Inn
2015 W. Third Street, OK 73644
Tel: 580-225-2331
Good-sized rooms with cable TV/HBO. Free continental breakfast, indoor pool, and airport transportation. **$**

Miami
Best Western Inn of Miami
2225 E. Steve Owens Boulevard,
OK 74354
Tel: 918-542-6681
This inn is set in landscaped grounds with many mature trees. All rooms are ground floor, with free cable and refrigerators. Outdoor pool, bar, and lounge. **$**

Oklahoma City
Biltmore Hotel
401 S. Meridian Avenue,
OK 73108
Tel: 405-947-7681
www.biltmoreokc.com
Large hotel with a mass of amenities, including three outdoor pools, one indoor pool, restaurant, café, three bars, and tennis courts – equipment can be hired. Free parking and complimentary shuttle service to fairground events. **$**

Colcord Hotel
15 N. Robinson Avenue,
OK 73102
Tel: 405-601-4300
www.colcordhotel.com
Downtown Oklahoma City's first boutique hotel occupies a restored 1910 Art Deco skyscraper, a former office building adjoining trendy Bricktown. Hushed, stylish, window-wrapped rooms and suites are party-sized; they have sofas, marble bathrooms, soaking tubs, 32-inch LCD TVs, and wireless internet. Gym, business center. No breakfast café onsite, but there's a lovely French dinner restaurant with loyal local following. **$$**
Grandison Inn at Maney Park
1200 N. Shartel, OK 73103
Tel: 405-232-8778
www.grandisoninn.com
Well-preserved, three-storey Victorian B&B. Eight rooms, each with their own bathroom, cable TV, and DVD player. Help yourself to drinks and home-baked dessert from the butler's pantry. **$$**

Stroud
Skyliner Motel
717 W. Main Street, OK 74078
Tel: 918-968-9556
Comfortable and well-kept Route 66 establishment dating from 1950. **$**

Tulsa
Desert Hills Motel
5220 E. 11th Street, OK 74112
Tel: 918-834-3311
www.deserthillstulsa.com
Classic Route 66 motor inn with obligatory neon sign on the outskirts of downtown Tulsa. Fifty basic rooms and laundry facilities, with very low rates. **$**
Hotel Ambassador
1324 S. Main Street, OK 74119
Tel: 918-587-8200
www.hotelambassador-tulsa.com
Originally built as accommodation for oil barons while they waited for their mansions to be built, this luxurious, ornate hotel in the city's uptown offers spacious rooms with Italian marble bathrooms.

ABOVE: classic Route 66 neon motel sign, Flagstaff, Arizona.

Restaurant, library, and extensive array of amenities. **$$**

Vinita
Park Hills Motel and RV Park
Highway 60/66 two miles west of Vinita, OK 74301
Tel: 918-256-5511
21 modest, clean, and serviceable rooms with refrigerator, microwave, and cable TV. Large fishing pond. **$**

Weatherford
Best Western Mark Motor Hotel
525 E. Main Street, OK 73096
Tel: 580-772-3325
Well-fitted guest rooms including free full breakfast, morning paper, cable TV, internet access, and refrigerator. Outdoor pool. **$**

Texas
Amarillo
Ashmore Inn & Suites
2301 I-40 E., Exit 72A, TX 79104
Tel: 806-374-0033
www.ashmoresuites-amarillo.com
New addition to the list of Amarillo's accommodation, this above-average hotel features all the usual room facilities, plus guest laundry, indoor pool, fitness center, and continental breakfast for a reasonable rate. **$**
Big Texan Motel
7701 I-40 E., TX 79118
Tel: 806-372-5000
www.bigtexan.com/motel
Old West themed motel with good rooms, next to the Steak Ranch. Texas-shaped outdoor pool. **$**

Canyon
Buffalo Inn
300 23rd Street, TX 79015
Tel: 806-655-2124
Run-of-the-mill rooms with

wireless internet, near the Panhandle-Plains Historical Museum. Restaurant nearby. **$**

Conway
Budget Host S&S Motel
I-40 and Highway 207 (Rt 2, Box 58), Panhandle, TX 79068
Tel: 806-537-5111
Standard motel rooms and restaurant. **$**

Vega
Vega Motel
1005 Vega Boulevard, TX 79092
Tel: 806-267-2205
Another good example of a vintage Route 66 motel. Worth a look and maybe an overnight stop. **$**

New Mexico
Albuquerque
Hi Way House
3200 Central SE, NM 87106
Tel: 505-268-3971
www.hiwayhousemotel.com
One of the last in the old Hi Way House chain seen frequently on the old Route 66. **$**
Hyatt Regency
330 Tijeras SW, NM 87102
Tel: 505-842-1234
http://albuquerque.hyatt.com
Elegant and contemporary downtown hotel, close to nightlife, galleries, and shopping. Pool, fitness room, restaurant, bar. **$$–$$$**

Gallup
El Rancho Hotel and Motel
1000 E. Highway 66, NM 87301
Tel: 505-863-9311
www.elranchohotel.com
You'll feel like a Hollywood star in the comfortable rooms at this historic hotel (see page 218). There is a variety of rooms and suites, some with balconies or kitchenettes, each decorated with signature

Southwestern artwork. Hotel amenities include fitness room, pool, business center. **$–$$**
Leisure Lodge
1204 E. Santa Fe Avenue, NM 87020
Tel: 505-287-2991
Time-honored and traditional Route 66 landmark. **$**

Las Vegas
Plaza Hotel
230 Old Town Plaza, NM 87701
Tel: 505-425-3591
www.plazahotel-nm.com
A fine historical hotel with attractive restaurant and saloon overlooking the Old Town Plaza. **$–$$**

Santa Fe
El Rey Inn
1862 Cerrillos Road, NM 87505
Tel: 505-982-1931
www.elreyinnsantafe.com
Set in lovely gardens, this 1930s motor court inn on the old Route 66 offers traditional and deluxe rooms, and Southwestern suites with fireplaces and kitchenettes. Amenities include pool, whirlpool, sauna, and complimentary continental breakfast. **$–$$**
Hotel Santa Fe
1501 Paseo De Peralta, NM 87501
Tel: 505-982-1200
www.hotelsantafe.com
Hotel Santa Fe is the city's only Native American-owned hotel, right in the buzzing new Railyard district. Stunning Indian artworks decorate the rooms and corridors, and the whole place oozes Southwestern style. The Amaya Restaurant makes Native American foods contemporary, and there is also Native American flute music here some nights. **$$–$$$**
La Fonda Santa Fe
100 E. San Francisco Street, NM 87501
Tel: 505-982-5511
www.lafondasantafe.com
Historic Pueblo Revival-style hotel on the Plaza rebuilt in 1919. The beautiful bedrooms have luxury mattresses, hand-painted wooden furniture, and New Mexican art, and some have fireplaces and balconies. Amenities include spa,

fitness center, outdoor hot tub, heated swimming pool, and free internet access. **$$–$$$**
St Francis
210 Don Gaspar Avenue, NM 87501
Tel: 505-983-5700
www.hotelstfrancis.com
Boutique hotel in a landmark building dating from the 1920s, fully restored with period decor. Restaurant, bar. **$$–$$$**

Tucumcari
Blue Swallow Motel
815 E. Route 66 Boulevard, NM 88401
Tel: 575-461-9849
www.blueswallowmotel.com
The landmark neon sign with its signature blue swallow is still a popular stop on old Route 66 (see page 213). It has comfortable rooms and the old motor court garages are still intact. **$**
Safari Motel
722 E. Route 66 Boulevard, NM 88401
Tel: 575-461-1048
Lovingly cared for landmark motel on Route 66, opposite the Blue Swallow (see above). Rooms are clean and comfortable, with period lamps and furniture mixed with modern amenities. **$**

Arizona
Flagstaff
Hotel Monte Vista
100 N.San Francisco, AZ 86001
Tel: 928-779-6971
www.hotelmontevista.com
A reasonably priced older hotel. The 50 rooms and suites cover four floors with beautiful views over Flagstaff, and are attractively furnished. Some are named after the many celebrity guests who have stayed here. **$–$$**
The Weatherford Hotel
23 N. Leroux Street, AZ 86001
Tel: 928-779-1919
www.weatherfordhotel.com

PRICE CATEGORIES
Price categories are based on the average cost of a double room for one night:
$ = under $110
$$ = $110–250
$$$ = more than $250

TRANSPORTATION
ACCOMMODATIONS
EATING OUT
ACTIVITIES
A – Z

A BOVE: the Wigwam Motel in Holbrook, Arizona.

Historic hotel reflecting Flagstaff's pioneer origins (see page 224). Rooms are charmingly decorated in period style. **$–$$**

Holbrook

Wigwam Motel
811 W. Hopi Drive, AZ 86025
Tel: 928-524-3048
www.wigwam-motel-arizona.com
Time your journey for an overnight stop in Holbrook and head for the Wigwam Motel. A night in a 1950s concrete tepee is a quintessential Route 66 experience. **$**

Jerome

Mile High Inn
309 N. Main Street, AZ 86331
Tel: 928-634-5094
www.jeromemilehighinn.com
A small, friendly inn occupying the 1899 Frontier-style Clinksdale Building. Compact rooms attractively furnished with period antiques. Relaxed dining downstairs at the Mile High Grill. **$–$$**

Peach Springs

Hualapai Lodge
900 Route 66, AZ 86434
Tel: 928-769-2230
www.destinationgrandcanyon.com
Basic but comfortable accommodation popular with rafters going down the canyon. **$**

Sedona

Adobe Village Graham Inn
150 Canyon Circle Drive, AZ 86351
Tel: 928-284-1425
www.sedonasfinest.com
A stylishly furnished inn

commanding spectacular views of the red rocks. In addition to the six de luxe guest rooms, there are four romantic *casitas* (cottages) with waterfall showers, bathroom fireplaces, and breadmakers. Includes early morning coffee, full breakfast, afternoon refreshments, and evening snacks. **$$–$$$**

Williams

Grand Canyon Railway Hotel
233 N. Grand Canyon Boulevard, AZ 86046
Tel: 928-773-1976
www.thetrain.com/grand-canyon-railway-hotel-williams-az-5686.html
Designed to resemble the historic Fray Marcos Hotel (see page 225) in the old train depot, this smart hotel has comfortable, classic rooms and suites with Southwestern accents. **$$**

Winslow

The La Posada Hotel
303 E. Second Street, AZ 86047
Tel: 928-289-4366
www.laposada.org
Built in 1929 for the Santa Fe Railroad and now restored to its original glory, La Posada reflects the architecture and decor of the bygone era of great railroad hotels. Rooms are named after the many famous guests who stayed here in its heyday. Standard rooms are attractively furnished with South-western style, and others have jacuzzis, balconies, and deluxe features. **$–$$**

Los Angeles

Bayside Hotel
2001 Ocean Avenue, Santa Monica, CA 90405
Tel: 310-396-6000
www.baysidehotel.com
Cozy rooms, comfy beds, oversized desks, and ocean views await guests at this affordable Santa Monica hotel, not far from the beach. **$$**

Hotel Oceana
849 Ocean Avenue, Santa Monica, CA 90403
Tel: 310-393-0486
www.hoteloceana.com
Sixty-three suites. Mediterranean-villa like, across from the ocean, a short walk to pier and promenade. Room service by Wolfgang Puck Café. Pool, laundromat, fitness center, car rental. **$$$**

Los Angeles Marriott Downtown
333 S.Figueroa Street, CA 90071
Tel: 213-617-1133
www.marriott.com.
Luxury hotel with 469 rooms on 4 acres (1.6 hectares) of landscaped grounds, near Music Center and Dodger Stadium. Executive floor, health club, business center, valet parking, airport bus service, restaurants, pool, courtesy coffee, babysitting, foreign currency exchange. **$$$**

O Hotel
819 S.Flower Street, CA 90017
Tel: 213-623-9904
www.ohotelgroup.com
Set in a historic 1920s building, the O is the first urban boutique hotel in downtown LA's financial district. The 67 rooms are well appointed in contemporary style with complimentary internet, plasma TVs, ergonomic designer chairs, and other amenities. **$$**

Residence Inn Santa Clarita
25320 The Old Road, CA 91381
Tel: 661-290-2800
www.residenceinn.com
Ninety suites, close to Magic Mountain, 20 miles (33km) to Downtown LA. Free breakfast, room

service, pool, exercise room, full kitchens, some fireplaces. **$$**

Sunset Tower Hotel
8358 Sunset Boulevard, West Hollywood, CA 90069
Tel: 323-654-7100
www.sunsettowerhotel.com
Art Deco landmark, and one-time home of such stars as Harlow, Gable, Monroe, and Flynn. Luxury rooms with period features and stylish lobby, bar, and restaurant, but it's the stunning rooftop pool that will take your breath away. **$$$**

Venice Beach House
15 30th Avenue, Venice, CA 90291
Tel: 310-823-1966
www.venicebeachhouse.com
Pretty, ivy-covered B&B near the beach built in 1911. Nine individually decorated rooms, full breakfast, some share bathrooms. **$$**

Needles

Best Western Colorado River Inn
2371 W. Broadway, CA 92363
Tel: 760-326-4552
www.bestwesterncalifornia.com/hotels/best-western-colorado-river-inn/
Spacious rooms and mini suites with large-screen TVs/HBO, microwaves, and refrigerators. Very nice indoor pool, sauna, and jacuzzi area. Restaurant adjacent. **$**

San Bernardino

San Bernardino Hilton
285 E. Hospitality Lane, CA 92408
Tel: 909-889-0133
www.hilton.com
Luxurious rooms. Fine dining, pool, and whirlpool. **$–$$$**

Wigwam Motel
2728 N. Foothill Boulevard, Rialto, CA 92376
Tel: 909-875-3005
www.wigwammotel.com
The seventh and last of the Wigwam Motel chain (see page 234), these Route 66 landmark tepees have wagon wheel headboards and checkered bedspreads, but have been updated with free internet and TV. Pool and barbecue grill on site. **$**

SOUTHERN ROUTE

Georgia

Atlanta

Atlanta Marriott Marquis
265 Peachtree Center Avenue, GA 30303
Tel: 404-521-0000
www.marriott.com/hotels/travel/atlmq-atlanta-marriott-marquis
This contemporary downtown landmark hotel designed by architect John Portman is a beauty: the atrium lobby, with the 50ft (15-meter) color-changing "sail" of its iconic cocktail bar Pulse, has a volume of 9.5 million cu ft (269,010 cu meters), and visitors feel they've entered the rib cage of some mythical beast. The upgraded suites and rooms all have spectacular city views. The high-end amenities include in-room large work spaces and granite-top counters in bathrooms. **$$$**

Beverly Hills Inn
65 Sheridan Drive NE, GA 30305
Tel: 404-233-8520
www.beverlyhillsinn.com
This B&B – Atlanta's first – is in a 1929 building in ritzy Buckhead. It's British-owned and filled with antiques. Some of the 18 roomy suites have canopy beds; all have kitchenettes, making this a good choice for longer stays. Breakfast in the lovely conservatory is Expanded Continental. Pets with deposit. **$$**

Glenn Hotel
110 Marietta Street NW, GA 30303
Tel: 404-521-2250
www.glennhotel.com
Located in a converted 1923 building, next to CNN Center, the Glenn is Atlanta's first downtown boutique hotel. With its see-and-be-seen bar and restaurant, dark night-club feel, and young, casual staff, it's aimed squarely at an urban hip crowd. An old-fashioned lift leads to low-lit corridors that feel more like art installations than thoroughfares. Rooms are tiny but well planned with large windows, built-in wardrobes, desks, and lighting, and bathrooms with rain-flow showerheads. Onsite parking is a big selling point. **$$**

Westin Peachtree Plaza
210 Peachtree Street, GA 30303
Tel: 404-659-1400
www.starwoodhotels.com/westin
With its 1,068 pie-shaped rooms, this 73-story, circular high rise is an Atlanta landmark, and the tallest hotel in America to date. Designed by famed architect John Portman, the structure is a must-see for its liberal use of glass, in rooms and in the domed pool. Small pets allowed. **$$$**

Juliette

Jarrell 1920 House
Jarrell Plantation State Historic Site, 715 Jarrell Plantation Road, GA 31046
Tel: 478-986-3972
www.jarrellhouse.com
A unique backwoods experience in rural Georgia, this atmospheric bed-and-breakfast is housed in a listed structure built from heart-pine lumber milled on the Jarrell family plantation. Two bedrooms have adjoining bathrooms, TVs, and ceiling fans; one room has an antique queen and the other two antique double beds. Breakfast buffet. **$$**

Macon

1842 Inn
353 College Street, GA 31201
Tel: 912-741-1842
www.1842inn.com
This European B&B, a ravishing beauty even among Macon's many historic antebellum mansions, both celebrates the finer things in life and makes you feel relaxed. Split between the main house and adjoining 1900 Victorian building, the 21 rooms retain their historic elements but also have wireless internet, push-button gas fireplaces, and whirlpool baths. The warm welcome from long-serving staff includes proper afternoon tea, a substantial happy-hour spread of appetizers complete with mint juleps, and elegant gourmet breakfasts. You can walk to Hay House from here. **$$$**

Best Western-Riverside
2400 Riverside Drive, GA 31204
Tel: 912-743-6311
www.bestwestern.com
This 120-unit motor inn is a good deal in Macon. It has an antebellum facade, reasonably comfortable rooms with fridges and other amenities such as high-speed internet, a pool, and restaurant. **$**

Palmetto

The Inn at Serenbe
10950 Hutcheson Ferry Road, Palmetto, GA 30268
Tel: 770-463-2610
www.serenbe.com
Expect gracious Southern hospitality, from afternoon tea to treats at bedtime and gourmet breakfast, at this romantic country retreat on 284 acres (115 hectares), 32 miles (51km) southwest of Atlanta. Elegantly furnished rooms are available in the 1905 farmhouse and four cottages and include hardwood floors, window seats, and canopy beds. Walking distance to Serenbe Village with 900 acres (365 hectares) of trails, farm, and lake. **$$**

Warm Springs

Callaway Gardens
17800 US Highway 27, Pine Mountain, GA 31822
Tel: 706-663-2281
www.callawaygardens.com
This huge mountain resort has the feel of a national park, with its nature trails, biking and fishing, botanical gardens, shops and restaurants, wood-surrounded Mountain Creek Inn, and elegant new Lodge and Spa. The reasonably priced inn sells out months in advance; rooms are usually available for the pricier Lodge. **$$$**

Mountain Top Inn and Resort
177 Royal Lodge Road, GA 31822
Tel: 706-663-4719
www.mountaintopinnga.com
You can rent a log cabin or stay in a lodge surrounded by Roosevelt State Park at this rustic retreat on Pine Mountain near Warm Springs. A popular place for weddings, this woodsy inn has a pool and restaurant. TVs but no telephones in cabins. **$$**

Alabama

Atmore

Royal Oaks Bed and Breakfast
5415 Highway 21, AL 36502
Tel: 251-368-8722
www.royaloaksbandb.com
This French-style country inn offers two-person apartments with private baths surrounded by gardens. The lovely peaceful setting is sometimes broken by the distinctive call of peacocks strutting near the pool. Farm-fresh eggs at breakfast in the morning. **$$**

Wind Creek Casino and Hotel
303 Poarch Road, AL 36502
Tel: 866-WIND360
www.windcreekcasino.com
This 17-story casino/hotel, near I-65 on the Poarch Creek Indian Reservation, is THE new luxury place to stay in the area. Its spacious rooms and suites have plump bedding, Native-made sweetgrass bathroom amenities, LCD TVs, and other extras. There are four

PRICE CATEGORIES

Price categories are based on the average cost of a double room for one night:
$ = under $110
$$ = $110–250
$$$ = more than $250

restaurants including a global buffet. **$$**

Bayou La Batre
Bayou La Batre Inn and Suites
13155 N. Wintzell Avenue, AL 36509
Tel: 251-824-2020
www.bayoulabatreinn.com
Close to the beach with 40 comfortable rooms, this motel offers continental breakfast, a pool, and in-room microwaves and refrigerators. Hot tubs in some rooms. Restaurant adjacent. **$**

Mobile
Azalea House
115 Providence Street, AL 36604
Tel: 251-438-9921
www.theinnkeeper.com/bnb/10808
This Colonial home was built in 1904. Each of the three bedrooms has an en suite shower, TV, ceiling fan, and queen bed. Full breakfasts served. There is a spacious porch overlooking the beautiful grounds. **$–$$**
Malaga Inn
359 Church Street, AL 36602
Tel/fax: 251-438-4701
www.malagainn.com
This unique downtown inn is set in a gas-lit courtyard and consists of two adjoining restored 1862 townhouses landscaped together with gardens and a patio. The 35 rooms and three suites are nicely decorated; many feature hardwood floors. Continental breakfast. **$$$**
Renaissance Battle House
26 N. Royal Street, AL 36602
Tel: 251-338-2000
www.marriott.com
Three hotels on this site have welcomed presidents and other history makers since 1852. The 1908 seven-story brick hotel, lavishly restored in 2007, has a massive circular lobby with spectacular stained-glass ceiling. Today's guests include many oil and shipping executives, and the 238 oversized rooms and suites feature masculine details such as dark-wood paneling and heavy brocade drapes as

well as oversized bathrooms with tub and shower. Two restaurants onsite, a spa, and guests can play nearby at the Magnolia Grove Golf Course at a discount as part of the Robert Trent Jones Golf Trail. **$$$**

Montgomery
Red Bluff Cottage
551 Clay Street, AL 36104
Tel: 334-264-0056
www.redbluffcottage.com
This B&B is in a well-designed, comfortable, bluff-top cottage. It's on the busy edge of the historic Downtown, near I-65, but is remarkably peaceful at night. A large porch offers views of the Alabama River and State Capitol. The five themed rooms celebrate local history; the Great Gatsby Room, in particular, with original mementos belonging to Montgomery resident Zelda Fitzgerald, will inspire writers. The hosts are anxious to please: guests can look forward to homecooked breakfasts, evening snacks, and lively discussions about the area. Phones and wireless internet but no TVs in rooms. **$$$**

Mississippi
Biloxi
Grand Biloxi Hotel
280 Beach Boulevard, MS 39530
Tel: 800-WIN2WIN
www.grandcasinobiloxi.com
This Harrah's-owned casino hotel has been rebuilt following Hurricane Katrina and has reasonably priced guest rooms with LCD TVs, beds with pillow-top mattresses, and high-speed internet. Spa, pool, and steakhouse onsite. **$**
Hard Rock Hotel
777 Beach Boulevard, MS 39530
Tel: 228-374-ROCK
www.hardrockbiloxi.com
The hotel's premium "crash pads" feature "sleep like a rock" beds, LCD TVs, plush robes, and Aveda toiletries. It's pet friendly and there are smoking and nonsmoking rooms. There are concerts by big-name acts of yesteryear in the Hard Rock Live venue

ABOVE: a Montgomery B&B.

near the casino, low-cost country music in the Roadhouse, and free entertainment in the Hard Rock Cafe along with the signature burgers. **$**

Gulfport
Crystal Inn
9379 Canal Road, MS 39503
Tel: 228-822-9600
www.crystalinngulfport.com
This chain has attractive rooms and excellent facilities, including complimentary hot breakfast, pool, spa. It's close to Gulf beaches and casinos. **$**

Long Beach
Red Creek Inn Vineyard and Racing Stable
7416 Red Creek Road, MS 39560
Tel: 228-452-3080
www.redcreekinn.com
Fans of this lovely 1899 raised French cottage on 11 wooded acres (4.5 hectares) – the first B&B on the Mississippi Gulf Coast – will be pleased to know it survived Hurricane Katrina. The three-story inn has three main rooms: a honeymoon suite and two attic rooms – areas between rooms can be used as spillover low-cost sleeping space for parties renting main rooms. There are antiques, old-fashioned wooden radios, and porch swings throughout. **$**

Moss Point
Moss Point Oaks Bed and Breakfast
4401 Welch Street, Moss Point, MS 39563
Tel: 228-474-1367
www.mosspointoaksbb.com
This eco-friendly B&B near

Ocean Springs has two guest rooms and is in one of the oldest buildings in Moss Point surrounded by lush gardens and wildlife habitat (this is a major migratory birding area). Rooms are airy and homey with antiques and four-poster beds. **$$**

Ocean Springs
Gulf Hills Hotel and Conference Center
13701 Paso Road, MS 39564
Tel: 866-875-4211
www.gulfhillshotel.com
This elegant hideaway hotel is on an 18-hole golf course. It was the summer home of Elvis from 1951 to 1957. It has 52 beautifully calm rooms and many amenities, including in-room microwaves, fridges, coffee makers, and wireless internet. Activities include golf, tennis, and there's a large pool. Snack bar. Deluxe continental breakfast. Pet friendly. **$$**

Louisiana
Abbeville
Sunbelt Lodge
1903 Veterans Memorial Drive, LA 70510
Tel: 337-898-1453
www.sunbeltlodge.com
This budget motel has 99 standard rooms and suites offering cable TV with HBO; wheelchair-accessible rooms are available. There's free continental breakfast in the morning, but the motel is close to shops and restaurants. **$**

Baton Rouge
Hilton Baton Rouge Capitol Center
201 Lafayette Street, LA 70801
Tel: 225-3-HILTON
www.hiltoncapitolcenter.com
The former Heidelberg Hotel – a favorite haunt of Governor Huey Long – has been reborn as a sumptuous Hilton near the State Capitol. It has 290 deluxe spacious rooms and suites with ample amenities, such as LCD TVs and sitting areas. The atmospheric brick-walled

Kingfish Restaurant serves steaks and seafood. **$$**

The Stockade Bed and Breakfast
8860 Highland Road
Tel: 225-769-7358
www.thestockade.com
Named after a Union stockade that occupied the site during the Civil War, this sweet B&B is located in a designated wildlife habitat near LSU. The owner is an artist, and each of the six comfortable guest rooms is decorated with antiques and Louisiana art and has a phone, fridge, TV, and coffeemaker. Traditional Southern breakfasts include grits, biscuits, and all the fixin's or continental – your choice. **$$**

Breaux Bridge

Bayou Boudin and Cracklin
100 W. Mills Avenue, LA 70517
Tel: 337-332-6158
www.bayoucabins.com
Breaux Bridge's first B&B is a collection of 13 charming 19th-century Cajun cabins with porches overlooking Bayou Teche. Homemade Cajun treats such as boudin sausage, hogshead cheese, and sweet pecan pralines welcome guests. **$**

Eunice

The Seale Guesthouse
125 Seale Lane, LA 70535
Tel: 337-457-3753
www.angelfire.com/la2/guesthouse
This pretty guesthouse sits on 60 acres (24 hectares) of tranquil wooded grounds. It has a large wraparound porch and a reception that was once robbed by Bonnie and Clyde. The rooms are tastefully decorated with antiques in the main guesthouse and a separate two-bedroom cottage. Full continental breakfast. **$**

Lafayette

Bois des Chênes
338 N. Sterling Drive, LA 70501
Tel: 337-233-7816
www.boisdechenes.com
Isn't it a joy to travel in rural America and witness so much of the French language? Award-winning historic inn Bois des Chênes

(the Oak Wood) is a lovingly converted Civil War-era Plantation carriage house close to the city center. Its five elegant rooms have four-posters and antiques. Louisiana country breakfast served family style, and yes, the host speaks French. **$$**

Lafayette Hilton and Towers
1521 Pinhook Road, LA 70503
Tel: 337-235-6111
www.hilton.com
This full-service high-rise Hilton is in downtown Lafayette on the banks of the Vermilion River. Some of its 327 luxurious rooms and suites have views of the bayou; bathroom toiletries are by Crabtree and Evelyn. There's a pool, exercise facilities, spa, and high-end restaurant Alexander's. **$$**

New Orleans

Bourbon Orleans
717 Orleans Street, LA 70116
Tel: 504-523-2222
www.bourbonorleans.com
This small French Quarter hotel is an old-fashioned gem. Each room and suite is uniquely decorated with traditional Southern furnishings and has amenities like satellite TV, high-speed internet, and ergonomic desk chairs. It's built around a courtyard where cabanas encircle the pool. Rooms with balconies overlook Bourbon Street, but it is quieter on the courtyard side. Restaurant and lounge. **$$**

Chateau Hotel
1001 Chartres Street, LA 70116
Tel: 504-524-9636
www.chateauhotel.com
This small, tastefully furnished corner motel has a charming courtyard and 45 rooms around a pool. It's located in the residential Lower Quarter – a good choice for budget travelers. Daily continental breakfast. **$–$$**

Lafayette Hotel
600 St Charles Avenue, LA 70130
Tel: 504-524-4441
www.neworleansfinehotels/#lafayette hotel.com
A 1916 gem, the very Gallic Lafayette's 44 beautifully

understated rooms have minibars, ottomans, easy chairs, and bookshelves; suites have wet bars, fridges, and some have four-posters and jacuzzi baths. A few on St Charles Avenue open on to wrought-iron balconies – great during Carnival season. Prices are surprisingly moderate. **$$$**

Westin New Orleans Canal Place
100 Rue Iberville, LA 70130
Tel: 504-566-7006
www.starwoodhotels.com/westin
It's hard to top the views from the 29-floor Westin overlooking the Mississippi River and French Quarter. Linked to the upscale Canal Place shopping mall, the hotel reception on the 11th floor is reached via glass elevator and opens onto a lobby with panoramic vistas. The calming decor of the hotel – especially its oversized rooms – provides a welcome respite from the 24-hour action in the Vieux Carre. It's also a great place to bring a client and seal a deal as you stare serenely at the Big Muddy. Rooftop pool, gym, onsite restaurant. **$$$**

Opelousas

Country Ridge Bed and Breakfast
169 Country Ridge Road, LA 70570
Tel: 337-942-3544
This is B&B in the traditional manner: the friendly owners offer weary travelers a laid-back setting and one of four spacious, super-clean guest rooms in their modern home. Three have bathrooms and access to a jacuzzi; all have wireless internet and TVs. The landscaped pool area adjoins a thoroughbred horse farm. **$–$$**

St Martinville

The Old Castillo Hotel
220 Evangeline Boulevard, LA 70582
Tel: 337-394-4010
www.oldcastillo.com
This beautiful historic inn is in a listed building

overlooking Bayou Teche and underneath the spreading branches of the famous Evangeline Oak. It has seven rooms with period antiques and wireless internet. Hot Cajun country egg breakfasts include bacon, beignets, and pain perdu with homemade jam. **$–$$**

Texas

Alpine

The Maverick Inn
1200 E. Holland Avenue, TX 79830
Tel: 432-837-0628
www.themaverickinn.com
This renovated historic motor court motel, complete with retro neon sign, poetically bills itself as a "Roadhouse for wanderers." The 18 rooms are small but exude a handsome West Texas *machismo*, with Mexican furnishings, and postmodern desert travel necessities like LCD TVs, fridges, microwaves, and wireless internet. Beds have high-thread linens and pillowtop mattresses. The lovely pool area is a great place to hang out. **$–$$**

Austin

Austin Motel
1220 S. Congress, TX 78704
Tel: 512-441-1157
www.austinmotel.com
Family owned since 1938, this authentic Fifties motel is retro-hip, green, and central, a few blocks south of Town Lake. A variety of rooms include small singles and two-room luxury suites. Onsite Mexican restaurant is a local favorite, and there's a kidney-shaped pool, of course. Two-night minimum on Fridays and Saturdays. **$$**

Driskill Hotel
604 Brazos Street, TX 78701
Tel: 512-474-5911
www.driskillhotel.com

PRICE CATEGORIES

Price categories are based on the average cost of a double room for one night:
$ = under $110
$$ = $110–250
$$$ = more than $250

This historic downtown landmark was built in 1886 as the showplace of cattle baron Jesse Driskill. Its huge columned lobby and stained-glass ceiling alone are worth a look. The 189 airy rooms span two wings and feature upscale amenities and unique hand-tooled furniture. There are workout facilities, business center, bar, a gourmet restaurant, and café. Kid extras include cookies and milk, a deputy sheriff badge, and coloring book; pets stay for a fee and receive their own special pet bed. **$$**

Intercontinental Stephen F. Austin Hotel
701 Congress Avenue, TX 78701
Tel: 512-457-8800
www.austin.intercontinental.com
The 189 rooms and suites in this chic, early 20th-century downtown hotel have dark-wood furniture, desk, couch, and coffee table, mini bar hidden in the TV cabinet, an enormous comfy pillow-top bed with fluffy linens and acres of pillows, and a spacious marble bathroom with vanity. High-speed internet in rooms; free Wi-fi in the lobby. A substantial breakfast buffet is served in a dedicated airy café. Dinner is available in a ground-floor western bistro. The second-floor bar, overlooking Congress, is a popular rendezvous for downtown businesspeople. Famous Intercontinental service doesn't disappoint: staff are knowledgeable, discreet, and friendly. **$$**

Castroville

Landmark Inn
402 E. Florence Street, TX 78009
Tel: 830-931-2133
www.landmarkinntx.com
Originally a mail stop on the Old San Antonio Road, this atmospheric 1870 inn is located in a state historic site and is less than a half-hour from San Antonio. Five romantically furnished suites have period decor and mostly shared bathrooms. There's good bird- and butterfly-watching here. **$–$$**

Columbus

Country Hearth Columbus
2436 Highway 71S, TX 78934
Tel: 979-732-6293
www.countryhearth.com
This pleasant motel chain offers double and queen rooms with sofa beds, desks, and free wireless internet and in-room movies; some have microwaves and fridges. Eco-rooms with low-energy-usage are also available. Pool, hot breakfast included. Pet friendly. **$$**

El Paso

Camino Real Hotel
101 S. El Paso Street, TX 79901
Tel: 915-534-3000
www.caminoreal.com/elpaso
Reason enough to stop in El Paso, this handsome and sophisticated Mexican-owned border hotel has parts dating to 1912, including a simply amazing Tiffany-glass domed lobby, on a par with any of the other stately hotels you'll see on this trip. There are 359 spacious rooms and suites, a pool, sauna, and the city's best bar and restaurant. **$$**

Fredericksburg

Magnolia House
101 E. Hackberry Street, TX 78624
Tel: 830-997-0306
www.magnolia-house.com
This 1923 home is very welcoming. It has five rooms and suites, each with private bath, nice linens and towels, robes, cable TV, and wireless internet; suites have private entrances and fireplaces. Hot breakfasts are served on elegant tableware and include locally made sausage. **$$**

Galveston

Gaido's Seaside Inn
3802 Seawall Boulevard, TX 77550
Tel: 409-762-9625
www.gaidosofgalveston.com
Gaido's survived Hurricane Ike intact and everyone is glad this popular family-run inn is still in business. Many of its 104 rooms have a sea

view and there's also a tiered flower garden. The adjoining restaurant is a local favorite for authentic gumbo. **$**

Moody Gardens Hotel, Spa, and Convention Center
7 Hope Boulevard, TX 77554
Tel: 800-582-4673
www.moodygardens.com
This huge resort adjoining the popular theme park is a good family option and, since it's on the quiet, residential, northwest side of the island, received less Hurricane Ike impact than downtown locations. It has spacious, kid-friendly rooms, a big outdoor pool and "beach," a gift shop, snack shop, two restaurants, a spa and workout room, and access to Moody Gardens and a seasonal waterpark. **$$**

Hondo

Stony Ridge Ranch
326 PR 2323
Tel: 830-562-3542
www.stonyridgeranch.com
Located near popular Lost Maples State Park, this remote and special B&B offers a romantic getaway in its four newly constructed wood cabins and custom log home but does all the cooking for you with its sumptuous gourmet cooked breakfasts. Fireplaces and views of the Hill Country in each rental. Two-night minimum; closed Mon–Tue. **$$**

Houston

St Regis
1919 Briar Oaks Lane, TX 77027
Tel: 713-840-7600
www.stregis.com
Enjoy luxury accommodations, including 52 suites, located between the exclusive River Oaks neighborhood and Galleria. The Astro Floor features maître d' and butler service and interpreters. **$$$**

Sara's Bed and Breakfast Inn
941 Heights Boulevard, TX 77008
Tel: 713-868-1130
www.saras.com
This lovely Queen Anne

mansion in the heart of the city has 14 beautifully designed rooms and suites with bathrooms, TVs, phones, wireless internet, and de luxe amenities. Extended continental breakfast, with breakfast buffet on weekends. **$–$$**

The Westin Galleria
5060 W. Alabama, TX 77056
Tel: 713-960-8100
www.specialoffers.starwoodhotels.com/westingalleria
This stylish hotel is in the ritzy Galleria mall. Its superb facilities include an ice rink, pool, restaurant, and gym. **$$**

Lajitas

Lajitas Resort and Spa
HC 70, Box 400, Terlingua, TX 79852
Tel: 432-424-5000
www.lajitas.com
Luxury and backcountry living coexist at this resort in a reconstructed frontier town just west of Big Bend National Park. Ninety-two surprisingly elegant western-themed rooms and suites occupy an Old West hotel and saloon and buildings along the main street. There's also a 3-bedroom adobe house for rent. Guests enjoy a pool, barbecues, float trips on the Rio Grande, and Country and Western dancing. There's an RV park, if you're camping. **$–$$$**

Marathon

Gage Hotel
101 Highway 90 W., TX 79842
Tel: 432-386-4205
www.gagehotel.com
Built as a private lodge by rancher Alfred Gage in 1927, this charming inn, a Texas Historical Landmark, is filled with western antiques; a modern adobe building was added in the early 1990s. Twenty brick rooms with private baths encircle a lovely courtyard with fountain, hacienda style; half have kiva-style fireplaces. The original lodge has 16 rooms with basins and private or shared bathrooms. Excellent onsite restaurant. **$$**

Marfa

El Paisano Hotel
207 N.Highland, TX 79843
Tel: 866-729-3669
www.hotelpaisano.com
The hacienda-style hotel that hosted Hollywood's finest during 1955's filming of *Giant* has dined out on its reputation for decades and is starting to look a little worn, which, depending on your perspective, may only add to its charm. Movie buffs will want to book the Rock Hudson Suite, where the actor enjoyed a rooftop terrace, fireplace, kitchen, sunroom, and a king-size bed. There's a lovely pool area, standard-fare dining room, lobby gift shops, and the pleasant Greasewood Gallery, where you can see Western art that appeals to locals more than the modern art found elsewhere in Marfa. **$–$$**

New Braunfels

Gruene Mansion Inn
1275 Gruene Road, TX 78130
Tel: 830-629-2641
www.gruenemansioninn.com
This former cotton plantation home has been converted to a luxury inn with 25 antique-filled rooms scattered throughout restored barns and sheds. It overlooks Guadalupe River and is adjacent to Gruene Hall, the oldest dance hall in Texas. Breakfasts are bountiful. **$$$**

Presidio

Three Palms Inn
Old Highway 67N, TX 79845
Tel: 432-229-3211
This motor inn is a little worn these days, but Presidio is so small, it's lucky there's a motel here at all. There's a pool and cable television and a diner next door. Easy on the wallet. **$**

San Antonio

Drury Plaza Riverwalk Hotel
105 S. St Mary's Street, TX 78205
Tel: 210-270-7799
wwws.druryhotels.com
The new star of the Drury Inn and Suites chain is located in the restored 1929 Alamo National Bank Building on the Riverwalk. Guests enjoy complimentary evening cocktails and hot breakfasts overlooking the Art Deco lobby, with its marble floors and inspiring art. Roomy suites have kitchens, sitting rooms, LCD TVs, free internet, and long-distance phone. New Terrace rooms above the expanded Riverwalk (donated to the city as part of the restoration) have views but are close to the action and often noisier. **$$**

The Historic Menger Hotel
204 Alamo Plaza, TX 78205
Tel: 210-223-4361
www.mengerhotel.com
Location, location: this 1859 hotel is located adjacent to the Alamo. Rooms are elegantly furnished with antiques, and several have jacuzzis. The hotel's player piano and Menger Bar are famous. There's also a pool, fitness center, and fine-dining restaurant. **$$**

La Mansion del Río
112 College Street, TX 78205
Tel: 210-518-1000
www.omnihotels.com
The Spanish mission architecture and wrought-iron balcony rooms overlooking a quiet portion of the Riverwalk make this exceptional small hotel, a former 1852 school, a superior destination. **$$**

Terlingua

Big Bend Resort
At junction of Routes 118 and 170, TX 79852
Tel: 432-371-2218
www.foreverlodging.com
Just west of the entrance to Big Bend National Park, this concessionaire-run resort offers 86 comfortable motel rooms and duplexes with kitchen facilities in several buildings; the VIP House, a full-facility rental; and an apartment. Conference center, pool, café, and RV park and campground. **$–$$**

New Mexico

Cloudcroft

The Lodge at Cloudcroft
1 Corona Place, NM 88317
Tel: 575-682-2566
www.thelodgeresort.com
Built in 1899 during the local timber-industry boom, this quaint lodge is a cool retreat for desert dwellers. The 59 finely appointed Victorian-style lodge rooms have antiques and romantic furnishings; the Governor's Suite is a favorite haunt for Rebecca, a former employee crossed in love. Rooms in the Pavilion, the original section of the Lodge, retain its rustic feeling with Adirondack log furniture, open rooms, and full breakfast. Pool, spa, restaurant onsite. **$$**

Las Cruces

Hotel Encanto de Las Cruces
705 S. Telshor Boulevard, NM 88011
Tel: 575-522-4300
www.hotelencanto.com
This luxury hotel is near all the main attractions in Las Cruces. It has 210 rooms and suites with Spanish Colonial decor, views, and full amenities such as comfy work areas, wireless internet, and fridges and microwaves on request. Onsite pool, spa, restaurant, bar, and salon. **$–$$**

Lordsburg

Comfort Inn and Suites
400 Wabash Street, NM 88045
Tel: 575-542-3355
www.comfortinn.com
Chains rule here but this one is newer than the others and has more attractive rooms and spacious suites with sitting areas. Indoor pool, hot tub, lobby fireplace, continental breakfast room, and free internet access. Book early: it's popular with Border Patrol. **$**

Mescalero

Inn of the Mountain Gods and Casino
287 Carrizozo Canyon Road, NM 88340
Tel: 888-324-0348
www.innofthemountaingods.com
Owned by the Mescalero Apache tribe, this famous resort hotel has been rebuilt on its original location on a lake facing 12,000ft (3,660-metre) Sierra Blanca peak, sacred to the Apache. Public spaces highlight Apache artwork. The 273 luxury view rooms and suites occupy their own tower. All are spacious with workspaces and soothing decor. The resort specializes in Indian-guided hunting, fishing, and horseback riding, boating, golf, and tennis. Onsite casino, fine-dining steak and seafood restaurant. No pets. **$$**

Old Mesilla

La Meson de Mesilla
1803 Avenida de Mesilla
Tel: 575-525-9212
www.mesondemesilla.com
Stay in a lovely boutique inn in historic Mesilla that also has one of the town's best restaurants. The newly remodeled rooms have pale walls, dark wood furnishings, and French doors leading to a wraparound veranda. Onsite pool, bocce ball court, fitness center, restaurant, bar. Breakfast included. **$$**

Pinos Altos

Bear Creek Motel and Cabins
88 Main Street, NM 88053
Tel: 888-388-4515
www.bearcreekcabins.com
Just north of Silver City, on the road to Gila Cliff Dwellings, these unique split-level cabins are built around trees in the Gila National Forest. Each has a kitchen or microwave, fridge, TV, phone, fireplace or heater, air conditioning, and patio with rustic furniture and barbecue grate. Two-night minimum on weekends. **$$**

Ruidoso

Swiss Chalet Inn
1451 Mechem Drive, NM 88345
Tel: 505-258-3333

TRANSPORTATION

ACCOMMODATIONS

EATING OUT

ACTIVITIES

A – Z

www.sciruidoso.com
This Swiss-style hotel is located in a cool, pine-clad forest and has 82 rooms with panoramic views of the Sacramento Mountains. Full breakfast, pool, hot tub, onsite steakhouse, and tavern. $

Silver City
Bear Mountain Lodge
2251 Cottage San Road, NM 88061
Tel: 575-538-2538
www.bearmountainlodge.com
This famous 1920s ranch hacienda has been completely remodeled and is now run as an ecolodge by The Nature Conservancy whose Gila Preserve is nearby. Ten romantic rooms in the main lodge and adjoining building and a guesthouse have been sensitively decorated with locally sourced furniture, handmade soaps, and nature items; several have jacuzzi tubs. The lodge is famous for its healthy gourmet breakfasts, guided nature hikes and talks, and birdwatching. $$

Arizona
Bisbee
Bisbee Grand Hotel
61 Main Street, AZ 85603
Tel: 520-432-5900
www.bisbeegrandhotel.com
Elegantly restored Victorian hotel with period decor in a small southern Arizona mining town. Amenities include parking, saloon, a billiard room with the only full-size pool table in Bisbee, and a free breakfast. $-$$
The Shady Dell
1 Douglas Road, AZ 85603
Tel: 520-432-3567
Vintage aluminum travel trailers have been kitted out with period 1950s kitsch at this one-of-a-kind motel on the edge of Bisbee. Old-style radios play big-band tunes and early rock 'n roll, and trailers have original working kitchens right down to the electric percolators. Dot's Diner on site serves breakfast and lunch. Great fun for overnight or weekly rentals. $

Gila Bend
Best Western Space Age Lodge
401 E. Pima Street, PO Box C, NM 85337
Tel: 928-683-2273
www.bestwesternspaceagelodge.com
The Space Age Lodge is like no other Best Western you've ever seen, the bedrooms having pictures from NASA on the walls and of course space-age lighting. There are even military aircraft in the public areas, alongside more conventional amenities like a pool and heated spa (see page 310). $-$$

Phoenix
Arizona Biltmore
2400 E. Missouri Avenue, AZ 85016
Tel: 602-955-6600
www.arizonabiltmore.com
An elegant grand hotel designed by Frank Lloyd Wright in landscaped grounds. Pools, fitness room, golf courses, biking, restaurants, bars, shops. $$$
Maricopa Manor
15 W. Pasadena Avenue, AZ 85013
Tel: 602-274-6302
www.maricopamanor.com
Spanish-style home built in the 1920s furnished with antiques and art and having just seven suites. All rooms are suites. Amenities include a pool with waterfalls, spa, and beautiful lush gardens. $$$

Scottsdale
The Phoenician
6000 E. Camelback Road, AZ 85251
Tel: 480-941-8200
www.thephoenician.com
The Phoenician is one of Scottsdale's premier resorts, set in 250 acres (100 hectares) and with no fewer than 10 restaurants and lounges to choose from, a spa, championship golf course, and numerous awards to its credit. $$$

Tombstone
Tombstone Motel
502 E. Fremont Street, AZ 85638
Tel: 520-457-3478
www.tombstonemotel.net

Clean, well-fitted rooms in historic 1880s building, a stay at the Tombstone Motel really lets you enter into the old western spirit of the town itself. $-$$

Tucson
Arizona Inn
2200 E. Elm Street, AZ 85719
Tel: 520-325-1541
www.arizonainn.com
A true hidden oasis in Tucson's desert landscape is the 14 acres (5 hectares) of gardens, fountains, and palms that surround this historic, luxury inn. Set in a quiet residential area, it's very central, when many of the other quality hotels in Tucson are on the outskirts. The casita-style rooms and suites are beautifully decorated and have writing desks, large private patios, wet bars, and many other features. There's a fabulous pool, and the restaurant is rated as one of the city's best. $$-$$$
Hotel Congress
311 E. Congress, AZ 85701
Tel: 520 622-8848
www.hotelcongress.com
Tucson's Hotel Congress is so historic that John Dillinger and his gang once stayed here. It's both idiosyncratic and inexpensive, with its own café and a music club that's been voted one of the 10 best rock clubs in the US. $$
Lodge on the Desert
306 N. Alvernon Way, AZ 85711
Tel: 520-320-2000
www.lodgeonthedesert.com
This in-town resort was first opened in 1936 and in summer 2009 received a massive make-over that has ensured it remains one of the top places to stay in the city. Most rooms have red-tiled patios and fireplaces, and facilities include a spa, pool, and outdoor hot-tubs. Its restaurant highlighting Southwest cuisine is recognized as one of the best in Tucson. $$-$$$

Yuma
Best Western Coronado Motor Hotel
233 S. 4th Avenue, AZ 85364
Tel: 928-783-4453
http://bwcoronado.com
One of the first Best Western hotels and the oldest still operating, the Coronado has comfortable rooms set around a flower-filled court. Still run by the same family, it has an atmosphere and charm all its own with a fascinating museum in the original reception building which doubled as the family's home. Rooms in one wing retain their 1950s-style furniture and there is a modern annex across the street. Features include a pool, great breakfast, free internet, and a vast free movie library. $-$$
La Fuente Inn and Suites
1513 E. 16th Street, AZ 85365
Tel: 928-329-1814
www.lafuenteinn.com
This contemporary inn has nicely landscaped gardens with fruit trees and flowers all surrounding a large pool. Other amenities include a fitness room, laundry, four BBQs, and a complimentary airport shuttle service. $$-$$$
Yuma Cabana Hotel
2151 S. Fourth Avenue, AZ 85364
Tel: 928-783-8311
www.yumacabana.com
The Cabana is an attractive little oasis with a quirky charm, due to the independent nature of the operation. It's very good value, relaxed, and the staff obviously enjoy working there. $-$$

California
Jacumba
Jacumba Hot Springs Spa
44500 Old Highway 80, CA 91934
Tel: 619-766-4525
www.jacumbasprings.com
Relaxing natural hot springs, pools, and private jacuzzis. All suites also have their own private patio area and jacuzzis. In addition there's a very good restaurant serving international dishes, and a beer and wine bar too. $$

California

Arcata

Fairwinds Motel
1674 G Street, CA 95521
Tel: 707-822-4824
www.fairwindsmotelarcata.com
The Fairwinds Motel is a basic and clean motel right by the highway and in the heart of Redwoods Country. Facilities include free wireless internet, and it's just a short walk to Arcata Square and to the Arcata campus. **$$**

Big Sur

Big Sur Lodge
47225 Highway One, Big Sur, CA 93920
Tel: 831-667-3110
www.bigsurlodge.com
Big Sur architect Mickey Muenning used the sea and the mountains as a backdrop to this lush resort, which is right in among the magnificent redwoods. At this lodge you will *not* find amenities like phones, TVs, or alarm clocks. **$$$**

Bodega Bay

Bodega Bay Lodge and Spa
103 Coast Highway One, CA 94923
Tel: 707-875-3525
www.bodegabaylodge.com
The Inn is in an idyllic location with all rooms having balconies that look out across marshland towards the sea, with birds, frogs, and other wildlife all around. Rooms are spacious and romantic, with fireplaces. Lovely gardens lead to the fitness center and ocean-view pool. **$$–$$$**

Cambria

Pelican Cove Inn
6316 Moonstone Beach Drive, CA 93428
Tel: 805-927-1500
www.moonstonehotels.com
Just across the road from the beach with its seal rocks and pathways, the Pelican Cove is a few minutes outside the center of the lovely little town of Cambria. Rooms are spacious and elegantly furnished. Most have ocean views of some

kind. Guests are treated to a substantial cooked breakfast, afternoon wine and tea, and dessert and coffee in the evenings. There is a pool and gardens. **$$–$$$**

Carmel-by-the-Sea

Cypress Inn
Lincoln & 7th, CA 93921
Tel: 831-624-3871
www.cypress-inn.com
Renowned for being co-owned by Hollywood legend Doris Day, who is also a great animal lover, the Cypress Inn is one of the most dog-friendly hotels on the Pacific Coast. Day's movie memorabilia lines the corridors, with some fun old film posters, and the Inn manages to be both chic and relaxed, with comfortable rooms and an excellent bar that's as popular with locals as with hotel guests. Downtown restaurants are a short walk away. **$$–$$$**

Vagabond's House Inn
4th & Dolores, CA 93921
Tel: 831-624-7738
www.vagabondshouseinn.com
The Vagabond Inn's 13 rooms, which are like luxury versions of rustic cabins, are grouped around a lovely, lush courtyard, where a waterfall plays day and night, a lovely sound to go to sleep to. The stylish rooms have king beds and cozy fires, and the complimentary breakfast is brought to your room. It's in a very quiet part of Carmel but only a short stroll to the town centre. **$$–$$$**

Eureka

Carter House Inn
301 L Street, CA 95501
Tel: 707-444-8062
www.carterhouse.com
The Carter House Inn is a collection of four romantic Victorian town houses on the edge of Eureka's historical district and a block back from the sea front. The Hotel Carter also contains the acclaimed Restaurant 301 *(see page*

435), where guests also enjoy the complimentary and very tasty breakfasts. Rooms are spacious and successfully combine style with period charm, and with all modern comforts too. Bell Cottage and Carter Cottage are exquisitely decorated private retreats. **$$–$$$**

Ferndale

Victorian Village Inn
400 Ocean Avenue, CA 95536
Tel: 707-786-4949
www.victorianvillageinn.com
This impressive inn was actually built from the local redwoods in 1890, and its Victorian style ensures high-ceilinged rooms that are filled with antique decor. The Village Inn also has its own on-site restaurant and bar. **$$**

La Jolla

The Lodge at Torrey Pines
11480 N. Torrey Pines Road, CA 92037
Tel: 858-453-4420
www.lodgetorreypines.com
The Lodge is a luxury retreat overlooking the Pacific Ocean and right next to the championship golf course at Torrey Pines. It has its own spa, swimming pool, and fine-dining restaurant. **$$$**

Laguna Beach

Casa Laguna Inn and Spa
2510 S. Coast Highway, CA 92651
Tel: 800-233-0449
www.casalaguna.com
Right on the Pacific Coast Highway, the Casa Laguna is a luxury mission-style inn with just 16 rooms, giving it an intimate and friendly feel. Some of the buildings used to be artists' studios, and the abundant greenery hides a pool, while inside there's a small spa and business center, free wine tastings, and a delicious gourmet breakfast. **$$–$$$**

Hotel Laguna
425 S. Coast Highway, CA 92651
Tel: 800-524-2927
www.hotellaguna.com

The Hotel Laguna is right on the beach and many of its 65 guest rooms have a view of either the ocean or the gardens. There is a complimentary newspaper and continental breakfast, and a choice of restaurants. **$$–$$$**

Mendocino

Stanford Inn by the Sea
Coast Highway and Comptche Ukiah Road, CA 95460
Tel: 707-937-5615
www.stanfordinn.com
At this peaceful and unique retreat, you can be indulgent and environmentally conscious at the same time. Pine and redwood paneling and wood fires are a rustic backdrop to the comfortable rooms, which look out over organic gardens towards Mendocino Bay from private balconies. There's a cozy lodge and bar, and an inviting heated covered pool, yoga sessions, and spa service. **$$$**

Montecito

Montecito Inn
1295 Coast Village Road, CA 93108
Tel: 805-969-7854
www.montecitoinn.com
On the edge of Santa Barbara and just two blocks from Butterfly Beach, but also with its own pool, spa, sauna, business centre, massage service, and exercise room. Some rooms have their own jacuzzi tubs

PRICE CATEGORIES

Price categories are based on the average cost of a double room for one night:
$ = under $110
$$ = $110–250
$$$ = more than $250

and some also have mountain views. **$$$**

San Ysidro Ranch
900 San Ysidro Lane, CA 93108
Tel: 805-969-5046
www.sanysidroranch.com
This is a truly special rural hideaway, which is why so many celebrities have sought some privacy there (see page 340). It has a fitness centre, a pool heated year-round, in-room massage services, yoga lessons, and 17 miles (27km) of hiking trails in the Santa Ynez Mountains from the front door. **$$$**

Monterey

Hotel Pacific
300 Pacific Street, CA 93940
Tel: 831-373-5700
www.hotelpacific.com
The Pacific is a luxury boutique hotel very close to Cannery Row, Fisherman's Wharf, and other Monterey attractions. The 105 guest rooms are all classified as suites, some being designated Romantic Fireplace Rooms. **$$–$$$**

Monterey Plaza Hotel and Spa
400 Cannery Row, CA 93940
Tel: 831-646-1700
http://montereyplazahotel.com
One of the largest and best hotels in Monterey, right in the heart of town on Cannery Row and overlooking Monterey Bay. It has its own spa, and a choice of bistro, grill or café dining. **$$–$$$**

Morro Bay

Embarcadero Inn
456 Embarcadero Street, CA 93442
Tel: 888-223-5777
www.embarcaderoinn.com
This peaceful inn features luxury rooms with private balconies, fireplaces, and attentive service. A good base for relaxing or touring local attractions. All rooms have bay view and some have hot tubs. **$$$**

Napa Valley

1801 First
1801 First Street, Napa, CA 94559
Tel: 800-518-0146
www.1801first.com

This luxury B&B inn is an indulgent treat, located right in Napa Town itself. The architect-designed interior is cool and contemporary, yet it fits right into the classic details of this Victorian house built in 1903. Suites have fireplaces, canopies, and other romantic touches, and there are private cottages in the lush garden. Modern comforts include free wine and hors d'oeuvres in the afternoon, and three-course breakfasts to set you up for a hard day's wine-tasting in Napa Valley. **$$$**

Wine Country Inn
152 Lodi Lane, St.Helena, CA 94574
Tel: 707-963-7077
www.winecountryinn.com
This gorgeous inn epitomizes Napa Valley's relaxed air of chic, with a friendly complimentary wine tasting in the afternoons and views over the neighboring vineyards. In addition to the luxurious guest rooms, several cottages offer the ultimate in privacy and pampering, with whirlpool baths beneath stained-glass windows, king-size beds, fireplaces, and patios. The Inn also has an outdoor pool and a hot tub, and superb fresh-cooked breakfasts. **$$–$$$**

Novato

Inn Marin
250 Entrada Drive, CA 94949
Tel: 415-883-5952
www.innmarin.com
There's a Southwestern feel to the rooms at the Inn Marin, which are decorated in warm reds and deep yellow colors. The bamboo coverlets and floors fit both with the hotel's design, and with its eco-friendly ethos. The 70 rooms and 4 suites border lovely spacious grounds with magnolia trees. Amenities include a swimming pool, complimentary Wi-fi and continental breakfast. Rickey's Restaurant (see page 435) is a must, with live jazz sessions at the weekend. **$$–$$$**

Pismo Beach

Spyglass Inn
2705 Spyglass Drive, CA 93449
Tel:805-773-4855
www.spyglassinn.com
Stylishly refurbished with panoramic ocean view, dining room, and lounge, the Spyglass Inn is dramatically situated on the cliffs near Pismo Beach, and has its own spa and pool too. **$$$**

Redondo Beach

Portofino Hotel & Yacht Club
260 Portofino Way, CA 90277
Tel: 310-379-8481
www.hotelportofino.com
Located on a private peninsula close to Redondo Beach, the Portofino Hotel and Yacht Club has its own pool, restaurant, views over the marina, and access to Gold's Gym nearby. **$$–$$$**

San Diego

Hotel del Coronado
1500 Orange Avenue, Coronado, CA 92118
Tel: 619-435-6611
www.hoteldel.com
World-famous Victorian-era landmark. As well as being a tourist attraction in its own right, the Coronado is also an exceptional hotel with its own tennis court, pool, spa, beachside cottages and villas, with nearby golf and boating. **$$$**

Sé San Diego
1047 Fifth Avenue, CA 92101
Tel: 619-515-3000
www.sesandiego.com
The chicest new hotel in the city, Sé San Diego oozes designer style and luxury. Upper-floor rooms have a grand view over the city at night. Guests enjoy a personal welcome rather than a check-in, and a hotel tour to show off its every impressive feature like the Sé Spa, the cool bar, the loanable laptops, or the Suite and Tender restaurant. **$$$**

U.S. Grant Hotel
326 Broadway, CA 92101
Tel: 866-837-4270
www.usgrant.net
Restored, grand old historic hotel dating back to 1910 and in the heart of the business, shopping, and

nightlife areas downtown. In keeping with the name, there are no less than two Presidential suites, and all rooms have marble bathrooms with stone sinks. Even if you don't stay here, you can eat at the Grant Grill, which is also a San Diego landmark. **$$–$$$**

San Francisco

The Archbishop's Mansion
1000 Fulton Street, CA 94117
Tel: 415-563-7872
http://thearchbishopsmansion.com
Exquisite French-style chateau/mansion in Alamo Square, built in 1904 for the Archbishop of San Francisco. An historical landmark, it closed for major renovations and reopened recently having had a major face-lift. **$$$**

Hotel Boheme
444 Columbus Avenue, CA 94133
Tel: 415-433-9111
www.hotelboheme.com
An abundance of bohemian charm and bags of history. Wonderful black-and-white photographs line the hallway. **$$**

Hotel Vertigo
940 Sutter Street, CA 94109
Tel: 415-885-6800
www.hotelvertigosf.com
The setting for the Hitchcock movie Vertigo is both sophisticated and comfortable. The Plush Room Theater, which was once a Prohibition-era speakeasy now known for its cabaret, is also located here. **$$–$$$**

Red Victorian Bed, Breakfast and Art
1665 Haight Street, CA 94117
Tel: 415-864-1978
www.redvic.com
Perfect for the budget traveler. Friendly and casual with each room reflecting a different theme, like the Flower Child Room, and there's also a Peace Café showing that the Summer of Love is not yet dead in some parts of San Francisco. **$$–$$$**

San Luis Obispo

Madonna Inn
100 Madonna Road, CA 93405
Tel: 800-543-9666
www.madonnainn.com

Well known for its eccentricity and bizarre decor, the Madonna Inn's 110 rooms are all totally different and have themes including Western, Hawaiian, Austrian, and even Safari and Sir Walter Raleigh! **$$–$$$**

Santa Barbara

The Cheshire Cat
36 W. Valerio Street, CA 93101
Tel: 805-569-1610
www.cheshirecat.com
This restored Victorian home offers a relaxed and pampered stay in the heart of Santa Barbara. Rooms are named after characters from *Alice in Wonderland*, including the Mad Hatter and the Queen of Hearts, and some have patios and in-room jacuzzis. **$$–$$$**

Franciscan Inn
109 Bath Street, CA 93101
Tel: 805-963-8845
www.franciscaninn.com
The tiled roofs and white walls give a Spanish-mission look to this 1920s collection of buildings in a quiet part of Santa Barbara but only one block from the beach. Rooms are comfortable and spacious, and there's a heated pool open year-round, free internet and video library, fresh-baked cookies and a freshly made continental breakfast – all welcome extras for a very reasonable price. **$$**

Santa Monica

The Embassy
1001 Third Street, CA 90403
Tel: 310-394-1279
www.embassyhotelapts.com
The Embassy Hotel Apartments have been in business since 1927 and the beautiful Mediterranean-style buildings sit among a lush garden where hummingbirds hover to greet arriving guests. The rooms are huge and have a kind of homely grandeur to them, with period furniture and kitchen facilities as there's no breakfast, but there are plenty of eating options nearby on the Third Street Promenade. **$$**

Sonoma

The Fairmont Sonoma Mission Inn and Spa
18140 Sonoma Highway, CA 95476
Tel: 707-938-9000
www.fairmont.com/sonoma
Pricey European-style spa in the heart of the wine country. Romantic rooms and suites with marbled baths and plantation shutters. Acclaimed fine dining and attentive service. **$$$**

Oregon

Astoria

Clementine's Bed and Breakfast
847 Exchange Street, OR 97103
Tel: 503-325-2005
www.clementines-bb.com
A classic Italianate Victorian building with pretty English cottage gardens and a small library. The inn has five rooms with queen-sized beds, private bathrooms. One room has a gas fireplace. **$–$$**

Cannon Beach

Ocean Lodge
2864 S. Pacific Street, OR 97110
Tel: 541-347-9441
www.theoceanlodge.com
This romantic lodge is tucked away in a quiet corner of Cannon Beach, right on the beach itself with views of the town's famous Haystack Rock from your private deck. It's a modern creation but modelled on 1940s-style rustic lodging, with all today's luxuries included in the lovely rooms, like a vast, free DVD library and wide-screen TVs, free internet, fireplaces, and jacuzzis in many of them too. An indulgent treat, right down to the homemade cookies in the lobby. **$$–$$$**

Gold Beach

Tu Tu' Tun Lodge
96550 N. Bank Rogue River Road, OR 97444
Tel: 541-247-6664
www.tututun.com
A few miles inland from Gold Beach on the banks of the Rogue River, this beautiful lodge has luxurious rooms,

an acclaimed restaurant, a sociable atmosphere, and opportunities for hiking, fishing, kayaking, golfing, or doing nothing but watching ospreys and bald eagles from your balcony. All rooms have relaxing river views, and some have fireplaces and an outdoor soaking tub. **$$–$$$**

North Bend

The Mill Casino Hotel and RV Park
3201 Tremont Avenue, OR 97459
Tel: 541-756-8800
www.themillcasino.com
The Mill is a former lumber mill that has been wonderfully converted into a hotel and casino by the local Native American tribe, the Coquille, whose tribal art can be seen in the gift shop. There are panoramic views of Coos Bay from every well-appointed suite; corner suites in the tower have huge baths with whirlpool tubs. The hotel has a fitness room, indoor pool and two outdoor spas, a business center, and several bars and restaurants in the casino. **$–$$**

Portland

The Benson Hotel
309 SW Broadway, OR 97205
Tel: 503-228-2000
www.bensonhotel.com
The Benson is a historic hotel, built in 1912, in the heart of Downtown and close to the Pearl District. There's a fitness center and a business center, and their London Grill is a full-service restaurant whose wine cellar has won a Wine Spectator Award of Excellence. **$$$**

Mark Spencer Hotel
409 SW 11th Avenue, OR 97205
Tel: 503-224-3293
www.markspencer.com
The Mark Spencer dates back to 1907 when it was opened in the Theater District, and it still attracts a lot of visiting actors and artists today. Guests have a complimentary continental breakfast, and a copy of the *New York Times* to read with it. **$–$$**

Rockaway Beach

101 Motel
530 Hwy 101, OR 97136
Tel: 503-355-2420
Well-fitted, good-value motel rooms with nice views, fireplaces, kitchens, and cable television. Hot tub. Wheelchair accessible. **$–$$**

Yachats

Overleaf Lodge
280 Overleaf Lodge Lane, OR 97498
Tel: 541-547-4880
www.overleaflodge.com
This relaxing lodge and spa is right on the beach a few minutes from the center of this appealing little town, one of the Oregon Coast's hidden gems. A variety of room styles feature fireplaces, whirlpool tubs, patios or balconies and big picture windows overlooking the sea. Outside the spacious lobby lounge you can walk out along the coastal footpath and enjoy the sandy bays and rock pools, while at night the sound of the pounding surf lulls you to sleep. **$$–$$$**

Washington

Grayland

Walsh Motel
1593 State Route 105, WA 98595
Tel: 360-267-2191
http://westport-walshmotel.com
This attractive little motel has 12 conventional motel units and a further 12 beachside units, some with fireplaces and jacuzzis, some with kitchens. **$$–$$$**

Raymond

Maunu's Mountcastle Motel
524 Third Street, WA 98577
Tel: 360-942-5571
Spotless rooms, some with microwaves and refrigerators, and right in the centre of Raymond. **$**

PRICE CATEGORIES

Price categories are based on the average cost of a double room for one night:
$ = under $110
$$ = $110–250
$$$ = more than $250

E ATING OUT

RECOMMENDED RESTAURANTS, CAFÉS, AND BARS

WHERE AND WHAT TO EAT

All-American

All-American (really German) mainstays like hot dogs and burgers and pretzels are associated with ballparks and corner stands like those found in New York. In Chicago, Polish-style sausages and Italian deep-dish pizza are local favorites. In Philadelphia, Philly Cheese Steaks explode out of hoagie rolls while in New Orleans, enormous muffaletta sandwiches, crammed with Italian sliced meats, olives, and dressing, are a specialty at Johnny's in the French Quarter.

Barbecue

Slow-cooked barbecue leans heavily on pork in the South and East but, invariably, beef in the West. Each region has its own style and fan base. You'll find aged beef with a smokey tomato sauce in Texas and vinegar-based sauces in the South: Memphis, Tennessee, famous for its barbecue, offers both wet and dry versions.

Coastal America

Coastal America is a haven for fresh seafood – from lobster and clams in New England and grouper on the Gulf to snapper in California and Dungeness crab and salmon in the Pacific Northwest. Inland mountain lakes, rivers, and streams in the Rockies and the Cascades and the Mississippi Delta support rainbow trout, striped bass, catfish, and

ABOVE: a Philly steak sandwich.

numerous other delicate freshwater fish.

The Pacific Coast's huge Asian population has led to a lighter fusion cuisine from California to Washington, combining traditional meat and fish with Chinese, Japanese, Vietnamese, and Thai flavors that linger in the mouth.

Southern Food

Southern food, while playing up deep-fried chicken, boiled ham, collard greens, hush puppies, grits, pecan and sweet potato pie, and other "po' folks" foods, has a fusion all its own. The region's Latin, Afro-Caribbean, and French roots are major influences, with the latter's rich Continental-style cuisine as the main fine-dining option.

Rich meets spicy in New Orleans, with its complex gumbo stews and smothered Cajun dishes like crawfish etoufée, and in Florida, where Floribbean cuisine – a sometimes-cloying combination of fresh fish,

coconut and nuts, cream sauces, tropical fruit, and fragrant spices – has many fans.

Mexican and Southwestern

Mexican food is ubiquitous, sometimes reaching gourmet heights. Typically, though, corn, beans, and squash are used to make corn tortillas, tamales, tacos, burritos, enchiladas, and other cheap dishes spiced with chili.

Huge cattle ranches along the border, particularly in Arizona and Texas, have led to spicy ranch-style Norteño cuisine. In Cowboy Country, blow-out steak dinners are accompanied by the fixings – baked potatoes, sweetcorn, and coleslaw.

Out West, look for delicious, low-fat, grass-fed bison, venison, elk, and other game accompanied by wild greens, pinyon nuts, and wild berries, mainstays of Native American cuisine that have a growing following.

Road Food

Road food is a subject unto itself. Never pass up a slice of homemade pie made from local fruit in farm states like Arizona, Georgia, and Washington; backwoods barbecue, fried green tomatoes, and boiled peanuts in the South; and filled pastries called kalaches in Texas Hill Country. Lastly, when you're traveling hundreds of miles a day, the most important meal of the day is breakfast. Even the lowliest truck stop or diner can fuel you properly for your travels with pancakes, waffles, chicken-fried steak, and creative egg dishes for under $10. Reason enough to get up in the morning.

ATLANTIC ROUTE

New York

New York City

Carnegie Deli
854 Seventh Avenue at 55th Street
Tel: 757-2245
A pilgrimage site in the heart of Midtown, this is one of New York's most famous Jewish delicatessens, where the corned beef sandwich is a must. No credit cards. **$$**

Excellent Dumpling House
111 Lafayette (just below Canal St)
Tel: 219-0212
Unpretentious, unadorned and on the outskirts of Chinatown proper; always packed with locals and devoted visitors who love its no-nonsense atmosphere, reasonable prices, and stellar dumplings (especially the vegetable dumplings, steamed or fried). No reservations, but there's sometimes a short wait; best for mid-afternoon lunch. No credit cards. **$$**

Oyster Bar
Lower level, Grand Central Terminal
Tel: 490-6650
A New York institution and a must for seafood lovers. The best fresh oysters and clam chowder in town, and you can sit at a counter, dining room or salon. **$$-$$$**

San Domenico
240 Central Park S.
Tel: 265-5959
One of the most highly rated Italian restaurants in the city, this Central Park South establishment offers unusual Bolognese fare, with a wide variety of Northern Italian pastas and an extremely large wine list. A fine place to take a big party, but not necessarily for an intimate romantic meal. Reservations required. **$$$**

Totonno's Napolitano Pizzeria
1524 Neptune Avenue, Brooklyn
Tel: 718-372-8606
Totonno's freshly baked brick-oven pizzas may well be the finest in the five boroughs. **$**

Union Square Café
21 E. 16th Street
Tel: 243-4020
Possibly the friendliest service in New York and some of the best new-American cuisine anywhere. Reservations are difficult as this very popular restaurant's innovative menu attracts a hip crowd. Definitely call ahead. **$$$**

New Jersey

Trenton

Mastoris Diner-Restaurant
144 Highway 130, Bordentown
Tel: 609-298-4650
Excellent prime rib and an impressive 77 varieties of sandwiches. For dessert choose from the many pies baked on the gigantic premises. **$**

Sal De Forte's Ristorante
200 Fulton Street
Tel: 609-396-6856
Romantic Italian – a little bit northern, a little bit southern – located in a century-old building with a Victorian floral-style dining room and wood-paneled bar. **$$**

Pennsylvania

Lancaster

Olde Greenfield Inn
595 Greenfield Road
Tel: 717-393-0668
www.theoldegreenfieldinn.com
Interesting, carefully prepared international seafood, poultry, steak, and pasta in a historic farmhouse just outside of town. **$$**

Philadelphia

La Famiglia
8 S. Front Street
Tel: 215-922-2803
An Old City favorite for high-class Italian food in a lovely formal setting. **$$$**

Le Bec-Fin
1523 Walnut Street
Tel: 215-567-1000
Regarded as one of the finest restaurants in the country, this very expensive French favorite near Rittenhouse Square garners rave reviews from critics and clients alike. Reservations required. A la carte menu served at the downstairs bistro. **$$$**

Jim's Steaks
400 S. Street
Tel: 215-928-1911
Many cheese-steak connoisseurs consider this funky little place the tastiest in town. **$**

Joe's Peking Duck House
925 Race Street
Tel: 215-922-3277
Many think this Chinatown standard, with non-existent decor and crowded ambiance, serves the best Chinese food in town. **$$**

Maryland

Annapolis

Carrol's Creek Restaurant
410 Severn Avenue
Tel: 410-263-8102
Critically acclaimed waterfront restaurant with fabulous views. **$$$**

Baltimore

4 West
4 W. University Parkway, Doubletree Inn at the Colonnade
Tel: 410-235-8200
A favourite with the business travelers looking for dependable fine dining. A raw bar offers a fresh selection of seafood. **$$**

Ixia
518 N. Charles Street
Tel: 410-727-1800
Baltimore's fresh seafood gets dressed up with a contemporary Asian flare. **$$$**

Obrycki's Crab House
1727 E. Pratt Street
Tel: 410-732-6399
Rich, well-flavored seafood dishes. Super-fresh Chesapeake Bay crab is often the star of the show. **$$**

Woman's Industrial Exchange
333 N. Charles Street
Tel: 410-685-4388
Well-prepared American home-style cooking. Wonderful egg and bacon breakfasts accompanied by fat clouds of "scratch" biscuits. For lunch try the well-seasoned crab cakes or an old-fashioned chicken salad. Welcoming atmosphere. **$$**

Virginia

Charlottesville

Blue Bird Café
625 W. Main Street
Tel: 434-295-1166
Appetizing lunches featuring steaks, fried chicken, and crab cakes. **$$**

C&O Restaurant
515 E. Water Street
Tel: 434-971-7044
Imaginative dishes with a French influence served in an attractively converted rail workers' layover. Try the sliced, marinated, and seared flank steak. Elegant but casual atmosphere. **$$**

Millers
109 W. Main Street
Tel: 434-971-8511
An old-style and pleasantly smoky atmosphere bar. Formerly a drugstore specializing in "Miller's Tonic" in the early 1900s. The current Millers dispenses great cheese-burgers and a nice grilled chicken salad. Sit on the outdoor patio with bubbling fountain and listen to live jazz. **$**

PRICE CATEGORIES

Price categories are for an average cost of dinner and a glass of wine, before tip:
$ = under $20
$$ = $20–40
$$$ = more than $40

Fredericksburg
Kenmore Inn
1200 Princess Anne Street
Tel: 540-371-7622
Good steak and seafood
restaurant with live
entertainment. **$$**

Lexington
Virginia House
722 S. Main Street, VA 24450
Tel: 540-463-3643
Mouthwatering Southern
cooking. **$**

Richmond
Bill's Barbecue
3100 N. Boulevard
Tel: 804-358-8634
Bill's is justly popular for
lavish portions of succulent
barbecue and excellent
breakfasts. **$**
Millie's Diner
2603 E. Main
Tel: 804-643-5512
Excellent New Southern
cooking in a remodeled
traditional diner. **$$**
The Tobacco Company
1201 E. Cary Street
Tel: 804-782-9555
www.thetobaccocompany.com
This restaurant features
creative New American
cuisine in a converted
tobacco warehouse. **$$**

Roanoke
Awful Arthur's
2229 Colonial Avenue SW
Tel: 540-777-0007
Much-loved seafood
restaurant, part of a chain,
in an attractive historic
location. Entrees include
steamed crab, oysters,
clams, and fresh fish. **$**
Roanoker
2522 Colonial Avenue
Tel: 540-344-7746
Short on atmosphere but
long on portions of delicious
Southern cooking. A wide
array of well-prepared
vegetable side dishes, rich
gravies, and other good
trimmings. **$**

North Carolina
Chapel Hill
Spanky's
101 E. Franklin Street
Tel: 919-967-2678
Buzzing restaurant serving
sandwiches, seafood, and

pasta. Spanky's club
sandwich is a favorite with
both locals and visitors. **$**

Mount Airy
Snappy Lunch
125 N. Main Street
Tel: 336-786-4931
The Snappy Lunch is known
for its hefty pork chop
sandwich – a cornucopia of
juicy meat, condiments, and
trimmings. Plenty of
atmosphere too. **$**

Wilmington
Elijah's Restaurant
2 Ann Street
Tel: 910-343-1448
Award-winning seafood
chowder and other
delectable, equally
praiseworthy dishes. The
adjoining oyster bar with
outdoor covered patio faces
onto Cape Fear. **$$**

Winston-Salem
Village Tavern
221 Reynolda Village
Tel: 336-748-0221
Popular family restaurant
offering pub-style food and
lively atmosphere. **$$**

South Carolina
Charleston
Cru Café
18 Pinckney Street
Tel: 843-534-2434
An imaginative menu
featuring fresh, well-cooked
seafood combined with a
pleasant terrace, relaxed
atmosphere, fragrant
coffees, and irresistible
desserts justify its
popularity. **$**

Georgetown
Pink Magnolia
719 Front Street
Tel: 843-527-6506
Fresh seafood salads,
creole, and crab cakes
served at your table right
on the harbor walk or
indoors. The non-seafood
specialty is a fried chicken
salad. **$$**

Jacksonboro
Edisto Motel Cafe
US Highway 17
Tel: 843-893-2270
Luscious fried seafood in a

casual setting. No credit
cards. **$$**

Myrtle Beach
**Omega Pancake and
Omelet House**
2800 N. Kings Highway
Tel: 843-626-9949
Favorite breakfast spot for
tourists and locals alike. **$**

Georgia
Brunswick
GA Pig
Exit 29 off I-95
Tel: 912-264-6664
Expertly prepared barbecue
dished up in pleasant
surroundings. A mighty fine
pit stop. **$**

Midway
**Ida Mae and Joe's North
Midway Restaurant**
US Highway 17
Tel: 912-884-3388
Very fresh, expertly fried
fish. **$**

St Simons Island
Dressner's Village Cafe
223 Mallory Street
Tel: 912-634-1217
A good choice for breakfast.
$

Savannah
The Chart House
202 W. Bay Street
Tel: 912-234-6686
Reserve a table and order
the prime rib in this three-
story nautical-themed
restored warehouse. **$$**
Downtown Cafe at Main
1 W. Broughton Street
Tel: 912-233-9666
A touch of seafood
enhances this mostly Italian
menu. Good location and a
wine list straight from the
Sonoma Valley. **$$$**
**Mrs Wilkes' Boarding
House**
107 W. Jones Street
Tel: 912-232-5997
Southern-style communal
dining, the old boarding
house way. Pass the biscuits
and fried chicken, and get
there early. Lunch only. **$**
The Pirates' House
20 E. Broad and Bay streets
Tel: 912-233-5757
Seafood galore at this
Savannah landmark. **$$$**

Florida
Bradenton
**Crab Trap and
Crab Trap II**
4815 Memphis Road, Ellenton
Tel: 941-729-7777
Highway 19, Palmetto
Tel: 941-722-6255
www.leescrabtrap.com
A local favorite for fine
fresh-catch and game
dishes. **$$**
Sandbar Restaurant
100 Spring Avenue, Anna Maria
Tel: 941-778-0444
www.sandbar-restaurant.com
Good food and excellent
views. **$$**

Clearwater Beach
**Kaiko Sushi Bar &
Japanese Restaurant**
2475 McMullen Booth Road
Tel: 727-791-6640
www.kaikosushibar.com
First-rate sashimi, sushi
and teriyaki. **$$**

Fort Myers
The Veranda
2122 Second Street
Tel: 239-332-2065
www.verandarestaurant.com
Continental cuisine served
in a mellow old mansion
with pleasant courtyard. Try
the rack of lamb. Mellow
atmosphere and steep
prices. **$$$**

Gainesville
Ti Amo!
12 SE Second Avenue
Tel: 352-378-6307
www.tiamogainesville.com
Fine Mediterranean dining
in a posh 19th-century
carriage house. **$$$**

Jacksonville
Matthew's
2107 Hendricks Avenue
Tel: 904-396-9922
www.matthewsrestaurant.com
Spare and stylish interior
with a top-notch wine cel-
lar. The five-course tasting
menu is an good intro-
duction to this innovative,
and varied menu. **$$$**

Key Largo
Crack'd Conch
105045 Overseas Highway
Tel: 305-451-0732
www.keysconch.com

A sublimely relaxed venue for soaking up a few beers with the local atmosphere and tucking into a heaped plateful of fried conch. **$**

Key West

Blue Heaven
729 Thomas Street
Tel: 305-296-8666
www.blueheavenkw.com
Relaxed, time-worn and popular café serving West Indian-style breakfasts, lunches, and dinners. **$**

Camille's
1202 Simonton Street
Tel: 305-296-4811
www.camilleskeywest.com
With a menu that changes daily, Camille's is one of the Keys' best budget eateries for breakfast, lunch, or dinner. Specialties include pecan waffles, stone crab cakes, smoked salmon, and garlic pork. **$$**

Louie's Backyard
700 Waddell Avenue
Tel: 305-294-1061
www.louiesbackyard.com
Fine American and Caribbean cooking in a romantic, seaside setting with old Key West ambience. One of Florida's finest. **$$$**

Pepe's Cafe
806 Caroline Street
Tel: 305-294-7192
http://pepescafe.net
Excellent grilled steak, succulent oysters, and fragrant, fresh-baked breads, indoor and outdoor dining and a very popular bar. **$$**

Marathon

Herbie's
Mile Marker 50.5
Tel: 305-743-6373
Great seafood and chowders. **$$**

Miami

Basil in the Grove
3301 Grand Avenue
Tel: 305-444-4848
Brazilian fusion café in the Grove offering authentic and house-created specialties. **$**

Bubba Gump Shrimp Company
401 Biscayne Boulevard,
Downtown-Miami
Tel: 305-379-8866
www.bubbagump.com

ABOVE: oysters on the half shell in Key West.

American food, shrimp, and other specialties. **$$**

Casa Juancho
2436 SW Eighth Street
Tel: 305-642-2452
www.casajuancho.com
Authentic Cuban/Spanish fare. **$$**

Joe's Stone Crab Restaurant
11 Washington
Tel: 305-673-0365
www.joesstonecrab.com
Regional specialties featuring the prized and delectably sweet stone crab. A Miami institution. **$$$**

News Cafe
800 Ocean Drive, Miami Beach
Tel: 305-538-6397
www.newscafe.com
Very fashionable 24hr café/restaurant with Middle Eastern dishes and good egg breakfasts. Outdoor dining. **$$**

Pacific Time
35 NE 40th Street
Tel: 305-722-7369
www.pacifictimerestaurant.com
A rotating menu that includes Pacific/Asian dishes

such as Mahi-Mahi in Szechwan sauce and local grouper in green curry. **$$$**

Scotty's Landing
33381 Pan American Drive, Coconut Grove
Tel: 305-854-2626
A salty shack with million-dollar views. Grilled dolphin sandwiches. **$**

Versailles
3555 SW 8th Street, Little Havana
Tel: 305-444-0240
Delicious Cuban cooking in a wonderfully gaudy atmosphere. **$**

Orlando

Fulton's Crab House
Aboard three-deck riverboat at Downtown Disney (priority seating)
Seafood specialties with fresh fish flown in daily. Raw seafood bar. **$$$**

Hard Rock Cafe
Universal Citywalk
Tel: 407-351-7625
Burgers and sandwiches, fries and shakes, in an over-the-top shrine to rock's biggest stars. **$$**

Kres Chop House
17 W. Church Street
Tel: 407-447-7953-7625
www.kresrestaurant.com
Very stylish restaurant serving one of the best steaks in Orlando. Good dessert (chocolate bread pudding) as well. **$$$**

Pom Pom's Teahouse & Sandwicheria
67 Bumby Avenue
Tel: 407-894-0865
Tiny café with excellent specialty sandwiches and a selection of gourmet teas, all served with a friendly smile by the owner herself. **$**

St Augustine

O'Steen's Restaurant
205 Anastasia Boulevard
Tel: 904-829-6974
Best fried shrimp that are worth a long wait. **$**

Raintree
102 San Marco Avenue
Tel: 904-824-7211
www.raintreerestaurant.com
Very good seafood with freshly baked breads and pastries served in a restored older home. **$$**

Tampa

Columbia Restaurant
2117 E. 7th Avenue
Tel: 813-248-4961
www.columbiarestaurant.com
Authentic Cuban cuisine and nightly flamenco dancing in an atmospheric building make this a Ybor City must. **$$–$$$**

Silver Ring Cafe
7419 US 301
Tel: 813-677-1487
http://silverringcafes.com
Heaped platters of authentic Cuban dishes. **$**

Venice

Saltwater Café
1071 Tamiami Trail South
Tel: 941-488-3775
www.saltwatercafe.com
Well-liked seafood restaurant. **$$**

NORTHERN ROUTE

Massachusetts

Boston

Durgin Park
30 N. Market Street
(Faneuil Hall Marketplace)
Tel: 617-227-2877/2038
Yankee cooking attracts
flocks of tourists to this
legendary old dining hall,
where they are seated with
others at long, picnic-cloth
covered tables and insulted
by the waiters. Try
brontosaurus-sized prime
ribs. No reservations; long
waits. **$$**

Imperial Seafood
70 Beach Street
Tel: 617-426-8439
Large, busy Cantonese
restaurant. Main attraction:
dim sum. **$–$$**

Legal Sea Foods
26 Park Plaza
Tel: 617-426-4444
Copley Place, 100 Huntington
Avenue
Tel: 617-266-7775
255 State Street
Tel: 617-742-5300
800 Boylston Street
Tel: 617-266-6800
What started as a small
Cambridge fish store now
has a justly deserved
international reputation.
Enormous variety. No
reservations and waits can
seem interminable. **$$–$$$**

Parker's
Omni Parker House,
60 School Street
Tel: 617-227-8600
A New England tradition
since 1854. Home of Parker
rolls and Boston Cream Pie,
with formal and attentive
service. **$$$**

BELOW: a hot dog with "everything on it" makes a filling meal.

Cambridge

East Coast Grill & Raw Bar
1271 Cambridge Street
(Inman Square)
Tel: 617-491-6568
www.eastcoastgrill.net
A stylish, wildly popular spot
for innovative grilled
seafood (often topped with
exotic spice rubs or fruit
salsas), creative salads,
barbecue and fiery "pasta
from hell." Margaritas help
ease the often long wait for
a table. **$$**

Rialto Restaurant
Charles Hotel, 1 Bennett Street
Tel: 617-661-5050
www.rialto-restaurant.com
Chef Jody Adams has
earned international
accolades for flavorful
Mediterranean cuisine in a
coolly elegant dining room.
$$$

Concord

Colonial Inn
48 Monument Square
Tel: 978-369-2373
A 1716 inn serving
traditional New England fare
as well as afternoon tea. **$$**

Gloucester

Dog Bar
65 Main Street
Tel: 978-281-6565
Cozy restaurant with a small
but varied choice of food,
from seafood to ciabatta
sandwiches and steak,
served in a dramatic
granite-walled hideaway.
Can dine alfresco in the
summer. **$$**

Franklin Cape Ann
118 Main Street
Tel: 978-283-7888

www.franklincafe.com
Upscale bistro with a
popular wine bar, blending
fresh fish and local produce
into intriguing French
creations. **$**

The Rudder Restaurant
73 Rocky Neck Avenue
Tel: 978-283-7967
A rollicking tavern in the
Rocky Neck artists' colony.
$$

Ipswich

Clam Box
246 High Street
Tel: 978-356-9707
One of the best places in
the region for fried clams.
You can't miss the place –
it's housed in a building
shaped like a clam box. **$**

Lexington

La Boniche
143 Merrimack Street, Lowell
Tel: 978-458-9473
www.laboniche.com
An intimate restaurant in a
landmark Art Nouveau
building with creative
French fare. Open for lunch
and dinner. Closed Sun–
Mon. **$–$$**

Olympia Restaurant
453 Market Street, Lowell
Tel: 978-452-8092
www.newolympia.com
A friendly, family-run Greek
restaurant. Lunch and
dinner daily. **$**

New Hampshire

Meredith

George's Diner
10 Plymouth Street
Tel: 603-279-8723
www.georgesdiner.com
No-nonsense, fresh New
England grub featuring such
staples as corn chowder
and red-flannel hash. B, L &
D daily. **$**

Portsmouth

**Portsmouth Gas Light
Company**
64 Market Street
Tel: 603-430-9122
www.portsmouthgaslight.com
In an attractive landmark
building, this is a local
favorite for its surroundings
and delicious brick-oven

pizza. Ground-floor
restaurant shares a lunch
and dinner menu with the
café on the open, upper
deck. Deck is open during
summer and features live
music. **$** (for the basement
pizza joint), **$$** (for the
restaurant)

Maine

Kennebunkport

The Clam Shack
2 Western Avenue (on the bridge)
Tel: 207-967-3321
Superlative fried clams and
lobster rolls dispensed to
appreciative locals from a
simple hut. Open May–Oct. **$**

Ogunquit Beach

**Barnacle Billy's
Perkins Cove**
Tel: 207-646-5575
www.barnbilly.com
Serves lobster galore plus
chicken and clam chowder.
Can dine on the outside
decking right on the edge of
Perkins Cove. L & D daily.
The next-door restaurant,
Barnacle Billy's Etc, is the
pricier option. **$–$$**

Portland

Back Bay Grill
65 Portland Street
Tel: 207-772-8833
www.backbaygrill.com
In an attractive century-old
building with high pressed-
tin ceilings. Imaginative
regional and New American
dishes are prepared fresh
daily in the open kitchen.
The wine list is extensive
and the desserts are
exquisite. Dinner only. **$$**

Becky's
390 Commercial Street
Tel: 207-773-7070
www.beckysdiner.com
Downtown diner with all-day
breakfasts and hearty
homestyle platters of fried
seafood, turkey, meatloaf,
and lobster rolls. Small,
friendly, and very popular.
Open daily. **$**

Wells

The Steakhouse
1205 Post Road/Route 1
Tel: 207-646-4200

www.the-steakhouse.com
Serves quality steak hand-cut on the premises, as well as a variety of chicken and seafood dishes. Voted one of the best steakhouses in the whole of New England. Open late March to mid-December. Closed Mon. **$$**

Vermont

Arlington

Arlington Inn
Route 7A
Tel: 802-375-6532
www.arlingtoninn.com
Fairly formal candlelit restaurant creating French Continental dishes – rack of lamb, roast duck – prepared with local meats and produce. Closed Mon. **$$$**

West Mountain Inn
River Road (off Route 313)
Tel: 802-375-6516
www.westmountaininn.com
New American fare featuring local and organic produce in a low-beamed paneled dining room at a romantic but family-friendly inn. Fixed-price, five-course meal. Reservations necessary. Dinner served daily. **$$$**

Dorset

Chantecleer Restaurant
Route 7a, E. Dorset
Tel: 802-362-1616
www.chantecleerrestaurant.com
The Swiss chef at one of the area's favorite restaurants prepares Swiss and French provincial cuisine in a handsomely renovated dairy barn. Reservations recommended. Dinner Wed–Sun. **$$$**

Dorset Inn
8 Church Street/Route 30
Tel: 802-867-5500
www.dorsetinn.com
Superb regional cooking: a choice of formal dining or tavern feasting in a 1796 hostelry. Part of the Vermont Fresh Network, thereby supporting farmers and serving the best local produce. **$$**

Fairlee

Fairlee Diner
Route 5
Tel: 802-333-3569

Neat little diner with a nicely balanced menu blending classic and current fare. **$**

Killington

Choices Restaurant
2808 Killington Road
Tel: 802-422-4030
Chef Claude specializes in rotisserie, with entrées such as filet mignon with Saga blue cheese, and prime rib. Lively 30-something bar scene. **$$**

Hemingway's
4988 Route 4
Tel: 802-422-3886
www.hemingwaysrestaurant.com
Inspired regional cuisine, consistently hailed as one of the nation's best. Prix-fixe options. D Wed–Sun. **$$$**

Manchester

Marsh Tavern
Equinox Resort, 3567 Main Street
Tel: 800-362-4747
Spectacular regional cuisine in a building that was one of the first lodging houses in the state. Live entertainment and drinks in the lounge. **$$–$$$**

Up for Breakfast
4935 Main Street
Tel: 802-362-4204
Fabulous pancakes, omelets and French toast. Freshly squeezed fruit juices. Jammed on the weekends but well worth the wait. **$**

Middlebury

Fire and Ice Restaurant
26 Seymour Street
Tel: 802-388-7166/800-367-7166
www.fireandicerestaurant.com
Prime rib, fresh fish and a huge salad bar with offerings ranging from crab salad to sushi are the highlights. VCR movie theater to keep children occupied. **$–$$**

Tully and Marie's
7 Bakery Lane
Tel: 802-388-4182
www.tullyandmaries.com
Unfussy regional American cuisine with Italian and Asian accents. No pre-packaged or processed food served. Art Deco-inspired interior with a deck overlooking Otter Creek and a congenial crowd. **$$**

Quechee

Parker House Inn & Restaurant
1792 Main Street
Tel: 802-295-6077
www.theparkerhouseinn.com
Tasteful continental cuisine in a brick Victorian mansion with grand views. **$**

Simon Pearce Restaurant
The Mill, 1760 Main Street
Tel: 802-295-1470
www.simonpearceglass.com
Fine country cuisine with Irish touches set in an old riverside mill. Dine on a covered terrace (glass-enclosed in winter) overlooking the falls. Extensive wine list. *(see page 109)* **$$**

Woodstock

White Cottage Snack Bar
462 Woodstock Road
Tel: 802-457-3455
(see page 111) **$**

New York

Buffalo

Anchor Bar
1047 Main Street
Tel: 716-884-4083
www.anchorbar.com
(see page 120) **$**

Encore
492 Pearl Street
Tel: 716-931-5001
www.encorebuffalo.com
Newly opened restaurant spead over two floors, specializing in steak and sushi. Located in the theater district near Shea's Performing Arts Center, with bare brick walls and a modern, casual feel. Closed Sunday. **$–$$**

Laughlin's Hearty Bistro
333 Franklin
Tel: 716-842-6700
www.laughlinsrestaurant.com
Varied range of upmarket salads, sandwiches, steak, and paninis. **$$**

Lockport

Cammarata's
6336 Robinson Road
Tel: 716-433-5353
www.cammaratas.com
This Italian restaurant offers a varied menu catering for everyone, with prime rib steak, seafood,

and pasta. Fish fry on Fridays. L Mon–Fri, D daily. **$–$$**

Rome

Teddy's Restaurant
851 Black River Boulevard
Tel: 315-336-7839
www.teddysrestaurantny.com
Popular family restaurant serving pizza, pasta, paninis, and seafood. L & D Mon–Sat. **$–$$**

Saratoga Springs

Wheatfields Bar and Restaurant
440 Broadway
Tel: 518-587-0534
www.wheatfields.com
Wholesome, freshly made pasta dishes ranging from chicken and seafood to vegetarian and gluten-free options. Pizza and salads also served. **$$**

Schenectady

Blue Ribbon Restaurant
1801 State Street
Tel: 518-393-2600
www.blueribbonrestaurant.com
Much-loved, family-run diner, known for its award-winning cheesecake. Open daily. **$**

Clinton's Ditch
112 S. College Street
Tel: 518-346-8376
www.onefortheditch.com
Casual place offering range of steak, burgers, pasta, pizza, and seafood, plus lighter bites for lunch. **$**

Syracuse

Empire Brewing Company
Armory Square, 120 Walton Street
Tel: 315-475-2337
www.empirebrew.com
Housed in a smartly converted old grocery warehouse with much exposed stone and brick, this popular microbrewery has a long list of beers and an eclectic menu with the focus on locally sourced ingredients. **$**

PRICE CATEGORIES

Price categories are for an average cost of dinner and a glass of wine, before tip:
$ = under $20
$$ = $20–40
$$$ = more than $40

The Mission
304 E. Onondaga Street
Tel: 315-475-7344
www.themissionrestaurant.com
Mix of Mexican and South American cuisine with tacos, enchiladas and quesadillas, including meat, seafood, and vegetarian choices. Formerly a Methodist church, this building sits on an underground tunnel which fugitive slaves on the Underground Railroad used as a refuge. **$–$$**

Pennsylvania

Erie
Stonehouse Inn
4753 West Lake Road
Tel: 814-838-9296
www.stonehouse-inn.com
Upmarket and romantic. The continental menu changes daily, and the wine list is one of the longest in the area. Smart dress required. D Tue–Sun. **$$$**

Ohio

Cleveland
Blue Point Grille
700 W. St Clair Avenue
Tel: 216-875-7827
www.hrcleveland.com/bluepoint
Located in the warehouse district and serving the best quality seafood, from scallops, oyster, and shrimp, to grouper, swordfish, and tuna. Good idea to book. **$$–$$$**
Pickwick & Frolic Restaurant
2035 E. 4th Street
Tel: 216-241-7425
Casual American dining with plenty of dishes designed for sharing. Array of pizza, pasta, and steak. **$$**

Toledo
Tony Packo's
1902 Front Street
Tel: 419-691-6054
www.tonypackos.com
Packo's hot dogs are a Toledo institution – don't leave uninitiated (see page 127). **$**

Indiana

South Bend
The Vine
103 W. Colfax
Tel: 574-234-9463
www.thevinesb.com
Pleasant, fairly upmarket restaurant with a menu designed to appeal to all palates, with an unfussy range of sandwiches, pizza, pasta, meat, and fish. Closed Sun. **$**

Valparaiso
Strongbow Inn
2405 E. US 30
Tel: 219-462-5121
www.strongbowinn.com
In business for over half a century. Good home-style steaks and seafood dishes and specializing in turkey. Few vegetarian options. **$$**

Michigan

Dearborn
Ciao Ristorante
1024 Monroe
Tel: 313-274-2426
www.ciaodearborn.com
Traditional Italian food. Wide range of pizza, pasta, meat, and fish for very affordable prices. **$–$$**
Crave Restaurant
22075 Michigan Avenue
Tel: 313-277-7283
www.cravelounge.com
Casual dining in the lounge or on the patio. Mediterranean and Asian fusion cuisine served in elegant surroundings where the young and fashionable go. Nightly entertainment varies from live jazz to DJs to dancers. **$$**

Illinois

Chicago
Everest
440S LaSalle Street
Tel: 312-663-8920
www.everestrestaurant.com
One of the top restaurants (and views) in the country, this outstanding restaurant is located on the 40th floor of the Chicago Stock Exchange and enjoys a fantastic reputation thanks to its French chef. Accompanying the dinner menu are tasting and pre-theater menus. Closed Sun–Mon. **$$$**
Pizzeria Uno
29 E. Ohio Street
Tel: 312-321-1000
Now part of the Uno Chicago Grill franchise, this was where Chicago Deep Dish pizza was born. Open daily. **$**
The Pump Room
Ambassador East Hotel,
1301 N. State Parkway
Tel: 312-266-0360
www.pumproom.com
A Chicago institution and the place to celebrate that special occasion. Known since the 1930s for its "Booth One" table frequented by celebrities from Humphrey Bogart and Lauren Bacall, to Frank Sinatra and Robert Redford. **$$$**
Twin Anchors Restaurant and Tavern
1655 N. Sedgwick Street
Tel: 312-266-1616
www.twinanchorsribs.com
Among the best ribs in Chicago. Great burgers too. Pleasant neighborhood watering hole in the old town. L Sat–Sun, D daily. **$–$$**

Wisconsin

Madison
Dotty Dumpling's Dowry
317 N. Frances Street
Tel: 608-259-0000
www.dottydumplingsdowry.com
Excellent burgers, fun decor and cheerful atmosphere. **$**
Essen Haus
514 E. Wilson Street
Tel: 608-255-4674
Excellent German food, a long list of beers, and staff in German national dress. Rollicking good fun. **$$**

Minnesota

Mankato
Mexican Village Restaurant
1630 E. Madison Avenue
Tel: 507-387-4455
www.mexicanvillagemankato.com
Pleasant, rustic-style restaurant featuring homemade fajitas (chicken, steak, and shrimp), chimichangas, and burritos, plus vegetarian options. **$**

Minneapolis
Buca di Beppo
1204 Harmon Place
Tel: 612-288-0138
Generous portions of Italian fare with hard-to-resist desserts. Friendly service; amusing decor. **$–$$**
Kramarczuk's East European Deli
215 E. Hennepin Avenue
Tel: 612-379-3018
www.kramarczuk.com
Founded by a Ukrainian couple in the '70s, this Eastern European deli specializes in cabbage rolls, varenyky, and sausages. On-site bakery. L daily, D Tue–Sat. **$**
Nye's Polonaise Room
112 E. Hennepin Avenue
Tel: 612-379-2021
Hearty Polish-American fare and live piano music in plush surroundings. **$$**

St Paul
Café Latte
850 Grand Avenue
Tel: 651-224-5687
www.cafelatte.com
Soups, salads, sandwiches, and fragrant hearth-baked breads, as well as full afternoon tea and award-winning desserts. Pizzas available in the attached wine bar. Open daily. **$**
Mickey's Dining Car
36 W. 7th Street
Tel: 651-222-5633
www.mickeysdiningcar.com
Classic, vintage diner in the heart of town serving up the usual fried and griddled fare. **$**
St Paul Grill
St Paul Hotel, 350 Market Street
Tel: 651-224-7455
www.stpaulgrill.com
Classy, upmarket restaurant with a select menu of mainly steaks, chops, and fish. Includes a bar serving rare scotches, whiskies, and cognacs, alongside an enviable wine list. Great view of Rice Park. **$$$**

South Dakota

Deadwood
Jakes
677 Main Street
Tel: 605-578-1555
www.themidnightstar.com

ABOVE: vintage metal soft drink sign in Point Reyes, California.

Casual dining on the top floor of Kevin Costner's casino, Midnight Star. Small, if varied, menu including cajun seafood and veal osso bucco. Strong wine list. **$$**

Lead

Cheyenne Crossing Cafe
21415 US Highway 14A
Tel: 605-584-3510
Scenic spot for tucking into a rib-sticking breakfast any time of day. Grocery store also on the premises. **$**

Mitchell

Chef Louie's Steak House
601 E. Havens Street
Tel: 605-996-7565
Not much to look at from the outside but don't let that put you off. This modern, family-friendly restaurant serves a varied menu, mainly steaks, which are excellent. **$$**

Pierre

La Minestra
106 E. Dakota Avenue
Tel: 605-224-8090
www.laminestra.com
Italian restaurant serving freshly made pasta and steaks handcut to order. Plenty of fish, calzone, and salad options for non-meat eaters. L Mon–Fri, D Mon–Sat. **$–$$**

Rapid City

Firehouse Brewing Company
610 Main Street
Tel: 605-348-1915
www.firehousebrewing.com
Microbrewery serving "pub-grub" and variety of hand-crafted beers. Located in the city's former fire station and spread over two floors.

Live music daily throughout the summer. **$**

Sioux Falls

K
8th Street and Railroad Center
Tel: 605-336-3315
Recently opened restaurant that has been garnering good reviews. Buzzy atmosphere, upmarket food and always busy. **$$**

Minerva's
301 S. Phillips Avenue
Tel: 605-334-0386
Popular with locals and serving a range of prime-cut steaks, seafood, and pasta. One of the few places in the city to get decent seafood. **$–$$**

Spearfish

Bay Leaf Café
126 W. Hudson Street
Tel: 605-642-5462
www.bayleafcafe.net
Friendly and informal café in historic building serving a variety of well-prepared dishes from Alaskan seafood and Greek favorites houmous and falafel, to rib-tickling and plate-filling buffalo steaks. **$–$$**

Wyoming

Cody

The Noon Break
927 12th Street
Tel: 307-587-9720
Cheerful breakfast and lunch spot serving Western, Mexican and Tex-Mex dishes. Beware of the chili. **$**

Gillette

Humphrey's Bar and Grill
408 W. Juniper Lane
Tel: 307-682-0100 or

877-360-6751
www.humphard.net
Lively sports bar with an excellent salad bar. Large array of snacks, sandwiches, fajitas, and burgers. **$**

Jackson

Blue Lion
160 N. Millward Street
Tel: 307-733-3912
www.bluelionrestaurant.com
Long-established local favorite in an older, renovated building. Excellent regional and continental dishes including elk, chicken, and vegetarian options. Dine indoors or alfresco. **$$$**

Snake River Grill
84 E. Broadway
Tel: 307-733-0557
American seafood and steak grill with an Asian influence. The menu varies with the season. **$$$**

Sundance

ARO Family Restaurant
205 E. Cleveland Street
Tel: 307-283-2000
Well-prepared food such as burgers, steaks, Mexican selections, served in warm atmosphere. Excellent value. **$**

Montana

Bozeman

John Bozeman's Bistro
125 W. Main Street
Tel: 406-587-4100
www.johnbozemansbistro.com
Eclectic menu featuring tapas, steaks, Thai, and Italian dishes. Relaxed, informal atmosphere. **$$**

Helena

Frontier Pies Restaurant and Bakery
1600 Prospect Avenue
Tel: 406-442-7437
Good food and freshly baked pies worth traveling for. Western decor. **$**

Windbag Saloon
19 S. Last Chance Gulch Street
Tel: 406-443-9669
Sample the lively atmosphere and range of microbrewery beers in this popular local spot. Good burgers and great pasta. **$–$$**

Kalispell

Moose's Saloon
173 N. Main Street
Tel: 406-755-2337
www.moosessaloon.com
The genuine article, with rustic tables and booths and sawdust on the floor. Great pizzas, sandwiches, and a soup and salad bar at lunchtime. **$**

Missoula

Food for Thought
540 Daly Avenue
Tel: 406-721-6033
Across the street from the University, this popular spot serves the biggest breakfasts in town, as well as lunches and freshly prepared salads. **$**

The Old Post
103 W. Spruce
Tel: 406-721-7399
www.oldpostpub.com
"Hey, it's more fun to eat in a bar than to drink in a restaurant" – that's the motto of this lively pub and it's definitely true at this downtown Missoula favourite. There's a wide choice of local beers on tap, good food like fish tacos, black beans and rice, surf 'n' turf, and teriyaki chicken stir-fry. A long bar down one side faces booths down the other wall, and in between are café-style tables and tons of atmosphere. **$**

Whitefish

Dos Amigos
6592 US Highway 93 S
Tel: 406-862-9994
Good choice of dishes. Mainly Mexican but with several Cajun and American dishes on offer. **$$**

Idaho

Bonners Ferry

Alberto's
6536 S. Main Street
Tel: 208-267-3410

Authentic, first-rate Mexican fare in gaily decorated surroundings. **$$**

Coeur d'Alene
Cedars Floating Restaurant
1 Marine Drive
Tel: 208-664-2922
www.cedarsfloatingrestaurant.com
Warm and welcoming restaurant moored on Lake Coeur d'Alene affording panoramic views. Extensive, nicely balanced menu featuring very fresh, expertly prepared fish. **$$-$$$**

Sandpoint
Forty-One South
41 Lakeshore Drive, Sagle
Tel: 208-265-2000
www.41southsandpoint.com
Next to but not part of the Lodge at Sandpoint, Forty-One South has a great location overlooking the lovely Lake Pend Oreille. The timber-framed building with wood-paneling provides a smart-casual background to some very smart cooking, with such dishes as a trio of salmon fillets, each prepared in a different way. There's also an array of desserts to die for – made by one of the waiters! **$$$**

Washington
Ellensberg
The Palace Café
4th and Main
Tel: 509-925-2327
http://thepalacecafe.net
The fact that this family-run café-restaurant has been in business since 1892 says a lot for its quality, and value for money. It's the kind of old-fashioned place that serves perfect versions of old favorites like a hot prime rib sandwich, or halibut and chips. There's only a short wine list but a good range of beers, with booths and a bar, friendly staff, and an easy-going atmosphere. **$$**

Forks
The In Place
320 S. Forks Avenue
Tel: 360-374-4004
This typical US diner is the kind of place we all need to

find on our road trips – serving good and simple food at good prices whether you want a pancake breakfast, a coffee or a steak dinner. There are pastas, salads, and seafood too, with wine and beer, no-frills booths, and friendly local service. **$**

Lake Quinault
Kelsey's Café
252 South Shore Road, Quinault
Tel: 360-288-2620
This casual café in the Quinault Mercantile, opposite the Lake Quinault Lodge, starts early with breakfast specials and keeps going all day providing good, inexpensive food, soft drinks, coffee, free Wi-fi, and dispensing all-round general advice on the area, thanks to the genial owner and his staff. There's also a gift shop attached. **$**

Roosevelt Restaurant
Lake Quinault Lodge,
345 South Shore Road
Tel: 360-288-2900
www.visitlakequinault.com
The formal dining room at the Lake Quinault Lodge is named for President Teddy Roosevelt, who was dining here when the idea for creating the Olympic National Park was first suggested. The feel is still old-fashioned, with romantic low lighting. The menu focuses on seafood with such dishes as Alaskan cod fillet with sweet potato chips, though meat-eaters can enjoy a pork loin or a steak. There's also a very good wine list, especially for wines by the glass. **$$$**

Leavenworth
Café Christa
801 Front Street
Tel: 509-548-5074
www.cafechrista.com
A pleasant café right on the city square, serving central European cuisine in an atmosphere of old-world charm. **$$**

Port Angeles
Destiny Seafood and Grill
1213 Marine Drive
Tel: 360-452-4665

Mediterranean and Middle Eastern cuisine. Nice baked goods. **$**

First Street Haven
107 E. First Street
Tel: 360-457-0352
Sweet-smelling cakes, muffins, and scones baked in-house. Breakfast served all day on Sundays. **$**

Port Townsend
Salal Cafe
634 Water Street
Tel: 360-385-6532
Wholesome meals served in pleasant surroundings. **$**

The Silverwater Café
237 Taylor Street
Tel: 360-385-6448
www.silverwatercafe.com
Well-prepared, fresh local seafood and produce. Easy ambiance. **$-$$**

Seattle
Cafe Campagne
1600 Post Alley
Tel: 206-728-2233
www.campagnerestaurant.com
In Pike Place Market, serving southern French cuisine with a rustic ambiance. Daily specials from seafood caught that day along with fresh local produce. **$$$**

Macrina Bakery and Café
2408 1st Avenue
Tel: 206-448-4032
www.macrinabakery.com
Pleasant coffee house with an extensive line of artisan breads and pastries, and a special lunch menu with full table service. **$**

Mitchelli's
84 Yesler Way
Tel: 206-623-3883
Long a Seattle favorite at Pioneer Square for its classic Italian dishes. Pizzas from the wood-fired oven and pasta dishes made to order. Old-fashioned tile floors and wooden lunch counter add to the charm. It's a lively spot and open into the wee hours on weekends. **$$**

The Pike Brewing Company
1415 First Avenue
Tel: 206-622-6044
www.pikebrewing.com
Top-rated brew-pub in the Pike Place Market district

serving classic pub fare. Entrees are made with fresh local ingredients, such as grass-fed burgers and raw milk cheeses, wild salmon and seafood. Take a tour of the traditional steam brewery producing great handcrafted beers. **$-$$**

Ray's Boathouse
6049 Seaview Avenue NW
Tel: 206-789-3770
www.rays.com
Truly a local establishment, from the wonderful view of Puget Sound to elegant preparation of local ingredients in this upscale eatery. **$$$**

Salty's on Alki
1936 Harbor Avenue SW
Tel: 206-937-1600
www.saltys.com
Alder-smoked salmon stuffed with Dungeness crab, but it's the view at night that steals the show. **$$-$$$**

Thoa's Restaurant and Lounge
96 Union Street
Tel: 206-344-8088
www.thoaseattle.com
Seattle chef Thoa Nguyen's smart downtown restaurant serves contemporary Vietnamese cuisine that combines Pacific Northwest ingredients with traditional flavors. Fresh, light, and inspiring. **$$**

Sequim
Three Crabs Restaurant
11 Three Crabs Road
Tel: 360-683-4264
www.the3crabs.com
Situated right on the beach, with a fine view of the harbor and freshest Dungeness crabs around. **$-$$**

Spokane
Fugazzi Bakery and Cafe
117 N. Howard Street
Tel: 509-340-2253
Nice sandwiches and pastries. **$**

Niko's
725 W. Riverside Avenue
Tel: 509-624-7444
www.nikosspokane.com
Excellent Greek food accompanied by a large, award-winning wine list. **$$**

Washington, DC

I Ricchi
1120 19th Street NW
Tel: 202-835-0459
Traditional Tuscan restaurant serving fresh, simple, and hearty cooking. Bread, meat, and fish cooked and grilled in the dining room's wood-burning stove. Wonderful sage and ricotta-stuffed tortellini, flavorful sauces for pastas and risottos, and excellent seafood. **$$**

La Brasserie
239 Massachusetts Avenue NE
Tel: 202-546-9154
The menu ranges from luxurious lobster to a variety of thick quiches to devilishly rich crème brûlée. In warm weather, the terrace makes a nice backdrop to the gastronomic delights. **$$$**

Market Lunch
225 Seventh Street SE
Tel: 202-547-8444
It's no surprise there's a fight to get in here for Saturday breakfasts. The crabcakes and homemade bread are superb, and the prices are cheap. You have a better chance of getting a seat for a weekday lunch. Don't expect to pay with plastic. **$**

Meskerem
2434 18th Street NW
Tel: 202-462-4100
Try for a table on the top floor, with basket tables under a tented ceiling. Best with a large group, so that many dishes can be ordered. For two, try the combination platter to sample an array of items presented on *injera*, the curious gray, spongy sourdough pancake bread that is ripped off and used as the utensil for the food. **$$**

Nora
2132 Florida Avenue NW
Tel: 202-462-5143
Sometimes trying a little too hard to be original, Nora's is nonetheless worth a visit for its audacious balancing of seemingly incompatible ingredients, served in an intimate dining room (and outdoor dining area in clement weather). It declares its produce organic and biodynamic, but those bored by the thought need not expect a diminution of interesting flavors. **$$**

Virginia
Arlington

Ray's Hell-Burger
1713 Wilson Boulevard, Arlington
Tel: 703-841-0001
Owner Michael Landrum couldn't have wished for better publicity than when President Barack Obama and Vice-President Joe Biden directed their motorcade to his well-regarded burger bar and ordered two 10-ounce burgers with spicy mustard for lunch. **$**

Front Royal

Soul Mountain
300 E. Main Street
Tel: 540-636-0070
www.soulmountainrestaurant.com
Varied Southern, Cajun, and Caribbean food, ranging from jerk chicken with coconut rice to lobster ravioli. Food is freshly prepared so you can dictate the level of spice required. Separate BBQ menu available. **$**

New Market

Southern Kitchen
Highway 11
Tel: 540-740-3514
Great fried chicken and regional favorites. **$**

North Carolina
Asheville

City Bakery Cafe
60 Biltmore Avenue
Tel: 828-252-4426
A popular all-rounder. Family-owned enterprise serving artisan, organic bread, European-style pastries and cakes. **$**

Tennessee
Cookeville

Crawdaddy's West Side Grill
53 W. Broad Street
Tel: 931-526-4660
www.crawdaddysgrill.com
Range of sandwiches, steak, chicken, pasta, and seafood dishes, some with a Cajun accent. Open-air courtyard and live music. **$$**

Knoxville

Calhoun's
400 Neyland Drive
Tel: 865-673-3355
www.calhouns.com
Enjoy excellent barbecue ribs (voted best in America) and a fine river view, being situated right on the riverfront. Outdoor deck. **$**

Memphis

Automatic Slim's
83 S. Second Street
Tel: 901-525-7948
www.automaticslimsmemphis.com
Menu offers lamb and pork chops, honey-glazed chicken, duck, and pasta, all with an exotic twist. Martini list as long as your arm. **$$**

Currents River Inn at Harbor Town
50 Harbor Town Square
Tel: 901-260-3300
www.riverinnmemphis.com
Rich continental food is executed with New Orleans-style flair and close attention to detail in this lovely corner dining room overlooking the Mississippi. The waitstaff – several drawn from Eastern Europe – is discreet and knowledgeable. The chef visits the farmers' market in season: look for local tomatoes, field greens, blue goat cheese, and Tennessee Cheddar. Try the Gulf bouillabaisse to start, followed perhaps by seared sea bass and scallop. Leave room for a Key Lime Tasting of pie, sorbet, and cheesecake. **$$$**

The Dixie Cafe
4699 Poplar Avenue
Tel: 901-683-7555
A great little place for Americana, serving old-fashioned food and with a nostalgic soda fountain. **$**

Nashville

Loveless Cafe
8400 Highway 100
Tel: 615-646-9700
www.lovelesscafe.com
Named after its founders, this café serves authentic Southern cooking using locally sourced ingredients. With a choice of first-class preserves, ham, and "red-eye" gravy, breakfast is a real treat. Generous portions and abundant atmosphere. **$**

Valentino's Ristorante
1907 West End Avenue
Tel: 615-327-0148
www.valentinosnashville.com
Fine Northern Italian cuisine at reasonable prices. Consistently voted one of Nashville's best Italian restaurants for its good service and elegant but casual atmosphere. **$$**

Sevierville

Applewood Farmhouse Restaurant
240 Apple Valley Road, off US 441
Tel: 865-428-1222
www.applewoodrestaurant.com
Very pleasant and reasonable family restaurant surrounded by orchards. Trout, catfish, meatloaf, and obligatory fried chicken all feature on the menu. Apple fritters with every meal. **$**

Arkansas
Hot Springs

Chef Paul's
Temperance Hill Square shopping center, 4330 Central Avenue
Tel: 501-520-4187
www.chefpaulsfinedining.com
Smart dining with Mediterranean-influenced menu, offering a wide choice ranging from Colorado lamb and prime rib-eye, to crab cake and snails. Reservations necessary for weekends. **$–$$**

McClard's Bar-B-Q
505 Albert Pike
Tel: 501-623-9665

Price Categories
Price categories are for an average cost of dinner and a glass of wine, before tip:
$ = under $20
$$ = $20–40
$$$ = more than $40

www.mcclards.com
Run by descendants of the founders, this place has been serving savory, well-seasoned barbecue since 1928. Everything is made from scratch on the premises, while the recipe for the sauce is a closely guarded secret. **$**

Little Rock
Doe's Eat Place
1023 W. Markham Street
Tel: 501-376-1195
www.doeseatplace.net
A favorite of Bill Clinton's in the early '90s. Choice-cut steaks. Choose from T-bone, porterhouse, and sirloin, accompanied by fries and Texas Toast. Tamales, shrimp, and salmon are also available on the dinner menu, while burgers and pasta dishes are an addition to the lunch menu. **$$**
The Faded Rose
1619 Rebsamen Park Road
Tel: 501-663-9734
www.thefadedrose.com
Steaks, burgers, garlic chicken, and a range of Creole dishes such as crawfish étouffée. **$–$$**

Oklahoma
Arcadia
Pops
660 W. Highway 66
Tel: 405-928-7677
www.pops66.com
Identified by a 66ft (20-meter) soda bottle and straw dominating its front, this place offers over 500 different drinks, including 54 varieties of root beer (Snoopy's favorite) and sinfully good milkshakes. Has a digital jukebox and convenience store. Chicken-fried steak, burgers, and usual fare served. **$**

Catoosa
Molly's Landing
3700 N. Highway 66
Tel: 918-266-7853
www.mollyslanding.com
Variety of steak and seafood in a log cabin by the river with the Blue Whale landmark. **$–$$**

Chandler
Steer Inn Family Restaurant
102 N. Oak Street
Tel: 405-258-3155
Range of burgers, sandwiches, steaks, and barbecued pork, ribs, and chicken. Lunch buffet Mon–Fri, plus evening all-you-can-eat buffets Tue–Sat, accompany the regular menu. **$**

Claremore
Hammett House Restaurant
1616 W. Will Rogers Boulevard
Tel: 918-341-7333
www.hammetthouse.com
Tasty, freshly prepared grub. Larger range of salads and soup alongside the steak and burgers than other establishments in the area. **$–$$**

Depew
Spangler's General Store
322 Main Street
Tel: 918-324-5472
Classic Route 66 landmark serving good burgers and sandwiches. **$**

El Reno
Robert's Grill
300 S. Bickford Avenue
Tel: 405-262-1262
Hometown of the original Fried Onion Burger, this tiny place has been operating since 1926 and has room for just 14 stools along the counter. Co-creators of the World's Largest Hamburger, annually on Memorial Day. **$**

Oklahoma City
Cattlemen's Steakhouse
1309 S. Agnew Avenue
Tel: 405-236-0416
www.cattlemensrestaurant.com
Excellent steaks served up in the middle of the stockyards. Relaxed atmosphere in the oldest restaurant in the city, that was once the stake in a bet. **$–$$**
Elephant Bar Restaurant
1845 NW Expressway Street
Tel: 405-879-1700
www.elephantbar.com
If you're in need of a break from steak and barbecued food, this safari-themed joint

serves a mix of pan-Asian and regional cuisine, such as Shanghai cashew chicken, pad thai, Vietnamese shrimp spring rolls, tempura, and fish with macademia nut sauce. **$**

Tulsa
New Atlas Grill
Atlas Life Building,
415 S. Boston Street
Tel: 918-583-3111
www.newatlasgrill.com
Salad, soups, and sandwiches in a casual, retro 1920s-style café. **$**
Ollie's Station Restaurant
W. 41st and Southwest Boulevard
Tel: 918-446-0524
www.olliesstation.com
Fun café-style place with good food and 10 model trains chugging merrily around and through scale-model cities. **$**
Warren Duck Club
DoubleTree Hotel, 6110 S. Yale Avenue
Tel: 918-495-1000
This club is on the dressy side of Tulsa, serving a healthy and well-prepared menu to the heirs of oil barons no doubt, and with wonderful views of the manicured lawns. **$$–$$$**

Vinita
Clanton's Cafe
319 E. Illinois Street
Tel: 918-256-9053
www.clantonscafe.com
Classic Route 66 eatery, known for its chicken-fried beefsteak. Also serves that "regional classic" of calf fries (aka testicles). **$**

Yukon
Sid's Diner
4 E. Main Street
Tel: 405-354-9702
Serves breakfast and lunch. **$**

Texas
Amarillo
Big Texan Steak Ranch
7701 I-40 E.
Tel: 806-372-6000
If you can eat a 72oz steak, plus side dishes, in under an hour you don't pay for it. More modest portions of

beef, fried rattlesnake etc. also available. **$$**
Zen 721
614 S. Polk Street
Tel: 806-372-1909
At the opposite end of the foodie spectrum is this locally owned, Asian-American restaurant with stir-fry, beef and chicken pad thai, soba noodles, and seafood dishes populating its menu. **$–$$**

Vega
Hickory Inn Cafe
1004 Vega Boulevard
Tel: 806-267-2569
Typical ranch fare. Steak burgers and homemade pies. **$**

New Mexico
Albuquerque
66 Diner
1405 Central Avenue NE
Tel: 505-247-1421
www.66diner.com
Spiffy old-time diner on old Route 66 near the university. Enjoy blue plate specials, burger platters, and other classics, along with a treat from the soda fountain **$**
Assets Grill Brewing Company
6910 Montgomery NE
Tel: 505-889-6400
Mixed ethnic cuisine in a lively country setting; great selection of beers and brew made in-house. **$**

Las Vegas
Adelia's Landmark Grill
230 Old Town Plaza
Tel: 505-425-3591
www.plazahotel-nm.com
Just off the lobby of the historic Plaza Hotel, this pleasant restaurant serves New Mexican favorites like chile rellenos and fajitas made from family recipes. Steak, seafood, and vegetarian entrees are also on the menu. **$**

Santa Fe
Cowgirl BBQ
319 S. Guadalupe Street
Tel: 505- 982-2565
www.cowgirlsantafe.com
The down-home Cowgirl BBQ is a Santa Fe favorite

that lies between the main Plaza and the Railyard district. Its food and margaritas have been widely praised in the media, but it remains an unpretentious place to enjoy affordable lunches and dinners, inside or on the small patio out front. You have to try their BBQ dishes, or maybe a steak or their spicy jerk chicken. **$$**

Coyote Cafe
132 W. Water Street
Tel: 505-983-1615
www.coyotecafe.com
American and New Mexican fare served in an imaginatively decorated site (a former bus depot). The restaurant menu features original Southwestern cooking. Cuban and Latino fare is served on the popular rooftop cantina. **$$–$$$**

Geronimo Maria's
555 W. Cordova Road
Tel: 505-983-7929
www.marias-santafe.com
Slightly out of the center and rather nondescript from the outside, Maria's is known more to locals than to visitors. They serve, without question, the best and strongest margaritas for miles, with a list of over 100 types – they also published a margarita recipe book. The authentic Mexican food is a match, with powerful spicy flavors especially in their signature dish of Carne Adovado. **$$**

Tomasita's
500 S. Guadalupe Street
Tel: 505-983-5721
Right next to the train station in the newly happening Railyard district, Tomasita's is always busy as it offers tasty Santa Fe-style Mexican food at good prices, with friendly service and in a relaxed café-like atmosphere. Try the excellent chile rellenos, the specialty of the house. **$$**

Arizona

Ash Fork

Route 66 Grill
322 Lewis Avenue
Tel: 928-637-2528

Another historic diner on the Mother Road, serving burgers, fries, and other classic fare. Indulge in a sundae from the ice-cream shoppe. **$**

Flagstaff

Black Bart's Steak House and Musical Revue
2760 E. Buner Avenue
Tel: 928-779-3142
www.blackbartssteakhouse.com
Oh go on, you know you want a big steak and some country music over your gravy and potatoes. Indulge. **$$**

Cottage Place Restaurant
126 W. Cottage Avenue
Tel: 928-774-8431
Set in a bungalow-style residence built in 1909, this is one of Flagstaff's best fine-dining establishments. Go all out for the 6-course tasting menu with wine pairings, or come early for the lighter Twilight menu. **$$–$$$**

Holbrook

Joe and Aggie's Cafe
120 W. Hopi Drive
Tel: 928-524-6540
www.joeandaggiescafe.com
Good Mexican dishes are prepared with homemade red and green chili from an old family recipe. The chile rellenos are a local favorite, and even the T-bone steaks are served with rice, beans, and chili on top. If that doesn't fill you up, polish it off with an apple burrito topped with ice cream. **$–$$**

Sedona

L'Auberge De Sedona Restaurant
301 L'Auberge Lane
Tel: 928-282-1661
www.lauberge.com/dining
So good they named a whole street (well, lane) after it. The French cuisine at this elegant restaurant at L'Auberge de Sedona Inn and Spa is top-notch, matched only by its delicious desserts and its delightful setting on Oak Creek. **$$$**

Shugrue's Hillside Grill
671 Highway 179
Tel: 928-282-5300
www.shugrues.com
A health-conscious American menu in the ideal

Sedona setting, looking onto the mountains. **$$**

Williams

Rod's Steak House
301 E. Route 66
Tel: 928-635-2671
www.rods-steakhouse.com
Much-loved Route 66 dining landmark. The menu is die-cut in the shape of a steer, one of many souvenir items at this all-American restaurant. **$$**

Twisters
417 E. Route 66
Tel: 928-635-0266
Great burgers and shakes at this 1950s soda fountain on Route 66. **$**

Winslow

Falcon Restaurant
1113 E. Third Street
Tel: 928-289-2628
Family restaurant serving awesome portions of down-home favorites like chicken-fried steak, accompanied by homemade salsa verde. **$**

California

Los Angeles

Chin Chin
8618 Sunset Boulevard
Tel: 310-652-1818
www.chinchin.com
This Chinese café in West Hollywood's Sunset Plaza is a prime people-watching spot, with indoor and outdoor dining. Great dim sum and noodle dishes are among the full Chinese menu. The Classic Shredded Chicken Salad is legendary. **$–$$**

Ciudad
445S Figueroa Street
Tel: 213-486-5171
www.ciudad-la.com
Latin and Southwest cross in a wild way in this downtown restaurant. From Salvadorean *pupusas* (corn meal puffs with cucumber *curtido* and mango *rocoto* sauce) to Colorado lamb steak with sweet-roasted *poblano* chili. Incredible desserts and liqueurs. **$$$**

Grand Central Market
317 S. Broadway
Tel: 213-624-2378
Bustling shoppers, neon signs, and varied produce – a feast for the eyes. Stalls

offer fish tacos and other cheap street food. **$**

JiRaffe
502 Santa Monica Boulevard
Tel: 310-917-6671
www.jirafferestaurant.com
Innovative California cuisine at this hip scene in Santa Monica. Good wine list. Interesting open architecture. **$$$**

Musso and Frank's
6667 Hollywood Boulevard
Tel: 323-467-7788
www.mussoandfrankgrill.com
Hollywood's oldest restaurant dates back to 1919. Its decor and its menu of old faithfuls, from steaks and chops to macaroni and cheese, would still be familiar to the Hollywood giants who have dined here over the decades. **$$**

A Thousand Cranes
120 S. Los Angeles Street
Tel: 213-253-9255
www.thousandcranesrestaurant.com
The classiest of three restaurants in the New Otani Hotel, this one overlooks the lovely third-floor garden. Refined Japanese cuisine with sushi and tempura bars and tatami rooms. **$$$**

Newberry Springs

Bagdad Café
46548 National Trails Highway
Tel: 760-257-3101
Decent café renamed after the Adlon film of the same name was shot here. **$**

Rancho Cucamonga

Magic Lamp Inn
8189 Foothill Boulevard
Tel: 909-981-8659
www.themagiclampinn.com
The eponymous magic lamp, lit up in bright neon, denotes another Route 66 landmark. The menu features prime aged steaks and inn favorites like chicken di angelo and stuffed shrimp, accompanied by its special hot cheese toast. **$–$$**

PRICE CATEGORIES

Price categories are for an average cost of dinner and a glass of wine, before tip:
$ = under $20
$$ = $20–40
$$$ = more than $40

SOUTHERN ROUTE

Georgia

Atlanta

The Dining Room
Ritz-Carlton Hotel
3434 Peachtree Road
Tel: 404-237-2700
www.ritzcarlton.com
One of only three US restaurants to receive Mobil's five stars, this elegant Buckhead eatery tops the list of Atlanta fine-dining places. Choose from an á la carte or six-course seasonal tasting menu paired with wines from the restaurant's award-winning wine list. A once-in-a-lifetime dining pleasure. **$$$**

The Varsity
61 N. Avenue
Tel: 404-881-1706
www.thevarsity.com
Opened in 1928, this drive-in burger-and-Coke joint is one of Atlanta's most famous restaurants. Their drive-in classics include chili dogs, onion rings, fried fruit pies and shakes. **$**

Jackson

Buckner Family Restaurant and Music Hall
I-75/US 36
Tel: 770-775-6150
Home-style fried chicken suppers and barbecue are served family style in a cavernous dining room in this rural restaurant where gospel music accompanies old-fashioned food. Dessert is usually peach cobbler. **$**

Macon

Marco Ristorante Italiano
4581 Forsyth Road
Tel: 478-405-5668
www.marcomacon.com
This elegant fine-dining restaurant's Italian owner has brought authentic Italian cuisine to Lil' Macon. Try branzino, Italian sea bass, veal ravioli with wild mushroom ragout, and end with a gelati sampler. **$$$**

Alabama

Mobile

Cafe 615
615 Dauphin Street

Tel: 251-432-8434
www.cafe615mobile.com
Popular with locals for its bottomless Champagne brunch on Sundays, 615 occupies a lovely, contemporary space on historic Dauphin Street. It's a great place to land for New Southern food that does inventive things with grits and seafood. The menu has a light touch, a boon after so much fried road food. **$$**

Wintzell's Oyster House
605 Dauphin Street, Mobile
Tel: 251-432-4605
www.wintzellsoysterhouse.com
Fresh oysters done every which way have starred on the menu of this corner pub in downtown Mobile for 70 years. A bit raucous but sidewalk dining makes for great people-watching, especially around Mardi Gras. Branches at eight locations in Mobile. **$**

Montgomery

Lek's Railroad Thai
300 Water Street
Tel: 334-269-0714
www.thaiemeraldleks.com
Vegetarians celebrate! This authentic Thai restaurant in the historic Union Station has lots of veggie offerings as well as sushi and traditional Thai dishes. **$$**

Martin's
1796 Carter Hill Road, Montgomery
Tel: 334-265-1767
A local favorite for 70 years, Martin's is famous for its fried chicken. Just the place when you want comfort food. Open lunch and dinner but closes very early and isn't open on Saturdays. **$**

Mississippi

Biloxi

Hard Rock Cafe
777 Beach Boulevard
Tel: 228-374-7625
www.hardrockbiloxi.com
The Hard Rock has seven restaurants to choose from, so if you're in a hurry, you should find something here

to suit your taste. The casual 24/7 offers huge breakfasts and the Hard Rock Cafe is, of course, famous for its trademark burgers and rock memorabilia. **$–$$$**

Gulfport

Port City Cafe
2418 14th Street
Tel: 228-868-0037
This storefront café serves traditional Southern food. The owner is always willing to stop and chat. **$**

Ocean Springs

The Shedd BBQ and Blues Joint
7501 Highway 57
Tel: 228-875-9590
www.thesheddbbq.com
This eclectic barbecue spot is nationally known for its pulled pork, smoked sausage, and other barbecue. The junkyard atmosphere offers a certain *je ne sais quoi*. **$**

Louisiana

Abbeville

Dupuy's Oyster Shop
108 S. Main Street
Tel: 337-893-2336
Established in 1869, this highly acclaimed oyster and seafood restaurant is the real deal for homecooked Cajun food. **$–$$**

Baton Rouge

Drusilla Seafood Restaurant
3482 Drusilla Lane
Tel: 225-923-0896
www.drusillaplace.com
A local favorite for seafood, steaks, and Cajun food. A good place to try shrimp remoulade, gumbo, crawfish etouffee, and their acclaimed seafood eggplant gratin. A real spirit of lagniappe (a little bit more). **$–$$**

Breaux Bridge

Cafe Des Amis
140 E. Bridge
Tel: 337-332-5273
www.cafedesamis.com
Famous for its Zydeco Breakfast on Saturdays,

featuring Cajun food, zydeco music, and dancing, Cafe Des Amis is a great place to sample local color. Its location in a historic building near the bridge is perfect. Try one of the many crawfish dishes and Cajun breakfast treats like *couche couche*, a corn cereal batter with sweetened milk and *oreilles de cochon*, cornmeal donuts shaped like pig's ears. **$–$$**

Eunice

Ruby's Cafe
221 W. Walnut Avenue
Tel: 337-457-2583
This tiny backstreet café is the real deal. It serves up generous portions of well-flavored Cajun food for next to nothing. Try an authentic ponce, pork roast stuffed with sausage, or fried shrimp over rice washed down with Louisiana-style coffee. **$**

Lafayette

Prejeans
3480 NE Evangeline Tramway
(1-49 N.)
Tel: 337-896-3247
www.prejeans.com
Famous for its live Cajun music and award-winning chicken and sausage, smoked duck, and seafood gumbos, Prejeans is touristy but the food is worth running the gauntlet of tour buses to sample. **$–$$**

New Orleans

Antoine's
713 St Louis Street, French Quarter
Tel: 504-581-4422
www.antoines.com
This French Creole restaurant has been run by the same family since 1840. Dishes such as Oysters Rockefeller originated at Antoine's. Many dishes are sensational, especially the Baked Alaska. **$$$**

Cochon
930 Tchoupitoulas Street
Tel: 588-2123
www.cochonrestaurant.com
A homage to everything porcine on the bayou, Cochon's chef-owner Donald

Link has a French-inspired way with *boucherie*. The menu showcases traditional Cajun hog dishes but you'll also find game and local seafood. It's located in a light-filled corner building in the Warehouse District. Unsuitable for vegetarians. **$$$**

St Martinville

Josephine's Creole Restaurant
830 S. Main Street
Tel: 337-394-8030
Bona fide Creole and Cajun cooking using time-honored family recipes are the secret to Josephine's success. Locals swear this is the best place to eat. Try the shrimp and chicken stews, stuffed turkey wings, and stuffed Creole bread. Expect a wait. It's always busy. **$$**

Texas

Austin

Threadgill's
6416 N. Lamar
Tel: 512-459-3855
www.threadgills.com
This famed Texan roadhouse café is located on the site of a 1933 gas station whose owner helped start the live-music scene in Austin. The original building was where Janis Joplin cut her musical chops. A branch, located next to the famous 1970s live-music venue Armadillo World Headquarters in South Austin, was opened in the 1990s. There are lavish servings of southern cuisine and live music at both venues. **$**

Wink
1014 N. Lamar
Tel: 512-482-8868
www.winkrestaurant.com
Wink is located in a quiet corner but still manages to make a lot of noise among foodies. Its chef-owners do clever things with seasonal game, fish, and produce from local sources, using herb-infused oils, emulsions, and vegetable purées to draw out the natural flavors. Try sautéed onaga with escarole and sorrel aïoli or grilled black

buck antelope. The elegant Wink Trio – lemon meringue pot, crème brûlée, and El Rey chocolate cake – makes a fitting finale. Reservations recommended. **$$$**

El Paso

The Dome Restaurant
101 S. El Paso Street
Tel: 915-534-3010
www.caminoreal.com/elpaso
This upmarket dining room is located in the elegant Camino Real Hotel, where the chef's innovative seafood and wild game creations have a huge following. They are matched by the majestic Tiffany glass dome that gives the restaurant its name. **$$$**

Leo's Mexican Food
5103 Montana Avenue
Tel: 915-562-5101
www.leosmexican.com
If you're going to eat Mexican on the US side of this border town, it had better be good. Leo's is a reliable bet for authentic Tex-Mex and Norteño food on a huge menu. The Caldo de Pollo (chicken soup) and steak fajitas have many fans. **$**

Fort Davis

Hotel Limpia Dining Room
100 State Street
Tel: 432-426-3241
This dining room has a country ambiance befitting its historic hotel setting. It serves Texas classics such as steaks, seafood, and homemade pies. **$$**

Fredericksburg

Altdorf Restaurant and Beer Garden
301 W. Main Street
Tel: 830-997-7685
www.altdorfbiergarten.fbg.com
Housed in an 1847 landmark building on Main Street, Altdorf's supplies plenty of oompah for the hordes. If you're looking for an atmospheric beer garden with German music, beer, and international grub, this is the place. **$**

Galveston

Mosquito Cafe
628 14th Street
Tel: 409-763-1010

www.mosquitocafe.com
This lovely bistro feels Californian, with its light-wood beams and excited foodie fervor. The owner is, in fact, Californian and has demonstrated his commitment to food and community by feeding clean-up crews from 2008's Hurricane Ike. The changing globally inspired menu includes creative salads, fresh fish tacos and mesquite-grilled salmon, and signature desserts. The Sunday brunch is a popular local hangout. **$–$$$**

Houston

Cafe Annie
1728 Post Oak Boulevard
Tel: 713-840-1111
www.cafeannie.com
Award-winning New Southwestern food is the big draw at this contemporary eatery, a Houston favorite when you want to push the boat out. Interesting fish choices, such as branzino with apple-fennel hash and a cinnamon-rubbed pheasant dish with wild mushrooms, are examples of the chef's use of seasonal foods. **$$$**

Dessert Gallery
Kirby and Richmond streets
Tel: 713-522-9999
www.dessertgallery.com
Sara Brook's original Dessert Gallery moved to new digs up the road in 2009 but she still makes some of the sexiest cupcakes, cakes, and cookies around. The Gallery also sells sandwiches, wraps, and box lunches, if sugar ain't your thing. Two other locations. **$**

The Grove Restaurant
1611 Lamar
Tel: 713-337-7321
www.thegrovehouston.com
Perfectly located in Houston's newest park, 11-acre (4.5-hectare) Discovery Green, the Grove has an enviable leafy treehouse setting. The blond-wood room makes an elegant backdrop for inspired dishes like duck meatloaf, Gulf fish in parchment, or shrimp and

scallop brochette, but basic burgers, soup, and sandwiches are done well, too. Closed Mondays. **$$–$$$**

Marathon

Cafe Cenizo in the Gage Hotel
10 Highway 90 W.
Tel: 432-386-4205
www.gagehotel.com
The elegant dinner restaurant in this historic hotel has won raves for its rustic New Southwestern food. Earthy dishes draw heavily on fresh game meats, such as buffalo tenderloin and grilled quail, and Gulf seafood, prepared using authentically Mexican cooking techniques to create salsas from fire-roasted tomatoes and chilis and dry spice rubs. The adjoining Buffalo Bar specializes in tequilas. **$$$**

Marfa

Cochineal
107 W. San Antonio
Tel: 432-729-3300
Marfa's best new dinner restaurant is owned by seasoned restaurateurs from NYC. Their creativity and expertise comes through in perfectly prepared steaks, flash-cooked Gulf seafood, and other globally inspired dishes made from fresh local ingredients. Reservations recommended. Closed Wednesdays and Thursdays. **$$$**

San Antonio

Casa Rio
430 E. Commerce Street
Tel: 210-225-6718
www.casaderio.com
This enduring Riverwalk favorite serves large portions of tasty Mexican food. Their tasty Tortilla Soup made with chicken is a nice light bite. **$**

PRICE CATEGORIES

Price categories are for an average cost of dinner and a glass of wine, before tip:
$ = under $20
$$ = $20–40
$$$ = more than $40

Chart House Tower of the Americas
701 Bowie
Tel: 210-223-3101
www.toweroftheamericas.com
Enjoy the Chart House's famously good steaks, prime rib, and seafood while taking in the spectacular views from the revolving Tower of the Americas in Hemisfair Park. $$$

New Mexico

Cloudcroft
Rebecca's
The Lodge at Cloudcroft,
1 Corona Place
Tel: 575-682-2566
Named after the resident ghost, Rebecca's features fine Southwestern and continental cuisine in an elegant dining room with a view into the meadows. $$

Mescalero
Wendell's Inn of the Mountain Gods
287 Carrizozo Road
Tel: 888-324-0348
www.innofthemountaingods.com
Located in the sumptuously rebuilt Inn of the Mountain Gods, Wendell's celebrates Apache cowboy country with the kind of awesome certified Angus beef steaks you'd expect. Fresh local elk, free-range chicken, and seafood options like sea bass are also available. $$$

Mesilla
Double Eagle Restaurant
On the Plaza, Old Mesilla
Tel: 575-523-6700
www.double-eagle-mesilla.com
Set in a historic building dating from the 1840s, this atmospheric restaurant is filled with antiques from the days of the Old West. The menu features steaks from the restaurant's own ageing room, as well as gourmet poultry and seafood dishes with New Mexican flavors. $$$
Torch Restaurant at Meson de Mesilla
1803 Avenida de Mesilla
Tel: 575-525-9212
www.mesondemesilla.com
Savor Spanish and French cuisine by acclaimed chef

Joseph Hilbert at this Pueblo-style boutique inn. Try the green chili corn chowder to start, followed by pistachio-crusted halibut or perhaps elk chop with seared foie gras. Open for dinner only Wed–Sat. $$$

Pinos Altos
Buckhorn Saloon and Opera House
32 Main Street
Tel: 575-538-991
An authentic Wild West setting greets diners at this famous historic spot en route to Gila Cliff Dwellings. White-linen-and-candlelight service in the main dining room enhances offerings such as buffalo burgers, New York strip steak with green chili, and prime rib. There's live blues or folk several nights a week in the dark bar, and melodramas in the adjacent Opera House on Friday and Saturday. $$–$$$

Ruidoso
Cafe Rio
2547 Sudderth Drive
Tel: 575-257-7746
Design a first-rate pizza from scratch at this hip little pizzeria. $

Silver City
Diane's Restaurant and Bakery
510 N. Bullard Street
Tel: 575-538-8722
www.dianesrestaurant.com
Lace curtains, hardwood floors, and starched white linens add refinement to this otherwise casual restaurant on the historic main street, an oasis of fine internationally inspired dining in southwestern New Mexico. At dinner, try an appetizer of spanokopita followed by Seafood Thai Curry. Lunch options include excellent quiche or green chili alfredo pasta. Diane's homemade bakery items are worth a special trip. Brunch on weekends. $$

Arizona

Phoenix
Aunt Chiladas
7330 N. Dreamy Draw Drive

Tel: 602-944-1286
www.auntchiladas.com
Set in an 1890s building made of desert stone and railroad ties, this landmark restaurant serves tamed-down Mexican food compared with what you'd find elsewhere, but it's won several "best of Phoenix" awards including one for its flour tortilla chips and fresh salsa. Enjoy them in the dining room with its hand-carved fountain or on the big garden patio. $
Christo's
6327 N.7th Street
Tel: 602-264-1784
www.christos1.com
One of the top Phoenix restaurants, dishing up elegant Italian food in a formal setting. $$

Tucson
El Charro
311N Court Avenue
Tel: 520-622-1922
www.elcharrocafe.com
The El Charro is legendary in Tucson and now has several outlets, but the restaurant in the historic Presidio district downtown dates back to the 1890s. Be sure to ask for their tequila list, and try their delicious sun-dried meat – their Carne Seca plate has been voted one of the best 50 dishes in the US. There's also a courtyard for outdoor dining. $$
The Grill at Hacienda del Sol
5601N Hacienda del Sol Road
Tel: 520-529-3500
www.haciendadelsol.com
Many Tucsonians say this is the city's best eating place, out at the intimate and historic Hacienda del Sol resort. Their Sunday brunch is definitely one of the best anywhere, and the romantic views of the foothills in the evening from the Terraza del Sol combine with dishes like Tasmanian ocean trout or expertly cooked rack of lamb, and one of the best wine lists in the country. $$$

Yuma
The Garden Cafe
250 Madison Avenue
Tel: 928-783-1491

These lush gardens punctuated with sweet-smelling flowers and bird-song were once part of the historic Sanguinetti House estate. Now they make a delightful setting for an alfresco lunch or breakfast. Dishes range from homemade quiche, soup and enormous salads to scrumptious tri-tip steak and grande burritos. Excellent desserts. $
Lutes Casino
221 S. Main Street
Tel: 928-782-2192
www.lutescasino.com
Lutes is a Yuma institution, not really a casino but a bar/restaurant with pool tables. The menu includes the Especial, Lutes' own hotdog/cheeseburger combo, and there are also standards like Philly cheese steaks, corn dogs, tacos, salads, and sandwiches. $
Market Wine Bar and Bistro
1501 S. Redondo Center Drive
Tel: 928-373-6574
This upscale but casual bistro and wine bar is in the new Radisson Hotel, a short drive from Downtown. The atmosphere is fun and colorful, with boutique wines and a menu inspired by Mediterranean cuisine with a fresh seafood catch flown in daily. $$–$$$

California

El Centro
La Hacienda Cafe
841 W. Main Street
Tel: 760-353-8118
Very good Mexican food. $

La Mesa
Brigantine Seafood Restaurant
9350 Fuerte Drive
Tel: 619-465-1935
www.brigantine.com
Enjoy the popular lounge and oyster bar, or a seafood meal in the nautical-themed restaurant or outdoors on the lush garden patio. $$
Marieta's Restaurant
8949 La Mesa Boulevard
Tel: 619-462-3500
Southwestern dishes and friendly service in a neighborhood restaurant. $$

PACIFIC ROUTE

California

Big Sur

Nepenthe
48510 Highway 1
Tel: 831-667-2345
www.nepenthebigsur.com
This landmark restaurant on Highway 1 opened in 1949 and is still operated by the same family. It serves simple but delicious favorites like Ambrosia Burger and Three Berry Pie. The real reason to come here is the fabulous views over Big Sur. **$$**

Bodega Bay

Lucas Wharf Restaurant
595 Highway 1
Tel: 707-875-3522
Fresh seafood is the specialty at this restaurant, with a range of dishes such as blackened snapper and risotto with jumbo prawns. Note that it can close as early as 8pm. **$$**

Calistoga

All Seasons Bistro
1400 Lincoln Avenue
Tel: 707-942-9111
www.allseasonsnapavalley.net
Black-and-white tile flooring and red ceiling give it a retro look, but the cuisine at this casual restaurant is anything but. The menu features creative dishes based on fresh seasonal ingredients from local producers, grown organically and chemical-free, paired with premium wines for a memorable meal. **$$$**

Cambria

West End Bar and Grill
774 Main St
Tel: 805-927-5521
If you want good burgers and good beer, the West End Bar and Grill is the type of Main Street place that does them both perfectly. There's a wooden bar, a cozy fireplace, background music, and a menu and drinks list that appeals to everyone, including families. Don't expect surprises or frills, but you will get decent food and friendly service. **$-$$**

Carmel-by-the-Sea

Dametra's Café
Between Dolores and Lincoln on Ocean
Tel: 831-622-7766
Diners queue every night of the week to sample the relaxed Mediterranean atmosphere created by the affable and charming owner and his team in the kitchen, who produce stunning versions of authentic Greek, Italian, Middle Eastern, and other dishes from the shores of the Mediterranean. The long, narrow dining room takes you back to the Med too, with ochre walls and a happy buzz from the close-set tables. **$$$**

Eureka

Restaurant 301
Carter House Inn, 301 L Street
Tel: 707-444-8062
www.carterhouse.com
Regarded as one of the best restaurants in northern California, and certainly with one of the best wine lists according to *Wine Spectator*, this small yet spacious restaurant is part of the Carter House Inn. It offers a changing menu of sophisticated cooking, with the option of taking a 5-course Discovery Menu which can include paired wines for each dish. **$$$**

Samoa Cookhouse
Off Highway 101 across the Samoa Bridge
Tel: 707-442-1659
Eat like a lumberjack at this northern California landmark on the outskirts of Eureka. Hefty breakfasts, lunches, and dinners are served family-style at long tables where you help yourself. Save room for the hot apple pie. **$**

Laguna Beach

Las Brisas
361 Cliff Drive
Tel: 949-497-5434
www.lasbrisaslagunabeach.com
Sit on the outdoor patio or indoor dining room, and enjoy excellent Mexican cuisine and seafood dishes with stunning views of the ocean. **$$-$$$**

Mendocino

Ravens Restaurant
Stanford Inn, Coast Highway and Comptche Ukiah Road
Tel: 707-937-5615
www.ravensrestaurant.com
The Stanford Inn's exceptional and acclaimed vegan restaurant is open to non-guests too, and even if you're not vegetarian, if you're interested in food you should dine here at least once. The rustic decor is smart but relaxing, the wine list extensive and the food startlingly original, like the signature dish of Sea Palm Strudel. **$$$**

Monterey

Abalonetti
57 Fisherman's Wharf
Tel: 831-373-1851
www.abalonettimonterey.com
The eating places on Fisherman's Wharf may look all the same but some are better than others. As well as some of the best clam chowder on Fisherman's Wharf, Abalonetti's stands out as one of the few to have really good terraces overlooking the bay, where you can watch the seals and sea lions swimming and also enjoying their own fish dishes. **$$**

Morro Bay

The Whale's Tail
945 Embarcadero
Tel: 805-772-7555
Whether you just want to warm up with a bowl of clam chowder, or fill up with a seafood platter, try this simple seaside restaurant serving seafood and pasta dishes. **$-$$**

Napa

The Bounty Hunter
975 1st Street, Napa Town
Tel: 707-226-3976
www.bountyhunterwine.com
The lively Bounty Hunter bar makes full use of the wines in its adjoining wine shop, with a list that includes 40 wines by the glass and over 400 you can purchase to drink or take home. The food's impressive too, especially their trademark Smokin' BBQ Platter. **$$**

Novato

Rickey's Restaurant and Bar
Inn Marin, 250 Entrada Drive
Tel: 415-883-5952
www.rickeysrestaurant.com
Part of the Inn Marin but livelier than any hotel restaurant you've ever seen, Rickey's has live jazz on Friday and Saturday nights (booking advised), lots of tables, a fun feeling, and food that isn't fancy but goes down well – like pan-seared scallops or filet mignon with bacon mashed potatoes. **$$-$$$**

Oceanside

101 Cafe
631 South Coast Highway
Tel: 760-722-5220
www.101Cafe.net
Oceanside's oldest restaurant is a real roadside diner decked out with 1950s memorabilia and serving great burgers, omelets and classic diner dinners from 6.30am till midnight daily. Try a peanut butter malt. It's the bee's knees! **$**

Pescadero

Duarte's
202 Stage Road
Tel: 650-879-0464
www.duartestavern.com
With a beautiful historic setting on a remote stretch of coast, this casual tavern serves everything from sandwiches for beachgoers to family Sunday dinners with all the trimmings, but *do not* miss the cream of artichoke and cream of green chili soups – get one of each. **$**

PRICE CATEGORIES

Price categories are for an average cost of dinner and a glass of wine, before tip:
$ = under $20
$$ = $20-40
$$$ = more than $40

San Diego

Rock Bottom Brewery
401 G Street
tel: 619-231-7000
www.rockbottom.com
Set in a former Studebaker showroom in the Gaslamp Quarter, this brew-pub serves great hand-crafted beers and great food to go with them. Live music and dancing every weekend. **$–$$**

Suite and Tender
1047 Fifth Avenue
Tel: 619-515-3003
www.suiteandtender.com
Choose your steak knife from a collection of knives from around the world at this sophisticated steakhouse in Downtown's Sé San Diego hotel (see page 418). There are plenty of fresh seafood options too. Both land and ocean choices bear the mark of Michelin 2-star chef Christopher Lee. **$$$**

San Francisco

Greens
Building A, Fort Mason Center in the Marina district
Tel: 415-771-6222
www.greensrestaurant.com
Organic produce, seasonal specials and a mesquite grill are the cornerstones of this vegetarian restaurant, one of the most renowned in the world. Plus spectacular views of the Golden Gate Bridge. **$$$**

House of Nanking
919 Kearny Street, Chinatown
Tel: 415-421-1429
The city's most popular Chinese, where the cramped seating and pushy service are part of the charm. **$**

Masa's
648 Bush Street,
north of Union Square
Tel: 415-989-7154
www.masasrestaurant.com
Perhaps the most expensive and critically lauded restaurant in all of San Francisco. The perennial winner in the city's restaurant lists. **$$$**

Santa Barbara

La Super-Rica Taqueria
622 N. Milpas Street
tel: 805-963-4940
Jaded taqueria aficionados meet their match here,

where almost every item on the menu would be the house specialty anywhere else. There's a varied and unusual mix of flavors, some quite intense (hot), and not a boring burrito to be seen. Eat in the covered patio along with the equally eclectic clientele and see why this landmark in Downtown's Latino quarter gets rave reviews. **$**

Olio e Limone
11 W. Victoria Suite 17
Tel: 805-899-2699
www.olioelimone.com
The wine cellar visible behind a glass wall in the dining room, combined with the white walls and tile floors, sets a cheerful Mediterranean scene at this always busy place. The mouthwateringly wonderful Italian food is perfectly prepared and presented, with dishes like pumpkin ravioli. Excellent service by Italian waiters. **$$$**

Santa Monica

Fig
101 Wilshire Boulevard
Tel: 310-319-3111
www.figsantamonica.com
The new restaurant in the Fairmont Miramar hotel is both intimate and casual, with cool classy modern lines, some private booths and some bar seating too. The food is what matters, though, and with dishes that are full of flavors, such as foie gras with a fig sauce, expertly prepared fresh fish and beef served with minty-tasting micro-greens and strawberry shortcake with strawberry ice cream for dessert, there's no problem on that score. **$$$**

Trinidad

Larrupin Cafe
1658 Patricks Point Drive
Tel: 707-677-0230
Truly a one-of-a-kind place, featuring unique West Coast/continental-inspired creations using organic meat and produce, with many vegetarian offerings. Hobbit comfort in an enchanting woodsy setting, it's a delight from appetizers to dessert.

Make reservations weeks in advance if possible, or you might miss out. **$$**

Oregon

Cannon Beach

The Warren House Pub
3301 S. Hemlock Street
Tel: 503-436-1130
You can eat either in the family-friendly restaurant at the front, where there's often a wait for a table, or in the simpler bar at the back, with its pool table. Both places have good wine and beer lists, and the menu has a lot of good plain but tasty seafood such as oyster burgers. **$$**

Coos Bay

Benetti's
260 S. Broadway
Tel: 541-267-6066
www.benettis.com
A family-run Italian restaurant with great service and fantastic food, Benetti's is always busy. There's family dining downstairs and an adult dining room upstairs, overlooking the bay and the boardwalk. **$$**

Fisherman's Wharf
Charleston Boat Basin, Dock D
Tel: 541-888-8862
There's no better place for fresh crab and seafood, which you can purchase right on the dock from local fishermen. They will pack you a box of crab to go – perfect for a picnic by the sea as you drive the Cape Arago beach loop. **$**

Gold Beach

Spinner's
29430 Ellensburg Avenue,
Highway 101
Tel: 541-247-5160
Good service and a buzzing atmosphere are the hallmarks of this seafood, steak and chophouse, set in a large, rustic wooden building with windows overlooking the shore. Great food, from bison burgers to prime rib to cedar-planked wild salmon. **$–$$**

Portland

Bread and Ink
3610 SE Hawthorne Boulevard
Tel: 503-239-4756

www.breadandinkcafe.com
Cheerful service and food cooked with fresh ingredients, locally sourced as much as possible. **$**

Jake's Famous Crawfish
401 SW 12th
Tel: 503-226-1419
www.mccormickandschmicks.com
Mouthwatering seafood and a Portland landmark for 110 years, this is one of the best and busiest seafood places along the Pacific Coast. **$$**

Yachats

The Drift Inn
124 Highway 101 N
Tel: 541-547-4477
www.the-drift-inn.com
The Drift Inn is one of the best and most popular eating places in the area, with a bar down one side, a small stage where musicians play every night, and seating in booths throughout the rest of the room. Their halibut fish and chips plate is perfect, and there are some unusual dishes such as figs in a blanket, and vegetarian choices in among the steak and seafood specials. **$$**

Washington

Chinook

Sanctuary Restaurant
794 State Route 101
Tel: 360-777-8380
www.sanctuaryrestaurant.com
Based in the unusual and beautiful surrounds of what was a Methodist church when it was built in 1906, the Sanctuary still has the antique purple and gold stained-glass windows – and thankfully food to compete with the surroundings. Opening hours vary. **$$**

Olympia

La Petite Maison
101 Division Street
Tel: 360-943-8812
Enjoy the fresh seafood and decadent desserts. **$$**

PRICE CATEGORIES

Price categories are for an average cost of dinner and a glass of wine, before tip:
$ = under $20
$$ = $20–40
$$$ = more than $40

A CTIVITIES

FESTIVALS, THE ARTS, NIGHTLIFE, SHOPPING, AND SPECTATOR SPORTS

FESTIVALS

January

First Peoples World's Fair and Powwow (Tucson, Arizona)
Tribes from all over the country converge on Tucson for this big powwow. Tel: 520-622-4900.

Orange Bowl (Miami, Florida)
The final game between Florida's two best college football teams. New Year's Day. Tel: 305-341-4700.

River City Bluegrass Festival (Portland, Oregon)
Big names like Ralph Stanley headline this annual fest in the rainy Northwest. Tel: 503-282-0877.

Westminster Kennel Dog Show (New York)
The US version of Britain's Crufts Dog Show, this two-day event at Madison Square Garden attracts the cream of the canine crop to the Big Apple; www.westminsterkennelclubshow.com.

February

San Antonio Stock Show and Rodeo (San Antonio, Texas)
The largest junior rodeo and stockshow in the US, and music, dance, storytelling, and poetry at the Texas Heritage Museum. Tel: 210-225-5851.

Groundhog Day (Punxsutawney, Pennsylvania)
Over 30,000 people descend on Gobblers Knob to see whether groundhog Punxsutawney Phil sees his shadow, denoting six more weeks of winter. Hayrides, parades, ice and chainsaw carving, and other entertainment. www.groundhog.org.

Mardi Gras (Mobile, Alabama; New Orleans, Louisiana; Galveston, Texas, etc.)
Gulf cities celebrate Mardi Gras. Mobile has the oldest Mardi Gras celebration (1703) but New Orleans is the most famous and long-running, from January 6 (Epiphany) to the day before Ash Wednesday in February. Highlights are parades of colorful, exotic floats created by competing "krewes," eating, drinking, dancing, and mayhem. Tel: 251-208-2000 (Mobile) and 504-522-1555 (New Orleans).

Madison Winter Festival (Madison, Wisconsin)
Madison's hardy residents descend on frigid Capitol Square to enjoy ice and snow sculptures, tubing hill, snowboard rail jam, and world-class cross-country ski racing and snowshoeing; www.winter-fest.com.

March

South by Southwest (Austin, Texas)
The 10-day live-music festival, the country's largest, welcomes more than 1,800 different acts on 80+ stages around Austin. A concurrent independent movie-making conference and festival and comedy showcase rounds out offerings. www.sxsw.com.

Tennessee Williams New Orleans Literary Festival (New Orleans, Louisiana)
Five days of readings, dramatizations, lectures, and walking tours featuring renowned actors celebrate the *Cat on a Hot Tin Roof* author. Tel: 1-800-990-FEST.

Miami International Film Festival (Miami, Florida)
A major movie love-in with emphasis on Ibero-American film. Tel: 305-237-FILM

National Festival of the West (Scottsdale, Arizona)
A four-day western extravaganza. It features a western music jamboree, concerts, a huge trade show, western film festival, the Cowboy Spirit Award, a cookout cookoff, mountain man rendezvous, cowboy mounted shooting, and Buffalo Soldiers re-enactment. Tel: 602-996-4387.

April

National Cherry Blossom Festival (Washington, DC)
Commemorating the 1912 gift of 3,000 cherry trees to the US, this festival heralds the advent of spring in the nation's capital. Tel: 877-44BLOOM.

Crossroads Film Festival (Jackson, Mississippi)
An inspiring cross-fertilization of Blues music and independent film makes this one of the biggest arts gatherings in Mississippi. Tel: 985-788-1306.

San Francisco Women's Film Festival (San Francisco, California)
A four-day festival honoring documentaries, animation, video, experimental films, and other movies made by women. Tel: 510-235-0709.

May

Beale Street Blues Festival (Memphis, Tennessee)
Three days of concerts by the top blues performers in the nation on the Mississippi River. Tel: 901-525-4611.

Cinco de Mayo
Festivals featuring parades, food, music, and folkloric dancing are held in Hispanic communities throughout the US to commemorate Mexican liberation from French occupation.

Key West Fishing Tournament (Key West, Florida)
A fish fest in Ernest Hemingway's old home town, held April to November. Tel: 800-970-9056.
Route 66 Fun Run Weekend (Seligman to Topock)
A classic car "run," with a festival in Kingman. Hualapai Indian barbecue, booths, entertainment, classic car judging, and a leisurely Sunday morning ride on Route 66. Tel: 928-753-5001.
Sweet Auburn Springfest (Atlanta, Georgia)
The largest African-American festival in the region features more than 300 entertainers in downtown Atlanta. Tel: 770-912-7221.

June

Corn Dances (Santa Ana, Tesuque, and other Pueblos, New Mexico)
One of the most important dances of the year prays for rain to ensure a good harvest. Tel: 505-843-7270.
Mariachi USA (Los Angeles, California)
Held at the Hollywood Bowl, this festival features a huge array of Mexican mariachi bands. Tel: 866-204-1873.
Juneteenth (various US cities)
Begun in Galveston, Texas, in 1865, Juneteenth is the oldest celebration in the US marking the end of slavery and celebrating African-American culture. Major celebrations in Texas. www.juneteenth.com.
Slug Festival (Eatonville, Washington)
The signature creature of the rainy Northwest, slugs are celebrated at Northwest Trek, south of Seattle, with displays, talks, and slimey games. Tel: 360-832-7152.
Solstice Celebration (Santa Barbara, California)
This wildly popular parade was the brainwave of local artists and has a free-spirited Mardi Gras-like feel, complete with gorgeous floats, extraordinary costumes and masks, dancing, face painting, and street food. Tel: 805-965-3396.

July

Fourth of July (throughout US)
Fireworks, cookouts, parades, and entertainment, from concerts to rodeos, mark American Independence Day celebrations.
Folkmoot USA (North Carolina)
More than 300 international performers highlight international folk arts in the mountains of western North Carolina. Tel: 877-FOLK USA.

Taste of Buffalo (Buffalo, NY)
The second-largest food festival in the country, attracting 60 restaurants and 450,000 visitors, takes place near Niagara Falls in upstate New York. Tel: 800-BUFFALO.
Olympic Peninsula Music Festival (Quilcene, Washington)
Starting in July, several months of weekend concerts in an old barn attract chamber music lovers to the remote Olympic Peninsula by ferry. Tel: 360-732-4800.

August

Burning Man Festival (Black Rock City, Nevada)
Throughout August, a temporary "city" of up to 25,000 campers arises in the scorching Mojave Desert to make art together and build community, culminating in the burning of a 52ft (15-meter) -high pagan effigy. Tel: 415-TO-FLAME.
Bumbershoot (Seattle, Washington)
The largest of its kind, Seattle's premier arts festival takes up residence below the Space Needle to offer three days of superb music on several stages, arts and crafts, food booths, and other activities over Labor Day Weekend. Tel: 206-816-6444.
116th Street Festival Carnival Del Barrio (New York City)
A fun two-day open-air festival celebrating Hispanic and Caribbean arts, food, and culture. Tel: 212-243-1177; 562-424-0013.
Retro on Roscoe (Chicago, Illinois)
A huge neighborhood weekend street festival featuring four stages of live entertainment, an antique car show, and an arts and crafts show. Tel: 773-665-4682.
Indian Market (Santa Fe, New Mexico)
Santa Fe's Plaza is transformed into the US's largest open-air market. About 1,000 Indian artists compete in a juried show; others set up booths along nearby streets. Book hotels well ahead. Tel: 505-983-5220.

September

Farm Aid (Chicago, Illinois)
This successful annual concert series raises funds for US small farms and features superb country rock music by founders Willie Nelson, John Mellencamp, Neil Young, Dave Matthews, and others.
Tel: 800-FARM AID.
Santa Fe Fiesta (Santa Fe, New Mexico)
The oldest such celebration in the US, this festival commemorating Santa

Fe's Spanish founding fathers features horseback parades, floats, a children's and pet parade – and the other Fiesta: the burning of Old Man Gloom, Zozobra – over Labor Day weekend. Tel: 505-988-3279.
East LA Mexican Independence Day Parade (Los Angeles, California)
The country's oldest Mexican independence day celebration. Tel: 310-914-0015.

October

Albuquerque International Balloon Fiesta (Albuquerque, New Mexico)
The world's largest gathering of hot-air balloons is staged over this nine-day festival. Tel: 800-733-9918.
New York City Underground Comedy Festival (New York)
For five nights, venues around Manhattan and Brooklyn host up-and-coming comics and seasoned veterans at legendary venues like the Bitter End. Tel: 212-563-7488.
Bluegrass FanFest (Nashville, Tennessee)
More than 60 musicians take to the stage to celebrate bluegrass music and choose a champion fiddler. Tel: 615-256-3222 .
Great Grapes! Wine, Food, and Arts Festival (Virginia, Maryland, North Carolina)
Visitors to Reston, Annapolis, Charlottte, and Cary on the East Coast raise a glass to fine local wines and enjoy gourmet foods and musical entertainment every October. www.uncorkthefun.com.
Rock Shrimp Festival (St Mary's, Georgia)
This one-day fest in historic St Mary's, off I-95, pays tribute to the Gulf's abundant rock shrimp with 5k/10k races, parade, entertainment, food, arts and crafts, and rock shrimp dinners. Tel: 912-552-1764.

November

New York Marathon (New York)
Watched by two million spectators, the largest marathon in the US attracts over 100,000 entrants competing for $600,000 in prize money. www.nycmarathon.org.
Sweet Auburn Heritage Festival (Atlanta, Georgia)
One of the largest outdoor festivals in the South attracts over 200,000 people to the Sweet Auburn neighborhood of Atlanta annually with its diverse musical offerings, from jazz to gospel.
Tel: 404-886-4469.

Doo Dah Parade (Pasadena, California)
This spoof parade features 1,500 participants. Some of the most famous include the Briefcase Marching Drill Team, the Hibachi Marching Grill Team, and the Invisible Man Marching Band. Berkeley also has its own Doo Dah Parade. Tel: 800-307-7977.
Dia De Los Muertos – Day of the Dead (Hispanic communities in the US)
Sugar skulls and food offerings adorn home altars and family grave sites in Hispanic communities on this day of celebrating those who have passed on.

December

Christmas New Orleans Style (New Orleans, Louisiana)
A month-long Christmas celebration featuring guided walks of the decorated French Quarter and Reveillon holiday meals reminiscent of those from the 1800s. Tel: 800-673-5725.
Canyon Road Farolito Walk (Santa Fe, New Mexico)
Farolitos (brown bag candle lanterns) show the way to the Holy Family on Christmas Eve. Attracts thousands to historic Canyon Road to stroll, sing carols, drink hot cider, and celebrate the holiday. Tel: 505-984-6760
New Year's Eve in Times Square (New York)
Viewers across the US count down to the New Year by watching televised musical acts and celebrities throwing the switch to start the ball drop in Times Square.

OUTDOOR ACTIVITIES

The United States has a huge number of national, state, county, and city parks; lakeside recreation areas; and nature preserves. There's plenty of scope for walking, swimming, fishing, cycling, boating, and participant sports.

Water and wind

Coastal areas are your best bet for water activities. **Deep-sea charters** offer fishing for grouper, sailfish, and tarpon in Florida and halibut, tuna, and salmon on the Pacific Northwest coasts. **Surfing** and **swimming** predominate along wave-pounded beaches in southern California and to some extent the Atlantic Coast.
Parasailing and **windsurfing** attract enthusiasts wherever there are prevailing strong winds. The

Windsurfing Capital of the World is actually inland, though, at Hood River in Oregon's Columbia River Gorge.
Diving and **snorkeling** are spectacular in Florida's Keys, where your companions are often dolphins. Limestone regions, such as Crystal River in central Florida, offer diving in crystal-clear spring-fed sinkholes frequented by manatees. Santa Rosa on the hot, dusty plains of eastern New Mexico is a unique find: its 80ft (25-meter) -deep, spring-fed Blue Hole is popular with desert divers.

Boating is virtually an artform in coastal regions, and along the US-Canada border regions of the Great Lakes in the Midwest and Finger Lakes of upstate New York. Boats are more than recreation on the calm Intracoastal Waterways and offshore islands of the Gulf Coast, New England, and Washington State: they are often residences and transportation. Above major dams, western mountain rivers, such as the Colorado through the Grand Canyon, and the Rio Grande in Big Bend National Park, have spectacular **whitewater** and **flatwater rafting**. Below the dams, flatwater sports are popular at Amistad Reservoir on the Rio Grande and Lake Powell on the Colorado, a good place to rent a houseboat or kayak.

Wherever there are bodies of water, people like to fish. Usually a state permit is required. **Fishing** next to highways, along canal banks or in small boats, is common in the South, particularly in the Everglades and in the bayous of the Mississippi Delta where fishing for crawfish has deep cultural roots. Fishing in high mountain streams and lakes requires a little more effort, with flyfishermen often hiking (or, these days, riding all-terrain vehicles) to catch rainbow trout and salmon. Resorts offering log cabins near stocked lakes and streams are popular in mountain regions of the US as summer vacation spots.

Hiking

Hiking is popular in every region. Many of the best-known trails follow historic American Indian and frontier trails through mountains, valleys, and open deserts. National parks, and other federally managed lands, usually offer the greatest diversity of trails for hikers, from short paved accessible trails to scenic overlooks for disabled users to short day hikes for families and longer cross-country trails.

Walkers and **joggers** in cities will increasingly find designated urban

trail networks linking the city and adjoining country in places such as Austin, Texas, and Flagstaff, Arizona.
Most challenging are **long-distance trails** like the Appalachian Trail in the East and the John Muir Trail in California's Sierra Nevada in the West. **Backcountry hiking** requires preparation, stamina, and time: many hikers split trails into segments hiked over years. Come well prepared and know your limits when you set out.

Desert cities

Cities such as Phoenix, Tucson, and Albuquerque and Florida locations (Tampa and Fort Myers for example), with their mild winter temperatures, are major destinations for **off-season outdoor activities** such as hiking, marathon training, bicycling, golf, tennis, and spring training for professional footballers and baseball players.

Mountains and "Sky Islands"

The Rockies, Cascades, Sierra Nevada, Appalachians, Smokies, and isolated desert "sky island" chains of southern deserts offer an escape from 90–100°F (32–38°C) summer temperatures at lower elevations. These same mountainous locales are even busier when winter snows hit, attracting downhill and cross-country skiiers and snowboarders to **ski resorts** as far south as Ski Apache in southern New Mexico's Sacramento Mountains.

The steady 58-degree temperature of subterranean limestone **cavern systems** such as Carlsbad Caverns in New Mexico makes them excellent for caving year round; Carlsbad offers wild-cave tours as well as main-cavern touring.

The Western States

The western states – particularly Arizona, Colorado, New Mexico, and Utah, where the mile-high Colorado Plateau has been carved into sinuous canyons by the Colorado River and its tributaries – have the country's most enchanting combination of outdoor activities and tourism on the largest federally managed acreage in the Lower 48. Professional tour companies in gateway communities next to parks are usually the best way of experiencing **remote wilderness areas** where vehicles aren't allowed, particularly if it's your first time in an area. They take care of all the planning, permits, transportation, and meals, and some use low-impact horses and llamas to carry equipment so you don't have to, freeing you up to enjoy the experience.

Extreme sports, such as backcountry canyoneering in Zion National Park, free- and roped climbing on cliffs in Yosemite National Park, and mountain climbing in North Cascades National Park in Washington are also available through adventure companies. These are aimed at very experienced and fit outdoorspeople, familiar with the local environments, and should never be attempted by beginners.

Bicycle tours of regions such as the Texas Hill Country, California's Wine Country, and New England in fall are both cultural as well as challenging, often incorporating upscale amenities such as bed-and-breakfasts, wine tastings, gourmet meals, and guided tours with pedal time. In urban areas, you can usually rent a bicycle (or rollerblades) to get around. Some cities offer designated bicycle trails through historic communities, such as the Pinellas Trail between St Petersburg and Tarpon Springs on Florida's Gulf and the Venice Boardwalk in southern California – the quintessential LA experience.

National Park System

America currently has 390 units in its vast National Park System. The seed of the national parks came when Yosemite Valley was set aside as a small land grant by Abraham Lincoln in 1864. The first federally mandated national park was Yellowstone, which was set aside in 1872 to protect its unique scenery followed rapidly by Yosemite, Mt Rainier, Glacier, and Mesa Verde national parks. In 1916 the **National Park Service** was founded with the challenging mission to both protect parks and make them accessible for the public to enjoy.

National parks are few in number and the crown jewels of the system. They preserve large, relatively intact ecosystems and the natural and cultural history associated with them; many also have pristine areas managed as wilderness that allow no mechanized transport within them. **National historic sites** and historical parks are more numerous and found in cities as well as the countryside. They focus on telling America's unique history through diverse stories. **Recreation areas** are reservoirs next to dams managed by the Army Corps of Engineers and operated by the Bureau of Reclamation.

National monuments are a special case: the US president may, at their discretion, unilaterally set aside areas of important scientific and archeological interest for preservation and research if they are in danger of being lost through destruction or overdevelopment.

Outdoor activities vary from park to park but most offer excellent opportunities for hiking, fishing, wildlife watching, horseback riding, and scenic drives. All of the National Parks listed in this book are open daily, year-round. For further information on the national parks, log on to www.nps.gov or visit the individual parks' websites listed below.

Atlantic Route

Everglades National Park
www.nps.gov/ever.
Permits & Licenses Backcountry camping permits required.
Camping Sites may be reserved at the Flamingo Campground online or by calling 877-444-6777 (international: 518-885-3639). All other sites are first-come, first-served only.
General Information Few parks conjure up more mystery or romance than the Everglades. This vast expanse of marshland, grasses, swamp, and cypress forest is the largest subtropical wilderness area in the US. Recently, the Everglades and nearby Big Cypress preserves have been a release point for jaguar, an endangered species that is teetering on the brink of survival here. Alligators are numerous, and drivers should be wary of reptiles crossing the road at all times.

Northern Route

Badlands National Park
Contact Tel: 605-433-5361, www.nps.gov/badl.
Permits & Licenses No.
Camping First-come, first-served.
General Information Be prepared for sudden changes in weather, high winds and sudden hail, rain or snowstorms. Hikers should carry adequate water – 1 gallon (4 liters) per day per person.

Grand Teton National Park
Contact Tel: 307-739-3300, www.nps.gov/grte.
Permits & Licenses Backcountry camping permits required.
Camping First-come, first-served.
General Information Park concessioners offer horseback rides at Colter Bay and Jackson Lake Lodge. The Teton Range offers many opportunities for climbers and mountaineers. The Jenny Lake Ranger Station is the center for climbing information, routes, conditions, etc. Contact Grand Teton Lodge Co. (tel: 307-543-2811) for Jackson Lake cruises, float trips on the Snake River, boat rentals, and horseback riding.

Yellowstone National Park
Contact Tel: 307-344-7381, www.nps.gov/yell.
Permits & Licenses Backcountry camping permits required.
Camping Some sites can be reserved in advance by contacting Yellowstone National Park Lodges, PO Box 165, Yellowstone National Park, WY 82190, tel: 307-344-7311.
General Information Do not try to approach or feed wildlife. Bison appear placid and slow-moving but can charge quickly and suddenly if irritated. Never approach closer than 100 yards (90 meters) to bears.

Glacier National Park
Contact Tel: 406-888-7800, www.nps.gov/glac.
Permits & Licenses Backcountry camping permits required.
Camping Fish Creek and St Mary campgrounds can be reserved in advance (tel: 800-365-CAMP); remaining campgrounds first-come, first-served.
General Information Never try to feed or approach wildlife. Glacier Park, Inc. (tel: 406-892-2525) offers a variety of guided bus tours. Glacier Park Boat Co. (tel: 406-257-2426) offers cruises on McDonald, Many Glaciers, Two Medicine, and St Mary lakes. Glacier Wilderness Guides & Montana Raft Co. (tel: 406-387-5555 or 800-521-RAFT) offer a variety of escorted trips, from one-day hikes to eight-day backpacking/rafting expeditions.

Olympic National Park
Contact Tel: 360-565-3130, www.nps.gov/olym.
Permits & Licenses Backcountry camping permits required (fee charged). In summer, some wilderness areas require reservations, tel: 360-565-3100. Washington fishing license.
Camping First-come, first-served.
General Information Crossing snowfields may require special skills and equipment. Hiking in high elevations can be extremely difficult, causing dizziness, nausea, and shortness of breath. Give yourself a few days to adjust. Obtain a tide table before hiking on the beach; incoming tides can trap hikers between headlands. Look for floating logs, too. An unexpected wave can send them hurtling toward the beach, crushing

anything that gets in the way. The ocean is cold and currents are fierce; swim in the lakes instead of the ocean.

Central Route
Shenandoah National Park
Contact Tel: 540-999-3500, www.nps.gov/shen.
Permits and Licenses Visitors may obtain a 5-day nonresident fishing license at Big Meadows Wayside or sporting goods stores. Camping in the backcountry requires a free permit, available online, at trailheads, and visitor centers.
Camping Most of the campsites in the park's four campgrounds are first-served basis and are very popular so get there early in the day to secure a site. Some 20 percent of sites may be reserved up to 180 days in advance through www.recreation.gov or by calling 1-877-444-6777.
General Information Shenandoah is known for its historic architecture as well as its scenic beauty. It has 340 structures on the National Register of Historic Places, many built in the 1930s by the Roosevelt-era Civilian Conservation Corps (CCC). Shenandoah's 105-mile (169km) -long Skyline Drive, linking the Front Royal with the Waynesboro-Charlottesville area, is a major through road for locals as well as visitors. A long-range repaving project is currently under way: be prepared for delays on weekdays.

Grand Canyon National Park
Contact Tel: 928-638-7888, www.nps.gov/grca.
Seasons The South Rim is open year-round. The North Rim is open mid-May–mid-October.
Camping First-come, first-served spaces on North and South Rim usually fill by noon May–September. Some sites can be reserved in advance by contacting 877-444-6677. RV sites are available on South Rim year-round at Trailer Village, tel: 303-297-2757 for reservations.
Permits & Licenses Arizona fishing license. Inexpensive backcountry permits (for overnight hiking; not required for day hikes) can be obtained by mail from Backcountry Information Center, PO Box 129, Grand Canyon, AZ 86023, fax: 928-638-2125. Reserve well in advance; popular trails tend to fill up early.
General Information The inner canyon is subject to extreme heat in summer. Hikers should carry adequate food and water, at least one gallon (4 liters) per person per day.

Southern Route
Big Bend National Park
Contact Tel: 432-477-2251, www.nps.gov/bibe.
Permits and Licenses Free backcountry camping permits required.
Camping Mainly first-come, first-served; 69 sites may be reserved Nov–Apr.
General Information Big Bend is over 800,000 acres (323,000 hectares) in size and extremely rugged and remote; you will need at least two days to see most of the park on main roads. Hikers and 4WD explorers should allow a week. The sun is intense all year: wear a high SPF sunscreen, sunglasses, and broad-brimmed hat. Carry high-energy food and water in the car and on every hike, no matter how short, taking care to eat and sip water in equal measures to avoid salt imbalances in the body. Allow 1 gallon (4 liters) per person per day. Don't overexert yourself: the nearest hospital is 100 miles (160km) away. Watch out for rattlesnakes, mountain lions, bears, and javelinas.

Pacific Route
Redwood National Park
Contact Tel: 707-464-6101, www.nps.gov/redw.
Permits & Licenses California fishing license and backcountry camping permits required.
Camping Camping fees at state park campgrounds. Campsites are available by reservation May–August, first-come, first-served at other times. Contact Reserve America, Rancho Cordova, CA, tel: 800-444-7275 or 916-638-5883.
General Information Access to the Tall Trees Grove is limited; summer shuttle bus transports visitors down the rugged 7-mile (11km) road to the trailhead. Otherwise, a limited number of private-vehicle permits are distributed on a first-come, first-served basis. Backpackers must secure a free permit at any information center. Animal-proof food canisters are available to borrow free of charge at Thomas H. Kuchel Visitor Center. Swimming can be extremely dangerous. Ocean water is cold, currents are strong, and no lifeguards are on duty.

SHOPPING

Shopping is a lot of fun in America! For lovers of kitsch, **Florida** and the **American West** won't disappoint, with their doctored postcards, fossil rocks, saltwater taffy, cactus jelly,

snowglobes, and other Americana. **Cities** such as New York, Los Angeles, San Francisco, and Houston are good places to buy contemporary art. Cowboy and pioneer art is easily found in towns adjoining **ranch country** in Arizona, New Mexico, Wyoming, and Colorado. Indian Market in Santa Fe offers Indian-made jewelry, pottery, carvings, sandpaintings, and other items. Mexican souvenirs are best purchased in **southern border towns** such as Tucson, Phoenix, San Antonio, and San Diego. Most American cities feature at least one large shopping mall, with chain stores, restaurants, cafés, and movie theaters on the outskirts of town.

More and more are also revitalizing their historic Downtowns with unique shopping areas featuring boutiques, restaurants, museums, and art galleries. **Small towns** in rural locations and roadside stands are often the most interesting places to find unique souvenirs of the region, from preserved foods to handmade clothing and crafts.

Atlantic Route
New York City
Shopping is a major pastime in New York City: there isn't much to be found anywhere that can't be found here, and usually more of it. **Art**, of course, is a good bet; apart from the major auctioneers, **Sotheby's** and **Christies**, there are hundreds of art galleries in which to browse and buy. **Antiques** can be found in Greenwich Village along Bleecker Street and on side streets off University Place; along Upper Madison Avenue, on 60th Street near Third Avenue. The city's famous **department stores** offer something for almost everyone: the most famous are the bustling **Bloomingdale's** (1000 Third Avenue at 59th Street) and **Macy's** (151 West 34th Street), **Lord & Taylor** (424 Fifth Avenue at 39th Street); and **Saks Fifth Avenue** (611 Fifth Avenue). Savvy New York shoppers also flock to Manhattan's **flea markets**, including the eclectic weekend **Chelsea antiques market** on Sixth Avenue between 25th and 27th streets and the **Sunday flea market** at Columbus Avenue and 77th Street on the Upper West Side.

New Jersey
At a time when downloaded music dominates, the **Princeton Record Exchange** (20 South Tulane Street) soldiers on, buying and selling CDs, DVDs and LPs, with more than 140,000 new, used and obscure

titles. The **Princeton Corkscrew Wine Shop** (49 Hulfish Street) offers an outstanding selection of hand-crafted, family-produced wines.

Pennsylvania

In Philadelphia, numerous haute couture boutiques line the streets around Liberty Place and Rittenhouse Square. The largest shopping district in the city is on Market Street east of Broad Street. Here you'll find **Lord & Taylor** (13th and Market), the grandad of Philadelphia department stores housed in a landmark building across from City Hall. Farther east on **Market Street**, past discount shops, sporting goods, electronics, shoes, and clothing stores, is **The Gallery**, a modern shopping mall which occupies three square blocks and four levels between 11th and 8th streets. There are over 200 shops and restaurants around the airy, sky-lit atrium including three department stores and a surprisingly interesting food court that's convenient for quick and inexpensive meals or snacks. **Market Place East** is next to **The Gallery** at 8th and Market streets. Housed in a magnificent cast-iron structure once occupied by **Lit Brothers Department Store**, this block-long mixed-use complex is now divided between offices and about 25 stores and restaurants. For more adventurous tastes, **South Street** is the place to go. The shops and eateries on or near South Street from 9th to Front streets include everything from punk shops and art galleries to rock bars and fine restaurants. This is the hip, edgy part of town, popular with, but certainly not limited to, young people. At one time, South Street ran through a large Jewish neighborhood. A remnant of those days can still be found on **Fabric Row**, which runs along 4th Street south of South Street. Mammoth **King of Prussia Mall** is beaten in size only by Minnesota's Mall of America.

Maryland

There are some fun shops along Baltimore's main avenue, 36th Street. **Harborplace & The Gallery** is a sensational atrium mall at 200 East Pratt Street, with over 100 shops, restaurants, and cafés.

Virginia

Outlet malls are a big attraction in Virginia. **Potomac Mills Mall** (2700 Potomac Mills Circle, Woodbridge), at exit 156 of I-95, has more than 200 stores featuring most of the big names, from Ralph Lauren to L.L.

Bean. Virginia's country roads are dotted with antique shops where it's sometimes possible to find good quality at a flea-market price. Craft shops display an impressive range of work by local artists.

North Carolina

Traditionally this state is known for the quality and range of its furniture, and you could easily furnish a house from one of the showrooms lining many highways. Fashion retailing is also strong in the main cities. One of the biggest shopping centers is **Hanes Mall** in Winston-Salem, with more than 200 stores and 7,861 parking spaces.

South Carolina

An unusual South Carolina craft is the handwoven Gullah sweetgrass basket, an art form of African origin that comes in many intricate designs. For traditional shopping, the **Market Common**, built on the former Myrtle Beach Air Force Base, creates the feel of an urban village community by including restaurants and residential properties in its mix.

Georgia

Savannah's cobblestoned River Street has many art galleries, Broughton and Bull streets are known for their antique shops, and the Ellis Square area surrounding the old City market is a center for artists' studios and specialty shops. Malls include **Oglethorpe Mall** (7804 Abercorn Street), **Savannah Festival Factory Stores** (11 Gateway Boulevard, South), and **Savannah Mall** (Rio Road and Abercorn Extension).

Florida

Shopping in Florida will either grab you or leave you shaking your head. Some people really do, apparently, need a collection of plastic flamingoes for their front lawn. More tasteful (literally) is the variety of fruits such as oranges, tangerines, limes, kumquats, and grapefruits that can be shipped home for a small fee. But if you look a little harder, Florida also has an array of quality goods to take home from a trip. There are shops worth seeking out that sell designer clothing at factory prices, primitive Haitian art, Art Deco, and old Florida antiques, Native Indian crafts, and shells that forever remind one of the sea.

The **Gold Coast** has the biggest choice of malls, particularly Miami, Fort Lauderdale, and Boca Raton. Just ask the staff in your hotel for details of the best malls in your area.

Miccosukee Indian Village, west of the Shark Valley entrance of Everglades National Park, sells Native American crafts at premium prices. Fort Lauderdale's **321 North** at Plantation's University Drive north of Broward Boulevard is a modern boutique mall built on the site of the popular Fashion Mall, which closed due to Hurricane Wilma.

Gingerbread Square Gallery at 1207 Duval Street, Key West, sells works by local artists. **Aventura Mall**, 19501 Biscayne Boulevard, is one of Miami's many malls. Over 200 shops with a half dozen of the major nationals including **Macy's**, **Abercrombie & Fitch**, and many other chains. Also in Miami.

Northern Route

Massachusetts

Three major shopping areas in Boston attract strollers as well as serious shoppers. The Back Bay's **Newbury Street**, which stretches for eight blocks from the Public Garden to Massachusetts Avenue, is lined with boutiques, salons, and galleries. The Public Garden end attracts the big spenders, while towards Massachusetts Avenue the atmosphere is more funky and shoppers are students, not international travelers. Also in Back Bay, **Copley Place** and the Shops at the **Prudential Center** are glass-enclosed malls with high-end retailers and specialty shops. **Downtown Crossing**, an outdoor pedestrian mall, is anchored by Macy's. The 150-plus shops and restaurants of **Faneuil Hall Marketplace** attract over 1 million visitors a month. Food stalls fill the Quincy Market Buildings, flanked by colorful pushcarts selling handmade crafts and souvenirs. In Cambridge, independently owned shops line **Massachusetts Avenue** and the squares; the **Harvard Square** area, however, with numerous chain and independent stores, is the city's predominant shopping district. It is claimed that here is the greatest concentration of bookshops in the nation. Most are in and around the Square, and some open until midnight.

New Hampshire

In Portsmouth, **New Hampshire Art Association-Robert Lincoln Levy Gallery** exhibits paintings, photographs and prints for sale. The non-profit, state-wide **League of NH Craftsmen** (open mid-May–mid-Oct) represents some of the state's finest artists. Their show each August at

TRANSPORTATION

Mount Sunapee is recommended. The **Dorr Mill Store** in Guild is a national craft center for hand hooking, braiding, and wool quilting. Shops fill Portsmouth's revitalized **waterfront area** near Market, Bow, and Ceres streets. Route 16 in North Conway, with more than 200 outlet stores, is one of the region's premier shopping destinations. No sales tax of 5–6 percent makes the deals even sweeter.

Maine

Portland's **Bayview Gallery** represents pre-eminent Maine artists, and **Stein Gallery Contemporary Glass** makes modern and functional glassware. There are free samples at Stonewall Kitchens in York, makers of sauces, preserves, and condiments, with stores in Portland and Camden, too.

Vermont

Woodstock's **North Wind Artisans' Gallery** exhibits a variety of excellent work, and its **Sugarbrush Farm** is one of the state's many sugarhouses open for tours. **Danforth Pewter** in Middlebury and Quechee is also worth a visit. The huge **Orvis** store in Manchester has everything necessary to take to the great outdoors. Although **Ben & Jerry's Ice Cream Factory** in Waterbury is now owned by the multinational Unilever, it still remains a big tourist attraction. To see ice cream being made, come on a weekday. Or you can stock up on java at **Green Mountain Coffee Factory Outlet** in Waterbury Village. Also in Waterbury is one of the state's premier co-operative cheese companies, the **Cabot Annex Store**, which lets visitors sample their wares. Cider is made all year at **Cold Hollow Cider Mill** where there's a huge retail store.

New York State

Regent Street Antique Center in Saratoga Springs represents numerous dealers within the region. For crafts, Saratoga Springs' Crafters Gallery has been showcasing the works of local artisans since 1993. For speciality produce, visit **Eagle Mills Cider Mill**, who have a waterwheel-powered mill and nature walks, or **Steiniger's** in Salem for their chocolates.

In the Leatherstocking District antique shops lie along every highway and in major cities. Among them is **Wood Bull Antiques** in Cooperstown. One-off shops in Cooperstown include **Collector's World**, selling baseball-related, autographed items, and **Brewey Ommegang**, which brews

authentic Belgian beer on the banks of the Susquehanna River.

Prime Outlets at Waterloo houses more than 95 stores. More than 100 vendors are at **Hanna Junction Farm and Craft Market** in Canandaigua Fri–Sat. **Windmill Farm and Craft Market** sells Mennonite and Amish items and is open Sat Apr–early Dec.

In the Greater Niagara region, antiques can be bought at **Canal Country Artisans** in Medina. **Prime Outlets** at Niagara Falls has 150-plus brand-name outlets. In Buffalo, visit Broadway Market where more than 40 vendors sell ethnic foods.

Pennsylvania

Saturday's market in Middletown sells everything from food to antiques. The outdoor part of the market is open Sat–Sun, with the indoor part open on Saturday. The landmark store and the "world's oldest bookseller," the **Moravian Book Shop**, is located in the historic area of Bethlehem.

Ohio

The **Hall China Company**, based in East Liverpool, has a factory outlet store, the most famous of their ceramics being the nautical teapot and donut jug. **Harry London Chocolates** have a factory store in Akron and offer tours, while **Malley's Chocolates** have 17 locations throughout the state – the hand-dipped strawberries are recommended. **Libbey Glass** has an outlet store in Toledo and is now the world's second-largest producer of glassware. Family-run **Longaberger** hand-crafted maple wood baskets can be bought at fairs and markets.

Indiana

Family-run **Clay City Pottery** produces traditional stoneware in Clay City, while **DeBrand Fine Chocolates**, a small, artisan chocolatier, has three locations in Fort Wayne. Baseball fans should stop by the **Hoosier Bat Company** in Valparaiso, whose bats are used by major and minor league players. The Aladdin's cave that is **Mundt's Candies** in Madison is unmissable. Founded in 1893 and known for its fish-shaped candy and soda fountain.

Illinois

Chicago has a number of vertical shopping malls, in particular along N. Michigan Avenue. It also has several of America's best department stores and a myriad of boutiques. There's no shortage of manufacturers' outlets in the suburbs. The **Magnificent Mile**

(Michigan Avenue from Chicago River to Oak Street) is the glamorous shopping area including **Tiffany** and **Cartier**. **Chicago Place Mall** (700 N. Michigan Avenue) houses fifty specialty shops including **Saks Fifth Avenue** and **Williams-Sonoma**. Oak Street's outstanding specialty shops emphasize diversity and quality. A fun place to window-shop. The antique district is on the North Side in Lakeview and there are a number of stores and malls on W. Kinzie as well, including **Chicago Antique Center**.

Wisconsin

Known as the "dairy state" and the "cheese capital of the nation," Wisconsin is the leading dairy farming state, so cheese and other dairy products are the obvious purchases. Also known for beer production, with the large producer **MillerCoors Brewing Company** based in Milwaukee. Two of the most popular beers are Coors Light and Miller Lite.

Minnesota

In Minneapolis, **Ingebretsen's** is situated in a quiet marketplace on East Lake Street, and sells Scandinavian foods and crafts. **Nicollet Mall** is on a Downtown pedestrian avenue, lined with boutiques and department stores – links to further shops by means of the city skyway system. The **World Trade Center** in St Paul, at 30 East Seventh Street, contains specialty shops and restaurants.

South Dakota

The **South Dakota Store**, on S. Holly Avenue in Sioux Falls, only houses products made or in some way linked to the state. These range from literature, Black Hills gold and buffalo leather to Native American crafts and music, Missouri river sapphires and prints of South Dakotan landscapes. Handmade crafts, such as jewelry, furniture, rugs and hand-rolled beeswax candles can be found in most towns and cities, not just the larger Sioux Falls and Rapid City.

Wyoming

Wyoming is the place to shop for snap-buttoned shirts, Western hats and boots, and all things cowboy. Sheridan's main street is lined with Western wear stores. Try **Dan's Western Wear** at 226 N. Main Street for Stetson and Resistol hats, Tony Lama boots, and other top brands. Down the block at **King's Saddlery**, 184 N. Main Street, you can buy a Western tack ranging from an authentic rancher's rope to a hand-

ACCOMMODATIONS

EATING OUT

ACTIVITIES

A – Z

tooled leather saddle; there is also a selection of lovely jewelry, wallets, and gifts. Jackson Hole has an interesting mix of stores ranging from Western wear, ski and outdoor gear to designer fashions, art and jewelry.

Montana

Montana is a good place to shop for outdoor gear such as skis, hiking boots, backpacks, sleeping bags, fishing tackle, tents, camping, and mountaineering gear, as well as the latest in outer wear. Most towns have outdoor and sporting goods retailers with a good selection.

In Missoula try **Pipestone Mountaineering**, 129 West Front, and The Trail Head, 221 East Front. Schnee's of Bozeman is renowned for its pac boots, sold at **Schnee's Boots and Shoes** at 121 West Main; it also sells hunting and outdoor gear at **Powder Horn Outfitters**, 35 East Main Street. Also in Bozeman is **Country Mall Antiques**, 8350 Huffine Lane, with around two dozen stalls selling antiques and collectables.

In Helena, **Reeder's Alley**, 100 South Park Avenue, has a shop selling restored antiques in a district that developed during the Gold Rush.

Idaho

The **Cedar Street Bridge Public Market** in downtown Sandpoint is set within a historic covered bridge spanning Sand Creek. It has arts and crafts gift shops, home decor, a jewelry boutique and apparel made from natural Alpaca wool at **Pedro's Pride Fashions**. Coeur d'Alene offers everything from large shopping malls to specialty shops in Downtown's quaint, cobbled **Sherman Avenue**.

Washington

The best shopping in Washington state is found in Seattle. In addition to its mind-boggling array of produce stalls, the popular **Pike's Peak Market** has shops selling gourmet goodies, cooking supplies, T-shirts, and souvenirs. **Westlake Center** and **Pacific Place** shopping malls, as well as **Macy's** and **Nordstrom's** department stores, cluster round the intersection of Fifth Avenue and Pine Street. Upscale boutiques such as **Louis Vuitton** and **Gucci** are found at Rainier Square, also part of the downtown shopping hub. The **Pioneer Square Antique Mall** has more than 60 dealers selling vintage jewelry, toys, and collectibles. Pioneer Square is also the heart of Seattle's art scene, with many galleries and artists' workshops to explore.

Washington, DC

Two of Washington's best shopping districts are on opposite sides of the Potomac, in **Georgetown** on the DC side and **Old Town** in Alexandria on the Virginia side. Both were busy ports well into the 19th century. The surviving weathered red-brick buildings have been converted into trendy shops, with lots of art galleries, antique shops, cafes, and more. Downtown stores include old reliables such as **Brooks Brothers** (1201 Connecticut Avenue), and **J. Press** (1801 L Street, NW). One of the best malls is **Georgetown Park** at M Street and Wisconsin Avenue; it is quaintly Victorian.

Virginia

The **Made in Virginia Store** on Caroline-Street in Fredericksburg brings the best of locally-made producst together. Choose from hams, wines, crafts, and cookbooks full of southern cooking recipies, amongst a host of Virginia-branded clothing. A similar style shop, the **Virginia Made Shop**, is located in Staunton.

North Carolina

The leading producer of tobacco in the States and known for its production of cotton, hogs, broiler chickens, and turkey, the best place for souvenirs, or a taste of this state, is the **Western North Carolina Farmers' Markets**, one of which is in downtown Asheville, with views of the Biltmore Estate. One of the five open-air sheds is reserved for farmers who sell directly to the consumer. A garden and plant nursery center and café are also present. Open daily.

Tennessee

Good buys include musical instruments (acoustic stringed instruments and amplified guitars) and studio recording equipment, and, of course, Tennessee whiskey, which must be produced within the state to make this claim. The two distilleries are **Jack Daniels** in Lynchburg, producing the famous Old No. 7 Brand, and George Dickel whisky, whose distillery lies in Normandy in between Nashville and Chattanooga.

Arkansas

Try Arkansas Black apples from **roadside stands** in the Ozark Mountains area, and mineral water from Hot Springs. **Whetstones** can also be bought from Hot Springs, while iron art from Mountain View and quartzite crystals from Mt Ida make good local buys.

Oklahoma

The quintessential **John Deere** Tractor (farm machinery manufacturer) baseball cap forms part of almost every farmer or agricultural worker's outfit, so if you find one of these at a flea market, buy it! Otherwise, wine from vineyards in Bristow, Geary, Stroud, and Vinita, and root beer from **Weber's Superior Root Beer** stand in Tulsa are worthwhile buys.

Texas

Route 66 throughout Texas offers perilously little to buy, apart from kitsch souvenirs.

New Mexico

Santa Fe is the second-biggest art market in the United States, after New York. Galleries selling world-class paintings and sculpture line **Canyon Road** and more can be found in the town center surrounding the **Plaza**, the city's main shopping district. Santa Fe is also a focus for Native American arts and crafts, particularly silver and turquoise jewelry, Pueblo pottery based on traditional designs, Navajo blankets and textiles and Kachina dolls. Native American artisans sell their work in an open-air market daily beneath the portal in front of the **Palace of the Governors**. The gift shop in the adjoining New Mexico **History Museum** has a good selection of regional art. In August, the **Santa Fe Indian Market** draws Native artists from around the country in the largest art show and sale of its kind, held on the Plaza. The **International Folk Art Market** and the **Traditional Spanish Market** are similar events, both held in July. You can also visit the pueblos north of Santa Fe and buy art directly from artists in their home workshops.

In Albuquerque, the **Old Town plaza** is the place to find a charming array of galleries and gift shops selling Native American jewelry and Southwestern arts and crafts.

Arizona

Sedona is one of the leading New Age centers in the US, which is reflected in the number of shops scattered throughout the town selling crystals, dreamcatchers and so on. It is also a leading art market with numerous galleries selling painting, sculpture, and other works by nationally known artists. With the Hopi and Navajo Nation lands covering much of northern Arizona, this is a prime place to buy Native American arts and crafts, baskets, jewelry, blankets, and textiles. There are trading posts and gift shops in Flagstaff and throughout the region. Some good outlets to try are the **Cameron Trading Post**, Highway 89N, approximately 4 miles (7km) outside Flagstaff, and **Navajo Arts and Crafts Enterprises**, off route 264 adjacent to Navajo Nation Inn in Window Rock.

California

For intrepid shoppers, Los Angeles can be right up there with the big guns like Paris and Hong Kong. Much of the high-class fashion, of course, can be found along that glitziest shopping street, Beverly Hills' renowned **Rodeo Drive**. Some of the world-class shops along the drive include **Chanel**, **Armani**, and **Ungaro**. Also in Los Angeles, a trip down **Melrose Avenue** is essential. First there's the **Pacific Design Center** – The Blue Whale – with its 200 designers' showrooms at the corner of San Vicente, and then there are several blocks of raffish shops between **Croft** and **La Brea**.

Lively **Chinatown**, rife with the aromas of herbs, dried fish, ginseng, and ginger, is the primary source of Asian imports. For mall lovers, Southern California is a shopper's Valhalla. Favorites include the **Beverly Center** with more than 200 stores, bordering Beverly Hills and West Hollywood, and **Westfield Century City Shopping Center**.

Further afield, the San Fernando Valley is renowned for its malls, the most famous and biggest of which are the **Glendale Galleria**, the **Northridge Fashion Center**, and the **Sherman Oaks Fashion Square**. Further still, in addition to Orange County's **South Coast Plaza**, are the **Del Amo Fashion Square** in Torrance, and the breezy Mediterranean-village type atmosphere of Newport Beach's **Fashion Island**. *See also* Santa Monica, page 446.

Southern Route

Georgia

Georgia is known for its peaches, tomatoes, and other fruits best purchased roadside in the Chattahoochee Hill Country or Atlanta's **Saturday Green Market**. Most of the good shopping in rural Georgia is in and around Atlanta. In Downtown, the **Mall at Peachtree Plaza** has more than 60 shops, restaurants, and services. Atlanta Underground occupies six historic blocks and has 100 shops and restaurants below and above ground, including **Brooks Brothers**, **Pendleton**, and a **B. Dalton**

bookstore. **Five Points** is a good place to go for unique gifts such as crystals. Midtown's **Atlantic Station**, a 140-acre live-work-play community, has hotels, stores, and restaurants. Lenox Square, in residential Buckhead, is a pleasant place to stroll and shop and has the city's toniest restaurants and a **Whole Foods Market**. **North Georgia Premium Outlets**, in Dawsonville 45 minutes north of Atlanta, offers an upscale village-style outlet center with 140 stores.

Alabama

A mainly rural farm state like Georgia, Alabama is known for its pecans and strawberries grown in small towns like Castleberry, which proclaims itself Home of the Alabama Strawberry. Muscadine grapes grown at Perdido Vineyards in Perdido produce mostly sweet wines for sale.

Montgomery's historic Downtown is a good place to find antiques; books, posters, cards, and other items promoting civil rights education at the **Southern Poverty Law Center**; and fresh produce, flowers, and home-prepared foods at the **Montgomery Curb Market** on Madison.

The state's most modern and affluent city is Mobile on the Gulf Coast, which has a number of big outlying shopping malls. The smaller residential communities on the other side of Mobile Bay, such as Fairhope, are known for their flowers, particularly azaleas, and small unique shops and restaurants. Downtown's historic district has interesting antiques and a candle factory.

Mississippi

Gulf Coast Mississippi was hard hit by Hurricane Katrina. The **Hard Rock Hotel/Casino** in Biloxi has reopened and is selling its famous T-shirts and other souvenirs but much of what you'll find are bland chainstore items.

The most interesting place to shop is Ocean Springs. The walkable Downtown has a number of charming art galleries, food purveyors, clothing boutiques, and gift shops. Art lovers will find reproductions of Walter Anderson's gorgeous paintings and ceramics in the terrific little store inside the **Walter Anderson Museum of Art**. **Shearwater Pottery**, begun in 1928 by Anderson's brother Peter, sells glazed ceramics by his son Jim. And award-winning **Miner's Doll and Toy Store** has classic toys and fine dolls.

Louisiana

Cajun Country offers many intriguing shopping possibilities. New Orleans is

the best one-stop shop, with its compact **French Quarter** a beehive of commerce. **Royal Streeet**, parallel to Bourbon Street, is a great place to find gorgeous antiques. Touristy **Decatur Street**, along the waterfront, has a number of souvenir shops selling Mardi Gras souvenirs, gumbo spices, jambalaya mixes, hot sauces, and its famous pralines. The ritzy **Canal Place Shops** has a movie theater and high-end clothing stores.

In Lafayette and the surrounding heartland of Arcadiana, you'll find tiny towns like Breaux Bridge selling wonderful antiques and fresh crawfish.

Texas

Houston's most visited destination is **The Galleria**, which has more than 375 department and specialty stores and restaurants. Historic Houston Heights, along Heights Boulevard and Yale Street, has Victorian buildings containing boutiques selling antiques, vintage clothing, and art galleries.

In the heart of Austin, you'll find many unique local boutiques in the 2nd Street District, including favorites like **Heritage Boot**, where owner Jerry Ryan designs each pair of his artsy footwear. The **23rd Street Renaissance Market**, across from UT, is a good place to pick up unique handicrafts. **Waterloo Records** is renowned for its knowledgeable staff and extensive selection of recordings by Texas musicians.

San Antonio is home to **Luchese Boots**, maker of fine hand-tooled cowboy boots. You'll find unique gifts and souvenirs at the **San Antonio Museum of Art**, and in other museum shops. At **North Star** mall (Loop 410 between San Pedro and MacCullough) there are over 200 stores, including many big names. **El Mercado** mall (514 West Commerce) offers specialty shops with Mexican arts and crafts. Several well-known artists make their home in Marathon and **Baxter Gallery** specializes in landscapes of Big Bend by local artists.

Marfa sells lots of contemporary art in the chicest galleries you'll ever see in a ranch town. One-of-a-kind offerings include minimalist furniture carved from juniper at **Benton/Garza**. **Marfa Book Company** has a great selection of books, including tomes on Marfa art guru Donald Judd. Several interesting artisans in Fort Davis sell handcrafted western items along State Street. Check out the beaver felt western hats at **Limpia Creek Custom Hats**. Several art galleries and bookstores in Alpine focus on the rugged beauty of the Big

Bend. **Bread and Breakfast Gallery** sells local artists' work. Books on Big Bend are the specialty of **Front Street Books**. El Paso is the home of the cowboy boot manufacturer, **Tony Lama**. There are four factory outlets in the city.

New Mexico

Options for shopping in southern New Mexico are more limited than the famous north. Alamogordo is famous for its pistachio orchards. At family-run **Eagle Ranch** north of town, you can tour the orchards, sample the produce, and take some home.

The small alpine village of Cloudcroft sells unique western art, such as antler furniture and large-scale chainsaw carvings of bears. Mescalero and the **Inn of the Mountain Gods** on the Apache reservation are good places to find authentic Apache crafts such as paintings and carvings of mountain *gaan* spirits, jewelry, beadwork, and tooled leather. There are numerous **art galleries** in or near Ruidoso. Dave McGary, known for his lifesize bronzes of Indians, has a gallery in Downtown, while artist Michael Hurd, son of the famed early 20th-century artists Peter Hurd and Henriette Wyeth, operates **Hurd/La Rinconada Gallery** and several guesthouses on the old family ranch in nearby San Patricio.

Those who want to try their hand at authentic Southwestern cooking should detour to tiny Hatch, the **chili capital of the world**, a few miles north of Las Cruces. Most of the region's *chile* is grown here, and you can buy it freshly ground or whole in colorful *ristras* (hanging bunches or rings) in small stands lining the road through town. **La Mesilla's central Plaza** is surrounded by gift shops and is an atmospheric place to browse.

Arizona

Phoenix has several large malls as well as the popular **Biltmore Fashion Park**, 2502 E. Camelback Road, and **Arizona Center**, Van Buren Street, in Downtown. A number of interesting shops are located in **Heritage Square**, which is also in the city center.

Scottsdale is known for its Western and contemporary art galleries, many of which are concentrated in the downtown Arts District. It adjoins Old Town, where you can buy everything from cowboy boots to Native American jewelry, rugs, and crafts. Scottsdale also has two of the metro area's finest shopping centers: Fashion Square at 7014 E. Camelback Road, and the

Borgata, with its galleries and specialty stores set amid a Tuscan-style village with fountains and courtyard. **Tucson** is a good center for Southwestern crafts. Downtown on North Court Avenue, behind the Tucson Art Museum, Old Town Artisans is a warren of small shops selling high-quality ceramics, painting, sculpture, photography and other arts in a block of adobe buildings from the mid-19th century, set around a shady courtyard. Nearby is the historic 4th Avenue shopping district, with more galleries and one-of-a-kind shops. A Tucson favorite is De Grazia's Gallery in the Sun, 6300 North Swan, where you can buy reproductions of the artist's distinctive Southwest paintings in the gallery gift shop.

About 30 miles (48km) south of Tucson, the artists' colony of **Tubac** is another popular shopping destination for everything from fine art to Southwestern crafts and imported Mexican decorative arts. Downtown **Yuma** is a pleasant shopping district with a number of interesting specialty shops.

Pacific Route

California

San Diego's **Gaslamp Quarter** is the place to browse for arts and crafts downtown. Here too is the multilevel **Horton Plaza** shopping center. **Seaport Village** has cute touristy shops on the harbor, while the **Old Town Esplanade** is lined with specialty shops, many selling Mexican crafts, blankets, embroidered shirts, and dresses, etc.

San Diego is also just a short hop away from the Mexican border town of Tijuana, where you can bargain for souvenirs (look for leather) at lower prices. Also at the border in San Ysidro is **Las Americas Premium Outlets**, the area's largest outlet center. Upscale art galleries and shops line the central village and main streets of Laguna Beach. The **Wyland Gallery**, 509 South Coast Highway, has works by this leading environmental marine life artist. Newport Beach is another shopping highlight with luxury shopping at **Fashion Island**, set around bougainvillea-lined courtyards and fountains, and charming boutiques along Balboa Island's **Marine Avenue**.

Santa Monica's **Third Street Promenade** is a pedestrian mall lined with whimsical topiaries between its popular chain stores and one-off outlets. It intersects with Arizona Avenue, where a fabulous **Farmers' Market** is held on Wednesdays and

Saturdays, with the colorful bounty of Southern California on display. Along Main Street you'll find everything from thrift shops to chic boutiques, while pricy Montana Avenue has designer apparel and furnishings. (*See also Los Angeles, page 445.*) **State Street** runs through the heart of downtown Santa Barbara, lined with trees, bright flags, and brick-paved sidewalks. Here you'll find an eclectic mix of shops selling shoes, fashions, art, and homewares. Look for the delightful **Retroville**, 521 State Street, with vintage clothes, accessories, art, and home furnishings. On either side of State Street are charming shopping enclaves such as **La Arcada Court**, a cheerful Spanish-style courtyard adorned with tile and ornamental ironwork and home to luxury jewelers and antiques shops, and **Paseo Nuevo**, an open-air mall of specialty shops set between adobe arches and palms.

There are 20 distinct shopping districts in San Francisco. You might want to start by exploring some or all of the following: **Union Square** includes the charming **Maiden Lane** with boutiques and galleries; **Chinatown**, between Stockton, Kearny, Bush, and Broadway, is good for fresh produce, fish, poultry, traditional herbs, antiques, and jewelry; **North Beach** offers a mix of book shops, Italian restaurants and delicatessens, cafés, vintage clothing, and designer boutiques; **Fisherman's Wharf** shopping extends from **Pier 39** to **Ghirardelli Square** in **The Cannery**.

Oregon

Shopping in Oregon is particularly good value, as the state has no sales tax. Resorts all along the coast feature shops selling art, crafts, and souvenirs. Lincoln City is a larger shopping city, with its **Tanger Outlet Center** in the business district along Highway 101, and many antiques stores also located here. Portland's **Farmers' Market** offers food, arts and crafts stalls amid a bustling, lively atmosphere. The main market is held on Saturdays from late spring to early autumn in the South Park Blocks of Portland State University. Other markets operate elsewhere in the city on other days. The **Old Town** district features specialty shops in a lovely setting.

Washington

The Washington coast offers little more than small specialty or souvenir shops. Your best bet for shopping is in Seattle, *see page 444*.

A – Z

A HANDY SUMMARY OF PRACTICAL INFORMATION, ARRANGED ALPHABETICALLY

A dmission Charges

Admission is usually charged at both private and public museums and attractions and national and state parks. As a rule, entrance fees are under $10 per person, although very popular sites, such as Grand Canyon and special traveling exhibits at nationally known museums, may charge as much as $20. Museums often offer free or reduced entrance fees certain days or evenings.

Consider buying **multi-site passes** for attractions in the larger cities, if available. Local visitor centers can assist you with planning and many also offer discount coupons, with excellent deals on local attractions, hotels, and dining.

Anyone planning to visit several national parks is strongly advised to buy an **$80 annual pass** that allows unlimited entry into federally managed public lands across the US. Passes are available at the entrance gate to national parks.

Age Restrictions

Few age restrictions are imposed at attractions. Theme parks, such as Disney World, may state age, weight, and height restrictions for safety reasons. To enter premises serving alcohol, you must be 21 or over in most states.

B udgeting for Your Trip

In early 2009, the dollar strengthened considerably against the pound and euro, so several unbroken years of rock-bottom prices for European travelers abruptly ended. Even so, the US remains a good buy for travelers, especially those on a road trip, where the main cost will be car rental, gas, lodging, and food, and you can search out bargains en route.

You can save considerably if you camp, stay in budget motels, eat in hometown cafés like the locals or bring your own food for picnics, and keep to a budget for visiting attractions. Allow $80–100/day for good-quality hotels for two people, although really

memorable hotels and bed-and-breakfasts tend to run you closer to $150/night. At the other end of the spectrum, you'll find an array of hostels and attractive campgrounds with full facilities for $16–18/night; bare-bones motel lodgings can be found for less than $50; and reliable chains are in the $60–80 range (look for AAA discounts and online deals at chains like Best Western and La Quinta). You can probably get away with $30/day per person for basic meals if you stick to diners, cafés, markets, and inexpensive restaurants and don't drink alcohol.

Meals in better restaurants cost a lot more (see Restaurant section), but if you're determined to visit that famous high-end establishment and don't have the cash, one insider trick is to eat lunch there: you'll find many of the items on the dinner menu at much lower prices and still get to say you've eaten at a hip eatery.

Budget at least $3 per gallon for gas costs for your rental car; most economy vehicles get over 30 miles per gallon. Trams, light rail, buses, and other public transportation in cities like Tampa,

Miami, San Francisco, and Atlanta are just a few dollars per ride, allowing you to get around for much less.

Children

Two words of advice about traveling with children: first, be prepared and, second, don't expect to cover too much ground. Take everything you need, along with a general first-aid kit: Western towns may be small and remote with supplies limited. If you need baby formula, special foods, diapers or medication, carry them with you along with a general first-aid kit and those wonderful all-purpose traveler's aids: wet wipes and Ziplock bags. Games, books, and crayons help kids pass time in the car. Carrying snacks and drinks in a day pack will come in handy when kids (or adults) get hungry on the road. Give yourself plenty of time, as kids do not travel at the same pace as adults.

Be sure wilderness areas and other backcountry places are suitable for children. Are there abandoned mine shafts, steep stairways, cliffs or other hazards? Is a lot of walking necessary? Are food, water, shelter, bathrooms, and other essentials available at the site? Avoid dehydration by having children drink plenty of water before and during outdoor activities. And particularly in summer, be sure they wear sunscreen with an SPF of 30, a hat, sunglasses, sturdy sandals or hiking boots, and layered clothing. Don't push children beyond their limits. Rest often and allow for extra napping.

Climate

The US climate is mostly temperate, but tropical in Hawaii, Florida, and the Deep South; arctic in Alaska; semi-arid in the great plains west of the Mississippi River – and arid in the Great Basin of the Desert Southwest.

Low winter temperatures in the Northwest are ameliorated occasionally in January and February by warm Chinook winds from the eastern slopes of the Rocky Mountains, but ice storms are common in the Columbia River Gorge, on the Washington-Oregon boundary, the only sea-level thoroughfare through the Cascade Mountains.

Hurricane season, which affects Florida and the Gulf Coast and runs from June 1 to November 30, has produced devastating hurricanes, storm surges, and torrential rain. Tornadoes, the bane of the Midwest, can strike very suddenly and specifically in spring, and even late

winter, if the right conditions arise. Between July and September in the Southwest, "monsoon" rainstorms can be dangerous, creating flashfloods that sweep away everything in their path.

Out west, the shift in jetstream in winter blows northwesterly winds onshore over mountain ranges that, along with frigid temperatures, bring heavy snows. Lake-effect snows also bedevil the Great Lakes region and East Coast, paralyzing some of the country's busiest areas in winter.

When to visit

With school out, long lazy summer days ahead, and vacation days piling up, summer is the traditional time for a US family road trip. Consider this only if you don't mind soaring temperatures, hot and humid conditions near water, desiccatingly hot, dry, dusty conditions in the desert, and crowded freeways, hotels, campgrounds, and attractions across the US. Far better is to time your road trip to enjoy the singular glories of spring and fall across the magical US landscape.

After Labor Day, the kids are back in school; roads, parks, and campgrounds are quieter; and weather conditions – usually warm days and cool nights – are perfect for outdoor activities. Winter has its own particular charm, but with frigid temperatures, heavy snows and winds, and road closures across the country, it's not the best time for a road trip.

Only the Southern, Atlantic, and Pacific routes are suitable for winter travel, and even then come prepared for bad weather that occasionally brings snow to low-desert areas like Tucson. Think twice before driving the Central, Northern, and Atlantic routes in this book in winter. If skiing is the main attraction, you'd do better to fly to a resort. Most winter travelers head for the Southern US, particularly Florida, where the sun shines 300 days of the year and winters are mild; the high season is January through April, rates plummet in summer. Many locals time their trips for the quieter, still pleasant "shoulder" seasons of May and June and October to December.

What to wear

The US climate is varied and quite intense, often changing rapidly from one extreme to another. Your best bet is to bring layers of lightweight clothing, which can cover exposed skin or be rolled up; a hat; polarized sunglasses; sturdy walking shoes or sandals; and a packable waterproof

shell in summer. In winter, long underwear made of silk or breathable technical fabrics can be slipped under fleece or wool for warmth. Don't forget wool gloves, scarf, and hat, and possibly a lightweight packable down jacket in high-elevation areas and those in the northern US. A sunscreen with an SPF of 30 or above is a good idea at any time of year.

Crime and Safety

If you are driving, never pick up anyone you don't know. Always be wary of who is around you. If you have trouble on the road, stay in the car and lock the doors, turn on your hazard lights and/or leave the hood up to increase your visibility and alert passing police. It's well worth carrying a sign requesting help. Do not accept a rental car that is obviously labeled as such. Company decals and special license plates may attract thieves on the look-out for tourist valuables.

Hitchhiking

Hitchhiking is illegal in many places and ill-advised everywhere. It's an inefficient and dangerous method of travel. Don't do it!

In the city

Most big cities have their share of crime. Common sense is your most effective weapon. Try to avoid walking alone at night – at the very least stick to livelier, more brightly lit thoroughfares and move about as if you know where you are going.

Keep an eye on your belongings. Never leave your car unlocked, or small children by themselves. Hotels usually warn that they do not guarantee the safety of belongings left in their rooms. If you have any valuables, you may want to lock them in the hotel safe.

Take particular care when using bank ATMs at night. If you are in doubt about which areas are safe, seek advice from hotel staff or police.

A little common sense goes a long way: Don't carry large sums of money or expensive video/camera equipment. Walk purposefully and don't make eye contact with unwelcome strangers or respond to come-ons. Don't travel alone at night.

Customs Regulations

You may bring in **duty-free gifts** worth **up to $800** (American citizens) or $100 (foreign travelers). Visitors over 18 may bring in **200 cigarettes** and **50 cigars** (not Cuban) or **2 kg of tobacco**. Those over 21 may bring in

34 fl. oz (1 liter) of alcohol. Travelers with more than **$10,000 in US or foreign currency**, travelers' checks, or money orders must declare these upon entry. Among the prohibited goods are meat or meat products, illegal drugs, firearms, seeds, plants, and fruits. For a breakdown of customs allowances write to: **United States Customs Service**, PO Box 407, Washington, DC 20044; tel. 877-227-5511; www.cbp.gov.

D isabled Travelers

The 1995 Americans with Disabilities Act (ADA) brought sweeping changes to facilities across America. Accommodations with five or more rooms must be useable by persons with disabilities. Older and smaller inns and lodges are often wheelchair-accessible.

For the sight-impaired, many hotels provide special alarm clocks, captioned TV services, and security measures. To comply with ADA hearing-impaired requirements, many hotels have begun to follow special procedures; local agencies may provide TTY and interpretation services.

Check with the front desk when you make reservations to ascertain the degree to which the hotel complies with ADA guidelines. Ask specific questions regarding bathroom facilities, bed height, wheelchair space, and availability of services.

Many major attractions have wheelchairs for loan or rent; most national parks today also offer paved "barrier-free" or "accessible" trails. Some provide visitor guides and interpreters for hearing- and sight-impaired guests. The **Society for Accessible Travel and Hospitality** (tel: 212-447-7284; www.sath.org) publishes a quarterly magazine on travel for the disabled.

E lectricity

Standard electricity in North America is 110–115 volts, 60 cycles AC. An adapter is necessary for most appliances from overseas, with the exception of Japan.

Embassies and Consulates

Australia: 1601 Massachusetts Avenue NW, Washington, DC 20036
Tel: 202-797-3000
Canada: 501 Pennsylvania Avenue NW, Washington, DC 20001
Tel: 202-682-1740
Great Britain: 3100 Massachusetts Avenue NW, Washington, DC 20008
Tel: 202-462-1340

Emergencies

Dial 911 (the operator will put you through to the police, ambulance or fire services). The call is toll free anywhere in the US, including on cellphones. If you can't get through, **dial 0** for an operator. In national parks, it's best to **contact a ranger**. For free emergency roadside assistance in Mexico, contact the **Green Angels** at 800-903-9200.

Ireland: 2234 Massachusetts Avenue NW, Washington, DC 20008
Tel: 202-462-3939
Mexico: 1911 Pennsylvania Avenue NW, Washington, DC 20006
Tel: 202-728-1600
New Zealand: 37 Observatory Circle NW, Washington, DC 20008
Tel: 202-328-4800

Etiquette

Visitors often associate the US with relaxed manners. While that may be true up to a point, particularly in dress and table manners, you should also be prepared for many Americans, particularly those who live in conservative areas of the Midwest and the South, to be surprisingly polite and formal, in speech, dress, and the intricate dance of social interaction.

Americans, as a rule, are positive, curious about others, generally accepting of differences, warm, effusive, and tactile. This being a nation of immigrants, care is generally taken in polite society not to give offence to any one group, and chauvinism and racism, though evident, are not tolerated in most social situations, so be careful about making off-color jokes or making assumptions about different regions of the country.

Visiting Indian reservations, which are sovereign lands within the US with their own laws and moral code, calls for unique sensitivity and cultural awareness. Make an effort to blend in, dress conservatively, behave modestly – particularly at Indian dances, which are religious rituals – and never enter a home without being invited (nor refuse a meal if invited on a feast day, as that is considered rude). Many tribes rely on tourism for their income and have developed luxury resorts on their scenic lands to rival any in Las Vegas. In remote areas, you will usually be asked to pay a small fee to take photos of family members.

G ay and Lesbian Travelers

On the whole, urban areas in the US are safer places to visit for gay and lesbian travelers than rural destinations away from the cities. Keep a low profile in such areas, particularly in the conservative Bible Belt in the South, to avoid problems. Having said that, the lucrative GLBT market is one of the hottest targeted markets in the US, and most states now offer information on gay-friendly travel within their communities. Cities like New York, South Beach (Miami), Seattle, San Francisco, Los Angeles, Phoenix, and Tucson roll out the red carpet. Smaller arts and university towns, such as Santa Fe, Austin, and Flagstaff, also have surprisingly large gay communities.

For more information, check out www.queeramerica.com and the **Gay and Lesbian Yellow Pages** (tel: 800-697-2812; www.glyp.com). **Damron Company** (tel: 415-255-0404; 800-462-6654; www.damron.com) publishes guides aimed at gay travelers and lists gay-owned and gay-friendly accommodations nationwide.

H ealth and Medical Care

Medical services are extremely expensive. Always arrange comprehensive travel insurance to cover treatment and emergencies. Check the small print – most policies exclude treatment for water, winter or mountain sports accidents unless excess cover has been included.

If you need medical assistance, consult the *Yellow Pages* for the physician or pharmacist nearest to you. The bigger hotels may have a resident doctor. In large cities, there is usually a physician referral service number listed.

If you need immediate attention, go directly to a hospital emergency room (ER); most are open 24 hours a day. You may be asked to produce proof of insurance cover before being treated. Walk-in medical clinics are much cheaper than hospital emergency rooms for minor ailments.

Care should be taken to avoid dehydration and overexposure to the sun. In the desert, or at high altitude, this can happen rapidly even on cloudy days. A cover-up, high-factor sun lotion, hat, and one-liter water bottle are essential accessories. Avoid excess alcohol, caffeine, and sugar to cut down on dehydration and pace yourself at high elevation. Allow a day or two to acclimatize to elevation that changes gradually.

TRANSPORTATION
ACCOMMODATIONS
EATING OUT
ACTIVITIES
A – Z

Internet and Websites

Many public libraries, copy centers, hotels, and airports offer high-speed (DSL) or Wireless internet (Wi-fi) email and internet access. Most charge a fee for access, either on their computer or your laptop. At Starbucks coffeehouses and airports, for example, you must first purchase a T-Mobile Hot Spot pass or Boingo Pass (currently about $9.95/day), before being able to log on; other coffeehouses and restaurants offer free Wi-fi as a customer incentive. Service providers such as Earthlink (www.earthlink.net) and Hotmail (www.hotmail.com) offer web mail accounts that will enable access while traveling. The modems of many foreign laptops and handheld computers won't work in the US. You may need to purchase a global modem before leaving home or a local PC-card modem once you arrive in the US. For more information, log on to www.teleadapt.com.

Luggage Storage

For security reasons, most airports and train stations in the US no longer operate luggage storage facilities for travelers, although some private companies do offer luggage lockers. Check with the individual location. Most hotels will allow you to check out and leave your luggage in a safe storage area. You will be taking a calculated risk if you leave your luggage in the car. In practice, though, if you lock all valuables (especially laptops and other electronic items) out of sight, you will probably be okay.

Lost Property

If you lose property, your best bet is to immediately report it to management of the attraction or hotel where the loss occurred, then file a report in person at the local police station; some police stations allow you to file an electronic report via email. All airlines have lost luggage desks and will usually forward any delayed bags to your destination.

Maps

A detailed road map is essential for any road trip. They are widely available from state welcome and city visitor centers, travel bookstores, outdoor stores, filling stations, supermarkets, and convenience stores. Cross-country travelers may find it useful to purchase a road-map book with maps of all 50 states, such

as the one published by American Maps. The American Automobile Association (AAA) provides excellent maps free of charge to members *(see page 389)*. Free maps of national parks, forests, and other public lands are usually offered by the managing government agency at entrance stations. Extremely detailed topographical maps of states are available from the US Geological Survey (www.usgs.gov/sales.html). Topo maps are usually available in higher-end bookstores and shops that sell outdoor gear shops.

Media

Newspapers

In this rapidly expanding era of electronic publishing and free information on the World Wide Web, print media has undergone a major contraction. Yet most communities across the US still publish print editions of newspapers, as well as electronic editions, and the opinions and endorsements of columnists and editorial boards continue to play an important role in American public life.

The **top 10 newspapers** by circulation in the US are: *USA Today*, the *Wall Street Journal*, the *New York Times*, the *Los Angeles Times*, the *Washington Post*, the *New York Daily News*, the *Chicago Tribune*, the *New York Post, Long Island Newsday*, and the *Houston Chronicle*.

Television

Unlike many countries, the US does not have national broadcasting. Instead, three major TV networks – ABC, CBS, and NBC – are carried in local markets by affiliates who also produce local programming and news that can usually be watched for free. In addition to the Big Three, the upstart conservative network Fox Broadcasting Corporation is gaining an increasing market share. Univision, a network of Spanish-language channels, is the fifth-largest TV channel.

Non-commercial broadcasting plays a much smaller role in American TV than in other countries, but what there is is excellent.

Among the most popular public interest channels on cable or satellite are CNN, ESPN, MSNBC, Discovery Channel, the Food Network, USA Network, TNT, TMC, TLC, BRAVO, Disney, National Geographic, and BBC America. Movie channels include HBO, Showtime, Stars, and pay-per-view movies through satellite providers such as DirecTV and Dish.

Radio

A good way to learn about American culture is to turn on the radio. Cities have a vast array of stations, from talk radio by right-wing host Rush Limbaugh to hip hop, contemporary, and classic rock music. On long, lonely highways, country music and religion predominate along with Spanish-language shows and AM talk radio. You'll find more cultural programming at the low end of the dial between 88 and 91 FM. National Public Radio, syndicated through local community radio stations, broadcasts the country's most listened-to public programs as well as opera, classical music, and often indigenous programming.

Hopi Radio (KUYI FM at 88.1) and Navajo Radio (660 KTNN AM) broadcast locally in their native languages. Cajun Radio (1470 AM) in Lake Charles belts out zydeco and cajun music throughout Cajun Country. You can tune in to Radio Sonora (101.3 FM) to enjoy lively polka-influenced Norteño music as you travel southern Arizona near the US-Mexico border. You'll find country music and headline news at KNFT 102.9 FM (Deming), KIXE 940 AM (Douglas), and KAVV 97.7 FM (Benson), and news and golden oldies at KBLU 560 AM (Yuma).

A radio show dedicated to Route 66 is broadcast on St Louis station KMOX (1120 AM) every Saturday from 8pm to 1am. Information about local road conditions and attractions can often be tuned in at 95 AM. Truckers with CB equipment talk to each other on dedicated channels, usually Line 19 in most of the country (Line 17 on the West Coast). There is also a truckers' channel among the large lineup on satellite radio Sirius and XM Radio, available in many rental cars.

Money

American dollars come in bills of $1, $5, $10, $20, $50, and $100, all the same size. The dollar is divided into 100 cents. Coins come in 1 cent (penny), 5 cents (nickel), 10 cents (dime), 25 cents (quarter), 50 cents (half-dollar), and $1 denominations. Credit cards are accepted almost everywhere, although not all cards at all places. Most hotels, restaurants, and shops take the major ones such as American Express, Diners Club, MasterCard, Visa, and En Route. Along with out-of-state or overseas bank cards, they can also be used to withdraw money at ATMs.

Travelers' checks are widely accepted, although you may have to provide proof of identification when cashing them at banks (this is not required at most stores). Travelers' checks in US dollars are much more widely accepted than those in other currencies. The best rates of exchange for them are in banks. Take along your passport.

Tipping

Although rarely obligatory, many service personnel in the US rely on tips for a large part of their income. Going rates are: **waiters and bartenders** 15–20 percent; **taxi drivers** 15 percent; **airport/hotel baggage handlers** around $1 per bag; **chambermaids** – for overnight stays, it is not necessary to tip, for longer stays a minimum of $1–2 per day; **doormen** 50¢–$1 for helping unload a car or other services; **hairdressers**, **manicurists, and massage therapists** 15 percent.

O pening Hours

Banks 9am–5pm, weekdays. Some stay open until 6pm and Saturdays.
Post Offices 8am–4 or 5.30pm, weekdays, Saturday closing earlier and opening later.
Shops 9am–5pm daily, later in tourist areas; shopping malls typically open 10am–9pm Mon–Sat, noon–5pm Sun.
All-hours services Most cities have 24-hour restaurants, convenience stores, and supermarkets.
Museums Usually open Tue–Sun, closed Mon.

P hotography

Even in this era of instant-view digital cameras, film is still widely available throughout the US. Business centers and discount chains often offer rapid development or conversion of digital to paper prints. The US is spectacularly photogenic. Some of the most rewarding photography is of cultural events such as costume parades, Indian dances, and wildlife events.

If you plan on photographing in the desert, avoid the flat, washed-out light in the middle of the day and shoot in the early morning or evening instead; cloudy days will offer better contrast than bright sunny days.

Observe appropriate etiquette when photographing American Indians. Pueblos in New Mexico usually require you to pay a fee to photograph within the pueblos and during dances. Native people will usually be happy to pose for

Public Holidays

Holidays celebrated no matter on what day they fall in the year are:
• **January 1** New Year's Day
• **July 4** Independence Day
• **November 11** Veteran's Day
• **December 25** Christmas Day

Other holidays are:
• **Third Monday in January** Martin Luther King Jr Day
• **Third Monday in February** Presidents' Day
• **March/April** Good Friday, Easter Monday
• **Last Monday in May** Memorial Day
• **First Monday in September** Labor Day
• **Second Monday in October** Columbus Day
• **Fourth Thursday in November** Thanksgiving

you for a small fee. Always ask permission and get a photo release, if it's for commercial purposes, before taking a photo of anyone.

Postal Services

Post offices

Even in the most remote towns are served by the US Postal Service. Stamps are sold at all post offices, plus at some convenience stores, filling stations, hotels, and transportation terminals, usually from vending machines. Postage rates in 2009 were 44 cents for a first-class domestic stamp up to 1 oz with 17 cents for each additional ounce. Postcards are 28 cents each. Postage for overseas letters is 98 cents for 1 oz; 79 cents to Mexico and 75 cents to Canada. Postage for overseas postcards is currently 98 cents; 79 cents to Mexico and 75 cents to Canada.

Public Toilets

Public toilets are rarely available in the US, unless you are visiting an attraction. Most businesses allow you to use their "bathroom." At special outdoor events, you will often find temporary Port-a-Potties brought in to serve large crowds.

R eligious Services

The majority of Americans believe in God and many attend religious or spiritual services regularly in their communities. Both high- and low-church Christianity is usually the most

visible religious expression across the US, but you'll also find Jewish temples, Mormon tabernacles and temples, Baptist chapels, Quaker meeting houses, Buddhist zendos, pagan Wicca ceremonies, evangelical tent revivals on Indian reservations, and other religious gathering places in the unlikeliest places, even remote national parks.

Visitors are welcome at most church services; however, whites attending Sunday services at black-majority gospel churches in the South should be prepared for a certain amount of suspicion of outsiders.

S moking

There are no federal bans on smoking, but many states and individual cities and towns in the US now ban smoking in workplaces, on public transportation, in bars, hotels, restaurants, airports, and in and around public buildings and public parks, so always check before lighting up.

Student Travelers

The **International Student Identity Card** (ISIC) is recognized throughout the world. Major cities across the US, such as New York and Atlanta, accept the card and offer substantial discounts on everything from entertainment and restaurants to lodging and airport parking. The **International Youth Travel Card** (IYTC) offers travelers under 26 low-cost fares on buses, trains, flights, and hotels. Both cards cost $22 a year. The ISIC includes a comprehensive travel insurance policy and ISIConnect, a complete communication tool with both calling card and cellphone options. For more information, tel. 800-223-7986 in the US or log on to www.myisic.com.

STA Travel (tel: 800-781-4040; www.statravel.com) also offers students discounts on airfares. Admission charges to attractions across the US are usually a couple of dollars less than full adult price for students, and children under 12 are often admitted free. Check at your destination.

T ax

Most states levy a sales tax. The amount varies from state to state (up to around 8 percent in some) and is invariably excluded from the marked price. You may also have to pay a local sales tax on top of this. When looking at prices, beware of other costs that may or may not be included in the stated price such as lodging or "bed tax" and taxes on restaurant meals, drinks and car rental. These are especially hefty in tourist towns like Miami. If in doubt – ask.

Telephones

In this era of cellphones, you'll find fewer **public telephones** in hotel lobbies, restaurants, drugstores, garages, roadside kiosks, convenience stores, and other locations. The cost of making a local call from a payphone for three minutes is 25–50 cents. To make a long-distance call from a payphone, use either a **pre-paid calling card**, available in airports, post offices, and a few other outlets, or your credit card, which you can use at any phone: dial 800-CALLATT, key in your credit-card number, and wait to be connected. In many areas, local calls have now changed to a 10-digit calling system, using the area code. Watch out for in-room connection charges in the more upmarket hotels; it's cheaper to use the payphone in the lobby. Ditto: wireless and broadband internet connections in your room: many hotel lobbies offer free wireless but charge for it in guest rooms. Inquire ahead of time.

Toll-free calls

When in the US, make use of toll-free (no-charge) numbers. They start with 800, 888, 866, or 877. You need to dial 1 before these numbers.

Cheaper rates

Long-distance rates are cheaper after 5pm on weekdays and throughout weekends. Many wireless plans offer unlimited free cellphone minutes on weekends and between 9pm and 6am.

Useful Numbers

Operator 0 (dial if you are having any problems with a line from any phone)
Local: 411
Long-distance: 1+area code+555-1212
Toll-free directory: 800-555-1212

Phone Codes

More than perhaps any other country, the United States has embraced the telephone. But now, with the proliferation of fax lines, modems, and cellphones, the system is seriously overloaded. To cope with these demands, the country has been forced to divide, then sub-divide, its existing telephone exchanges, in some cases every six months. Although every effort has been made

Time Zones

The continental US spans four time zones. These are divided as follows:
•**Eastern** (Greenwich Mean Time minus five hours)
•**Central** (Greenwich Mean Time minus six hours)
•**Mountain** (Greenwich Mean Time minus seven hours)
•**Pacific** (Greenwich Mean Time minus eight hours)

Daylight Saving Time

This begins each year at 2am on a Sunday in March when clocks are advanced one hour ("spring forward"), and ends on the first Sunday in October ("fall back."). Arizona and Indiana do not observe Daylight Saving Time; however, confusingly for travelers, the huge Navajo Indian reservation, spanning Arizona and New Mexico, does.

to keep the telephone prefixes listed here up to date, it's always a good idea to check with the operator if you're in any doubt about a number.

Tour Operators and Travel Agents

The US has a huge variety of travel agents and tour operators to assist with both general and specialty travel packages. Even if you are planning on doing the driving yourself, you may want to hook up with a local tour operator to let someone else show you around for a few days. You can locate a US tour operator by checking listings on the websites of the **US Tour Operator Association** – USTOA (www. ustoa) and the **National Tour Association** (www.ntaonline.com) or contacting the visitor center at your destination for official listings.

Top tour operators serving all of the US include top-rated **Tauck Tours** (tel: 800-788-7885; www.tauck.com), a family-run company that has been in business since 1924, and **Abercrombie and Kent** (tel: 800-554-7016; www.abercrombiekent.com), both of which specialize in small-group luxury tours. **The Smithsonian Institution** (tel: 877-338-8687; www. smithsonianjourneys.com) offers educational study tours to sites of archeological, historic, and scientific interest in the US, such as the ancient Indian ruins of the Southwest, guided by authorities in the field. National park

concessionaires, such as **Fred Harvey** at Grand Canyon National Park, offer bus tours, mule rides, and other guided tours; park staff have listings of individual outfitters. Check individual parks for more information.

Specialty tour operators offer guided trips tailored to your interests, from tours of ghost towns in Arizona to historic walking tours in cities like Santa Fe, Seattle, and Boston. Outfitters offer guided trips of the outdoors. You can enjoy hunting, fishing, river rafting, horseback riding, and skiing with outdoor outfitters in the Mountain West; rock climbing and bicycle and Jeep touring in the Southwest; wildlife watching in Florida; ballooning and wine tours in California; heritage tours on private ranches, Indian reservations, and archeological sites in the West; tours of Civil War battlefields and communities in the South; and tours aimed at those with special needs, health issues, disabilities, singles, women only, and the gay and lesbian community, among others.

Tourist Information

Check the website www.usa.gov or call 800-FED INFO for links to government-run tourist offices, including tribal government offices, for all 50 states. **Welcome Centers** are usually located at the state line. They are staffed by volunteers who can give you maps and general advice on your stay and have rest rooms, water, and often hot coffee. Most communities have visitor centers that offer information and trip planning. When visiting national parks, be sure to stop at the visitor center first. Rangers there can help you get the most out of your time in the park.

The website **www.usa.gov** has helpful information for tourists. In addition to serving as a clearing house for tourist information bureaus across the US, it displays travel warnings and information on road conditions and highways, gas prices, and public transport, and offers tips on driving. The website **www.byways. org** has information on America's designated **scenic byways** – a little-known resource of great interest to road trippers meandering America's inspiring Blue Highways.

Route 66

National Historic Route 66 Federation
Tel/fax: 909-336-6131
www.national66.com

State Tourism Offices

Alabama Tourism Department
Tel: 800-252-2262
www.800alabama.com

Arizona Office of Tourism
Tel: 866-275-5816
www.arizonaguide.com

Arkansas Department of Parks and Tourism
Tel: 800-628-8725
www.arkansas.com

California Tourism
Tel: 877-225-4367
www.visitcalifornia.com

Connecticut Commission on Culture and Tourism
Toll free: 888-288-4748
www.ctvisit.com

Visit Florida
Toll free: 888-735-2872
www.visitflorida.com

Georgia Department of Economic Development
Toll free: 800-847-4842
www.exploregeorgia.org

Idaho Division of Tourism Development
Toll free: 800-VISITID
www.visitidaho.com

Illinois Bureau of Tourism – Chicago Office
Toll free: 800-406-6418
www.enjoyillinois.com

Indiana Office of Tourism Development
Toll free: 800-677-9800
www.in.gov/visitindiana

Louisiana Office of Tourism
Tel: 225-342-8119
www.louisianatravel.com

Maine Office of Tourism
Toll free: 888-624-6345
www.visitmaine.com

Maryland Office of Tourism Development
Toll free: 866-639-3526
www.mdisfun.org

Massachusetts Office of Travel and Tourism
Toll-free: 800-227-MASS
www.massvacation.com

Explore Minnesota Tourism
121 7th Place E, Metro Square, Toll free: 888-868-7476
www.exploreminnesota.com

Mississippi: Division of Tourist Development
Toll free: 866-733-6477
www.visitmississippi.org

Travel Montana
Toll free: 800-847-4868
www.visitmt.com

New Hampshire Department of Resources and Economic Development
Toll free: 800-386-4664
www.visitnh.gov

New Jersey Division of Tourism and Travel information
Toll free: 800-VISIT NJ
www.state.nj.us/travel

New Mexico Department of Tourism
Tel: 505-827-7400
www.newmexico.org

New York State tourist information
Toll free: 800-225-5697
www.iloveny.com

North Carolina Division of Tourism
Toll free: 800-847-4862
www.visitnc.com

Ohio Division of Travel and Tourism
Toll free: 800-BUCKEYE
www.consumer.discoverohio.com

Oklahoma Tourism And Recreation Department
Toll free: 800-652-6552
www.travelok.com

Oregon Tourism Commission
Toll free: 800-547-7842
www.traveloregon.com

Pennsylvania Tourism Office
Toll Free: 800-847-4872
www.visitpa.com

South Carolina Department of Tourism
Toll free: 866-224-9339
www.discoversouthcarolina.com

South Dakota Office of Tourism
Toll free: 800-952-3625
www.travelsd.com

State of Tennessee Department of Tourist Development
Tel: 615-741-2159
www.tennesseeanytime.com

Texas Tourism
Toll free: 800-8888-TEX
www.traveltex.com

Vermont Deptartment of Tourism and Marketing
Toll free: 800-vermont
www.800-vermont.com

Virginia Tourism Corporation
Toll free: 800-847-4882
www.virginia.org

Washington State Tourism Division
Toll free: 800-544-1800
www.experienceWA.com

Washington, DC: Destination DC
Tel: 202-789-7000
www.washington.org

Wisconsin Department of Tourism
Toll free: 800-432-8747
www.travelwisconsin.com

Wyoming Travel and Tourism
Toll free: 800-225-5996
www.wyomingtourism.org

Visas and Entry

For entry into the US, most foregin nationals require a machine-readable passport, a passport-sized photograph (note: the size required in Britain is different from that in a US passport), a visitor's visa, proof of intent to leave the US after your visit and (depending upon your country of origin) an international vaccination certificate. Under the **Visa Waiver Program** (VWP), visitors from certain countries, such as the UK, staying less than 90 days no longer need a visa. However, as of January 12, 2009, non-US residents from VWP countries are required to submit information about themselves online to the Department of Homeland Security and be pre-approved for travel to the US at least three days before they travel. It is compulsory for short-term visitors to the US to register via the website of the Electronic System for Travel Authorization (www.esta.us/travel_authorization.html) before traveling.

Vaccination certificate requirements vary, but proof of immunization against smallpox or cholera may be necessary. US citizens traveling by air between the US, Canada, Mexico, the Caribbean, and Bermuda must present a current passport; a birth certificate and photo ID are no longer valid proof.

Check current entry requirements on www.travel.state.gov/visa_services.html.

Weights and Measures

The US operates on the imperial system of weights and measures.

Women Travelers

Driving is a wonderful, generally safe way for a woman to travel across the US. You are unlikely to have any trouble, and, from the safety of your vehicle, you will enjoy an unaccustomed, and possibly addictive, feeling of true adventure and freedom.

Although it's fun to meet new people on the road, if you are a lone female, be a little cautious to avoid unwarranted attention. Be conservative in dress and avoid engaging with anyone partying hard, especially groups of men in bars, where things can rapidly get out of control. Don't go home with strangers or pick up hitchhikers if you're a female traveling alone.

Plan on staying in slightly more expensive motels and public campgrounds, and get in the habit of keeping your car doors locked at all times. Avoid walking around at night in poorly lit areas, whether in the city or the country, and keep to public places. Try to let someone know your planned itinerary.

For further tips see Open Road Survival Skills, page 388.

FURTHER READING

General

Great Plains by Ian Frazier. A thoughtful travelogue by the British writer on his 25,000-mile odyssey through the historic American heartland.

The Great Deluge: Hurricane Katrina, New Orleans, and the Mississippi Gulf Coast by Douglas Brinkley. Historian Brinkley, a New Orleans resident and survivor of the hurricane, captures the experience and politics of the deadly storm.

Legends of the American Desert by Alex Schoumatoff. An unusually well-written account of the real New Mexico by an outsider with curiosity to burn.

Fiction

The Border Trilogy by Cormac McCarthy. McCarthy captures the feeling of Border Country, *macho* cowboys, and their love of horses.

Black Cherry Blues by James Lee Burke. Former New Orleans policeman Dave Robicheaux grapples with an illegal Mafia takeover of Indian lands in Montana.

Brokeback Mountain by Annie Proulx. This poignant short story of enduring love between two cowboys evokes the real American West of the 1960s with its spare prose, haunting characters, and authentic sense of place.

Death Comes to the Archbishop by Willa Cather. Based on the life of Santa Fe's 19th-century Archbishop Lamy who worked to "civilize" New Mexico's capital.

The Grapes of Wrath by John Steinbeck. This classic novel follows an Oklahoma family's experiences as migrant field workers in California during the Dust Bowl years of the Great Depression. It still resonates today.

Gone With The Wind by Margaret Mitchell. Mitchell's masterpiece is a tale of love and redemption with the changing South of the Civil War era as backdrop.

Ernest Hemingway: Many of Hemingway's novels and short stories were written in the 10 years he lived in Key West, but *To Have and Have Not* is the only one set in the town

(published in 1937).

Carl Hiassen: *Miami Herald* journalist Hiassen writes bestselling comic thrillers set in Florida, including *Native Tongue* (1992), which makes fun of theme parks.

Tony Hillerman: The former journalist's novels about Navajo policemen Sgt Joe Leaphorn and detective Jim Chee offer insights into the Navajo people and their vast reservation.

Lake Wobegon Days by Garrison Keillor. Charming stories about daily life in a mythical Minnesota burg based on the popular radio show *Prairie Home Companion.*

The Friends of Eddie Coyle by George Higgins. Set among Boston's criminal fraternity, this novel is celebrated for its dialogue and authenticity.

Tales of the City by Armistead Maupin. A series of stories set among San Francisco's gay community.

Send Us Your Thoughts

We do our best to ensure the information in our books is as accurate and up to date as possible. The books are updated on a regular basis using local contacts, who painstakingly add, amend and correct as required. However, some details (such as telephone numbers and opening times) are liable to change, and we are ultimately reliant on our readers to put us in the picture.

We welcome your feedback, especially your experience of using the book "on the road." Maybe we recommended a hotel that you liked (or another that you didn't), or you came across a great bar or new attraction we missed.

We will acknowledge all contributions, and we'll offer an Insight Guide to the best letters received.

Please write to us at:
   Insight Guides
   PO Box 7910
   London SE1 1WE
Or email us at:
   insight@apaguide.co.uk

On the Road

Blue Highways: A Journey into America by William Least Heat Moon. This exploration of life along the blue-lined highways on the map is still essential road-trip reading.

Driving to Detroit: An Automotive Odyssey by Lesley Hazleton. An expat Brit explores personal love and loss against the backdrop of a US road trip.

The Lost Continent: Travels in Small Town America by Bill Bryson. Hysterical look at growing up in the Midwest by an expat American living in the UK.

Lost Highway: Journeys and Arrivals of American Musicians by Peter Guralnick. America viewed through the lens of roots musicians like Elvis, Howling Wolf, and Merle Haggard.

On the Road by Jack Kerouac. A syncopated-jazz wild ride of a tale capturing the romance of the road and crazy, amped-up lifestyles of 1950s Beat poets.

Route 66 Magazine quarterly from PO Box 1129, Port Richey FL 34673-1129, tel: 928-853-8148, www.route66magazine.com.

Route 66 Adventure Handbook: Expanded Third Edition by Drew Knowles. An exhaustive tome with lots of personal charm.

Travels with Charley: In Search of America by John Steinbeck. A classic road-trip book featuring the author's standard poodle companion and a vast continent.

Other Insight Guides

For more detailed information about particular cities, states and regions, Insight Guides publishes a comprehensive range of titles. Companion titles to the present book include **Arizona and the Grand Canyon, Boston, California, Chicago, Florida, Las Vegas, New England, New York City, Orlando, San Francisco, Seattle, Texas** and **Washington, DC.** Durable and practical Insight Fleximaps include **Atlanta, Boston, Los Angeles, Miami, New York, San Diego, Seattle,** and **Washington, DC.**

ART & PHOTO CREDITS

INDEX

Central Route

	Washington, DC	Memphis, TN	Joplin, MO	Amarillo, TX	Gallup, NM	Flagstaff, AZ	Los Angeles, CA
Washington, DC		940	1371	1850	2270	2452	2922
Memphis, TN	940		431	910	1330	1512	1982
Joplin, MO	1371	431		479	899	1081	1551
Amarillo, TX	1850	910	479		420	602	1072
Gallup, NM	2270	1330	899	420		182	652
Flagstaff, AZ	2452	1512	1081	602	182		470
Los Angeles, CA	2922	1982	1551	1072	652	470	

Northern Route

	Boston, MA	Buffalo, NY	Chicago, IL	Pierre, SD	Cody, WY	Seattle, WA	Cape Flattery, WA
Boston, MA		872	1419	2309	2891	3961	4095
Buffalo, NY	872		547	1437	2019	3089	3223
Chicago, IL	1419	547		890	1472	2542	2676
Pierre, SD	2309	1437	890		582	1652	1786
Cody, WY	2891	2019	1472	582		1070	1204
Seattle, WA	3961	3089	2542	1652	1070		134
Cape Flattery, WA	4095	3223	2676	1786	1204	134	

Atlantic Route

	New York, NY	Baltimore, MD	Roanoke, VA	Savannah, GA	Orlando, FL	Miami, FL	Key West, FL
New York, NY		202	543	811	1170	1597	1761
Baltimore, MD	202		341	609	968	1395	1559
Roanoke, VA	543	341		268	627	1054	1218
Savannah, GA	811	609	268		359	786	960
Orlando, FL	1170	968	627	359		427	591
Miami, FL	1597	1395	1054	786	427		164
Key West, FL	1761	1559	1218	960	591	164	

Pacific Route

	San Diego, CA	Los Angeles, CA	San Francisco, CA	Eureka, CA	Crescent, OR	Newport, OR	Seattle, WA
San Diego, CA		124	504	785	867	1108	1399
Los Angeles, CA	124		380	661	743	984	1275
San Francisco, CA	504	380		281	363	604	895
Eureka, CA	785	661	281		82	323	614
Crescent, OR	867	743	363	82		241	532
Newport, OR	1108	984	604	323	241		291
Seattle, WA	1399	1275	895	614	532	291	

Southern Route

	Atlanta, GA	New Orleans, LA	Houston, TX	San Antonio, TX	Lordsburg, NM	Phoenix, AZ	San Diego, CA
Atlanta, GA		473	825	1070	1989	2213	2572
New Orleans, LA	473		352	597	1516	1740	2099
Houston, TX	825	352		245	1164	1388	1747
San Antonio, TX	1070	597	245		919	1143	1502
Lordsburg, NM	1989	1516	1164	919		224	583
Phoenix, AZ	2213	1740	1388	1143	224		359
San Diego, CA	2572	2099	1747	1502	583	359	

Atlantic Route
New York (NY) - Key West (FL)

Northern Route
Boston (MA) - Cape Flattery (WA)

Central Route
Washington, DC - Los Angeles (CA)

Southern Route
Atlanta (GA) - San Diego (CA)

Pacific Route
San Diego (CA) - Seattle (WA)

All distances shown are in miles.

Central Route

	Washington, DC	Memphis, TN	Joplin, MO	Amarillo, TX	Gallup, NM	Flagstaff, AZ	Los Angeles, CA
Washington, DC		940	1371	1850	2270	2452	2922
Memphis, TN	940		431	910	1330	1512	1982
Joplin, MO	1371	431		479	899	1081	1551
Amarillo, TX	1850	910	479		420	602	1072
Gallup, NM	2270	1330	899	420		182	652
Flagstaff, AZ	2452	1512	1081	602	182		470
Los Angeles, CA	2922	1982	1551	1072	652	470	

Northern Route

	Boston, MA	Buffalo, NY	Chicago, IL	Pierre, SD	Cody, WY	Seattle, WA	Cape Flattery, WA
Boston, MA		872	1419	2309	2891	3961	4095
Buffalo, NY	872		547	1437	2019	3089	3223
Chicago, IL	1419	547		890	1472	2542	2676
Pierre, SD	2309	1437	890		582	1652	1786
Cody, WY	2891	2019	1472	582		1070	1204
Seattle, WA	3961	3089	2542	1652	1070		134
Cape Flattery, WA	4095	3223	2676	1786	1204	134	

Pacific Route

	San Diego, CA	Los Angeles, CA	San Francisco, CA	Eureka, CA	Crescent, OR	Newport, OR	Seattle, WA
San Diego, CA		124	504	785	867	1108	1399
Los Angeles, CA	124		380	661	743	984	1275
San Francisco, CA	504	380		281	363	604	895
Eureka, CA	785	661	281		82	323	614
Crescent, OR	867	743	363	82		241	532
Newport, OR	1108	984	604	323	241		291
Seattle, WA	1399	1275	895	614	532	291	

Atlantic Route

	New York, NY	Baltimore, MD	Roanoke, VA	Savannah, GA	Orlando, FL	Miami, FL	Key West, FL
New York, NY		202	543	811	1170	1597	1761
Baltimore, MD	202		341	609	968	1395	1559
Roanoke, VA	543	341		268	627	1054	1218
Savannah, GA	811	609	268		359	786	960
Orlando, FL	1170	968	627	359		427	591
Miami, FL	1597	1395	1054	786	427		164
Key West, FL	1761	1559	1218	960	591	164	

Southern Route

	Atlanta, GA	New Orleans, LA	Houston, TX	San Antonio, TX	Lordsburg, NM	Phoenix, AZ	San Diego, CA
Atlanta, GA		473	825	1070	1989	2213	2572
New Orleans, LA	473		352	597	1516	1740	2099
Houston, TX	825	352		245	1164	1388	1747
San Antonio, TX	1070	597	245		919	1143	1502
Lordsburg, NM	1989	1516	1164	919		224	583
Phoenix, AZ	2213	1740	1388	1143	224		359
San Diego, CA	2572	2099	1747	1502	583	359	

Atlantic Route
New York (NY) - Key West (FL)

Northern Route
Boston (MA) - Cape Flattery (WA)

Central Route
Washington, DC - Los Angeles (CA)

Southern Route
Atlanta (GA) - San Diego (CA)

Pacific Route
San Diego (CA) - Seattle (WA)

All distances shown are in miles.

Interstate Route Marker

Even numbers indicate east-west routes: odd show north-south routes.

US Highway Marker

Four-way Stop Sign

Traffic from all four directions must stop. The first vehicle to reach the intersection should move first.

Yield Ahead

Reduce speed and allow vehicles crossing your path right-of-way.

One tr

Traffic Merges (from right)

Traffic flows merge from indicated direction.

2-Way Traffic

Traffic flows in both directions.

Traffic Lane Joins

Traffic enters carriageway with new lane.

Yield Ahead

A yield sign is ahead.

D

Di to

Dead End

Not a through road, no access to other streets.

Crossing Traffic

Highway is crossed by road. Look to left and right for cars.

Stop sign ahead

Stop sign ahead, prepare to stop.

Slippery Surface

Road surface is slippery when wet. First half-hour of rain is most hazardous.

Be c

Construction Ahead

Distance given until construction begins. Watch for further signs.

Railroad Crossing Ahead

Slow and prepare to stop at crossing ahead.

Left Turn

All traffic must turn left.

Keep Right

Traffic is required to keep to the right of medians or obstructions.

The certai Req us

One Way

One-way traffic in direction of arrow.

Camping

Direction to camping site.

Rest Area

Roadside park and rest area.

Hospital

Watch for pedestrians and emergency vehicles.

School Zone

Follow speed limit displayed when lights above sign flash.

School

Children crossing road.

Lane Control

Travel in lane.

Lane Control

Clear the lane. If flashing, left turn is permitted.

Lane Cont

Don't use lane approachi